CANADA'S POLITICS

Democracy, Diversity, and Good Government | Third Edition

Eric Mintz
Grenfell Campus, Memorial University of Newfoundland

Livianna Tossutti
Brock University

Christopher Dunn
Memorial University of Newfoundland

PEARSON

Toronto

CONTENTS

PREFACE

Politics affects many aspects of our lives, such as students' ability to afford higher education; the safety of the food we eat; how well the natural environment is protected; the quality of our communities; and the peace, prosperity, and security of our country. Canadian politics is particularly interesting because the great diversity of Canada provides important challenges for the practice of democracy and the good government that Canadians expect.

Reading this book should give you a good understanding of the major features of Canadian politics, including the workings of the parliamentary system of government, the protection of rights and freedoms, the competition among political parties, the federal system, and the ways in which citizens try to influence government policies. Highlighted throughout the book are a variety of important issues, problems, and controversies. These include national unity and Quebec sovereignty, Aboriginal self-government, the increasing inequality in wealth and income, the concentration of power in the hands of the prime minister, the major changes in the contemporary political party system, the representation of women and minorities in politics, whether Canada should strive to be an "energy superpower," and Canada's role and responsibilities in international politics.

There are many features that make this textbook interesting and easy to understand:

- Each chapter opens with a *vignette* that provides an interesting and often provocative story that relates to the content of the chapter. Among other topics, the vignettes address the struggle of women to be recognized as "persons," student protests against tuition increases, and whether prisoners and 16-year-olds should have the right to vote.
- *Boxes* in each chapter provide examples that illustrate the material in the text. These boxes deal with such topics as same-sex marriage; the controversy concerning the Northern Gateway pipelines; and Canada's recent combat missions in Afghanistan, Iraq, and Syria.
- To guide students in understanding the textbook, each chapter includes *Chapter Objectives* at the start and a *Summary and Conclusion* at the end.

- *Key terms* are printed in bold in the text, defined in the margin for instant reference, and compiled in the end-of-book glossary.
- The *Discussion Questions* at the end of each chapter are designed to spark critical thought and discussion.
- The *Further Reading* section at the end of each chapter provides suggestions for those who would like to explore further the topics in the chapter.
- *Weblinks* in the margins provide additional research resources.
- The *graphics*—photos, figures, and tables—illustrate concepts discussed in the text and illuminate some features of Canadian politics.

NEW TO THIS EDITION

We have made many changes to the third edition of this text, both to improve the textbook and to discuss a variety of important recent events. These changes include the following:

- A new section on social democracy (Chapter 1)
- Discussion of reforms of the Citizenship Act and the treatment of refugees (Chapter 3)
- Examination of new and proposed free trade and foreign investment protection agreements (Chapter 4)
- The development of the "Idle No More" and "SlutWalk" movements (Chapter 6)
- The removal of the charitable status of some advocacy groups (Chapter 7)
- The 2015 Canadian election and its implications for Canada's party system (Chapter 8)
- Changes to the Canada Elections Act and explanations of the 2015 election results (Chapter 9)
- Expanded discussion of Aboriginal land claims and modern treaties including the Tsilhqot'in ruling (Chapter 11)
- The increased potential power of party caucuses in the House of Commons, omnibus budget bills, and the issue of Senate reform (Chapter 14)
- Analysis of the clash between the Harper government and the Supreme Court of Canada over various laws, and the controversies concerning the appointment of Supreme Court of Canada judges (Chapter 16)
- An entirely new chapter on domestic public policy that includes an analysis of the factors affecting the context of public policy and examination of social, health, economic, and environmental policy-making (Chapter 17)
- Expanded discussion of foreign policy perspectives, terrorism, and development assistance (Chapter 18)

In addition, the organization of the textbook has been modified. Discussion of the Charter of Rights and Freedoms has been incorporated into

Chapter 10 on the Constitution. Chapter 6 "Canada's Place in the World" has been moved to Chapter 18 and renamed "Foreign Policy". As well, the ordering of Chapter 3 (renamed "Canada and the Challenge of Cultural Diversity") and Chapter 4 (renamed "The Canadian Economy and the Challenges of Inequality") has been reversed.

SUPPLEMENTS

The supplements package for this book has been carefully created to enhance the topics discussed in the text.

- **PowerPoint Presentations.** This instructor resource contains key points and lecture notes to accompany each chapter in the text.
- **Test Item File.** This test bank contains multiple-choice, true/false, short answer, and essay questions.
- **Computerized Test Bank.** Pearson's computerized test banks allow instructors to filter and select questions to create quizzes, tests, or homework. Instructors can revise questions or add their own, and may be able to choose print or online options. These questions are also available in Microsoft Word format.

peerScholar

Firmly grounded in published research, peerScholar is a powerful online pedagogical tool that helps develop students' critical and creative thinking skills through creation, evaluation, and reflection. Working in stages, students begin by submitting written assignments. *peerScholar* then circulates their work for others to review, a process that can be anonymous or not, depending on instructors' preferences. Students immediately receive peer feedback and evaluations, reinforcing their learning and driving development of higher-order thinking skills. Students can then re-submit revised work, again depending on instructors' preferences.

Contact your Pearson representative to learn more about *peerScholar* and the research behind it.

Technology Specialists

Pearson's technology specialists work with faculty and campus course designers to ensure that Pearson technology products, assessment tools, and online course materials are tailored to meet your specific needs. This highly qualified team is dedicated to helping schools take full advantage of a wide range of educational resources, by assisting in the integration of a variety of instructional materials and media formats. Your local Pearson Education Canada sales representative can provide you with more details on this service program.

ACKNOWLEDGMENTS

Many people at Pearson Canada took great care in turning the authors' drafts into a very readable and interesting textbook. In particular, we acknowledge Matthew Christian, Madhu Ranadive, Daniella Balabuk, Pippa Kennard, and Laurel Sparrow.

Eric Mintz would like to thank Diane Mintz, who put up with the many long hours he spent working on this book and provided much-needed support and encouragement.

Livianna Tossutti would like to thank her parents, Victor and the late Therese Tossutti, and Pawel Cimek, for their love and encouragement. Mike, it has been a year since you died. I think of you every day and miss you.

To the memory of my dear son Aaron (1985–2015)

E.M.

To my parents, Victor Tossutti and Therese Gallery Tossutti

L.T.

To my sister Catherine Dunn, for her activism and example

C.D.

CHAPTER 1

Introduction

CHAPTER OBJECTIVES

After reading this chapter, you should be able to

1. Define some basic political concepts.
2. Examine and evaluate the basic features of Canadian democracy.
3. Discuss alternative approaches for enhancing Canadian democracy.
4. Examine the political significance of Canadian diversity.
5. Outline the criteria for good government.
6. Discuss the importance of interests, ideas, identities, institutions, and external influences in understanding Canadian politics.

On October 17, 2013, near Rexton, New Brunswick, RCMP officers in riot gear carrying some assault weapons and accompanied by German Shepherd dogs attacked protesters who ignored a court injunction against their blockade of an SWN Resources Canada facility. This American-owned company was engaged in seismic testing that could lead to hydraulic fracturing ("fracking") to produce natural gas on land claimed by the Elsipogtog First Nation. In the clashes that followed, six RCMP vehicles were torched, some homemade explosives were found, beanbags and possibly rubber bullets were fired at protesters, and 40 protesters were arrested (Lukacs, 2013; Strapagiel, 2013).

Fracking involves the high-pressure injection of water, soil, and a variety of chemicals into shale formations to extract oil or natural gas that cannot be produced by conventional drilling. Fracking has greatly increased petroleum production in North America in recent years, resulting in lower oil and gasoline prices. It has also made the United States less dependent upon imported oil. For the government of the relatively poor province of New Brunswick, fracking was seen as an important potential source of revenue and jobs. However, fracking has also raised concerns about human health, the potential for earthquakes, and the contamination of soil and water. It has also slowed down the shift to renewable energy sources, including solar and wind power, and thus contributed to the serious problem of global climate change.

The New Brunswick protests were led by persons from the Mi'kmaq and Maliseet First Nations. They claim that the peace and friendship treaties their ancestors signed centuries ago mean that they never gave up their legal right to their traditional territories and that development on their lands should not proceed without their consent. As the Supreme Court of Canada ruled in a somewhat different situation in British Columbia: "Aboriginal title confers on the group that holds it the exclusive right to decide how the land is used." If the title has not yet been established, the government "is required to consult in good faith . . . about proposed uses" (*Tsilhqot'in*, 2014). On the fracking issue, the New Brunswick government had not engaged in meaningful consultation with First Nations or with the general public.

Fracking is just one important case where the reconciliation of economic growth and environmental protection presents difficult political challenges. Meaningful public discussion of controversial issues helps to ensure that government decisions are based on scientific evidence and community support. Democracy and good government involve more than simply electing a government every few years. Furthermore, despite being ignored for generations, the rights of Aboriginal peoples (founders of Canada's diverse society) need to be taken seriously.

In the end, the Liberal party (which promised a moratorium on fracking) defeated the Progressive Conservative government in the 2014 New Brunswick election. Likewise in neighbouring Nova Scotia, the Liberal provincial government continued a moratorium (initiated by the previous NDP government) that was recommended after an extensive scientific review and public consultations by an independent panel. Fracking may eventually be allowed under strict conditions in these provinces.

POLITICS

Political actions by individuals and groups and the decisions of governing institutions have important effects on our lives; on the interests of various groups; and on the quality of our country, province, and local community. Consider, for example, the actions of student organizations to try to persuade governments to lower or eliminate tuition fees, the Supreme Court of Canada's decision that resulted in the legalization of same-sex marriage, and the efforts of environmental groups to try to convince governments to adopt effective policies regarding global climate change.

Politics can be thought of as all of the activities related to influencing, making, and implementing collective decisions.[1] Political activity usually

POLITICS
Activities related to influencing, making, and implementing collective decisions.

---

[1]"Politics," like many other terms used in political science, is subject to different contending definitions that often reflect different political perspectives. In particular, some prefer to think about politics in terms of any relationship that involves the use of power. A distinction between public, collective decisions and private decisions, it is argued, obscures the use of power to dominate subordinate groups in society.

involves controversy because different people have contrasting interests, values, and priorities when collective decisions are at stake. As well, controversy and conflict characterize politics because of the relentless competition for positions of political power and the potential for misuse of power.

Politics, particularly in stable, democratic countries such as Canada, often also involves activity aimed at resolving conflicts or at least playing down their significance. For example, after Quebec's divisive 1995 independence referendum, the Canadian government made some overtures to appease those Quebecers who voted "yes" because they wanted changes to Canada's federal system but did not necessarily believe in outright independence. The gestures included presenting a resolution to the House of Commons recognizing "that the Québécois form a nation within a united Canada" (CBC News, 2006).

Power is a key feature of politics. Power involves the ability to affect the behaviour of others, particularly by getting them to act in ways that they would not otherwise have done. For example, take a student group that succeeds in pressuring its provincial government to lower tuition fees. If the government would not have taken action without pressure from the students, we can say that the group has exercised its power—and done so effectively.

> **POWER**
> The ability to affect the behaviour of others, particularly by getting them to act in ways that they would not otherwise have done.

The collective decisions of a political community mirror, to a considerable extent, the distribution of political power. Those who have scant political power will likely find that collective decisions do not reflect their interests or values. For example, through much of Canada's political history, Aboriginal peoples, women, and some minority ethnic, racial, and religious groups enjoyed almost nothing in the way of political power. It is hardly surprising, then, that Canadian governments barely paid attention to the needs and aspirations of these groups and, indeed, adopted policies that discriminated against or even oppressed these groups. Although the right to vote in elections now gives some political power to all citizens, the reality is that some people, groups, and interests are much better equipped to influence government than is the "ordinary" citizen. For example, the Canadian Council of Chief Executives, whose membership comprises the leaders of Canada's largest corporations, has demonstrated a considerable ability to shape government policy on a variety of important issues such as the pursuit of free trade agreements.

STATE AND GOVERNMENT

Canada is a sovereign (independent) **state** whose governing institutions are able to make and enforce rules that are binding on the people living within its territory. The national and provincial governments that are currently in office act on behalf of the state (legally referred to as "the Crown"). "The state" also refers to all of the institutions and agencies that act on behalf of the state, including the police and military forces and state-owned (Crown) corporations.

At the centre of political life is the **government**: the set of institutions that have the authority to make executive decisions; present proposed laws, taxes,

> **STATE**
> An independent, self-governing country whose governing institutions are able to make and enforce rules that are binding on the people living within a particular territory.
>
> **GOVERNMENT**
> The set of institutions that have the authority to make executive decisions; present proposed laws, taxes, and expenditures to the appropriate legislative body; and oversee the implementation of laws and policies.

and expenditures to the appropriate legislative body for approval; and oversee the implementation of laws and policies. When we talk about the Canadian government (also called the "national" or "federal" government), we are usually referring to the prime minister and cabinet along with the variety of departments and agencies that fall under their direction. However Parliament, the court system, and the monarch and governor-general are also part of the overall system of the Canadian government. Provincial and territorial governing systems are organized in a separate but similar manner.

In analyzing the power of governments, political scientists often make use of the related concepts of *authority* and *legitimacy*. **Authority** refers to the right to exercise power. Those in governing positions in Canada claim the right to make and implement decisions under the authority of the constitution. **Legitimacy** refers to the acceptance by the people that those in positions of authority have the right to govern. Governments can exercise power through their ability to direct the major means of force—the police and military. However, since those in positions of authority have usually been able to establish their legitimacy in the eyes of the public, governments in Canada have rarely needed to rely heavily on the use of force to exercise power. In this respect, Canada contrasts sharply with countries such as Egypt and China, where authorities often depend on force to maintain their power.

Without free and fair elections to select the governing party, the legitimacy of Canadian governing institutions would be compromised. In addition, the willingness of those in government to abide by constitutional rules helps to preserve the legitimacy of governmental authority while placing some limits on how government acts. However, the legitimacy of a government may weaken among those who feel that the government is systematically unfair to their group or unjust in its policies.

Legitimacy also comes into play in analyzing the state. If some groups feel the state was forced on them or is controlled by and acts in the interests of others, then the legitimacy of the state may be challenged. For example, some Aboriginal First Nations claim that they never gave up their right to sovereignty (i.e., their right to govern themselves and their territory without outside interference). The Canadian state in this view is an illegitimate colonial power. This raises the question as to whether, or to what extent, they should be subject to the laws of Canadian governments. In another example, if a majority of Quebecers had voted for independence in 1995 and the Canadian government refused to recognize Quebec's sovereignty, the Quebec government might have challenged the legitimacy of the Canadian state.

Governments not only have the power to make and implement decisions, but also have some ability to persuade the society they govern about the desirability of their policies. They may be able to influence society by controlling information, gaining media exposure for their views, and carrying their messages to the public through advertising. For example, in 12 weeks in 2011, the Canadian government spent $26 million on television and radio advertising to

AUTHORITY
The right to exercise power.

LEGITIMACY The acceptance by the people that those in positions of authority have the right to govern.

support the claim that its economic action plan was benefiting the public. Politics thus involves not only the attempts of various groups and individuals to influence government, but also a two-way relationship between society and government.

In thinking about the power of government, it is important to keep in mind that Canada has a variety of governments, including federal, provincial, territorial, municipal, and Aboriginal. As will be discussed in Chapter 12, Canada's federal system is characterized by quite a high level of conflict, as well as considerable cooperation, between the Canadian government and provincial governments. The power of the Canadian government is limited because provincial governments enjoy considerable power that they are determined to use. Action on a number of policies relies on negotiation and agreement between national and provincial governments.

Although governments and legislatures have the authority to make binding, collective decisions, a variety of other organizations, groups, and individuals also have a hand in making and implementing some decisions. For example, Canadian governments often consult with interest groups representing different elements of society or sectors of the economy to help develop policies on topics that affect them. Similarly, businesses and community organizations are sometimes involved as partners with government in developing and carrying out specific programs.

DEMOCRACY

If you were asked to describe the basic nature of Canadian politics, how would you respond? For most people, democracy is the key feature of Canadian politics. But what exactly does it mean to describe Canada as a "democratic" country? While Canada is undoubtedly more democratic than Iran, Saudi Arabia, or Cuba, can Canada be considered fully democratic?

The term **democracy** originated with two words of ancient Greek that can be interpreted as "rule by the people." In the **direct democracy** system of some of the ancient Greek city–states, such as Athens, citizens took charge of the governing decisions, especially by discussing the issues and then voting on laws in an open forum that all citizens could (and were expected to) attend. Democracy was viewed as putting power in the hands of ordinary citizens (other than women, slaves, and the foreign born) rather than in the hands of an elite group, particularly the wealthy few.

DEMOCRACY
Rule by the people either directly or through the election of representatives.

DIRECT DEMOCRACY
A form of democracy in which citizens are directly involved in making the governing decisions.

Representative Democracy

In modern times, **representative democracy** has served as the primary method of implementing the democratic ideal of rule by the people. In this system, most citizens are not directly involved in making governing decisions. Instead, citizens elect representatives to make governing decisions on their behalf. In electing a representative nominated by a political party,

REPRESENTATIVE DEMOCRACY
A form of democracy in which citizens elect representatives to make governing decisions on their behalf.

Canadian voters in effect are determining which political party will form the government.[2] In most cases, the leader of the party that wins the greatest number of legislative seats in the House of Commons will become the prime minister and will select cabinet ministers from members of his or her political party.

Representative democracy is often viewed as the most practical way of applying the democratic ideal to large, modern, complex societies. Voters may get a sense of what those vying to be elected will do by studying the campaign platforms of political parties and carefully following coverage of the campaign in the media. Thus, they may be able to have some influence on the general direction of the government by choosing among the competing parties. If citizens are disgruntled with the policies of the governing party, they can vote for a representative of a different party in the next election. Admittedly, the people may have only limited control over those they elect. Yet the desire to get re-elected can lead politicians and governing political parties to act in ways that will help them achieve that goal, particularly by meeting the expectations of a sufficient number of voters to win an election. Furthermore, we can hope that our elected representatives will devote their knowledge, skills, and energies toward deciding what is in the public interest, thus freeing up the rest of the population from much of that responsibility.

Critics of representative democracy argue that elections are imperfect vehicles for ensuring that representatives act according to the wishes of the people. There is the ever-present danger that those we elect will be preoccupied with their own interests or those of their supporters rather than the interests of the public as a whole. As well, those we elect may act on their own perspectives and values, which may diverge from those of the population they represent. Furthermore, political parties often do not offer clear choices to voters or spell out exactly how they will act in office. And those we elect do not always respect the positions taken or fulfill the promises made during election campaigns.

Furthermore, to some extent Canada does not fully meet the ideal of representative democracy. As discussed in Chapter 14, the unelected Canadian Senate has to approve all legislation, although it has rarely rejected legislation passed by the House of Commons in modern times. As well, because of the nature of our electoral system (see Chapter 9), the governing party rarely has obtained a majority of the votes in an election, even if it wins a majority of seats in the House of Commons. Furthermore, as discussed in Chapters 13 and 14, the power of government has tended to be concentrated in the hands of the prime minister, the prime minister's advisers, and a few key cabinet ministers. Strict party discipline in the House of Commons curbs the ability of elected members to vote according to the

---

[2]A coalition of parties could also form the government, but this has been much less common in Canada than in many other democratic countries.

wishes of their constituents, and debate in the House of Commons is often limited on controversial legislation.

More generally, some argue that political power in Canada is very unevenly distributed. Members of elite groups and large corporations along with lobbyists having inside connections to government policymakers play a leading role in affecting major decisions (Carroll, 2004; Clement, 1977; Olsen, 1980; Porter, 1965). Others, however, suggest that the development of a vast array of groups representing different sectors of society and contrasting political perspectives has provided an avenue for the general public to try to influence public policies—a way to exercise power beyond the choices made in an election. Nevertheless, greater social and economic equality may be needed if Canada is to become more fully democratic. Greater equality would reduce the power of the wealthy and might encourage more effective participation in political life by all individuals.

Liberal Democracy

In addition to being a representative democracy, Canada can also be described as a **liberal democracy**. In a liberal democracy, all individuals are able to express their views freely, organize for political action, compete for public offices in regular, fair elections, and access a variety of sources of information and opinions that are not controlled by government. Liberal democracies also feature **constitutional government**—that is, a government that consistently acts according to established fundamental rules and principles. An independent judicial system that protects the rights of individuals and upholds the constitution is an essential feature of a liberal democracy. Thus, liberal democracy is based on the rule of law.

Liberal democracy involves protecting rights and freedoms both from arbitrary governments and from majorities who might seek to curb the rights of unpopular individuals or groups. Liberal democracy not only guarantees protection of the political rights needed for a meaningful democracy, but also ensures that individuals are entitled to live as they choose, as long as they do not significantly harm others or interfere with their rights. In other words, the "liberal" aspect of liberal democracy means maintaining a substantial area of private activity where government should not intervene (although what should be considered "private" is often controversial). Thus, liberal democracy protects diversity within society by allowing people to follow their own values and practise their own beliefs, even if the majority view these values and practices as undesirable (see Box 1-1, Banning the Kirpan: Religious Rights and Public Safety in Schools).

Despite the characterization of Canada as a liberal democracy, the rights of minorities have not always been protected. During times of heightened awareness of real or imagined threats to national security and public order, governments and security forces have sometimes acted in illiberal ways.

LIBERAL DEMOCRACY
A political system in which the powers of government are limited by law, the rights of the people to engage in political activity freely are well established, and fair elections are held to choose those who make governing decisions.

CONSTITUTIONAL GOVERNMENT
A government that consistently acts in keeping with established fundamental rules and principles.

BOX 1-1

Banning the Kirpan: Religious Rights and Public Safety in Schools

In 2001, 12-year-old Gurbaj Singh Multani dropped the sheathed steel knife, or kirpan, he was wearing at a Montreal elementary school. As required by his Khalsa Sikh faith, he had made a spiritual commitment to carry a kirpan (which is only to be used as a weapon of defence) at all times. When Gurbaj dropped the kirpan while playing in the schoolyard, the mother of another student complained to school officials (Timeline: The Quebec *kirpan* case, 2006). Although Gurbaj's family accepted a school board request that the kirpan be securely covered, higher school authorities resolved that the kirpan, like other weapons, should be banned from schools. When this decision was overturned in a court challenge, some parents picketed the school and refused to send their children to class. Because of the taunts that pursued him, Gurbaj left to attend a private school.

Eventually, the question of whether kirpans should be banned in schools went before the Supreme Court of Canada. Its ruling in 2006 allowed Gurbaj to wear the kirpan, as long as it was under his clothes and sewn into a sheath. In the court's view, a complete ban could not be justified because of the right to freedom of religion enshrined in the Charter of Rights and Freedoms. As well, Justice Louise Charron argued that a ban is "disrespectful to believers in the Sikh religion and does not take into account Canadian values based on multiculturalism."

Many Canadians favoured the banning of kirpans in schools. While the Supreme Court decision may

© Fred Chartrand/Canadian Press Images

When 12-year-old Gurbaj Singh Multani dropped his kirpan (a sheathed steel knife) at school in 2001, he had no idea that he would become central to a Charter case about freedom of religion that would not be decided by the Supreme Court until 5 years later.

not have reflected the opinion of the majority of Canadians, it did uphold the right of a minority group to follow their religious beliefs while trying to ensure that practices based on those beliefs did not harm or endanger others.

In particular, concerns about terrorism can lead to challenges to liberal rights and freedoms, including the surveillance of various forms of communications.

Plebiscitary Democracy

Some Canadians have pushed for modifications to the system of representative democracy to give the people greater control of their representatives and the decisions that governments make. In particular, the Progressives in the 1920s (a farmers-based political party) and the Reform Party[3] that originated in Western Canada in the 1980s advocated **plebiscitary democracy**: the use of referendums, initiatives, and recall procedures. This, it was argued, would help to ensure that decisions were based on the interests, values, and common sense of ordinary people rather than the wishes of elites and "special interests."

A **referendum** is a vote by citizens on a particular question asked by the government or a legislative body. The Canadian government has resorted to referendums only three times (for the prohibition of alcohol, the imposition of conscription, and a package of constitutional changes known as the Charlottetown Accord). Provincial and local governments have turned to referendums[4] on such issues as the fixed link (bridge) to the mainland (Prince Edward Island), Sunday shopping (Nova Scotia), and video lottery terminals (New Brunswick and various municipalities in Alberta).

An **initiative** is a proposed new law or changes to an existing law drafted by individuals or groups rather than by a government or a legislature. Initiatives are put to a vote by citizens after enough signatures have been collected. In Canada, only British Columbia has set up a procedure for initiatives.[5] In 2011, the first successful initiative involved the collection of 557 383 signatures (easily surpassing the requirement that at least 10 percent of registered voters in each of the province's 83 electoral districts sign the petition within a 90-day period). This was followed by a mail-in ballot in which 57.43 percent of those voting supported rescinding British Columbia's adoption of the harmonized sales tax (HST). A 2013 initiative that would, in effect, largely decriminalize marijuana possession obtained over 200 000 signatures in 90 days, but fell far short of meeting the 10 percent requirement in every electoral district.

Recall procedures allow citizens to recall their representative and require that a new election be held. Again, British Columbia is the only province that provides this opportunity. At least 40 percent of registered voters in a district have to sign a recall petition within a 60-day period for a recall election to be called. From 1995 to October 2015, all of the 26 petition applications were withdrawn or did not receive sufficient valid signatures, although one representative resigned rather than face a probable recall election.

Plebiscitary mechanisms give citizens a chance to vote for more than the election of a representative every few years. However, there are some potential problems. The wording of a referendum question or initiative proposal may be misleading or manipulative. For example, the Canadian government

---

PLEBISCITARY DEMOCRACY
The use of referendums, initiatives, and recall procedures as an alternative to what some view as the elite-oriented nature of representative democracy.

REFERENDUM
A vote by the people on a particular question asked by the government or legislative body.

INITIATIVE
A proposed new law or changes to an existing law drafted by an individual or group rather than by a government or legislature. The proposal is put to a vote by the people after enough signatures have been collected.

RECALL
A procedure that allows citizens to recall their representative and require that a new election be held, provided sufficient names are obtained on a petition.

---

[3]Although members of the former Reform Party (and its successor, the Canadian Alliance) played a leading role in the founding of the new Conservative Party in 2004, the Conservatives dropped the plebiscitary proposals from their party's platform.

[4]Referendums are also known as plebiscites. In the past, *plebiscite* was used to refer to a vote that was not binding on government or legislatures. This distinction has generally disappeared.

[5]Alberta provides for citizen initiatives at the municipal level.

criticized the 1995 Quebec referendum question on the grounds that the phrasing did not provide voters with a clear question about independence. As well, almost all referendums and initiatives allow voters to respond only "yes" or "no" to a particular proposition; more nuanced ways of dealing with an issue are not presented. As with elections, those with money or influence may be able to sway voters in referendums. Furthermore, turnout for referendums and initiatives is often low. For example, although 93.5 percent of Quebecers voted in the 1995 sovereignty (independence) referendum, only about 54 percent of registered voters participated in the BC HST vote. As well, if voters are called upon to decide several issues at the same time (as frequently occurs in some American states), they may not pay enough attention to all of the complexities involved. Referendums and initiatives may also be used to trample the rights of unpopular minorities. For example, in the past many American states held referendums that led to banning same-sex marriage. Finally, the recall procedure does not fit easily into Canada's parliamentary system, in which individual representatives are expected to vote along party lines rather than in keeping with the wishes or interests of their constituents.

Deliberative Democracy

DELIBERATIVE DEMOCRACY
A form of democracy in which governing decisions are made based on discussion by citizens.

Unlike plebiscitary democracy, which gives citizens extra opportunities to vote, **deliberative democracy** engages citizens in deliberating about governing decisions through discussion (Mendelsohn & Parkin, 2001). The underlying idea is that ordinary citizens can make recommendations that are in the public interest, provided they have the opportunity for free and equal discussion and have access to the information, ideas, and time needed for intelligent deliberation. Unlike politicians, whose decisions are often based on seeking advantage in the ongoing struggle for power, ordinary citizens may be able to reach a consensus on some key issues despite having different interests, values, and viewpoints. Deliberative democracy can, therefore, be a means to accommodate the diversity of society, provided that those actively involved in the deliberation reflect that diversity. Citizens' assemblies consisting of a random selection of citizens were used in British Columbia and Ontario to deliberate and make recommendations about changes to those provinces' electoral systems (see Chapter 9).

The idea of deliberative democracy faces the hurdle that interest in politics is not generally high. Many people may not be willing to devote the time and energy needed to discuss and deliberate on complex issues. However, although many people are not deeply engaged in competitive partisan politics, they are likely to take an interest in those political issues and problems that concern or affect them. Indeed, active participation in politics has increased substantially through participation in various groups seeking to influence public policy, bring about social change, or protest the actions of government. Contemporary communications technologies, combined with a more educated population, can facilitate informed discussion of political issues. However, those most likely to actively participate in public deliberations are typically the best-educated people and those with higher social and economic status, as well as spokespersons for particular interests. Unless major efforts are made to involve a wide diversity of people, deliberative democracy may result in recommendations that do not adequately take into account the views and interests of many elements of society.

Social Democracy

Critics of liberal democracy argue that it is not fully democratic, particularly if liberal values include a defence of property rights and income inequality. Large corporations and members of elite groups, it is argued, have a strong ability to affect major government decisions. Further the owners of the mass media tend to promote the values and interests of the corporate world. The less advantaged members of society have much less ability to participate effectively in the political process and thus do not have an equal voice. From the perspective of **social democracy**, greater social and economic equality is needed for Canada to become more truly democratic. For social democrats, various social rights such as health, education, and child care should be equally available to all persons in addition to political and civil rights. Thus, social democrats favour a greater role for government than do those who focus on protecting the property rights associated with a free market economy.

SOCIAL DEMOCRACY
The perspective that greater social and economic equality is needed for a country to be fully democratic.

DIVERSITY

A key characteristic of Canada that has great political importance is the diversity of its peoples. Accommodating Quebec's distinct society within the Canadian federal system has been the subject of considerable attention in Canadian politics. Other provinces and territories also vary in their economic characteristics, their historical experiences, the cultural and linguistic characteristics of their populations, and the identities, values, and political perspectives that are widely held by their residents. Aboriginal First Nations have been searching for a new relationship with Canadian governments that respects what they view as their inherent right to self-government—that is, the ability to govern their own people and lands. Immigrants from many parts of the world have added greatly to the diversity of Canada by bringing different cultures, values, beliefs, identities, and political perspectives. Furthermore, differences in interests, values, and identities are found among those in different social classes, regions, genders, and religions.

The diversity of Canada raises questions about not only how to accommodate different cultures, values, perspectives, and identities, but also how to deal with the problems and injustices that different groups have experienced or continue to experience. Aboriginal people, women, those of different sexual orientations, immigrants, and various minority cultural, ethnic, and religious groups have suffered discrimination and face continuing social and economic barriers to full equality. As well, many provincial governments have emphasized real or perceived unfair treatment of their province at the hands of the national government.

The diversity of Canada also raises issues concerning how democracy is applied in Canada. Democracy is often thought to involve the equality of all citizens. For some, this means that all persons should be treated the same and the wishes of the majority should be the basis of public policies. However, as discussed in Chapter 11, Canada's Aboriginal peoples claim special rights based on their cultural differences and the treaties that were signed with French, British, and Canadian governments. French Quebecers often argue that the Quebec government needs special powers to protect and develop their distinct culture. Controversies also arise concerning whether governments should encourage new and recent immigrants to Canada to adopt Canadian customs and values, or encourage them to maintain their own languages, customs, and traditions.

Accommodating diversity can occur in a variety of ways. Protecting individual freedoms is essential to ensuring that those with different beliefs, cultures, and values can live according to their own convictions. Providing equal rights and benefits for those with different characteristics or lifestyles is important in accommodating diversity. For example, legalizing same-sex marriage has accommodated gays and lesbians. The Charter of Rights and Freedoms and human rights codes prohibit various forms of discrimination based on such characteristics as race, ethnic origin, religion, sex, age, and disability. A more active approach (as discussed in Chapter 4) involves adopting policies that promote an equitable representation of persons with different characteristics in employment and political positions.

Providing rights, freedoms, and opportunities for individuals does not necessarily take into account the importance of the community in shaping how we live our lives. At the collective level, allowing a community that differs from the mainstream to govern itself affords a way of accommodating diversity. By that means, the values and interests of the group can lay the foundation for the policies and laws of the community. However, all of the members of a community will not necessarily share the same values and interests. For example, the government of Quebec views itself as representing the entire Quebec community, yet the English-speaking minority in that province has fought against the government's measures to make French the sole public language. As well, there are some very small groups whose practices (such as polygamy) are at odds with the values of the Canadian community.

Diversity and Unity

In the past, diversity often triggered negative thoughts and feelings. People from foreign or minority cultures were expected to assimilate to the dominant Canadian culture by adopting the language, customs, and values of the

The diversity of Canada's population has great political significance. Those of different social classes, ethnic groups, genders, and sexual orientations as well as those with different religious beliefs often have different political interests, values, and ideological perspectives.

© Calgary Herald

majority. Those who did not "fit in" and looked or acted differently from the majority were often scorned, discriminated against, and shut out of positions of political power. Although many people continue to believe that assimilation is necessary to create a unified country, efforts to assimilate people into the dominant culture are likely to cause tension and political conflict. Nevertheless consensus about the basic political values and laws of the country is needed to maintain a degree of unity among members of diverse groups. Even though many people have a strong sense of identification with their cultural groups or their province, to varying degrees most also have a sense of attachment to Canada and its democratic political system. Thus, a significant degree of unity exists in Canada despite considerable diversity.

GOOD GOVERNMENT

We cannot assume that governments, even in a democratic country, will necessarily act in the public interest. Because of the competitive struggle for power, those in governing positions may be more preoccupied with staying in power than with doing what best serves the country and its people. The governing party may act in ways that are designed to discredit the opposition, dupe the public, or provide perks and benefits to those expected to support it in the next election. Furthermore, those in governing positions may be tempted to act in ways that reward themselves and their families personally. Although recent efforts have tried to ensure that public office-holders act ethically, some individuals will inevitably abuse their positions of authority. Even if most of those in governing positions are dedicated to serving the public interest, competing views exist as to what the public interest entails. Different interests, values, and ideological perspectives shape perceptions of the public interest. For example, some people argue that "the government that governs best governs least," while others believe that government should supply a wide variety of services, play an active role in economic development, and reduce inequalities.

Many people assess the actions of government in terms of their particular interests, values, and identities. That is, they may focus more on the well-being of their province, local community, cultural group, social class, or gender than on the well-being of the country as a whole. It is natural to be concerned with our own well-being and that of our family, friends, and groups with which we identify. However, in a diverse country like Canada, this tendency to judge the broader effects of government primarily in terms of those groups or localities we identify with seems firmly entrenched; it may be stronger than in some countries where people generally view themselves as part of a single national community. Canada's federal system, which divides governing authority between national and provincial governments, tends to reinforce or heighten the assessment of actions taken by the Canadian government in terms of the benefits or costs for particular provinces.

Even if we set aside the interests of the groups we identify with, there remains the issue of whether we should evaluate government actions primarily in terms of the public interest of Canada or that of the world as a whole. For example, if government policies encouraged the conversion of land from growing food crops to growing crops for biofuel, this might benefit Canadian farmers and the Canadian economy, but could contribute to higher food prices, food shortages, and even starvation in other parts of the world. Should we assess good government only in terms of what's advantageous for Canadians? Or should good government also involve actions and initiatives such as protecting the global environment, assisting the development of poorer countries, promoting global human rights, and working toward a peaceful world?

Finally, there is the issue of the relative importance of the public interests of Canadians in the present and Canadians in the future. For example, degradation of Canada's natural environment may fuel prosperity in the present while harming opportunities for future generations. Likewise, a high level of government debt today (unless it involves investments in the future) may become a lasting burden to new generations.

Democracy and Good Government

Democracy can help foster good government, particularly if those in positions of authority are held accountable for their actions and are responsive to the needs and desires of the people.

ACCOUNTABILITY   Accountability includes the following:

- providing valid justifications for the actions and policies of government,
- responding to criticisms, and
- moving swiftly to remedy problems resulting from government actions and policies.

For accountability to be effective, legislators, the media, and interested members of the public should be able to investigate and scrutinize the activities of government. As discussed in Chapter 14, governments have made considerable use of procedures to severely limit parliamentary debate on proposed legislation. Furthermore, the increasing use of "omnibus bills" that bundle together a large number of often unrelated legislative proposals limits the scrutiny of legislative proposals. For example, the 2012 Budget Implementation Act proposed major changes to more than 70 laws dealing with a wide variety of topics, including environmental assessment, employment insurance, immigration, fisheries, and old age pensions, most of which were not directly related to the government's budget. This prevented detailed scrutiny of major policy changes by the standing House of Commons committees that are familiar with particular policy areas.

Public inquiries headed by independent individuals, as well as independent court systems, are also key to dealing with allegations of illegal or improper behaviour by government. Likewise, independent review and investigative processes are needed to ensure that various government agencies operating somewhat independently of government—such as the RCMP and other police, military, and national security agencies—do not abuse the power vested in them. For example, the death of Polish immigrant Robert Dziekanski after being repeatedly tasered by four RCMP officers at Vancouver International Airport in 2007 was revealed by an amateur video uploaded to YouTube. A public inquiry led by retired judge Thomas Braidwood concluded that the taser use was unjustified and that the officers misrepresented their actions. However, while the RCMP made a public apology and the victim's mother received financial compensation, it is not clear that inappropriate use of tasers by police forces has changed.

TRANSPARENCY   For the accountability of government to be meaningful, government must be as *transparent* (open) as possible. Governments have a strong tendency to withhold information that may reflect negatively on them. However, hiding information can hinder governments from making use of constructive criticism to correct their mistakes and better their performance. Transparency facilitates informed public participation in politics. Access to information (also known as freedom of information) legislation, backed up by the ability of the courts or an independent body to require that information be released in a timely manner, is important in making transparency more than mere rhetoric. Although some limits on transparency are needed to protect national security, individual privacy, ongoing negotiations, and the functioning of cabinet, governments often go far beyond justifiable limits.

RESPONSIVENESS   Governments should be *responsive* to the needs and wishes of the people they govern. Governments can easily lose touch with ordinary people, and elections every few years may not be enough to ensure responsiveness. Governments do frequently use public opinion polls, although, on occasion, it is more to craft messages for electoral advantage than to respond to public opinion and concerns. Opposition parties are quick to exploit opportunities to raise awareness of the problems people face. However, sometimes they (and the media) focus on trivial issues (e.g., criticizing a cabinet minister for using her expense account to buy a $16 glass of orange juice). Governments are often reluctant to act on issues raised by opposition parties or to consider alternative policy ideas they present.

Does good governing simply entail doing what the majority of people want the government to do? In a liberal democracy, the wishes of the majority need to be balanced by protections for the rights of minorities and individuals. Furthermore, some people expect government to provide leadership, which may involve creating a vision for the country. This may involve trying to convince people that a certain course of action will, in the long run, achieve important, widely shared values.

PARTICIPATION AND INCLUSIVENESS   The informed *participation* of the public, including groups that represent all sectors of society, helps those in governing positions to grasp and be responsive to the needs, wishes, and perspectives of those being governed. Of particular importance is participation by marginalized groups in society whose views and interests are often ignored because of their limited power and organizational capabilities. Ideally, public participation should be meaningful, with government and legislators taking the views of the public seriously. Likewise, the *inclusiveness* within governing, legislative, judicial, and administrative institutions of diverse elements of society allows different voices with contrasting needs and values to be taken into account. Developing a broad consensus based on participation and inclusiveness helps to shore up the legitimacy of the state and its governing institutions among all elements of society.

ANALYZING POLITICS

In analyzing politics, it is useful to examine the:

- contending interests that seek to benefit by influencing what government does;
- major political ideas and perspectives;
- extent to which people identify themselves with different groups and political communities;
- development and characteristics of political and governmental institutions; and
- external and global influences on the country.

As well, it is important to understand the historic, economic, and social context of politics. Of particular importance in affecting the decisions of governments is the relative capability of various groups, individuals, and institutions to exert power effectively (see Box 1-2: Dam Politics).

BOX 1-2

Dam Politics

Across northern Canada, many recent and potential hydroelectric projects hold the promise of relatively clean energy. Amid concerns about pollution and global climate change caused by the burning of fossil fuels, building dams seems to be an ideal solution for sourcing clean power. However, many large-scale hydro projects have come under criticism. Large concrete dams often flood forests that store carbon dioxide, and the decaying, submerged forests and other vegetation eventually releases methane, a highly potent greenhouse gas. The building of transmission lines that run thousands of kilometres results in a significant removal of forest while potentially harming migratory animals. Furthermore, dams may cause a buildup of poisonous mercury in rivers, which can have serious effects on fish and human health.

Among the interests concerned with promoting dams that can cost billions of dollars are major construction companies, unions representing building trades, and corporations (such as aluminum producers) that require large amounts of inexpensive energy. Those opposing dam construction are typically environmental and conservation groups, wilderness outfitters, hikers, and trappers. Aboriginals, who may be displaced from their traditional land and find their traditional way of life harmed, often view damming a river as a threat to their livelihood, identity, and spiritual values. There is also often conflict between those who primarily value economic growth and development and those who place a higher value on preserving the natural environment.

Governments are often advocates of these "megaprojects," which they see as opportunities to create jobs and stimulate economic growth. Likewise, the Crown (government-owned) corporations responsible for energy production and distribution are often forceful advocates of dam building. In the past, Aboriginal peoples were often ignored when power projects were developed that flooded their traditional territories. However, the Supreme Court of Canada has ruled that Canadian and provincial governments have a "duty to consult" Aboriginal peoples when proposing developments on lands where they have rights or land claims. This can lead to lengthy and difficult negotiations.

As well, if the dam or the transmission lines affect other provinces, it may be difficult to reach agreements between provincial governments. For example, the construction of the Churchill Falls Generating Station dam in Labrador has resulted in many decades of intense and bitter tensions and lawsuits between the government of Newfoundland and Labrador and the government of Quebec, because Quebec gained the vast majority of the financial benefits of the electricity generated that passes through its territory. Finally, there may be some foreign influence, particularly if energy needs to be sold to the United States to make the projects economically viable. For example, the Cree in Quebec sought support for their campaign against dams by asking various state governments in the United States to refuse to buy power from northern Quebec until their demands were met.

Although there are complex economic, financial, engineering, and environmental considerations involved in decisions to build dams, there are also important political considerations that may involve different interests, ideas, identities, institutions, and external influences.

© Locke, Greg

Interests

A classic definition of politics is "who gets what, when, how" (Lasswell, 1935). In this view, politics is basically a struggle among contending groups and individuals to promote their own interests, particularly in terms of how the benefits and costs of government policies are distributed. For example, poorer people will likely seek government programs that provide free health care and education as well as insurance against unemployment, disability, and old age. Business owners and corporate executives, on the other hand, will typically seek to have lower taxes, fewer business regulations, and fewer costly government-funded social services.

Ideas

The ideas, values, and beliefs that people (including both the public and those in governing positions) hold often affect how they act in political life. For example, discussions of Senate reform (or abolition) are often framed in terms of which proposal is most likely to improve the quality of Canadian democracy.

In addition, as discussed in Chapter 5, the political ideologies of liberalism, conservatism, and democratic socialism (and variations of each of these classic ideologies) have influenced the way Canadians think about government and politics and the policies governments should adopt. In recent decades, the perspectives of feminism and environmentalism have also influenced politics in Canada. To some extent, the politically relevant values and beliefs that people hold relate to their position in society and the economy. It is not surprising, for example, that workers are more likely to favour a stronger role for government in providing various social benefits, while business managers and entrepreneurs generally are more likely to favour a smaller role for government in regulating the economy. Nevertheless, political ideas are not simply a product of interests. For example, some workers have the same free market perspective as corporate executives, and a few multimillionaires favour higher taxes for the rich.

Different religious perspectives also have a substantial effect on political views. The majority of Canadians tend to view laws and public policies as separate from religious doctrine. Nevertheless, religious beliefs affect the way many people think about political issues. For example, the social gospel (associated with the Methodists and other religious groups in the late nineteenth and early twentieth centuries) promoted the idea of social justice and advocated for various policies to aid the disadvantaged. Although the social gospel movement faded away many decades ago, it helped to lay the foundation for the acceptance of a variety of social policies and the continued engagement of many religious groups in the pursuit of social justice at home and abroad.

Identities

An individual's identity refers to that person's perception of his or her characteristics and sense of belonging to a particular group, culture, or political community.

Many of those who voted for Quebec sovereignty in the 1995 referendum had a strong sense of Québécois identity. This typically included a strong attachment to, and identification with, the language and culture of French Quebec as well as sharing the common ethnicity (ancestry) as the majority of Quebecers. Similarly, the identity of Aboriginal peoples as members of a First Nation, Métis Nation, or Inuit group has stimulated their struggle for recognition of their right to self-government and self-determination.

Identities are based not only on ethnicity and culture, but also on geography and history. Many Canadians have a strong sense of provincial identity (and, in some cases, an identity from an area within a province, such as Cape Breton) based on a sense of place and, to varying extents, cultural and ethnic differences. This is often combined with a sense that their province has not been well treated by the policies of the Canadian government and a feeling that their province or region has been dominated or ignored by other parts of the country. In addition, many Canadians have a sense of identification with their religion, social class, gender, and country of birth or ancestry as well as being proud to be Canadian.

Identities do not necessarily determine one's beliefs and political actions. For example, many people with a Roman Catholic identity do not agree with their church's positions on contraception, abortion, or euthanasia. Neither will they necessarily prefer to vote for a Catholic candidate in an election. Furthermore, most Canadians have multiple identities, including both a provincial and a Canadian sense of identification, as well as an identification with one or more ethnic groups. In addition, the nature and relevance of different identities can change over time. For example, in the past many people of French ancestry in Quebec identified themselves primarily as Catholic French Canadians. This has changed to a Québécois identity, with language replacing religion as the major basis of identification for many Quebecers. The significance of Aboriginal identities has increased in recent years, as many Canadians now take pride in their Aboriginal ancestry whether or not they are recognized members of an Aboriginal group.

Identity politics has become increasingly important. Groups that view themselves as oppressed by government or by dominant groups in society have sought recognition of their distinctiveness. As well, they have sought changes in society and government policy to overcome the injustices they face. Among the groups involved in identity politics in Canada are women; those with a gay, lesbian, bisexual, or transgender sexual orientation; Aboriginal peoples; and various racial and ethnic minorities. Identity politics tends to differ from interest politics in its focus on culture, respect, and group equality.

As discussed in Chapter 3, the importance of Canadian diversity is particularly evident when we examine national identity. People often use the term "nation" to refer to the country and its citizens as a whole (as, for example, "national government," "national flag," and "national anthem"). However, a nation can also be thought of as a group of people who have a strong sense of common identity based on some shared characteristics and history and a belief that they should be self-governing within their homeland (Suny, 2006). Although the majority of people living in Canada view Canada as their nation, this is not the case for many Quebecers and Aboriginal peoples. Those who identify themselves primarily as Québécois or as a member of a particular First Nation may think of Canadian democracy more in terms of equality between nations and the right to govern their own nation than in terms of equality among all individual Canadian citizens.

Institutions

A variety of political institutions (such as political parties, interest groups, and the media) affect the ways in which people are mobilized to try to exert influence on those in governing positions. Political parties have very gradually become somewhat more democratic in their organizational structure (particularly in their processes for leadership selection) and in the diverse characteristics of their members. In recent decades, there has been a proliferation of groups that promote the interests and causes of large numbers of citizens. For example, many groups have been established to promote environmental protection, civil rights, the equality of women, and gay and lesbian rights. These and many other politically active groups have helped to move Canada in a more democratic direction and brought greater political attention to the diversity of the country and the problems faced by various segments of society.

A wide variety of governing institutions are involved in making and implementing policies and laws. For example, as will be discussed in Chapter 12, Canada's federal system divides and shares power between the Canadian and provincial governments, which has a major effect on what governments do. Reaching agreement among these governments, which often have different interests and perspectives, has often proven difficult. Furthermore, laws passed by Parliament and provincial legislatures as well as actions taken by the executive (prime minister or premier and their cabinets) can be invalidated by the courts if deemed to be in violation of the Constitution. For example, Canada's abortion law was struck down by the Supreme Court of Canada as it was deemed to be a violation of the constitutional Charter of Rights and Freedoms (see Chapter 10). In addition, there are a variety of agencies (e.g., the Bank of Canada, the Canadian Radio-television and Telecommunications Commission, and the RCMP) that have been established by government but operate with a considerable degree of independence. Even within the governmental organizations that are directly controlled by the prime minister and cabinet, there are often different goals pursued by different departments.

Thus, different institutions, each with its own history, goals, values, interests, and operating procedures, are involved in the processes of raising issues, mobilizing the public, and making and implementing governing decisions. In turn, these institutions will often attempt to influence the public. Although institutions tend to be long-lasting, the desire of many Canadians for greater democracy and the challenges posed by Canada's diversity have affected, to varying degrees, the development and evolution of Canada's political and governmental institutions.

External Influences

Finally, we cannot understand Canadian politics and government simply by examining what goes on within Canada, as this country and its people have always been strongly influenced by external forces and cultures. Canada developed from a colony to a sovereign country over a lengthy period of time, and its governing institutions continue, in many respects, to reflect their British heritage, modified by the adoption of a federal system. Canada's geographical closeness and economic and cultural ties to the United States have great importance for Canadian politics and government. As well, a large and growing number of international organizations, treaties, and laws influence how Canadian governments act. For example, the North American Free Trade Agreement (discussed in Chapter 4) has major implications for Canada's economic policies, as does Canada's participation in the global economic system. Membership in the North Atlantic Treaty Organization (NATO) affected Canada's decision to participate in military actions in Yugoslavia, Afghanistan, and Libya (see Chapter 18).

Summary and Conclusion

Politics involves controversy and conflict because of the different interests, ideas, and identities that exist within any political community. Controversy and conflict also result from the competition to exercise political power. The distribution of power is important in determining what decisions are made.

The Canadian political system can be classified as basically a liberal representative democracy. Voters elect representatives to make decisions on their behalf, and people are free to express their concerns, organize for political action, and try to influence the decisions of

government. Clearly, each Canadian citizen has some potential political power through the ability to cast a vote in elections. Yet questions arise as to whether some powerful groups are in a strong position to influence government for their own advantage. Some people favour a fuller realization of the democratic ideal of rule by the people through greater involvement by all members of the public in political debate and decision making, as well as through greater social and economic equality.

Canadian politics is strongly affected by the diversity of the country, particularly the different ethnic, cultural, and linguistic communities and the distinctive provincial societies. This diversity has meant that many Canadians do not have an overriding or exclusive Canadian political identity. Treating all Canadians similarly, as equal citizens, is but one perspective in Canada; controversy has arisen over whether distinctive groups or distinctive provinces should enjoy different statuses, powers, and laws to protect and develop their own identities and cultures.

Good government requires governing institutions and policymaking processes that are directed to achieving the public interest of the political community. Ensuring that governments are accountable for their actions, transparent, and responsive to the needs and aspirations of all people by facilitating public participation is important in trying to achieve good government.

The policies and actions of governments are a product of a complex set of factors. The conflicting interests of different elements of society—the different ideas, perspectives, and identities that people have; the workings and interactions of a variety of political and governmental institutions; and external influences on Canada—are all significant. Of particular importance is the distribution of power and how effectively those with greater potential power use it to achieve particular objectives.

Discussion Questions

1. How should decisions be made about controversial issues such as hydraulic fracturing ("fracking")?

2. Should a province have the right to secede from Canada if a majority of its population votes in favour of secession?

3. Do you think that political power is widely dispersed or highly concentrated in Canada?

4. Should the Canadian government try to promote a common set of values and a common national identity?

5. Should Canada move in the direction of greater democracy? If so, how might this be achieved?

CHAPTER 2

The Historical Context

CHAPTER OBJECTIVES

After reading this chapter, you should be able to

1. Outline the key political events in Canada prior to Confederation.
2. Explain the significance of responsible government.
3. Discuss the reasons for Confederation.
4. Examine the opposition to Confederation.
5. Discuss the major challenges faced by Canada since 1867.

Delegates from the legislatures of Canada, New Brunswick, Nova Scotia, and Prince Edward Island pose for a photo during the September 1864 convention in Charlottetown at which it was agreed to consider the union of the British North American colonies.

© Library and Archives Canada

On July 1, 1867, many flags were flown at half-mast in Nova Scotia. Buildings were draped in black crepe. Premier Charles Tupper was burned in effigy alongside a rat. A newspaper described "young and fair Nova Scotia" being forced into an "unhappy union" by "an old, crabbed and almost bankrupt" Canadian suitor, while her numerous friends "intend shortly to take prompt and decided steps to procure a divorce" (quoted in "Married," 1867/2005).

Although Ontarians greeted the formation of Canada in 1867 with enthusiasm, this was not the case in other parts of the new country, particularly in Nova Scotia and New Brunswick. The Nova Scotia government agreed to join Canada against the wishes of the majority of its population. In the first Canadian election, the Anti-Confederates, advocating seceding from Canada, won 18 of Nova Scotia's 19 seats in the Canadian Parliament. Likewise, in November 1867, Anti-Confederates won 36 of the 38 seats in the Nova Scotia legislature. Thirty-one thousand Nova Scotians signed a petition in favour of separation (almost as many as voted in the 1867 election), and in 1868 the Nova Scotia legislature passed a motion to secede from Canada. The British government refused to accept this request. Bowing to the inevitable, Joseph Howe, leader of the Anti-Confederates, accepted a position in the Canadian cabinet after having been given a promise of "better terms" for Nova Scotia by Sir John A. Macdonald, Canada's first prime minister.

In neighbouring New Brunswick, there was also considerable opposition to Confederation. In 1865, the government of Samuel Tilley, which supported joining Canada, was defeated by the Anti-Confederates, who claimed that Tilley had sold the province for 80 cents a person—the customs revenues the province would receive for joining Canada (Morton, 2006). However, the British government was determined to persuade New Brunswick to join Canada.

The British-appointed governor forced an election in 1866 to oust Premier Albert J. Smith, who opposed the terms of Confederation, and Tilley's pro-Confederation party was returned to power. A raid on New Brunswick by the Fenians (Irish Americans opposed to British rule in Ireland) helped to convince many New Brunswickers that union with Canada was necessary for their security, as the British government claimed that it was unwilling to continue to provide military protection indefinitely (Conrad & Finkel, 2007).

In Quebec, there was also significant opposition to Confederation. However, the defeat of the Rebellion of 1837–1838 had resulted in political apathy and passivity among much of the population. With the powerful Catholic Church preaching that legitimate authority had to be obeyed, the Conservative Bleus who supported Confederation decisively beat the anti-Confederate Rouges in the first Canadian election. Nevertheless, except among the English-speaking business community in Montreal, there was not much enthusiasm for the new country.

Now a country of more than 35 million people, Canada has successfully developed a stable and peaceful political system despite its precarious start in 1867. Of course, survival over a period of nearly a century and a half does not guarantee a smooth path for the future. Indeed, some of the tensions that Canada struggled with in the past are reflected in the political challenges of the present.

INTRODUCTION

Canada today is very different from how it was in the distant past. However, Canada's historical political development has been in the form of evolutionary rather than revolutionary change. The development of responsible government (the basis of the parliamentary system) in the 1840s and the Constitution Act, 1867, continue to have relevance to contemporary politics and government. In addition, historic events, achievements, and grievances continue to affect how people act politically. For example, the history of oppression of Aboriginal peoples and broken treaty promises are important in understanding the difficulties in achieving reconciliation with the rest of Canada. The battle on the Plains of Abraham (1759), the Durham Report (1839), the hanging of Louis Riel (1885), the conscription crisis (1917), and Bill 101 (1977) are of lasting significance for French–English relations in Canada. Thus, the historical context is an important aspect of understanding contemporary Canadian politics.

EARLY SETTLEMENT AND HISTORY

Canada was first settled more than 10 000 years ago by the ancestors of contemporary First Nations (misleadingly called "Indians" by European explorers) who crossed from Asia. About 1000 years ago, the ancestors of the Inuit spread from western Alaska to the Canadian Arctic. Aboriginal groups developed a variety of different languages and cultures. While some had hunter–gatherer economies, others established settled communities based on agriculture and fishing and developed intricate cultures and governing systems prior to European settlement.

European settlement began in the seventeenth century. The colony of New France developed along the St. Lawrence River, and the smaller French colony of Acadia was established in what are now the Maritime provinces. Britain set up colonies in what is now the Atlantic region of the United States. There were also small British and French colonies in Newfoundland. The Hudson's Bay Company, which was granted a British royal charter in 1670 covering the vast territory known as Rupert's Land, had a few trading posts in the North. Native (indigenous) peoples provided knowledge that helped the first Europeans survive in the harsh climate. Many French males were involved in the fur trade and spent part of their time living in Native communities. This resulted in a substantial population of people of mixed French and Native heritage known as the Métis.

Britain and France vied for control over Canada. By the Treaty of Utrecht (1713), France ceded control of mainland Nova Scotia, Newfoundland, and lands surrounding Hudson Bay to Great Britain. Conflicts persisted in the Maritimes with many Acadians and their Native allies resisting British rule. The final British conquest of Acadia began in 1755, with Britain eventually deporting about four-fifths of the French-speaking Acadians from the region to the American colonies, France, and Britain. During the subsequent global Seven Years' War[1] between Britain and France and their European allies, the British army captured Quebec City, the capital of New France, in the Battle of the Plains of Abraham in 1759. By the Treaty of Paris (1763), New France and Acadia were ceded to Britain.[2]

After British Conquest

THE FATE OF THE "INDIANS" AND THE FRENCH   The **Royal Proclamation, 1763,** established British rule over the former French colonies. It placed "Indians" under the protection of the British Crown, stated that they were to be left undisturbed, established their exclusive hunting rights over a vast territory, and provided that their lands could not be sold without the approval of authorized representatives of the monarch. The Royal Proclamation is often cited as providing recognition of Aboriginal rights, including the ownership of lands they inhabited. However, its protection of Aboriginal peoples from the inroads of settlers was often not enforced by the colonial governments (Dickason, 2009).

ROYAL PROCLAMATION, 1763
Established British rule over the former French colonies and placed "Indians" under the protection of the British Crown.

---

[1] The nine-year conflict in North America is referred to in the United States as the French and Indian War.
[2] France retained the islands of St. Pierre and Miquelon off the south coast of Newfoundland and, until 1904, had fishing rights along the "French Shore" of Newfoundland.

Britain hoped that settlers from the American colonies and from Britain would turn Quebec into a colony composed largely of people of British ancestry. However, Quebec remained primarily French-speaking and Catholic, with the exception of several hundred American merchants who followed in the wake of the British conquest. Thus, although the British legal system was introduced, in practice the British governors recognized the need to be conciliatory to the leaders of the French-speaking Catholic population and left most laws and practices from the French regime intact. The **Quebec Act, 1774,** passed by the British Parliament, formalized this arrangement with guarantees that Catholics would be able to freely practise their religion, the privileges of the Catholic Church would be maintained, and the French system of civil (private) law would be used alongside British criminal law.

QUEBEC ACT, 1774 An act of the British Parliament that guaranteed that Catholics would be able to freely practise their religion, the privileges of the Catholic Church would be maintained, and the French system of civil (private) law would be used alongside British criminal law.

AN INFLUX OF IMMIGRANTS   Support in Quebec and the other northern colonies for the American War of Independence (1775–1783) was limited, and an American invasion of Quebec in 1775–1776 was eventually repulsed by the British army. The success of the American revolutionaries in gaining independence from Britain resulted in many Americans who had remained loyal to the British Crown (the **Loyalists**), those who had fought in the British army, and Indians who had fought against the Americans seeking refuge in the British North American colonies. The British authorities provided land and subsidies for the Loyalists and former soldiers to settle in the colonies of Nova Scotia (particularly in the area that later became New Brunswick) and Quebec (including what is now southern and eastern Ontario).

LOYALISTS Americans who remained loyal to the British Crown at the time of the War of Independence. Subsequently, many Loyalists migrated to the British North American colonies.

The newcomers to British North America not only added to the population of the colonies but also gave it a somewhat greater diversity. Among the Loyalists and former soldiers were significant numbers of Scots, Germans, and people of other nationalities. Many of the new settlers came from a variety of Protestant groups. As well, a sizable number of black Americans settled in Nova Scotia, although discriminatory treatment by that colony soon resulted in about one-half leaving for Sierra Leone. In addition, the Iroquois and some other Indian nations that had fought against the Americans were resettled in what is now southern Ontario. The settlement of refugees from the United States was followed in subsequent decades by a substantial number of Americans who sought to take advantage of the available land in British North America.

The influx of new settlers led to important changes in the politics of the British North American colonies. In response to Loyalist demands, New Brunswick was separated from Nova Scotia in 1784. The settlement of a large number of English speakers created problems for the colony of Quebec. In particular, the settlers expected to be governed by British laws and to have an elected representative assembly as had been established in the other British North American colonies (except Newfoundland, which did not have an assembly until 1832). To some extent this was resolved when the British Parliament passed the **Constitutional Act, 1791,** dividing Quebec into two

CONSTITUTIONAL ACT, 1791 An act that divided Quebec into two separate colonies: Upper Canada and Lower Canada.

colonies: Upper Canada (the forerunner of Ontario) and Lower Canada (Quebec), with each having its own elected representative assembly.

THE WAR OF 1812   In 1812, the United States declared war on Britain. This was a result of the British blockade of European ports during the Napoleonic Wars that cut off American trade with Europe, and the actions of the British navy in boarding American ships in international waters. As well, Americans were angered by British support for the Indian Nations in the territories that Britain had ceded to the United States at the end of the War of Independence. Some members of the U.S. Congress in areas bordering British North America wanted to annex the British colonies (Bumsted, 2003). British soldiers, regiments and militias from the British North American colonies, and First Nations warriors successfully resisted the American invasions into Canada. The War of 1812 ended in 1814 without a clear victory for either side. Nevertheless, it has been argued that the success in defending Canada against invasion by much larger American forces contributed to the development of a Canadian identity and sense of patriotism (Taylor, 2010). Subsequent large-scale immigration to Canada from the British Isles in the nineteenth century contributed to the country's English, Irish, Scottish, and Welsh character, although many immigrants subsequently left Canada to pursue economic opportunities in the United States.

Rebellions

Despite having elected assemblies, the British North American colonies were far from democratic. The British governors of the colonies were expected to follow the orders of the British government. In turn, the governor appointed powerful local elites as members of the Legislative Council (which had the right to reject any legislation proposed by the elected Assembly) and the Executive Council responsible for administration. Democratic reform movements developed to challenge the powers of the elites that dominated the colonies. In particular, they demanded greater power for the elected Assembly. Ultimately this led to rebellions in both Canadian colonies in 1837. The rebellion in Upper Canada was small, lacked broad support, and was quickly suppressed. The rebellion in Lower Canada was more serious, as it not only involved a struggle for greater democracy but also reflected tensions between the English-speaking minority who controlled most of the economic and political power in the colony and the French Canadian majority who had come to dominate the Quebec Assembly. Nevertheless, after a few bloody clashes, the rebellion in Lower Canada was quashed in 1838.

The Durham Report, Unification, and Responsible Government

As a result of the rebellions, the British government sent Lord Durham to investigate the causes of the conflicts in the Canadian colonies. His report was telling: "I expected to find a contest between a government and a

Report of Lord Durham
http://faculty.marianopolis.edu/c.belanger/quebechistory/docs/durham/

people. I found two nations warring in the bosom of a single state." To end "the deadly animosity that now separates the inhabitants of Lower Canada into the hostile divisions of French and English," he recommended that Upper and Lower Canada be reunited (quoted in Bumsted, 2003, p. 349). This, he hoped, would lead to the gradual assimilation of the French-speaking population and their acceptance of "superior" English values. In addition, the **Durham Report, 1839** (*Report on the Affairs of British North America*) recommended that a more democratic system, known as **responsible government**, be adopted. In a system of responsible government, the executive (cabinet) is responsible to an elected, representative legislative body and can only remain in office as long as it maintains the support of a majority of that body.

Based on Durham's recommendation, the British Parliament passed the **Act of Union, 1840**, creating the United Province of Canada. Each of the two parts, called "Canada East" (Quebec) and "Canada West" (Ontario), was awarded equal representation in the Province of Canada's elected Legislative Assembly (despite the larger population of Canada East at the time). English was made the language of the Assembly, although later the right to use French in the Assembly was added. This recognition of two official languages was a significant feature in the subsequent Confederation agreement.

With Canada East and Canada West each electing half of the Assembly, power was shared between the English and the French. Joint leaders—an English-speaking politician from Canada West and a French-speaking politician from Canada East—headed the government. As well, although Canada East and Canada West had no separate governing structures, ministers from each part were responsible for matters within their half of Canada. Indeed, Canada East and Canada West continued to have different legal and educational systems. Furthermore, the practice developed that laws were expected to be passed by a "double majority"—that is, by majorities of representatives in each of the two regions. Thus, the governance of the Union reflected, to a considerable extent, the distinctiveness of its two components.

Durham's recommendation concerning responsible government did not come into effect with the Act of Union. The British governor was not prepared to surrender his power. He continued to reject bills (proposed legislation) passed by the Legislative Assembly, interfered in elections to the Assembly, and decided upon appointments to the Executive Council. This caused tension with the Reformers in the elected Assembly who pressed for the adoption of responsible government. The principle of responsible government was accepted in Nova Scotia in 1848 after a vigorous campaign by Joseph Howe and shortly thereafter in New Brunswick (1848) and the Province of Canada (see Box 2-1: The Struggle for Responsible Government in Canada). A few years later, responsible government was adopted in Prince Edward Island (1851) and Newfoundland (1858).

DURHAM REPORT, 1839
A report by the British governor Lord Durham that recommended the union of Upper and Lower Canada and the adoption of responsible government.

RESPONSIBLE GOVERNMENT
A governing system in which the executive is responsible to an elected, representative legislative body and must retain its support to remain in office.

ACT OF UNION, 1840
An act that united Upper and Lower Canada, creating the United Province of Canada.

The Struggle for Responsible Government in Canada

Governor General Lord Elgin is often associated with the struggle for responsible government in Canada. In 1848, Lord Elgin, on instructions from the British government, appointed a cabinet nominated by the majority grouping of Reformers in the Legislative Assembly, which was led by Robert Baldwin and Sir Louis-Hippolyte Lafontaine. Both men were key advocates of responsible government.

In 1849, the principle of responsible government was tested and then confirmed when Lord Elgin did not veto the highly controversial Rebellion Losses Bill that had been passed by the Legislative Assembly and the Legislative Council. The objective of the bill was to compensate those individuals, including most of the rebels, who had suffered property losses in the 1837–1838 Rebellion in Lower Canada. The "Tories" (conservatives), supported by many prominent members of the English-speaking community in Lower Canada, demanded that Lord Elgin refuse to give royal assent. Although Lord Elgin had his misgivings about the bill, he did not yield to their demands; royal assent was granted.

Infuriated by the decision, a crowd of English Montrealers pelted Lord Elgin's carriage with rotten eggs and burned down the Parliament buildings in Montreal. Some English Montreal merchants, already dismayed by the lack of a free trade agreement with the United States, circulated a petition demanding the annexation of Canada to the United States. Curiously, they found some support among radical French Canadians who believed they, too, would be better treated by their neighbour to the south (Gillmor & Turgeon, 2000).

After the burning of the Montreal Parliament buildings, later sessions of the Legislative Assembly had to be held in Toronto and Quebec City. The final session in 1866 was held in Ottawa, the new capital of Canada.

Despite the controversy over the Rebellion Losses Bill, the principle of responsible government became the cornerstone of the governing system in Canada—one that has survived into the twenty-first century.

The shared governing of the Province of Canada brought a number of successes, including involvement in negotiating a partial free trade treaty (Reciprocity Treaty, 1854) with the United States, reform of the school system in Canada West, modernization of the land tenure system in Canada East, and the building of a railway system. Less satisfactorily, the shifting coalitions of political factions meant frequent changes of government, and the need for a "double majority" often led to a stalemate that made legislative decisions difficult to achieve.

Differences between Canada West and Canada East were heightened as the population of Canada West surpassed that of Canada East. The Clear Grits, a radical reform movement in Canada West, demanded representation by population rather than the equal representation of West and East. In addition, reflecting their evangelical Protestant beliefs, the Clear Grits favoured the separation of church and state and opposed the privileges granted to the Anglican Church. Furthermore, they tended to express negative views about French Canadians (Bumsted, 2003).

Figure 2-1 shows a timeline depicting some of the important events in Canada's political history before Confederation.

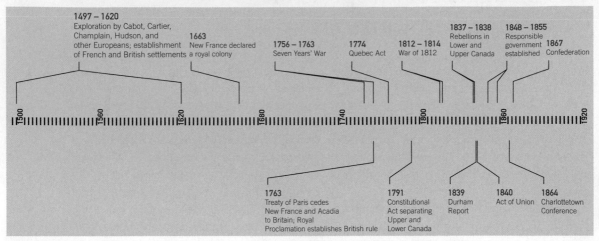

FIGURE 2-1
TIMELINE: KEY HISTORICAL
EVENTS TO 1867

CONFEDERATION

The political problems of governing the colony of Canada encouraged some, particularly in Canada West, to look to a larger union to avoid the political problems of the Province of Canada. The uniting of the British North American colonies was also seen as economically advantageous, as it would create a larger domestic market by financing a railway link between the Maritimes and central Canada. This became particularly important when the United States, a key market for Canadian exports, cancelled the Reciprocity Treaty that had allowed unprocessed goods to trade freely without customs duties between British North America and the United States.

A larger union was also seen as facilitating the opening up of the West to settlement and mitigating security concerns that included the potential for the large army mobilized in the American Civil War to be turned against Canada. Threats also came from the Fenians, an Irish-American group that conducted raids on the colonies as part of their nationalist campaign to free Ireland from British rule. A union of the British North American colonies was seen as a way to allow the colonies to better defend themselves against potential American invasion.

The idea of uniting the British North American colonies had been talked about for a long time and was supported by the British government. However, it took a proposal by George Brown, leader of the Reformers, to get the process under way. Brown suggested forming a "Grand Coalition" with the Conservatives, led by John A. Macdonald, and the Bleus, the major political grouping in Canada East, led by George-Étienne Cartier. From the start, the politicians put forward different models for the union. Macdonald preferred a legislative union (i.e., a single legislature) rather than a federal union (one in which each province would have its own legislature in addition to the Canadian Parliament). In Macdonald's view, the American Civil War showed that its federal system had failed because each state had sovereign powers. However, Macdonald realized that a legislative union would not gain the support of Quebec and the Maritime colonies, and thus he looked to the establishment of a strong Parliament having all of the major legislative powers needed to develop a great nation while provincial legislatures dealt with local matters (LaSelva, 1996). His ally Cartier had a somewhat different view. He believed that maintaining ethnic and religious diversity would benefit the new country. Canadians would create a "political nationality," rather than one based on a particular ancestry or religion. A federal system in which provincial governments had substantial powers, along with protection for minority rights, was, in Cartier's view, essential for the formation of Canada (LaSelva, 2009).

In September 1864, delegates from Canada attended a conference of Maritime leaders who had planned to discuss uniting the Maritime colonies. The Canadian delegation was able to convince the Maritime leaders at this **Charlottetown Conference, 1864** to put aside the idea of a regional union in favour of discussing a broader union of all the British North American colonies. A month later at a closed-door conference in Quebec City, 72 resolutions were adopted "to establish a federal union under the Crown of Great Britain, provided such union can be effected on principles just to the several provinces" (quoted in McNaught, 1969). The delegations from Prince Edward Island and Newfoundland, however, did not think that the terms of union provided them with sufficient benefits. After further discussion in London, England (1866), by delegates from Canada, Nova Scotia, and New Brunswick, the British Parliament passed the **British North America Act, 1867**, based on the resolutions of the colonial leaders. This established what was then called the Dominion of Canada (see Figure 2-2).

CHARLOTTETOWN CONFERENCE, 1864 A meeting of the leaders of Canada and the Maritimes at which it was decided to hold further discussions about uniting the British North American colonies.

BRITISH NORTH AMERICA ACT, 1867 An act of the Parliament of the United Kingdom establishing the Dominion of Canada. In 1982 it was renamed the Constitution Act, 1867.

FIGURE 2-2
CANADA IN 1867

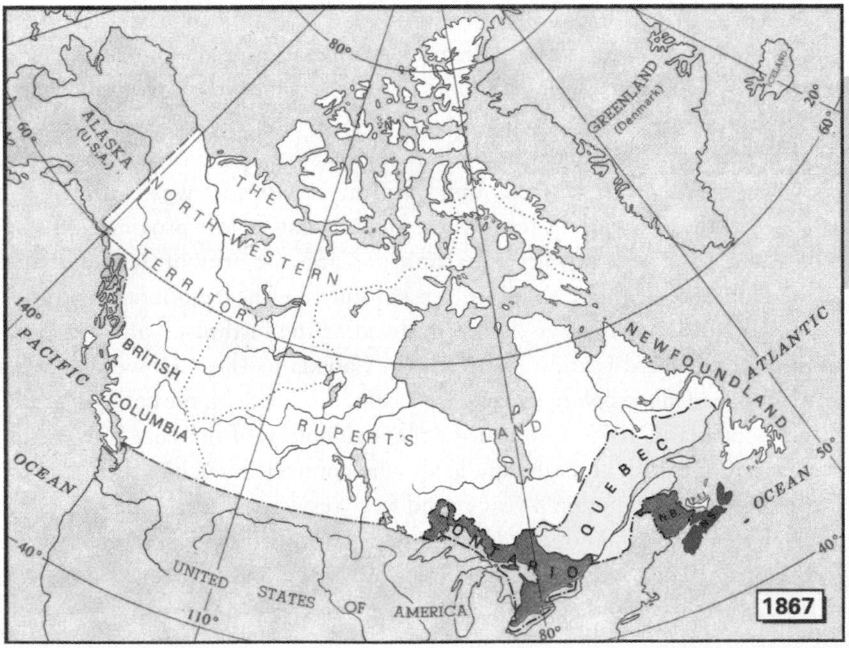

New Brunswick, Nova Scotia, and Canada are united in a federal state, the Dominion of Canada, by the British North America Act (July 1, 1867). The province of Canada is divided into Ontario and Quebec. The United States proclaims the purchase of Alaska from Russia (June 20).

SOURCE: "Territorial Evolution of Canada, 1867," *Atlas of Canada, Map Archives History, 1639 to 1949 Territorial Evolution of Canada (1667 to 1949).* © Department of Natural Resources Canada. All rights reserved. http://atlas.nrcan.gc.ca/site/english/maps/archives/historical/mcr_2306

Opposition

The union of the British North American colonies did not enjoy widespread popularity. As discussed in the opening vignette, the majority of the public in Nova Scotia opposed the union, and considerable opposition surfaced among French Quebecers as well. For Maritimers, the fear was domination by Canada, meaning Ontario and Quebec, and loss of their own identities. For French Quebecers, the worry was that their culture, language, and religion would be threatened by their minority status in the newly expanded Canada. As for Canada's first inhabitants, the Aboriginal peoples of British North America were neither consulted nor considered in the establishment of the new country.

EXPANSION OF CANADA

From this contentious beginning, Canada grew over time "from sea to sea to sea." In 1868, to expand westward and northward, the Canadian government negotiated an agreement to purchase Rupert's Land (the large Hudson Bay drainage area) and the North-Western Territory from the Hudson's Bay Company.[3] The residents and governing council of the Red River settlement (in what is now southern Manitoba) were not consulted about this annexation. A Métis rebellion led by Louis Riel forced the Canadian government in 1870 to agree to the establishment of the Manitoba provincial government initially in the area around the Red River Valley (see Box 2-2: The Métis Rise Up: Louis Riel and the Rebellion of 1869–1870).

In 1871, British Columbia (which had been created by a merger of the colonies of Vancouver Island and British Columbia in 1866) became a Canadian province. Opposition to joining Canada was overcome when favourable terms were negotiated; these included a large subsidy and the assumption of the impoverished colony's debts, as well as the promise of a railway to link the province with the rest of the country within 15 years (it was completed in 1885), and the adoption of responsible government for the province. As elsewhere, the Aboriginal peoples who formed a large majority of the population at the time were neither considered nor consulted in the negotiations.

Although Charlottetown is often viewed as the birthplace of Confederation, Prince Edward Island refused to join Canada in 1867. However, after a costly railroad in the colony created an unsupportable debt, the colony decided to join Canada in 1873 in return for the assumption of the debt by Canada, the buyout of British absentee landlords who controlled much of the land, and a commitment to maintain a year-round ferry service to the island.

Newfoundland did not join Canada until 1949. Although acceptable terms for joining Canada were negotiated in 1869, Newfoundland voters decisively defeated their pro-Confederation government in 1869.

---

[3]These vast territories became the North-West Territories (now Northwest Territories) in 1870.

BOX 2-2

The Métis Rise Up: Louis Riel and the Rebellion of 1869–1870

French Quebecers were not the only minority who feared for their language and culture. Farther west, in the Red River Valley, lived many Métis, descendants of French fur traders and Aboriginal women. When the Métis learned that Canada planned to annex the North-Western Territories, including the Red River Valley, they began to mobilize. Above all, they wanted to prevent the loss of their land and the large-scale immigration that would threaten their language, culture, and Catholic religion.

To prepare for the formal annexation of the North-Western Territories, the Canadian government appointed William McDougall, an Ontario Member of Parliament with notoriously anti-French views, as governor-designate. The Métis banished McDougall from their settlement and formed a provisional government with Louis Riel as its president. Their goal was to negotiate with the Canadian government to create a provincial government in southern Manitoba (rather than being administered by the Canadian government as part of a territory) and to gain protection for their rights.

Opponents of the provisional government who threatened to take up arms were arrested, and Thomas Scott, convicted of insubordination, was executed by a Métis firing squad. In 1870, the Canadian government agreed to establish the provincial government of Manitoba, and a military force was sent to Manitoba to enforce Canadian authority. Fearing for his life, Louis Riel fled to the United States. He was subsequently elected three times to the House of Commons but prevented by the Canadian government from assuming his seat in Parliament. After returning to

© Glenbow Museum

Louis Riel and the members of his provisional government (1869–1870) wished to create a provincial government in southern Manitoba and to gain protection for their rights from the Canadian government.

Canada in 1885 to lead the North-West Rebellion (discussed later in this chapter), Riel was captured and tried for treason. Although the jury that convicted him recommended mercy, Riel was sentenced to be hanged. While Quebec Catholics pleaded for the prime minister to spare Riel from the noose, Ontario Protestants demanded his execution. In the end, Prime Minister Macdonald refused to commute the sentence, saying, "He shall hang though every dog in Quebec bark in his favour."

Over time, Riel has come to be seen by many Canadians as a defender of his people rather than a murderous traitor. Manitobans now have a holiday in February to celebrate Louis Riel Day, and there have been attempts to have the Canadian Parliament overturn Riel's conviction. Although Riel was hanged more than a century ago, his defence of minority rights resonates with many Canadians today.

During the Great Depression of the 1930s, the government of Newfoundland faced bankruptcy. Based on the recommendation of a royal commission, the Newfoundland legislature agreed to suspend responsible government until self-sufficiency was restored. In 1934, an appointed Commission of Government was formed with three commissioners from the United Kingdom and three from Newfoundland. In effect, Newfoundland reverted to the status of a British colony.

At the end of World War II, the British government decided that an elected national convention should consider options for the future of Newfoundland, with the people to choose between those options in a referendum. Although the Newfoundland National Convention rejected putting confederation with Canada as an option on the ballot, the British government, which favoured confederation, insisted that it be included in the referendum. On June 3, 1948, a return to responsible government (i.e., independence) received 44.6 percent of the vote, confederation with Canada 41.1 percent, and continuation of Commission of Government 14.3 percent. With no option gaining a majority, a second referendum held on July 22, 1948, resulted in 52.3 percent voting for confederation and 47.7 percent for responsible government. Negotiations with the Canadian government on the terms of union (including the assumption of the Newfoundland government's debt, subsidies, and the guarantee of steamship service to Nova Scotia) succeeded, and on March 31, 1949, Newfoundland became Canada's tenth province.[4]

The British Arctic Territories (islands in the high Arctic) were ceded to Canada in 1880 and became part of the North-West Territories. As a result of its growth during the Klondike Gold Rush, the Yukon became a separate territory in 1898. The provinces of Alberta and Saskatchewan were created out of the North-West Territories in 1905. The territory of Nunavut was separated from the Northwest Territories in 1999, reflecting the wishes of Nunavut's mainly Inuit population.

Canada has grown not only in territorial size, but also in population (see Figure 2-3). Canada's population today is almost 10 times larger than in 1867.

FIGURE 2-3
POPULATION GROWTH, 1851–2011

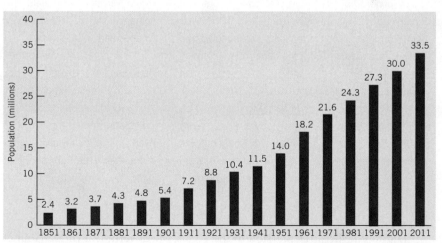

SOURCE: Based on Statistics Canada (2012). *Census of population. Population and growth components (1851–2011 Censuses)*. Retrieved from http://www.statcan.gc.ca/tables-tableaux/sumsom/l01/cst01/demo03-eng.htm

---

[4]In 2001, the province's name officially changed to Newfoundland and Labrador.

In the decades after Confederation, more people emigrated from Canada (primarily to the United States) than immigrated to Canada. However, since the beginning of the twentieth century, immigration has substantially exceeded emigration (except during the Great Depression of the 1930s). Indeed, in recent years immigration has contributed to more than one-half of Canada's total population growth.

POLITICAL INDEPENDENCE

Canada did not become a completely sovereign (independent, self-governing) country in 1867. The British government retained important controls, including the right to overturn Canadian legislation, extend British laws to Canada, and control Canada's foreign policy. The British government's involvement in Canadian affairs was not always in Canada's interests. For example, in 1903 the British representative on a tribunal to settle the dispute over the boundary between Alaska and British Columbia sided with the Americans, depriving Canada of coastline for northern British Columbia.

The major contribution of Canada to the British effort in World War I and the heavy sacrifices of Canadian soldiers helped to make the case for greater Canadian independence. Canada (along with other British dominions) signed the peace treaties that ended the war, participated in the Paris Peace Conference, and became a member of the League of Nations (the forerunner of the United Nations). In 1926, an Imperial Conference recognized Canada (along with the other dominions) as being completely self-governing and not subordinate to the United Kingdom in any aspect of domestic or external affairs. The governor general was no longer an agent of the British government, but rather a representative of the Crown. The ending of British imperial control of Canada was formalized in the **Statute of Westminster, 1931**, passed by the Parliament of the United Kingdom. Nevertheless, the Judicial Committee of the Privy Council (consisting of British law lords) continued to be the highest court of appeal for some Canadian cases until 1949. Furthermore, because of disagreements between the Canadian and provincial governments about the procedures for formal constitutional amendments, the Constitution did not come entirely under Canadian control until 1982 when the British Parliament, at the request of the Canadian Parliament, passed the Canada Act, 1982, which ensured that any future British laws did not apply to Canada.[5] The Constitution Act, 1982, technically an appendix to the Canada Act, included a number of important constitutional provisions (see Chapter 10). The Quebec government objected to constitutional changes made without its approval.

Although Canada became, in effect, independent from 1926, Canada was slow to adopt all of the symbolism of a sovereign country because of the

STATUTE OF WESTMINSTER, 1931
An act of the Parliament of the United Kingdom ending British control of Canada.

---

[5] In carrying out her formal duties related to Canada, Queen Elizabeth II acts as Queen of Canada and not as Queen of the United Kingdom.

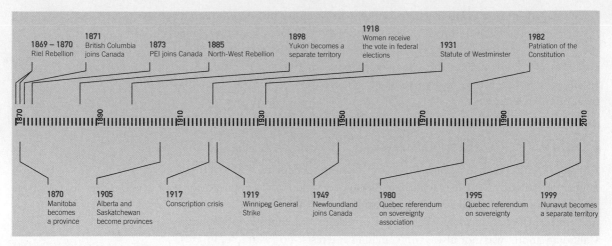

FIGURE 2-4
TIMELINE: KEY HISTORICAL
EVENTS AFTER 1867

continuing strength of emotional ties to Britain of many Canadians. Canadians remained "British subjects" until Canadian citizenship was adopted in 1947. A distinctive Canadian flag was adopted in 1965 only after considerable controversy among those who wanted to retain the British Union Jack. In 1967, "O Canada" replaced "God Save the Queen" as the national anthem (although it was not officially recognized until 1980). And, Canada continues to use the British monarch as the formal symbolic head of state. Indeed, the Conservative government led by Stephen Harper emphasized the royal connection by, for example, restoring the names "Royal Canadian Navy" and "Royal Canadian Air Force" and requiring that all Canadian embassies prominently display a portrait of Queen Elizabeth II.

Figure 2-4 shows a timeline of key Canadian historic events since Confederation in 1867.

POLITICAL ISSUES IN POST-CONFEDERATION CANADA

Regionalism

Prime Minister William Lyon Mackenzie King once said that "if some countries have too much history, we have too much geography." Given the vastness of Canada; the uneven dispersal of the population; the different economic activities of different regions; and the diverse characteristics, cultures, and identities of people that have settled in different areas, it is not surprising that regional and provincial differences have always been an important feature of Canadian politics.

THE MARITIMES   As noted in the introductory vignette, the new Dominion of Canada faced an immediate challenge from a separatist movement in Nova

Scotia. However, despite the election victories of the anti-Confederation forces in the first Nova Scotian elections, the British government refused to entertain a petition for separation. In 1886, Premier W.S. Fielding won a Nova Scotia election on a promise to lead the three Maritime provinces out of Confederation, but he did not carry out his promise.

The Maritime provinces did not fully share in the growth of the Canadian economy. The shift from cross-Atlantic trade with Britain to north–south trade with the United States placed the Maritime provinces on the periphery of the country. Furthermore, the sale of many leading Maritime businesses to central Canadians reduced Maritimers' control of their own economies and contributed to the out-migration of skilled personnel. As well, the development and expansion of Ontario and Quebec and the rapid growth of the West reduced the political influence of the Maritime provinces.

Dissatisfaction with the declining economic and political position of the Maritimes in Canada resulted in a **Maritime Rights Movement** in the 1920s, which sought better terms for the Maritimes within Canada. However, the historical differences and competing interests of the Maritime provinces made unified political action difficult. Although the Canadian government implemented some of the recommendations of the Royal Commission on Maritime Claims (1926) that was established in response to the demands of the Maritime Rights Movement, these measures were insufficient to reverse the decline of the region.

MARITIME RIGHTS MOVEMENT
A political movement in the 1920s that sought better terms for the Maritime provinces within Canada.

DISSATISFACTION IN THE WEST   Western alienation has been and continues to be a significant theme in Canadian politics. In the first decades of the Prairie provinces' existence, the Canadian government treated them somewhat like colonies to be exploited. Unlike other provincial governments, the Alberta, Saskatchewan, and Manitoba governments did not gain control of their natural resources until 1930. Macdonald's **National Policy** (1879), which involved placing a high **tariff** on manufactured goods coming into Canada so as to encourage the development of industry located primarily in Ontario and Quebec, did little to assist Westerners who had to sell their products on international markets. Subsequently, many Western Canadians demanded that the Canadian government pursue a free trade agreement with the United States. Furthermore, railway freight rates established by the Canadian government tended to discourage the location of manufacturing and processing in Western Canada. When in 1980 the Canadian government incensed Albertans (and some other Western Canadians) by adopting the **National Energy Program,** the government was thus exacerbating long-established resentment in the West.

The National Energy Program, adopted at a time of high international oil prices and concerns about energy shortages, included keeping oil prices below the international level, increasing the Canadian government's share of oil revenues, establishing a federal Crown corporation to be involved in the oil industry, and encouraging and subsidizing oil exploration on federal lands in the Arctic and

NATIONAL POLICY
A Canadian government policy adopted in 1879 that included a high tariff on the import of manufactured products, railway construction, and the encouragement of immigration to Western Canada.

TARIFF
A tax or customs duty on imported goods.

NATIONAL ENERGY PROGRAM
A Canadian government program adopted in 1980 that included keeping oil prices below the international level, increasing the Canadian government's share of oil revenues, establishing a federal Crown corporation to be involved in the oil industry, and encouraging and subsidizing oil exploration on federal lands in the Arctic and offshore Newfoundland.

offshore Newfoundland to reduce dependence on Alberta oil. Although the National Energy Program was scrapped a few years later, it symbolized Ottawa's catering to the manufacturing interests in Ontario and Quebec (that benefited from lower energy costs) at the expense of the oil-producing provinces.

Many Western Canadians have also been annoyed with the emphasis of much of Canadian politics on central Canadian issues. In particular, there was considerable opposition in Western Canada to the adoption of bilingualism and to the various efforts since the 1960s to accommodate the distinctiveness of Quebec.

NEWFOUNDLAND AND LABRADOR   Many Newfoundlanders are critical of the "giveaways" of the province's resources and question whether the province has benefited from joining Canada. The mismanagement by the Canadian government of cod stocks and disputes concerning offshore oil revenues have led to considerable dissatisfaction with the Canadian government. In addition, the unwillingness of the Canadian government to require that Quebec allow Labrador power to be transmitted through Quebec led to the sale of Labrador power to Quebec Hydro. This provides a benefit to Quebec of $1–2 billion per year, while the province of Newfoundland and Labrador receives minimal revenues from its Upper Churchill hydro power (Feehan, 2009). At times, the government of Newfoundland and Labrador has demanded greater provincial powers. However, although many people have a strong sense of Newfoundland identity, a significant independence movement has not developed.

ONTARIO   Unlike other areas of the country, Ontario has not usually been considered to have important regional grievances. With its economic and political power, Ontario has been the most influential province in Canada. Nevertheless, Ontario premiers have often been at odds with the Canadian government and have complained that their province contributes much more to Canada than it receives in return. The decline in Ontario's manufacturing base has caused considerable concern about the province's economy, the provincial government's growing debt, and its ability to provide services to its population.

Provincial Rights

Macdonald's vision of a strong central government was reflected, to a considerable extent, in the Constitution that was approved by the Parliament of the United Kingdom in 1867 (see Chapter 10). The expansion of Canada to the Pacific coast, the massive undertaking to build a transcontinental railroad, the National Policy of high tariffs to encourage manufacturing to locate in Canada, and recruitment of immigrants to settle the West reflected his vision of creating a great country matching the growth of the United States, but based on different values.

The idea of the Canadian government leading the development of a centralized Canadian nation was opposed by some provincial governments

seeking to protect and promote provincial rights. The Ontario Liberal government led by Sir Oliver Mowat (1872–1896) challenged the centralizing orientation of Conservative prime minister Macdonald (1867–1873 and 1878–1891). The hanging of Riel stirred nationalist feelings in Quebec, contributing to the election victory of the Parti National led by Honoré Mercier in 1887. Premier Mercier called an interprovincial conference (attended by representatives of the governments of Ontario, New Brunswick, and Nova Scotia, but not Prince Edward Island or British Columbia), which he hoped would "safeguard the autonomy of every province in the federation by guaranteeing their independence" (quoted in Ryan, 2003). Although there was agreement about greater provincial autonomy among those attending, the conference was not followed by subsequent meetings. Nevertheless, tensions between various provincial governments and the Canadian government have been and still are a regular and prominent feature of Canadian politics (as discussed in Chapter 12).

English–French Relations

The relationship between English- and French-speaking Canadians has often been at the centre of Canadian political controversy. In the past, this often had strong religious overtones as many French Canadians viewed their Roman Catholic faith as a key element in protecting their culture from the large Protestant majority in North America. In more recent times, language has been a key issue, with French-speaking minorities outside Quebec striving to maintain their language, while many francophone Quebecers focus their attention on ensuring that French is the dominant language in Quebec.

LANGUAGE AND EDUCATION   The Constitution that was adopted in 1867 included only limited provisions protecting the rights of the French Canadian minority. English or French may be used in the Canadian Parliament and courts established by Parliament. The records and acts of Parliament must be published in both languages. Similar provisions in the Constitution for the use of English and French in the Quebec legislature and courts were designed to protect the English minority in that province. Catholic and Protestant denominational school systems in provinces where they had been established in law at the time of Confederation were also protected by the Constitution. Although the Constitution made education the exclusive responsibility of provincial legislatures, the Canadian Parliament was given the right to pass remedial legislation if those denominational rights were violated.

The establishment of new provinces raised controversial issues about language, religion, and education. The Manitoba Act, 1870, reflecting the roughly equal numbers of French- and English-speaking persons, made both English and French the languages of the provincial legislature and the province's courts. However, as the English-speaking population swelled (primarily with Protestants from Ontario), the Manitoba legislature in 1890 passed the

Official Language Act making English the sole language of the legislature and courts.[6] As well, the Manitoba Schools Act, 1890, eliminated public funding for denominational schools (including French-language Catholic schools) and established a public school system with English as the language of instruction.

To avoid the use of remedial federal legislation that would interfere with provincial control of education, Liberal prime minister Wilfrid Laurier worked out a compromise with Thomas Greenway, the Manitoba premier in 1896. This agreement allowed for some religious education in public schools after hours and for the right of parents to have their children educated in English and another language. However, in 1916 the right to educate children in a language other than English was lost due to wartime animosity toward Germans and those of some other continental European ancestries.

The language of education was also a controversial issue in Ontario. In 1912 Ontario's Ministry of Education adopted Regulation 17, which made English the language of instruction in all Ontario schools (modified slightly in 1913 to allow some limited teaching of French). This regulation was dropped in 1927, although the right to a French-language education was not guaranteed in Ontario until 1968.

Language issues have also been very controversial in Quebec. In particular, in 1977 the Quebec legislature passed Bill 101, which made French the official language of the province and prevented most children from enrolling in a publicly funded English-language school unless at least one of their parents had been educated in English in Quebec (see Chapter 3).

CANADA AND THE BRITISH EMPIRE   In the late nineteenth and early twentieth centuries, Canadians struggled to define themselves in relation to the British Empire. English Canadian imperialists promoted the idea that Canada and the other former colonies settled by those of British ancestry should unite with Great Britain in an Imperial Federation. This would allow Canada "its proper place in the councils of the Empire and in the destiny of the world" (Stephen Leacock, quoted in Bumsted, 2008, p. 162). Others looked to the development of a fully independent Canada. For example, Henri Bourassa, founder of the newspaper *Le Devoir,* promoted an independent bilingual and bicultural Canada based on the mutual respect of English and French Canadians. Still others viewed closer ties or some sort of union with the United States as desirable and inevitable (Bumsted, 2008).

While many English Canadians favoured Canadian participation in Britain's imperialistic war against the Boers (Dutch-speaking settlers) in South Africa (1899–1902), French Canadians were generally opposed to involvement in this British war against a threatened minority in a distant land. Faced with strong divisions in his Liberal party on the issue, Prime Minister Laurier

---

[6] Although various courts ruled the Official Language Act unconstitutional, it was not until the 1980s that the Manitoba government began to translate its acts into French.

avoided taking the issue to Parliament. Instead he arranged for Canadian volunteers to be organized, equipped, and sent to South Africa with their pay covered by the British government (Morton, 2007). Several years later, Laurier was less successful in finding a compromise between imperialists and Quebec Nationalists. Conservative imperialists wanted Canada to build two dreadnaughts (large battleships) for the British Royal Navy. Quebec nationalists were critical of Laurier's proposal (the Naval Services Bill) to build a small Canadian navy; they feared it would lead to Canadian participation in British wars, while imperialists mocked the idea of a "tin pot" Canadian navy. The Conservatives and Quebec Nationalists joined forces to defeat the Liberals in the 1911 election. However, the Liberal majority in the Senate subsequently defeated a Conservative bill to contribute money to build three dreadnaughts for Britain.

THE CONSCRIPTION CRISIS   Canada's entry into World War I was widely supported, even by French Canadian Nationalists, in the House of Commons. However, the lengthy war eventually resulted in controversial calls for conscription despite the large number of volunteers that had enlisted. Many French Canadians, as well as many people of other non-British ancestries, opposed compulsory military service.[7] Violent anti-conscription demonstrations in

© Library and Archives Canada

Anti-conscription demonstration by Université de Montréal students prior to 1942 referendum to release the Canadian government from its promise not to impose conscription.

---

[7]There was also considerable opposition to conscription among some groups of English Canadians when various exemptions from compulsory military service (such as the exemption for farmers' sons) were removed in 1918.

Quebec City resulted in Canadian troops being sent to that city, and four people were killed when the troops opened fire (Torrance, 1986). Nevertheless, conscription was imposed by a Union government composed of Conservatives, along with most of the Liberal Members of Parliament from English Canada. The Union government won the 1917 election by a substantial margin, although Quebecers elected anti-conscription Liberals in every district that had a French-speaking majority. To help ensure a solid victory, the Union government extended the right to vote to women serving overseas as nurses in the army and to women with close relatives fighting in the war. The **conscription crisis** reinforced the negative feelings that many English Canadians harboured toward French Canadians. It also had a long-term effect on Canada's party system, contributing to the difficulties the Conservative party experienced in appealing to Quebecers for decades afterward.

CONSCRIPTION CRISIS
The imposition of compulsory military service during World War I that sharply divided many English and French Canadians.

The conscription issue arose again during World War II. To gain support from French Canadians for the war effort, Liberal prime minister Mackenzie King promised that there would be no conscription for overseas service. Conscription for Home Guard duty was introduced in 1940. Then, in 1942, the Canadian government held a national referendum asking to be released from its promise not to impose conscription. The cautious prime minister promised "conscription if necessary but not necessarily conscription." Outside Quebec 72.8 percent voted in favour of allowing conscription, while in Quebec only 27.9 percent voted in favour. Nevertheless, conscription for overseas service was not implemented until November 1944,[8] and a relatively small number of conscripts ended up on the front lines before the end of the war. Despite the controversy over conscription, the Liberals managed to get re-elected shortly after Victory in Europe Day, albeit with a substantially reduced popular vote. The Bloc Populaire, which was formed by Quebec's anti-conscriptionists, managed to win only two seats and disappeared soon afterward.

QUEBEC INDEPENDENCE   In the early 1960s, a variety of groups and political parties were formed to pursue independence for Quebec. One of the most radical groups, the Front de libération du Québec (FLQ), was inspired by liberation movements in countries such as Algeria and engaged in violence to pursue its cause. The October Crisis of 1970 involved the kidnapping of British trade commissioner James Cross and the murder of labour minister Pierre Laporte by the FLQ. At the request of the Quebec government, the Canadian government invoked the War Measures Act (which suspended civil liberties) and rounded up hundreds of Quebecers, most of whom had no connection to the FLQ. Support for revolutionary political and social change disintegrated after the October Crisis.

Much more important was the formation of the Parti Québécois (led by a former Liberal cabinet minister, René Lévesque) in 1968 which sought

---

[8]Some Home Guard conscripts were sent to Alaska's Aleutian Islands in 1943 to fight the Japanese, who had captured two islands. However, this was not considered overseas service.

"sovereignty-association" (Quebec political sovereignty with an economic association with the rest of Canada). The Parti Québécois formed the government of Quebec after the 1976 provincial election, but failed to gain a majority for sovereignty in a 1980 Quebec referendum. In a second referendum in 1995, 49.42 percent of Quebecers voted in favour of sovereignty. Since then, support for Quebec independence has declined substantially. Nevertheless, the position of Quebec within Canada remains an important issue.

Aboriginal Peoples and the Canadian Government

In the decades after Confederation, there was a flurry of activity as the Canadian government signed treaties with First Nations to open up vast areas of land for settlement by those of European ancestry. Diseases brought by European settlers weakened and decimated Aboriginal peoples and starvation became a serious problem on the Prairies as a result of the near extinction of the bison. Thus, First Nations had little choice but to sign unequal treaties based on promises of assistance from the Canadian government. Although relations between Aboriginal peoples and the Canadian government were generally more peaceful than in the United States, desperate circumstances did lead to conflict, as discussed in Box 2-3: Aboriginal Unrest: The North-West Rebellion of 1885.

Shunted off to reserves and subjected to oppressive Canadian government control by the Indian Act, 1876, Aboriginal peoples were generally excluded from political life (although they participated in Canada's wars). Indeed it was not until 1960 that First Nations people had the right to vote without giving up their Indian status. In recent decades, First Nations have been active in pursuing their rights. In addition to using the legal system (see Chapter 11), civil disobedience (such as blocking highways and railways) has been used to draw attention to their grievances. Occasionally confrontations have turned violent. For example, in 1990 Mohawk opposition to the expansion of a golf course on land they claimed at Oka, Quebec, led to a brief gun battle in which a Quebec provincial police officer died. In 1995, an Ontario provincial police officer fired on unarmed Aboriginal protesters occupying Ipperwash Provincial Park, killing Dudley George. At a public inquiry held 11 years later, a former attorney general testified that Premier Mike Harris had told him to get the Indians out of the park (an allegation denied by Harris). The land that had been taken from the Kettle and Stony Point band in 1942 using the War Measures Act was returned to the Cheppewa in 2009.

Racial, Ethnic, and Religious Minorities

Canada is often thought of as a country that is tolerant of racial, ethnic, and religious diversity. However, those with characteristics different from the majority's have often suffered from discrimination and exclusion from political life. For example, exclusion of persons of Chinese, Japanese, and East

BOX 2-3

Aboriginal Unrest: The North-West Rebellion of 1885

Faced with starvation and the destruction of their traditional way of life in the 1870s and early 1880s, Prairie Cree leaders, including Big Bear and Poundmaker, reluctantly agreed to sign treaties with the Canadian government and moved to reserves. The Department of Indian Affairs provided little assistance, even after Cree leaders wrote to Prime Minister Macdonald about their desperate situation. Tensions developed as some starving Aboriginals stole cattle from settlers, while others considered protest actions including armed rebellion (Bumsted, 2008; Conrad & Finkel, 2007).

Many Métis moved to what is now Saskatchewan after being denied title to the lands they had been promised in the Red River area. Here, the Métis (as well as white settlers) faced problems concerning land grants, assistance for farming, and services such as schools and local police (Conrad & Finkel, 2007). When the Canadian government ignored their petitions, the Métis invited Louis Riel to return from the United States to take up their cause. Believing he had a divine mission to save God's chosen people, the Métis, Riel consented.

Riel's peaceful attempts to persuade the Canadian government to improve the circumstances of people in the region were unsuccessful. He and his Métis supporters set up a provisional government of Saskatchewan with Gabriel Dumont as military leader. After the Métis had some success in a clash with the North-West Mounted Police at Duck Lake, Cree warriors, upset about broken treaty promises, attacked the community of Frog Lake, killing nine settlers including the Indian agent. The Canadian government quickly sent a military force over the newly built Canadian Pacific Railway. In the final Battle of Batoche, the Métis were easily defeated by the larger Canadian force. Riel was arrested and Dumont fled to the United States where he became a star performer in the Wild West Show. A few weeks later, the Cree were defeated in the Battle of Loon Lake. Eight Cree were hanged and many others were imprisoned, including Big Bear and Poundmaker, who had opposed the armed uprising.

Although the North-West Rebellion was short-lived, it challenges the popular myth that the Canadian West was settled peacefully.

Indian ancestry from voting existed in some cases until 1948, and certain religious groups were excluded from the right to vote until 1955.

In the nineteenth century, sympathetic Canadians assisted thousands of black slaves who fled to Canada from the United States on the "Underground Railroad." However, after settling in Canada, the refugees faced discrimination and social exclusion. For example, in 1946 Viola Desmond, a Nova Scotia businesswoman, was forcibly removed from a movie theatre in New Glasgow and arrested when she refused to move from the white section and sit in the black balcony, where she said she could not see the film.[9] This incident led to a lengthy political struggle to end Nova Scotia's segregation law, which was finally revoked in 1954.

---

[9]Because Viola Desmond had paid for a ticket in the balcony, she was convicted and jailed for defrauding the Canadian government of one cent—the difference in the amusement tax between the black and white seats.

Prejudice against Asian immigrants was common, particularly as other workers feared the loss of jobs to those willing to accept low wages. A "head tax" was imposed on Chinese immigrants after the Canadian Pacific Railroad (to which Chinese workers had made a major contribution) was completed. In 1907, the Asiatic Exclusion League was formed in Vancouver to try to stop Asian immigration. Riots occurred as thousands of members and supporters of the racist league marched through Chinatown and Japantown smashing windows. The areas were placed under martial law and, for days, fearful Chinese and Japanese residents avoided going into the streets.

In recent times, the Canadian government has adopted a policy of multiculturalism and the more blatant forms of discrimination against racial, ethnic, and religious minorities have ended. Nevertheless, persons of colour often face discrimination in finding employment and some black youth claim that they are harassed by the police.

The religious divide between Catholics and Protestants has been an important feature of Canadian politics. In the 1880s and 1890s, strong anti-Catholic and anti-French sentiment was politicized through such groups as the Equal Rights Association and the Protestant Protective Association, which called for an end to the Catholic Church's privileges and publicly funded Catholic schools, while raising fears about a Catholic takeover of Canada. In the 1920s and 1930s, anti-immigrant sentiment was fuelled by concerns that large-scale immigration from southern and eastern Europe would increase the influence of Catholicism and undermine efforts to assimilate newcomers to the dominant British-oriented culture.

In the 1920s, the Ku Klux Klan, notorious for its violence against blacks and its hatred of Catholics, established "klans" in many Canadian communities. In Saskatchewan, where it claimed to have 40 000 members, the Klan campaigned against Liberal premier Jimmy Gardiner, burning crosses at his rallies among other activities. The Conservatives defeated the Liberals in the 1929 provincial election, aided by support from the Klan. However, the Klan, which had no platform other than bigotry and conspiracy theories, quickly faded from the scene and did not influence the Conservative government (Robin, 1992).

Anti-Semitism has also had a significant presence in Canada, with Jewish people suffering various forms of discrimination. In 1933, a six-hour violent brawl occurred at Christie Pits (Willowvale Park) in Toronto after an anti-Semitic club displayed a large Nazi swastika and shouted "Heil Hitler" at a softball game in which a mainly Jewish team participated. As Jews fled Nazi oppression and extermination in Europe, the Canadian government was willing to accept only a tiny number of Jewish refugees—even forcing a boat carrying refugees to return to Europe in 1939 (Abella & Troper, 2000). In more recent times, synagogues and Hebrew schools have continued to be vandalized and desecrated. Likewise, Canada's growing Muslim population faces considerable animosity. In particular, the face-covering and other clothing of some

Muslim women along with the wearing of religious symbols by public sector employees has been controversial.

Women

Women have engaged in a lengthy struggle to try to end discriminatory laws and practices. For example, until the early twentieth century in most provinces,[10] married women did not have the right to make legal agreements and buy property. Indeed, it wasn't until the late 1970s that provincial legislatures passed laws guaranteeing women an equal division of property after a divorce. Women were excluded from the right to vote and hold public office from the time of Confederation. They were expected to be responsible for home and family, while leaving the "dirty" business of politics to men. Through peaceful protests, the women's suffrage movement challenged the exclusion of women from political life. They were successful first in persuading male politicians to grant women the right to vote in the three Prairie provinces in 1916, followed by British Columbia in 1917 and federal elections in 1918. However, it was not until 1940 that women could vote in Quebec provincial elections and until 1951 that the Indian Act was amended to allow women to vote in First Nations elections. Despite winning the right to vote and hold elected office, only a handful of women were elected to Parliament and provincial legislatures until recent decades (see Figure 2-5). Although 76 women were elected in 2011, this was still only 24.7 percent of the members of the House of Commons. In 2015, 88 women were elected (making 26 percent of the House). Likewise, women comprise about one-quarter of the members of provincial legislatures. As of May 2015, three provinces had female premiers.

Women were also limited in their educational opportunities and found it difficult or impossible to enter certain professions. Until the 1970s, job advertisements were often classified in terms of being for men or for women.

Women have entered the paid labour force, including professions, in large numbers in recent decades. The equality of women is now constitutionally protected through the Charter of Rights and Freedoms. Nevertheless, as will be discussed in Chapter 4, women face various hurdles in the pursuit of full equality. And women continue to be greatly underrepresented in many senior political and business positions.

Farmers and Workers

The struggle of farmers and workers to improve their position has also played a key role in Canada's political history. In the pre-Confederation British North American colonies, reformers with support based in farming communities

---

[10]Full legal equality for women was not established in Quebec until changes in the Civil Code were made in 1964.

FIGURE 2-5
**THE REPRESENTATION
OF WOMEN IN THE HOUSE
OF COMMONS**

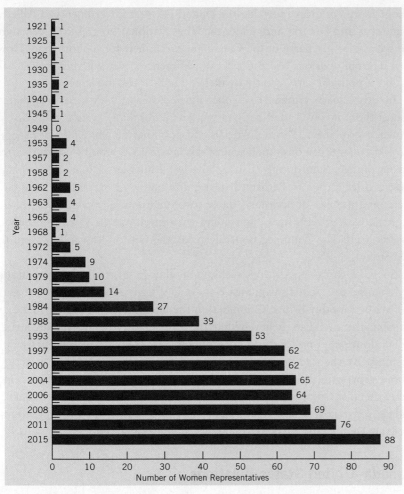

SOURCE: Compiled from Parliament of Canada. (2011). Women candidates in general elections—1921 to date. Retrieved from www.parl.gc.ca/About/Parliament/FederalRidingsHistory/hfer.asp?Search=WomenElection& Language=E. CBC News. (2015). Canada votes. Retrieved from http://www.cbc.ca/news2/interactives/results-2015/#women.

struggled against the wealthy, privileged elite who dominated government, the economy, and society. In the first decades of the twentieth century, farmers' movements developed throughout Canada, with particular strength on the Prairies and in rural Ontario. Both major political parties—the Conservatives and the Liberals—were seen as beholden to the interests of big business. Many in the farmers' movement advocated plebiscitary democracy so that ordinary people could have direct control over their representatives and the policies adopted by governments.

Following World War I, the farmers' movement entered the arena of electoral politics, with farmers nominating candidates who pledged to act on the wishes of their constituents. The collection of farmers' representatives achieved considerable success (in combination with a small number of independent labour representatives), forming the United Farmers governments of Alberta, Manitoba, and Ontario and, under the label National Progressives, becoming the second-largest party in the Canadian Parliament for a short time. However, internal divisions based in part on differences over whether they should act like a political party greatly weakened the farmers' movement.

In early Canada, criminal laws concerning conspiracy were used to lay charges against those involved in organizing workers and taking strike action. George Brown, a prominent Liberal politician and publisher of *The Globe* newspaper, provoked a large demonstration against this law in 1872 after he used it to arrest striking printers. Subsequently, Conservative prime minister Sir John A. Macdonald presented legislation to Parliament to legalize unions. Nevertheless there have been, on a number of occasions, bitter confrontations between employers and workers, with governments often siding with employers (see Box 2-4: Labour Asserts Itself: The Winnipeg General Strike, the On-to-Ottawa Trek, and the GM Strike).

Socialist parties and groups seeking, in some cases, radical or revolutionary changes to Canada's capitalist economic system developed in some parts of Canada (notably British Columbia) in the late nineteenth century. Like the farmers, the socialists believed that the Conservative and Liberal parties, which dominated politics and government, represented the interests of big business. By the late nineteenth and early twentieth centuries, a variety of labour representatives were elected provincially and nationally. The democratic socialist Co-operative Commonwealth Federation was formed in 1933 and elected to govern Saskatchewan in 1944. In 1961 it transformed itself into the New Democratic Party as "the political voice of labour."

Canada–United States Relations

Canada's relations with the United States have often been a subject of controversy among Canadians. For some, developing a close relationship with Canada's prosperous and powerful neighbour is seen as essential for Canada's economy and security. As well, a close relationship is often advocated based on the shared values and personal ties of Canadians and Americans. Others worry about the potential for the United States to dominate and exploit Canada, undermine Canadian culture and identity, and commit Canada to supporting the United States in its military activities.

Some concerns about American expansion into Canada persisted in the decades following Confederation. However, American expansionism and imperialism in the nineteenth and early twentieth centuries were directed at the Caribbean, Mexico, Central America, Hawaii, and the Philippines rather than Canada. Instead, debate raged in Canada about the identity and future of the country. Influential British-born intellectual Goldwin Smith, in his book *Canada and the Canadian Question* (1891), argued that Canada was an "unnatural country" with no real reason to exist, and that it should unite with

BOX 2-4

Labour Asserts Itself:
The Winnipeg General Strike, the
On-to-Ottawa Trek, and the GM Strike

THE WINNIPEG GENERAL STRIKE

During World War I, industrial employment and union membership increased substantially. Some individuals in the divided labour movement were striving to create One Big Union that would fundamentally transform the capitalist system. In 1919, building and metal trades workers in Winnipeg went on strike when their employers rejected collective bargaining. As an act of solidarity, the Winnipeg Trades and Labour Council (as well as workers in various other Western communities) decided to strike. With socialism on the rise and the Bolshevik (Communist) Revolution having recently occurred in Russia, governments and business leaders raised fears of revolution in Canada led by non-British "aliens." Although the General Strike was non-violent, the city police who showed some sympathy for the strikers were replaced and the militia and RCMP were called in. When the strike supporters held a peaceful march in defiance of the city's ban on parades, the RCMP and militia broke up the march, killing one spectator and wounding others. The strike leaders were thrown in jail and charged with seditious conspiracy (McNaught, 1969).

THE ON-TO-OTTAWA TREK

During the Great Depression of the 1930s, the federal government established work camps for desperate, hungry, unemployed men and paid them 20 cents a day for hard labour. A communist-led Relief Camp Workers' Union was established to protest the conditions at the camps. Four thousand men left the relief camps in British Columbia and went on strike in Vancouver (Gillmor, Michaud, & Turgeon, 2001). One thousand left Vancouver on boxcars, and many others joined the "On-to-Ottawa Trek" en route. Among the demands made were first aid equipment for the camps, coverage by workers' compensation, and the right of the relief workers to vote.

After a bitter, unsuccessful meeting between the strike leaders and Conservative prime minister R.B. Bennett, the trekkers held a public meeting in Regina. RCMP riot squads battled with the strikers and their supporters for four hours. Many were wounded, and one plainclothes police officer and one striker died. The protesters were encircled with barbed wire and denied food and water. The premier of Saskatchewan accused the RCMP of instigating the riot. Subsequently, the prime minister and his party were decisively defeated in a general election, the federal work camps were disbanded, and wages for workers on relief increased slightly.

THE GM STRIKE

In 1937, a strike began at the General Motors automobile plant in Oshawa, Ontario, when the company refused to recognize the United Auto Workers as the bargaining agent for the workers. Ontario premier Mitch Hepburn, an opponent of industrial unions, organized a special force of 400 men with plans to set up machine guns and instructions to shoot strikers at the knees, if ordered. "I'd rather walk with the workers than ride with General Motors," retorted David Croll, an Ontario cabinet minister. Later, he and another cabinet minister resigned in protest. Fortunately, a compromise was reached and a contract was signed between General Motors and the union local.

As a result of the determined actions of workers, the right to organize, bargain collectively, and take strike action has become well established. Nevertheless, labour is often at odds with business and government, not only about wages, working conditions, and "back to work" legislation, but also about what social and economic policies should be adopted.

the United States because there were no major differences between Canadians and Americans. However, no significant movement for a political union between Canada and the United States developed. Instead, the issue of free trade with the United States became, at times, a focal point for intense political controversy.

FREE TRADE   In the decade after Confederation, both Conservative and Liberal governments tried to persuade the American government to re-establish the Reciprocity Treaty. However, the United States, which established high tariffs to encourage the development of its industries, was not interested in free trade. In 1879 Conservative prime minister Macdonald placed a high tariff on manufactured products (averaging 30 percent) coming into Canada from the United States to promote the development of industries in Canada.

In 1888, with a global recession hurting Canada and with the United States proposing to increase tariffs on some important Canadian exports, Wilfrid Laurier's Liberal party advocated unrestricted reciprocity (i.e., free trade) with the United States. This became the centrepiece of the 1891 election campaign. With his government plagued by scandals, tensions between English and French, and opposition from provincial governments, Prime Minister Macdonald accused the Liberals of "veiled treason" and taking part in a "deliberate conspiracy . . . to force Canada into the American Union" (quoted in Beck, 1968, p. 64). Furthermore, he played to the sentiments of many English Canadians by proclaiming that "A British subject I was born—a British subject I will die." These emotional appeals helped the Conservatives win the election.

The issue of free trade with the United States was also central to the 1911 election. Prime Minister Laurier and U.S. president William Howard Taft reached an agreement regarding free trade in many natural products and lower tariffs on some manufactured products (Conrad & Finkel, 2007). When the House of Commons failed to approve the agreement because of a Conservative filibuster (a tactic to prevent proposed legislation coming to a vote), Laurier requested an election. A group of 18 prominent businessmen, the Canadian Manufacturers Association, and some Liberal Members of Parliament bolstered Conservative opposition to the agreement. In addition to the self-interest of those Canadian businesses that had benefited from the National Policy, opponents raised concerns about being absorbed by the United States. "No truck or trade with the Yankees" was a popular slogan in the campaign. Fears about the intentions of the United States were reinforced by Champ Clark, the Speaker of the U.S. House of Representatives, who asserted in the American debate that "I hope to see the day when the American flag will float over every square foot of the British North American possessions, clear to the North Pole" (quoted in Beck, 1968, p. 125). In the end, the Conservatives defeated the Liberals in the 1911 election and the agreement was not signed.

The Canada–United States Free Trade Agreement reached in 1987 under the direction of Progressive Conservative prime minister Brian Mulroney and

U.S. president Ronald Reagan was extremely controversial. The 1988 election was fought almost exclusively on this issue, with Liberal leader John Turner promising to tear up the agreement which, Liberals claimed, would in effect wipe out the border between the two countries. Although slightly less than one-half of Canadians supported the free trade agreement, the PCs won the election and implemented the agreement. In 1993, a broader **North American Free Trade Agreement** (NAFTA) between Canada, the United States, and Mexico was ratified (see Chapter 4).

NORTH AMERICAN FREE TRADE AGREEMENT
An agreement between Canada, the United States, and Mexico that established a high level of economic integration in North America.

Summary and Conclusion

The story of Canada's past takes many forms. Some describe Canadian historical development as the evolution from colony to independent country. Likewise, Canada gradually became a democratic country as the right to vote moved from a minority of the population to include all adult citizens. Others view the development of a close relationship with the United States as limiting the independence of contemporary Canada or even making Canada, in effect, a colony of the United States. Still others look at Canadian history as the continuing struggles for equality, respect, and justice, and a more substantial democracy by diverse groups, including women, Aboriginal peoples, French Canadians, ethnic and racial minorities, and the working class.

Canadian politics has often focused on relations between English and French, the grievances of various provinces and regions, and the relationships between the Canadian government and provincial governments. These tensions are frequently seen as creating challenges to "national unity."

This chapter has highlighted some serious political conflicts that have threatened Canadian unity. However, Canada has, for the most part, enjoyed a peaceful existence since Confederation despite the challenges of integrating a large country with a growing, increasingly diverse population. While maintaining Canadian unity and sovereignty continues to be a relevant concern, other issues, including environmental degradation, Aboriginal self-government, equality for women, the accommodation of those with different cultures and religious practices, and inequalities in income and wealth have become increasingly important.

Discussion Questions

1. If you had lived in British North America in the 1860s, do you think you would have supported or opposed Confederation?

2. What have been the most serious challenges Canada has faced? What challenges do you think will be most important in the coming years?

3. Is regionalism a serious threat to national unity?

4. Why has Canada's relations with the United States been a major topic of political controversy?

5. Should Canada establish its own head of state?

Further Reading

Ajzenstat, J., Romney, P., Gentles, I., & Gairdner, W.D. (Eds.). (2003). *Canada's founding debates.* Toronto, ON: University of Toronto Press.

Brandt, G.C., Black, N., Bourne, P., & Fahmi, M. (2011). *Canadian women: A history.* Toronto, ON: Nelson.

Bothwell, B. (2007). *The Penguin history of Canada.* Toronto, ON: Penguin Canada.

Bumsted, J.M. (2011). *A history of the Canadian peoples* (4th ed.). Toronto, ON: Oxford University Press.

Conrad, M., Finkel, A., & Fyson, D. (2012). *Canada: A history* (3rd ed.). Toronto, ON: Pearson Education Canada.

Dickason, O.P. (with McNab, D.T.). (2009). *Canada's First Nations: A history of founding peoples from earliest times* (4th ed.). Toronto, ON: Oxford University Press.

Gillmor, D., & Turgeon, P. (2000). *Canada: A people's history* (Vol. 1). Toronto, ON: McClelland & Stewart.

Gillmor, D., Menaud, A., & Turgeon, P. (2001). *Canada: A people's history* (Vol. 2). Toronto, ON: McClelland & Stewart.

Marsden, L.R. (2012). *Canadian women and the struggle for equality.* Toronto, ON: Oxford University Press.

Mensah, J. (2010). *Black Canadians: History, experiences, social conditions.* Winnipeg: Fernwood Publishing.

Morton, D. (2006). *A short history of Canada* (6th ed.). Toronto, ON: McClelland & Stewart.

Palmer, B.D., & Sangster, J. (Eds.). (2008). *Labouring Canada: Class, gender and race in Canadian working class history.* Toronto, ON: Oxford University Press.

Saul, J.R. (2008). *A fair country. Telling truths about Canada.* Toronto, ON: Viking Canada.

CHAPTER 3

Canada and the Challenge of Cultural Diversity

CHAPTER OBJECTIVES

After reading this chapter, you should be able to

1. Define and distinguish between an ethnic nation and a civic nation.
2. Discuss the significance of identities and the different ways of understanding the Canadian identity.
3. Discuss how and why Canada became one of the most culturally diverse states in the world.
4. Define and distinguish between a national minority and an ethnic group.
5. Discuss the evolution of French Canadian and Québécois nationalism and how Canada has responded to the challenge of minority nationalism.
6. Discuss Canada's response to polyethnicity, as shown by its immigration and integration policies.

Tensions caused by the growing presence of new cultures, religions, and social practices have been at the centre of high-profile disputes about the extent to which public institutions should accommodate religious diversity.

One of those disputes took place in February 2015, when a Court of Quebec judge told Rania El-Alloul, who had applied to get her car back after it had been seized by Quebec's automobile insurance board, that the judge would not hear her case until she removed her hijab. The hijab is a traditional covering for the hair and neck that is worn by millions of Muslim women around the world. During the proceeding, Judge Marengo cited a regulation stating that "any person appearing before the court must be suitably dressed." Although the regulation makes no specific reference to headscarves or other garments, the judge told El-Alloul that "in my opinion, the courtroom is a secular place" where religious symbols were not permitted. After El-Alloul refused, the case was suspended indefinitely. The single mother's case made national headlines and led to a crowdfunding campaign that raised more than $50 000 to help her buy a new car. El-Alloul, a welfare recipient, decided not to accept the money, noting that the funds could be put to better use by promoting human rights (CBC News, March 13, 2015).

In 2011, the Supreme Court of Canada heard arguments in a legal matter pitting a Muslim woman's religious beliefs against the rights of defendants. The woman was appealing a lower court ruling that she had to remove her niqab while testifying against two male relatives in a sexual assault case in Ontario. The niqab is a full veil worn by some Muslim women that covers the entire face save for the eyes. The defendants said they should be able to see her facial expressions for the purpose of cross-examination. A representative from the Canadian Council on American–Islamic Relations worried that banning the niqab could lead to fewer Muslim women reporting crimes or agreeing to testify in court (CBC News, 2011b). In 2012, the Supreme Court ruled that judges should neither ban outright nor routinely allow face coverings. Judges would have to consider the veiled witness's "sincerity of belief," any risk to trial fairness, ways to accommodate those beliefs by using alternative measures, such as allowing evidence to be given behind a screen, and whether the harm of veiled testimony in a particular case outweighed the benefit to society of encouraging victims to testify in court (MacCharles, 2012).

In 2013, Zumera Ishaq, a high school teacher from Pakistan, challenged a 2011 policy that prevented anyone from taking the citizenship oath with their face covered. In February 2015, the Federal Court ruled that it was "unlawful" for the Canadian government to require new citizens to remove religious face coverings while taking the oath. Ms. Ishaq uncovered her face in private before a citizenship judge to prove her identity and took the oath while wearing her niqab at a public citizenship ceremony in October. This became a hotly contested issue in the 2015 Canadian election (as discussed in Chapter 9). Prime Minister Stephen Harper asserted that covering one's face while being sworn in is "not how we do things here" and is "offensive." While polls show that most Canadians do not find the niqab personally offensive, a poll commissioned by the government found that 82 percent of Canadians supported the requirement that women remove their niqabs or burkas at citizensip ceremonies (Vincent, March 17, 2015; Beeby, September 24, 2015).

CANADA'S DEEP CULTURAL DIVERSITY

If you used Google Earth to zoom in over Canada, you would notice the country's distinctive physical features: a huge landmass bounded by three oceans and traversed by long rivers, lakes and bays as vast as small seas, and soaring mountain ranges. If you could use a different Google engine to observe the country's social features, you would notice that Canadians come from myriad cultural backgrounds. Canadians trace their ancestral origins to more than 200 different ethnic groups and report more than 200 different languages as the language they first learned at home. More than one-fifth of the total population was born in another country. The breadth and depth of the country's cultural diversity defines Canada as much as its spectacular landscape.

Cultural diversity is both a source of pride for many Canadians and a challenge for public officials who are striving to build a cohesive political community. Canada's Aboriginal peoples have pressed for more power in governing their own affairs, as well as territorial, economic, and resource rights. The predominantly francophone province of Quebec has held two referendums on whether it should establish an independent state. Canadians across the country are debating whether and to what extent public institutions should be adapted to accommodate the different traditions of increasingly multicultural citizens.

The vast majority of Canadians express pride in their country, but they also identify with, or feel a sense of belonging to, their language group, ethnic ancestry, province, region, Aboriginal group, and other affiliations. The persistence of linguistic, ethnic, and regional identities in Canada and other advanced capitalist states has surprised integrationist theorists, who expected these allegiances to weaken as societies modernized (Deutsch & Foltz, 1963; Tilly, 1975). They predicted, prematurely, that scientific and technological progress, the spread of mass education and communications, the geographic concentration of economic activities, urbanization, and secularism would narrow differences between people and encourage cultural uniformity. To the contrary, since World War II, indigenous movements and regional languages and cultures have enjoyed a renaissance in many liberal democratic states. This has led to the growth of nationalist or regional movements making separatist claims or clamouring for more political autonomy.

The persistence of cultural differences raises the question of how liberal societies should go about building a unified political community out of disparate parts. **Classical liberalism** is based on the idea that the state should remain neutral in cultural and religious matters and concentrate on protecting individual rights and freedoms and the life, liberty, and property of its citizens. Some contemporary liberals, however, argue that the state can endorse the survival and flourishing of a particular national, cultural, or religious group, as long as the basic rights of citizens who do not belong to that group or who do not share its goals are protected. In Canada, supporters of these contrasting perspectives on liberalism debate whether the state should grant special rights to cultural minorities or whether it should treat all Canadians the same regardless of their ancestry. Charles Taylor (1992) has argued that the recognition of group identities and differences is consistent with liberal principles, providing the state protects the basic rights and freedoms of all citizens. In practice, this would

CLASSICAL LIBERALISM
An ideological perspective based on a belief in a minimal role for government, leaving individuals free to pursue their interests and follow their own beliefs as long as they do not seriously harm others.

entitle members of certain cultural groups to specific rights and powers that are not enjoyed by other Canadians. In contrast, former prime minister Pierre Trudeau (1968), a supporter of the classical liberal tradition of individual rights and freedoms, adamantly opposed the organization of any political society along ethnic lines.

A LOOK AHEAD   This chapter begins with an exploration of the nature of Canada's nationhood and identity. It then takes a closer look at how Canada has dealt with two important sources of cultural diversity within its borders: the presence of more than one nation within the boundaries of the Canadian state, and polyethnicity. Canada is a **multination state** because its historical development involved the English, French, and Aboriginal nations.[1] In this context, the term **nation** refers to a historical community with its own institutions, occupying a given territory, and sharing a distinct language and culture. Canada is also a **polyethnic state** because it is composed of many ethnic groups formed by immigrants who left their countries of origin to live in another society (Kymlicka, 1995).

When discussing Canada's approach to building one political community out of a multinational state, we will focus on how it has responded to the claims of many in the French Canadian, and subsequently Québécois, national minority for language rights and sovereignty. The position of Aboriginal peoples that seek self-government or some form of sovereignty will be discussed in Chapter 11. This chapter will also examine the decisions Canada has made with respect to admitting immigrants to the country and integrating members of ethnic groups into broader society. As Canada's policy responses have changed over time, the project of building the Canadian political community is best viewed as an interesting work in progress.

CANADA AND NATIONHOOD

Is Canada a nation? The answer to this provocative question depends on how one defines this concept. Anthony Smith (1976, 1999) distinguishes between two types of nations: ethnic and civic. An **ethnic nation** describes a community with a distinctive culture and history, which operates primarily for the benefit of that cultural group. Members of the ethnic nation can trace their roots to common ancestry, language, customs, and traditions. The **civic nation** is not based on its members' sharing a common ancestry or culture, but on their sharing a common territory. Also integral to the civic nation is a community of laws and institutions, a sense of legal equality among the members

---

MULTINATION STATE
A state that contains more than one nation.

NATION
A historical community with its own institutions, occupying a given territory or homeland, and sharing a distinct language and culture.

POLYETHNIC STATE
A state that contains many ethnic groups.

ETHNIC NATION
A community with a distinctive culture and history, which operates primarily for the benefit of that cultural group. Members of the ethnic nation share common ancestry, language, customs, and traditions.

CIVIC NATION
A community based on a common historic territory, a community of laws and institutions, a sense of legal equality among community members, and a measure of common values, sentiments, and aspirations that binds the population together.

---

[1]The Canadian Constitution recognizes three distinct groups of Aboriginal peoples: Indians (commonly referred to as First Nations), Métis, and Inuit, each with their own histories, languages, cultural practices, and spiritual beliefs. The First Nations people alone represent more than 50 nations or cultural groups.

of the community, and a measure of common values, sentiments, and aspirations that binds the population together.

Canada is not, and never was, an ethnic nation. When European settlers made first contact with the original inhabitants of North America, they met indigenous peoples from many cultural backgrounds. Each Aboriginal group had a unique economic organization, language, religion, and set of values. The Aboriginal peoples were in turn confronted with predominantly French and British settlers who imported their unique political and legal structures and cultural traditions. The migration of 40 000 to 50 000 Loyalist settlers during and shortly after the American War of Independence further diversified the cultural mix in the British North American colonies.

Between 1815 and 1867, a massive exodus of emigrants from the British Isles escaping Old World poverty sought new opportunities in British North America. From Confederation until the first decade of the twentieth century, the Canadian government heavily promoted immigration from the United States, Central and Eastern Europe, and Scandinavia to develop Canada's economy and population base. As early as 1901, the census recorded about 25 ethnic groups living in Canada. People who reported Aboriginal ancestries and British and French origins comprised the majority of the population at the time, although German, Ukrainian, Polish, Japanese, Chinese, and other ethnic groups formed sizable communities. They were joined in the latter half of the twentieth and early twenty-first centuries by large numbers of immigrants from across Europe, Asia and the Middle East, South America, and Africa (see Figure 3-1).

Immigration and a growing number of mixed marriages and common-law unions between people from different cultural backgrounds have contributed

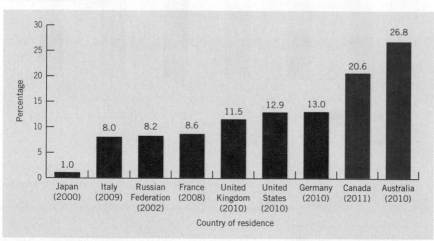

FIGURE 3-1
FOREIGN-BORN POPULATION AS A PROPORTION OF THE TOTAL POPULATION, G8 COUNTRIES AND AUSTRALIA (PERCENTAGE)

SOURCE: *Organization for Economic Cooperation and Development, International Migration Outlook 2012. OECD Publishing, 2012 and Statistics Canada, National Household Survey, 2011.* Immigration and Ethnocultural Diversity in Canada, National Household Survey, 2011 (Catalogue no. 99-010-X2011001).

to the large number of Canadians reporting multiple ethnic origins. In 2011, 57.9 percent of the population reported more than one ethnic origin. The most commonly reported ethnic origin was Canadian (10 563 800), either alone or with other origins. This was followed by English (6 509 500), French (5 065 700), Scottish (4 715 000), Irish (4 544 900), and German (3 203 300). Other origins that surpassed the 1 million mark were: Italian, Chinese, First Nations, Ukrainian, East Indian, Dutch, and Polish (Ministry of Industry, 2013).

By the early twenty-first century, Canada was home to the proportionately largest foreign-born population among G8 countries[2] (see Figure 3-1). Policy reforms in the 1960s that eliminated explicitly discriminatory admissions criteria have contributed to a dramatic shift in the source countries of immigration (see Figure 3-2). More than three-quarters (78.3 percent) of immigrants who came to Canada before 1971 were from Europe, primarily the United Kingdom, Italy, Germany, and the Netherlands. Asia has emerged as the main source of recent immigration. Among immigrants who arrived between 2006 and 2011, about 57 percent came from Asia (including the Middle East), 13.7 percent came from Europe, 12.5 percent from Africa, and 12.3 percent from the Caribbean and Central and South America. The leading countries of birth among people who immigrated during that period were the Philippines, China, and India (Ministry of Industry, 2013).

FIGURE 3-2
REGION OF BIRTH OF IMMIGRANTS BY PERIOD OF IMMIGRATION, CANADA, 2011

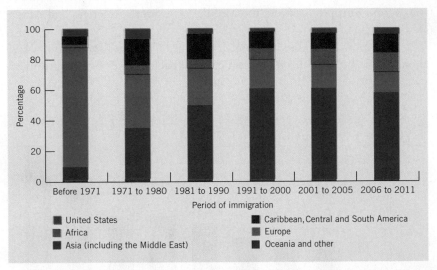

SOURCE: *Statistics Canada, National Household Survey, 2011.* Immigration and Ethnocultural Diversity in Canada, National Household Survey, 2011 (Catalogue no. 99-010-X2011001). Reproduced and distributed on an "as is" basis with the permission of Statistics Canada.

---

[2]The G8 (G7 with the suspension of Russia's membership in 2015) is a group of the heads of state or government of major industrial democracies that have been meeting annually since 1975 to deal with major economic and political issues facing their domestic societies and the international community.

Although immigrants have settled across Canada, in 2011 the vast major-ity (94.8 percent) of the country's 6.8 million immigrants lived in Ontario, British Columbia, Quebec, and Alberta. They were also much more likely to live in the nation's largest urban centres (91 percent) than people born in Canada (63.3 percent) (Ministry of Industry, 2013). These settlement patterns have reinforced the multiracial profile of Canadian cities (see Figure 3-3). In 2011, visible minorities accounted for about one out of every five (19.1 percent) people in the total population. The three largest visible minority groups were South Asians, Chinese, and blacks, who accounted for 61.3 percent of the visible minority population. They were followed by Filipinos, Latin Americans, Arabs, Southeast Asians, West Asians, Koreans, and Japanese (Ministry of Industry, 2013). By 2031, just under one-third of the population could belong to a visible minority group (Malenfant, Lebel, & Martel, 2010).

Canada has always been a country of linguistic diversity, and immigra-tion is contributing to a polyglot population where more than 200 languages are reported as a **mother tongue**. In 2011, more than one-third of the total population (36.6 percent) spoke more than one language. Three-quarters (74.5 percent) of immigrants spoke more than one language, and roughly

MOTHER TONGUE
The first language a person learned at home in childhood and still understands.

FIGURE 3-3
FOREIGN-BORN AND VISIBLE MINORITY POPULATIONS BY CENSUS METROPOLITAN AREAS (2006 AND 2031)

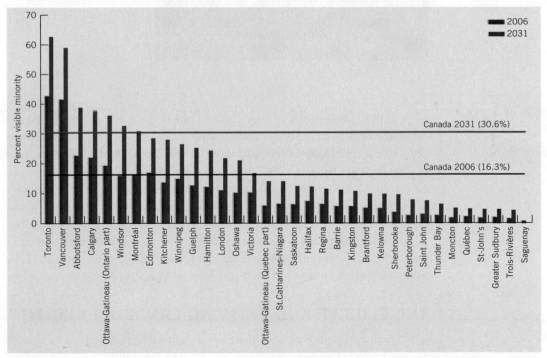

SOURCE: Malenfant, E., Lebel A., & Martel, L, (2010). *Projections of the diversity of the Canadian population, 2006 to 2031* (Catalogue no. 91-551-XWE). Ottawa, ON: Statistics Canada. Retrieved from www.statcan.gc.ca/bsolc/olc-cel/olc-cel?catno=91-551-x&lang=eng. Reproduced and distributed on an "as is" basis with the permission of Statistics Canada.

Canadians increasingly have diverse ethnic and racial characteristics.

© Courtesy Simon Fraser University

61 percent spoke one official language and one or more non-official languages (Ministry of Industry, 2013). Canada's religious make-up is simultaneously becoming increasingly diverse, and more secular. In 2011, the largest religion in Canada was Christianity (67.3 percent), with Roman Catholics as the largest group. Consistent with changing immigration patterns, more Canadians are reporting non-Christian religious affiliations. Roughly 7 percent of the population reported an affiliation with the Muslim, Hindu, Sikh, and Buddhist religions, up from about 5 percent in 2001. A large and growing segment of the population also expressed no religious affiliation (23.9 percent) in 2011, up from 16.5 percent a decade earlier (Ministry of Industry, 2013).

THE ELUSIVE AND EVOLVING CANADIAN IDENTITY

IDENTITIES
Individual and group self-understandings of their traits and characteristics.

Individuals and groups possess **identities,** or self-understandings of their traits and characteristics. A country may also be associated with a unique identity that is understood by the people who live within and outside its borders. Identities are crucial because they affect how people interpret the world; how they interpret the past, present, and future; how they understand other groups and states; and how they perceive their political and economic interests (Abdelal, Herrera, Johnston, & McDermott, 2005).

Journalist Andrew Cohen has observed that the Canadian national identity "is as elusive as the Sasquatch and Ogopogo. It has animated—and frustrated—generations of statesmen, historians, writers, artists, philosophers, and the National Film Board . . . Canada resists easy definition" (Cohen, 2007, p. 105). Some view loyalty to the larger political community as a measure of the strength of the Canadian identity. If this is true, then the national identity is among the strongest in the world as almost 96 percent of Canadians saw themselves as citizens of their country in 2006 (World Values Survey, 2006). Some observers relate the national identity to feelings of attachment to or pride in the country. Here again, 30 years of survey data suggest that the Canadian identity is healthy. In 2012, the vast majority (93.5 percent) said they were very proud or somewhat proud to be Canadian. When Canadians were asked what they liked about Canada (see Table 3-1), they expressed the greatest pride in the country's freedom and democracy, its humanitarian and caring people, multiculturalism, and the beauty of its land (Environics Institute, 2012b).

This does not mean that feelings of strong pride are shared uniformly across the country. Surveys taken since the mid-1980s have shown that Quebecers have always been less likely to be very proud to be Canadians, but that gap widened in 2012, when just 34 percent of Quebecers expressed strong pride in Canada, compared to 83 percent of respondents living in the rest of Canada (Environics Institute, 2012a).

Writers and commentators have also associated Canada's identity with the land, its people, and its history. For celebrated author Pierre Berton, an essential part of the Canadian identity lies in the way many Canadians embrace the harshness of the northern winter (Bumsted, 2004). The Canadian identity has

	1994	2003	2006	2010	2012
Free country/freedom/democracy	31	28	27	27	26
Humanitarian/caring people	9	13	9	9	9
Multiculturalism	3	6	11	6	7
Beauty of the land	7	4	4	4	6
Quality of life	5	6	3	10	5
Health care system	–	3	2	6	4
Respected by other countries	4	3	4	2	4
Peaceful country	7	5	6	4	3
Social programs	3	2	1	3	2

TABLE 3-1
BASIS OF PRIDE IN BEING CANADIAN, TOP MENTIONS 1994–2012

SOURCE: Environics Institute. (2012). *Focus Canada 2012*. Retrieved from http://www.environicsinstitute.org/uploads/institute-projects/environics%20institute%20%20focus%20canada%202012%20final%20report.pdf (p. 15). Used with permission.

also been linked to symbols such as the flag and national anthem, to its national parks, or to the accomplishments of the country's authors and artists, musicians, and athletes. Others believe the Canadian identity is rooted in important events, institutions, laws, and public policies.

Canadians often define themselves in terms of their differences from Americans (Lipset, 1990). Canadians view their country as less violent and more compassionate to the less fortunate. Canadians are also more likely to hold more liberal attitudes on the abolition of the death penalty, access to abortion, gay marriage, and the legalization of marijuana (Resnick, 2005).

Multiple and Overlapping Identities

Capturing the complexity of the Canadian identity is complicated by the fact that Canadians also identify with their province, region, class, gender, religion, and sexual orientation, among other affiliations. In 2006, almost 96 percent of Canadians saw themselves as citizens of their country *and* their provinces or regions (World Values Survey, 2006). These identities are politically salient because they influence perceptions of the role the regions play in the broader Canadian political community. Subnational territorial identities are particularly strong. Western Canada has long harboured resentment toward the federal government and a belief that federal politicians have been preoccupied with the concerns of Ontario and Quebec (Cooper, 1984; Gibbins & Arrison, 1995). Leaders in the Atlantic provinces have also criticized what they have seen as unjust treatment by Ottawa. Since 2004, a growing number of Ontarians feel that the province has not been treated with the respect that it deserves, that its influence on important national decisions has declined, and that Ontario has received less than its fair share of federal dollars. Nevertheless, this has not altered Ontarians' traditional sense of identification with Canada. Ontarians still demonstrate the highest levels of Canadian identity and the lowest levels of provincial identity in the country (Mendelsohn & Matthews, 2010; Environics Institute, 2012a).

On balance, Canadians were more likely to consider themselves a citizen of their country (57 percent) than their home province (39 percent) in 2012 (see Figure 3-4). Quebecers have consistently identified more with their province than with Canada. Residents in Alberta and Saskatchewan are increasingly likely to identify more closely with the country, while those living in British Columbia and Manitoba have shifted toward identifying with their province (Environics Institute, 2012b).

Globalization theorists have argued that we live in an era in which identities are no longer inherited at birth but can take shape as a result of the deliberate choices that people make during their lives (Castells, 1997; Giddens, 1994). This opens up possibilities for the flourishing of more identities based on political struggles to achieve major social and cultural

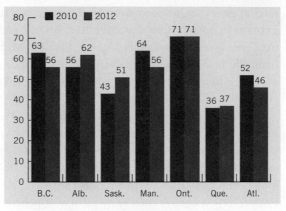

SOURCE: Environics Institute. (2012). *Focus Canada 2012*. Retrieved from http://www.environicsinstitute.org/uploads/institute-projects/environics %20institute%20%20focus%20canada%202012%20final%20report. pdf. Retrieved from www.mowatcentre.ca/pdfs/mowatResearch/8.pdf.

FIGURE 3-4
IDENTIFY MORE WITH COUNTRY THAN WITH PROVINCE, 2010–2012

changes. Since the early1960s, a wave of new social movements, including the women's, environmental, and lesbian and gay movements, contributed to the growth of identities based on gender, environmentalism, and sexual orientation (Smith, 2005).

Changing English Canadian and French Canadian Identities

Both the English Canadian and French Canadian identities—essential components of the Canadian identity—have shifted from a model of nationhood based on common ancestry to a more inclusive civic model (Resnick, 2005). After control over New France was transferred to the British in 1763, French Canadian society promoted a collective identity based on Roman Catholicism, the French language and ancestry, and agricultural vocations. This ethnic-based identity extended beyond the borders of the new colony of Quebec to include everyone of French Canadian ancestry.

On the English Canadian side, the British connection was the primary source of identity for people of English ancestry. During the interwar period in English Canada, a stronger brand of Canadian nationalism emerged as the country became more autonomous from Great Britain. After World War II, the economic and military prestige of Great Britain declined and Canada became a major industrial and diplomatic player on the world stage (Bumsted, 2004). Correspondingly, the British roots of the English Canadian identity also began to wither. The government set up a legally separate Canadian citizenship in 1947, ended appeals to the British Judicial Committee of the Privy Council in 1949, replaced British-born with Canadian-born governors general, and adopted the maple leaf flag in 1965 in place of the red ensign with the Union Jack. In 1967, the federal government put a stop to the discriminatory elements of an immigrant selection system that favoured British and other white immigrants over immigrants from Asia, Africa, and the Middle East. The move away from the British connection was reinforced by the adoption of a policy of official bilingualism in 1969 and **official multiculturalism** in 1971 (discussed later in this chapter).

Resnick (2005) argues that the French Canadian identity has also evolved into a more civic and inclusive identity that can be embraced by all Quebecers, regardless of their ancestral origins. Even sovereignists generally insist that the Quebec nation includes people of any ethnic, racial, or religious origin, as long as they conform to the common public language of French. Sovereignists thus contend that Québécois society includes francophone blacks with roots in Haiti, francophone Jews and Muslims with roots in Egypt or Morocco, bilingual anglophones, and immigrants whose first language is neither English nor French (Howard, 1998). This interpretation of the modern Quebec identity competes with the views of some who have argued that there is a gap between inclusive official discourse and the persistence of exclusion and discrimination against religious minorities in the province (Potvin, 2011).

CANADA: A MULTINATION AND POLYETHNIC STATE

William Kymlicka (1995) has described Canada as a multination state built on a federation of three distinct national groups: English, French, and Aboriginal. Aboriginal Canadians and the Québécois are each considered a **national minority** because each constitutes a nation (historical community with its own institutions, occupying a given territory, and sharing a distinct language and culture) that has been incorporated into a larger state. Canada is also a polyethnic state composed of many **ethnic groups**, which Kymlicka defines as groups of immigrants who have left their countries of origin to enter another society. Although such groups establish their own religious, commercial, cultural, and educational institutions (e.g., churches or mosques, specialty food shops, community centres, and schools), they are not considered "nations" because they do not occupy a separate territory. Furthermore, their members participate within the public institutions of the dominant culture, and most of them speak English or French (although some may speak their own language within their own communities).

Canada, like other multination and polyethnic states, has been confronted with the challenge of responding appropriately to the claims of national minorities and ethnic groups for recognition of their cultural distinctiveness. One way to meet such demands is by extending legal protections for civil and political rights to individuals. Guarantees of rights of freedom of association, religion, speech, mobility, and political organization allow individual members of national minorities and ethnic groups to

OFFICIAL MULTICULTURALISM
A policy introduced in 1971 that encouraged individuals to embrace the culture and tradition of their choice while retaining Canadian citizenship.

NATIONAL MINORITY
A culturally distinct and potentially self-governing society that has been incorporated into a larger state.

ETHNIC GROUPS
Groups of immigrants who have left their countries of origin to enter another society, but who do not occupy a separate territory in their new homeland.

protect and promote their rights and interests (Kymlicka, 1995). Another approach is to grant **differentiated citizenship** (Young, 1989), or special group-based legal or constitutional rights, to national minorities and ethnic groups. Kymlicka has identified at least three forms of group-based measures for accommodating national and ethnic differences: self-government rights, polyethnic rights, and special representation rights.

Self-Government Rights

Many multination states have met the demands of national minorities for recognition by giving them **self-government rights**—some kind of territorial jurisdiction or autonomy over their political and cultural affairs. One way of achieving this is through federalism, an institutional arrangement that divides power between the central and regional or provincial governments. Federalism can effectively provide self-government for a national minority if the national minority is geographically concentrated. For example, the federal division of powers in Canada gives the provinces, including Quebec, control over issues such as education, language, and social services that are crucial to the survival of minority cultures.

States may also redraw territorial boundaries so that national minorities living within a particular geographic area can acquire self-government. This is what occurred in 1999 when the Northwest Territories was divided into two and the territory of Nunavut was created in its eastern half. This arrangement in effect gave the predominantly Inuit population the right of self-government. Aboriginal self-government is discussed in Chapter 11.

Polyethnic Rights

Polyethnic rights give ethnic groups and religious minorities the right to express their cultural distinctiveness without discrimination. These rights would include public funding of ethnic cultural practices and the teaching of immigrant languages, as well as exemptions from laws that disadvantage minorities (Kymlicka, 1995). Following the introduction of official multiculturalism in 1971, the federal government established a multiculturalism program that was oriented toward helping ethnic groups maintain their cultural traditions and languages. Many federal institutions have also implemented policies that exempt minorities from dress codes that offend their religious traditions. For example, the Canadian Air Transport Security Authority, which employs screening officers at airports across the country, has a policy that recognizes its duty to respond to individual uniform requests by respecting the need for accommodation based on, but not limited to, race, national or ethnic origin, colour, religion, age, sex, or disability. The Employment Equity Act, 1995, and the Charter of Rights and Freedoms, 1982, provide the basis for the extension of some group-based rights for members of ethnic groups, as discussed later in this chapter.

DIFFERENTIATED CITIZENSHIP
The granting of special group-based legal or constitutional rights to national minorities and ethnic groups.

SELF-GOVERNMENT RIGHTS
Group-based rights that grant a national minority some kind of territorial jurisdiction or autonomy over its political and cultural affairs.

POLYETHNIC RIGHTS
Group-based rights that allow ethnic groups and religious minorities to express their cultural distinctiveness without discrimination.

Special Representation Rights

Special representation rights may also be given to national minorities and ethnic groups so that they can participate in the political process. For example, unlike New Zealand, which has established electoral districts in which only the indigenous Maori population can vote, Canada does not reserve seats for the representation of national minorities in the House of Commons and Senate.

MINORITY NATIONALISM AND THE CANADIAN STATE

According to the 2011 National Household Survey, more than 5 million people, or 16 percent of the total population, reported a French ancestry. Canadians of French ancestry share a common linguistic, religious, and historical heritage. They live in communities across Canada but are largely concentrated in Quebec, northern New Brunswick, and Ontario. Ninety percent of all Canadian francophones live in Quebec, where about 79 percent of the population reports French as a mother tongue (Statistics Canada, 2012b). Quebec's distinctive cultural makeup explains why the province has vied for more control over matters that it considers vital to the preservation of the French language and its social institutions.

Conquest and the Will to Survive

The Conquest of New France in 1759 marked a tragedy for French speakers and the central event in the history of Canadians of French ancestry. British governors replaced French officials, and English-speaking merchants from Britain and the American colonies quickly assumed control of Quebec's economic affairs (Cook, 1977). The Roman Catholic Church was the only important institution in Quebec to remain outside of British control, and it became the principal defender of the French Canadian way of life. French Canadian clerical and political leaders urged their people to resist **assimilation** into the anglophone culture through a strategy of *la survivance*, or survival. The French Canadian nation was to be preserved by resisting the anglicizing pressures of Protestantism, liberal democracy, and commercial occupations, and by remaining fiercely loyal to the Catholic religion, the French language, and the traditional mores of rural life. Supporters of traditional nationalism portrayed French Canada as an ethnic nation whose boundaries reached beyond Quebec to include all French Canadians.

British colonial authorities passed the Quebec Act in 1774 to secure the allegiance of French Canadian clerical and civic leaders to the British Crown. The Quebec Act granted formal protection to the status of the Roman Catholic religion and the system of civil law. In the meantime, French Canadians found a means of strengthening their ranks that involved neither military manoeuvres nor government proclamations—the high fertility rate among French Canadians enabled them to continue to outnumber English-speaking colonists, even after the immigration of Loyalists from the United States and English speakers from the British Isles.

The strategy of *la survivance* ensured the cultural survival of the French nation in Quebec, but it also contributed to the relative dearth of French Canadians in industry and finance. Discrimination against francophones was also a recognizable feature of the Quebec economy until the 1960s (McRoberts, 1988). Some francophones ran small- and medium-sized businesses, but anglophones controlled most of the province's wealth and high-paying managerial and technical jobs. The processes of economic and social modernization that unfolded from the early to mid-twentieth century placed increasing pressure on traditional French Canadian nationalism. By 1921, Quebec's urban population had surpassed the rural population, and manufacturing workers outnumbered farm workers by the mid-century (McRoberts, 1993). Quebec's economic modernization prompted groups representing cultural, academic, labour, and other interests to challenge the monopoly on power held by clerical elites, English Canadian and foreign business interests, and Maurice Duplessis's Union Nationale government that ruled during 1936–1939 and 1944–1959. The goal of these groups was to bring Quebec's society, economy, and government up to date—a goal that became known as *rattrapage,* or catching up.

Modern Quebec Nationalism and the Role of Language

The early 1960s marked a turning point in the province's history. The election of the provincial Liberals under Jean Lesage in 1960 ushered in a series of political, institutional, and social reforms referred to as the **Quiet Revolution**. The modern nationalism of the Quiet Revolution identified the French Canadian nation with the territory of Quebec. Instead of defining the nation in terms of language and religion, modern nationalism promoted the idea that the Québécois should assume control of their own affairs through the government of Quebec. The provincial government replaced church-run institutions in the areas of education, health, and social services, and took over a broader range of economic functions. It established a ministry of education; nationalized privately owned hydroelectric companies; created Crown corporations such as La Caisse de dépôt et placement, which manages public pensions and insurance funds; set up a Quebec Pension Plan; and provided career opportunities for the growing number of francophones. The provincial government also succeeded in persuading the federal government to give it more powers over social policy and immigration.

LINGUISTIC CLAIMS   In the face of declining birth rates and the tendency for immigrants to adopt English as their home language, several Quebec governments introduced language policies aimed at ensuring that francophones

QUIET REVOLUTION
A series of political, institutional, and social reforms ushered in under Quebec Liberal leader Jean Lesage beginning in 1960.

would not become a linguistic minority in the province. The Official Language Act of 1974 (Loi sur la langue officielle), also known as Bill 22, made French the sole official language of Quebec. It was replaced by the controversial Charter of the French Language (also known as Bill 101) in 1977. The Charter's main features stated that:

- French would be the sole official language in Quebec, the exclusive official language for proceedings of the provincial legislature and the courts, and the main language for public administration;
- businesses with 50 or more employees would need to receive a "francisation certificate" as a condition of doing business in the province;
- commercial signs and advertisements would be in French only; and
- children could enroll in English school if one of three conditions were met: if a child's parents had been educated in English in Quebec and the child had a sibling already going to an English school; if the child's parents were educated in English outside of Quebec but were living in the province when the law was passed; or if the child was already enrolled in an English school when the law came into effect.

Three of these provisions prompted court challenges from organizations in the anglophone community that strenuously objected to the restrictions on the use of English in the province. In 1979, the Supreme Court of Canada ruled that the provision making French the sole official language of the provincial legislature and the courts violated Section 133 of the Constitution Act, 1867, which guaranteed the equality of both languages in the Quebec National Assembly and in the courts of Quebec. The provisions concerning the language of commercial signage (modified in 1983 to make an exception for bilingual advertising by "ethnic businesses") were also challenged in court. In 1988, the Supreme Court of Canada ruled that the prohibition of all languages other than French in public signs, posters, and commercial advertising violated the right to freedom of expression guaranteed in the Canadian and Quebec Charters of Human Rights and Freedoms.

In response to the court's decision, the government of Quebec passed Bill 178, which invoked Section 33, the "notwithstanding" clause, of the Canadian Charter of Rights and Freedoms.[3] It reaffirmed the ban on languages other than French for commercial signs outside a business while permitting the use of other languages on interior signs, providing the French language was more prominently displayed. Just as the five-year limit on the application of the notwithstanding clause was set to expire, a less controversial law was put in place. In 1993, Bill 86 was passed, stating that more flexible government regulations, rather than laws, would determine when signs must be in French only or when other languages would be permitted.

[3]The "notwithstanding" clause allows federal or provincial governments to pass legislation that infringes on fundamental freedoms and legal and equality rights.

Bill 101's provisions concerning access to English-language education generated the most opposition from anglophones and immigrant groups who were upset that they could not send their children to English-language public schools and who were worried about the long-term viability of English-language schools in the province. In 1984, the Supreme Court ruled that the Bill 101 provision that guaranteed access to English-language education only to those children of Canadian citizens who had been educated in English in Quebec was unconstitutional because it violated the Canadian Charter of Rights and Freedoms. The Charter guarantees the right of Canadian citizens to have their children receive primary and secondary school instruction in English, providing they have received their primary school instruction in Canada in English, or if they have a child who has received or is receiving primary or secondary school instruction in English in Canada.[4] This right applies wherever in the province there is sufficient demand to warrant the provision of minority language instruction out of public funds. In 1993, the education provisions of Bill 101 were brought in line with the Charter.

THE CANADIAN STATE AND LANGUAGE RIGHTS   In contrast to the unilingual approach of the Quebec government, Canada has dealt with the issue of language claims by embedding the principle of linguistic duality in the country's Constitution, laws, and policies. Section 133 of the *Constitution Act, 1867*, states that English and French have equality of status in the federal Parliament and the Quebec National Assembly, and in federally established courts and all courts in Quebec. Language rights were extended in the 1982 Charter of Rights and Freedoms, enshrining English and French as the two official languages of the Canadian Parliament, the federal courts and federal public institutions, and the legislature, courts, and public institutions of New Brunswick, the only province that is officially bilingual. It also guarantees the rights of Canadians to have their children educated in their own official language where numbers warrant. This helps to protect and preserve both English and French and the cultures associated with them throughout Canada.

The principle of linguistic duality can also be seen in the federal government's policy response to the rising tide of Quebec nationalism in the 1960s. In 1963, the Liberal government of Lester B. Pearson established the Royal Commission on Bilingualism and Biculturalism to inquire into and report on the state of bilingualism and biculturalism in the country and to recommend what steps should be taken to develop Canada on the basis of an equal partnership between the English and French, taking into account the contributions made by other ethnic groups. The government followed up on the commission's recommendations by

---

[4]Except in Quebec, the Charter right also applies to Canadian citizens "whose first language learned and still understood is that of the English or French linguistic minority of the province in which they reside."

passing the Official Languages Act (OLA) in 1969, which regulates bilingualism in the federal public service and federally regulated industries in the private sector. The Act was designed to address the issue of francophone underrepresentation in the public service and to transform the language of the public service, which was, in most parts of the country, English. It reflects a philosophy of a Canada in which language rights are guaranteed to individuals and are safeguarded by national institutions.

The OLA (as amended in 1985) gives individual members of the public the right to communicate with and to be served by the federal government in English or French within the National Capital Region or elsewhere in Canada where there is significant demand for communications with and services from that office in that language, it requires that francophones and anglophones have equal opportunities to obtain employment and advancement in federal institutions, and it guarantees the ability of public servants from both language groups to work in the language of their choice. To strengthen the bilingual character of the federal bureaucracy, language training has been provided for public servants and an increasing share of positions have been designated as bilingual. About one-third of federal offices and service points across Canada communicate with and provide services in either English or French to Canadians. About 40 percent of positions in the public service require knowledge of both official languages (Treasury Board of Canada Secretariat, 2014a). The federal government has also promoted bilingualism through the financial assistance it provides for minority language education and second language instruction delivered by the provincial and territorial school boards. Although the goal of encouraging bilingualism across the country has yet to be realized, rates of bilingualism have grown among anglophones in every province and territory since 2001 (Corbeil & Blaser, 2007). In 2011, about 18 percent of Canadians reported being able to conduct a conversation in both English and French (Statistics Canada, 2012b).

Public opinion seems to favour continuing support for minority French- and English-language communities and bilingualism. A 2006 poll found that slightly more than 63 percent of Canadians felt that federal institutions should support the development of the official language minority community in their province, an increase of 17 percent over 2002 (Canadian Heritage/Decima, 2006). In 2012, a strong majority of Canadians (63 percent) favoured bilingualism for all of Canada and for their province, with support for a national policy of bilingualism most widespread in Quebec and among Canadians aged 18 to 29 (see Figure 3-5).

Self-Government and Sovereignty Claims

ORIGINS During the Confederation debates, most English Canadian leaders from the province of Canada favoured a unitary system of government that would assign all legislative powers to a national parliament. Yet French

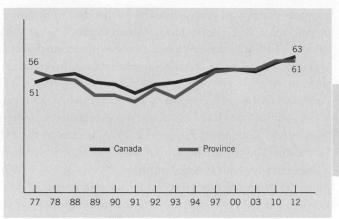

FIGURE 3-5
SUPPORT FOR
BILINGUALISM FOR
CANADA AND PROVINCE,
1977–2012 (PERCENTAGE)

Respondents were asked, "As you know, English and French are Canada's two official languages. Are you, personally, in favour of bilingualism for all of Canada? Are you in favour of bilingualism for your province?"

SOURCE: Environics Institute. (2012). *Focus Canada 2010*. Retrieved from http://www.environicsinstitute.org/uploads/institute-projects/environics%20institute%20%20focus%20canada%202012%20final%20report.

Canadian representatives from Canada East wanted a federal system that would give the provinces jurisdiction over linguistic and cultural matters. Politicians from the Maritimes also preferred the federal option because they had developed strong local identities, and some politicians from Canada West felt that the conflict between English Protestant and French Catholic communities, which had led to government instability in Canada, would subside if local affairs were assigned to the provinces.

The Constitution Act, 1867, established a federal system in which the authority to make laws and to tax was divided between a national government and provincial governments. Provincial governments were given exclusive jurisdiction over matters such as hospitals, municipal institutions, and property and civil rights, as well as shared jurisdiction over immigration. Each province could also make laws in relation to education, providing they did not overstep the existing religious education rights of the Protestant or Roman Catholic minority communities in their provinces. In the middle of the twentieth century, the federal government became more involved in provincial affairs through its controversial power to spend money in policy areas under provincial jurisdiction. At the same time, successive Quebec governments became more protective of what they argued were their exclusive powers under the Constitution.

The Quest for Independence

Before the mid-1960s, the idea of Quebec independence did not enjoy broad support. Quebec's quest for independence, or "sovereignty," became a crucial issue with the victory of the Parti Québécois (PQ) in the 1976 provincial election —a victory that sparked the exodus of many anglophones from the province. In May 1980, Quebecers were asked to vote yes or no—*oui ou non*—on a proposal that would give the province a mandate to negotiate a new agreement with Canada. The referendum proposal explained that the agreement would "enable Quebec to acquire the exclusive power to make its laws, levy its taxes and establish relations abroad—in other words, sovereignty—and at the same time, to maintain an economic association with Canada, including a common currency" (LeDuc, 2003, p. 104). It was defeated by 59.6 percent of provincial voters, with a majority of francophones voting against independence.

Some 15 years later, on June 12, 1995, leaders of the PQ, the federal Bloc Québécois, and the provincial Action démocratique du Québec (ADQ) signed an agreement which stated that after a "yes" victory in a provincial referendum, the National Assembly would be able to proclaim the sovereignty of Quebec and the provincial government would propose to Canada a treaty on a new economic and political partnership (Government of Canada, 2000). If negotiations succeeded, the treaty would provide for a customs union, a monetary policy, citizenship, and the mobility of people, capital, and services. If negotiations failed, the stalemate would empower the National Assembly to declare sovereignty.

In September 1995, the government of Quebec publicized the wording of the referendum question: "Do you agree that Québec should become sovereign, after having made a formal offer to Canada for a new Economic and Political Partnership, within the scope of the Bill respecting the future of Québec and of the agreement signed on June 12, 1995?" Ninety-four percent of eligible voters turned out to vote, and they narrowly defeated the proposal by a 50.6 percent to 49.4 percent margin. However, Quebec's PQ premier, Jacques Parizeau, declared that the separatists had not really lost because more than 60 percent of francophones had voted for independence. To the consternation of many, he added that the sovereignist forces had been defeated by money and the ethnic vote, raising the spectre that Quebec nationalism was not civic in character.

In the wake of the second referendum, many of the sovereignist movement's more charismatic leaders abandoned politics. The 2003 provincial election returned the Liberals to power, meaning that debates about independence no longer dominated Quebec politics. In the 2011 federal election, voters in Quebec backed the federalist New Democratic Party in historic numbers and reduced the separatist Bloc Québécois to just four seats in the House of Commons. In 2012, the PQ returned to power with a minority government following a campaign in which corruption allegations were raised against the incumbent Liberals, and in which PQ leader Pauline Marois campaigned on controversial measures to boost French culture, language, and identity. These included new language laws that would force small businesses to work in French, and laws banning public employees from wearing religious symbols such as Muslim headscarves and Jewish kippas in the workplace (Campion-Smith & Woods, 2012).

An early election was triggered in 2014 when Premier Marois asked the lieutenant governor to dissolve the legislature. The PQ entered the election

BOX 3-1

Culture Wars

In 2013, the Parti Québécois government introduced Bill 60, the charter affirming the values of state secularism and religious neutrality and of equality between women and men, and providing a framework for accommodation requests. If passed, the legislation would have banned public sector employees from wearing conspicuous religious symbols such as crosses, kippas, and hijabs while on the job. It would also have required anyone providing public services (with some exceptions) or receiving them to remove religious face coverings. While initially enjoying substantial public support, Bill 60 drew strong criticism from politicians, religious leaders, and civil liberties associations inside and outside Quebec, who argued that the measures were unconstitutional infringements of religious freedoms. Some have even partly attributed the victory of the Quebec Liberals in the 2014 provincial election to the controversial bill.

While Bill 60 died with the election defeat of the PQ, divisive debates about the accommodation of religion in public institutions have not. The newly elected Quebec Liberal government introduced Bill 62, which would require people who work in the public sector or who do business with government officials to remove their face coverings. The bill also established the conditions under which accommodations on religious grounds could be granted (National Assembly, 2015). During the 2015 federal election, Prime Minister Harper announced that, if re-elected, a Conservative government would consider banning federal civil servants from wearing niqabs.

with a realistic prospect of winning a majority government. However, the party's support began to collapse after it announced Pierre Péladeau, president and CEO of media conglomerate Quebecor, as a star candidate. Péladeau's outspoken support for a third referendum on Quebec sovereignty, and an anti-union background that was at odds with the party's social democratic history, sidelined another issue that the PQ had identified as its main campaign theme: the controversial Bill 60, often referred to as the Quebec Charter of Values (see Box 3-1: Culture Wars) and questions about the integrity of the Quebec Liberal Party. The Liberals under Philippe Couillard were elected with a majority government, and the incumbent PQ finished second with 30 seats, marking the lowest seat total for the party since 1989. After losing her own riding, Premier Marois stepped down as party leader and Péladeau was elected leader in May 2015. In the wake of declining support for parties committed to Quebec independence and the fading prominence of jurisdictional disputes between the federal and provincial governments, divisions between those favouring state secularism and those supporting the accommodation of religious identities in public institutions have flared up in Quebec and federal politics.

Canada's Response to Claims for Self-Government and Sovereignty

During the 1980 Quebec referendum campaign, Prime Minister Pierre Trudeau promised that his government would begin the process of renewing the federal system if Quebec voted no to the sovereignty-association proposal. The federal government and nine provinces reached an agreement in 1981 on constitutional reform that would become the Constitution Act, 1982. The Act included formal procedures for amending the Constitution and a Charter of Rights and Freedoms, but did little to satisfy the requests for change that Quebec governments, both federalist and separatist, had presented since the Quiet Revolution. Specifically, the PQ government of René Lévesque refused to sign the 1981 agreement on the grounds that it failed to meet the following conditions:

- It did not recognize the character of Quebec as a distinct society.
- It restricted the provinces' exclusive rights in linguistic matters.
- The amending formula removed what Quebec considered its traditional veto over constitutional changes.
- The amending formula did not guarantee financial compensation for provinces that chose not to participate in shared-cost federal–provincial programs other than education and culture.

Despite Quebec's refusal to sign the 1981 agreement, the Constitution Act, 1982, applies to the province. Subsequently, the prime minister and all provincial leaders reached agreements on constitutional changes—the Meech Lake Accord, 1987, and the Charlottetown Accord, 1992—that included recognition of Quebec as a distinct society. However, as discussed in Chapter 10, both accords were not approved, ending efforts to achieve comprehensive constitutional reform.

FEDERAL PLANS A AND B   The razor-thin victory for the federalist side in Quebec's 1995 sovereignty referendum led the federal government to develop two strategies to defuse Quebec nationalism. The first approach, dubbed "Plan A," was designed to convince Quebecers about the benefits of staying in Canada. It consisted of non-constitutional initiatives that responded to some of Quebec's traditional demands. In 1996, the House of Commons passed a resolution recognizing the distinct character of Quebec's unique culture, civil law tradition, and French-speaking majority in the province. The 1996 Constitutional Amendments Act gave Quebec a form of veto over future constitutional changes.

Intergovernmental agreements that decentralized powers to the provinces were also part of the federal government's strategy following the Quebec referendum (Russell, 2006). Beginning in 1996, more powers over forestry, mining, recreation, tourism, and social housing were devolved to the provinces. The second thrust of Ottawa's post-referendum strategy, dubbed "Plan B," was aimed at clarifying the terms for secession to make it very difficult for future referendums on Quebec's sovereignty to succeed. In April 1996, the federal government sought a ruling from the Supreme Court on three questions:

- Under the Constitution of Canada, can the National Assembly, legislature, or government of Quebec effect the secession of Quebec from Canada unilaterally?

- Is there a right to self-determination under international law that would give the National Assembly, legislature, or government of Quebec the right to effect the secession of Quebec from Canada unilaterally?
- In the event of a conflict between domestic and international law, which would take precedence?

The court ruled in 1998 (*Reference re Secession of Quebec,* 1998) that while Quebec did not enjoy a right under international or domestic law to unilateral secession, the federal government would be obligated to negotiate with Quebec if a clear majority of Quebecers responded to a clear question that they no longer wished to remain in Canada.

In response to the ruling, the Canadian Parliament passed the Clarity Act in 2000. The Clarity Act sets out the rules by which the government and Parliament would react to future referendums. It states that the government will not negotiate the terms of separation with a province unless the House of Commons has determined that the question is clear and that a clear expression of will has been obtained by a clear majority of the population. Negotiations would have to include the division of assets and liabilities, changes to the borders of the province, the "rights, interests and claims" of Aboriginal peoples, and the protection of minority rights. Finally, a constitutional amendment approved by all provincial governments would have to be passed before separation could occur. This would, undoubtedly, make it extremely difficult for a province to separate from Canada. The Quebec government retaliated with its own act respecting the exercise of the fundamental rights and prerogatives of the Quebec people and the Quebec state. It states that "the Québec people has the inalienable right to freely decide the political regime and legal status of Québec," and that a simple majority of 50 percent plus one of the valid votes cast in a referendum counts as an expression of the people's will (Statutes of Quebec, 2000, Ch. 46).

The Conservative government of Prime Minister Stephen Harper pursued non-constitutional measures in a bid to temper support for Quebec independence. These have included allowing Quebec to take a formal role at the United Nations Educational, Scientific and Cultural Organization (UNESCO) and persuading the House of Commons to support a motion recognizing "that the Québécois form a nation within a united Canada." Supporters of the motion argued that it would help defuse Quebec nationalism by recognizing that Quebec is a distinct sociological nation within the united civic nation of Canada. Others worried that the recognition of nationhood might legitimize future claims for sovereignty.

SUPPORT FOR INDEPENDENCE   Public opinion polls over the past several decades have rarely found that a clear majority of Quebecers support independence.[5] In 2014, one poll estimated 39 percent of Quebecers would vote "yes"

---

[5]Support for independence peaked at 70 percent in 1990 after the defeat of the Meech Lake Accord.

in a referendum on sovereignty (CBC News, March 9, 2014), while another suggested less than 30 percent of 18–24-year-olds supported Quebec independence (Mennie, June 2, 2014)

POLYETHNICITY AND THE CANADIAN STATE

Wave after wave of immigration has transformed Canadian cities into polyethnic communities that are home to hundreds of ethnic groups with different cultural traditions and practices. The urban character of Canadian immigration extends beyond Toronto, Montreal, and Vancouver, as large numbers of immigrants and their families have settled in Edmonton, Calgary, Winnipeg, Ottawa, and Brampton.

Canada's multicultural model of integrating immigrants into the broader political community supports cultural pluralism within a constitutional and legislative framework that grants rights and protections primarily to individuals. Some group-based polyethnic rights are guaranteed in certain laws and policies. The most significant laws and policies that support the multicultural model of integration—the shift from an assimilationist to a multicultural integration model in 1971, the Human Rights Act (1977), the Canadian Charter of Rights and Freedoms (1982), the Multiculturalism Act (1988), and the Employment Equity Act (1995)—are discussed below.

Immigration

From Confederation until the 1960s, Canada's immigration policy was designed to sustain the primarily white, European character of the population. Between 1880 and 1884, when the transcontinental Canadian Pacific Railway was being constructed, Chinese labourers were recruited to work on the most dangerous and least well-paid jobs. Once the railway was completed, the federal government tried to discourage the labourers from settling permanently in Canada. It passed the Chinese Immigration Act, 1885, which introduced the "head tax" system through which Chinese admission to Canada was made more expensive. The 1923 Chinese Exclusion Act later banned all but a trickle of Chinese immigration.

In the early twentieth century, the Liberal government of Prime Minister Wilfrid Laurier (1896–1911) embarked upon a plan to recruit Eastern Europeans to populate and develop the agricultural potential of the Prairie provinces. In the same era, the government put measures in place to discourage black Americans and South Asians from entering Canada. During the two world wars and the Depression era, immigration to Canada was greatly reduced in response to these crises. Following the end of World War II, an economic boom favoured the opening up of Canadian immigration policy. In 1947, Prime Minister Mackenzie King stated that the government would encourage population growth through immigration, but that immigration was not to change the fundamental character of the population and that any considerable "Oriental" immigration would give rise to social and economic problems—sentiments that are far removed from today's policy of promoting diversity. The 1952 Immigration Act gave preferential status to immigrants from the United Kingdom, some Commonwealth countries, France, and the United States (Kelley & Trebilcock, 1998).

Several developments led to a more open and inclusive immigrant selection system in the 1960s. These included the country's post-war participation in international organizations and agreements committed to the protection of human rights, the need for labour in a rapidly expanding economy, and a decline in applications from traditional regions as European economies recovered from wartime upheaval. In 1962, the Progressive Conservative government of John Diefenbaker issued new regulations that eliminated the provisions for preferred countries for independent immigrants, that is, people with specific occupational skills, experience, and personal qualifications. For the first time in the history of Canada's immigration policy, the admission criteria would be based solely on factors such as education, work experience, and other skills, rather than on a candidate's race or nationality. In 1967, a new points system for independent immigrants was adopted that assessed prospective immigrants on their occupational experience and training, educational background, knowledge of the official languages, and related criteria. The Immigration and Refugee Protection Act (IRPA), which came into effect in 2002, amended the points system to give more weight to education and knowledge of English or French.

IMMIGRATION TODAY   In 2013, Canada ranked among the world's major immigrant-receiving countries, admitting close to 259 000 **permanent residents** (Citizenship and Immigration Canada, 2014b). Canadian public opinion generally supports immigration (see Figure 3-6), in contrast to the negative attitudes prevailing in the United States and various European countries (German Marshall Fund of the United States, 2011). A 2012 survey found that a strong majority (83 percent) agree that immigration has had a positive impact on the Canadian economy and disagree (72 percent) that immigrants take jobs from other Canadians (Environics Institute, 2012a). Canadian support for high levels of immigration has been relatively unaffected by recessions, the threat of terrorism, and negative coverage of certain immigrant groups (Reitz, 2011). However, there are signs that Canada's openness to diversity and immigration is in flux. The percentage of Canadians who think that too many immigrants and members of visible minorities are coming to Canada has doubled between 2005 and 2015 (Ekospolitics.com, 2015).

The Immigration and Refugee Protection Act identifies four major categories under which permanent immigrants are admitted into the country: economic, family class, refugees, and other immigrants. The number of people admitted in each category shows that Canada has prioritized economic over family reunification and humanitarian policy objectives. Every year since 1995, more than half of all immigrants to Canada were from the economic category, which includes

PERMANENT RESIDENTS
Immigrants who are allowed to live in Canada and receive certain rights and privileges, while remaining a citizen of their home country. Permanent residents must pay taxes and respect all Canadian laws.

FIGURE 3-6
CANADIAN ATTITUDES
ABOUT IMMIGRATION
LEVELS, 1977–2012

Notes: In your opinion, do you feel there are too many, too few, or about the right number of immigrants coming to Canada?

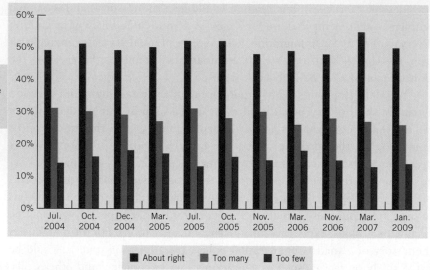

SOURCE: Environics Institute. (2012). *Focus Canada 2012.* Retrieved from http://www.environicsinstitute.org/uploads/institute-projects/environics%20institute%20%20focus%20canada%202012%20final%20report.pdf

PROVINCIAL/TERRITORIAL NOMINEES

Permanent immigrants who are nominated by provinces or territories on the basis of their skills, education, and work experience.

REFUGEES

People living in or outside Canada who fear persecution in their home country or whose removal from Canada to their country of origin would subject them to torture, a risk to their life, or a risk of cruel and unusual treatment.

skilled workers, business immigrants (i.e., investors, entrepreneurs, self-employed), caregivers, **provincial/territorial nominees**, and their dependants. The family class was the second largest category of immigrants in 2013 at about 31 percent of total immigration, and is composed of spouses, partners, children, and other relatives of Canadian residents who want to reunite with their families.

Refugees comprise the third largest category and include people living in or outside Canada who fear persecution in their home country or whose removal from Canada would subject them to torture, a risk to their life, or a risk of cruel and unusual treatment (Milan, 2011). In 2013, the refugee category represented about 9 percent of all immigrants (Citizenship and Immigration Canada, 2014a), lower than the annual shares of refugees admitted throughout the 1980s and early 1990s (Milan, 2011).

Immigration has long been used to develop the labour market—an approach that can be seen in the increasing number of foreign workers who have been admitted to Canada on a temporary basis. Temporary foreign workers (TFWs) include those who are recruited to work as live-in caregivers or to fill jobs in farming, in the manufacturing and service industries, and in certain professions. Between 2004 and 2013, the number of TFWs increased from 86 570 to 176 613, as the number of refugee claimants in the temporary immigration stream dropped from 25 526 to 10 350 over the same period. International students also make up a growing share of temporary immigration. Their numbers have increased from 104 986 in 2004 to 284 050 in 2013 (Citizenship and Immigration Canada, 2014b).

In response to criticisms about Canada's increased reliance on TFWs and of measures allowing employers to pay them less than the average wage for their occupation, the government reformed the Temporary Foreign Worker program in 2013 to place a cap of 10 percent on the proportion of an employer's workforce that can consist of low-wage TFWs,[6] to require employers who are applying to bring TFWs to Canada to report the number of Canadians who applied for and were interviewed for an available job, and to explain why those Canadians were not hired. The government has also refused to process TFW applications for selected low-wage/lower-skilled occupations from employers in the accommodation and food services sector and the retail trade sector in economic regions that have an unemployment rate of 6 percent or higher (Employment and Social Development Canada, 2014). However, the proposed Trans-Pacific Partnership (see Chapter 4) is expected to facilitate the entry of TFWs although the details were not available at the time of writing.

REFUGEE POLICY   At times, Canada has been a haven for **asylum seekers,** including providing sanctuary to American slaves travelling the Underground Railroad, displaced persons arriving from Europe following World War II, more than 37 000 Hungarians after the communist suppression of the Hungarian Uprising in 1956, about 60 000 Vietnamese in the late 1970s, and 5000 airlifted from Kosovo. As well, American war resisters were welcomed

ASYLUM SEEKERS
Individuals who have sought international protection and whose claim for refugee status has not yet been determined.

Three year old Alan Kurdi's body was washed up on a beach in Turkey after an overloaded boat of Syrian refugees seeking to reach Greece capsized. Although the Canadian government rejected Kurdi's aunt application to sponsor the family in June 2015, the sponsorship application for seven family members was approved in November 2015.

© Nilufer Demir/AFP/Getty Images

---

[6]On-farm primary agriculture and the Live-in Caregiver Program are exempt from these caps.

during the Vietnam War, Chileans during the brutal dictatorship of Augusto Pinochet, and persecuted Africans from Uganda more recently.

Accepting refugees has been controversial. In the 1930s, Canada begrudgingly accepted just 4000 Jewish refugees fleeing Nazi persecution. More recently, about 4 million people fled the horrific conflict in Syria, including nearly 1 million seeking refuge in Europe in 2015. However, Canada had resettled only 2374 Syrian refugees by September 2015 (Fine, 2015, September 4). Among those seeking refuge in Canada was Alan Kurdi, whose family has relatives in Canada. A picture of the three-year-old boy lying dead on a Turkish beach after an overloaded boat of refugees capsized went viral around the world. The new Liberal government promised to accept 25 000 Syrian refugees by March 2006.

By law, anyone who enters Canadian territory has the right to an in-person hearing on Canadian soil to determine the legitimacy of his or her asylum claim. During the first six months of 2014, Canada was the 15th largest recipient of asylum claims in 44 industrialized countries, with Germany, the United States, and France as the top three (United Nations High Commission on Refugees, 2014).

In recent years, Canada's refugee system has been criticized for being too lax in allowing rejected asylum seekers to remain in the country for too long, and for being soft on allowing "bogus" refugees to enter Canada. In 2012, the Protecting Canada's Immigration System Act brought reforms to Canada's refugee system. The legislation aims to provide faster protection to bona fide refugees and faster removal of those who are not (Citizenship and Immigration Canada, 2012). Supporters of the legislation argue that the existing refugee system had been encouraging people to make unfounded claims, knowing they would be able to live and work in Canada for many years, while genuine refugees are forced to wait. One of the more contentious aspects of the law sorts refugee claimants into two groups: those from democratic countries deemed safe and those from more dangerous spots. Designated safe countries of origin include countries that do not normally produce refugees, that have a robust human rights record, and that offer strong state protection. Critics have argued that safe-country lists are politically motivated and flawed, since even well-established democracies sometimes fail to protect their citizens from persecution (Schmitz, 2010). Human rights organizations have argued that countries such as Hungary, which has been designated as a safe country, have done little to protect the Roma and other minorities from violence and discrimination (see Box 3-2: Is None Too Many for the Roma?).

The Protecting Canada's Immigration System Act also contains measures to combat human smuggling, a global criminal enterprise in which smugglers charge people large sums of money to help them reach Canada illegally. These were prompted by the arrival off the British Columbia coast in 2009 and 2010 of two cargo ships carrying hundreds of Tamil-speaking refugee claimants. The arrival of the MV Sun Sea in 2010 raised questions about the reasons why the passengers had made the perilous voyage across the Pacific Ocean. The arrivals responded that they were refugees seeking asylum under the 1951 United

"None Is Too Many" for the Roma?

The passage of the Protecting Canada's Immigration System Act in 2012 ushered in a new system that sorts refugee claimants into two groups: those from democratic countries deemed safe and those from more dangerous spots. As of 2015, Canada had designated 37 countries as safe places that should not generate many legitimate refugee cases. Refugee claimaints from "safe" countries have a few weeks to prepare for the hearings that determine the legitimacy of their refugee claims. If their claims are unsuccessful, they lose their right of appeal to the Immigration and Refugee Board and are deported faster. The government says reducing the number of claims from countries determined to be safe will help the refugee claimants who are most in need of protection. But the new system remains unpopular with refugee advocates who say that valid claims are being turned down.

From 2010 to 2012, Hungary was the largest source of asylum claims and is one of the countries on the "safe" list. The Roma in Hungary, who have often been labelled as "gypsies," face poverty, discrimination, and violence from extremist groups (Human Rights Watch, 2014), and have been a major source of refugee claimants. Leaders of the Roma community in Canada have strongly criticized Hungary's designation as a "safe country" and government moves to discourage asylum claims from the Roma.

In 2013, the Canadian government funded a billboard, bus shelter, and radio ad campaign in Hungarian cities with large Roma populations, announcing that to deter abuse, people with unfounded refugee claims will be returned quickly to Hungary. After the changes were brought in, the number of people claiming refugee status reached historic lows in 2013 (Wingrove, 2014). The drop in asylum claims raises the question of whether "none is too many" for the Roma. "None is too many" refers to a statement by a senior Canadian immigration official in 1945 commenting on the number of Jewish people who should be allowed into the country.

Nations Refugee Convention, which Canada has signed. They said they were in danger of being killed by the Sri Lankan government, which had carried out violent reprisals against many Tamil civilians following the end of a 25-year civil war against Tamil separatists. Some questioned this version of the story, suggesting that the passengers were not genuine refugees but terrorists and criminals, or that they were economic migrants trying to jump the immigration queue (Literary Review of Canada, 2011). Some called for them to be sent back to sea, recalling what Canada did in 1939 when it forced more than 900 Jewish refugees aboard the *MS St. Louis* to return to Nazi-dominated Europe.

In an attempt to discourage a repeat of other dramatic incidents, the new Act gives the Minister of Public Safety the power to designate the arrival of a group of people as an "irregular arrival" and a "human smuggling event." It also imposes mandatory minimum prison sentences for those convicted of human smuggling and allows prosecutors to apply greater penalties to ship owners and operators involved in smuggling. In addition, it makes it mandatory to detain those deemed to have arrived in an irregular manner until the identity of a claimant has been established and a refugee claim approved (Citizenship and Immigration Canada, 2011a).

In 2012, the government introduced a new policy denying health care to failed refugee claimants and to refugee claimants from countries deemed safe by Ottawa. Refugee and medical advocacy groups challenged the policy and, in 2014, the Federal Court struck it down on the grounds that it was a form of "cruel and unusual treatment" that intentionally targeted vulnerable children and adults, violating Section 12 of the Canadian Charter of Rights and Freedoms. In the case, the government argued that it had the right to try to deter bogus claimants from coming to Canada by denying them medical care. It said the cuts would save $80 million over four years, and those denied care could turn to charity, emergency rooms, or private insurance.

Citizenship: Defining "Who Belongs"

Canadian citizenship was not established until 1947, marking another significant symbol of independent nationhood. Prior to that, both native-born and naturalized citizens were British subjects. Canadian citizenship means having legal status, sharing equally in the rights and responsibilities that belong to each Canadian, and taking an active part in Canadian society. Citizens possess important rights that are not enjoyed by permanent residents, such as the right to vote and to run for political office in federal and provincial elections, the right to hold certain public offices, and the right to hold a Canadian passport. Canadian citizenship is highly valued around the world. In 2013, more than 333 000 people applied for citizenship, the highest number in Canada's history. The country also has the world's highest rate of naturalization—85 percent of immigrants become Canadian citizens (Citizenship and Immigration Canada, 2014a).

Under current laws, citizenship remains relatively open to new immigrants. In addition, Canadians can take on citizenship in another country without automatically losing their Canadian citizenship. Applicants must be at least 18, but parents may apply on behalf of their minor children. They must also be able to speak English or French and to demonstrate knowledge of Canada and the rights and responsibilities of citizenship. This knowledge is evaluated in a written test or oral interview. The final step in becoming a citizen is to take the oath of citizenship at a public ceremony where a citizenship judge administers the oath and presents each new Canadian with a Certificate of Canadian Citizenship. Citizenship applications will be turned down for various reasons, including: being charged with or convicted of certain crimes in Canada or abroad; being investigated for, charged with, or convicted of a war crime or a crime against humanity; and posing a security risk (Citizenship and Immigration Canada, 2014b).

The passage of the Strengthening Canadian Citizenship Act in 2014 made key changes to the Citizenship Act that have expanded the grounds for revoking Canadian citizenship and tightened access to citizenship for some, while making it easier for others to become a Canadian citizen. They include:

- new rules that allow the government to revoke Canadian citizenship from dual citizens who are convicted of terrorism, treason, or spying, or from dual citizens who have served as members of an armed force of a country or an organized armed group engaged in armed conflict with Canada. This would include even those individuals born in Canada.

- new rules of residency that require citizenship applicants to live in the country for at least four of the six years prior to applying for citizenship, and for at least 183 days per year in four of the six years. Previously, citizenship applicants had to reside in Canada for three out of four years, with the term "residency" undefined.
- new language and knowledge requirements that expand the age group required to take the citizenship test to 14–64, from 18–54;
- reducing the qualifying period for citizenship by one year for individuals serving or on exchange with the Canadian Armed Forces.
- extending citizenship to "Lost Canadians" who were born or naturalized in Canada, as well as to those who were British subjects residing in Canada, prior to January 1, 1947 (or April 1, 1949, for Newfoundland and Labrador), and to the children of "Lost Canadians" who were born abroad.

A new guide has been developed to help newcomers prepare for their citizenship test. The guide emphasizes the importance of obeying the law, voting in elections, volunteering, and knowing the country's military history. It includes new items intended to articulate Canadian values to prospective citizens (Citizenship and Immigration Canada, 2011b):

- Canada's openness and generosity do not extend to "barbaric cultural practices that tolerate spousal abuse, honour killings, female genital mutilation, forced marriage or other gender-based violence."
- Canada's diversity includes gay and lesbian Canadians, who enjoy the full protection of and equal treatment under the law, including access to civil marriage.

When the guide was released, Liberal party leader Justin Trudeau suggested that the government should have qualified violence against women as "absolutely unacceptable" rather than belittling other cultures with the word "barbaric." The criticism did not deter the majority Conservative government from introducing legislation aimed at preventing certain cultural practices that it deemed to be "barbaric." In June 2015, the Zero Tolerance for Barbaric Cultural Practices Act received Royal Assent. It creates new measures under the Immigration and Refugee Protection Act that will render permanent and temporary residents inadmissible to Canada if they practise polygamy, will criminalize conduct related to early and forced marriages, and will limit the defence of provocation so that it would not apply in "honour" killings and many spousal homicides (Government of Canada, 2015). During the 2015 federal election, the Conservatives pledged that they would establish a tip line for reporting "barbaric cultural practices" to the RCMP.

Immigrant Integration

Since the 1970s, governments have grappled with the major issue of how to integrate immigrants into Canadian society (Frideres, 2008). The concept of **integration** can be understood as both an outcome and a process. Integration may imply a desirable result that is reflected in low levels of conflict between native-born and immigrant Canadians and in mutual respect and understanding between these groups (Ruspini, 2005). Integration can also describe the process through which an immigrant becomes a member of the host society. Moreover, within these two broad definitions, there are different types of integration. For example:

- social integration describes the participation of immigrants in Canadian institutions;
- cultural integration describes the processes of learning about the host culture and its values and norms (Heckmann, 1997);
- economic integration refers to the process of finding a job and earning an income that matches one's educational and experiential background; and
- political integration refers to participation in electoral processes and other forms of political engagement.

Until 1971, Canada generally encouraged immigrants to assimilate into the dominant—usually anglophone—culture. Classical models of assimilation expect that immigrants, ethnic minorities, and members of the majority group will become similar over time in their norms, values, behaviours, and characteristics (Brown & Bean, 2006). Since Canada adopted a policy of official multiculturalism (discussed below), recognizing cultural diversity has become a cornerstone of the Canadian identity and the model for integrating members of cultural groups into the political community. Until the mid-twentieth century, immigrants to Canada were considered responsible for their own integration. Today, prospective immigrants and newcomers benefit from federal and/or provincial settlement and integration programs and services before and after their arrival in Canada.

Immigration presents economic, demographic, and cultural development opportunities for countries, but it also challenges their capacity to come up with the best mix of programs and services that will help newcomers adjust to a new homeland. Despite the programs discussed above, injustices persist in Canadian society. Members of certain visible minority groups feel that they are more likely to be the target of discriminatory or unfair treatment than white Canadians. A related tension that surfaces frequently in public discourse is the question of racial profiling used by police and security agencies. Studies have shown that members of the black community are both subject to greater police surveillance and more likely to get caught when they do break the law (Wortley & Tanner, 2004). Muslim Canadians also feel they are often subject to tighter-than-justified security surveillance (Kahn & Saloojee, 2003).

INTEGRATION
The multidimensional process through which an immigrant becomes a member of the host society.

The economic integration of newcomers is another source of strain. Critics argue that Canada needs to do more to inform newcomers about labour market conditions and society before people make the decision to migrate. Questions arise, too, about the emphasis that the points system places on selecting immigrants with high levels of formal education and language skills. Supporters of the points system argue that it offers a more objective and non-discriminatory method of selecting potential citizens and ensures that Canada has a highly educated and skilled labour pool. Critics feel that the new system favours wealthier immigrants who can pay for education and training or make investments. Others are increasingly concerned about the emphasis on selecting highly educated and skilled immigrants, only to see many of them under-employed in low-wage jobs following their arrival because their foreign education credentials and work experience are not recognized (Grant & Sweetman, 2004; Picot & Hou, 2003).

"REASONABLE ACCOMMODATION"   Conflicts between established members of a community and newcomers are not uncommon in polyethnic societies. Debates in Quebec about how to accommodate the requests of cultural and religious minorities for differential treatment illustrate how easily these tensions may be ignited. Beginning in 2006, sometimes incendiary or exaggerated media reports of "excessive" accommodations prompted calls from the public for a tougher approach to immigrants and minorities. Part of the population felt that some minority group practices threatened Quebec's core values. In response to perceptions of a growing crisis, Premier Jean Charest appointed the Bouchard–Taylor Commission in 2007 to examine accommodation practices in Quebec and other societies, to conduct public consultations, and to recommend accommodation practices that conformed to Quebec's values.

The commission report discussed numerous controversies that had arisen over the accommodation of minority religious practices. One such incident involved a spat in 2006 between members of a Montreal YMCA and leaders of a neighbouring Hasidic Jewish congregation. The trigger was a decision by the YMCA management to install frosted glass windows in place of the regular glass in the windows of its exercise room. The congregation had asked and paid for the frosted windows because it was concerned that its younger male members could view "scantily clad" women exercising through the regular glass. The installation of the frosted windows prompted a complaint from YMCA members who objected to the accommodation. The conflict was resolved when the YMCA announced that it would replace the frosted glass with regular glass equipped with blinds.

After conducting research, public consultations, and hearings on accommodation controversies and practices, the Bouchard–Taylor Commission concluded that Quebec society had made significant strides in accommodating cultural diversity and that there was no indication of a crisis in public institutions. Nevertheless, it noted the need for improved intercultural understanding and pointed out the existence of xenophobic and even racist sentiments against Muslims and Jews. It made recommendations for providing cultural sensitivity training for journalists and the staff of all public institutions, encouraging state and partly state-controlled institutions to adopt policies on accommodating cultural and religious diversity, and reinforcing the principle of state neutrality and the separation of church and state. In late 2008, the Quebec government announced that new immigrants in the economic and family reunification categories must sign a pledge to "respect the common values of Quebec society." These include gender equality, the rule of law, and the separation of church and state.

MULTICULTURALISM   For many Canadians, multiculturalism is seen as an important part of the Canadian identity (Kymlicka, 2009). In 1971, Canada became the first country in the world to adopt a policy of official multiculturalism. The landmark policy marked a new approach to nation-building that encouraged individuals to embrace the culture and tradition of their choice while retaining Canadian citizenship. It was introduced in response to the recommendation from the Royal Commission on Bilingualism and Biculturalism that Canada adopt an official policy of multiculturalism and multilingualism as a means of integrating immigrants into Canadian society. Prime Minister Pierre Trudeau instead chose to promote a policy of multiculturalism within a bilingual framework. The main objectives of the policy were to:

- help cultural groups to retain and foster their identity;
- help members of all cultural groups to overcome cultural barriers to their full participation in Canadian society;
- promote creative exchanges among all Canadian cultural groups; and
- assist immigrants in learning at least one of Canada's official languages.

The Canadian government followed through by providing financial grants to ethnic and immigrant organizations and funding ethnic studies programs at universities, official language training, and initiatives to help ethnic minorities in the areas of human rights, racial discrimination, citizenship, and cross-cultural understanding (Mahtani, 2002). The policy gained further momentum after ethnic groups successfully lobbied for the inclusion of a clause in the Charter of Rights and Freedoms (Section 27) recognizing Canada's multicultural heritage. In 1988, the Progressive Conservative government passed the Multiculturalism Act, which included the objectives of assisting in the preservation of culture and language, reducing discrimination, enhancing cultural awareness and understanding, and promoting culturally sensitive institutional change at the federal level. Until 1990, the federal government also provided support to ethnocultural organizations to offer **heritage language** instruction in German, Italian, Ukrainian, and other languages.

Funding for multicultural programs was cut back in the 1990s as part of the government's overall debt and deficit reduction strategy—and in response

HERITAGE LANGUAGE
Any language other than the Aboriginal languages of the First Nations and Inuit peoples and the official languages of English and French.

to criticisms that the existing program was undermining the development of immigrant attachments to Canada. Beginning in the 1990s, the program's focus shifted to removing discriminatory barriers for the growing number of visible minority immigrants whose main concerns were finding employment, housing, and education and fighting discrimination (Dewing & Leman, 2006). New program objectives place more emphasis on promoting what the government refers to as Canadian values: democracy, freedom, human rights, and the rule of law (Citizenship and Immigration Canada, 2009).

Since the adoption of multiculturalism, Canadians have debated its impact on the integration of immigrants and their children. Supporters have argued that multiculturalism helps newcomers feel more welcome, leading to a stronger sense of belonging in Canada. Critics have countered that it has weakened national identity and could lead to the possible infringement of human rights, and in particular, women's rights (Jedwab, 2005). In his book *Selling Illusions: The Cult of Multiculturalism in Canada*, Trinidad-born novelist Neil Bissoondath (1994) argued that the government encouraged immigrants to isolate themselves in distinct enclaves and away from "mainstream" culture. Quebecers have also expressed uneasiness about federal multiculturalism policy since its beginnings. Many have viewed multiculturalism as an attempt to dilute the French fact in Canada and to weaken the status of francophones.

Various publications and polls suggest that Canadians generally support a multicultural society, at least in principle. In fact, a growing body of research suggests that the process of immigrant and minority integration is working better in Canada than in other countries, and that multiculturalism policy has played a role in this success (Kymlicka, 2009). Immigrants and minorities express high levels of pride in Canada and praise the country's freedom, democracy, and multiculturalism (Adams, 2007). Immigrants to Canada and visible and religious minorities also fare better than most, if not all, foreign-born populations in other Western democracies. For example, the children of immigrants have better educational outcomes in Canada than in other countries (OECD, 2006 cited in Kymlicka, 2009) and earn more than Canadians whose parents were born in this country (Corak, 2008). Canadian neighbourhoods with a high concentration of immigrants are not characterized by the same levels of poverty and social isolation that can be found in the "ghettos" of major American or European cities (Hiebert, Schuurman, & Smith, 2007).

In terms of political integration, immigrants in Canada are much more likely to become citizens than are immigrants in other Western democracies (Bloemraad, 2006). Furthermore, more foreign-born citizens are elected to Parliament than in any other country (Adams, 2007). Political parties run minority candidates in competitive ridings, and once they are nominated there is no evidence that Canadian voters in general discriminate against these candidates. Nevertheless, visible minorities remain underrepresented in the House of Commons (Tossutti & Hilderman, 2015). However the 2015 election saw record numbers of visible minority MPs elected and appointed to the cabinet.

Protection of Minorities under the Law

HUMAN RIGHTS ACT   The Human Rights Act, 1977, is a key piece of federal legislation that supports multiculturalism by granting rights to individuals. It prohibits discriminatory practices against individuals based on their race, national or ethnic origin, colour, religion, age, sex, sexual orientation, marital status, family status, disability, or conviction for an offence for which a pardon has been granted. The current law applies to the employment, business, and service delivery practices of the federal government and federally regulated industries, such as the airlines, banks, television and radio stations, interprovincial communications, telephone and transportation companies, and First Nations. Throughout the 1960s and 1970s, the provinces also put in place human rights codes or charters to protect individuals from various forms of discrimination by a business, non-business organization, government department, public agency or institution (e.g., school board), or individual.

In recent times, political opponents have clashed over the Act's hate speech provisions. In 2013, a Conservative private member's bill was passed to scrap Section 13, which banned the communication of messages by telephone or on the Internet that expose a person or persons to hate on the basis of their race, national or ethnic origin, colour, religion, age, sex, sexual orientation, marital status, family status, disability, or conviction for an offence for which a pardon has been granted or in respect of which a record suspension has been ordered. Proponents of the bill argued that Section 13 limited freedom of speech, while human rights lawyers and groups such as the Canadian Bar Association argued that removing it would allow the proliferation of hate speech on the Internet (Canadian Bar Association, 2012). Criminal Code provisions against hate speech remain in place. In 1983, the Royal Commission on Equality in Employment (the Abella Commission) called for legislated employment equity to provide employment opportunities not just for women but also for visible minorities, people with disabilities, and Aboriginal people. This led to the passage of the first Employment Equity Act in 1986.

The 1995 Employment Equity Act, which still applies today, aims to achieve equality in the workforce so that no one is denied employment opportunities for reasons that are not linked to ability. It covers several types of employers: the federal public service; federally regulated employers in the private sector and Crown Corporations with more than 100 employees; and other public sector employers with 100 or more employees (e.g., Canadian Forces, Royal Canadian Mounted Police, Canada Revenue Agency).[7] The Act's principal goal is to correct the disadvantage in employment experienced by women, Aboriginal peoples, people with disabilities, and members of

---

[7]The omnibus Budget Implementation Act, 2012, removed the requirement that an organization with 100 or more employees that wants to bid on a federal government contract must sign a contract to implement employment equity in the workplace (Human Resources and Skills Development Canada, 2012; Parliament of Canada, 2012).

visible minorities. Employment equity requires employers to eliminate employment barriers against people in designated groups and to institute policies to
ensure that people in the designated groups achieve a degree of representation
in the employer's workforce that reflects their representation in the Canadian
workforce. Employment equity does not require that the employer hire or promote people who are not qualified for the work (Department of Justice, 2009).

Employers have to produce an employment equity plan, including goals and a
timetable, as well as progress reports detailing the measures they have undertaken
to improve the workforce representation of the four designated groups. The
reports are forwarded to the Canadian Human Rights Commission and a fine can
be imposed on employers for failure to file. Since the extension of the law on
employment equity in 1995 to all departments and agencies, there has been a significant increase in the representation of women, persons with disabilities, Aboriginals, and visible minorities in the federal public service. As a result of new hires,
the representation of visible minorities increased from 9.8 percent in 2006–2007
to 13.3 percent in 2011–2012 (Treasury Board of Canada Secretariat, 2013).[8]

THE CHARTER OF RIGHTS AND FREEDOMS, 1982   The Charter of Rights
and Freedoms supports Canada's multicultural model of integration by granting rights to individuals and groups. Section 15 of the Charter guarantees
individual equality while allowing for affirmative action to assist individuals
and groups that have been disadvantaged because of their personal characteristics, including race, national or ethnic origin, colour, and religion. In addition, the Charter's recognition of Canada's multicultural heritage has been
used by the Supreme Court to uphold legislation aimed at preventing the
expression of hatred against religious and racial minorities.

Summary and Conclusion

Canada has never been an ethnic nation made up of people from a single linguistic or cultural group. This will continue as international migration and intercultural
relationships deepen the country's longstanding cultural
diversity. In general, Canada is best described as a civic
nation based on a common territory, a community of laws
and institutions, and the legal equality of its members.
Canadians attach different meanings to the Canadian identity and express multiple and often overlapping allegiances

to other identities. Consequently, characterizing the
Canadian identity is an elusive endeavour. That may satisfy
Canadians who are comfortable with ambivalence, while
others will desire more clarity on the question.

The challenge of building a unified political community
in a state that is home to a multinational and polyethnic
population is closely tied to questions of democracy and
good government. Each day, public officials must determine whether the principles of freedom and equality that

[8]The official report on the representation of the four employment equity groups in the public service,
including visible minorities, has been criticized for relying on out-of-date information about workforce availability. Some observers argue that visible minorities remained underrepresented in the
public service in 2012 (Agocs, 2012; Said, 2013).

underpin democratic values are best served by treating all citizens in the same way, regardless of their cultural background, or whether national minorities and ethnic groups should enjoy special group rights so that they may fully participate in the broader society. Their decisions reflect whether Canadians agree that "good government" includes the accommodation of the requirements of minorities.

Canada's response to fulfilling the lofty goals of democracy and good government in a multinational and polyethnic state has been to grant a combination of group-based and individual rights to national minorities and ethnic groups. Official attitudes about the desirability of cultural diversity have undergone fundamental shifts throughout Canadian history. The Canadian nation-building project has evolved from relying on racially exclusionary immigrant selection criteria and an assimilationist integration model to adopting more open immigration and citizenship policies and a multicultural approach to admitting and accommodating newcomers. Right now, Canada is under strain as it struggles to respond to ever-growing diversity in a way that upholds liberal democratic values. How Canadians resolve these tensions will be fascinating to behold, and will be watched closely both at home and abroad in other states facing similar challenges.

Discussion Questions

1. How would you describe the Canadian national identity?

2. Are the Québécois an ethnic or a civic nation?

3. Should Canada grant group-specific rights to national minorities and to ethnic groups? Why or why not?

4. Should Canada change its laws, institutions, or policies to accommodate the cultural and religious needs of ethnic groups? Why or why not?

5. What is your opinion about recent changes to Canada's Citizenship Act?

6. Does multiculturalism strengthen or undermine the Canadian identity?

Further Reading

Adams, M. (2007). *Unlikely utopia: The surprising triumph of Canadian pluralism.* Toronto, ON: Penguin Group Canada.

Biles, J., Burstein, M., & Frideres, J. (Eds). (2008). *Immigration and integration in Canada in the twenty-first century* (Queen's Policy Series #52). Kingston, ON: McGill-Queen's University Press.

Bouchard, G. (Trans. By H. Scott) (2015). *Interculturalism: A view from Quebec.* Toronto: University of Toronto Press.

Gagnon, A. (2014). *Minority nations in the age of uncertainty: New paths to national emancipation and empowerment.* Toronto, ON: University of Toronto Press.

Kelley, N., & Trebilcock, M. (2010). *The making of the mosaic: A history of Canadian immigration policy* (2nd ed.). Toronto, ON: University of Toronto Press.

Kymlicka, W. (2001). *Politics in the vernacular: Nationalism, multiculturalism and citizenship.* Toronto, ON: Oxford University Press.

Lécours, A. (2014). *Multinationalism and accommodation: Analysis of a Canadian success.* The Federal Idea: A Quebec Think Tank on Federalism. http://ideefederale.ca/documents/Lecours_ang.pdf

Leuprecht, C., & Russell, P. (Eds.). (2011). *Essential readings in Canadian constitutional politics.* Toronto, ON: University of Toronto Press.

McRoberts, K. (1997). *Misconceiving Canada: The struggle for national unity.* Toronto, ON: Oxford University Press.

Taylor, C. (2012). *Multiculturalism: Examining the politics of recognition* (expanded ed.). Edited and introduced by Amy Gutmann. Princeton, NJ: Princeton University Press.

CHAPTER 4

The Canadian Economy and the Challenges of Inequality

CHAPTER OBJECTIVES

After reading this chapter, you should be able to

1. Outline the basic features of the Canadian economy.
2. Discuss the issues relating to foreign ownership and investment.
3. Evaluate the North American Free Trade Agreement.
4. Examine the changing role of government in the economy.
5. Discuss the extent of inequality in Canada.
6. Outline the political significance of various divisions in Canadian society.

As winter approached in November 2011, Chief Theresa Spence declared a state of emergency in the First Nation community of Attawapiskat, located near the shore of James Bay in Northern Ontario. The community was in desperate need of shelter as many people were living in tents, uninsulated sheds, and mouldy one-room houses. There was also a lack of toilets and running water, and the school was contaminated with oil. Although the community is near the billion-dollar De Beers diamond mine, which uses the band's traditional lands for $2 million per year and has hired some Aboriginals, 60 percent of adults in the community were unemployed.

With little response from the Canadian government, area NDP Member of Parliament Charlie Angus repeatedly raised the issue in the House of Commons, and the story of "third world" conditions received national and international media attention. The Red Cross responded to the emergency by supplying wood stoves, toilets, plastic sheeting, and other essentials. The Canadian government claimed that $90 million in funds that had been given to the community over a period of five years had been mismanaged (a claim vigorously rejected by Chief Spence). The Canadian government appointed an outside manager to control finances for several months for a fee of $1300 per day charged to the band council (the appointment of an outside manager was later ruled "inappropriate" by the Federal Court). As public outrage mounted, the Canadian government agreed to send 22 modular homes to the community.

The situation of Attawapiskat is not unique. As Canada's auditor general reported in 2011: "conditions have generally not improved for First Nations. . . . The education gap between First Nations living on reserves and the general Canadian population has widened, the shortage of adequate housing on reserves has increased, comparability of child and family services is not ensured, and the reporting requirements on First Nations reserves remains burdensome." Indeed, the Canadian government's payments for reserve housing declined substantially from 1996 to 2011 (Wells, 2011), resulting in a high level of substandard, unhealthy housing on First Nations reserves across Canada.

Unlike provincial and municipal governments that provide many services such as education, health care, and quality drinking water to most Canadians, the Canadian government has not legislated support for such services for First Nations reserves. Adequate funding and accountability for these services have not been clearly established. Funding agreements for the delivery of services by First Nations have to be renewed annually, and funds are often not provided in a timely manner. Thus, First Nations are faced with uncertainty about funding, making it difficult to make long-range plans to improve services (Office of the Auditor General of Canada, 2011).

INTRODUCTION

Canada is one of the most prosperous, economically developed countries in the world. Canadians generally enjoy a high standard of living, are well educated, have a long life expectancy, and are satisfied with their lives (Organisation for Economic Co-operation and Development, 2011). Nevertheless, the conditions in many First Nations communities have been compared to those of poor "third world" countries, and inequalities between the rich and the rest of society are larger than in a number of other developed countries. Economic growth often benefits some regions and groups of people more than others, resulting in social and political tensions. Furthermore, the pursuit of rapid economic growth, particularly through mining and oil and gas production, can have damaging effects on the natural environment.

THE CANADIAN ECONOMY

Canada has a basically free market, capitalist economy. Most businesses are in the hands of privately owned companies and corporations. Some businesses (termed Crown corporations) are government-owned including the Canadian Broadcasting Corporation, VIA Rail, and, in some provinces, companies that generate and distribute electric power. Many Crown corporations (such as Air Canada and Petro-Canada) have been privatized. Governments have looked to public–private partnerships to provide some public services. For example, the Public Transit Fund announced in the 2015 Canadian government budget requires that projects have a private partner (Curry, 2015). As well, in recent times, governments have reduced regulation of business activities and lowered corporate taxes.

Canadian governments do not generally directly involve themselves in the decision making of private businesses and corporations other than through laws and regulations concerning matters of public interest such as product and worker safety, environmental protection, and competition policy. Nevertheless, national and provincial governments are often involved in encouraging and assisting business development. Canadian governments try to influence the overall functioning of the economy, particularly by adjusting the level of government spending (which accounts for slightly over two-fifths of Canada's gross national product) and taxation to stimulate or cool down the economy. Likewise, the Bank of Canada (a Crown corporation that operates at arm's length from government) has important effects on the Canadian economy through its responsibility for monetary policy (the supply of money), which affects interest rates and the level of inflation.

ECONOMIC DEVELOPMENT

Economic historians often describe Canada as a country whose financial well-being has relied on the export of a few resource staples: the near-unparalleled riches of its seas, forests, mountains, and plains. Europeans first became interested in what is now Canada for the abundant cod as well as whale oil for lamps. Next, the export of furs to Europe became a leading source of revenues from the early seventeenth century until the early nineteenth century. In the nineteenth century, timber from New Brunswick and Quebec, as well as wheat from Ontario, became major export commodities. Early in the twentieth century, Prairie wheat came to the fore as a major export. More recently, oil, natural gas, and minerals have become some of Canada's major exports.

Canada's dependence on a few staples has often been viewed as undesirable for long-term economic development. Resource commodities are subject to sharp fluctuations in world demand and prices, leading to cycles of "boom" and "bust." Exporting unprocessed or lightly processed materials does not create many long-lasting jobs, particularly with the development of labour-saving modern technology. For example, prior to the sharp drop in oil prices in 2014, Newfoundland and Labrador's booming offshore oil industry provided about 34 percent of the province's gross domestic product and about 31 percent of provincial government revenues but only 2.4 percent of its employment (*St. John's Telegram*, 2011).

Some natural resources (such as oil and minerals) are non-renewable and thus of declining importance over time. Some renewable resources (such as fish and forest products) have become depleted because of overexploitation. Natural resource exploitation can also damage the environment. For example,

Alberta's huge oil (tar) sands developments use large quantities of water and can release toxins into one of the world's major freshwater river systems. The extraction of bitumen from the sands releases more carbon dioxide (a major source of greenhouse gas emissions) than conventional oil production and thus adds to the problem of global climate change. Although resource developments (and other pollution-creating activities) add to the country's gross domestic product (GDP), this standard indicator of prosperity is an imprecise measure of how the country is doing as it does not take into account the costs of damage to the environment and human health.

Canada's economy began to diversify in the latter part of the nineteenth century with the production of consumer goods, such as clothing and shoes. Toward the end of the nineteenth century and in the first decades of the twentieth century, "heavy industries" such as iron and steel, pulp and paper plants, machinery, and chemical plants were established (Conrad & Finkel, 2007). In the last decades of the twentieth century, Canada's manufacturing sector, aided by a low exchange rate for the Canadian dollar (allowing goods to be produced more cheaply than in the United States), flourished in areas such as automobile production and telecommunications. More recently, however, employment in manufacturing has tended to decline while employment in health care, professional services, and public administration has increased. As Table 4-1 indicates, the bulk of employment is now in the broadly defined service sector. In recent

TABLE 4-1

EMPLOYMENT BY INDUSTRY, 2014 (IN THOUSANDS)

ALL INDUSTRIES	17 802.2
Goods-producing sector	3 897.1 (21.9%)
Agriculture	305.1 (1.7%)
Forestry, fishing, mining, oil and gas	372.6 (2.1%)
Utilities	136.9 (0.8%)
Construction	1 371.5 (7.7%)
Manufacturing	1 711.0 (9.6%)
Services-producing sector	13 905.1 (78.1%)
Trade	2 729.3 (15.3%)
Transportation and warehousing	896.8 (5.0%)
Finance, insurance, real estate, and leasing	1 083.8 (6.1%)
Professional, scientific, and technical services	1 333.3 (7.5%)
Business, building, and other support services	734.8 (4.1%)
Educational services	1 236.9 (6.9%)
Health care and social assistance	2 219.7 (12.5%)
Information, culture, and recreation	757.2 (4.3%)
Accommodation and food services	1 207.5 (6.8%)
Other services	795.1 (4.5%)
Public administration	910.7 (5.1%)

SOURCE: Statistics Canada. (2015). *Employment by industry* (Catalogue no. 71F0004XCB). Retrieved from http://www.statcan.gc.ca/tables-tableaux/sum-som/l01/cst01/econ40-eng.htm. Calculations by the authors.

Energy products	24.3%
Motor vehicles and aircraft	18.2%
Minerals and mineral products	14.4%
Consumer products	11.1%
Forest products	7.0%
Basic and industrial chemical, plastic, and rubber products	6.8%
Farm, fish, and food products	5.9%
Industrial machinery	5.6%
Electronic and electrical equipment	4.6%
Special transactions and adjustments	2.2%

TABLE 4-2
EXPORT OF GOODS ON A BALANCE-OF-PAYMENTS BASIS BY PRODUCT, 2014

SOURCE: Calculated from Statistics Canada. (2015a). *Export of goods on a balance-of-payments basis, by product.* Retrieved from http://www.statcan.gc.ca/tables-tableaux/sum-som/l01/cst01/gblec04-eng.htm.

years, services (particularly services provided by banks and insurance companies) have become Canada's fastest-growing exports (Greenwood, 2015).

The Canadian economy has always relied heavily on international trade. Before the United Kingdom adopted free trade policies in the 1840s, Canadian exports benefited from the preferential treatment given to British colonies. After British preferential treatment ended, Canadian trade shifted toward the United States, which became, by far, Canada's largest trading partner. For example, in 2014, 75.6 percent of Canada's exports went to the United States, while 66.9 percent of Canadian imports came from that country (Statistics Canada, 2015a). Although China has become Canada's second largest trading partner in recent years, the value of Canadian imports from China is larger than the value of exports to China.

As Table 4-2 indicates, energy products along with automobiles and minerals are Canada's major export goods.

ECONOMIC GLOBALIZATION AND THE CANADIAN ECONOMY

Economic globalization is an important feature of the contemporary world. Canada, like most other countries, has become increasingly embedded in the global economic system, which has powerful effects on the Canadian economy and government policies. There has been a greatly increased international free flow of goods, services, money, and investment along with the growth of multinational corporations. Free trade and foreign investment agreements have important effects on the Canadian economy and have led to important political controversies.

Free Trade

The idea of free trade—that there should be no barriers to trade among the countries of the world—tends to dominate economic thought and strongly influences government policy. Free trade encourages countries to specialize in the production of goods and services on which they have a comparative advantage, and benefits consumers by giving them a choice of a wider range of goods with lower prices. Although in the past many businesses sought protection from foreign competition, generally business interests today (and multinational corporations in particular) push for free trade to take advantage of a globalizing world economy. Labour interests are often critical of unrestricted free trade, fearing that global competition leads to lower wages and a loss of jobs as business moves to countries with low-cost labour. Businesses may try to drive down employee wages and benefits to remain competitive and profitable. With business and finance being much more mobile than workers, globalization and free trade tend to enhance the power of business in the marketplace and its influence on governments, while reducing the power and influence of workers.

The Canadian government has pursued many free trade agreements. However, in understanding such agreements, it is important to note that these agreements do not only involve removing tariffs (taxes) and restrictions on goods that are traded and services that foreign corporations and producers can provide. Rather, they often establish binding rules and compliance measures that may affect such matters as environmental protection, labour rights, the affordability of patent medicines, government's ability to regulate the country's economy, and the protection of foreign investors (Johnson, 2015). In effect, many free trade agreements could be described as establishing "managed trade" in goods and services that protect or enhance the profitability of some businesses while limiting the ability of governments to legislate for the common good (Stiglitz & Hersh, 2015).

CANADA, THE UNITED STATES, AND THE NORTH AMERICAN FREE TRADE AGREEMENT   Free trade with the United States has, at times, been a very controversial Canadian political issue. Historically, Canadian manufacturers feared that cheap American products would devastate their businesses. Canadian nationalists have been concerned that Canadian culture would be threatened and that American influence would make Canada a virtual satellite of the United States.

In the decades after World War II, the majority of goods flowed between the United States and Canada free of tariffs, particularly after the Canada–United States Automotive Agreement (the "Auto Pact") was adopted in 1965. Nevertheless, many Canadian businesses worried that the United States would apply its trade remedy laws against imports from Canada. Specifically, U.S. countervailing duties can be levied on government subsidized imports to the United States, and anti-dumping duties can be levied on imports that are sold in the United States at less than their "fair value."

In 1988, the Canada–United States Free Trade Agreement was signed after the Progressive Conservative government that had negotiated the deal won an election that was fought on the issue. This was followed by the signing in 1992 of the **North American Free Trade Agreement (NAFTA)** by Canada, the United States, and Mexico, which included many of the same provisions. These agreements go beyond free trade in goods to establish a high level of economic integration in North America.

NAFTA Provisions

The provisions of NAFTA include:

- eliminating tariffs on goods traded among the three countries;
- eliminating restrictions on the export of almost all goods;
- forbidding new laws and regulations to protect service industries;
- requiring that investments from the other countries be treated the same as domestic investments (although allowing the screening of proposed take-overs of large domestically owned companies);
- forbidding Canada from placing higher taxes on energy exported to the United States than it levies on energy consumed in Canada (and prohibiting the Canadian government from imposing restrictions that reduce Canadian energy exports to the United States);
- allowing the retention of agricultural marketing boards that set production quotas to protect farmers; and
- allowing Canada to continue its existing protection of its cultural industries, with the United States retaining the right to retaliate against new cultural protection measures.

Although Canada had hoped to be exempted from American trade remedy laws, the American government refused this concession, and no agreement was reached on what constituted an "unfair subsidy" that could result in special duties. A decision to impose special countervailing or anti-dumping duties can be appealed to a binational dispute settlement tribunal made up of persons chosen by the countries involved in the dispute. However, the tribunal's powers are limited. It can determine only whether the rules of the country levying the duty were correctly applied using the judicial review standards and precedents of that country. Although the provision has helped to resolve some trade disputes, the United States was unwilling to accept the tribunal's verdict regarding Canada's exports of softwood lumber. The United States government refused to give back the billions it had improperly collected from Canadian lumber companies for what it claimed to be unfair subsidies. In the end, the Harper government settled for the return of $4.5 billion—part, but not all, of the money withheld (Clarkson, 2008).

Furthermore, NAFTA has not prevented the United States from adopting protectionist policies such as its "Buy America" law. For example, steel makers based in Canada have found themselves largely shut out of bidding on U.S. government-funded projects, while American companies can generally bid on

NORTH AMERICAN FREE TRADE AGREEMENT (NAFTA) A 1992 agreement between Canada, the United States, and Mexico that established a high level of economic integration in North America.

Canadian projects. Indeed, Canadian iron and steel companies could not bid on a major overhaul of a British Columbia ferry terminal that was funded by the United States and Alaska governments that sublet the facility (McKenna, 2014, November 25).

A particularly controversial provision of NAFTA is its investor–state dispute resolution mechanism. NAFTA's Chapter 11 allows foreign companies to sue governments that they allege are harming their investments through expropriation or actions "tantamount to expropriation." Claims for compensation may be based on government actions that affect "the company's future profitability or opportunities for growth" (Boyd, 2003, p. 257). Decisions are made in a private tribunal rather than a public court. For example, a NAFTA tribunal in 2012 upheld a case by Exxon Mobil and Murphy Oil against the Canadian government because the government of Newfoundland and Labrador had required that the oil companies developing the province's highly profitable offshore oil resources increase their spending in the province on research, education, and training. The petroleum companies took their case to a NAFTA tribunal after losing in Canadian courts. Likewise, the Quebec government's moratorium on fracking for oil and gas under the St. Lawrence River resulted in Lone Pine Resources (based in Canada but incorporated in the United States) launching a $250 million lawsuit in September 2013 against the Canadian government. At the time of writing, the tribunal panel lawyers had not reached a decision.

In general, NAFTA tends to reflect the interests of the major corporations that lobbied governments to negotiate the agreement and that were consulted by governments throughout the negotiations. In particular, Chapter 11 gives corporations unprecedented powers to challenge governments through binding international arbitration (Boyd, 2003). Critics argue that the right of corporations to profit takes precedence over the public good and protection of the environment. Although NAFTA includes labour and environmental "side agreements," these are generally viewed as weak.

Despite its significance in integrating the economies of Canada, the United States, and Mexico, NAFTA is not a "supranational" government (Clarkson, 2008). NAFTA has not led to the establishment of any meaningful governing institutions to develop, oversee, and enforce rules for North America. Unlike the European Union, it offers no guidelines for social policies and human rights and barely addresses the environment or the mobility of workers across national borders. Reflecting a business-oriented free market agenda that seeks to limit the ability of governments to adopt policies that interfere with trade and investment, NAFTA could be viewed as restricting the scope of democracy. Furthermore, with tribunals that typically conduct their business in secret and committees that are generally invisible to the public, NAFTA cannot be characterized as transparent and accountable (Clarkson, 2008).

OTHER FREE TRADE AGREEMENTS   Although NAFTA has been by far Canada's largest and most important free trade agreement, the Canadian government has free trade agreements in force with several countries (including Korea, Chile, and Israel) and is actively pursuing agreements with some other countries (including India, Japan, and Ukraine). Of particular importance are three potential wide-ranging multilateral agreements.

The **Canada–European Union Comprehensive Economic and Trade Agreement (CETA)** was signed in 2014, and is expected to go into effect in 2016 if approved by the European Union (EU) Council and the EU Parliament. CETA (which will eliminate virtually all tariffs) is broader than NAFTA as it includes access to services such as transportation, travel, insurance, and communications as well as professional certification and product standards. Of particular concern are the intellectual property provisions that include an extended period of protection for patented prescription drugs that will increase costs for Canadian health care. As with NAFTA, the investor–state dispute settlement provisions in CETA will allow corporations to challenge domestic laws through independent tribunals. However while the Canadian government has supported the inclusion of investor–state provisions in CETA, the French and German governments have looked for changes to these provisions (Mazereeuw, 2015). Complicating the issue, the similar European Union–United States Transatlantic Trade and Investment Partnership that was to be signed after the Canada–European Union agreement also faced opposition to the investor–state dispute settlement provision (Gurzu, 2015).

The **Trans-Pacific Partnership (TPP)** was announced on October 6, 2015, by 12 countries (representing about 40 percent of the world's economy): Australia, Brunei, Canada, Chile, Japan, Malaysia, Mexico, Peru, New Zealand, Singapore, the United States, and Vietnam.[1] After signing, countries have two years to ratify the TPP. It comes into effect when most of the signatory countries have ratified the agreement.

The announcement of the TPP agreement during the 2015 Canadian election campaign raised considerable controversy. The Conservative party strongly supported the agreement, the NDP wanted a better deal, and the Liberal party promised a full and open debate in Parliament if elected. Among the issues raised about the TPP were the partial opening of the dairy, chicken, and egg market to foreign competition (offset by a promise to provide farmers with $4.3 billion in assistance over 10 years), and the substantial reduction of the protection of the North American automobile and auto parts industry. This could result in serious job losses, particularly in Ontario, even with a promise of $1 billion in assistance to the auto industry. On the positive side, the agreement would provide greater access to the Japanese

CANADA–EUROPEAN UNION COMPREHENSIVE ECONOMIC AND TRADE AGREEMENT (CETA)
An agreement between Canada and the European Union that was signed in 2014 and will be implemented in 2016 if formal agreement is approved.

TRANS-PACIFIC PARTNERSHIP (TPP)
A proposed free trade agreement involving 12 countries including Canada.

---

[1]Commentators attributed the exclusion of China from the TPP as a deliberate effort to contain China's growing power in the Asia–Pacific region.

market. Although President Obama supported the TTP agreement, leading Democratic presidential candidate Hillary Clinton announced that she "was not in favour of what I have learned about it" (Merica & Bradner, 2015, October 7). It was not clear whether the required legislation to approve the agreement would have enough support to be passed by the American Congress.

A proposed **Trade in Services Agreement (TiSA)** involves the European Union and 24 countries including Canada, the United States, Pakistan, Mexico, and Turkey. If adopted, this would establish free trade in services. It could limit government regulation of services, including financial regulations, give foreign corporations the same national treatment as domestic corporations, include a version of investor–state provisions, and encourage the privatization of a number of government services. At the time of writing, little was known about the secretive negotiations (Dayen, 2015).

Canada is also a member of the **World Trade Organization (WTO)**, which establishes global rules of trade for 160 countries. As well as lowering tariff and non-tariff trade barriers, the WTO has established dispute settlement procedures. Discussion of further trade liberalization in services and agricultural products began in 2001, but as of 2015 had not been successful, in part because of disagreement concerning the agricultural subsidies used by rich countries to protect their farmers.

Overall, international trade agreements reduce the ability of individual countries to impose tariffs and other limitations on imported goods and services. They can also affect government policies concerning business subsidies, environmental protection, food safety, intellectual property, cultural promotion, public services, and domestic and local preference in government purchasing that may be viewed as barriers to trade and investment.

Foreign Investment and Ownership

Canada's economy has relied quite heavily on foreign investment. In the nineteenth century, Canadian governments borrowed intensively through bond issues to finance the building of canals, railways, and other infrastructure essential to the growth of the new country. British financiers were a key source of loans for Canadian governments and businesses. Beginning late in the nineteenth century, many American companies set up **branch plants** in Canada to avoid the tariffs on manufactured products established by the National Policy and produce goods for the growing Canadian market. Other American companies started Canadian operations to obtain the raw materials needed for American industry. Thus, American companies became owners of many larger Canadian businesses.

Foreign ownership of Canadian business has, at times, been a hotly contested political issue. Although Canadian governments have generally welcomed foreign investment, they have placed limitations on foreign ownership

TRADE IN SERVICES AGREEMENT (TISA)
A potential agreement being negotiated by 24 countries including Canada, the United States, and the European Union that would establish free trade in services including a major reduction in government regulation of services.

WORLD TRADE ORGANIZATION (WTO)
An organization of more than 150 countries (including Canada) that establishes global rules of trade, including the lowering of trade barriers and procedures for dispute settlements.

BRANCH PLANTS
Factories set up outside the United States by an American company to produce and sell products in a foreign market.

in certain key sectors of the economy, such as banking and insurance, the mass media, airlines, and telecommunications.

In the 1960s, concerns were raised about the high level of American ownership of the Canadian economy. At the time, about one-half of Canada's manufacturing, mining, and petroleum industries were foreign-owned (largely American-owned). Some saw foreign investment as desirable, arguing that it brought increased economic activity and employment to Canada, facilitated access to modern technology and markets outside Canada, and increased competitiveness for Canadian industry leading to greater efficiency and lower prices. Critics argued that the American branch plants often purchased their parts and supplies in the United States, concentrated their research and development activities as well as their management functions in the United States, and were often limited by their American parent companies to producing only for the Canadian market. Furthermore, they noted that most of the funds to buy out Canadian companies or to establish new enterprises came from Canadian financial institutions, while foreign ownership led to an outflow of profits, dividends, and management fees from Canada. Critics also registered concerns that American-owned companies operating in Canada were subject to American laws such as the Trading With the Enemy Act that prevented American-owned companies and executives from doing business with Cuba. More generally, Canadian nationalists feared that the high level of American ownership limited Canadian independence by increasing American political and cultural influence on Canada.

SCREENING FOREIGN INVESTMENT In 1973, the Canadian government established the **Foreign Investment Review Agency (FIRA)**. This allowed the Canadian government to reject proposals by foreigners to take over Canadian businesses or set up new businesses that were not of significant benefit to Canada. Although few investment proposals were rejected outright, the agency gave the Canadian government some ability to negotiate with foreign firms to achieve more benefits for Canada.

The 1989 Canada–United States Free Trade Agreement and the 1994 NAFTA limited the ability of the Canadian government to screen American investment or to adopt policies that give preferential treatment to Canadian-owned companies. In 1985, FIRA was converted to **Investment Canada** with a mandate to attract foreign investment. Nevertheless, it retained the power to recommend that proposals for foreign takeovers and mergers that do not provide a "net benefit" to Canada be rejected. Furthermore, since 2009, the Canadian government has had the authority to block foreign investment (and foreign mergers with Canadian companies) that are viewed as threats to national security. Since national security reviews are secret, it is unknown how many foreign investments have been rejected for this reason (Gray, 2015).

FOREIGN INVESTMENT REVIEW AGENCY (FIRA)
A Canadian government agency established in 1973 to review proposals from foreigners to take over Canadian businesses or to set up new businesses.

INVESTMENT CANADA
A Canadian government agency established in 1985 with a mandate to attract foreign investment.

BOX 4-1

The Government of China's Appetite for Canadian Resources

On February 26, 2013, the China National Offshore Oil Company (CNOOC) purchased Nexen, a major Canadian oil producer, for US$15.1 billion. The takeover was controversial particularly because CNOOC is a Chinese state-owned enterprise. To gain the approval of the Canadian government, CNOOC promised to keep Nexen's headquarters in Calgary, increase its investment in Alberta's oil (tar) sands, and keep Nexen's 3000 employees and senior management. Despite this promise, many employees lost their jobs in 2014 as a result of a major cost-cutting program (Cattaneo & Lewis, 2014). In 2013, Petronas, a Malaysian state-owned enterprise, purchased Progress Energy Resources, a major owner of Canadian shale gas properties, for $6 billion. Although the Canadian government initially rejected the Petronas purchase, it approved the deal after the company made promises to build a large liquefied natural gas (LNG) facility in British Columbia.

Faced with considerable public concern about the takeover of a significant proportion of Canada's natural resources, the Canadian government declared that foreign state-owned investors would be barred (other than in exceptional cases) from new takeovers in the oil sands. As well, the threshold for review of investments by foreign state-owned enterprises would remain at $330 million rather than the new threshold of $1 billion for review of other foreign investments.

Although investment by foreign-based corporations has often led to concern and opposition in Canada, some of the largest foreign investors today are state-owned enterprises, including enterprises controlled by undemocratic governments. While ownership by companies such as CNOOC may facilitate increased Canadian exports to China, it also raises concerns about maintaining Canada's control of important natural resources.

Overall, the Canadian government has rarely intervened to keep a home-grown company in Canadian hands. It has also been reluctant to penalize companies such as Stelco (a major employer in Hamilton) that do not live up to their promises of "net benefit." The takeover of major Canadian companies by corporations owned or controlled by foreign governments, especially undemocratic governments, has been controversial (see Box 4-1: The Government of China's Appetite for Canadian Resources).

FOREIGN INVESTMENT PROMOTION AND PROTECTION AGREEMENTS The total amount of investment by Canadian companies in foreign countries now exceeds foreign investment in Canada. For example, about three-fifths of the international mining exploration and development companies are Canadian-based Canadian International Development Platform, 2013. To protect foreign investment by Canadian companies, the Canadian government has negotiated foreign investment promotion and protection agreements (FIPAs) designed to ensure that foreign investors are not treated worse than domestic investors and have the same rights and obligations. As of June 2015, Canada had FIPAs with 36 countries, and negotiations with 18 other countries were either concluded or ongoing.

The Canada–China FIPA was adopted by the cabinet without parliamentary debate or scrutiny. This treaty, which came into effect in 2014, allows Chinese corporations operating in Canada to challenge any law or regulation passed by any government that threatens their profitability. A panel of independent arbitrators decides whether the claim is justified and decides on the compensation the government will have to pay, even if it involves billions of dollars. There is no recourse to the judicial system, and the Canadian government retains the right to avoid making documents public. Unlike NAFTA, which can be terminated with six months' notice, the Canada–China FIPA agreement lasts a minimum of 15 years and, even if terminated, claims against the government can be pursued for an additional 16 years. International Trade Minister Ed Fast argued that "investment agreements provide the protection and confidence Canadian investors need to expand, grow, and succeed abroad" (quoted in Isfeld, 2014). However, critics claim that the treaty favours China and threatens Canadian laws and regulations concerning environmental protection, natural resource conservation, labour rights, and Aboriginal treaties, as these could be challenged particularly by Chinese resource investments in Canada (Van Harten, 2012, 2014; Martin, 2012).

GOVERNMENT AND THE ECONOMY

The Canadian state has played a significant role in helping to shape the Canadian economy. The formation of Canada was an act of faith—a belief that a country could be built across northern North America despite the costs involved. To build links across a sparsely populated landmass, substantial Canadian government subsidization of the railway system was required. For example, the Canadian Pacific Railway Company was awarded 10 million hectares of land, a 20-year monopoly, exemption from tariffs on imported materials, and a 20-year exemption from taxation, as well as substantial government cash grants and loan guarantees (Conrad & Finkel, 2007). Later, the Canadian government got directly involved by consolidating various bankrupt rail companies into the government-owned Canadian National Railway (privatized in 1995 and now called CN). Likewise, the Canadian government owned and operated Air Canada (formerly Trans-Canada Airlines) until it was privatized in 1988. Canada's first national radio and television network, the Canadian Broadcasting Corporation (CBC), continues to be a Crown corporation. Government involvement proved essential in some cases because private business did not have the capability to provide the service or because the service was not likely to turn a profit.

Business Regulation

Governments affect various sectors of the economy through the regulation of business activity. For example, regulations under the authority of the Consumer Packaging and Labelling Act help consumers by requiring accurate and meaningful labelling of prepackaged consumer products. The Canadian Radio-television and Telecommunications Commission (a semi-independent government agency) determines which companies will receive broadcasting and cable licences and establishes various conditions (such as Canadian content requirements) for the use of broadcasting licences.

Regulations often help to protect consumers and ensure that large corporations do not restrict free competition. Regulations are also very important in protecting the natural environment. Because the costs of producing goods do not normally take into account the consequences of damaging the natural environment, regulations (including environment assessments before major new projects are approved) can help to limit environmental damage.

Many regulations have been criticized by business interests for being costly, time-consuming, and interfering with economically efficient business decisions. In recent decades, there has been a tendency to move away from mandatory regulations (a process known as deregulation). Instead, guidelines, voluntary agreements between business and government, self-regulation by the businesses involved in a particular sector of the economy, and certification of products and processes by independent organizations (such as the Forest Stewardship Council for forest management) have become more common. The 2012 Conservative government's budget substantially reduced environmental regulations, particularly to try to speed up approval of new oil production and transportation proposals. In addition, Environment Canada suffered serious cuts to its staffing, and a variety of government and government-funded scientific research programs regarding the environment were terminated.

Assistance to Business

Canadian governments have participated in the economy to try to foster economic growth by providing assistance to business. Although we often think of business as being opposed to government intervention in the economy, in fact many businesses have sought government assistance. For example, in 2009 the Canadian and Ontario governments contributed $10.6 billion to help prevent the bankruptcy of General Motors and gave $3.8 billion to Chrysler—corporations that were also bailed out by the American government. Likewise, governments have provided incentives for companies to locate in Canada or in particular communities. Assistance has also often been provided to companies to modernize their facilities and processes and to export their products abroad.

Governments also help business through their support for education and research. An educated workforce is essential for business to be productive and globally competitive. Provincial government funding has helped Canada to have one of the highest proportions of university graduates in the world. The Canadian government is also a major funder of research and development that can be used for economic advantage. Canadian businesses, on the other hand, have tended to lag behind other advanced countries in the proportion of their expenditures devoted to research and development, making the Canadian economy somewhat less innovative and productive than some of its leading competitors (Council of Canadian Academies, 2009).

MANAGEMENT OF THE ECONOMY

Even though Canadian governments in the late nineteenth and early twentieth centuries were active in the development of the economy through such measures as tariffs on imported manufactured goods and involvement in building essential infrastructure, it was not until the post–World War II period that governments played a more active role in managing the functioning of the overall economy. The severe consequences of the Great Depression of the 1930s and the government's mobilization of the economy during World War II contributed to a move away from the classical liberal belief in a pure free market economy. Instead, the ideas of British economist John Maynard Keynes became influential, including that government should smooth out the tendencies of a free market economy to go through cycles of boom and bust. Rather than trying to balance the government's budget each year so that government spending did not exceed government revenues, Keynes argued, governments should run a deficit when the economy needed stimulus and a surplus when cooling down was needed. The Canadian government's White Paper on Employment and Incomes (1945) echoed the themes of **Keynesian economics**, with its call for government to ensure that a "high and stable level of employment" was maintained (quoted in Bothwell, Drummond, & English, 1989, p. 57).

To achieve this, a centralization of taxing and spending authority in the hands of the Canadian government was needed. A broad consensus in support of Keynesian economic policies and the development of a modest welfare state helped to diminish conflicts between business and labour interests in the generally prosperous decades after World War II.

KEYNESIAN ECONOMICS
A perspective on managing the economy through government stimulation of the economy when business investment is weak and cooling the economy when inflation is rampant.

A Shift in Economic Perspectives

In the 1970s, the Keynesian economic doctrines that had guided policy in Canada and other Western countries were challenged. A combination of economic stagnation and inflation (termed "stagflation") ended the long period of economic growth. The growth of government spending was blamed for "crowding out" private investment. Government regulations, it was claimed, were "interfering" with the efficiency of the free market. High taxes and government programs such as social assistance and unemployment insurance were reducing the incentives for hard work and investment. And excessive union demands were disrupting the economy. In the ideological perspective of **neoliberalism** (adopted by many conservatives), a purer free market system would restore prosperity. To achieve this, the role of government in regulating business activity and managing the economy should be greatly reduced, individuals should be responsible for their own well-being, taxes should be

NEOLIBERALISM
An ideological perspective based on a strong belief in a free market system with the role of government reduced to a bare minimum, individuals responsible for their own well-being, taxes substantially reduced, global free trade pursued, and barriers to the international flow of finance and investment removed.

substantially reduced, global free trade should be pursued, and barriers to the international flow of finance and investment should be removed. Such measures, it was argued, would help Canadian corporations to become more competitive internationally.

In the mid-1990s, the Liberal government of Jean Chrétien slashed government spending in response to a perceived financial crisis related to a series of high federal government deficits that had resulted in a large total government debt. A decade later, the Conservative party, led by Stephen Harper, expressed a strong commitment to smaller government, reduced government spending, less government regulation, lower taxes, and an end to government deficits. Nevertheless, substantial budgetary deficits were incurred by the Conservative government in response to a global recession in 2008. Overall, however, the Conservative government reduced taxes from 2006 to 2015, resulting in one of the world's lowest business tax rates (World Bank Group, 2014). This led to cuts to many government programs and to the federal public service.

THE ECONOMY AND THE ENVIRONMENT

Canada's wealth does not include only the country's gross national product or national income. Canada's abundant supply of fresh water, forests, lakes, farmlands, areas of natural beauty, and parks and wilderness areas could also be considered an important part of Canada's wealth as well as contributing to the happiness and well-being of its peoples.

A wide variety of environmental laws and policies were adopted in the last three decades of the twentieth century to protect the natural environment. More recently, however, environmental protection was reduced. For example, in 2012, provisions in an omnibus finance bill greatly reduced the protection of fish habitats, limited the number of projects requiring federal environmental assessment, weakened the protection of endangered species, and placed restrictions on public consultation for proposed projects such as new pipelines that might endanger the environment.

The pursuit of economic growth, particularly by promoting and assisting the fossil fuel industry, has been a major feature of Canadian government policies. Clean energy industries—including the development of wind, solar, run-of-river hydro, and biomass power—have been supported by some provincial governments, including the governments of Quebec, Ontario, and British Columbia. However, the Canadian government has thus far done little to support renewable energy industries (Blackwell, 2014, December 2).

Global climate change (the result particularly of burning fossil fuels that release carbon dioxide) is a serious threat to all ecosystems and, indeed, the future of humanity (International Panel on Climate Change, 2014). Unfortunately, even though most industrialized countries and some less developed countries have reduced their carbon emissions, Canada's emissions have increased substantially in recent decades.

As the world gradually moves toward reducing and perhaps eventually have zero net carbon emissions, Canada may find that its economic wealth, being based to a considerable extent on fossil fuel extraction and production, is in jeopardy. Although the Canadian government along with other members of the G7 made a commitment in 2015 to achieve a carbon-free economy by 2100, this would require fundamental changes in the Canadian economy. In fact, long before then, global warming will likely lead to the release of large quantities of carbon dioxide and methane (a highly potent greenhouse gas) that are sequestered in the Canadian Arctic tundra and Canada's forests as well as in the oceans.

THE CHALLENGES OF INEQUALITY AND SOCIAL DIVISIONS

Income inequality has increased in recent decades. Economic globalization and technological innovations have increased the total amount of income generated by the Canadian economy. However, this increase in income has benefited the upper class much more than the lower middle or working class (Banting & Myles, 2014). For example, the richest 1 percent of Canadians increased their share of national income from 8.1 percent in 1981 to 12.2 percent in 2010 (Organisation for Economic Co-operation and Development, 2014b). Using a different source of data, the top 1 percent of taxpayers reported 10.3 percent of total income (Statistics Canada, 2014, November 18). The 100 top chief executive officers of major corporations earned an average of $7.9 million in 2012—171 times that of the average income earner (Mackenzie, 2014).

Inequality in total wealth (net worth) is particularly dramatic. The top 20 percent of families has 67.5 percent of total wealth (with the top 10 percent accounting for 47.9 percent of total wealth), while the bottom 40 percent has only 2.1 percent of total wealth (Statistics Canada, 2014, February 25). The concentration of wealth has tended to increase. From 1999 to 2012, the 20 percent of families with the highest incomes increased their wealth by 80 percent, while the 20 percent of families with the lowest incomes increased their wealth by 38 percent (Statistics Canada, 2015c). The general increase in wealth particularly reflects the rising value of housing, which has made it difficult or impossible for most people to buy their first house in Vancouver or Toronto.

A reduction in taxes on higher-income earners and reduced government spending on social benefits has increased inequality in disposable (after-tax) income. A variety of tax breaks (including registered retirement savings plans and tax-free savings accounts) are used to a greater extent by higher-income earners than by other Canadians.

Depending on the measure used, between 9.6 percent and 13.3 percent of Canadians could be considered low-income or poor (Conference Board of

Supporters of the Occupy Toronto movement gather on October 15, 2012, in Toronto's St. James Park to mark the first anniversary of their 39-day occupation of the park.

Canada, 2011). As indicated in Box 4-2, Income Inequality and Poverty in Canada: An International Comparison, the Canadian incidence of poverty is higher than in most high-income countries.

Particularly high proportions of people with low incomes are found among unattached persons aged 18–24 (58.1 percent in 2008), unattached females (29.0 percent), Aboriginals, the disabled, and recent immigrants (especially

Do you know where your next meal is coming from? Extreme poverty has become more visible as the number of homeless people and the use of food banks have increased in Canada in recent decades.

BOX 4-2

Income Inequality and Poverty in Canada: An International Comparison

On a scale from A to D, the Conference Board of Canada (2014) has graded Canada's performance on a number of indicators compared with the performance of other high-income countries.

A GRADE:

Level of poverty among the elderly
(3rd of 17 countries)

Intergenerational income mobility
(4th of 11 countries)

Income of disabled persons
(8th of 16 countries)

B GRADE:

Joblessness among youth (9th of 16 countries)

C GRADE:

Income inequality (12th of 17 countries)

Gender inequality (11th of 17 countries)

Child poverty (15th of 17 countries)

Working age poverty (15th of 17 countries)

D GRADE:

None

those who are visible minorities). On the positive side, the rate of poverty among seniors (5.8 percent) has declined substantially, although it is still relatively high among unattached senior women (17.1 percent) (House of Commons Standing Committee on Human Resources, Skills and Social Development and the Status of Persons With Disabilities, 2010). Despite a 1989 House of Commons resolution to end child poverty by 2000, child poverty increased from 15.8 percent in 1989 to 19.1 percent in 2012. Four in 10 Aboriginal children live in low-income families (Ogrodnik, 2014).

Another indicator of the extent of poverty is the increasing use of food banks. In March 2014, at least 841 191 individuals used food banks (based on 1217 food banks reporting). This was an increase of 24.5 percent from 2008. Of those using food banks, 36.9 percent were under 18 years old, 13.6 percent were Aboriginal, and 12.3 percent were immigrants or refugees. Indeed, 45 percent of households in Nunavut used food banks. The increase in the use of food banks can be attributed to the fact that social assistance (welfare) generally has not matched increases in the cost of living (Hunger Canada, 2014). On any given night, an average of 235 000 people are homeless (Monsebraaten, 2015).

Government policies have important effects on the extent of inequality and poverty. Canadian government transfers (such as employment insurance and social assistance) and taxes reduce income inequality and poverty less than in other Western countries (with the exception of the United States and Switzerland). For example, eligibility for employment insurance has decreased substantially in recent decades and most provinces have not increased social assistance (welfare) to match increases in the cost of living. The income tax system has become less progressive as high-income individuals no longer face much higher tax rates than the middle class and benefit from reduced taxes on investments. As well, the tendency to shift taxation from incomes to consumption (the GST/HST) reduces the redistributive effect of taxation (Banting & Myles, 2014).

Why have governments (both Liberal and Conservative) been less likely in the past few decades to adopt social policies and taxation measures to offset the tendency of the economy to create greater inequality? Banting & Myles (2014) cite a variety of factors including:

- the pressures resulting from economic globalization;
- the influence of the ideology of neoliberalism that emphasizes the desirability of a free market system with limited government interference in the economy;
- the declining political influence of groups (including labour unions and civil society organizations) promoting the interests of the less well-off and the greater influence of organizations promoting the interests of corporations and the wealthy;
- the increasing importance of the Department of Finance rather than government departments focused on social policy in affecting government policy;
- at times, the high level of government debt; and
- the decentralization of the federal system that reduces the ability of the Canadian government to affect social policy.

Not only has the Canadian government been less likely in recent decades to reduce income inequality than most other comparable countries, but also there are substantial differences among provincial governments in addressing this issue. In particular, the Quebec government has done much more to reduce inequality than other Canadian governments (Haddow, 2014). This has been attributed to the greater power of unions, the women's movement, and various social and community organizations in Quebec (Banting & Myles, 2014).

Social Class

Social class refers to a large category of people who hold a similar position in the hierarchy of society and in the economy. Some analysts define social class primarily in terms of different positions in the capitalist economic system, distinguishing particularly between capitalists and the working class as well as middle classes of professionals, administrators, and small business owners. Often this approach to thinking about class is connected to **Marxist theory,** which views the relationship between capitalists and workers as inherently antagonistic. Others define class (often called **socioeconomic status**) in terms of a combination of income (or wealth), education, and occupational status.

SOCIAL CLASS
A large category of people who hold a similar position in the hierarchy of society and in the economy.

MARXIST THEORY
The theory that a fundamental feature of capitalist societies is an antagonistic and exploitative relationship between the capitalist class and the working class that leads to class conflict.

SOCIOECONOMIC STATUS
A combination of income (or wealth), education, and occupational status.

THE SIGNIFICANCE OF CLASS DIVISIONS   Political conflict in many countries is based, to a considerable extent, on issues that affect the distribution of wealth and income and the level of government services and assistance available to those with lower incomes. The political significance of social class is related to **class consciousness**, the awareness within a social class of their common interests and a willingness to act collectively on those interests.

It has often been argued that class divisions and class consciousness are not very significant in Canada. Canadians enjoy a considerable level of social mobility, with many persons of working class background able to move into middle class positions. Identities such as those based on province, ethnicity or nationality, race, religion, gender, or sexual orientation are often stronger than class-based identities. As well, the relatively low level of working-class consciousness in Canada is sometimes attributed to the weak political organization of the working class (Brodie & Jenson, 1988).

However, when compared to the United States, the importance of labour unions in Canada is striking. Since the mid-1960s, the proportion of workers represented by unions in the United States has declined sharply while it has declined very slightly in Canada. Only about 12 percent of American workers are unionized compared to about 30 percent of Canadian workers. Eidlin (2015) argues that unions have been incorporated into Canadian politics as a representative of the working class, noting that Canada (unlike the United States) adopted a tripartite system of labour relations involving business, unions, and government. Likewise, unions have promoted working class interests by generally adopting a close relationship with the NDP. By contrast, labour unions are incorporated into American politics more as an interest group competing with other interest groups, particularly within the Democratic Party. Nevertheless, the growth of unionization in the public sector (including many in professional and semi-professional positions) means that a substantial proportion of union membership in Canada could be considered middle class.

The Supreme Court of Canada has upheld the fundamental right of unions to strike (*Saskatchewan Federation of Labour v. Saskatchewan*, 2015, SCC 4). However, a private member's bill (Bill C-377) supported by the Conservative government was passed by Parliament in July 2015 that requires unions to post publicly all of their expenses of $5000 or more on a Canada Revenue Agency website. Union leaders saw this as an attack on the labour movement. Seven provincial governments objected to this costly measure (which does not apply to corporations and private businesses) as a violation of provincial jurisdiction over labour law. Both the NDP and the Liberal party promised to repeal the legislation if elected.

Overall, Canada is often described as primarily an affluent middle-class society. However, the depiction of Canada's workforce as mainly holding permanent jobs that provide wages supporting a middle-class lifestyle is changing. Part-time and temporary jobs that often have no health, pension, paid sick

CLASS CONSCIOUSNESS
The awareness within a social class of their common interests and a willingness to act collectively on those interests.

leave, and other benefits have become increasingly common. In fact, in 2014, part-time jobs accounted for 80 percent of new jobs (Jackson, 2014). The proportion of the workforce with low-wage jobs has increased substantially in recent years (Block, 2015).

Young persons are finding it increasingly difficult to find full-time, long-lasting jobs after they complete their education. Many are now taking low-paying, part-time jobs even though they have large student debts to repay. Indeed, Stephen Poloz, governor of the Bank of Canada, suggested that young persons should work for free to gain some real-life experience (Grant, 2014). The shortage of good jobs also affects immigrants to Canada, making it more difficult for many of them to integrate into Canadian society.

Region

There are substantial differences in the economies of different regions, which lead to inequalities in wealth, income, and employment opportunities. This has contributed to dissatisfaction with the Canadian government in various provinces. Canada's industrial, commercial, financial, and cultural activities have tended to be concentrated in southern Ontario and in the Montreal region. For example, 35 percent of the 500 largest Canadian corporations have their headquarters in greater Toronto, compared to 16.2 percent in Montreal, 15 percent in Calgary, and 9.8 percent in Vancouver (Gainer, 2011). In addition, the concentration of over three-fifths of Canada's population in Ontario and Quebec provides considerable political power to these provinces. In contrast, other provinces (as well as the northern areas of Ontario and Quebec) have depended heavily upon the extraction and export of commodities such as forest products, minerals, and petroleum. Such commodities tend to fluctuate sharply in demand and price and generally provide less employment than other economic activities.

Past Canadian government policies that negatively affected the economies of Western Canada, such as the National Policy (1879) and the National Energy Program (1980), left a legacy of regional dissatisfaction often referred to as "Western alienation." The introduction of official bilingualism and the focus of Canadian politics from the 1960s to the 1990s on accommodating Quebec also caused resentment among many Western Canadians. The dominance of the federal government until 2006 by the Liberal party, which had little representation from Western Canada, left Westerners as outsiders.

The election of the Conservative party in 2006, with its strong Western Canadian representation including its Calgary-based leader, contributed to a decline in Western alienation. For example, while 55.8 percent of Western Canadians in 2004 believed that the federal government treats their province worse than other provinces, 34.7 percent held this belief in 2008.

By this measure, Atlantic Canadians were the most alienated in 2008 (44.5 percent), while the proportion of Ontarians thinking their province was treated worse increased from 15.5 percent to 28.7 percent. In contrast, the proportion of Quebecers feeling their province was treated worse than other provinces declined from 30.9 percent to 23.8 percent in 2008 even though Quebec had little representation in the governing Conservative party (Berdahl, 2010).

Canadian governments have devoted considerable attention to regional economic disparities. Beginning in 1957, the Canadian government provided equalization payments to the governments of the poorer provinces to enable them to provide their population with a comparable level of services to that of other provinces. In the 1960s, the Canadian government set up various programs to promote rural regional economic development, most notably through the establishment in 1969 of the Department of Regional Economic Expansion, which focused on Atlantic Canada and eastern Quebec. However, the success of these programs in promoting economic development was limited. In 1987 a somewhat more decentralized approach was adopted, with the establishment of agencies to galvanize economic development in Atlantic Canada, Western Canada, Northern Ontario, and, beginning in 1991, Quebec. In 2009, a development agency was established for Southern Ontario, a region that traditionally boasted a robust economy but has suffered from the decline of its major manufacturing industries. Thus, there has been a movement away from the original focus on bolstering development in the poorest areas of the country.

The median income of people in the poorer provinces has moved closer to the national average in the past few decades, while Alberta residents have enjoyed significantly higher incomes than the national average. Atlantic Canada continues to have higher unemployment rates than the national average, and the unemployment rate in the northern and remote areas of provinces is often much higher than in the cities in the south. Residents of Nunavut not only have lower median incomes and higher rates of unemployment, but also have a much higher cost of living (see Table 4-3).

Canada's federal political system tends to encourage a focus on provincial and regional differences as powerful provincial governments often highlight grievances of their province. Furthermore, as discussed in Chapter 9, Canada's electoral system tends to exaggerate provincial and regional differences in party support.

Gender

Although women have made significant advances in recent decades, equality between women and men is still far from achieved. Relatively fewer women hold top positions in major corporations. Likewise, despite some gains, women are substantially underrepresented in legislative bodies. There has only

TABLE 4-3

MEDIAN TOTAL FAMILY INCOME (2012) AND RATE OF UNEMPLOYMENT BY PROVINCE AND TERRITORY (2015)

Notes: Census families include couples, with or without children, and lone-parent families. The unemployment rate is seasonally adjusted except for the territories, where a three-month moving average, not seasonally adjusted, is used.

	INCOME	PERCENT OF NATIONAL	PERCENT AVERAGE UNEMPLOYED
Canada	$74 540	100.0%	6.8%
Newfoundland and Labrador	70 900	95.1	12.6
Prince Edward Island	69 010	92.6	10.5
Nova Scotia	67 910	91.1	9.2
New Brunswick	65 910	88.4	9.9
Quebec	70 480	94.6	7.4
Ontario	74 890	100.5	6.8
Manitoba	70 750	94.9	5.5
Saskatchewan	80 010	107.3	4.3
Alberta	94 460	126.7	5.5
British Columbia	71 660	96.1	6.3
Yukon	94 460	126.7	8.1
Northwest Territories	106 710	143.2	8.1
Nunavut	65 530	87.9	14.9

SOURCES: Median total income, by province and territory (all census families). Statistics Canada, 2014; Statistics Canada Daily, Labour force characteristics by province (April 2005) seasonally adjusted. Statistics Canada, May 8, 2015; Labour force characteristics, unadjusted, by territory (three-month moving average). Retrieved from http://www.statcan.gc.ca/tables-tableaux/sum-som/l01/cst01/lfss06-eng.htm

been one female prime minister (Kim Campbell for a few months in 1993). Although 6 of the 13 premiers were female in 2013, two years later there were only 3 (Kathleen Wynne, Ontario; Christy Clark, B.C.; and Rachel Notley, Alberta). However in 2015 prime minister Trudeau carried out his promise to appoint an equal number of women and men to his cabinet.

Women have become an important part of the paid workforce, although they are still underrepresented. As of March 2015, 60.9 percent of women 25 years of age and older were in the paid workforce compared to 71.8 percent of men. Although men were slightly more likely to be unemployed than women (6.2 percent vs. 5.4 percent), women were more likely than men to work part-time (21.6 percent vs. 7.9 percent) (Statistics Canada, 2015b).

The proportion of women obtaining higher education has increased greatly in recent decades. Indeed, young women are now more likely than young men to obtain a university degree and are at least as likely as young men to work as doctors, lawyers, and business administrators. In fact, 28 percent of employed women aged 25–34 work in professional occupations compared to only 18 percent of employed men of the same age group (Uppal & LaRochelle-Côté, 2014).

Nevertheless, there continue to be substantial inequalities in employment earnings between women and men. To some extent, this results from women being more likely to have part-time rather than full-time employment. Even so, as Table 4-4 indicates, the earnings of women in full-time employment are still considerably below those of men. In part, this is a result of differences in

FULL-YEAR, FULL-TIME WORKERS YEAR	WOMEN	MEN	EARNINGS RATIO (%)
2001	41 400	59 300	69.9
2002	41 700	59 400	70.2
2003	41 500	59 200	70.2
2004	42 800	61 100	70.1
2005	42 700	60 600	70.5
2006	44 100	61 300	71.9
2007	44 900	63 100	71.2
2008	45 500	64 000	71.1
2009	47 300	63 500	74.4
2010	47 300	64 200	73.6
2011	47 300	65 700	72.0

TABLE 4-4
AVERAGE EARNINGS BY SEX AND WORK PATTERN ($ CONSTANT 2010)

SOURCE: Statistics Canada. (2013). *Average earnings by sex and work pattern*, CANSIM Table 202-0102. Retrieved from http://www.statcan.gc.ca/tables-tableaux/sum-som/l01/cst01/labor01b-eng.htm.

the occupations of women and men. Less educated men are more likely to have jobs in higher-paying occupations, such as mining, oil drilling, and construction, while less educated women are more likely to hold lower-paying jobs in retail sales, clerical work, and personal services. Likewise, university-educated women are more likely to pursue careers in lower-paid female-dominated professions such as nursing, education, and social work than in some higher-paid male-dominated occupations such as engineering and computer science. Income inequality is particularly evident at the highest-income levels. Women account for only 29.8 percent of the top 10 percent of income tax filers and 21.3 percent of the top 1 percent (Statistics Canada, 2014, November 18). Nevertheless, these proportions of high-income women are about double those of three decades ago.

Income inequality between women and men is substantially higher among workers in the private sector than among workers in the public sector.[2] To a considerable extent, this reflects the much higher rate of union membership in the public sector than in the private sector (McInturff & Tulloch, 2014). Collective bargaining tends to promote greater equality in wages. As well, pay equity (discussed below) is more prevalent in the public than in the private sector.

There undoubtedly continues to be some discrimination against women, particularly in senior executive and non-traditional occupations, and a reluctance of some employers to take into account the different circumstances of women in hiring, pay scales, and promotion. As well, although the division of household duties has moved somewhat in an egalitarian direction, women still tend to devote more time to caring for other family members than men. In particular, the scarcity of affordable, quality child care creates important

---

[2]Visible minorities and Aboriginals also face a higher level of income inequality in private sector employment than in the public sector (McInturff & Tulloch, 2014).

obstacles in the pursuit of employment equality for many women. Sexual harassment in the workplace can affect the willingness of women to pursue promotions or remain with an employer.

ADDRESSING GENDER INEQUALITY For many decades, national and provincial laws have required that employers pay men and women equal wages for carrying out the same or substantially similar work (although differences can be based on such factors as experience, qualifications, and merit). This requirement does not, however, remedy the overall inequality in wages between men and women because women tend to be employed in lower-paying occupations. To overcome gender-based inequalities in wages, women's groups have sought government action to pass and enforce **pay equity** laws. Pay equity requires that equal pay be given for work of *equal value*. Specifically this involves increasing the pay of those working in occupations that are staffed primarily by women to the level of pay of equivalent occupations that are primarily staffed by men. The equivalency of different occupations is determined by a combination of the skill, effort, responsibility, and working conditions involved in each occupation. For example, if the occupation of school secretaries is determined to be equivalent to that of school janitors, then pay equity would require that a school board raise the salary of school secretaries to match that of school janitors.

Most jurisdictions in Canada have adopted some form of pay equity legislation for public servants and, in some provinces, the broader public sector. Only Ontario and Quebec have legislated pay equity for the private sector. Even where legislation has established pay equity, questions have been raised as to whether the legislation (particularly if it relies on individual complaints) is effectively applied and enforced. Many business leaders oppose pay equity because of its costs and argue that wages and salaries should be determined by the market.

Women's groups have also advocated that **employment equity** (affirmative action) programs be established to encourage or require the hiring and promotion of women for positions in which they are underrepresented. For example, the Canadian government requires that government departments set targets to increase the proportion of women (as well as Aboriginals, visible minorities, and people with disabilities) in senior positions. Employment equity has had considerable success in changing the gender composition of the federal public service, as 54.1 percent of all jobs, including 46.1 percent of executive positions, are now held by women (Treasury Board of Canada Secretariat, 2015). Federally regulated companies and companies having or seeking contracts worth at least $1 million from the Canadian government are also required to set up employment equity programs. Most universities and colleges have adopted employment equity policies, and many professional programs have adopted measures to try to increase the diversity of their student body. Still, despite major increases in the proportion of women in some traditionally male occupations, gender segregation remains surprisingly evident. Furthermore,

PAY EQUITY
A requirement that equal pay be given for work of equal value, in particular by increasing the pay of those working in occupations staffed primarily by women to the level of pay of equivalent occupations primarily staffed by men.

An Overview of Pay Equity in Various Canadian Jurisdictions
www.payequity.gov.on.ca/en/about/ pdf/pe_survey.pdf
Status of Women Canada
www.swc-cfc.gc.ca

EMPLOYMENT EQUITY
Programs that encourage or require the hiring and promotion of women (or other groups) for positions in which they are underrepresented.

although many more women now hold managerial positions in business, top-level executives are still predominantly male. For example, only 17.1 percent of the directors of the largest corporations are female (MacFarlane, 2014).

Critics of employment equity and other measures to increase the proportion of women and minorities in various positions argue that they involve "reverse discrimination" against men (particularly young men). Merit, rather than such characteristics as gender or colour, should be the basis for hiring and promotion. Others argue that promoting diversity has positive effects as various groups who have been underrepresented bring different perspectives to business and politics. Furthermore, what seem to be merit-based decisions for hiring and promotion, or for selecting candidates for public office, may in fact be decisions of an "old boys' network" that emphasizes fitting in, personal or social connections, and a willingness to avoid family responsibilities.

Gender Minorities

Those with different gender identities and sexual orientations (including lesbian, gay, bisexual, transgender, and questioning) have long faced discrimination, harassment, and oppression in Canada and throughout the world. Until 1969, homosexual behaviour was a criminal offence that, in at least one case, resulted in a life sentence. Even after decriminalization, gays and lesbians faced continued harassment, notably the police raid on gay bathhouses in Toronto in 1981 that resulted in more than 300 arrests. This action led to public protests and the development of a gay and lesbian activist movement. Annual gay pride parades and festivals have become major events in many cities and towns. Court decisions based on the Charter of Rights and Freedoms along with federal and provincial human rights legislation gradually expanded the rights of gays and lesbians. Although only a relatively few politicians have "come out of the closet," those who have publicly declared their sexual orientation (including the premiers of Ontario and PEI) have succeeded in gaining support from voters.

Despite the recognition of the equal rights of gays and lesbians and acceptance by a majority of the public of same sex marriage and homosexuality (Rayside & Wilcox, 2011), serious problems remain. Homophobia, bullying, and violence are still prevalent. Some religious leaders and politicians continue to publicly speak out against homosexuality. In 2012, Ontario's Roman Catholic bishops opposed the formation of support groups for gay students in Catholic schools if they were called "gay–straight alliance clubs." However, as part of Ontario's Accepting Schools Act, publicly funded schools could not refuse to allow clubs with this name.

Egale Canada
www.egale.ca

Aboriginal Peoples

Undoubtedly, Aboriginal peoples are most likely to suffer from inequality, particularly those who live on reserves or in remote northern communities. In many cases, a large majority of the adult population is unemployed, with the band council often being the only source of employment. Inadequate housing, poor food supplies, contaminated drinking water, and limited health care and social services are common features of many Aboriginal communities. Even among Aboriginals living off reserves, the employment rate is more than 10 percent lower than that of non-Aboriginals. This difference is particularly evident among those without a high school diploma (Statistics Canada, 2011a).

The legacy of harsh treatment in residential schools and the removal of many Aboriginal children from their homes and communities have resulted in what might be termed "cultural genocide." Faced with continuing racism, discrimination, and violence directed at Aboriginals, it is not surprising that many Aboriginals face severe challenges and hardships in their lives.

Ethnic, Religious, and Racial Minorities

Canada is a highly diverse country with a variety of different cultures and identities. About half of Canada's population has a strong sense of belonging to an ethnic or cultural group (Statistics Canada, 2003). Despite the adoption of official multiculturalism and the ending of discriminatory laws, various ethnic, religious, and racial minorities still face difficulties in gaining full acceptance in mainstream Canadian society. A large survey conducted in 2002 found that 24 percent of visible minority persons felt uncomfortable or out of place because of their ethnocultural characteristics at least some of the time. Twenty percent of visible minority members (including 32 percent of black Canadians) said that they had "often" or "sometimes" experienced discrimination or unfair treatment in the past five years because of their ethnicity, race, skin colour, language, accent, or religion[3] (Statistics Canada, 2003). This treatment occurred most often at work or in applying for a job or a promotion. Furthermore, the average earnings of visible minority people are substantially less than those of whites, they are more likely to be poor, and they are less likely to be called for a job interview (Reitz & Banerjee, 2007; Grant, 2011).

In Toronto, the police practice of "carding" (stopping people on the street for no specific cause and asking for identification and personal information that is then entered into a large database) has been controversial. This practice, of dubious legality, involved at least 2.1 million cards being filled out between 2008 and 2013. Particularly targeted were young black males, some of whom were stopped numerous times (MacLelland, 2015). In Fall 2015, the Ontario government announced that random and arbitrary carding would end.

---

[3]An additional 15 percent (17 percent of blacks) said that this had occurred "rarely." The survey was conducted among those 15 years of age or older, but did not include Aboriginals. No comparable survey has been conducted more recently.

Summary and Conclusion

Canada is fortunate in being a prosperous country. However, Canada has depended on natural resources for more of its wealth than most other developed countries. The Canadian economy also relies heavily on trade with the United States, and many of the country's major industries are owned by foreign (particularly American) companies. The North American Free Trade Agreement has resulted in a high level of economic integration in North America and, along with economic globalization, has tended to enhance the power of corporations. A variety of major new trade and investment agreements will likely also increase the power of corporations and reduce the ability of Canadian governments to regulate trade, investment, and the provision of government services. The secretive nature of negotiations about major international economic agreements and their tendency to focus on the interests of business (including multinational corporations) raises important questions about the quality of democracy in Canada. Likewise, the use of independent tribunals to decide on important disputes raises issues about the accountability and transparency of the tribunals.

Canadian governments have often played an active role in developing the Canadian economy. Although government policies continue to have an important influence on the economy and business activities, privatization and deregulation in recent decades have reduced the role of government. The focus of governments on facilitating rapid economic growth, particularly through large-scale natural resource developments, can have long-term negative environmental effects. Canadian governments are going to have to take major steps to move the country to a low carbon and, eventually, a zero net carbon emission world.

The adoption of various social and health care programs has helped improve the quality of life of all Canadians. Nevertheless, the development of a "welfare state" has been limited by concerns about government deficits and the development of the neo-liberalism perspective, which views many government social programs as interfering with the efficiency of the free market. The growth of income inequality and the concentration of power in the hands of large corporations have been criticized, particularly by those who believe that Canadian democracy should strive for greater equality.

Canada has generally avoided the severe social divisions that afflict many countries. Nevertheless, divisions based on class, region, gender, sexual orientation, ethnicity, nationality, race, religion, and Aboriginality continue to create important challenges to the cohesion and solidarity of Canadian society.

Overall, good government involves ensuring that Canada's economic prosperity is sustainable and benefits all Canadians, that the natural environment is protected, and that different groups and individuals in society are treated fairly and equitably.

Discussion Questions

1. Is a focus on developing Canada's natural resources desirable? What are the political implications of moving toward a low or zero net carbon emission economy?

2. Should Canada try to limit foreign ownership of Canadian businesses?

3. What are the advantages and disadvantages of Canada's free trade and investment protection agreements?

4. Which divisions in Canadian society have the most important effects on Canadian politics? Is this likely to change in the future?

5. Should governments be more active in pursuing greater social and economic equality? If so, what policies should be adopted?

Further Reading

Banting, K., & Myles, J. (Eds.). (2014). *Inequality and the fading of redistributive politics*. Vancouver, BC: UBC Press.

Bashevkin, S. (2009). *Women, power, politics. The hidden story of Canada's unfinished democracy*. Don Mills, ON: Oxford University Press.

Berdahl, L., & Gibbins, R. (2014). *Looking west: Regional transformation and the future of Canada*. Toronto, ON: University of Toronto Press, 2014.

Clarkson, S. (2008). *Does North America exist? Governing the continent after NAFTA and 9/11*. Toronto, ON: University of Toronto Press.

Hamilton, R. (2005). *Gendering the vertical mosaic: Feminist perspectives on Canadian society* (2nd ed.). Toronto, ON: Pearson Education Canada.

Howlett, M., & Brownsey, K. (Eds.). (2008). *Canada's resource economy in transition: The past, present, and future of Canadian staples industries*. Toronto, ON: Emond Montgomery.

McDougall, J.M. (2006). *Drifting together: The political economy of Canada–US integration*. Peterborough, ON: Broadview Press.

McMullin, J. (2010). *Understanding social inequality: Intersections of class, age, gender, ethnicity, and race in Canada* (2nd ed.). Toronto, ON: Oxford University Press.

Rayside, D., & Wilcox, C. (Eds.). (2011). *Faith, politics and sexual diversity in Canada and the United States*. Vancouver, BC: UBC Press.

Rice, J.J., & Prince, M.J. (2012). *Changing politics of Canadian social policy* (2nd ed.). Toronto, ON: University of Toronto Press.

Vickers, J., & Isaac, A. (2012). *The politics of race: Canada, the United States, and Australia* (2nd ed.). Toronto, ON: University of Toronto Press.

Tommy Douglas, the "father of medicare," in Ottawa in 1983. Chosen as the "Greatest Canadian" during a 2004 CBC contest, he was devoted to social causes that improved the lives of all Canadians.

© Chris Schwarz/Canadian Press Images

CHAPTER 5

Political Culture

CHAPTER OBJECTIVES

After reading this chapter, you should be able to

1. Explain the meaning of political culture and how it is analyzed.
2. Discuss how founding fragments theory has been applied to understanding Canadian political culture.
3. Examine the usefulness of formative events theory in assessing the differences between the Canadian and American political cultures.
4. Explain post-materialist theory.
5. Discuss whether there is a single, distinctive Canadian political culture.

In 2004, CBC Television held a contest to select the "Greatest Canadian." The response was tremendous as Canadians nominated thousands of individuals for this honour. The names of the top 100 nominees were posted on a CBC website. Each week an advocate for one of the top 10 nominees presented his or her nominee's case in an hour-long show. Finally, after over 1.2 million votes were cast through a website and by telephone, Tommy Douglas was declared the "Greatest Canadian"—beating out runners-up Terry Fox, Pierre Trudeau, Frederick Banting, David Suzuki, Lester B. Pearson, Don Cherry, Sir John A. Macdonald, Alexander Graham Bell, and Wayne Gretzky.

Just who was this man Canadians rated more highly than eminent inventors and hockey legends? As a young boy growing up in a family that could not afford proper medical care, Tommy Douglas would have lost his right leg as a result of osteomyelitis if not for the compassion of a visiting doctor who treated him for free. As premier of Saskatchewan from

1944 to 1961, Douglas fought tirelessly to bring free public medical care to the people of his province. Later, as leader of the New Democratic Party (NDP), he successfully persuaded the minority Liberal government of Lester B. Pearson to institute a national medicare system in 1966. Finally, in 1971, his lifelong campaign for free medical care for all residents of Canada was fully achieved.

U.S. President Barack Obama faced a difficult battle to pass legislation that would reduce the large number of Americans (nearly 50 million) without health insurance coverage. "Obamacare" continues to be a very contentious issue, with many Republican members of Congress calling for its repeal. In contrast, Canada's medicare system has become a source of pride for most Canadians and is often referred to when Canadians describe their country as having superior values to those of the United States. Despite some problems with Canada's health care system (such as wait times for some treatments), most Canadians react negatively when basic changes to the system are suggested, such as allowing patients to pay for faster diagnosis and treatment in privately run clinics.

Do such differences indicate that the neighbouring countries have different political cultures based on different fundamental political values, beliefs, and orientations to politics? As is often the case in political analysis, there is no easy answer. Many Americans have been unhappy with their largely private health care system, although misleading portrayals of the Canadian system have created confusion about alternatives. In Canada, many people were opposed to the introduction of medicare in the 1960s; private insurance companies fought against the loss of their lucrative business and doctors in Saskatchewan went on a lengthy strike in protest against medicare. Furthermore, although medicare in Canada has become a "sacred trust" in which politicians of all political persuasions hasten to proclaim their belief, other elements of the Canadian welfare state (such as social assistance and employment insurance) have suffered from criticism and cutbacks. As well, unlike other rich countries that have comprehensive public hospital and medical insurance, Canada lacks equivalent coverage for pharmaceutical drugs (Boothe, 2015).

Despite being voted the "Greatest Canadian," Tommy Douglas, as national leader of the NDP, did not succeed in gaining widespread electoral support, and he twice lost his seat in federal elections. However, his contribution to the well-being of Canadians won him enduring respect and admiration.

WHAT IS POLITICAL CULTURE?

POLITICAL CULTURE
The fundamental political values, beliefs, and orientations that are widely held within a political community.

The term **political culture** refers to the fundamental political values, beliefs, and orientations that are widely held within a political community. Measuring the proportion of individuals who hold particular political attitudes and orientations to political objects can provide indicators of political culture. However, political culture generally refers to the collective attributes of a political community (Stewart, 2002), not just the distribution of individual political attitudes.

Political culture differs from public opinion—the views of the public about specific political issues, political parties, and political figures. To some extent, public opinion is affected by the more fundamental values, beliefs, and orientation of the political culture. However, public opinion is also influenced by the media, family, friends and other individuals, the groups one associates with or identifies with, and the circumstances surrounding the particular issue. In other words, political culture is a long-term feature of a political community, while public opinion can change more quickly.

In Canada, medicare, the Charter of Rights and Freedoms, and the Mountie in uniform are all associated with a political culture (see Box 5-1:

Symbols of Canadian Identity). They are among the various symbols, myths, meanings attached to widely used terms, and interpretations of important events that help to shape **political discourse**—the ways in which politics is discussed and the rhetoric that is used in political persuasion. Political culture affects the politics of a political community and the general kinds of policies that are adopted. It does this by setting some broad limits to the actions governments consider desirable and what the public is willing to accept. A country's political culture helps to explain why similar political institutions (such as a parliamentary system of government) may operate in quite different ways in countries with different political cultures (Bell, 1992).

Through a process called **political socialization**, new generations and immigrants are socialized into the political culture through the educational system; the media; exposure to the ideas of parents, friends, and associates; and various organizations such as religious institutions, political parties, community groups, and labour unions. A political culture usually evolves gradually as new circumstances or important events lead to changes in political thinking.

Key to political culture are the dominant values of a society—for example, views concerning freedom, equality, order, security, justice, and prosperity. Such values serve as popular buzzwords and influence our thinking about politics. But which are most important and influential when different values conflict? For example, when faced with the possibility of terrorism, should we be concerned with maintaining everyone's civil liberties or take tough measures to protect our safety and security, even if those measures involve curbing

POLITICAL DISCOURSE
The ways in which politics is discussed and the rhetoric that is used in political persuasion.

POLITICAL SOCIALIZATION
The process by which new generations and immigrants are socialized into the political culture.

individual rights and freedoms? Should economic growth through projects such as the development of Alberta's oil sands be promoted even if there are serious environmental consequences?

As well, certain terms used in political discourse, however popular, may be interpreted in different ways. For example, equality may represent a popular value, but its meanings are many and diverse: an equal sharing of wealth and income; ensuring that every individual has an equal opportunity to get ahead in life; protecting the equal legal rights of everyone; or requiring that there be an equal number of women and men in Parliament, the cabinet, and the boards of directors of corporations.

It is often assumed that each country has its own distinct political culture based on such factors as its historical political experiences, the characteristics of its population, its economy, and its geographical characteristics. However, broad similarities often exist among different countries. Canada's political culture bears general similarities to that of other Western liberal democracies and, in particular, countries such as Australia and New Zealand originally colonized by the United Kingdom (Inglehart, 2009). Furthermore, the political values, beliefs, and orientations of a particular country do not usually develop in a void, isolated from the political ideas of other countries. American political values, in particular, are often thought to have an important influence on Canadian thinking because of the close ties between the two countries and the tremendous influence of the American mass media.

The assumption that each country has its own, broadly shared political culture can also be questioned because genuine differences often exist within a single country. Different groups or areas of a country may hold contrasting— even clashing—values and beliefs. Most countries have **subcultures** that are variations on the national political culture. However, in some countries differences in basic values and beliefs among different groups or regions may be so large and fundamental that we cannot consider the country to have a single unified political culture.

SUBCULTURES
Variations on the national political culture.

ANALYZING POLITICAL CULTURE

There are two major approaches to analyzing political culture. The first involves examining a country's historical experiences; its constitution and governing institutions; the general policies that governments adopt; and the writings of its leading thinkers, political figures, and political observers. Analyzing the effects of the British conquest of New France, the Confederation debates, the operation of the parliamentary system, Macdonald's National Policy, or the writings of Margaret Atwood, John Ralston Saul, and Pierre Trudeau could reveal something about Canada's political culture. Yet this approach has limitations—it may depict the political culture of the past rather than the present. For example, the Canadian Constitution was written at a time when democratic values were not fully accepted, and thus Canada's governing institutions (particularly the Senate) do not reflect the democratic political values of contemporary Canada. There may be significant differences between the political values, beliefs, and orientations characteristic of those most deeply committed to political life and the political thinking of the general public. The public policies adopted by governments may tend to reflect the views of the more powerful and politically engaged elements of society.

The second major approach to analyzing political culture involves the use of sample surveys. Well-designed surveys can quite accurately capture the views of a population at a given moment, even though only about 1000 or 2000 people are normally sampled. However, it is not always clear whether the responses to surveys reveal the deeply held values of the population, or fleeting and hasty opinions in response to a battery of questions. Public opinion on particular issues may reflect deeply held values and beliefs or simply a temporary or knee-jerk reaction to current events.

THEORETICAL APPROACHES TO UNDERSTANDING POLITICAL CULTURE

A **political ideology** is a set of ideas, values, and beliefs about politics, society, and the economic system often based on assumptions about human nature. Of particular importance in understanding the political culture of Canada and other Western democracies are the ideologies of **liberalism**, **conservatism**, and **socialism**[1] (see Box 5-2: Major Political Ideologies and Perspectives). Two major theoretical approaches to understanding Canadian political culture—founding fragments theory and formative events theory—focus on the historical development of ideological perspectives. It should be noted, however, that political culture is a broader concept than a political ideology, which is held in consistent form primarily by an educated elite.

Founding Fragments Theory

American political scientist Louis Hartz (1955) pointed out that each of the classic political ideologies became an important element of European political cultures. Liberalism developed to challenge the traditional conservative ideas often associated with the feudal era and the aristocracy. Socialism provided a synthesis of liberal ideas about individual freedom and traditional conservative ideas about the collective good of society.

Hartz's **founding fragments theory** suggests that in the founding of new societies, such as Canada, the United States, and Australia, only a fragment of

POLITICAL IDEOLOGY
A set of ideas, values, and beliefs about politics, society, and the economic system often based on assumptions about human nature.

LIBERALISM
An ideological perspective that emphasizes the value of individual freedom based on a belief that individuals are generally capable of using reason in pursuit of their own interests.

CONSERVATISM
An ideological perspective that generally looks to laws based on traditional (religious) moral values and established institutions to maintain an orderly society.

SOCIALISM
An ideological perspective that emphasizes the value of social and economic equality and generally is critical of the capitalist economic system.

FOUNDING FRAGMENTS THEORY
The theory that in the founding of new societies, only a fragment of the political culture of the "mother country" formed the basis for the political culture of the new society.

---

[1]The terms "left" and "right" are often used to depict ideological positioning. Those on the left (including socialists) seek greater social and economic equality and generally favour laws based on universal human rights. Those on the right (including conservatives) view inequality as a natural feature of human society and often favour laws based on traditional moral values and free market capitalism.

BOX 5-2
Major Political Ideologies and Perspectives

Liberalism, conservatism, and socialism represent the three classic political ideologies that developed in Western societies.

LIBERALISM

Liberalism emphasizes the value of individual freedom based on a belief that individuals are generally capable of using reason in pursuit of their own interests. Classical liberals challenged government restrictions on business activity, the privileged position of the aristocracy, and state support for established religions. Government, they argued, should be concerned only with protecting life, liberty, and property, leaving individuals free to pursue their own interests and follow their own beliefs as long as they do not seriously harm others.

CONSERVATISM

Conservatism holds a less positive view of individual capabilities, and thus places less emphasis on the rights and freedoms of individuals. Instead it generally looks to laws based on traditional (often religious) moral values and to established institutions to maintain an orderly society. Traditional conservatives typically view the elites of society as having a responsibility to maintain the civilized values of the community, and seek to avoid radical changes that could threaten the collective good of society.

SOCIALISM

Socialism places high value on social and economic equality. Believers in the idea that human beings are naturally social and cooperative, socialists are critical of what they view as the excessive competition and greed associated with the capitalist system. In place of the inequality and exploitation of the capitalist system, socialists traditionally looked to the establishment of some form of social (or governmental) ownership of the major means of production. In addition, to move toward equality of condition, socialists generally look to government to provide a wide variety of services freely to all and to reduce inequality by redistributing wealth and income.

Each of the ideological perspectives has evolved over time, and many variations exist. Reform or welfare liberalism favours an active role for government in ensuring that all individuals have the means and opportunity to develop their capabilities. Neoliberalism has a strong belief in the free market system and advocates free trade, major reductions in government regulation, lower taxes, and the privatization of many government services. Contemporary conservatism generally combines neoliberal advocacy of limited government with tough measures to fight crime and maintain military strength. Social conservatism focuses on upholding traditional moral and religious values. Contemporary socialists (often termed social democrats) no longer advocate the nationalization of industry. Instead, they oppose the privatization of government services and favour government action to reduce inequality, regulate the economy, provide various social programs, and promote human rights.

Other perspectives are also important in Canada. Feminism challenges the male-dominated power relations throughout society and politics and seeks to end the subordination of women. Environmentalism challenges the pursuit of unsustainable economic growth and seeks to develop a more harmonious relationship with nature. Nationalism emphasizes the importance of the people being able to govern themselves so that the interests, culture, and values of their nation (whether Canada, Quebec, or a First Nation) can be promoted.

BOX 5-3

Is Canada a Métis Civilization?

Canadian political culture has often been viewed in terms of the influence of English- and French-speaking settlers. Some scholars add to this the influence of subsequent waves of immigrants, while others focus on the influence of the United States on Canadian political culture.

A very different perspective is provided by John Ralston Saul (2008). In his view, Canada is "a métis civilization" that "has been heavily influenced and shaped by the First Nations" (p. 3). In particular, Saul claims that Canadian acceptance of diversity is derived from "the First Nations idea of an inclusive circle that expands and gradually adapts as new people join us" (p. 4). In addition, he suggests that Aboriginal influence has contributed to the distinctiveness of the Canadian political culture in terms of its orientation to fairness and equality, the balancing of group and individual rights, environmental consciousness, and the preference for negotiation rather than violence.

Aboriginal peoples interacted quite extensively with Canada's early European settlers. However, the significance of Aboriginal cultures for Canadian society was reduced greatly in the past two centuries as Aboriginals were largely confined to the margins of society and their proportion of Canada's population declined sharply. Nowadays, the Aboriginal population is increasing faster than the non-Aboriginal population. Many Canadians who are not officially recognized as First Nations (Indian), Inuit, or Métis are rediscovering and taking pride in having some degree of Aboriginal heritage. Thus, even if the description of Canada as a "métis civilization" is contentious, Canada's political culture is more diverse than those who focus on British and French immigrants suggest.

the "mother country" formed the basis for the political culture of the new society. The leading ideological perspective in the mother country at the time of colonization tended to become the dominant or sole ideology of the new society. In particular, Hartz characterized the United States as being a classical liberal fragment. Without a significant presence of traditional conservative ideas and lacking an aristocracy, the interaction of liberalism and conservatism that he viewed as necessary for the development of socialist ideas could not occur. Instead, ideological development would only take place within the framework of the liberal perspective. Indeed, Hartz claimed that classical liberal ideas had become the unthinking dogma of the United States and the basis for nationalistic views of American superiority, creating a lack of tolerance for those daring to express different ideological views.

DIFFERENT PERSPECTIVES As applied to Canada, Hartz's founding fragments theory suggests that the Canadian political culture should be analyzed in terms of two separate "fragments"—French and English Canada. Although Hartz takes note of Aboriginal peoples, the original founders of Canada, he does not view them as significant in the development of Canadian political culture. (For a different view, see Box 5-3: Is Canada a Métis Civilization?)

French Canada was established in the seventeenth and eighteenth centuries when authoritarian conservative values still dominated in France, although questions have been raised about whether Quebec was ever really a "feudal fragment" (Forbes, 1987). Even if the dominant ideas of French Quebec were authoritarian conservatism, at times some liberal ideas were also present. Liberal ideas that became more significant in the 1950s and 1960s could be viewed, in accordance with fragment theory, as allowing for the development of socialist ideas through the interaction of conservative and liberal ideas (Wiseman, 1988).

English Canada was viewed by Hartz and Kenneth McRae (1964) as similar to the United States in terms of being a classical liberal fragment. However, this depiction of the English Canadian political culture is controversial.

The United Empire Loyalists who fled the American Revolution because of their ties to the British government and their opposition to American independence are often viewed as major founders of English Canada. Some view the Loyalists as similar to other Americans in sharing classical liberal individualistic views (Ajzenstat, 2003).

Others view the Loyalists (and others with British ancestry) as bringing a **"tory touch"** or "tory streak" to Canada. This "tory touch" was an element of traditional conservatism that included the defence of a hierarchical rule by a privileged elite on behalf of what they viewed as the collective good of the nation and a greater concern for order than for individual rights. Gad Horowitz (1966) argues that the Loyalist "tory touch" was significant in allowing socialist ideas to gain some acceptance in Canada (unlike the United States). The idea that government should act for the collective good of society as a whole (an important aspect of socialism as well as traditional conservatism) has not been rejected as an "alien" perspective as it has in the United States. The presence of some conservative ideas laid the foundation for some degree of acceptance of the socialist ideas that later were brought to Canada by British immigrants (and Canadians studying in British universities). Canadian political culture, in this perspective, is more diverse than the American political culture. Liberalism is the leading ideology, but conservative and socialist ideas also contribute to the diversity of the political culture.

One problem with Horowitz's analysis is that socialist ideas found acceptance in those areas of the country where the "tory touch" is weak or nonexistent. Socialist ideas have played a more significant role in the political culture in parts of Western Canada than in parts of Ontario and the Maritimes, where the Loyalist influence is most strongly felt. As well, it has been pointed out that the social democratic version of socialism that has gained popular support in Canada is not that different from welfare liberalism—the version of liberalism that is characteristic of the left wing of the Liberal party (Forbes, 1987).

Nelson Wiseman (2007) argues that fundamental features of political culture did not become fixed at the time of early settlement. Rather, wave after wave of immigration brought new ideas to Canada that became incorporated into the political culture. After the first wave of immigrants from France prior

TORY TOUCH
An element of traditional conservatism that includes the defence of a hierarchical rule by a privileged elite on behalf of the collective good of the nation.

to 1760 and the second wave of Loyalists in the 1780s, a third wave of immigrants from 1815 to 1851 brought reform-minded workers and artisans from Britain who pushed for responsible government (i.e., a government in which the executive is responsible to elected representatives). A fourth wave of immigrants from the 1890s to the 1920s, who settled primarily in the West and Ontario, included socialists influenced by the development of the British Labour Party, populists from the United States who favoured more direct control by ordinary people over government, and continental Europeans. Finally, a fifth wave of immigration since the end of World War II has brought people from many parts of the world who have a variety of different perspectives.

Formative Events Theory

Formative events theory, associated with American political scientist and sociologist Seymour Martin Lipset, emphasizes the importance of a crucial formative event in establishing the basic character of a country's political culture. The American political culture was shaped by its revolutionary experience, while the Canadian political culture was shaped by its counter-revolutionary stance in reaction to the American Revolution. Similarly, French Canada under the influence of the Catholic Church rejected the radicalism of the French Revolution of 1789 (Lipset, 1996).

The revolutionary experience of the United States resulted, in Lipset's view, in a political culture that emphasized the values of individual freedom, minimal government, and equality of opportunity associated with classical liberalism. In contrast, Canada's counter-revolutionary experience gave rise to a traditional conservative ("tory") political culture that emphasized the rule by an elite, deference to those in positions of authority, and a strong state (Lipset, 1990). Both political cultures have since evolved. The Canadian political culture has adopted some of the individualistic and democratic values of the American political culture. In addition, the Canadian political culture has become more egalitarian in that Canadians have become favourable to the use of government to create greater social and economic equality. To some extent, the American political culture also has come to accept a role for government in dealing with social and economic problems and to support some group-oriented policies, such as affirmative action for minorities. Nevertheless, Lipset argued that there continue to be "fundamental distinctions" between the two countries resulting from the American Revolution; these have been "reinforced by variations in literature, religious traditions, political and legal institutions, and socioeconomic structures" (Lipset, 1990, p. 8).

Lipset tended to view the Canadian political culture as more conservative (in the traditional sense of that term) because of its counter-revolutionary past. However, like Horowitz, he saw the collectivist orientation of traditional conservatism as contributing to the development of a socialist strain within the Canadian political culture. For example, he views the substantially higher

FORMATIVE EVENTS THEORY
A theory that emphasizes the importance of a crucial formative event in establishing the basic character of a country's political culture.

level of unionization in Canada than in the United States (other than in the 1930s) as a reflection of the collectivist element in the Canadian political culture. In turn, the union movement has been important in pressuring governments to develop welfare state policies and in supporting democratic socialist parties that have, at times, governed various provinces.

Lipset argued that the tendency of Canadians to take more liberal positions on moral and social issues (such as abortion and homosexual rights) can be explained, at least in part, by long-standing differences in the religious makeup of the two countries. In modern times, the leading religious organizations in Canada have promoted social justice as advocates for the disadvantaged. The United Church (formed in 1925 out of a variety of Protestant groups) has tended to be quite liberal on moral issues. In the United States, however, the development of influential fundamentalist and evangelical movements that take a literal view of the Bible as the word of God hold a strongly moralistic view of the need to eradicate evil. Furthermore, Canada has become a more secular society than the United States in that religious observance and belief play a less important role in the lives of many Canadians. Canadians are also less likely to favour religious influence in political life (see Table 5-1). In its largely secular, rather than religious, approach to politics, the Canadian political culture has come to resemble that of a number of countries in Western Europe.

Overall, Lipset likened Canada and the United States to two trains "that have moved thousands of miles along parallel railway tracks. They are far from where they started, but they are still separated" (1990, p. 212). Questions can be raised about Lipset's claim that Canada is "still Tory" (1990, p. 212). For example, some surveys indicate that Canadians are now less deferential to authority than Americans and more critical of government than Americans (Nevitte, 1996). Some scholars argue that there is a significant "Red Tory" element in the Canadian political culture. Red Tories (such as philosopher George Grant and former Progressive Conservative party leader Robert Stanfield) favour the use of the state for nation-building purposes, are critical of unregulated capitalism, often emphasize the importance of Canada's British heritage as a way of countering American influence, value social

TABLE 5-1
THE POLITICAL IMPORTANCE OF RELIGION IN CANADA AND THE UNITED STATES

VALUE	CANADA	UNITED STATES
Religious leaders should not influence government	70.9%	49.4%
Politicians who don't believe in God are unfit for public office	17.3	32.0
Better if more people with strong religious beliefs are in public office	22.8	31.8
Religious leaders should not influence how people vote	77.6	60.5
Attend religious services at least once a month	34.2	48.9

SOURCE: World Values Survey, 2006. World Values Survey Association (www.worldvaluessurvey.org).

The Canada–United States border: Does this line separate two countries that have different political cultures?

harmony more than individualism, and stress the responsibility of privileged elites to contribute to the common good (Ball, Dagger, Christian, & Campbell, 2010). However, many Canadian conservatives (including the contemporary Conservative party) have rejected the Red Tory perspective in favour of a more individualistic, free market, limited government perspective similar to that of many American conservatives.

Overall, Canadians have become more liberal than Americans on some social issues, such as male–female equality (Adams, 2003). As Table 5-2 indicates, Canadians are also slightly more egalitarian than Americans and more likely to support increased government ownership of business. On the other hand, Canadians are slightly less likely to feel that government should take more responsibility to ensure that everyone is provided for. More recently, the AmericasBarometer also found that Canadians are more egalitarian than Americans; 51 percent of Canadians compared to 29 percent of Americans strongly agreed with the statement that "government should implement strong policies to reduce income inequality," while 6 percent of Canadians and 36 percent of Americans strongly disagreed.[2] However, when asked what should be done to reduce poverty and inequality, only 31 percent of Canadians suggested increasing taxes on the rich and 7 percent offering assistance to the poor, compared to 40 percent suggesting creating jobs or improving the economy (Environics Institute, 2012a).

---

[2]"Strongly agree" represents 6 and 7 on a 7-point scale, while "strongly disagree" represents 1 and 2 on this scale; 66 percent of Quebecers strongly agreed compared to 36–38 percent of those in the three Prairie provinces.

TABLE 5-2

VIEWS ON EQUALITY AND THE ROLE OF GOVERNMENT IN CANADA AND THE UNITED STATES

Notes: Respondents were asked to state their opinion to each pair of statements on a scale of 1 to 10. Intermediate responses (5 and 6) are not shown in this table. Scale means represent the average position of all responses. A lower number indicates stronger tendency to support the first statement.

	CANADA	UNITED STATES
Incomes should be made more equal	29.0%	19.1%
We need larger income differences as incentives	44.3%	46.3%
Scale mean	5.8	6.1
Private ownership of business should be increased	52.4%	62.2%
Government ownership of business should be increased	17.4%	6.0%
Scale mean	4.4	3.7
Government should take more responsibility to ensure everyone is provided for	25.9%	28.3%
People should take more responsibility to provide for themselves	47.5%	44.2%
Scale mean	6.0	5.9

SOURCE: World Values Survey, 2006. World Values Survey Association (www.worldvaluessurvey.org).

Generally, the Canadian political culture appears to be more moderate than that of the United States, where Tea Party extremists (a movement largely within the Republican party that includes anti-government right wing populists, libertarians, and social conservatives) have been an influential political force in recent years.

Post-Materialist Theory

POST-MATERIALIST THEORY
A theory that those who have grown up in relative security and affluence are more likely to give priority to post-materialist values rather than materialist values.

POST-MATERIALIST VALUES
Values such as self-expression, participation in economic and political decisions, emphasis on the quality of life, tolerance of diversity, and concern for environmental protection.

Ronald Inglehart (1977, 1990) developed a **post-materialist theory** about changes in political culture related, in part, to the economic changes since the 1940s. His theory contends that those who have grown up in relative security and affluence (as has been the case for Canada and other Western countries since World War II) are more likely to give priority to **post-materialist values** such as self-expression, participation in economic and political decisions, emphasis on the quality of life, tolerance of diversity, and concern for environmental protection. Earlier generations tend to prioritize materialistic values such as a concern for economic growth, order, and physical security.

Inglehart and his colleagues argue that post-materialism—combined with the development of a post-industrial, knowledge-based economy, greater access to higher education, and more effective means of mass communications—has led to a number of significant political trends. These include greater citizen activism, the questioning of authority, the development of new political parties and new social movements, the raising of new types of issues (such as issues related to the environment and gender equality), and the development of more liberal social values (Dalton, 2006). For example, there has been a substantial decline in recent decades in moral traditionalism (particularly reflecting a greater acceptance of homosexuality) in Canada. Feminist and environmentalist perspectives have also become increasingly important.

	1982 (N = 1186)	1990 (N = 1647)	2000 (N = 1882)	2006 (N = 2164)
Materialist	22.3%	11.9%	8.6%	10.3%
Mixed	61.8	62.5	62.9	58.5
Post-materialist	16.0	25.6	29.4	31.2

TABLE 5-3
POST-MATERIALISM INDEX: CANADA

SOURCE: Calculated from World Values Survey, 2006. World Values Survey Association (www.worldvaluessurvey.org).

Note: The index is based on responses to two questions: "If you had to choose, which one of the things on this card would you say is most important? And which would be the next most important?"
1. Maintaining order in the nation.
2. Giving people more say in important government decisions.
3. Fighting rising prices.
4. Protecting freedom of expression.
Those responding #1 and #3 were classified as "materialist"; #2 and #4 as "post-materialist," and other combinations as "mixed."

At the same time, the extent of value change should not be exaggerated. The majority of the population exhibits a mixture of materialist and post-materialist values (see Table 5-3). Nevertheless, when faced with a hypothetical choice between "giving priority to protecting the environment even if it causes slower economic growth and some loss of jobs" or "making economic growth and job creation . . . the top priority even if the environment suffers to some extent," 72.2 percent of Canadians chose the environmental priority over the more materialist one. In comparison, only 54.1 percent of Americans chose the environmental priority (World Values Survey, 2006).

DEMOCRATIC VALUES

Canadian political culture is often described in terms of the values of liberal democracy. As noted in Chapter 1, liberal democracy includes the ideas of a free society, tolerance of different viewpoints, equal rights for all, competitive elections, limited government, and the rule of law. Table 5-4 indicates that

CHARACTERISTIC	NOT ESSENTIAL (1)	ESSENTIAL (10)	MEAN
Women have the same rights as men	1.1%	66.2%	9.1 (8.5)
People choose their leaders in a free election	1.4%	50.2%	8.7 (8.3)
Civil rights protect people's liberty against oppression	0.9%	32.6%	8.1 (8.0)
People receive state aid for unemployment	1.4%	19.8%	7.4 (5.8)
People can change the laws in a referendum	4.0%	20.7%	7.2 (7.4)
Criminals are severely punished	5.0%	23.2%	7.1 (6.6)
The economy is prosperous	2.9%	17.3%	7.1 (6.9)
Governments tax the rich and subsidize the poor	4.1%	6.7%	6.1 (5.0)
The army takes over when the government is incompetent	29.9%	5.1%	4.0 (3.9)
Religious authorities interpret the law	33.6%	1.1%	3.0 (3.2)

TABLE 5-4
CANADIAN VIEWS OF THE ESSENTIAL CHARACTERISTICS OF DEMOCRACY

Note: Respondents were asked to rank each characteristic on a scale from 1 (not essential) to 10 (essential). Mean scores for American respondents are shown in brackets.

SOURCE: Calculated from World Values Survey, 2006. World Values Survey Association (www.worldvaluessurvey.org).

FIGURE 5-1
IMPORTANCE OF
DEMOCRACY

V162: Question: How important is it for you to live in a country that is governed democratically? On this scale where 1 means it is not at all important and 10 means absolutely important, what position would you choose?

Number of respondents: 2165
Mean: 9.0

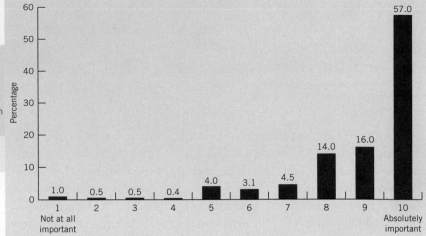

SOURCE: Data for Canada, World Values Survey, 2006. World Values Survey Association (www.worldvaluessurvey.org).

almost all Canadians view liberal democratic values as highly important. There is also considerable support for government's role in aiding the poor and unemployed in Canada.

About seven-eighths of Canadians agree that democracy is the best form of government (Dalton, 2006; Pérez, 2008). Likewise, most Canadians consider it very important to live in a country that is governed democratically (see Figure 5-1). Over three-quarters of Canadians said that "having a strong leader who does not have to bother with Parliament and elections" was a bad or very bad idea (World Values Survey, 2006).

Views about Government and Politics

Most Canadians are very satisfied (13.7 percent) or fairly satisfied (51.5 percent) with the way Canadian democracy works, with only 11.2 percent not at all satisfied (Canadian Election Study, 2011).[3] However, the general satisfaction with democracy does not extend to positive evaluations of government, politicians, and political parties. A majority of Canadians said they had not very much or no confidence at all in the government (60.7 percent), Parliament (61.9 percent), and political parties (76.5 percent). On the other hand, a majority of those surveyed expressed a degree of confidence in the civil service (55.7 percent), the justice system (65.7 percent), the environmental protection movement (72.8 percent), the women's movement (72.9 percent), and the police (81.7 percent) (World Values Survey, 2006). Only one-fifth of

---

[3]Satisfaction with democracy was quite high in all provinces except Quebec, where 48.7 percent of francophones expressed satisfaction with democracy in Canada (Tanguay, 2014).

Canadians indicated that they trust the government in Ottawa to do what is right always or most of the time (Docherty, 2002). While 93 percent of Canadians rated firefighters and 87 percent rated nurses as trustworthy, only 12 percent rated local politicians and 7 percent rated national politicians as trustworthy (Galt, 2007). About three-quarters of Canadians give political leaders a low or very low rating on ethics and honesty. About the same proportion feels that political leaders do not tell the truth or keep their promises (Centre for Research and Information on Canada, 2002). Similarly, 59 percent of those polled said that they thought that most politicians are mainly in politics "because they want to advance their own ambitions" rather than "because they want to do something good for the country" (CBC, 2004).

Associated with the low level of confidence and trust in government and politicians, the majority of people do not have a strong sense of **political efficacy**—that is, a belief that government is responsive to the people and that they can influence what government does. For example, 64.9 percent of Canadians agreed or strongly agreed with the statement that "I don't think that the government cares much about what people like me think," compared to 33.0 percent who disagreed or strongly disagreed. Likewise, 66.5 percent strongly or somewhat agreed with the statement: "Once elected to Parliament, MPs soon lose touch," compared to 29.1 percent who disagreed or strongly disagreed (Canadian Election Study, 2011).[4]

How have we reached a point where the general distrust of government and politicians is so widespread? In some cases, political scandals and broken promises have sparked negative attitudes toward politicians. As well, the mass media has generally become more critical of politicians and the failures of government. Likewise, criticism of politicians and governments is widespread in the social media. A more educated and informed public has higher expectations of government. This leads to disappointment when those expectations are not fulfilled. In addition, the decline in trust and confidence in politicians and political institutions may be part of a general decline in deference toward authority in various forms.

Overall, the combination of a general belief in the value of democracy—along with a critical attitude toward government, political parties, and politicians—characterizes not only Canada but also other Western democratic countries. Citizen demands for a greater voice in decision making and expectations that politicians should be more responsive and accountable to the public suggest that the political culture of the Canadian population places a high value of democracy. However, as discussed in Chapter 6, participation in conventional political activities such as voting is rather low.

POLITICAL EFFICACY
A belief that government is responsive to the people and that they can influence what government does.

---

[4]For both statements, a small proportion answered "don't know" or refused to answer.

Rights and Freedoms

There is a strong consensus among Canadians about the desirability of democratic rights and freedoms. For example, 98 percent of Canadians agreed with the statement, "No matter what a person's political beliefs are, he or she is entitled to the same legal rights and protections as everyone else." However, when asked "whether members of extreme political groups should be allowed to hold a public rally," the proportion agreeing dropped to 61 percent. Only 35 percent of respondents supported this freedom for a specific group that they disliked the most (such as communists or fascists) (Sniderman, Fletcher, Russell, & Tetlock, 1996, pp. 20–22). Generally, the majority of Canadians do not take the libertarian position that advocates very few restrictions on individual freedom. Instead, the majority of Canadians tend to favour controls on the rights and freedoms of those they view as promoting hatred, advocating the revolutionary overthrow of government, or posing a potential threat to public safety and national security. However, polls in 2015 indicated that the majority of people who were aware of the anti-terrorism law (Bill C-51) disapproved of the legislation despite the widespread publicity given to terrorist attacks in Canada and around the world (Maloney, 2015).

Tolerance

As discussed in Chapter 3, the Canadian government has adopted a policy of multiculturalism and has ended discrimination against those of non-European ancestry in its immigration policies. Nevertheless, a majority of Canadians think that immigrants should adopt Canada's culture (Macdonald, 2007). However Canada has avoided the anti-immigrant demonstrations, violence, and growth of far right political parties in many European countries that seek to bar or even expel persons of a particular religion, ethnicity, race, or nationality.

Equality

There is little doubt that Canadians today favour political equality in the sense of all citizens having the right to vote and hold office. Likewise, the vast majority support equal rights for women and men. Canadians generally have become much more accepting of the rights of gays and lesbians than in the past. For example, 60 percent of Canadians strongly agree with the right to same sex marriage while only 15 percent disagree. Likewise 70 percent strongly agree with their right to run for public office while only 6 percent strongly disagree. Although Americans are nearly as accepting of the right of gays and lesbians to run for public office, only 47 percent strongly agree with the right to same-sex marriage. Support for gays and lesbians is much weaker in the rest of the Americas than in Canada and the United States (Environics Institute, 2014).

However, there appears to be less support for special treatment (such as affirmative action programs or hiring quotas) for disadvantaged groups to promote equality (Sniderman et al., 1996). As well, when asked to choose whether personal freedom ("that is, everyone can live in freedom and develop without hindrance") or equality ("that is, nobody is underprivileged and that class differences are not so strong") is more important, only about one-third of Canadians chose equality (World Values Survey, 1982, 1990).

DIVERSITY AND POLITICAL CULTURE

Does Canada have a single national political culture, or are there several distinctive political cultures in Canada? It could be argued that concern about establishing a Canadian identity different from that of the United States has encouraged the development of a distinct Canadian political culture (Nevitte, 1995). Various opinion leaders (such as novelists, journalists, academics, and politicians) have sought to define what is distinctive about Canadian political orientations, policies, and institutions. Indeed, Canadian governments have sought to promote Canadian culture by financing the Canadian Broadcasting Corporation and the National Film Board, and establishing Canadian content rules for the broadcast media. However, protecting Canadian culture has become more difficult in the Internet age. The Harper government reduced its financial support to the CBC.

The development of a single, distinctive Canadian political culture is limited not only by Canada's strong economic and cultural ties to the United States and the influence of American media, but also by a number of important divisions within Canadian society. Whether the fundamental values, beliefs, and orientations widely held within a particular group should be considered to constitute a distinctive political culture rather than a subculture within a broader Canadian political culture is not always clear.

Provincial and Regional Political Cultures

Researchers have often focused on differences in basic political attitudes among the residents of different provinces or groupings of provinces (particularly the Western Canadian and Atlantic Canadian provinces). Given the importance of provincial governments in Canada's federal system, differences in provincial histories and economic, social, and ethnic differences as well as the vast geography of Canada, it would not be surprising to find substantial variations in the attitudes commonly held by the residents of different provinces. Provincial education systems and provincially based media may also contribute to provincial differences in political attitudes and opinions (Henderson, 2010).

There is a considerable difference across Canada in people's views about Canada's federal system: 65 percent of Ontario residents favour a strong federal government, 30 percent of Quebecers and 37 percent of Newfoundlanders favour more provincial power, and residents of the Prairie provinces are divided equally between the two options (Canadian Election Study, 2011, cited by Harell & Deschâtelets, 2014, p. 238).

Focusing on political efficacy and political trust, Elkins and Simeon (1980) found that "there are strong differences among the citizens of Canadian provinces and among those of different language groups" (p. 68). In particular, based on surveys in 1965 and 1968, residents of the Atlantic provinces tended to be "disaffected" (i.e., low in political efficacy and political trust). Residents of Ontario, British Columbia, and Manitoba tended to have higher levels of trust and efficacy. However, a subsequent analysis found that provincial and regional variations in levels of political efficacy (and political interest) were "minimal" (Clarke, Jenson, LeDuc, & Pammett, 1996).

Although regional differences on various public policy issues were generally diminishing from 1949 to 1975 (Elkins & Simeon, 1980), regional differences on policy issues increased from 1979 to 2006 (Anderson, 2010). Not surprisingly, regional differences were strongest on issues relating to Quebec's place in Canada, which was a key concern in this time period. Nevertheless, regional differences (particularly, but not exclusively, based on differences between Quebec and the rest of Canada) were significant on several policy issues. However, gender had a greater effect than region on social spending, and education level had the strongest effect on views about moral issues. Aggregating six different policy issues, regional differences (including the differences between Quebecers and persons in the rest of Canada) were more significant than nonterritorial differences based on sociodemographic differences such as gender, age, and social class (Anderson, 2010). Using a different method of analysis and a different data set, Cochrane and Perrella (2012) found that differences in support for government intervention in the economy could be better explained by language than by region (French-speaking persons were more likely to support government intervention whether they lived in Quebec or elsewhere).

Henderson (2004) suggests that regional political cultures should be examined not only in terms of provinces and groups of provinces. Instead, areas that have similarities in terms of such characteristics as ethnicity, race, religion, language, proportion of immigrants, and social structure (such as education, occupation, and dependence on natural resources) should be compared. Using these criteria, she identified "nine relatively homogeneous clusters" (p. 604), including urban Canada, rural and mid-northern, suburban Toronto and Vancouver, and the manufacturing belt. Based on data from the 2000 Canadian Election Survey, she found that these regional clusters accounted for variations in attitudes such as political efficacy and left–right political ideology nearly as well as differences based exclusively on province. In particular, she concluded that in analyzing political culture, attention needs to be given to the differences between north and south and between urban, suburban, and rural areas.

Quebec Political Culture

The political culture of French Quebecers tends to be markedly different from that of the rest of Canada. French settlers brought different ideas to the New World than did settlers from Britain and the United States. The Catholic Church was influential in persuading many French Canadians that they had a mission to protect their culture and avoid the dominant individualistic, materialistic, and capitalist ideas of English-speaking North Americans. However, the influence of conservative, religious ideas was challenged (particularly during the Quiet Revolution of the early 1960s) by liberal and socialist ideas, and the significance of religion among French Quebecers has declined sharply.

French Quebecers have become quite similar to other Canadians in their levels of education and economic status. However, linguistic differences play an important part in maintaining the distinctiveness of the political culture of Quebec. Language is a crucial aspect of culture, as the words we use affect our understanding of the world we live in. People in different language groups tend to think about and discuss politics somewhat differently. For example, discussion between English and French speakers about whether Quebec is a "nation" can be difficult because the word "nation" has different connotations in the two languages. For English-speaking Canadians, a nation is often thought of in terms of the people of a sovereign country; for French speakers, it may refer to the culture and identity of people living in a particular area. Controversy thus arises when Quebec is called a "nation" (Bell, 1992).

As discussed in Chapter 3, the development of a secular form of Quebec nationalism focused on building a strong Quebec "state" has also helped to ensure that the Québécois political culture differs from that of the rest of the country. The Quebec government's efforts to rectify historic inequalities between French and English Quebecers and to steer the social and economic development of the province have given a somewhat greater collectivist character to Quebec politics than is the case in the rest of the country. The contemporary Quebec political culture can also be considered as somewhat more egalitarian and social democratic than that of the rest of Canada.

Quebecers have tended to become more liberal than English Canadians in their social and moral attitudes. Indeed, in their analysis of survey data, Grabb and Curtis (2005) found that differences between Quebecers and English Canadians tended to be greater than differences between English Canadians and Americans.[5] For example, they found that Quebecers tended to be more liberal than English Canadians (and Americans) in the proportion favouring the equality of women, same-sex marriage and gay rights, and less harsh

---

[5]Grabb and Curtis (2005) view Canada and the United States as consisting of "four societies". Just as Quebec has a different political culture from the rest of Canada, the southern states have a political culture that makes them distinct from the rest of the United States.

treatment of criminal behaviour. However, liberal attitudes do not necessarily extend to those of very different cultures such as Muslim women wearing face-covering clothing.

Aboriginal Political Cultures

Discussions of Canadian political culture have focused on the values of those of European (particularly British and French) ancestry who have dominated political life. Canadian governments have tried to force or persuade Aboriginals to adopt Western values, beliefs, and practices. In particular, the system of residential schools removed Aboriginal children from their parents and communities and forced them to adopt Christianity. Students were routinely beaten for speaking their native language. In fact, many Aboriginal languages are no longer used or will soon be lost. Those Aboriginal peoples who were nomadic were persuaded or forced to move to permanent settlements, thus changing their traditional lifestyles. Instead of self-sufficient communities, dependence on government handouts became the way of life for many Aboriginal communities.

Important cultural changes also have occurred as many Aboriginal people moved to the cities. Although some Aboriginals have succeeded in pursuing middle-class professional careers, other urban Aboriginals have become part of an "underclass" of low-paying casual labour.

Despite fundamental changes in the lives of Aboriginals, their political cultures generally continue to differ from those of other Canadians. Persons living in Aboriginal communities tend to think about politics in terms of seeking a consensus, rather than the adversarial and competitive view of politics that is incorporated in Canadian political institutions and practices. For example, in the Northwest Territories and Nunavut, where Aboriginals make up a substantial proportion of the population, political parties are absent from territorial politics and government. As well, First Nations and Inuit tend to have a collectivist rather than an individualistic orientation, reflecting both their traditional practices and the system of collective ownership of land and resources that have been maintained by the system of "reserves." First Nations also often combine the election of community leaders with traditional practices of drawing on the wisdom of community elders to guide decision making.

A survey of political attitudes in Nunavut (where Inuit predominate) found substantial differences as compared to other Canadians. Nunavut residents were more likely than residents of the provinces in the south to feel they "don't have any say about what government does" and that "politics and government seems so complicated that a person like me can't really understand what's going on." On the other hand, they were somewhat less likely to agree that MPs soon lose touch with the people. They were also more likely to agree that they were satisfied with the way democracy works

Former Governor General Michaëlle Jean, middle, uses an ulu to skin a seal during a community feast in Rankin Inlet, Nunavut, on May 25, 2009.

© Sean Kilpatrick/Canadian Press Images

in Canada. In terms of political values, they were much more likely to view protecting the environment as more important than creating jobs. They were also more likely to favour returning to traditional family values and were more critical of the welfare state. Finally, Nunavut residents were slightly less likely to choose materialist value priorities than other Canadians (Henderson, 2007).

Social Class

Surveys have found substantial class differences on a number of political attitudes. Not surprisingly, working-class persons are more likely than middle- and upper-class persons to take "left-wing" positions in favour of greater economic equality, a greater role for government in the economy, and greater support for various social programs that aid the less advantaged. On the other hand, those in higher social classes tend to have a more favourable view of civil liberties and a more tolerant view of minorities.

Gender

To some extent, women think about politics in different ways than men based on differences in socialization, circumstances, and experiences. Brenda O'Neill (2002) suggests that there is a women's political culture that "is distinctive in its political priorities and the degree to which an ethic of care and concern for responsibility permeate it" (p. 52). This is apparent, for example, in a tendency to have a less favourable attitude toward the use of military force, a less positive attitude toward the competitive capitalist system, and a more favourable attitude toward an active role for government in providing assistance to the disadvantaged. Younger women in particular, reflecting the influence of feminism, are more likely to be critical of traditional views about the role of women in the family, society, and politics.

Ethnicity

Given the large number of ethnic groups and the diversity of views that often exists among the members of an ethnic group, it is difficult to analyze the impact of ethnicity on political attitudes and perspectives. To generalize, those whose families immigrated to Canada many decades ago tend to be more likely to adopt the values of the Canadian mainstream than more recent immigrants. New Canadians from some cultures and religions are more likely than other Canadians to hold traditional moral and patriarchal attitudes regarding family, sexuality, and the position of women. There is often some tension in immigrant families between young persons who want to be more like most Canadians their age and other family members who seek to maintain the values and practices of their country of origin.

Youth

There are also significant differences between different generations in politically relevant values and orientations. In particular, younger persons tend to be more liberal in their views on moral issues (such as same-sex marriage) and somewhat more likely to have post-materialist value priorities than older persons. Younger persons are also more likely to participate in politics through involvement in social movements and protest activities than by voting and membership in a political party. Similarly, they are more likely to follow and discuss politics through new technology like social media rather than using traditional media such as newspapers and magazines. Although younger persons tend to have different political values and orientations, to some extent this may represent a generational change. That is, younger persons may retain their different values and orientations as they grow older, thus modifying the overall Canadian political culture.

Summary and Conclusion

The study of political culture provides a useful antidote to a commonly expressed view that ideas, beliefs, and values are not relevant to understanding Canadian politics. The struggle for power, position, and privilege is important, but politics also involves a contest of ideas and values among those who hold different perspectives.

Both Louis Hartz's founding fragments theory and Seymour Martin Lipset's formative events theory look to the past for the foundations of political culture. However, there are differences as to how the past has shaped Canadian political culture. Hartz views English Canada as having a basically liberal political culture similar to that of the United States. In contrast, Lipset sees opposition to the American Revolution as setting Canada in a somewhat more "Tory" conservative direction. Gad Horowitz views the presence of both liberal and some conservative elements as providing the basis for the development of an element of socialism. Post-materialist theory sees Canada (like other countries) as undergoing major changes in value priorities in recent decades. This has resulted in the Canadian political culture becoming less traditionalist, less deferential to authority, and more geared to self-expression and tolerance of diversity.

Nelson Wiseman (2007) argues that there is no "single unifying thread in contemporary Canadian political culture." In his view, "the country is too complex, its regions and peoples too varied, and its history too contentious to unequivocally assert the existence of a singular Canadian identity" (p. 264). Although the political culture of diverse groups of Canadians differs markedly, some political values and orientations are widely held. In common with other Western countries, the Canadian political culture has as its basis the values of liberal democracy. Nevertheless, there are many ways of interpreting the values of liberal democracy, and different priorities may be given to these values.

The political cultures of Aboriginal peoples and the Québécois have developed in substantially different ways than the political culture of the Canadian majority and continue to be distinctive. Likewise there are significant regional differences in political culture. Moreover, the immigration of many people of non-European origin has added considerably to the diversity of Canadian political culture or cultures. Despite the diversity of Canada, many Canadians are reluctant to recognize Quebec as a "distinct society" or "nation" or accept that Aboriginal peoples want to be self-governing nations with historic rights to their lands.

Many Canadians share a common heritage with Americans, interact with Americans, and are influenced by the culture of our powerful neighbour. Still, Canadians often view themselves as differing from Americans and consider Canadian values superior to those of the Americans. Canadians have become somewhat more liberal than Americans on various moral issues and more willing to favour government provision of various programs, including universal health care.

Discussion Questions

1. How would you describe your basic political values and beliefs? Are they similar to or different from those of your family, your friends, and other influences on your life?

2. How different are the political cultures of Canada and the United States? How can the similarities and differences best be explained? Is the Canadian political culture becoming more similar to that of the United States?

3. Is the political culture of your province or region substantially different from that of other areas of Canada?

4. Does Quebec have a distinct political culture and, if so, what are the implications for Canadian politics?

5. How do the political cultures of Aboriginal peoples differ from those of the rest of Canada?

6. Is the Canadian political culture changing rapidly, or does it still basically reflect its historic roots?

Further Reading

Ball, T., Dagger, R., Christian, W., & Campbell, C. (2013). *Political ideologies and the democratic ideal* (3rd Canadian ed.). Toronto, ON: Pearson Education Canada.

Bell, D.V.J. (1992). *The roots of disunity. A study of Canadian political culture* (rev. ed.). Toronto, ON: Oxford University Press.

Fierlbeck, K. (2006). *Political thought in Canada: An intellectual history.* Peterborough, ON: Broadview Press.

Grabb, E., & Curtis, J. (2010). *Regions apart: The four societies of Canada and the United States.* Toronto, ON: Oxford University Press.

Hartz, L., et al. (1964). *The founding of new societies.* New York, NY: Harcourt Brace.

Henderson, A. (2007). *Nunavut. Rethinking political culture.* Vancouver, BC: UBC Press.

Kaufman, J. (2009). *The origins of Canadian and American political differences.* Cambridge, MA: Harvard University Press.

Lipset, S.M. (1990). *Continental divide: The values and institutions of the United States and Canada.* New York, NY: Routledge.

Nevitte, N. (1996). *The decline of deference.* Peterborough, ON: Broadview Press.

Resnick, P. (2005). *The European roots of Canadian identity.* Peterborough, ON: Broadview Press.

Thomas, D.M., & Biette, D.N. (Eds.) (2014). *Canada and the United States: Differences that count* (4th ed.). Toronto, ON: University of Toronto Press.

Wesley, J.J. (2011). *Code politics: Campaigns and cultures on the Canadian Prairies.* Vancouver, BC: UBC Press.

Wiseman, N. (2007). *In search of Canadian political culture.* Vancouver. BC: UBC Press.

CHAPTER 6

Political Participation and Civic Engagement

Slutwalk, an annual protest march that started in Toronto in 2011 is an example of the peaceful unconventional forms of political participation that are an important aspect of contemporary politics.

© Mark Blinch/Reuters

CHAPTER OBJECTIVES

After reading this chapter, you should be able to

1. Identify different forms of political participation and civic engagement.
2. Discuss levels of political participation and civic engagement in Canada, and how they compare with other democracies.
3. Identify which Canadians are more likely to participate in political and civic affairs and why.
4. Discuss the significance of political participation and civic engagement to Canadian democracy and to individual Canadians.

SlutWalk is a global movement of protest marches that started in Toronto in 2011 after a police officer advised students attending a safety forum at York University that one way women could avoid being sexually assaulted—a major problem on Canadian university campuses—was to "avoid dressing like sluts." As far back as 1450, the word "slut" almost exclusively referred to a sexually promiscuous woman. The comments spurred thousands of outraged women and men to take to the streets in a highly publicized "SlutWalk." Women donned a range of attire, from jeans and T-shirts to lingerie, fishnet stockings, and stilettos. The revealing clothing was intended to raise awareness about "slut shaming," or shaming women for being sexual, and about the treatment of sexual assault victims. For the protesters, sexual assault is not about what a woman wore or did, it is about consent. "Because we've had enough" became the movement's official rally cry (Whyte, 2014). Global news coverage of the protest and social media inspired follow-up marches around the world.

The movement has been praised for challenging the myths that feed rape culture and for its success in mobilizing supporters. While the SlutWalk did not associate itself with **feminism**, an ideology that seeks to define and achieve equal political, economic, social, cultural, and personal rights for women, it drew attention to the broader women's movement and feminist messages. Rallies typically ended "with speakers and workshops on stopping sexual violence and calling on law enforcement agencies not to blame victims after sexual assaults." The movement's ideology and methods have been criticized by some, particularly women of colour and feminists in the Global South, who do not see their lived experiences reflected within "SlutWalk," or who regard the "slut" label as a male-defined term or foreign to their vocabulary (Dobrowolsky, 2014).

Since the inaugural event, SlutWalk marches have been held annually around the world, and have been described as the most successful feminist actions of the past few decades (Valenti, 2011). In an era where participation in formal political activities is on the wane, SlutWalk illustrates the power of grassroots actions and the social media to spread a clear message and mobilize people across borders.

FEMINISM
An ideology that seeks to define and achieve equal political, economic, social, cultural, and personal rights for women.

POLITICAL PARTICIPATION AND CIVIC ENGAGEMENT

Beginning in late 2010, a wave of mass demonstrations across the Middle East and North Africa led to the toppling of regimes in Tunisia, Egypt, Libya, and Yemen, and to civil uprisings in many other countries across the region. The protesters, motivated by a desire for democracy, human rights, transparency in government, and better living conditions, had relied on sustained campaigns of mass marches and demonstrations and the social media to organize and raise awareness about state attempts to repress the uprisings. In most of these countries, civil resistance associated with the "Arab Spring" has been met with violent responses from state authorities.

In contrast, the vast majority of Canadians can express their opposition to government policies and participate in other political activities without risking their personal security or their lives. They enjoy the right to freely express their views about political issues and to pursue their political goals through various means. Canadians may also participate in civic affairs by contributing to community life. This chapter looks at the extent to which Canadians exercise rights that are denied to many people elsewhere.

Political participation refers to the actions people take to raise awareness about political issues, influence the selection of government personnel, and shape the laws and policies that affect their lives. Canadians can participate in formal political activities by contacting an elected official about an issue that concerns them, attending a political meeting, volunteering in an election, joining a political party or interest group, donating money to a party or candidate, or running for public office (Milbrath & Goel, 1977; Verba & Nie, 1972; Verba, Nie, & Kim, 1971).

Some Canadians turn to **protest activities** outside of formal institutions like elections, parties, and Parliament, as a means of achieving political change. Protesting can encompass peaceful forms of political expression such as signing a petition, boycotting or **buycotting** products and services (Stolle, Hooghe, &

POLITICAL PARTICIPATION
Actions people take to raise awareness about issues, to influence the choice of government personnel, and to shape the content of legislation and public policies.

PROTEST ACTIVITIES
Political acts that include non-violent actions such as signing a petition, boycotts, peaceful marches, demonstrations, and strikes. They may sometimes involve the use of violence to damage property or harm the opponents of the cause.

BUYCOTTING
The act of buying goods and services based on political or ethical considerations, or both.

Micheletti, 2005), or participating in marches, demonstrations, and strikes. Some protest actions involve violence, resulting in damage to property or, very occasionally, physical harm to opponents of the cause.

Cyberactivism, or online political activism, is an increasingly popular way for people to express their opinions and to mobilize like-minded others to act through social networking sites, emails, and blogs. Conversations about politics also take place offline; people who feel strongly about an issue might discuss it with their friends and family in person or over the phone, write a letter to the editor, or organize a public event or meeting (Samara Canada, 2014).

Civic engagement, or participation in community affairs, refers to actions such as joining or volunteering for a civic organization, helping other individuals directly, or giving financial donations to charitable causes. There are many categories of civic organizations, including student associations, sports and recreation clubs, religious-based groups, ethnocultural associations, service clubs, environmental and human rights groups, and business or professional associations. Although voluntary organizations focus on improving the quality of community life or serving their members' needs, some of them are active in politics. For example, a local animal rights group might raise money to help subsidize a low-cost spay and neuter clinic for pet owners of limited means, but its activities might also extend to lobbying local governments and businesses to adopt cruelty-free policies and practices.

Canadians who are busy with school, jobs, families, and hobbies get involved in political or civic affairs for different reasons. One of the principal reasons is that they have been touched by an issue. They may feel strongly about a particular subject—youth unemployment, environmental protection, poverty, gun control, or women's rights, for instance—and want to express their opinion about it, or influence the decisions that public officials make. They may volunteer at a food bank or raise money for cancer research because they want to give back to their communities or because they know someone who needs assistance.

Because Canada is a liberal democratic country, citizens may also choose not to get involved in political and civic life. The extent to which Canadians participate in political and civic affairs and the ways in which they get involved paint a telling portrait of the state of Canadian democracy. Are Canadians activists or apathetic? How do they compare with citizens living in other democratic states? To answer these questions, this chapter tracks long-term trends in political participation and civic engagement, whether some of us are more likely than others to participate, and whether Canadians are more or less active than people living in other established democracies.

Canadian and International Trends in Public Affairs Involvement

In general, most of us do not get involved in political activities beyond voting, and a small minority take part in the most demanding activities that require

CYBERACTIVISM
Political activism that employs online communications tools such as websites, emails, blogs, and social networking services.

CIVIC ENGAGEMENT
A set of activities in the community, such as joining a voluntary organization, volunteering for the organization, helping others directly, or giving financial donations to charitable causes.

extra time, skills, and knowledge, such as joining political parties or working on a campaign. This makes Canadians very much like citizens living in other democratic countries. Furthermore, people who are active in political affairs do not represent the broader Canadian society; they are generally older, better educated, and better off than non-participants—more likely to be school principals or CEOs than squeegee kids or holders of McJobs.

However, as more people turn away from voting and party involvements in Canada, the United States, much of Europe, Australia, New Zealand, and Japan, protest activity has grown in some of these very same countries. In particular, Canada, the United States, Great Britain, and France have seen more and more protest activity over the past few decades. Cyberactivism is also gaining in popularity as a form of political participation in Canada and around the world. Since the late 1980s, counter-globalization and social justice groups have relied heavily on the World Wide Web and social media to raise awareness about issues and to mobilize members to take online and offline action.

Despite declining or low levels of formal political participation, as we discuss later in this chapter, a large number of Canadians take part in civic affairs. In fact, the country boasts one of the highest rates of participation in voluntary organizations in the Americas, and more than 80 percent of Canadians have volunteered to help others directly (Vézina & Crompton, 2012) or have given money to charitable causes (Turcotte, 2015). As is the case with political participation, certain types of Canadians are more engaged in civic affairs than others. The people who join civic groups tend to be middle aged, university educated, and affluent. Furthermore, although many Canadians give their time to help others, a relatively small percentage is responsible for the vast majority of volunteer hours that are contributed each year.

The trends summarized above inspire questions about the meaning of democratic citizenship in contemporary Canada. Is it necessary for a large number of people to get involved in politics to make democracy work, or can a democracy still thrive if relatively fewer people are engaged? Does it matter if certain types of Canadians are more likely to participate in political and community life than others? What, if anything, should the state do about plummeting levels of involvement in certain activities?

POLITICAL PARTICIPATION AND DEMOCRACY

Classical Democratic Theory

What level of political participation is ideal in a democracy? Who should try to influence the decisions of public officials? Two broad perspectives exist on these questions. **Classical democratic theory** is based on the idea that it is desirable to have a large number of citizens from different backgrounds participating in political affairs. In *Considerations on Representative Government,* philosopher John Stuart Mill argued that broad citizen participation guarantees that everyone's interests are protected from arbitrary rule. He also suggests that political participation changes citizens for the better, giving them a sense of control over their own lives, making them less likely to devote all their energies to private life, broadening their interests, and making them better informed (Mill, 1872/1991; Thompson, 1976). When individuals join in, they gain skills and knowledge about public affairs so that they can make good decisions. Participation is also said to promote tolerance. When individuals join a group to achieve a political goal, they are exposed to the opinions of others and must respect the decision of the majority, even if they do not agree with the outcome.

Over the past decade, governments and private organizations in Canada and around the world have become more and more interested in deliberative democracy, discussed in Chapter 1. Classical theorists are optimistic about the potential for individuals from diverse backgrounds to participate in politics. They assume that citizens are the best judges of their own interests and that political activity is the best way to express those interests and to judge how public officials respond to them. Classical democrats also generally feel that there should be equal levels of participation among members of different social and economic groups. **Deliberative democracy** involves citizens deliberating about government decisions through "fair and open" community discussion of the merits of competing political arguments (Uhr, 1998). Interest in forums that encourage people to participate in all stages of the policymaking process has been developed for several reasons. As citizens express weaker attachments to political parties and less confidence in politicians, some governments are looking for new ways to reinvigorate public involvement in political affairs. Internet technology has made it easier to hold discussions between people in far-flung locations about political ideas. The citizens' assemblies set up by the provincial governments of British Columbia and Ontario to examine the question of electoral reform are examples of deliberative democracy. (See Box 6-1: Citizens Decide: Deliberative Democracy in the Provinces.)

DELIBERATIVE DEMOCRACY
A form of democracy in which governing decisions are made based on discussion by citizens.

Classical Elite Theory

In contrast to classical democratic theory, **classical elite theory** is based on the idea that a small minority of individuals with more education and political experience are better positioned to decide what is in the public interest than the relatively uninformed, apathetic, and less tolerant electorate (Michels, 1915; Mosca, 1965). Elite democratic theorists feel that widespread participation by members of the public could trigger a conflict between social groups and political instability. Because they believe that not everyone possesses the virtues to make sound decisions about politics, they are more willing than classical democratic theorists to tolerate vast differences in the political involvement of people from different social and

CLASSICAL ELITE THEORY
The belief that only a small ruling class has the knowledge and skills necessary to decide what is in the public interest, and that mass political participation is undesirable.

BOX 6-1

Citizens Decide:
Deliberative Democracy in the Provinces

In 2003, the government of British Columbia undertook a bold new experiment: letting ordinary citizens decide whether the province should retain the single member plurality (SMP) electoral system or replace it with a new one that would be proposed by the assembly (see "Voting" later in this chapter, and also Chapter 9 for an explanation of different electoral systems). Nowhere else in the world had such power over the development of an electoral system been given to unelected citizens.

The Citizens' Assembly on Electoral Reform had 161 members, 1 man and 1 woman from each of British Columbia's 79 electoral districts, plus 2 Aboriginal members and a chairperson. Members were picked at random, by a computer, from the province's voters' list. The assembly was diverse in its demographic makeup, with gender, age, and regional representation being reflected. Those who agreed to serve received an honorarium of $150 for each meeting day, plus any expenses associated with their work for the assembly.

Participation in the assembly was not for slackers: the members began their task by studying the pros and cons of different electoral systems used throughout the world. In 2004 they attended 50 public hearings held across the province, where they listened to British Columbians' views on electoral reform. More than 1600 written submissions from members of the public were also made available to the assembly participants for their consideration. After the hearings were over, the assembly members considered what they had studied and what British Columbians had told them, and discussed different options.

The assembly ultimately recommended that British Columbia switch to the single transferable vote system (a system in which voters rank candidates in multimember districts in order of preference, with votes not needed by one candidate transferred to the next preferred candidate). This recommendation was brought to the public for approval in a province-wide referendum on May 17, 2005. Although supported by 58 percent of voters, it failed to reach the required 60 percent level of approval. A second referendum on electoral reform was held together with the 2009 provincial general election. This time, the proposal received only 39 percent support.

In 2006, Ontario set up a similar citizens' assembly to evaluate whether the province should replace its electoral system with a form of proportional representation. It was made up of a chairperson and 103 randomly selected citizens—1 from each of the province's electoral districts. The assembly membership was evenly divided between males and females, and at least one member was Aboriginal. Once again, the task was arduous. The members spent an entire year studying various election systems, talking to people in their communities, holding public consultation meetings, reading public submissions, and using online forums to discuss the issues between meetings. In spite of their efforts, the issue received relatively little attention from the media, and ordinary citizens struggled to grasp the concepts. The final recommendation to replace SMP with a mixed member proportional (MMP) system was rejected in a referendum held in October 2007: just under 37 percent of those who cast a vote supported MMP.

Although the reform proposals were rejected in both provinces, the assembly participants agreed that they benefited enormously from their personal involvement in the process (Turnbull & Aucoin, 2006). How do you feel about the idea of citizen involvement in the policymaking process? Should important political decisions be left only to professional politicians and bureaucrats? Do the examples from British Columbia and Ontario suggest that deliberative democracy is a viable way of engaging the broader public in politics?

economic backgrounds (Mishler, 1979). Some scholars have argued that Mill himself was often skeptical about the benefits of public participation. In *On Liberty,* he worried about the tendency of the majority to impose its own ideas and practices on those who dissent from them. He thought that democracy would encourage mass conformity and intolerance and inflame factional rivalries (Zakaras, 2007).

In their groundbreaking study of political cultures in five contemporary democracies, Gabriel Almond and Sidney Verba (1963) argued that the majority of citizens expressed only a weak commitment to democratic norms and that their active involvement in politics could lead to political instability and the emergence of authoritarian politics. They favoured a civic culture—a society in which only a small group of well-educated citizens participates actively in politics and where most citizens leave politics to the experts. As discussed in Chapter 5, Canadians strongly support democratic values and there is little indication that political elites are much more committed to liberal democratic values than the rest of the population.

Which of these two perspectives on the number and types of individuals who participate in political affairs best describes democratic life in Canada? The following section tackles this question by examining trends in political participation, as well as the personal characteristics and attitudes of the Canadians who get involved and those who do not. Since a certain level of political interest is necessary for political action, the section also considers whether Canadians are interested in, and knowledgeable about, politics.

CANADA: A NATION OF POLITICAL ACTIVISTS?

Canada, like many other democracies, is not a nation of political activists. By international standards, Canadians are moderately interested in politics, but not very knowledgeable about it. Only a small minority of people take part in political activities beyond voting and signing petitions. However, a growing number of Canadians are turning to interest groups and social movements, protest activities, or cyberactivism to raise awareness about new or neglected issues and to change public policies. Young Canadians and the disadvantaged are an integral part of this phenomenon, although they still do not constitute the majority of participants in protest activities.

Political Interest and Knowledge

People who are interested in political affairs are motivated to spend the time and energy to keep informed so that they can discover what they want, evaluate the government's performance and the options presented by the opposition, and act upon that information. In general, Canadians are only moderately interested in politics and only occasionally discuss politics with their family and friends. When compared with people living in other established Western democracies, however, Canadians are actually more interested in politics and discuss it more frequently than average. As in other countries, television is the leading source of political information for Canadians. Certain Canadians—men, university graduates, and the affluent—are more likely to express an interest in politics and in media coverage about policies (Gidengil, Blais, Nevitte, & Nadeau, 2004).

Canada is one of the Anglo-American countries that political scientist Henry Milner has diagnosed as suffering from relatively low levels of political knowledge, in contrast to the Netherlands, Sweden, Norway, Denmark, and Germany, where civic literacy is more robust (Howe, 2006). Significant numbers of Canadians do not know the names of the prime minister, party leaders, prominent cabinet ministers, or the premiers, and cannot identify political parties with their issue positions and whether the federal parties occupy the ideological left, right, or centre (Gidengil et al., 2004). Whereas many Canadians may recognize American president Barack Obama and pop star Katy Perry, they may be tongue-tied when asked about Bill Morneau or Kathleen Wynne. Political knowledge is also not distributed evenly across the population. University graduates, older Canadians, and the affluent know more about politics than Canadians with less formal education, the young, and the less well-off (Gidengil et al., 2004).

Voting

The right to vote is the cornerstone of democracy. When you cast a ballot, you have an opportunity to hold your elected representative accountable and to support or reject a political party's policies. Voting also symbolizes your connection to the political community. Virtually all citizens aged 18 years and over have the right to vote. However, this was not always the case in Canadian history (see Table 6-1). At the time of Confederation, only male property owners aged 21 years and over and who were British subjects by birth or naturalization could vote. Women, racial minorities, most Aboriginals, and the poor were excluded from voting. These laws reflected commonly held views based on the British tradition that certain groups were unsuited to participate in democratic affairs (Courtney, 2004).

World War I and the women's suffrage movement led to the doubling of the electorate by 1918. In 1917, Parliament passed the Wartime Elections Act and the Military Voters Act. These laws were designed to increase the number of voters who would support conscription and disqualify those who were opposed to it. The Military Voters Act extended the right to vote to all British subjects, male or female, who were active or retired members of the Canadian forces. Some 2000 military nurses—the "Bluebirds"—became the first women to get the vote. The Wartime Elections Act gave the vote to close female relatives of people serving in the armed forces. It also took away the vote from likely opponents of conscription: conscientious objectors, pacifist religious minorities, individuals born in an enemy country who became naturalized

YEAR	GROUP ENFRANCHISED
1917	Serving members of the armed forces (including women)
1918	Women aged 21 years and over, not alien-born, who meet property requirements in provinces where those requirements exist
1948	Disqualifications on the basis of race eliminated
1950	Inuit granted the right to vote
1955	Last vestiges of religious discrimination removed from federal elections
1960	Franchise extended unconditionally to "registered Indians"
1970	Voting age lowered to 18
1982	Canadian Charter of Rights and Freedoms entrenches the right to vote
1992	Legislation to ensure access to vote for people with disabilities
1993	Removal of voting disqualifications for federally appointed judges, people with mental disabilities, and inmates serving less than two years in correctional institutions
2002	Supreme Court decision in *Sauvé v. Canada* repeals the Canada Elections Act restriction of voting rights for inmates serving sentences longer than two years

TABLE 6-1
A TIMELINE OF THE FEDERAL FRANCHISE

SOURCE: *A history of the vote in Canada.* Elections Canada. (2010). This is an adaptation of the version available at www.elections.ca. Reproduced with the permission of Elections Canada, but adaptation rests with the author.

British subjects after March 31, 1902 (with the exception of those born in France, Italy, or Denmark and who arrived in Canada before the date on which their country of origin was annexed by Germany or Austria), and British subjects naturalized after March 31, 1902, whose mother tongue was that of an enemy country (Elections Canada, 1997).

Some women of property were able to vote in the colonies until pre-Confederation legislatures passed laws (1849 in the Province of Canada) explicitly preventing women from voting—a restriction that was maintained by the British North America Act, 1867 (Elections Canada, 1997). Within a decade after Confederation, a women's suffrage movement had taken root in most of the former colonies. In 1916 and 1917, Canada's suffragists and their allies successfully petitioned provincial governments in British Columbia, the Prairies, and Ontario to allow them to vote in provincial elections. The broadening of the provincial **franchise** and the extension of the municipal franchise to propertied women created pressure for change at the federal level. In 1918, women 21 years of age and over were given the right to vote, provided they met the same property requirements that applied to male electors. The property requirement was dropped in 1920 (Elections Canada, 1997).

Following World War II, racial and religious restrictions on voting were lifted as social attitudes toward minority groups began to change (Elections Canada, 1997). In 1950, Canada restored the vote to the Inuit, who had been disenfranchised in 1934. This was one of several measures taken to protect the country's sovereignty in the Arctic following the onset of the Cold War. In

FRANCHISE
The right to vote.

1960, Status Indians[1] were allowed to vote without having to give up their status and the benefits associated with it. By 1948, the last vestiges of property qualifications and laws excluding the Chinese, Japanese, and South Asians from voting had been removed. In 1955, all remaining voting restrictions against certain religious minorities were dropped. In 1970, Parliament lowered the voting age from 21 years to 18 years to discourage the student strikes and unrest that had been taking place in the United States and parts of Europe. The electorate grew once more with the adoption of the Canadian Charter of Rights and Freedoms in 1982. Section 3 of the Charter states that "every citizen of Canada has the right to vote in an election of members of the House of Commons or of a legislative assembly and to be qualified for membership therein." This provision opened the door to a series of successful court challenges that resulted in the extension of the vote to people who had previously been denied it: federally appointed judges, people with mental disabilities, and inmates serving sentences of two years or more.

Although in the past Canadians have fought tirelessly for the right to vote, many Canadians today are more complacent about this hard-won right. In countries such as Afghanistan, Iraq, and Zimbabwe, people have died or have risked their lives to vote. Although Canadian citizens do not have these worries, turnout in national elections has not been high by international standards. In the five elections held since 2000, turnout has hovered around the 60 percent mark. As of 2014, Canada ranked 130th out of 198 countries in terms of the proportion of registered voters who actually voted in the most recent parliamentary elections (Institute for Democracy and Electoral Assistance, 2015). Some observers argue that Canada's single member plurality (SMP) electoral system accounts for the country's mediocre ranking. Election turnout tends to be lower in SMP systems than in systems based on proportional representation (Blais & Carty, 1990). With SMP, the victorious party usually wins more seats in the legislature than the popular support it receives in the election. In proportional representation (PR) systems, a party's representation corresponds more closely to its popular support. For example, if a party wins 20 percent of the vote in a PR system, it will receive about 20 percent of the seats to be distributed. Some experts have argued that turnout is higher in countries that use PR because voters are more likely to think that every vote counts and that their votes will not be "wasted" (LeDuc, 2005). Another institutional factor that has been associated with higher turnout is compulsory voting. In 29 countries, voting is compulsory and is regulated by the constitution or electoral laws. Some of these countries impose sanctions on non-voters, ranging from fines and the removal of civil and social

---

[1]Status Indians are members of First Nations who are listed on the official registry maintained by the Canadian government and who are entitled to a range of programs and services funded by the federal and provincial governments. These benefits do not extend to the Métis or several hundred thousand "non-status" persons who trace their ancestry to a First Nation.

rights, to disenfranchisement and prison time. Countries with enforced compulsory voting have, on average, turnout rates that are 15 points higher than countries such as Canada, where individuals make up their own minds about whether or not to go to the polls (Gratschew, 2002).

Although nearly every Canadian citizen aged 18 years and over can vote in federal elections, turnout rates have plummeted since the late 1980s (Elections Canada, 2008). Between 1945 and 1988, voter turnout rates averaged 75.4 percent. After turnout sank to a historic low of 58.8 percent in 2008, preliminary estimates pegged turnout in the 2015 federal election at 68.5 percent, an increase of 7 percent over 2011 (see Figure 6-1). Trends showing voter disengagement are not unique to Canada. Between 1990 and 2000, the median average turnout for 15 Anglo-American, Nordic, and West European countries was 77 percent, down 9.2 percentage points compared with the 1945–1989 period.

As turnout in federal elections has declined precipitously since 1988, the same trend has occurred in all provinces since the 1970s or early 1980s (see Table 6-2). Turnout reached historic lows in provincial elections held in Newfoundland and Labrador, New Brunswick, Nova Scotia, Prince Edward Island, Ontario, and British Columbia between 2009 and 2014. In Quebec and Alberta, turnout rebounded in 2012 after record lows were reached in their respective 2008 provincial elections.

Participation rates in municipal elections are even lower than federal or provincial elections, despite the fact that local governments are responsible for essential services that touch our daily lives—policing and emergency services, public health, parks and recreation, roads and sewers, garbage collection, and recycling. The average turnout in the 1990s for some of Canada's largest cities—Vancouver, Edmonton, Winnipeg, Hamilton, Toronto, Ottawa, and

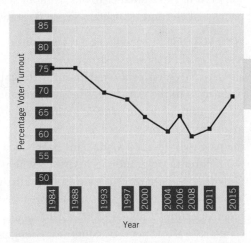

FIGURE 6-1
TURNOUT RATE IN FEDERAL ELECTIONS, 1984–2015*

*Official turnout in Canada is based on the number of electors on the final lists of electors.

SOURCE: *Voter turnout at federal elections and referendums.* Elections Canada. (2015). This is an adaptation of the version available at www.elections.ca. Reproduced with the permission of Elections Canada, but adaptation rests with the author.

TABLE 6-2
TURNOUT TRENDS IN PROVINCIAL ELECTIONS, 1965–2014

*The 2014 turnout rate was calculated based on the addition of 51 701 electors to the official register following the 2010 provincial election. Since the 2010 turnout rate of 69.6 percent was calculated prior to these revisions, the real decline in turnout between 2010 and 2014 will be smaller than 5 percent.

PROVINCE	MAXIMUM TURNOUT (YEAR)	MINIMUM TURNOUT (YEAR)	TURNOUT IN MOST RECENT ELECTION (YEAR)
New Brunswick	82.1% (1967)	64.7% (2014)*	64.7% (2014)*
Nova Scotia	78.2% (1978)	57.9% (2009)	58.2% (2013)
Prince Edward Island	87.3% (1970)	76.5% (2011)	85.9% (2015)
Newfoundland and Labrador	83.6% (1993)	58.0% (2011)	58.0% (2011)
Quebec	85.3% (1976)	57.4% (2008)	71.4% (2014)
Ontario	73.5% (1971)	48.2% (2011)	51.3% (2014)
Manitoba	78.3% (1973)	54.2% (2003)	55.8% (2011)
Saskatchewan	83.9% (1982)	64.6% (1999)	66.0% (2011)
Alberta	72.0% (1971)	40.6% (2008)	54.2% (2015)
British Columbia	77.7% (1983)	55.1% (2009)	57.1% (2013)

SOURCES: Based on Wesley, J. (2010). *Slack in the system: Turnout in Canadian provincial elections, 1965–2009.* Paper presented at the Annual Meeting of the Canadian Political Science Association. Desserud, D. (2011). The 2010 provincial election in New Brunswick. *Canadian Political Science Review 5*(1). Official websites of various provincial electoral agencies. Brousseau-Pouliot, V., & Santerre, D. (2012, September 5). Le taux de participation le plus haut depuis 1998. Retrieved from www.lapresse.ca/actualites/elections-quebec-2012/201209/05/01-4571267-le-taux-de-participation-le-plus-haut-depuis-1998.php. CBC News. P.E.I. voter turnout up in provincial election (2015, May 5). Retrieved from http://www.cbc.ca/news/elections/prince-edward-island-votes/p-e-i-voter-turnout-up-in-provincial-election-1.3061315.

Montreal—was 43.2 percent (Gidengil et al., 2004). Municipal turnout may be higher in smaller towns than larger cities because politics is less complicated and impersonal; citizens know each other and how politics works, and know whom to contact when they have a problem (Verba & Nie, 1972). This has been true in Ontario, where turnout in towns with fewer than 10 000 people was, on average, higher than in cities with a population over 100 000. But even in those smaller towns, turnout was still lower than in national and provincial elections (Kushner, Siegel, & Stanwick, 1997).

WHO VOTES?   Although legal restrictions on voting have been virtually eliminated for adult citizens, participation rates in federal elections are lower in the early twenty-first century than in historical periods when fewer Canadians had access to the franchise. The sharp declines witnessed since the late 1980s raise questions about who is voting and who is not. **Generational replacement** has been pinpointed as the main reason for the decline in turnout over the past two decades. Canadians born since 1970 are less likely to vote than their parents or grandparents were when they were the same age (Blais, Gidengil, Nevitte, & Nadeau, 2004). Furthermore, younger generations of voters are also less likely than their predecessors to start voting as they grow older (Elections Canada, 2008). This generational pattern is not confined to Canada. In 21 democratic countries, young people born in 1980 or later voted at lower rates than the national average (Milner, 2005).

Several demographic characteristics influence electoral participation. Age is the most important factor, as young Canadians are less likely to vote than

GENERATIONAL REPLACEMENT
The process through which younger-age cohorts enter the electorate and replace their older predecessors.

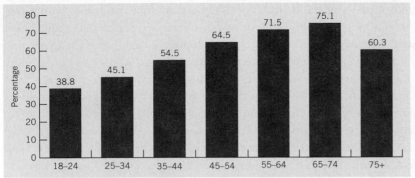

FIGURE 6-2
TURNOUT IN THE 2011 CANADIAN FEDERAL ELECTION BY AGE GROUP

SOURCE: *Estimates of voter turnout by age group, 2011 federal general election.* Elections Canada. (2012). This is an adaptation of the version available at www.elections.ca. Reproduced with the permission of Elections Canada, but adaptation rests with the author.

older citizens. In the 2011 federal election, just 38.8 percent of young adults aged 18–24 voted, compared with 54.5 percent of those aged 35–44, and 75.1 percent of those aged 65–74 (see Figure 6-2). **Life-cycle effects** have been identified as one reason for the dismal turnout rates of young people around the world; as people grow older, they get more involved in their social milieu and develop stronger preferences over time, and they are more likely to vote (Baum, 2002). This is because as they settle down with a partner, become parents, and find a job, they become more aware of how political issues such as taxes, economic development, and access to social and health services affect their lives.

LIFE-CYCLE EFFECTS
The tendency for people to vote at higher rates as they age.

Voters also tend to be wealthier and more educated than non-voters. People with higher household incomes may be more likely to vote because the poor have less time and energy for politics, or because they feel that the political system does not address their concerns (Blais, 2000). People with more formal education may be more likely to vote because it is easier for them to understand complex political messages. In the 2011 election, women aged 18–64 voted at higher rates than men in their same age group (Elections Canada, 2012). Recent immigrants are also less likely to vote than more established immigrants and the Canadian-born (Tossutti, 2007; Uppal & LaRochelle-Côté, 2012). This may be because relative newcomers have to attend to their most pressing needs—finding employment, housing, and schools for their children and learning a new language—before they can get involved in the political life of their new country.

Attitudes are also linked to electoral participation. Canadians who are more interested in and knowledgeable about politics vote at higher rates than citizens with less interest and knowledge (Blais, Gidengil, Nadeau, & Nevitte, 2002; Gidengil, Blais, Everitt, Fournier, & Nevitte, 2005; Howe, 2003; Pammett & LeDuc, 2006). This is because awareness of the issues, where the parties stand, and who their leaders are makes it easier to decide how to vote. Not everyone agrees that Canadians who do not vote are uninterested in and uninformed about the political system. Focus groups conducted with disengaged Canadians from different backgrounds—lower-income Canadians, less-educated youth, urban Aboriginal people, women, new Canadians, and rural Canadians—found that their political disengagement was driven more by disappointing experiences interacting with government, civil servants, and politicians, and by a perception that the political system does not work for them (Bastedo, Chu, Hilderman, & Turcotte, 2011). Voters are also more likely than non-voters to express trust in their elected representatives, a sense of civic duty or moral obligation to vote, and a belief that their vote will affect the outcome (LeDuc, Pammett, & Bastedo, 2008). Lifestyle circumstances also make a difference. Many non-voters report they are too busy with work, school, or family obligations to make time to vote (Pammett & LeDuc, 2006).

YOUNG CANADIANS AND FEDERAL ELECTIONS   Why do some young people vote while others abstain? Young voters and non-voters tend to be distinguished by their attitudes, lifestyles, and demographic characteristics. Following the 2011 election, Canadians aged 18–34 were asked why they voted. Many pointed to the importance of voting as a civic duty and to their desire to express their opinions and views. A majority of those who did not vote said they were too busy with school, work, or taking care of their families. Those with higher levels of education and household income and who were employed were also more likely to have voted than young people who were unemployed and who had less education and income (Statistics Canada, 2011b). A study of the turnout rates of 18- to 30-year-olds during 1997–2008 found that youths who were informed and interested in politics were also more likely to vote than those who were not (Blais & Loewen, 2011).

Studies comparing the voting habits of younger to older Canadians have found that the former are less likely than Canadians aged 30 years and over to agree that they have a duty to vote, and are less interested in and knowledgeable about politics (Blais et al., 2002; Gidengil et al., 2005; Howe, 2003). Political scientist Henry Milner (2002, 2005) has argued that low levels of political knowledge are linked to declining newspaper readership and watching too much television, and that young Canadians are less likely to read newspapers. During the 2004 election, only 60 percent of Canadians in their twenties could name Paul Martin as Liberal party leader, only 47 percent of young Canadians could name Stephen Harper as leader of the Conservative party, and just 34 percent correctly identified Jack Layton as leader of the NDP (Gidengil et al., 2005). One international survey asked young adults in nine countries to identify countries on a map. Americans, Canadians, and Mexicans posted the lowest scores, far behind the Swedes, Germans, and Italians (Milner, 2005).

Another survey found that young Canadians were slightly more knowledgeable about politics than young Americans (Milner, 2008). The biggest difference was on international matters: 55 percent of young Americans were unable to name one permanent member country of the UN Security Council (including the United States), compared with only 30 percent in Canada. People were also ignorant about domestic matters; 56 percent of young Americans were unable to identify citizens as the category of people having the right to vote, compared with 43 percent in Canada. Young Canadians did not score as well as youth in Finland, where 14- and 15-year-olds in the last year of compulsory school must complete a full-year civic education course to graduate. Many then go on to complete upper secondary school, where they are given two compulsory and two optional civic education courses (Milner, 2008).

Concerned citizens and groups have come up with creative ways to encourage higher youth voter turnout. During the 2011 election, university students borrowed from the "flash mob" idea, in which groups use social media to plan large gatherings, and shot videos of "vote mobs," or crowds of students walking or running through campus carrying messages encouraging youth turnout. These videos, often set to music, were then uploaded to social networking sites such as Facebook and YouTube, and in some cases were viewed as many as 20 000 times (CTV News, 2011).

The Student Vote program (run by the non-partisan group Civix, in partnership with Elections Canada) holds mock provincial and federal elections in elementary and secondary schools that coincide with federal, provincial, municipal, and territorial elections. During the 2015 federal election, more than 850 000 students in 6000 schools used newspapers and online media to follow the political parties and leaders and learn about the campaign issues. Participating schools organized all-candidate debates and encouraged students to share their political knowledge with their peers, families, and the community. During the week before official Election Day, students took on the roles of deputy returning officers, poll clerks, and scrutineers, and organized a vote

The Memorial University's Students' Union organized a "vote mob" to encourage young people to vote in the 2015 Canadian election and actively participate in politics.

© Canadian Federation Of Students/Newscom

using authentic election ballot boxes, voting screens, and ballots. As in the official election process, they could vote for the local candidates in their electoral district. The results of the Student Vote were released publicly on Election Night (Student Vote, 2015). Participants in previous mock elections have reported that their knowledge about politics and the electoral process had improved as a result (Elevate Consulting, 2011).

ABORIGINAL CANADIANS AND FEDERAL ELECTIONS   Voter turnout among Aboriginal Canadians is lower than among non-Aboriginals (Bedford, 2003; Guérin, 2003; Loewen & Fournier, 2011), although turnout varies dramatically among on-reserve Aboriginals living in different regions of the country (Bedford & Pobihushchy, 1996; Guérin, 2003). In the 2011 federal election, the estimated turnout on First Nations reserves was 44.8 percent, about 16 points lower than the national turnout rate (Bargiel, 2012).

Three broad perspectives have been used to explain the gap in participation rates. The first explanation is that many First Nations question the legitimacy of the Canadian state and the relevance of Canadian elections. Some observers have argued that Aboriginals do not trust Canada's electoral system because the federal government used it to try to assimilate them (Cairns, 2003; Ladner, 2003). Before 1960, the government's enfranchisement policy gave Indians (as defined under the Indian Act) the right to vote, but only if they gave up their Indian Status and the benefits associated with it. For some treaty First Nations who see themselves as sovereign nations, voting and Canadian citizenship conflict with their desire to deal with Canadian governments on a nation-to-nation basis. For these reasons, many Aboriginal leaders have used their influence to dissuade their people from going to the polls. That view softened during the 2015 federal election campaign, when the Assembly of First Nations, a national advocacy organization representing more than 900 000 people living in 634 First Nation communities and in cities and towns across Canada, urged Aboriginal people to vote, arguing they could influence the outcome in 51 swing ridings.

Some have also noted that Aboriginals have been less likely to vote in federal or provincial elections because they feel that non-Aboriginals cannot represent their interests and identities (Cairns, 2003; Ladner, 2003). In fact, turnout increases when there are Aboriginal candidates or when political issues are raised that resonate with Aboriginal communities (Guérin, 2003). Aboriginal voting rates are also higher in band or territorial elections, suggesting that these elections are perceived as more legitimate or relevant to Aboriginal interests than federal or provincial elections (Bedford, 2003; Henderson, 2007).

A second view attributes much of the voting gap to differences in the social profile and living conditions of Aboriginal and non-Aboriginal Canadians (Howe & Bedford, 2009). On average, Aboriginal peoples are younger, have lower levels of income and education, and are in poorer health than the general population. As discussed earlier in this chapter, younger Canadians, the less well-off, and those without a university education are less likely to vote. In the 2011 election, younger Aboriginals reported lower turnout rates than non-Aboriginal youths (Statistics Canada, 2011c). Poor health can make it harder for a person to get around (Prince, 2007), which could also affect electoral participation.

A third perspective focuses on the role of the electoral system and laws, as well as the efforts of political parties to reach out to Aboriginal populations. The nature of the electoral system, along with the fact that most on-reserve Aboriginals live in thinly populated communities scattered across the country, may discourage Aboriginals from voting. This is because the electoral system favours federal ridings that are densely populated by a single cultural group; in other words, cultural groups are better able to influence the outcome of an election or to elect representatives from their communities when they are concentrated in large numbers within a federal riding (Barsh, 1994). Since very few ridings have large numbers of Aboriginals, they have fewer opportunities to influence riding and national election results. Aboriginal organizations have argued that the Fair Elections Act—which ended the practice of "vouching" in which voters with acceptable identification could attest to the identity and addresses of those who lacked it—will create barriers for Aboriginal participation. This is because many Aboriginals used vouching as a form of voter identification (Krackle, 2015). Other possible reasons for lower Aboriginal turnout include a lack of information about the election and contact with the candidates, as well as general feelings of being left out (Barsh, Fraser, Bull, Provost, & Smith, 1997).

A study of Aboriginal turnout in federal elections held during 2004–2011 found that Aboriginal electors who are more interested in politics, who follow it closely, who are familiar with the party platforms, and who feel strongly that voting is a duty are more likely to vote than those who do not. The social profile of the Aboriginal population is also relevant, as turnout increases among Aboriginals who live off-reserve, who are older, and who have more education and income (Loewen & Fournier, 2011).

ETHNOCULTURAL DIVERSITY AND FEDERAL ELECTIONS   In the United States, the United Kingdom, and the Netherlands, turnout varies across members of different ethnic groups (Clark, 2003; Electoral Commission, 2005) and eligible immigrants have been shown to vote less than others in the United States (United States Census Bureau, 2010). Is the same also true in Canada? Some studies have shown that established immigrants are less likely to vote than the Canadian-born (Uppal & LaRochelle-Côté, 2012). Recent immigrants who have lived in Canada for 10 years or less are also less likely to vote than both their more established counterparts and the Canadian-born (Tossutti, 2007; Uppal & LaRochelle-Côté, 2012). In the 2000 federal election, immigrants who were under 30, single, and earning less than $50 000 voted at lower rates than older, wealthier immigrants who were married or involved in common-law relationships (Tossutti, 2007).

Visible minorities generally vote at lower rates than Canadians of European origin. Among Canadian-born voters, blacks reported the lowest turnout rates in the 2000 federal election. Among foreign-born voters, the Chinese voted at a lower rate than South Asians, blacks, and Canadians of European ancestry. However, the differences in the electoral participation of members of different ethnocultural groups disappear when other demographic factors are taken into account (Tossutti, 2007). The lower turnout rates that have been reported by Canadians of East Asian ancestry have been attributed to a history of discriminatory state policies against the Chinese (Li, 1998), discussed in Chapter 3; community orientations that do not place a high priority on voting (Lapp, 1999); language barriers; a lack of awareness of democratic rights or the electoral process; negative attitudes about politics; and the relative recency of mass immigration from East Asia (Elections BC, 2005).

Turnout also differs among citizens who have immigrated to Canada from different parts of the world (see Figure 6-3). Canadian citizens who

FIGURE 6-3
VOTING RATES BY IMMIGRANT STATUS AND COUNTRY/REGION OF BIRTH

Note: Voter turnout is based on individual responses to a survey question. Actual turnout rates are typically lower.

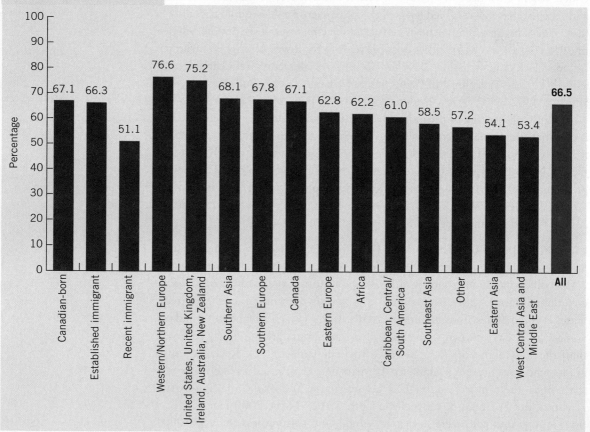

SOURCE: *Labour Force Survey, May 2011* Statistics Canada. Reproduced and distributed on an "as is" basis with the permission of Statistics Canada.

were born in Western/Northern Europe, the United States, the United Kingdom, Ireland, Australia, New Zealand, and Southern Asia were more likely to cast a ballot than citizens born in the Caribbean, Central/South America, Southeast Asia, Eastern Asia, West Central Asia, and the Middle East (Uppal & LaRochelle-Côté, 2012). Explanations for these differences include a lack of democratic traditions in their countries of origin, a lack of trust in institutions, and differences in political culture (Bevelander & Pendakur, 2007, 2009).

Political Party Membership and Campaign Activism

Political parties play a key role in Canadian democracy. They develop positions on issues and dominate political debates in Parliament and in the media. Party members also choose the leaders and candidates in each electoral district who run for the House of Commons. If elected, they decide whether Canada should send armed forces to participate in a war or risky peacekeeping missions; how much should be spent on job creation, the environment, health, and other important policy areas; and how much Canadians should pay in taxes. Parties offer their supporters several incentives to join and get involved, including opportunities for socializing, access to jobs, and political education. They may also give their members a role in party decision making or introduce them to public officials who can help them when they have a problem.

There are few barriers to joining a political party; non-citizens and people who are at least 14 years old can join, and membership fees are quite low. Nevertheless, parties have not attracted large numbers of Canadians to their fold. About 10 percent of Canadians report that they have belonged to a political party in the last five years (Samara Canada, 2014). In other countries, too, party membership is becoming a less appealing form of political participation. During the mid-to-late twentieth century, party membership declined in 12 of 15 democracies (Scarrow, 2000). While there is some debate as to whether fewer people are joining the federal political parties than 50 years ago, it is clear that Canadian parties do not have strong membership bases and do not inspire much confidence. In 2006, more than 58 percent of Canadians said they did not have very much confidence in parties, while another 17.9 percent said they had none at all (World Values Survey, 2006).

The small minority of Canadians who do join parties are not typical of broader society. In 2012, just 9 percent of Canadians aged 18–34 had belonged to a party in the last five years (Samara Canada, 2014). Young Canadians in particular are more likely to commit to groups concerned with various causes such as protecting the environment and human rights, voluntary organizations, or protest activities. This "greying" trend in political parties has also been observed in Denmark, Ireland, and Great Britain. The Canadians who do join parties are also more likely to be well educated, male, Canadian born, and of European ancestry (Cross, 2004). This profile resembles party membership patterns in the United States, the United Kingdom, and Ireland.

Federal election campaigns in Canada are relatively short and low-budget affairs when compared with elections in the United States. Because of this, political parties need to attract volunteers to attend campaign events, ask for donations, contact voters at their homes, drive voters to the polls on Election Day, and perform other campaign tasks. In the 1960s and 1970s, between 20 percent and 40 percent of Canadians reported that they had worked on a campaign activity (Mishler, 1979). By 2012, just 10 percent said they had volunteered in an election in the last five years (Samara Canada, 2014). These low levels of involvement mirror declining trends in campaign involvement in Australia, the United States, and six European countries (Dalton, McAllister, & Wattenberg, 2000).

It is widely believed that fewer people are volunteering to help candidates and parties because campaign styles have changed (Gidengil et al., 2004). Since the 1960s, parties have relied more and more on professional public relations consultants, pollsters, advertising agencies, and media specialists to run their campaigns, and on automated dialling software to contact voters. The professionalization and centralization of campaigns have meant that local party members are left with menial tasks that do not give them a great deal of influence on party policies.

Interest Group and Social Movement Involvement

Interest groups (also known as advocacy groups) are organizations that seek to influence government policy by raising issue awareness, communicating their members' views, and in some cases negotiating the details of policies with public officials. In 2004, about 14 percent of Canadians reported that they had joined an interest group at some point in their lives (Canadian Election Study, 2004). More Canadians, particularly younger Canadians, feel they have a better chance to influence public policy by joining an interest group rather than a political party (Howe & Northrup, 2000). As with other vehicles of political participation, interest group membership does not represent society as a whole. Older, affluent university graduates and Canadians of European ancestry are most likely to belong to these groups (Gidengil et al., 2004).

Social movements are networks of groups and individuals that seek major social and political changes, often by acting outside established political institutions. Some examples include the women's, environmental, lesbian and gay rights, human rights, and animal rights movements. Ronald Inglehart (1971, 1990) has attributed their growth in many advanced capitalist democracies since World War II to changes in cultural values. For a fuller discussion of interest groups and social movements in Canada, see Chapter 7.

Protest Activities

While most types of formal political participation have been withering, protest activities have been growing over the past few decades in Canada, Great Britain, the United States, and France (Hall, 2002; Maloney, 2006; Putnam, 2000; Worms, 2002). Political scientist Neil Nevitte (1996) has attributed this cross-national phenomenon to the shift to a postindustrial economy and the rise of postmaterialist values that have produced a growing number of citizens who possess the skills, knowledge, and information to challenge public authorities. As is the case with formal political participation, certain individuals are more likely to engage in political protest. They include university-educated Canadians, the relatively affluent, public sector employees, people from union households, and a core of young Canadians born after 1970 (Gidengil et al., 2004).

When Canadians protest, they tend to engage in actions that do not require a lot of time and effort. According to the 2012 Samara Citizens' Survey, 51 percent of Canadians had signed a petition and 49 percent had boycotted or bought products for ethical or political reasons ("buycotting") in the last 12 months. In comparison, just 14 percent had taken part in a protest or demonstration (Samara Canada, 2014). Although relatively fewer Canadians participate in more time-consuming protest activities, even modest efforts can have a major impact on public opinion or business practices. In the 1970s, thousands of Canadians took part in mass demonstrations against the war in Vietnam and nuclear testing off the coast of Alaska. During the 1990s, protests and blockades set up by environmental groups and First Nations drew the world's attention to industrial logging in British Columbia's ancient temperate rainforests, while information campaigns alerted consumers to the cost of buying wood and paper products from this ecosystem.

The early twenty-first century has seen significant mass protests organized by environmental, student, and indigenous and social justice movements. A few examples include the thousands of Americans and Canadians who demonstrated for two weeks in front of the White House in 2011 to protest the Keystone XL Pipeline project. Protesters included people from all walks of life—students, grandmothers, celebrities—concerned about the damage that could be caused by pumping oil from the Alberta tar sands across environmentally sensitive land to refineries in Texas (Scharper, 2011). In 2012, about 185 000 postsecondary students in Quebec went on strike, stopped attending classes, and took to the streets to protest planned tuition increases (see Chapter 8).

In 2012, four women from Saskatchewan held a conference called "Idle No More." They set up a website and Facebook page outlining their opposition to a budget implementation bill that threatened to erode Indigenous sovereignty and environmental protections. Supporters of the movement staged rallies across the country, held flash mob-style protests in shopping malls, and

Protest against the G20 leaders meeing in Toronto, 2010.

blocked passenger rail lines. Attawapiskat chief Theresa Spence began a 43-day hunger strike and a group of young people from a Cree community in Quebec trekked 1600 kilometres to Ottawa (CBC News, October 4, 2013). The movement also spread beyond Canadian borders as rallies were staged as far off as Texas, Hawaii, and New Zealand (CBC News, January 1, 2013).

Although violent protests are not common, they have had a significant impact on Canadian history. In 1837 and 1838, an estimated 40 000 to 200 000 French Canadians participated in the Lower Canada rebellions. In 1869, Louis Riel, the leader of about 10 000 Métis in the Red River area, seized Fort Garry and established a provisional government of Manitoba. More than 15 000 Canadians took part in the conscription riots of 1917, and another 30 000 workers left their jobs in support of the Winnipeg General Strike in 1919. The 1960s and early 1970s saw the Front de liberation du Québec (FLQ), a Quebec secessionist group, carry out bombings and kidnappings that culminated in the deaths of at least five people.

In 1990, Mohawks near the town of Oka, Quebec, organized a peaceful blockade to oppose the development of a golf course on sacred land. The protest escalated into a 78-day armed siege at Kanesatake and Kahnawake between Mohawks, the Quebec police, and the Canadian army. In 2010, downtown Toronto became "ground zero" in a violent clash between police and demonstrators outside a meeting of leaders of the world's 20 major economies. Prior to the summit, protests against poverty, globalization, climate change, and the plight of Aboriginal peoples, among other issues, had unfolded in the city streets without a major incident. That changed on June 26, when a peaceful march of 4000 protesters erupted into violence. A small group of masked, black-clad protesters broke away from the march; stormed onto the streets armed with hammers, rocks, and other objects; set parked police cruisers on fire; and smashed the windows of banks, retail stores, fast food chains, and some local businesses (Kidd, 2010).

During the three-day summit, police detained more than 880 people in a temporary jail. Those detained say they were subjected to inhumane conditions: overcrowded cells; bathrooms with no doors; strip searches; and little access to water, food, or legal counsel (Yang, 2011). On the second day of the summit, police "kettled" a group of peaceful protesters and local bystanders for several hours because they suspected members of the Black Bloc were still in the crowd. "Kettling" is a controversial tactic used by police to contain a large crowd, which prevents protesters from leaving the cordoned area. An independent review of summit policing found that while most officers carried out their duties in a professional way, numerous others used excessive force in dealing with the protesters. It also found that the makeshift jails were not prepared for the mass arrests, leading to violations of prisoner rights (Office of the Independent Police Review Director, 2012).

Cyberactivism

The growth of computers and connectivity since the early 1980s has paved the way for another form of political involvement dubbed "cyberactivism," or online activism. Web-based platforms such as Facebook, Twitter, and YouTube have radically altered how groups and social movements raise awareness about issues that are not reported or are underreported in the mainstream media, how political activists circulate information to their followers and organize campaigns, and how Canadians discuss politics with each other. The mainstream media and political parties are also using Twitter, the social media site in which people talk back and forth in 140-character bursts, to converse about politics (Baran, 2011; Small, 2010).

In Canada and abroad, the global social justice movement has relied heavily on websites and email lists to contest trade and investment liberalization, the privatization and deregulation of public health care and other welfare state institutions, and "sweatshop" practices by major clothing companies, among many other issues. Those involved in the demonstrations at the G20 summit used Facebook and Twitter to coordinate the protest and YouTube to upload images of police actions against the protesters. Social media played an important role in the spread of the global Occupy movement in 2011 to protest income inequality between the wealthiest 1 percent of the world's population and the "99 percent." A Wall Street journalist observed that the outpouring of support for the movement through video, photos, text messages, audio, and other messaging using Facebook, Twitter, Tumblr, and other online services had given the movement a sense of legitimacy (Preston, 2011).

Social media have opened up new avenues of political engagement for Canadians, particularly young Canadians (see Box 6-2: The Social Media and

The Social Media and Political Protest

The Occupy movement, which encouraged protesters to converge on the financial centres of the world to protest income inequality, began with a single tweet. In 2011, the Vancouver-based anti-consumerism magazine *Adbusters* posted a suggestion for a march on Wall Street against the gap in wealth between the richest 1 percent and the "99 percent." As Occupy encampments spread to 130 countries, protesters used cellphones and social media sites like Twitter, Facebook, and YouTube to produce daily images and live-streaming videos of their activities (Preston, 2011). Between July and October 2011, the movement had generated more than a half million Twitter posts, with Canada emerging second only to the United States in terms of Twitter chatter (*National Post*, 2011). Although local authorities eventually broke up the encampments, the movement had successfully placed the issue of social inequality on the political and media agenda.

The battle against income inequality is just one example of cyberactivism. In the future, the greater sophistication and availability of new information technologies, along with innovations in how to apply them, could make these already powerful tools for political expression and change even more effective.

Political Protest). According to a 2012 survey, 18- to 34-year-olds were more likely than Canadians in general to circulate or report political information on social networking sites, use email or instant messaging to discuss societal/political issues, blog about a political issue, and participate in an online group about a societal/political issue in the last 12 months (see Figure 6-4).

There are different perspectives on whether the interactive setting of the Internet and World Wide Web will revitalize political participation. Optimists argue that "chatrooms, radio and video streaming, personalized websites, as well as access to databases, government documents and unfiltered news sources" give people the freedom to create and interpret information in their own way (Deibert, 2002, p. 11). The Internet can also connect people in

FIGURE 6-4
THE TWITTERING CLASS: ONLINE DISCUSSION

ONLINE DISCUSSION	CANADIANS	18 TO 34 YEARS	35 YEARS AND OVER
Have you done the following on (Facebook, Twitter, Google+, Blogging Site, Other) in the last 12 months?: circulated, (re)posted or embedded political information or content?	17%	30%	12%
In the last 12 months, have you: used email or instant messaging to discuss a political or societal issue?	30%	42%	26
In the last 12 months, have you: blogged about a political issue?	15%	26%	11%
In the last 12 months, have you: participated in an online group about a political or societal issue?	25%	40%	20%

SOURCE: 2012 Samara Citizens' Survey. (Samara Canada, 2014).

isolated communities to the outside world. However, there are concerns that the lack of face-to-face interaction in a virtual environment and the ease with which identities can be forged will undermine trust between people (Barney, 2000). There are also inequalities in Internet access and usage in Canada. In addition to the fact that the Internet remains a minor source of information about politics and elections, a narrow spectrum of Canadian society—university graduates, the affluent, and the young—are more likely to rely on it for information than Canadians who are older, less educated, and less well-off. The "digital divide," whereby wealthier individuals in urban areas are more likely to live in households with access to high speed broadband connections than the poor and residents of rural and remote communities, mirrors the participation gap between the affluent and less well-off that has been observed in many conventional political activities.

CIVIL SOCIETY, CIVIC ENGAGEMENT, AND DEMOCRACY

Democracy, as Alexis de Tocqueville (1969) argued in his observations of nineteenth-century America, requires civic associations that are not specifically political, but that provide meaning for people and opportunities for them to become involved in their communities. He concluded that voluntary organizations strengthened democracy because they encouraged people to cooperate with each other to achieve the common good. **Civil society** consists of the voluntary associations and non-governmental organizations that bring people together to achieve a common goal. Some examples of voluntary organizations include the following:

CIVIL SOCIETY
The voluntary associations and non-governmental organizations that bring people together to achieve a common goal.

- sports and recreation clubs;
- religious associations;
- student or campus clubs;
- community/service organizations (e.g., Lions, Canadian Legion);
- ethnocultural associations;
- environmental groups;
- human rights organizations; and
- business and professional associations and labour unions.

Although most voluntary associations are not primarily political in nature, many of them become involved in political actions while representing their members' interests. Some examples include student associations that lobby postsecondary institutions and provincial governments for lower tuition fees, religious groups that take public stands on moral issues such as abortion and euthanasia, and ethnocultural organizations that lobby the federal government on foreign policy and immigration matters.

Political scientist Robert Putnam (2000) has argued that voluntary associations provide modern democracies with a crucial supply of **social capital**.

SOCIAL CAPITAL
The networks, norms of generalized reciprocity, and trust that foster coordination and cooperation for mutual benefit.

Social capital refers to the social networks, norms of generalized reciprocity, and interpersonal trust that foster coordination and cooperation for mutual benefit. Generalized reciprocity refers to the understanding that "I will do this favour for you now without expecting anything specific back from you, in the expectation that someone else will do something for me down the road" (pp. 20–21). This idea was captured in the movie *Pay It Forward*, in which a young boy is asked in his social studies assignment to propose an idea that will improve humankind. The boy decides to do good deeds for three new people. If they can also do good deeds for others, or "pay it forward," then positive changes should and do occur. According to social capital theorists, mutual cooperation and trust between individuals living in the same society are necessary for democracies to thrive. Others are skeptical about the potential for social capital to support democracy. For example, members of groups that promote racial hatred or gang members may also cooperate with and trust each other, but they can hardly be described as supporting democracy and tolerance.

Why do many people believe that it is a good thing for a country to have a strong civil society in which many people participate in voluntary groups? One reason is that people who get involved in these associations are more likely to get involved in political activities. This happens because people meet new friends in these groups. They may end up talking about politics or asking new acquaintances to attend a political party meeting, to help out on a campaign, or to join a protest. Furthermore, members of voluntary groups take an interest in community affairs, and often learn how to plan a meeting; cooperate with others to achieve a common goal; and acquire the attitudes, leadership, and social skills that are necessary to participate in politics. In Italy, regions with dense networks of amateur soccer clubs, choral societies, community service organizations, and the like, were found to be more prosperous and better governed (Putnam, 1993). In the United States, youths are better off and healthier in states with more voluntary organizations, higher rates of participation in them, and higher rates of volunteering (Putnam, 2000). These states are also safer, more tolerant of civil liberties, and more committed to racial and gender equality. Income gaps between the rich and poor in these states are also lower than in states with fewer civic groups.

Civic Engagement in Canada

Civic engagement refers to different forms of community involvement such as **volunteering** for a civic group or organization, helping others directly, or donating money to charities. While relatively fewer Canadians participate in most types of political activities, the country's civic life is healthy. Civic engagement, unlike voting and campaign involvement, has not declined over time. The amount of time that Canadians spend on civic acts such as attending

VOLUNTEERING
Providing unpaid service to help others.

community, political, church, or trade union meetings; tutoring; coaching; or organizing community events held steady between 1971 and 1998 (Andersen, Curtis, & Grabb, 2006). Despite these positive signs, civic life is also characterized by inequalities. Older, university-educated, and relatively affluent Canadians are more likely to join or volunteer for civic groups. Furthermore, a small minority of Canadians account for most volunteer hours (Hall, Lasby, Ayer, & Gibbons, 2009; Hall, Lasby, Gumulka, & Tryon, 2006; Turcotte, 2015) and charitable giving (Turcotte, 2015).

In 2013, 12.7 million Canadians or 44 percent of people aged 15 years and older volunteered for a group or organization at least once during the previous 12 months. This represents a decrease from 47 percent in 2010. Women, middle-aged adults who were often parents of school-aged children, and young adults aged 15–19 were the most likely to volunteer for these groups. Volunteer rates varied across the country because of differences in the economic conditions of provinces and territories, as well as the social and cultural values of the people who make up subnational populations (see Table 6-3). Residents of Saskatchewan, Manitoba, and Nova Scotia were more likely to volunteer for organizations than residents of Quebec and New Brunswick (Turcotte, 2015).

The vast majority of Canadians (83 percent) also help others directly, without working through an organization, according to the 2010 Canada Survey of Giving, Volunteering and Participating (Vézina & Crompton, 2012). By helping out with household tasks, providing personal care, offering unpaid coaching or tutoring, or caring for the elderly and children on an informal basis, they are helping to fill gaps in the welfare state. Young people aged 15–24 were the most likely to help others directly, as were people with higher incomes and a postsecondary education. The provinces with the highest rates

PROVINCE/TERRITORY	VOLUNTEERING FOR ORGANIZATIONS	CHARITABLE GIVING
Canada	44	82
British Columbia	49	78
Alberta	50	85
Saskatchewan	56	85
Manitoba	52	84
Ontario	44	83
Quebec	32	81
New Brunswick	41	83
Nova Scotia	51	84
Prince Edward Island	50	84
Newfoundland and Labrador	46	87

TABLE 6-3
VOLUNTEER AND CHARITABLE DONATION RATES BY PROVINCE (PERCENTAGE)

SOURCES: Turcotte, M. (2015). *Volunteering and charitable giving in Canada.* Ottawa, ON: Minister of Industry, pp. 5, 16. Statistics Canada: General Social Survey on Giving, Volunteering and Participating, 2013. This does not constitute an endorsement by Statistics Canada of this product.

BOX 6-3

Students at Work: Mandatory Community Service in High Schools

In response to declining levels of youth engagement in political or civic activities, educational institutions around the world have introduced community service requirements. Their goal is to help students develop an understanding of civic responsibility and the contribution they can make to their community. In British Columbia, students must participate in 30 hours of work or community service to graduate from secondary school (BC Ministry of Education, 2008). The Ontario requirements are slightly more demanding. Since 1999, high school students in Ontario have been required to take a civics class and complete a minimum of 40 hours of community involvement activities to graduate (Ontario Ministry of Education and Training, 1999). Service can involve activities such as cleaning up a local park, volunteering at a local hospital or animal shelter, coaching a young athlete, or any other activity that is not done for pay and that improves the quality of community life.

These curriculum changes were introduced because research has shown that community service can lead to improvements in political knowledge and political efficacy (Niemi, Hepburn, & Chapman, 2000); to higher rates of volunteering during high school (Henderson, Brown, Pancer, & Ellis-Hale, 2007); and to volunteering involvements later in life (Janoski, Musick, & Wilson, 1998).

But not everyone agrees that mandatory community service is a good idea. Shortly after the requirement was introduced in Ontario, one principal commented that it "ticks off those students who had no intent of volunteering before, who will act out in defiance of being told what to do and say they're not going to volunteer, possibly putting their graduation prospects at risk" (Volunteer Canada, 2006). Students who are forced to volunteer may also come to view community service as an activity that should be done only when it is required or rewarded (Batson, Janoski, & Hanson, 1978). The effectiveness of community service programs also depends on whether students have meaningful placements, are well supervised, and have the opportunity to share their experiences in the classroom (Meinhard & Foster, 1999, 2000).

If you were designing the high school curriculum in your province, would you require that students perform community service in order to graduate? What are the benefits of mandatory community service? Are there any drawbacks?

---

of one-on-one volunteering were Saskatchewan and Prince Edward Island. The lowest rates of helping others directly were reported in the Northwest Territories and Quebec.

Canadians volunteer because they want to give back to their communities and use their skills and experience, and because they were personally affected by the cause supported by the organization. Other Canadians performed community service in response to requests by schools, employers, or non-profit and charitable organizations. In 2013, one in five young adults aged 15–19 reported that they were required to volunteer (Turcotte, 2015). The provinces of British Columbia and Ontario are among those jurisdictions that require high school students to perform community service to graduate (see Box 6-3: Students at Work: Mandatory Community Service in High Schools).

For many Canadians with busy lives, giving money to a charitable or non-profit organization is less arduous than volunteering their time. In 2013, 82 percent of Canadians donated $12.8 billion to improve the well-being of their communities (Turcotte, 2015). Their donations helped shelters and food banks deliver their services; helped universities and hospitals carry out medical research; and helped political, religious, and environmental groups have their voices heard, among many causes. Older donors gave more on average, and donation rates were highest in the provinces of Newfoundland and Labrador, Alberta, and Saskatchewan (see Table 6-3).

Summary and Conclusion

This chapter has drawn a portrait of democratic life in Canada by examining levels of political participation and civic engagement, how Canadians choose to get involved in these activities, and whether some people are more likely than others to participate. Although there are numerous opportunities to get involved on a local, provincial, national, and international scale, we found that Canadians are not fervent political activists, and that several forms of conventional political involvement are in decline. In this respect, Canadians have much in common with citizens living in other democratic states. Furthermore, the individuals who take part in most types of political and civic activities do not reflect the country's diverse social makeup. A small core of individuals tend to dominate political and civic affairs. The attitudes, personal characteristics, and living conditions of Canadians explain these differences. With some exceptions, voice, power, and influence tend to be concentrated among those who are better off, well educated, and older.

There are some bright spots in this portrait of individual and group participation in democratic life. A large majority of Canadians give back to their communities through volunteering, and growing numbers are finding new ways to become engaged in politics through interest groups, social movements, protest activity, and cyberactivism. Thus, as Canadians become more disillusioned with their elected representatives and wonder, increasingly, whether good government is an achievable goal, they are developing alternative ways of bringing their ideals and values into the public arena. These vehicles of participation have not replaced formal political activism and offline political communication, but they have already changed public opinion, policies, laws, and the ways Canadians learn about issues, express their views, and take action.

Discussion Questions

1. Classical democratic theorists argue that high levels of political participation by a broad cross-section of society are desirable in a democracy. Elitist theories are based on the premise that participation should be limited to those who have the education and resources to understand complex political issues. Where do you stand?

2. What is your opinion about deliberative democracy? Should citizens play a larger role in the policymaking process?

3. Why are young people less interested in voting than older citizens?

4. What can be done to revitalize youth engagement in political activities such as voting and party membership?

5. Is voting a civic duty?

6. Has the increasing popularity of online communications tools as a means of political expression and mobilization bolstered or undermined democracy?

7. Can violent protest activity ever be justified?

8. Should high schools or colleges and universities institute mandatory community service for students to graduate?

Further Reading

Everitt, J., & O'Neill, B. (Eds.). (2002). *Citizen Politics: Research and theory in Canadian political behaviour.* Toronto, ON: Oxford University Press.

Fournier, P., & Loewen, P. (2011). *Aboriginal electoral participation in Canada.* Ottawa: Elections Canada. http://www.elections.ca/content.aspx?section=res&dir=rec/part/abel&document=index&lang=e

Gidengil, E., & Bastedo, H. (Eds.). (2014). *Canadian democracy from the ground up: Perceptions and performance.* Vancouver, BC: University of British Columbia Press.

Gidengil, E., Blais, A., Nevitte, N., & Nadeau, R. (2004). *Citizens.* Vancouver, BC: UBC Press.

Howe, P. (2010). *Citizens adrift: The democratic disengagement of young Canadians.* Vancouver, BC: UBC Press.

Milner, H. (2010). *The Internet generation: Engaged citizens or political dropouts.* Hanover, NH: University Press of New England.

Putnam, R.D. (Ed.). (2002). *Democracies in flux: The evolution of social capital in contemporary societies.* New York, NY: Oxford University Press.

Samara Canada. (2014). *Lightweights? Political participation beyond the ballot box.* Toronto, ON: Samara Canada. http://www.samaracanada.com/research/current-research/lightweights

Tossutti, L. (2007). *The electoral participation of ethnocultural communities.* Ottawa, ON: Elections Canada.

CHAPTER 7

Political Influence: Interest Groups, Lobbyists, and Social Movements

CHAPTER OBJECTIVES

After reading this chapter, you should be able to

1. Discuss the importance of interest groups.
2. Distinguish between the types of interest groups.
3. Assess the ability of interest groups to influence public policy.
4. Discuss whether lobbying should be strictly regulated.
5. Explain the significance of social movements.

In February 2012, Quebec student associations began a lengthy strike to protest the provincial government's plan to raise tuition fees by $325 in each of the following five years, amounting to a 75 percent increase. Although Quebec university tuition fees are lower than all provinces except Newfoundland and Labrador, many students still face large loan debts and difficulties finding well-paying jobs after graduation. Following the example of some Western European countries, some Quebec students argued that education was a right that should be free.

Influenced by the anti-globalization protests, the "Arab Spring" democracy movement, and the Occupy movement that challenged the wealth and power of the top 1 percent, student activists viewed themselves as part of a movement seeking a different social order (Hébert, 2012). In particular, the militant organization CLASSE, representing about one-half of the students, viewed the struggle as not only about education, but also about the imposition of neoliberalism on Quebecers.

Every night, tens of thousands of students and their supporters gathered and marched in the streets of Montreal and other Quebec cities. In some neighbourhoods, people banged pots and pans to show their support as demonstrators walked by. Despite the generally peaceful nature of the demonstrations, some protesters clashed with police, smashed windows, and prevented students from attending classes. As the protests continued, Jean Charest's Liberal government responded with emergency legislation that required police be informed at least eight hours in advance of the time, duration, and route of any demonstration and limited the number of participants to 50. Heavy fines were established for individuals and student organizations that didn't comply with the legislation. Many legal experts viewed the law as a violation of the right to peaceful assembly guaranteed by the Canadian Charter of Rights and Freedoms.

Protesters responded with an illegal demonstration in Montreal that attracted hundreds of thousands of participants and media attention from around the world. Nevertheless, the Quebec government stood firm against what it viewed as a threat to its authority despite the large costs to the province in lost tourism revenue. Likewise, students and their supporters continued their civil disobedience with daily demonstrations despite arrests and fines. Indeed, anger at what they viewed as an oppressive law provoked more aggressive actions by some protesters, such as attempts to disrupt the annual Grand Prix race in Montreal.

After the Liberal government lost the September 2012 election, the new Parti Québécois government initially cancelled tuition fee increases, but later announced that tuition fees would increase by 3 percent each year. This was continued by the Liberal government elected in 2014.

For some, an elected representative government should be able to make the decisions that it views as being in the best interests of the community. Through interest groups, people can express their opinions and try to influence government by presenting specific policy proposals. If government doesn't act in the public interest, voters can replace it in the next election. Others argue that elected governments often act in the interests of the powerful. Mobilizing people through a social movement to challenge the powerful may be needed to create a more democratic society.

INTRODUCTION

A key feature of liberal democracy is the ability of people to freely organize and join groups to express their views and to influence the decisions of government. Through involvement in interest groups and social movements, individuals can try to make their voices heard. To what extent does government listen and take into account the ideas, proposals, and demands of various groups of people? Are some groups more influential than others? How can groups representing the interests of students best achieve their objectives, and what obstacles do they have to overcome?

INTEREST GROUPS

Interest groups (also known as pressure groups[1] or advocacy groups) are organizations that pursue the common interests of groups of people, particularly by trying to influence the making and implementation of public policies. Because individuals have differing interests (including those based on region, ethnicity, gender, occupation, age, values, religious affiliation, and recreational activities), each person may join or be represented by many groups. A group formed to promote a particular interest or issue position will often stimulate the creation of other groups to promote different interests or other positions on the same issue. In this way, competing interest groups can represent the diversity of interests present in society.

Often, several organizations claim to represent the same interest. For example, both the Canadian Federation of Students (CFS) and the Canadian Alliance of Student Associations (CASA) claim to represent the interests of post-secondary students. The organizations differ not only in the tactics they use (the CFS has been more likely to engage in protest activity, while the CASA focuses on developing good relations with politicians), but also in their general ideological perspective—the CFS has tended to lean to the left while the CASA tends to be more conservative. Francophone students in Quebec are represented by yet other student organizations.

Overall, contemporary Canada features a very large number of interest groups. Some are regularly active in politics, while others are only occasional participants in the political process.

Theoretical Perspectives

Pluralist theory assumes that governments in liberal democracies are influenced by a wide variety of interest groups. Politicians will try to find compromises among the positions brought forward by competing interest groups to satisfy as many groups as possible. Government, in the pluralist view, is not biased toward a particular interest, but rather reacts to the pressures placed on it by different groups. Of course some interest groups are more influential than others. However, while some groups may have plentiful financial resources that help them to exert influence, other groups may be able to make use of the voices of their large membership or the expertise they possess. Furthermore, the pattern of group influence will vary from one policy area to another. For

INTEREST GROUPS
Organizations that pursue the common interests or values of groups of people, particularly by trying to influence the making and implementation of public policies.

Canadian Federation of Students
www.cfs-fcee.ca

Canadian Alliance of Student Associations
www.casa-acae.com

PLURALIST THEORY
The theory that the freedom of individuals to establish and join groups that are not controlled by the government results in a variety of groups having an ability to influence the decisions of government, with no group having a dominant influence.

---

[1]The term "pressure group" is sometimes used to distinguish groups that are primarily devoted to influencing government from the broader category of "interest groups" that share a common interest or goal but do not necessarily focus on political action. The term "advocacy group" is also used to describe "any organization that seeks to influence government policy but not to govern" (Young & Everitt, 2010, p. 170).

example, business groups may be more influential when it comes to economic policies (such as the pursuit of free trade agreements), but may be less influential than other groups when government is considering education or health care policies.

Overall, then, pluralist theory (which was developed in the United States) suggests that no one group or interest has a dominant influence over public policy. As long as people are free to form and join groups, it is assumed that the differing interests in society will be able to influence public policy. Thus, interest groups play a major role in creating a liberal democratic political system in which power is widely dispersed. Furthermore, it is assumed that free competition among the groups, each promoting a particular set of interests, will generally result in policies that are in the public interest.

Critics argue that pluralist theory is unrealistic in its depiction of political influence. **Neo-pluralism**, a modification of pluralist theory, views business interests as having a privileged position in influencing government policy-making. Not only do corporations have substantial financial resources and organizational capabilities, but they also largely determine the economic well-being of countries that have free market economic systems (Lindblom, 1977). Because of their economic clout, large corporations have a "guaranteed access" to key government decision makers that empowers them to influence governments (Macdonald, 2007, p. 181).

Marxist theory views capitalist countries, such as Canada, as inherently biased toward the interests of capitalism and the capitalist class. Even if governments provide some benefits to the working class, this is viewed as an attempt to shore up the legitimacy of the capitalist system and prevent serious challenges to capitalism. The working class may not know what is in their true interests, thus allowing a system that is inequitable for the majority to be maintained even in a liberal democracy.

Rational choice theory (also known as public choice theory) works from the assumption that individuals rationally pursue their own self-interest. Interest groups that seek special benefits from government for their members are more likely to be better organized and influential than groups that are concerned about the general good of the country or of a large part of the population. For example, dairy farmers have organized themselves and pressured government to create marketing boards that limit production and make it difficult for new operations to be established. Higher prices for consumers are the result. However, consumers are difficult to organize into a strong interest group because the benefit to each consumer is small.

Finally, **state-centred theory** views the state (all the institutions involved in governing) as largely independent of social forces. Thus, politicians and bureaucrats are relatively free to act on their own values and interests and try to shape the political context in which they operate. This may include encouraging and supporting certain interest groups, selecting which interest groups to include in the policy-making process, and using interest groups as a means

NEO-PLURALISM
A modification of pluralist theory that views business interests as having a privileged position in influencing government policy-making.

MARXIST THEORY
A theory that views capitalist countries as inherently biased toward the interests of capitalism and the capitalist class.

RATIONAL CHOICE THEORY
A theory based on the assumption that individuals rationally pursue their own self-interest.

STATE-CENTRED THEORY
The theory that the state is largely independent of social forces and thus state actors are relatively free to act on their own values and interests.

to persuade the public of the merits of the policies government plans to adopt. State-centred theory does not assume that the Canadian state is a single-minded actor. Rather, in this perspective, public policy is shaped to a substantial degree by the interaction between, or conflict among, governing institutions (such as the competing interests of national and provincial governments and of different government departments and agencies). In state-centred theory, then, interest groups are not viewed as having a strong independent effect on public policy.

Types of Interest Groups

Some interest groups, termed **self-interest groups**, are primarily concerned with gaining **selective benefits** from government for their members. For example, more than 100 members and 150 associate members of the Canadian Association of Petroleum Producers (CAPP), representing most of the $110 billion a year industry, have a variety of objectives, including "eliminate/modify costly regulations," "streamline approval processes" for new developments, and "promote the industry's economic well-being and sustainability" (Canadian Association of Petroleum Producers, 2012).

Another type of interest group, termed a **public interest group** or citizens' group, pursues goals that can be viewed as advocating for what it believes to be for the public good rather than only benefiting members of the group. Examples include the Sierra Club, which campaigns for environmental protection, and the Council of Canadians, which fights to protect Canadian independence. Although the policies championed by various public interest groups may be controversial, public interest groups believe the policies they promote will provide **collective benefits** for society. Groups seeking to improve conditions in other parts of the world may also be considered public interest groups. For example, the Canadian Council for International Co-operation, a coalition of about 75 voluntary organizations, aims to "end global poverty and to promote social justice and human dignity for all."

The distinction between self-interest and public interest groups can be contentious as almost all interest groups will claim that they are pursuing the public good. The Canadian Association of Petroleum Producers, for example, in its extensive advertising, emphasizes its commitment to protecting the environment and operating in a sustainable fashion as well as noting its importance to jobs and Canadian prosperity. Nevertheless, business groups are primarily concerned with the profitability of the corporations they represent.

On the other hand, a number of organizations that are generally considered public interest groups are focused on improving the position of a sector of society (rather than just their dues-paying members). For example, many groups that represent women, the poor, and those of different sexual orientations may be considered public interest groups since they are primarily concerned with achieving equality and social justice. Similarly, groups representing

SELF-INTEREST GROUPS
Interest groups that are primarily concerned with selective benefits that are directed toward their members.

SELECTIVE BENEFITS
Particular benefits that are made available to the members of an interest group but are not available to the public as a whole.

Canadian Association of Petroleum Producers
www.capp.ca

PUBLIC INTEREST GROUP
A group that pursues goals that can be viewed as being for the public good and do not benefit members of the group exclusively.

COLLECTIVE BENEFITS
Benefits to society as a whole.

Sierra Club Canada
www.sierraclub.ca

Council of Canadians
www.canadians.org

Canadian Council for International Co-operation
www.ccic.ca

a particular ethnic group might be considered to be basically public interest groups as they are not generally focused on gaining specific, selective material benefits for their members. Rather they may seek changes in public policies that reflect the concerns, values, and identities of the sector of society that they represent.

Overall, distinctions between self-interest groups and public interest groups can be useful. Yet claims that the policies sought by any group, corporation, union, or individual are in the public interest are often controversial and need to be examined carefully to assess their validity.

Interest Group Activities

Political activity is often only one aspect of the activities of interest groups. For example, in addition to pursuing the interests of their profession through political activity, many professional associations (such as lawyers, doctors, and social workers) also devote considerable attention to activities such as the following:

- educating and informing their members;
- arranging conferences for their members;
- assessing the qualifications of those who seek accreditation to practise their profession; and
- determining whether members should be disciplined for violating the ethics and rules of their profession.

Similarly, business associations may be involved in helping members find export markets, developing certification standards for products, and working with community colleges to ensure potential workers are properly trained. Labour unions, although often active in politics, are primarily concerned with collective bargaining and ensuring that employers honour collective agreements. The Royal Canadian Legion provides social gathering places for veterans, is involved in community activities, and reminds Canadians of the sacrifices made in times of war, as well as lobbying government to improve veterans' pensions.

Interest groups also vary in whether they seek to influence the policies adopted by governments on one particular issue or a range of issues. For example, pro-life and pro-choice groups focus on whether abortion should be legal and accessible. The Canadian Council of Chief Executives and the Canadian Labour Congress, on the other hand, try to influence government on a variety of issues that relate directly or indirectly to the interests of big business and labour unions.

The Organization of Interest Groups

The organizational structure of interest groups is as varied as the groups themselves. A group of neighbours who attempt to get their city to fix the potholes

Canadian Bar Association
www.cba.org

Canadian Medical Association
www.cma.ca

Canadian Association of Social Workers
www.casw-acts.ca

Canadian Council of Chief Executives
www.ceocouncil.ca

Canadian Labour Congress
www.canadianlabour.ca

on their street has quite a different organization than the Canadian Manufacturers & Exporters Association or the Canadian Nurses Association. The neighbours will not likely bother setting up a formal organization, other than perhaps deciding on a spokesperson, and the group will probably be temporary. A group that is formed to express views on a particular issue, but has little organizational capacity and usually is not long-lasting, is termed an **issue-oriented group** (Pross, 1992). In contrast, an **institutionalized interest group** such as the Canadian Medical Association has a formal organizational structure, a well-established membership base, paid professional staff, executive officers, and permanent offices. This provides the capability for an institutionalized group to respond to members' interests by developing policy positions and pursuing the goals of the group through regular contact with government policy-makers (Pross, 1992). Institutionalized interest groups are typically concerned with promoting their views and proposals on various issues, building their organization for the long term, and developing close working relationships with key government policy-makers. Of course, many groups fall between the example of an informal group of neighbours and a well-established institutional group. For example, pro-life and pro-choice groups have successfully developed long-lasting organizations and membership bases.

Many institutionalized groups have adopted procedures for members to elect a board of directors to oversee the operations of the group, hold an

ISSUE-ORIENTED GROUP
A group formed to express views on a particular issue, concern, or grievance, but with little organizational capacity and usually not long-lasting.

INSTITUTIONALIZED INTEREST GROUP
A group that has a formal organizational structure, a well-established membership base, paid professional staff, executive officers, permanent offices, and the capability to respond to the interests of its members by developing policy positions and promoting them through regular contact with government policy-makers.

© Native Women's Association of Canada

Institutionalized interest groups, such as the Canadian Teachers' Federation (shown here), often monitor government policies and work to promote their members' interests to key government policy-makers.

annual meeting, and provide information to members about the organization's activities. Beyond this, member involvement is often limited to paying dues while the professional staff runs the organization with some oversight by the board of directors. Some organizations, such as the Canadian Automobile Association and the Canadian Federation of Independent Business, poll their members on particular issues, while others encourage members and supporters to sign petitions to back their causes. A few interest groups set up local chapters so that members can discuss issues regularly. For example, the Council of Canadians, which claims to be "Canada's largest public advocacy group," features about 60 local chapters pursuing social justice issues such as protection of water resources, fair trade, public health, climate change, and democracy.

Some groups, such as the Canadian Taxpayers Federation, have "supporters" rather than members (Young & Everitt, 2004), while Greenpeace Canada considers anyone who has donated to the group to be a "member." In such cases, the staff or the leaders of the organization are not directly responsible to supporters, and supporters do not have a formal voice in the group's decisions. Instead, the organization's functioning depends on its ability to raise funds from its supporters for its causes. By purchasing mailing lists and keeping track of past donors, some groups are able to raise substantial amounts of money through direct mailings and email appeals for funds.

Peak associations are organizations representing a particular major interest based on a number of related interest groups rather than individual members (E. Montpetit, 2010). For example, the Canadian Federation of Students consists of about 80 student unions on individual university and college campuses. Indirectly it represents more than 500 000 students. Likewise, the Canadian Federation of Agriculture is composed of groups representing dairy, chicken, pork, and other farmers as well as provincial agricultural associations.

To what extent does an interest group actually represent the interests and views of its members or supporters? Groups that focus on interacting with government officials risk losing touch with members. Of course, sharp declines in membership or financial support will likely encourage a group to be more responsive to members. However, the need of some groups to devote great efforts to fundraising may detract from their ability to pursue the interests of their members and supporters. Furthermore, appeals used to raise funds do not always reflect the group's major goals. Groups that mobilize members around their causes through such activities as petitions, letter-writing campaigns, and demonstrations are more likely to be attentive to the views of their members and supporters. Yet groups that have a guaranteed membership may take positions that do not reflect members' views, unless organizers are worried about a campaign to oust the leadership or to break from the association or union. Likewise, groups that people join primarily for non-political reasons (such as religious and recreational groups) may take some political positions

Canadian Automobile Association
www.caa.ca

Canadian Federation of Independent Business
www.cfib-fcei.ca

Canadian Taxpayers Federation
www.taxpayer.com

Greenpeace Canada
www.greenpeace.ca

PEAK ASSOCIATIONS
Organizations representing a particular major interest based on a number of related interest groups rather than individual members.

Canadian Federation of Agriculture
www.cfa-fca.ca

that are at odds with the views of the majority of members. However, their ability to influence government officials may be compromised if the credibility of the group's leaders in representing their members' political views is questioned.

Canada's federal system has important implications for interest group organization. Because many decisions are made by provincial governments, interest groups often want to influence provincial governments as well as the federal government. This may involve setting up offices in some or all provincial capitals. Moreover, many interest groups are established as federations of provincial associations. Furthermore, given the distinctiveness of Quebec and the concentration of the francophone population in that province, there is often a special relationship between the Quebec branch of the interest group and the interest group in the rest of the country. In some cases, Quebec has a separate organization that is not part of the national organization. For example, the two Quebec teachers' associations (teaching in French and English school boards) are not members of the Canadian Teachers' Federation.

Canadian Teachers' Federation
www.ctf-fce.ca

Why Do People Join Interest Groups?

Pluralist theory assumes that individuals will join with like-minded people to form groups in order to advance their interests, particularly through political action (Smith, 2005). As Table 7-1 indicates, a significant proportion of Canadians say that they are members of voluntary groups, although organizations that are not primarily political (such as religious and recreational groups) attract larger numbers of members than those formed to take up a political cause. Even so, the limited data available indicates that some types of politically

ORGANIZATION	INACTIVE MEMBER	ACTIVE MEMBER	TOTAL
2000 Survey			
Human rights			5.1
Women's group			8.1
Peace group			2.1
2006 Survey			
Environmental	9.9	6.6	16.5
Professional association	10.1	18.7	28.8
Charitable/humanitarian	11.7	23.2	34.9
Consumer	7.4	4.5	11.9
Church/religious	22.2	27.9	50.5
Sports/recreational	14.2	29.1	43.3
Art/music/educational	12.6	23.2	35.8
Labour union	12.5	13.6	26.1
Any other voluntary	6.9	4.8	11.7

TABLE 7-1

PERCENTAGE OF CANADIANS INVOLVED IN PARTICULAR TYPES OF GROUPS

Note: The 2000 survey did not ask respondents if they were active or inactive members.

SOURCES: WORLD VALUES SURVEY, 2000, 2006. World Values Survey Association (www.worldvaluessurvey.org).

active groups, such as environmental organizations, attract larger memberships than political parties.

Questions have been raised as to why individuals would find it in their interest to join and be active in an interest group. Working from the rational choice perspective, Mancur Olson (1965) noted that individuals acting in their own self-interest may not find it worthwhile to devote time and money to join and be active in a group if they know that they can benefit from the actions of other group members. Why bother to be active in a student organization demanding lower tuition fees if thousands of others will do the work for you? Instead, you can be a **free rider** on their activity. Thus "rational, self-interested individuals will not act to achieve their common or group interests" (Olson, 1965, p. 2).

In Olson's analysis, groups will likely form and have the membership needed to pursue collective action in certain specific circumstances. First, coercion may be used to ensure that those benefiting from group action act in their common interest. This is particularly the case where membership is compulsory. Unions, including student unions and associations, generally have compulsory membership, or at least compulsory dues, once a majority of workers or students have voted to form a union. Likewise, to practise many professions, a person must become a member of the professional association. Second, groups that represent the interests of small numbers of individuals or individual companies will find it easier to form and maintain an active membership. In this case, individuals realize that if they do not support the group that aims to represent their interest, the group will fail and they will not gain the benefits they seek. In a small group (particularly one in which members have regular personal contact), peer pressure can help to sustain it. Third, a group may be able to provide some selective incentives to its members that are not available to non-members. For example, many interest groups provide useful information to members and arrange for member discounts on insurance, travel, and other purchases.

Since Olson wrote his book, the number of public interest groups and the size of their membership has increased considerably, and most groups do not have much in the way of exclusive benefits for their members. For example, it has been estimated that between 1500 and 2000 environmental groups exist in Canada (Wilson, 2002). To some extent, people may join an interest group for social reasons, such as the opportunity to attend meetings and interact with others (termed **solidary incentives**). A more compelling reason is the sense of satisfaction that people gain by joining or supporting a group that gives voice to their values or promoting a cause in which they believe (termed **purposive incentives**).

Overall, Olson's analysis seems hard to sustain in an era in which public interest groups have flourished. However, such groups can face problems in keeping up their membership and support base. While business and professional groups can maintain a strong membership and financial base over time,

FREE RIDER
An individual who enjoys the benefits of group action without contributing.

SOLIDARY INCENTIVES
Incentives to join a group for social reasons, such as the opportunities to attend meetings and interact with others.

PURPOSIVE INCENTIVES
Incentives to join a group based on the satisfaction that is gained by expressing one's values or promoting a cause in which one believes.

public interest groups may suffer from sharply fluctuating membership and support as public interest in particular issues and causes goes through a cycle of ups and downs (Downs, 1972).

Are All Sectors of Society Adequately Represented by Interest Groups?

The growing array of interest groups has meant that almost every interest has one or more groups claiming to represent it. Interest groups have been formed to represent those elements of society that have in the past been marginalized or excluded from politics—for example, Aboriginal peoples, women, and the poor. Nevertheless, taking the interest group system as a whole, some sectors of society are better represented than others. In particular, those with university education are more likely to join interest groups while younger persons and, to some extent, those with lower incomes are less likely to join. Almost the same proportion of women and men reported membership in interest groups in a 2008 national survey (Young & Everitt, 2010). Business interest groups have always been well represented in Canadian politics, while groups representing the less privileged elements of society often struggle to survive.

Interest groups need money and expertise to be effective. It takes considerable financial resources to keep an organization running smoothly, keep its members informed, and develop the expertise needed to sway policy-makers. Public interest groups often have to rely on unpaid volunteers and devote considerable time and resources to fundraising. A Canadian interest group may need to have provincial offices if it wants to affect the many policy areas in which provincial governments play a key role. Furthermore, the bilingual character of Canada means that expensive translation services may be necessary to operate in both official languages. In addition, the increasing use of the courts to advance or protect interests results in expensive legal costs. Indeed, strategic lawsuits against public participation (SLAPPs) have been used by some corporations to intimidate environmental and consumer groups that speak out or take a position on controversial issues. Even if the public interest group wins the court case (e.g., by invoking its right to freedom of expression), it will have expended considerable time, money, and energy to defend itself[2] (Lott, 2004).

However, Canadian tax laws limit the ability of interest groups to raise funds. If a group wishes to have registered charity status so that it can give donors a deduction on their income tax, the group cannot spend more than 10 percent (or up to 20 percent for charities that have low revenue) of its resources on political advocacy and cannot involve itself in partisan activities[3] (Canada Revenue Agency, 2003). Amendments to the Canada Revenue

Voices-Voix—Defending advocacy and dissent in Canada
http://voices-voix.ca

---

[2]Quebec and Ontario have adopted legislation to try to limit this abuse of the legal process.

[3]This limitation does not apply to businesses who receive a tax deduction for lobbying government or paying membership dues to a business association that lobbies government.

Agency Act have been designed to discourage registered charities from engaging in political activities (even if not partisan) and working against the "national interest" (Plecash, 2012). Indeed, beginning in 2012 the Harper government gave considerable amounts of money to the Canada Revenue Agency to conduct audits aimed at removing charitable status from groups deemed to be undertaking political advocacy. In particular, environmental, international development, and human rights organizations and left-wing policy institutes were targeted for audits, while conservative groups and institutes were not targeted (Beeby, 2014, September 15). Even a small birdwatching society received a warning about political activity from the Canada Revenue Agency (Beeby, 2014, October 16).

Government Sponsorship and Support

Prior to the 1960s, Canadian governments generally assumed that interest groups and government should be strictly separate (Pal, 1993). The development and activities of interest groups were considered a private matter, although governments did grant some professional groups (such as doctors and lawyers) the right to regulate their own professions. Governments were also often involved in controversies concerning the right of unions to organize, engage in collective bargaining, and take strike action.

In the mid-1960s, the Canadian government, through the Secretary of State Department, began to provide support and encouragement for official language minority groups as part of its campaign to promote bilingualism (and counter Quebec nationalism). Subsequently, Prime Minister Pierre Trudeau expressed an interest in "participatory democracy" and asserted that "counterweights" were needed to offset the power of the dominant interests (such as business interests) that influenced government policy. As a result, the Canadian government began to encourage and support the development of groups representing various sectors of society and viewpoints that had previously had little or no influence, such as Aboriginal groups, equality-seeking women's organizations, and environmental groups (Pal, 1993). Eventually, most Canadian government departments developed programs to fund interest groups related to their areas of policy-making, either in the form of sustaining grants (core funding) or, more typically, grants for specific projects. Indeed, in a few cases, the Canadian government could actually take credit for establishing interest groups. For example, the Canadian government set up the National Council of Welfare in 1962 to advise the government on welfare and poverty issues. However, its small budget was eliminated in the Canadian government's 2012 budget and the organization folded.

Providing support for interest groups can be useful to government. Interest groups can be a source of information and policy advice. Government officials may be better able to gain an understanding of the views of an element of society and thereby develop policies less likely to be criticized. Interest groups can also be a channel of communication to the public for government proposals and policies. If an interest group publicly supports the policy and carries the government's message to its members and to the public, effective criticism of the policy is less likely. Interest groups can also be useful in providing support for the positions of government in international politics. For example, the Canadian Coalition on Acid Rain, supported in part by Environment Canada, played an important role in successfully lobbying the American government (as well as Canadian governments) to reduce emissions causing acid rain (Doern & Conway, 1994).

The involvement of a variety of interest groups in discussing options for government policy on controversial topics can also be useful in developing a consensus among different or conflicting "stakeholders." In some cases, the stakeholders may agree to take voluntary action (e.g., managing a forest) rather than have government adopt a law or regulation. It can also be a way to defuse criticism and add legitimacy to the final government policy decision (see Box 7-1: "Talk and Dig": The Alberta Oil Sands).

Interest groups can also be useful for particular departments and agencies. An interest group may further departmental objectives by mobilizing public support for more resources and by supporting the efforts of that department to be considered a higher policy priority. For example, the Conference of Defence Associations, which promotes the need for greater military spending, receives $100 000 a year from the Department of National Defence (Taylor, 2012). As governments seek to reduce their program spending and balance their budgets, various groups have been encouraged to undertake activities that had previously been carried out by government.

However, providing support to interest groups carries the risk to government of mobilizing the demands, grievances, and criticisms of various segments of society. Some interest groups are reluctant to accept compromises to their basic values and thus tend to be critical of government policies. Equality-seeking groups, for example, have often criticized what they consider to be very limited measures to improve the situation of disadvantaged members of society.

Government funding of interest groups has been controversial. Critics argue that governments should not be funding "special interests" that may be demanding benefits that increase the costs of government and increase the role of government in the society and economy. Criticisms have also been raised about the choice of groups that have received funding. In the past, the Canadian government awarded substantial funding to the National Action Committee on the Status of Women (NAC), which represented a large number of women's groups, while usually denying funding to REAL Women, a conservative anti-feminist group that promotes traditional family values. However, as NAC became more confrontational in its relations with government, its funding was reduced. The Harper government eliminated core funding to NAC (and a number of other advocacy groups). Without regular government funding and

BOX 7-1

"Talk and Dig": The Alberta Oil Sands

Developing Alberta's bitumen-rich sands is highly controversial. On the one hand, they have become a major source of economic growth, royalties, and tax revenues for governments, and have created many thousands of high-paying jobs. On the other hand, the production of "dirty oil" has serious environmental effects on major rivers and wildlife as well as contributing to the increase in carbon emissions that cause global climate change. Major social issues have also arisen from the influx of workers to communities near the oil sands.

A close relationship developed between the major oil companies and the Alberta government in establishing a variety of policies related to oil sands projects. Other interests were not part of the policy process. However, as the initial projects transformed into a number of massive undertakings, many individuals and groups in Canada, the United States, and elsewhere took strongly critical positions on the developments. In response, the Alberta government set up several multi-stakeholder bodies to involve a larger set of groups in consultations about oil sands policy.

An analysis of the Oil Sands Consultation Advisory Group found that the expansion of consultation to include new actors, including environmental and Aboriginal groups, had little effect on the policies adopted. On almost all issues government and industry were in agreement. A consensus could not be reached on issues raised by other groups such as capping emissions, limiting the amount of land that could be disturbed, and water conservation. Thus, important issues were not effectively dealt with (Hoberg & Phillips, 2011). Likewise a non-governmental multi-stakeholder group examining the cumulative effects of the large number of developments did not affect the decision of regulatory bodies to approve more oil sands projects. However, a report from a multi-stakeholder committee that recommended the need for improved infrastructure to support oil sands development resulted in the Alberta government committing to spend substantial sums of money on health care, water treatment, and affordable housing for the local communities where the oil sands were being developed, along with a much smaller amount for agencies dealing with environmental impacts (Hoberg & Phillips, 2011).

The inclusion of environmental and Aboriginal groups in developing policy recommendations appears to have been intended to increase the legitimacy of the policy process. But consultation did not change the basic structure of power dominated by government and the oil industry. Instead, it was a strategy of "talk and dig" (Hoberg & Phillips, 2011, p. 524). In the end, the frustrated environmental groups ended their participation in the multi-stakeholder processes.

weakened by internal divisions related to differences concerning race, ethnicity, and sexual orientation, the once-influential NAC faded from the political scene (Dobrowolsky, 2008).

Overall, state-centred theory points out that interest groups are not necessarily an autonomous product of concerns among different interests in society. Governments have, at times, encouraged and supported the development of interest groups and included them in the policy process. In some cases, interest groups have been involved in promoting or carrying out the agenda of government, and have been used by some departments of government in their struggles with other government departments. The danger for interest groups is that they may lose their outspokenness if they depend too heavily on government for financing.

With government funding for most interest groups (including consumer-based advocacy groups) reduced or eliminated in recent decades, interest groups have had to devote much effort to fundraising and writing proposals for specific grants. In the health care field, major drug companies have provided grants and sought partnerships with organizations such as the Canadian Cancer Society, Canadian Diabetes Association, and the Heart and Stroke Foundation. Whether this support is simply charitable or whether pharmaceutical companies seek to gain support for weaker drug regulation, less rigorous safety standards, speedier approval of new drugs, or longer drug patent protection against generic drugs is unclear (Batt, 2005).

INFLUENCING PUBLIC POLICY

Direct Influence

Interest groups can try to affect the policies that governments develop and implement in many ways. The most effective way is to directly influence those responsible for developing public policies. It is generally thought that "getting in on the ground floor"—that is, exerting influence at the early stages of developing a policy—is most effective. At the early stages of policy development, government officials may be looking for information about a problem and examining possible alternatives. An interest group that is able to interact with key policy developers, typically within the public service, may be able to supply the information and policy ideas that will be considered.

Influencing a cabinet minister who is responsible for the relevant policy area can also be useful because the minister will likely encourage or instruct departmental personnel to give priority to a particular problem and set out the goals to be achieved. As well, the minister will be involved in assessing the alternative policies that may be provided by public servants, and will present recommendations to the relevant cabinet committee and, if necessary, to the cabinet as a whole. Even so, influencing departmental policy developers and persuading the cabinet minister who heads the department may not be enough to achieve the interest group's objectives. Various central agencies (such as the Privy Council Office and the Prime Minister's Office) play a key role in determining what government does. In addition, the prime minister, along with the central agencies, sets the overall direction of the government. Access to the prime minister is tightly controlled, however, and central agencies are less open to influence than departments.

Generally, interest groups receive a more sympathetic hearing, and will find it easier to develop a close working relationship with key people, in the department that most closely matches their interests. Although public servants are often thought to be insensitive to political considerations and thus largely free of outside influence, this is not entirely the case. As noted above, public servants often value contact with key interest groups because such groups provide information and ideas that can be useful in developing policy proposals. By interacting with people representing major interests, public servants can benefit in several ways. They can gauge the potential reaction to new policies, and try to avoid potential criticism from these interests by involving them in the formulation of policies. As well, consultation with major interest groups can add legitimacy to government decisions.

Political scientists have found that public policies can be developed through the collaboration of a **policy community**[4] of government officials responsible for a particular policy area and relevant institutionalized interest groups (Coleman & Skogstad, 1990; Pross, 1992). In this situation, interest groups not only promote the interests of their members, but also draw on their information and expertise to engage in deliberation with groups representing different interests and with government officials to develop policies acceptable to the policy community (Montpetit, 2004).

ADVISORY COUNCILS AND "THINK TANKS"   In some cases, the interactions between interest groups and key policy-makers have been formalized through the establishment of advisory councils and committees that include representatives of those interest groups or individuals that the government department or agency considers important. Royal commissions and government task forces that are set up to examine issue areas and make recommendations often include people associated with various interests. Some royal commissions, such as the ones on bilingualism and biculturalism (1963–1967) and the status of women (1967–1970), had important long-term effects on public attitudes and government policy.

Governments have also established or funded various organizations that provide independent policy advice as an alternative to the advice provided by powerful self-interest groups. However, in 1992, Brian Mulroney's Progressive Conservative government eliminated five such organizations that operate at "arm's length" from government, including the Economic Council of Canada, the Science Council, and the Law Reform Commission. Likewise, the Chrétien Liberal government closed the Canadian Advisory Council on the Status of Women in 1995[5] and some other advisory organizations. In the 2012 budget, the Harper government announced the cancellation of funding for the National Round Table on the Environment and the Economy, the National Council of Welfare, the First Nations Statistical Institute, and the Rights and Democracy agency.

With many independent policy advisory bodies no longer in existence, "think tanks," many of which promote the interests of their wealthy corporate backers, have become an important source of policy research and advice.

POLICY COMMUNITY
Collaboration of government officials responsible for a particular policy area and relevant institutionalized interest groups in developing public policies.

---

[4]Policy communities are also often referred to as policy networks, with policy communities sometimes analyzed as a particular type of policy network.

[5]Some provincial governments have continued to maintain their own advisory councils on the status of women.

Interest groups often take part in the public consultations organized by the Canadian government to discuss various proposals. However, if government has already committed itself to a proposed policy, it appears unlikely that interest group representation will result in major changes to the proposal. Convincing the government to change its mind often takes strong action and the support of a variety of interests.

MEMBERS OF PARLIAMENT   The most powerful institutionalized interest groups generally do not devote a great deal of attention to influencing ordinary Members of Parliament (MPs). MPs play a limited role in policy development; instead, they are involved primarily in the passage of legislation presented to Parliament by the government, although they do propose modifications to legislative proposals in House of Commons committees. As well, parliamentary committee members do involve themselves, to some degree, in developing policy recommendations that are, on occasion, picked up by policy-makers in government. However, party discipline restricts the ability of individual MPs or groups of MPs to take an independent role in policy-making. John Bulloch, founder of the Canadian Federation of Independent Business, noted that he was initially "very naive" in trying to influence MPs, but came to the conclusion that it was generally a waste of time "to talk to people who have no influence" (quoted in Pross, 1992).

Nevertheless, interest groups do present their cases to MPs and participate in the public hearings of parliamentary committees. As well, there have been situations in which influencing MPs has proven effective. For example, in 1996 the Insurance Bureau of Canada (an interest group representing insurance companies) successfully mounted a campaign against allowing the major banks to enter the insurance business. By mobilizing insurance agents in each electoral district to contact their MP, the Insurance Bureau was able to convince the governing Liberal party caucus to oppose the plan promoted by the Canadian Bankers Association (Clancy, 2008). Because the big banks are unpopular among the public, it was in the political interests of the Liberal caucus, prime minister, and finance minister to go against the wishes of the banks (Havro, 2004). Likewise, in 2009, Canada's 33 000 insurance agents successfully lobbied MPs, particularly those of the governing Conservative party, to prevent banks from marketing insurance policies on their websites (Chase & Perkins, 2009).

Insurance Bureau of Canada
www.ibc.ca

Canadian Bankers Association
www.cba.ca

INFLUENCING THE PUBLIC   Interest groups often take their case to the public as an indirect way of influencing government. They may get the word out through press releases, advertising, websites, social media, and participating in public forums. Petitions and mass emails to politicians may be used to show that a group enjoys substantial support for its positions on particular issues. Public interest groups, in particular, sometimes use protest techniques to attract media attention. More than most, Greenpeace is known for its dramatic protest activities. For example, in July 2009, Greenpeace activists chained themselves to the front door of the Quebec Ministry of Natural Resources, set up a banner proclaiming "Boreal Forest: The Destruction Starts Here," and dumped a load of lumber at the building's entrance. Similarly, President Obama was greeted on his first visit to Ottawa with large Greenpeace banners on the Alexandra Bridge: "Welcome President Obama" and "Climate Leaders Don't Buy Tar Sands."

Public techniques are often the only way of trying to influence public policy for the many groups that lack effective access to policy-makers. However, institutionalized groups influential in the policy process sometimes also take their case to the public to try to counter the influence of other groups in the public eye, and to try to demonstrate to politicians that they have public support. For example, in 2012, the Canadian Association of Petroleum Producers mounted an extensive multimedia advertising campaign featuring pictures of clean lakes and forests to counter criticism of oil sands development. It has also developed a variety of classroom resources, including the Energy in Action program for Grade 4 and 5 students emphasizing the importance of oil and gas resources and environmental stewardship.

POLITICAL PARTIES AND ELECTIONS   Canadian interest groups generally avoid direct involvement in political parties. Interest groups hope to influence whichever political party is in power, and thus most interest groups do not want to be perceived as being "in bed" with one political party. A key exception is the Canadian Labour Congress (CLC), which was involved in the formation of the New Democratic Party. Although the Canadian Labour Congress is not formally affiliated with the NDP, many individual CLC unions are affiliated with the NDP. The relationship between labour unions and the NDP is not always harmonious. For example, Buzz Hargrove, then president of the Canadian Auto Workers Union (CAW), was expelled from the NDP after he publicly advised CAW members to vote for the Liberal candidates in districts where the NDP had little chance of winning in the 2006 election, and appeared to publicly endorse Liberal leader Paul Martin. After his expulsion, the CAW ended its affiliation with the NDP. Instead it supported individual NDP and Liberal candidates (as well as the Green party leader) in the 2008 and 2011 elections. Likewise Unifor, the largest private sector union formed through the amalgamation of the CAW with the Communications, Energy, and Paperworkers Union in 2013, decided to encourage its 305 000 members to vote strategically in the 2015 election to defeat the Conservative government. This involved voting for the NDP or Liberal candidate in each district who had the best chance of being elected.

Interest groups are banned (along with corporations and unions) from making financial contributions to political parties. Nevertheless, a number of interest groups publicize their views during election campaigns, with some spending more than $100 000 on campaign-related advertising expenses.

LEGAL ACTION   Increasingly, interest groups have used legal action to promote their causes. Aboriginal groups have made major advances over time through gaining legal recognition of Aboriginal rights. Women's groups have challenged a range of laws and policies that they view as violating the protection of female–male equality entrenched in the Charter of Rights and Freedoms. Gay and lesbian groups have used the courts to gain the same rights and benefits for same-sex couples as heterosexual couples. And environmental groups have, at times, forced reluctant governments to undertake some environmental reviews of projects in accordance with environmental laws and regulations. Overall, however, corporate interests have been the largest users of the court system to pursue their agendas (Hein, 2000).

In addition to initiating legal actions, interest groups frequently present briefs in cases before higher-level courts. For example, in 2006 non-governmental interveners participated in over two-fifths of the cases heard by the Supreme Court of Canada. Particularly active as interveners have been the Women's Legal Education and Action Fund (LEAF) and the Canadian Civil Liberties Association, although many other groups have also presented briefs to the Supreme Court (Hausegger, Hennigar, & Riddell, 2015).

Women's Legal Education and
Action Fund
www.leaf.ca

Canadian Civil Liberties Association
www.ccla.ca

A drawback of using the courts to pursue group causes is the high cost of legal action. To help, in 1978 the Canadian government established the **Court Challenges Program**, which provided some money for individuals and groups seeking to challenge Canadian laws and government actions that violated the equality rights of historically disadvantaged groups and the rights of official language minorities. However, the Conservative government shut down this program in 2006.[6] The Liberal party promised to restore the program in the 2015 election campaign.

**COURT CHALLENGES
PROGRAM**
A federal government program that provided some money for individuals and groups seeking to challenge Canadian laws and government actions that violate equality rights and minority language rights.

The Potential for Successful Influence

Interest groups vary considerably in their potential ability to influence public policy. Well-financed groups are able to hire qualified and knowledgeable people or firms that can monitor government activities, provide detailed policy analyses and proposals, develop ongoing relationships with key government officials, maintain an effective organization, and mount public relations campaigns.

Group members can be useful in persuading politicians and government officials to consider the policies the group is advocating. What matters here is not only the number of members, but also the group's ability to mobilize members in support of its positions. Credibility is also important. For example, professional associations, such as the Canadian Medical Association and

---

[6]In 2008, the Canadian government established the Language Rights Support Program to clarify and advance the constitutional rights of official language minorities and provide some financial assistance to resolve disputes.

the Canadian Bar Association, are usually taken seriously when they speak out on issues related to their profession.

A group's success in influencing government is also affected by its ability to develop close relationships with key officials. It is important for a group to be viewed as the legitimate representative of a particular element of society. If other groups claim to represent the same interest and put forward different policy proposals, the group's influence may be undermined.

It is not only the resources and capabilities of an interest group that matter. The governing political party is much more likely to listen to proposals from a group whose perspective is similar to its own and whose proposals fit in with the government's agenda and plans. For example, environmentalist and feminist groups found it very difficult to influence Stephen Harper's Conservative government.

For groups that have trouble gaining effective access to policy-makers, attracting the attention of the media and receiving favourable coverage for their cause is important. Groups that cultivate relationships with sympathizers in the media can sometimes gain free publicity for their views. However, the media generally focus on dramatic events, particularly those that have a strong visual component for television. This can make it difficult for a group to explain its viewpoint and proposals.

Finally, if a group can form coalitions with other groups to advance its causes, particularly groups representing different interests or different elements of the population, this can be very useful in successfully influencing policy-makers. By gaining support from other groups, the interest group may no longer appear to be pursuing benefits only for its own members or reflecting a particular point of view. For example, in 1995, the Canadian Federation of Students successfully challenged the government's proposed income contingent repayment plan for student loans. By building a coalition of support from a variety of interest groups (including those representing seniors, women, labour, and poor people), as well as mounting a "National Day of Strike and Action," the federation was able to demonstrate widespread support for its cause (Temelini, 2008).

Overall, business groups have a particularly strong ability to influence public policy, not only because of the resources at their disposal, but also because of their ability to make the case that the policies they advocate (such as lower taxes, less regulation, and free trade) are essential for a prosperous economy and for remaining competitive in a globalized marketplace. Nevertheless, other groups have been able to persuade governments to provide a variety of social programs, often over the objections of business interests. Many Canadians do not have a positive view of "big business," and thus its interests have, at times, been successfully challenged. For example, in 1998, the Council of Canadians successfully mobilized opposition to defeat the government's plan, backed by big business, to ratify the Multilateral Agreement on Investment, which the council argued would enhance the power of large multinational corporations. In addition, politicians need to be responsive to various social interests if they are to succeed in their political careers. Even though governments do not always act as the majority of people want and do not always act in keeping with the wishes of many interest groups, it would be misleading to assume that Canadian governments ignore interest groups or that business interests always prevail (Young & Everitt, 2004).

LOBBYISTS

Lobbying has been defined as "the practice of communication, usually privately, with government officials to try to influence a government decision" (Young & Everitt, 2004, p. 88). The term originated from the historic practice (by those seeking benefits from government for themselves or for the members of the group they represent) of contacting MPs in the lobby of the British House of Commons.

The practice of lobbying has become professionalized. Many institutionalized interest groups and business corporations employ people who specialize in developing contacts within government and can represent the interests of their group or corporation. In addition, a number of companies (as well as individuals) provide lobbying services for a hefty fee. These services include trying to persuade government officials on a particular topic and monitoring government activities that may affect an interest group or corporation. Moreover, lobbyists typically provide advice on whom to contact in government, what approach to take if the group or corporation wishes to lobby itself, and how to win public support for the group and the positions it wishes to promote. Overall, there are close to 800 lobbyists at the national level—an 85 percent increase since 2005 (Kirby, 2014).

Many professional lobbyists have held important positions in government or have been key political "insiders" who have a close relationship with important political figures. There is often a "revolving door" between those working in senior government positions and firms that provide advice for those seeking to influence government. For example, upon leaving government, Jason MacDonald (Prime Minister Harper's director of communications) was appointed vice-president of Hill and Knowlton Canada (a leading lobbying firm), while Rob Nicol (a lobbyist for Canadian Tire) became the prime minister's new director of communications (Maher, 2015). Although the Accountability Act places some limitations on the lobbying activities of former government officials, this does not prevent them from making use of the knowledge and contacts they obtained in government.

While maintaining contacts with key people in government is still a central feature of successful influence, lobbying companies have increasingly broadened their activities to include advertising, social media, public opinion analysis, building relations with stakeholders and communities, and public engagement. This can help build a stronger case to politicians and counter opposition to their policy positions.

LOBBYING
An effort to influence government decisions, particularly through direct personal communication with key government decision makers.

F-35 Stealth Fighters:
Keeping Parliament and the Public in the Dark

In 2010, the Canadian government signed a memorandum of understanding to purchase 65 American F-35 single engine stealth fighter jets to replace Canada's aging CF-18s. Defence Minister Peter MacKay told Parliament that the cost of the jets would be $9 billion, and the Department of National Defence (DND) said that the jets, including their full operating costs over 20 years, would cost $14.7 billion. Two years later, Canada's auditor general, Michael Ferguson, reported that the DND's internal estimates (which were not reported to Parliament) had been $25 billion for the full operating costs of the 65 jets (Office of the Auditor General of Canada, 2012). Defence Minister MacKay claimed that the $10 billion difference was simply an "accounting error" (Stechyson, 2012).

In his report and in media interviews, Ferguson was strongly critical of the DND's handling of the military purchase and its failure to respond to Parliament's repeated requests for the full cost of the jets (Payton, 2012). Unlike most government purchases, there was no competitive bidding for the purchase of fighter jets, and the DND did not take due diligence in choosing the single-engine jets. Furthermore, while Prime Minister Harper promoted the F-35s as creating thousands of jobs across Canada, the reality was that there were, unlike with other major military purchases, no guarantees that there would be benefits to Canadian industries such as contracts related to the maintenance of the jets.

Instead, Canada would have to compete with other countries for such contracts.

The auditor general noted that the rush to announce the deal in 2010 was "partly in response to pressure from the industry." To pursue the contract, Lockheed Martin, the primary contractor, used two lobbying firms: CFN Consultants, a specialist in lobbying for military purchases, and Prospectus Associates, lobbyists with strong connections to Defence Minister MacKay and the Conservative party. Other industries that would benefit from the F-35 purchase also lobbied the government.

Was industry lobbying on behalf of the F-35s a major influence on the government's decision to purchase the jets, or was it the eagerness of the DND to have the most advanced fighter jets? Determining what influences government decisions is not an easy task. However, with the public and parliamentarians kept in the dark about the full costs in this case, informed public discussion of a major government decision was stifled.

As of 2015, the Canadian Department of National Defence (DND) planned to continue to use the aging F-18 jets for another decade and was considering whether alternatives to the F-35s (estimated by the DND in 2014 to cost $45.8 billion over their life-cycle) would be more suited to Canada's military tasks. Liberal leader Justin Trudeau promised to hold an open competition to choose a more affordable fighter jet and focus more on rebuilding Canada's navy (CBC News, 2015, September 20).

Lobbying activities have frequently aroused suspicion and sparked debate (see Box 7-2: F-35 Stealth Fighters: Keeping Parliament and the Public in the Dark). Seeking selective benefits from government behind closed doors raises questions about whether the public interest is being ignored. Treating government officials and politicians to expensive dinners and inviting them on expense-paid holidays can create the impression of unfair or illegal influence. The "sponsorship scandal" that contributed to the defeat of the Liberal government in 2006 included evidence that advertising agencies connected to the Liberal party paid lobbyists to seek contracts for which little work was actually done.[7] In return, substantial sums of money were given to those involved in the Quebec branch of the Liberal Party of Canada.

The practice of senior public officials and cabinet ministers of leaving government and becoming employed as lobbyists also creates legitimate concerns. Not only do such people enjoy unfair advantages in influencing their former colleagues, but also their decisions while in public office might be influenced by the hopes for subsequent employment or contracts. For example, shortly after he stepped down as prime minister in 1993, Brian Mulroney received three cash payments totalling at least $225 000 from lobbyist Karlheinz Schreiber. Mulroney eventually admitted that he received money from Schreiber, including an envelope containing $100 000 in cash that he pocketed in a New York City hotel room. Accusations were made that the money related to lobbying efforts to persuade Air Canada (then a Crown corporation) to purchase Airbus jets. Mulroney claimed that he had accepted the money to help Schreiber (accused but not convicted of large-scale fraud, bribery, and tax evasion in Europe) to promote the sale of German armoured vehicles to foreign governments.

Lobbyist Regulation

Efforts have been made to clean up the process of lobbying. In particular, the Lobbying Act, 2008, requires that those who are paid to communicate with government officials on various matters or who arrange a meeting with a public office are required to file reports indicating the following:

- on whose behalf they are acting;
- the name of the department or other government institution that they are communicating with; and
- the subject matter of the communication.

As well, paid lobbyists who ask the public to communicate directly with public officeholders must file reports on this activity. Lobbyists are not allowed to receive contingency payments from their clients based on the outcome of their persuasive efforts. In addition, cabinet ministers, their staff, top public servants (such as deputy ministers and assistant deputy ministers), and MPs and senators are forbidden to act as paid lobbyists for five years after leaving their office. The Lobbying Act is overseen by a commissioner of lobbying, an officer of Parliament. The Lobbying Act makes the commissioner responsible for developing a code of conduct for lobbyists and allows the commissioner to grant exceptions to the rules in certain circumstances.

---

[7]The sponsorship program, initiated after Quebec's 1995 sovereignty referendum, was intended to promote Canadian unity at various Quebec events.

Democracy Watch
www.democracywatch.ca

Canadians for Responsible Advocacy
responsible advocacy.org

Although the Lobbying Act is stricter than previous laws, the public interest group Democracy Watch (2011) has pointed out that some loopholes still exist. For example, unpaid lobbyists and lobbyists who spend less than 20 percent of their time lobbying on behalf of corporations are not required to register as lobbyists. Only formal meetings have to be reported. Lobbyists can also take leading positions in the election campaigns of political parties. The enforcement of the Lobbying Act is difficult since politicians and public officials being lobbied are not required to report when they have been lobbied. Indeed, the commissioner cannot levy any penalties against those who fail to register as lobbyists, and there have been no prosecutions to date for violating the Lobbying Act (LeBlanc, 2011).

SOCIAL MOVEMENTS

SOCIAL MOVEMENT
A network of groups and individuals that seeks major social and political changes, particularly by acting outside of established political institutions.

A **social movement** can be thought of as a network of groups and individuals that seeks major social and political changes, particularly by acting outside established political institutions (Martell, 1994). It is not always easy to distinguish between interest groups and organizations based on social movements. However, interest groups tend to focus on affecting a range of specific public policies. In contrast, social movements embrace broader goals, such as challenging and transforming the values, power relationships, and institutions of society and politics. For example, the environmental movement is not only concerned with spurring government to act on environmental problems. It also aims to persuade individuals to change their lifestyles and relationship to nature and to convince businesses to change their practices to reduce their impact on the natural environment. Likewise, the women's movement has challenged traditional male–female relationships and tried to raise women's consciousness, pride, and assertiveness. Similarly, the gay and lesbian movement has sought to forge a sense of collective identity and solidarity among those of different sexual orientations. Nevertheless, social movements have stimulated the formation of many public interest groups.

Social movements have often played an important role in Canadian politics. For example, the women's suffrage movement that began in the late nineteenth century eventually succeeded in achieving the right of women to vote and hold public office, as well as changing laws that gave women an inferior legal status. Its tactics included circulating petitions as well as holding mock parliamentary debates to illustrate the political competence of women. The Canadian suffrage movement had connections to other influential early social movements, such as the temperance movement (which promoted abstinence from alcoholic beverages and advocated banning the making and sale of alcohol) and the social purity movement (which emphasized traditional moral and family values) (Smith, 2005). Likewise, the farmers' and labour movements have had considerable importance in Canadian politics and society.

New Social Movements

Beginning in the late 1960s, a number of social movements developed in Canada (and other countries). Among these **new social movements** were the women's movement, the environmental movement, the Aboriginal movement, and the gay and lesbian rights movement. Many Canadians have also been involved in the global social justice movement (often labelled the "anti-globalization" movement) and the "Occupy" movement. These new movements tend to have different goals, values, organizational structures, and types of participants than the social movements developed in earlier times. For example, many of the new social movements are concerned with developing a collective sense of identity among those who are deemed to suffer from oppression. The women's movement, in promoting a new sense of women's identity, has made public issues out of what were traditionally viewed as private matters and challenged the power relationships involved in personal relations (Smith, 2008). Generally, the tendency of new social movements to focus on identities, values, participation, and the quality of life may be viewed as reflecting the shift toward post-materialism discussed in Chapter 5.

New social movements have tended to avoid involvement with conventional political institutions such as political parties. Because those involved in new social movements have often criticized the hierarchy, bureaucracy, and power politics of conventional political organizations, they have sought to create an alternative—more informal organizations or networks based on grassroots participation by those who share the movement's goals. Indeed, the Occupy movement lacked both leaders and organization. This trend, along with the exclusion of new social movement activists from the policy-making

NEW SOCIAL MOVEMENTS
Social movements concerned particularly with developing a collective sense of identity among those who are deemed to suffer from oppression, along with adopting new cultural values and lifestyles.

This march in downtown Vancouver was organized by We Love This Coast which fights against fossil fuel projects such as proposed oil pipelines that could damage the B.C. coast

© Ben Nelms/Reuters/Landov

BOX 7-3

Save Our Forest: Civil Disobedience

In 1993, protesters at Clayoquot Sound on Vancouver Island stood in front of logging trucks every morning for several months to block loggers from entering the old-growth forest—this despite a court injunction banning the action.

As early as 1979, residents of Tofino, British Columbia, had begun to protest against clear-cut logging of the old-growth forests at Clayoquot Sound. Yet in 1993 the British Columbia government decided to allow MacMillan Bloedel, a major forestry company, to raze over half the forest. The protesters who gathered in response came from various elements of the environmental movement. About 12 000 people were involved overall, and 857 protesters were arrested, with some sentenced to 45 days in jail and $1500 in fines. The protest attracted global attention, with Hollywood celebrities such as Barbra Streisand, Robert Redford, Martin Sheen, and Oliver Stone supporting the action and the Australian band Midnight Oil putting on a concert at the protest camp (Bantjes, 2007).

Environmental groups such as Greenpeace, the Rainforest Action Network, and the Sierra Club launched a boycott of companies selling products made from the old-growth forests of British Columbia. The boycott's success eventually persuaded MacMillan Bloedel to agree to a compromise involving a joint venture with the local Nuu-chah-nulth First Nations to harvest parts of the old-growth forest in a more ecologically sound manner. Later MacMillan Bloedel withdrew, and in 2008 the First Nations Isaak Forest Resources Ltd. became the sole owner of timber rights after buying Weyerhaeuser's 49 percent share. Isaak (which means "respect") adopted the strict environmental and social standards of the Forest Stewardship Council. However, the burden of debt has posed difficult financial challenges (Bunsha, 2013) and Isaak applied for a permit to cut old growth forest on Flores Island (Sierra Club BC, 2012).

The blockade at Clayoquot Sound was one of the largest acts of civil disobedience in Canadian history. Groups involved in the environmental movement succeeded in raising public awareness about threats to old-growth forests and pressuring companies and governments to change forest management practices. However, the future of Canada's old-growth forests remains uncertain.

CIVIL DISOBEDIENCE
The deliberate and public breaking of a law to draw attention to injustice.

process, has meant that various forms of public protest have served as an important tool for new social movements to draw attention to their causes. Included in the repertoire of some new social movements has been **civil disobedience**—deliberately and publicly breaking the law to draw attention to injustice (see Box 7-3: Save Our Forest: Civil Disobedience). Taking their cue from the successful use of non-violent civil disobedience by the civil rights movement in the United States in the 1960s, Aboriginal groups have used civil disobedience to blockade highways and rail lines to bolster their claims to lands that they view as having been unjustly taken from them, women's groups have organized sit-ins at government offices to protest cutbacks to women's programs, and anti-poverty groups have jammed traffic in Toronto's financial district.

Although civil disobedience is usually non-violent, clashes between protesters and police or between protesters and affected members of the public have occurred in some cases. Because protests may involve a range of groups and individuals without a disciplined organization, some individuals and small groups that prefer throwing stones at police, smashing windows, and other violent acts have drawn attention away from the message of the protest.

For example, during the G20 protests in Toronto in 2010, small groups of masked "Black Bloc" anarchists smashed business windows and torched police cars. This served to divert attention away from the messages of the much larger number of protesters, provided an excuse for the security forces to arrest a substantial number of protesters not involved in the violence, and allowed the Canadian government to defend spending close to $1 billion on security measures for the G20 summit in downtown Toronto.

Although it is often small groups within a movement that initiate violence, there have been occasions where police or security forces have used force to disperse peaceful protests. For example, some of those peacefully protesting the presence of the Indonesian dictator at the 1997 Asia-Pacific Economic Cooperation summit held on the University of British Columbia campus were pepper sprayed by the RCMP. Indeed, *agents provocateurs* have sometimes been used to make it appear as if protests were violent. For example, when protesters congregated at Montebello, Quebec, in 2007, where the Canadian prime minister and the American and Mexican presidents were discussing the Security and Prosperity Partnership, three young men carrying rocks whose faces were covered joined the protest. When the men refused a demand from protest organizers to uncover themselves, they pushed through the police line and were "arrested." However, a video posted on YouTube and broadcast on television revealed that the three "protesters" were wearing the same boots as the police! The Sûreté du Québec (Quebec's provincial police) then admitted that the three "protesters" were in fact police officers—although denied that they were trying to instigate violence.

The distinction between old and new social movements is sometimes exaggerated. Some of the old social movements used various means of protest, including civil disobedience, and some tried to avoid rigid organizational structures. Some early Canadian social movements, such as the temperance and moral purity movements, were middle-class movements focused on values and lifestyles, albeit of a traditional, conventional nature. Moreover, some new social movements, such as the Aboriginal and women's movement, are concerned about materialist goals such as employment and social programs as well as seeking recognition for their identities.

As new social movements mature, more conventional public interest groups have been formed to pursue their causes. Such groups have a better chance of influencing specific policies while potentially alienating the more idealistic movement activists. For example, most of the larger organizations associated with the Canadian environmental movement have become institutionalized interest groups with professional staff and a conventional organizational structure. This has allowed them to become a regular part of the policy communities that interact with government officials, business, and other interest groups in policy development.[8] However, some groups like Greenpeace

---

[8]However, even moderate environmental groups were ignored by the Harper government and generally excluded from participation in environmental reviews (McCarthy, 2012b).

have resisted becoming a conventional interest group. While some criticize the more "radical" groups for giving the environmental movement a negative image, such groups can be useful in encouraging government to work with the more "moderate" groups. Also, the radical groups are more likely to be able to mobilize activists in support of the cause, keep issues in the public eye, and prevent moderate groups from straying too far and compromising the movement's goals.

Although the new social movements have not achieved all their goals, they have affected Canadian politics. In particular, they have raised awareness of important problems and issues such as climate change, the inequalities between women and men, and the rights of Aboriginals that have often been ignored. Even if effective policies to deal with many of the issues raised by the new social movements are often still lacking, there has been increased recognition that these issues are important and need to be resolved.

Summary and Conclusion

Interest groups offer an important way for people to try to influence public policies. Well-organized groups that are able to cultivate ongoing relationships with key policy-makers are most likely to affect government decisions. Nevertheless, groups not involved in the policy-making process may be able to make a difference if they can mobilize strong public support behind their cause and win the support of other influential groups.

From the perspective of pluralist theory, the growth of interest groups representing a variety of interests and causes suggests that the decisions and policies adopted by governments are likely to reflect the diverse interests of Canadians, rather than the interests of a small group of powerful people inside or outside government. Critics of pluralist theory argue that business interests, because of their economic clout, continue to have a privileged position from which to influence government despite the development of many groups representing other interests.

Governments do not simply respond to the pressures placed on them. Whether as a result of their view of what is in the public interest, a calculation of what is needed to win the next election, or a desire to maintain their power in federal–provincial or international relations, governments do, at times, adopt

policies that cannot be explained in terms of interest group pressures.

Interest groups are sometimes viewed as a threat to democracy and good government. Because many interest groups pursue the particular interests of their members, or of one narrow segment of society, there is a risk that powerful interest groups could achieve benefits for some elements of society at the expense of the general public interest.

However, the development of groups representing diverse interests and ideas can be viewed as a positive feature of political life. Deliberations involving government officials and groups with a variety of different perspectives may result in a better understanding of problems and consideration of a broader range of solutions (Montpetit, 2010). The development of public interest groups has provided increased opportunities for public involvement in the political process and enhanced public discussion of policy issues. Thus, interest groups are an important component of democracy.

Although interest groups representing disadvantaged elements of society have been established, their ability to influence policy-makers is limited. Cutbacks in government funding for equality-seeking groups add to the imbalance of influence and make the quest for a fully democratic society more difficult.

The activities of lobbyists tend to advance the interests of large corporations and some well-funded interest groups. Despite the passage of laws regulating lobbyists, their activities will likely continue to raise concerns about unfair influence, secret backroom deals, and the need for greater transparency in the policy-making process.

Social movements may be viewed as enhancing the quality of democracy by mobilizing large numbers of people to participate in collective actions intended to better society and the world at large. By challenging embedded structures of social and economic power as well as political power, social movements can encourage debate about fundamental issues and values, and voice the concerns of disadvantaged and marginalized groups (Philips, 2004). However, the strident positions and disruptive or even violent actions taken by some of those participating in social movement actions may alienate potential supporters and make it difficult for social movements to influence governments. Nevertheless, social movements can have a long-term effect by influencing the thinking of the public and by raising issues that might otherwise be ignored.

Discussion Questions

1. Are interest groups an essential feature of democracy?

2. Are you active in an interest group? Why or why not?

3. Does your student union or student association effectively represent your interests?

4. Why are social movements an important aspect of Canadian politics?

5. Are social movement activists justified in engaging in civil disobedience to advance their cause?

Further Reading

Clement, D. (2009). *Canada's rights revolution: Social movements and social change, 1937–82.* Vancouver, BC: UBC Press.

Coleman, W. (1988). *Business and politics: A study of collective action.* Montreal, QC: McGill-Queen's University Press.

Hale, G. (2006). *Uneasy partnership: The politics of business and government.* Toronto, ON: University of Toronto Press.

Hammond-Callaghan, M., & Hayday, M. (Eds.). (2008). *Mobilizations, protests and engagements: Canadian perspectives on social movements.* Halifax, NS: Fernwood.

Macdonald, D. (2007). *Business and environmental politics in Canada.* Peterborough, ON: Broadview Press.

Pross, A.P. (1992). *Group politics and public policy* (2nd ed.). Toronto, ON: Oxford University Press.

Smith, M. (2005). *A civil society? Collective actors in Canadian political life.* Peterborough, ON: Broadview Press.

Smith, M. (Ed.). (2008). *Group politics and social movements in Canada.* Peterborough, ON: Broadview Press.

Young, L., & Everitt, J. (2004). *Advocacy groups.* Vancouver, BC: UBC Press.

CHAPTER 8

Justin Trudeau led the Liberal party to a majority government in the 2015 election.

© Paul Chiasson/Canadian Press Images

Political Parties

CHAPTER OBJECTIVES

After reading this chapter, you should be able to

1. Assess the role of political parties in Canadian democracy.

2. Discuss different types of party systems and their impact on government formation, accountability, and the representation of diverse interests.

3. Discuss changing patterns of party competition.

4. Compare the ideas and policies of the most significant parties in federal politics.

5. Discuss how much influence party members have over party platforms and the selection and removal of their leaders and local candidates.

When Conservative prime minister Stephen Harper emerged from Rideau Hall on a hot and hazy August 2015 long weekend to confirm that he had asked the governor general to dissolve Parliament for a general election on October 19, few political observers would have predicted the dramatic conclusion to the longest campaign held since 1872. A long campaign was originally seen as benefiting the Conservatives, who had the biggest war chest. But early polls showed the Conservative party, New Democratic Party, and Liberal party jockeying for first place in a tight three-way race. With no clear front-runner, it appeared that Canadians were poised to elect a minority government.

Party leaders and candidates jostled over issues ranging from the criminal trial of Conservative senator Mike Duffy, the government's handling of the Syrian refugee crisis, Canada's role in the fight against the Islamic State, the newly signed Trans-Pacific Partnership, to Harper's statement that he would consider banning federal civil service workers from wearing the niqab.

As the campaign wore on, public opinion polls indicated that voting intentions were shifting. Support for the official opposition New Democratic Party (NDP), which had high hopes of forming the government based on its historic second place finish in the 2011 election, began to drop, while support for the Liberal party, which had been reduced to third party status after its disastrous showing in 2011, began to grow. Many pundits interpreted the shifting fortunes of the opposition parties as a sign that voters who wanted change were deciding which party was best placed to defeat the Harper government.

After a lengthy 78-day campaign in communities, on the airwaves, and in cyberspace, more than 17.5 million Canadians delivered their verdict at the ballot box. Although Liberal party leader Justin Trudeau had been the target of negative Conservative party advertising depicting him as "just not ready" for the job of prime minister, the Liberals won a strong majority with 184 seats based on 39.5 percent of the vote. The Liberal "red wave," which began in Atlantic Canada and swept across much of the country, prompted comparisons to the "Trudeaumania" phenomenon in 1968, when Pierre Trudeau's Liberals won a majority that was broad in geographic scope.

The Liberals swept all 32 seats in Atlantic Canada, placed first in Quebec, Ontario, and British Columbia, and won ridings in large urban centres in western Canada. The Conservatives finished second with 99 seats, as they saw the evaporation of many of the electoral inroads they had made between 2006 and 2011 east of the Ontario–Manitoba border. The government party's support had contracted mainly to Alberta and rural ridings in Ontario, the Prairies, and BC. The NDP "orange crush" that had captivated Quebec four years earlier faded in 2015. Thomas Mulcair's NDP saw the 59 seats it had won in that province in 2011 cut to 16. Support for the sovereignist Bloc Québécois, the leading party in Quebec between 1993 and 2008, dropped to its lowest proportion of Quebec's votes since its foundation. Gilles Duceppe, who had come out of retirement to lead the Bloc again, lost his own riding. Although the Bloc won more seats than it had in 2011, this was insufficient to gain official party status in the House of Commons.

The 2015 election demonstrated that campaigns matter and that the potential for electoral volatility, in an era of declining and weak party attachments, remains high.

POLITICAL PARTIES AND CANADIAN DEMOCRACY

Federal election campaigns are intense and unpredictable events that provide most Canadians with their main exposure to political parties. During election campaigns, parties battle online, on the airwaves, and in local communities to elect their candidates and win the right to form a government and implement their policies. Parties are the cornerstone of representative democracy and play a central role in the governance of the country. The Canada Elections Act underscores their primary role as electoral machines. Under Canadian law, a **political party** is "an organization one of whose fundamental purposes is to participate in public affairs by endorsing one or more of its members as candidates and supporting their election."

The high profile of parties at election time tends to overshadow the other functions they perform that sustain democratic life. When elections are not underway, parties develop policies on key issues and provide their members with opportunities to influence those policies and select their leaders and local candidates. Since Canada's largest parties have local organizations in communities

POLITICAL PARTY
An organization that endorses one or more of its members as candidates and supports their election.

across the country, they have also been expected to promote national unity and represent the country's diversity by ensuring that the interests of Canadians from different territorial, linguistic, socioeconomic, ethnocultural, and gender backgrounds are reflected in their policies, organizational structures, and personnel.

How much political parties have lived up to their promise as agents of representative democracy and nation-building has been debated since Confederation. Parties in Canada, as in most democracies, have had trouble recruiting members. Between 1989 and 2004, fewer and fewer Canadians joined parties. Just 10 percent of Canadians said that they had belonged to a political party in the last five years (Samara Canada, 2014). Those who do join these organizations tend to be dissatisfied with their influence on policy development (Cross & Young, 2006). A decline in the Canadian public's attachments to these parties was also observed between the mid-1960s and late 1990s (Dalton, 2000). By 2011, 25 percent of Canadians said they did not identify with any of the federal parties (Clarke, Scotto, Reifler, & Kornberg, 2011). Canadians believe they need political parties, but they do not like or trust them (Howe & Northrup, 2000; World Values Survey, 2006).

Canadian parties have also been criticized for failing to offer voters distinct policy choices (Carty, 2006). Since the 1970s, their role as policy innovators has been largely usurped by other institutions, including the Prime Minister's Office, the bureaucracy, royal commissions, the courts, interest groups, and think tanks (Meisel & Mendelsohn, 2001). In the late 1980s and early 1990s, the ability of the country's more established parties to unite Canadians was challenged by the Reform and Bloc Québécois parties that championed regional rather than national causes.

This chapter explores the role of political parties in Canadian democracy. It discusses the ideas and policies they have championed, why some parties have thrived while others have failed, and whether they have given their members a powerful voice in party affairs. It will show that party competition has changed over time and that the federal parties have also adapted to changing social and political circumstances to appeal to voters and potential members. Whether they have evolved enough to engage Canadian citizens in the future will be for you to judge.

POLITICAL PARTIES AND PARTY SYSTEMS

Political Parties

BROKERAGE THEORY
A perspective that maintains that parties are not differentiated by ideology and that they do not adopt consistent policy positions over time.

One way of understanding political parties is to examine how they try to appeal to voters. Many students of Canadian politics have described the federal parties as "brokers." **Brokerage theory** maintains that the parties are not differentiated by principled stands on issues or ideologies, and do not attempt to appeal to a single region, language group, religious community, or economic class over time. According to this perspective, federal elections are a competition between teams of office-seekers that present middle-of-the road platforms and discuss issues in a way that will help them attract the greatest number of voters (Thorburn, 1991), rather than events where voters are presented with a clear choice between competing worldviews.

The reasons why brokerage parties strike these compromises have been attributed to their desire for electoral success (Clarke, Jenson, LeDuc, & Pammett, 1984, 1991, 1996) and the need to maintain national unity and social stability in a deeply divided society (Siegfried, 1966). According to Ken Carty, the Liberal party has operated as a "big tent" party that provided a forum for balancing the many competing interests in Canada, and a political home for all kinds of Canadians (2015). Both the Liberal and Progressive Conservative parties have been described as brokerage parties that adopted similar, middle-of-the-road programs and routinely shifted their policy positions.

Not all scholars agree that the federal parties fit this mould. They argue that Canada's major parties have been divided ideologically (Christian & Campbell, 1990; Benoit & Laver, 2006), particularly in the late twentieth century (Cochrane, 2010). For example, the NDP has been characterized as a social democratic party (Brodie & Jenson, 2007) and party activists have labelled themselves as social democrats or socialists (Whitehorn, 2007). Parties such as the Bloc Québécois and the Reform party, which have directed their appeals to specific regional or linguistic groups, have also challenged brokerage politics (Carty, Cross, & Young, 2000). One question in Canadian politics is whether the Conservative party formed in 2003 governed from the centre or the ideological right (see Box 8-1: The Conservatives: Moderate or Ideological?).

Party Systems

Almost every democracy has a **party system,** or a pattern of electoral competition that emerges between two or more parties. Party systems can be assessed and compared across countries in several ways. The simplest method for classifying a country's party system involves counting the number of parties that compete for office (Duverger, 1954). If there are two or primarily two parties, we can speak of a **two-party system.** If there are three or more parties, Duverger (1954) speaks of a multiparty system. Two-party systems, such as those in the United States, in the United Kingdom between 1945 and 1979, and in most of the former British colonies of the Caribbean, typically produce single-party governments (Siaroff, 2005). The party that wins a majority of seats in a legislature following an election forms a single-party government.

Single-party governments tend to enhance government accountability because it is easier for voters to identify which party is responsible for public policies. Alternation in power between two relevant parties is also more common in two-party systems. If electors are unhappy with the performance of the governing party, they can vote for its rival in the next election. Parties in two-party competitive environments also tend to adopt moderate, centrist policies (Mair, 2002).

PARTY SYSTEM
A pattern of electoral competition that emerges between two or more parties.

TWO-PARTY SYSTEM
A pattern of competition in which there are two, or primarily two, parties.

The Conservatives: Moderate or Ideological?

Do the policies of the Conservative party reflect a middle-of-the-road orientation characteristic of brokerage parties, or a vision grounded in the ideologies of classical liberalism and social conservatism? The former refers to a preference for a smaller, free market-oriented government, while the latter refers to traditional views about family and morality. A review of their record in government provides support for both interpretations (Farney & Malloy, 2011).

With respect to government spending, the Conservatives inherited a budgetary surplus but ran record budget deficits until 2015. Meanwhile, their approach to taxation and regulatory powers shows a preference for limited government. They cut the GST and small business and corporate income tax rates, and supported measures curtailing the role of the state. These include cutting public sector jobs, rolling back the age of eligibility for Old Age Security from 65 to 67, cancelling the 2005 Liberal national child care plan, abolishing the long gun registry and long-form census, and opposing most climate change and environmental assessment regulatory measures.

Political observers have also debated the prominence of social conservatism in a party where many oppose abortion and same-sex marriage. Once again the evidence is mixed. In 2009, the Conservative government cut funding to gay pride parades, and in 2010 it announced that it would not fund abortions in its child and maternal health care initiatives for developing countries. Several backbench Conservative MPs have introduced private member's bills to reopen the abortion debate, but Prime Minister Harper did not pursue new abortion laws in Canada or revisit the same-sex marriage law.

Farney and Malloy (2011) argue that social conservatism is buried within a broader agenda to appeal to traditional families through a direct child care allowance to parents and income-splitting tax policies that favour single-breadwinner families (but not single parents). The "tough on crime" measures of the Conservative government (including mandatory minimum jail sentences) despite a decline in the crime rate could also be viewed as evidence of a social conservative agenda.

Multiparty systems are those in which three or more parties compete for power. Since it is less likely that a single party will win an outright majority of seats in the legislature, these systems are more likely to produce coalition governments. Coalition governments are formed when two or more parties enter into a formal agreement to share power. Coalitions have ruled many democratic countries, including Germany, the Netherlands, Italy, Australia, New Zealand, and the United Kingdom. Canada has had just one coalition government at the federal level (1917–1920), although Ontario, Manitoba, Saskatchewan, and British Columbia have been governed at times by coalitions.

Multiparty systems have been praised for allowing for a more diverse range of voices to be heard. Critics of multiparty systems say they may undermine government accountability and the possibility of alternation in government, since coalition partners often do not change from election to election. Extreme ideological political parties with narrow bases of support are also more likely to thrive in multiparty systems.

Party systems may also be classified according to the relative strength of the parties, the ideological spread between them, and their support bases

(Blondel, 1968; Lipset & Rokkan, 1967; Sartori, 1976). Jean Blondel (1968) identified four distinct patterns of party competition that take into account the relative strength of parties. In **two-party systems**, two major parties win 90 percent or more of the popular vote and the gap between their vote share is small. In the **two-and-a-half party system**, there are two major parties that win 75–80 percent of the vote, and one or more much smaller third parties. Multiparty systems in which four or more parties play a significant part in the political process may be subdivided into two types. In a **multiparty system with a dominant party**, there is one large party that receives about 40 percent of the vote, and the two largest parties together win about two-thirds of voter support. In a **multiparty system without a dominant party**, there is no dominant party and three or four parties are well placed to form coalitions.

The Evolution of the Canadian Party System

Over the course of Canadian history, party competition has evolved from a two-party contest to a multiparty system like those commonly found in European democracies. Until 1921, Canada had a two-party system that produced a series of stable majority governments. Power alternated between the Conservatives (subsequently renamed the Progressive Conservatives) and the Liberals, and both parties won similar shares of the popular vote in most provinces. However, Canadian society was changing rapidly in the early twentieth century, and the parties came under pressure to respond to the demands of people who felt shut out from decision-making processes. As well, the conscription crisis in World War I contributed to the Conservatives' electoral weakness in Quebec for much of the twentieth century.

Between 1921 and 1993, Canada had a two-and-a-half party system with the two leading parties regularly winning more than three-quarters of the popular vote combined. Smaller parties including the Progressives, Co-operative Commonwealth Federation (CCF), Social Credit, NDP, Reform, and Bloc Québécois emerged during this period to give voice to regional, class or ethno-linguistic grievances. While these and other smaller parties attracted enough support to reduce the combined vote share for the Liberals and Progressive Conservatives (PCs), they never formed a government on their own. The Liberals dominated electoral competition for most of the twentieth century, save for brief periods when they lost power to the PCs (see Table 8-1).

Some political observers have suggested that Canada moved to a multiparty system in 1993 (Carty, Cross, & Young, 2000). The elections held between 1997 and 2000 could be interpreted as having produced a multiparty dominant system, with the Liberals as the dominant party winning an average 40 percent of the vote; their principal competitors were divided among four smaller parties. The elections held between 2004 and 2008 produced three minority governments in which no single party won 40 percent of the vote and three parties were in a position to form an alternative governing coalition.

TWO PARTY SYSTEMS
Two major parties win 90 percent or more of the popular vote and the gap between their vote shares is small.

TWO-AND-A-HALF PARTY SYSTEM
Pattern of competition whereby two major parties win at least three-quarters of the vote, and a third party receives a much smaller share of the vote.

MULTIPARTY SYSTEM WITH A DOMINANT PARTY
One large party receives about 40 percent of the vote, and the two largest parties together win about two-thirds of voter support.

MULTIPARTY SYSTEM WITHOUT A DOMINANT PARTY
Competition where there is no dominant party and three or four parties are well placed to form coalitions.

FIGURE 8-1
PARTY POSITIONS IN 2015 CAMPAIGN, BY ISSUE AREA

	CONSERVATIVE	NEW DEMOCRAT	LIBERAL	GREEN	BQ
Economy and Taxation	Balance budget Income splitting for families with minor children Reduce small business taxes Expand free trade agreements and support Trans-Pacific Partnership	Balance budget Raise corporate income tax rates Reduce small business taxes Institute $15/hour federal minimum wage Oppose Trans-Pacific Partnership Cancel income-splitting for families	Run deficit until 2019 Cut middle income tax rate Raise taxes on wealthiest 1% Cancel income splitting for families Encourage free trade	Invest in renewable energy, expand passenger rail, improve infrastructure Oppose Trans-Pacific Partnership Reduce taxes for small and medium size business & raise corporate tax rate Guarantee liveable income at 65	Increase taxes on major corporations, for big banks, oil companies and high income earners
Infrastructure	Commit $53 billion over 10 years in funding for infrastructure	Give cities an extra cent of gas tax Spend $1.5 billion per year for cities and $1.3 billion per year for national public transit Boost municipal funding to $3.7 billion per year	Spend $60 billion on infrastructure over 10 years	Commit $6 billion a year for urban projects	Invest in more federal infrastrucutre in Montreal
Environment	Oppose carbon tax and cap-and-trade Buy international credits to meet greenhouse gas emissions goals	Institute a cap-and-trade emission reduction plan	Set national targets for carbon pricing and develop climate change strategy with provinces	Institute a carbon "fee and dividend" regime Plan 40% GHG reduction by 2025	Support Quebec's cap-and-trade plan
Social Issues & Health Care	Spend $250 million over two years to train skilled workers Set 2015 budget committing $567 million over five years for Aboriginal people and northerners Increase health care funding after 2017 based on economic growth	Develop $15 per day national child care program Restore old age security at 65 Conduct public inquiry on missing and murdered Aboriginal women Spend $1.8 billion over four years for First Nations education Restore home mail delivery and long-form census Spend $2.6 billion over four years toward universal drug coverage; restore annual 6% increase in health care transfers	Restore old age security at 65 Make new child benefit based on household income Require no repayment of student loans until earning at least $25 000 per year Conduct public inquiry on missing and murdered Aboriginal women Spend $2.6 billion over four years for First Nations education Restore home mail delivery and long-form census Spend $3 billion over four years to improve health care system	Increase social housing, reduce homelessness Make a national pharmacare plan Eliminate all tuition fees by 2020 Create new child care programs with provinces; give a tax credit for employers creating workplace day care Restore $5.1 billion commitment to First Nations	Restore home mail delivery Restore full health care transfers to provinces

	CONSERVATIVE	NEW DEMOCRAT	LIBERAL	GREEN	BQ
Justice	Pass "life means life" legislation Establish "barbaric cultural practices" tipline	Decriminalize possession of small amounts of marijuana	Legalize marijuana	Legalize and regulate marijuana	
Security and Anti-Terrorism	Support providing CF-18 jets in fight against Islamic State Support Bill C-51	Oppose Canadian role in fight against Islamic State Oppose Bill C-51	Oppose sending CF-18 jets to fight Islamic State Support Bill C-51 but with more oversight of security agencies	Support more oversight of security agencies	Tighten security measures surrounding rail transport of hazardous materials
Foreign Affairs and Defence	Increase escalator in national defence budget to 3% Support combat role against ISIS in Iraq and Syria Spend $193 million over five years to improve veterans services	Participate only in UN-mandated operations Increase contribution to UN peacekeeping Reopen veterans services offices End bombing in Iraq and Syria	Support multinational institutions Reopen veterans services offices End bombing in Iraq and Syria	Focus on UN peacekeeping contributions Oppose military mission against ISIS Increase spending on disaster assistance Reopen veterans services offices	Support military intervention in Syria and Iraq
Governance	Elect or abolish Senate	Abolish Senate Adopt mixed-member proportional representation electoral system	Make non-partisan appointments to Senate Change current electoral system	Eliminate single member plurality electoral system	Support Quebec sovereignty

Sources: Whittington, Les. 2015, June 20. "Federal Parties rolling out the election pledges." *Toronto Star*, p. A4; The Canadian Press. 2015, September 28. "Bloc Québécois election promises from the campaign trail so far." Retrieved from: http://www.cbc.ca/news/politics/canada-election-2015-bloc-election-promises-1.3246596; CBC News (October 9, 2015). Read the political parties' 2015 platforms, www.cbc.cca/news/politics/Canada-election-2015-party-platforms-1.3264887; Maclean's magazine (2015, October 26). Ultimate issue primer cheat sheet.

For this reason, this period conforms to a multiparty system with no dominant party. The 2011 and 2015 elections produced two majority governments led by the Conservative and Liberal parties, respectively. The multiparty system persists for the time being. Future elections will tell us whether any one party can establish or reestablish electoral dominance in that multiparty system, or whether Canada will revert to a two-and-a-half party system.

Party System Instability Since 1993

The federal party system has seen considerable instability since the "electoral earthquake" of 1993. The Liberals were returned to power with a majority and the distinction of being the only party that was able to elect members from every province and territory. Two parties that were mainstays of the third era of party competition were nearly decimated. Neither the Progressive Conservatives nor the NDP elected enough MPs to qualify for official party status.[1] The election was also remarkable for the breakthrough made by new regional parties. The Bloc Québécois, created in 1990 by the defections of Progressive Conservative and Liberal MPs who were unhappy with the failure of the Meech Lake Accord, won 54 seats and became the Official Opposition. Bloc leader Lucien Bouchard campaigned on a platform of Quebec sovereignty and ran candidates only in Quebec. Astoundingly, Canada had an Official Opposition whose goal was to take the country apart. The West, too, was raising its voice in protest against the established system. The Reform party, formed in 1987 to express feelings of political and economic alienation in the West, won 51 of its 52 seats in Western Canada.

The newcomers challenged the brokerage politics practised by the Liberals and Progressive Conservatives. The leadership of the older parties had generally supported the growth of the social welfare state, an active role for government in managing the economy, official bilingualism and multiculturalism, and the constitutional reform initiatives in the 1980s and early 1990s. However, this public consensus wore thin in the 1980s as issues such as deficit reduction, welfare reform, and lower taxation began to attract more support within state institutions and the general public. The Reform party benefited from voter dissatisfaction with parties that were perceived to be giving in too much to Quebec's constitutional demands. In contrast, the Bloc capitalized on anger about the failure of constitutional reform efforts to recognize Quebec's distinctiveness and transfer more powers to the provinces.

The Liberals continued to draw on their strength in Ontario and Atlantic Canada to win majority governments in 1997 and 2000. Liberal dominance

---

[1]Recognition of official party status in Parliament allows parties certain privileges. In the House of Commons, a party normally must have at least 12 seats to be recognized as an official party. Recognition means that the party will get more time to ask questions during question period in the House, be represented on committees, and be provided money for research and staff.

was assured by the splitting of the right-of-centre vote between Reform and the Progressive Conservatives. The Bloc Québécois remained the leading party in Quebec, and the Reform party continued to dominate the West. After the Reform's failure to win a single seat east of the Manitoba–Ontario border in the 1997 election, party leader Preston Manning proposed that the PCs and Reform run joint candidates in the next election. Progressive Conservative leader Joe Clark rejected this proposal, as well as Manning's invitation to form a new party that would unite "right-wing" forces and mount a stronger opposition to the Liberals. In 1998, Manning launched the United Alternative (UA) movement with the support of some members of the national and provincial Progressive Conservative parties. At a UA convention in 2000, the Reform party dissolved itself to create a new party called the Canadian Conservative Reform Alliance.

Attempts to unseat the Liberals seemed destined for failure. The Liberals were re-elected in 2000 with an even larger majority and the Canadian Alliance managed to win just two seats in Ontario, bolstering the perception that the Alliance was yet another Western Canadian protest party. After facing an internal party revolt, Alliance leader Stockwell Day called a leadership race for 2002. Stephen Harper, a former Reform MP and president of the National Citizens Coalition, defeated Day to become the new leader of the Alliance. Some Alliance and Progressive Conservative MPs dreamt of merging the two parties. Together, they believed, they might defeat the Liberals. However, many PCs opposed a merger because they felt that the Alliance shunned the pragmatic and more moderate positions of the Progressive Conservatives. Moreover, new Progressive Conservative leader Peter MacKay had promised a rival candidate during the 2003 PC leadership convention that, in exchange for his support on the final ballot to select the leader, no merger with the Alliance would take place. MacKay did not keep his word. In 2003, Harper and MacKay agreed to a merger that would create a united Conservative party.

THE LIBERALS LOSE GROUND   The once-dominant Liberals won just one minority government in the four elections held between 2004 and 2011. Over this same period, the Conservatives built on their support in rural and small town Ontario and made significant gains in urban and suburban centres, and with ethnic communities and new Canadians who were once mainstays of Liberal support. The NDP enjoyed a steady rise in popular support and parliamentary representation under the leadership of the late Jack Layton, with a major breakthrough in 2011 and became the offical opposition in the House of Commons.

The erosion of Liberal support can be traced to the release in 2004 of the auditor general's report on the misallocation of public funds on federal government advertising in Quebec. The scandal severely damaged the Liberals' reputation, and they were scaled back to a minority government following the 2004 election. In November 2005, the Liberal minority government was defeated on a non-confidence motion and voters headed back to the polls in January 2006.

The Conservatives set the election agenda in the early weeks by announcing new policies each day, including a cut to the GST, a modest child care allowance for parents, and a promise to introduce new legislation on government accountability. Right in the middle of the campaign, the Royal Canadian Mounted Police announced a criminal investigation into finance minister Ralph Goodale's office for potentially engaging in insider trading before making an announcement on the taxation of income trusts. The probe later cleared Goodale's office of wrongdoing, but the allegations distracted attention from the Liberals' policy announcements and allowed the Conservatives to mount further attacks on Liberal corruption. On January 23, 2006, Canadians elected a Conservative minority government, ending 13 consecutive years of Liberal rule.

THE BATTLE FOR A MAJORITY   The next election was not scheduled to take place until October 2009.[2] However, Stephen Harper made a controversial request to the governor general on September 7, 2008, to dissolve Parliament and call another election for October 14, hoping to secure a majority mandate. During the campaign, the opposition parties attacked the government for backing out of Canada's commitments under the Kyoto Protocol to cut greenhouse gas emissions, for corporate tax cuts, and for its tough stance on sentences for young offenders convicted of murder. In the final weeks of the campaign, the economy emerged as the most important issue as a financial crisis that had begun in the United States spread to Canadian and world stock markets. Stock market indices plummeted and Canadians became increasingly anxious about their investments, pension plans, and the possibility of an impending recession. On October 14, the Conservatives won a second minority government with 143 seats. They consolidated their hold in the West and displaced the Liberals as the leading party in Ontario. However, they fell short of their bid for a majority. The Liberals held on to Official Opposition status, but were reduced to 77 seats.

The minority Conservative government was defeated in March 2011 on a non-confidence motion after a House committee found the government in contempt for refusing to reveal the cost of budget plans, including the purchase of fighter jets and the construction of new prisons. Tapping into Canadians' frustrations with having a fourth election in seven years, the Conservatives appealed for a "strong, stable, national, majority government." They invoked warnings about the instability that would follow from a Liberal-led coalition backed by socialists and separatists (Dornan, 2011).

---

[2]In November 2006, Parliament passed a law to hold elections on the third Monday in October every four years, starting in October 2009. At the time, Harper argued that the law would prevent governing parties from calling snap elections when public opinion polls favoured them.

They ran a series of negative attack ads painting Liberal leader Michael Ignatieff as a snob and opportunist who was out of touch with the concerns of Canadians after being out of the country for 30 years. The strategy worked and gave the Conservatives their coveted majority. The geographic breadth of the Conservative victory was impressive: They increased their vote share in every province except Quebec and advanced their urban growth strategy by winning 21 seats in the suburban region around Toronto and 9 seats in Toronto, where no Conservative candidate had been elected since 1988 (Ellis & Woolstencroft, 2011).

The results for the opposition were no less dramatic. The historical positions of the Liberals and NDP were reversed; the Liberals were reduced to 34 seats, losing seats in every region of the country. For the first time in its history, the NDP won more seats and a higher vote share than the Liberals. Fifty-nine of its MPs were elected in Quebec, a province where the party only ever elected one NDP MP in a general election. The "orange" wave in Quebec all but sank the Bloc, which was reduced to just four seats in the House. Finally, although support for the Green party dropped significantly from 2008, its leader became the first elected Green party member.

The 2015 election results, as summarized in Figure 8-1, saw the Liberal party rise from the ashes of its disastrous showing in 2011 to win 39.5 percent of the national vote and increased support across the country. For Prime Minister Harper and the Conservatives, the loss ended their nearly 10-year hold on power, which had seen taxes cut, crime punished more severely, and a more combative role for Canada on the world stage. The New Democrats had entered the campaign with high hopes, having won 103 seats in 2011 including 59 in Quebec. After leading in opinion polls for most of August, the party stumbled at the end, winning only 16 seats in Quebec and 8 in Ontario. The results were also disappointing for the Bloc, which finished a distant third in popular support in Quebec and failed to gain official party status. Popular support for the Green party remained virtually unchanged from 2011, with the party electing just one MP—leader Elizabeth May.

POLITICAL PARTIES: IDEAS AND ELECTORAL PERFORMANCE

The Roots

The origins of party competition date back to the early nineteenth century and the struggle to achieve responsible government in British North America (see Chapter 2). Two political tendencies gradually emerged out of this political conflict. The privileged members of the executive and legislative councils led the conservative or Tory element. Tories believed in the need for a strong executive authority that could check democratic assemblies and promote economic development. Their rivals were the Reformers, who aimed to make the

TABLE 8-1
VALID VOTES CAST (%) AND CANDIDATES ELECTED (*N*) BY POLITICAL PARTY IN CANADIAN GENERAL ELECTIONS, 1945–2015

YEAR (N)	CONS.	PROG. CONS.	REFORM/ ALLIANCE	LIBERAL	NDP	CCF	BQ	SOCIAL CREDIT	GREEN	OTHER
1945 (245)		27.7 (67)		41.4 (125)		15.7 (28)		4.1 (13)		11.1 (12)
1949 (262)		29.7 (41)		50.1 (190)		13.4 (13)		2.4 (10)		4.4 (8)
1953 (265)		31 (51)		50 (171)		11.3 (23)		5.4 (15)		2.3 (5)
1957 (265)		38.9 (112)		40.9 (105)		10.7 (25)		6.6 (19)		2.8 (4)
1958 (265)		53.7 (208)		33.6 (48)		9.5 (8)		2.6 (0)		0.6 (1)
1962 (265)		37.3 (116)		37.4 (99)	13.4 (19)			11.7 (30)		0.2 (1)
1963 (265)		32.9 (95)		41.7 (129)	13.1 (17)			11.9 (24)		0.4 (0)
1965 (265)		32.4 (97)		40.2 (131)	17.9 (21)			3.7 (5)		5.8 (11)
1968 (264)		31.4 (72)		45.5 (155)	17 (22)			0.9 (0)		5.2 (15)
1972 (264)		35 (107)		38.5 (109)	17.7 (31)			7.6 (15)		1.2 (2)
1974 (264)		35.4 (95)		43.2 (141)	15.4 (16)			5.1 (11)		0.9 (1)
1979 (282)		35.9 (136)		40.1 (114)	17.9 (26)			4.6 (6)		1.5 (0)
1980 (282)		32.5 (103)		44.3 (147)	19.8 (32)			1.7 (0)		1.7 (0)
1984 (282)		50 (211)		28 (40)	18.8 (30)			0.1 (0)		3 (1)
1988 (295)		43 (169)	2.1% (0)	31.9 (83)	20.4 (43)			0.03 (0)		4.7 (0)
1993 (295)		16 (2)	18.7% (52)	41.3 (177)	6.9 (9)		13.5 (54)			3.6 (1)
1997 (301)		18.8 (20)	19.4 (60)	38.5 (155)	11 (21)		10.7 (44)		0.4 (0)	1.2 (1)
2000 (301)		12.2 (12)	25.5 (66)	40.8 (172)	8.5 (13)		10.7 (38)		0.8 (0)	1.5 (0)
2004 (308)	29.6 (99)			36.7 (135)	15.7 (19)		12.4 (54)		4.3 (0)	1.3 (1)
2006 (308)	36.3 (124)			30.2 (103)	17.5 (29)		10.5 (51)		4.5 (0)	1 (1)
2008 (308)	37.7 (143)			26.3 (77)	18.2 (37)		10 (49)		6.8 (0)	1 (2)
2011 (308)	39.6 (166)			18.9 (34)	30.6 (103)		6.1 (4)		3.9 (1)	1 (0)
2015 (338)	31.9 (99)			39.5 (184)	19.7 (44)		4.7 (10)		3.4 (1)	1 (0)

SOURCE: Based on data retrieved from the Library of Parliament, 2009. http://www2.parl.gc.ca/Parlinfo/compilations/ElectionsAndRidings/ResultsParty.aspx?Language=E. Results for 2015 are unofficial.

government more democratic and responsive to the popular will (Thorburn, 2001). They planned to achieve their ideal through responsible government, whereby the governor would choose his advisers in the executive council from men who had the confidence of the elected assembly. The achievement of responsible government in Nova Scotia in 1848, and in the Province of Canada in 1849, created the need for more, well-organized parties to support or oppose the governor's policy.

After the adoption of responsible government, loose alliances of politicians sharing similar tendencies gradually coalesced into parties. By 1854, John A. Macdonald and George-Étienne Cartier had forged an alliance of commercial and industrial interests from English-speaking Canada East, conservative French Canadians from Canada East, Tories and moderate Reformers from Canada West, and members of the Family Compact and Château Clique elites,[3] which became the Liberal–Conservative party. After Confederation, the Liberal–Conservative party lost its Liberal elements and by 1878 became known as the Conservative party. English- and French-speaking Reformers from Canada West and Rouges from Canada East opposed the Conservatives. After Confederation this loose coalition welcomed allies from the Maritime provinces, but did not coalesce into a united Liberal party until 1887. The modern-day Liberals are the successors of these nineteenth-century politicians who advocated responsible government (Cook, 1977; Pickersgill, 1962).

Canadian Election Results by Party, 1867–2008
**www.sfu.ca/~aheard/elections/
1867-present.html**

Progressive Conservative Party

The Conservative party (renamed Progressive Conservative in 1942) was the country's oldest party until it merged with the Canadian Alliance in 2003 to form a new Conservative party. Early Conservatives dominated the electoral contests of the nineteenth century, but the twentieth century belonged to the Liberals; between 1921 and their demise, the Conservative/Progressive Conservative (PC) party formed the government on just eight occasions. Just as a party's electoral fortunes rise and fall over time, its ideas change too. Whereas early Canadian conservatism was based on support for a strong central government, close ties with Britain, and protectionist trade policies, by the late twentieth century the PCs championed the decentralization of powers to the provinces and free trade with the United States. The party's failure to manage the resurgence of Western alienation and Quebec nationalism in the late 1980s and early 1990s ultimately led to its disappearance from the federal scene.

Canada's first government was formed by the Liberal–Conservative party headed by John A. Macdonald, the leading instigator of Confederation. Its National Policy favoured a protective tariff for Canadian industry,

---

[3]The Family Compact and the Château Clique comprised members of wealthy families in Upper Canada and Lower Canada, respectively. They controlled the government through their roles as members of the executive council and legislative council.

government support for railway building, immigration, and Western settlement. The Conservatives' success hinged on Macdonald's skills at building a stable coalition of French–English and Protestant–Catholic interests. However, his decision not to commute the death sentence of Louis Riel—the Catholic, French-speaking leader of the Métis uprising of 1885—eroded the party's popularity in Quebec (see Chapter 2). The party's appeal in Quebec was further undermined by its support for compulsory enlistment during World War I. By the early 1920s, the Conservatives' high tariff policy had also alienated Western farmers.

The Great Depression, a severe economic depression that originated in the United States and spread worldwide, struck in 1929. The Conservatives, led by New Brunswick–born self-made millionaire R.B. Bennett, demanded that the Liberal government raise tariffs to kick-start Canadian industry and provide jobs to unemployed Canadians through public works projects. These arguments convinced enough Canadians that the Conservatives could solve the country's economic hardships, and the Conservatives were elected to office in 1930. The Bennett government drew on the power of government to battle the Depression, but many Canadians thought the government had done too little too late and re-elected the Liberals in 1935.

The Conservatives remained shut out of power until 1957. During two decades of Liberal dominance, the Conservatives had six leaders and underwent three name changes (National Conservative, National Government, and Progressive Conservative). In 1956, the Progressive Conservatives chose John Diefenbaker, a firebrand prairie populist from Saskatchewan, as their leader. In the 1957 election, Diefenbaker campaigned on a platform attacking Liberal arrogance and insensitivity to the economic problems of Western and Atlantic Canada. The strategy paid off and he won a minority government. He followed this up in 1958 with the largest landslide victory in Canadian history.

During the Diefenbaker era (1957–1963), the government increased old-age pensions and unemployment insurance benefits, provided financial assistance to regions outside central Canada, and helped boost Western Canadian agriculture by arranging wheat sales to China. While in office, his government passed a statutory Bill of Rights, granted the vote to First Nations Canadians, and helped force South Africa out of the Commonwealth for its system of racial apartheid. However, a series of fumbles in nuclear and defence policy and a faltering economy eroded Diefenbaker's popularity, and the Progressive Conservatives' brief interlude in power ended with a Liberal minority victory in 1963.

The Progressive Conservative government headed by Brian Mulroney (1984–1993) pursued an ambitious agenda of economic and political reform. It launched two ill-fated attempts at constitutional change designed to meet Quebec's conditions for signing the Constitution Act, 1982, and to address provincial demands for the decentralization of powers. It also abandoned its historic resistance to closer ties with the United States after a royal commission appointed by the previous Liberal government recommended that Canada seek a free trade agreement (FTA). Although Mulroney had opposed the idea when he was vying for his party's leadership, he changed his mind and campaigned for an FTA with the United States during the 1988 federal election. In the end, more Canadians voted for parties that opposed the FTA, but the PCs won the largest number of seats and a second consecutive majority. By the early 1990s, a recession, unpopular policies such as the goods and services tax and free trade, and widespread dissatisfaction with the government's approach to constitutional reform contributed to mounting voter discontent. Although all three federal parties supported the constitutional overtures that had been made to Quebec and the other provinces through the Meech Lake Accord, many English-speaking Canadians objected to constitutional recognition of Quebec as a distinct society. Meech Lake ran into opposition in the Manitoba and Newfoundland legislatures and was not ratified by the 1990 deadline. The PC government's next attempt at constitutional reform—the Charlottetown Accord—was defeated in a national referendum in 1992. Mulroney resigned in 1993 and was succeeded by Kim Campbell, Canada's first (and, to date, only) female prime minister.

In the 1993 election, the PCs suffered the worst electoral defeat for a governing party in Canadian history. The results could not have been more humiliating: They were reduced to two MPs. Between 1993 and 2003, the PCs had four different leaders but failed to win back the support they enjoyed in the 1980s. In an effort to end the vote-splitting on the right that helped the Liberals win three majority governments between 1993 and 2000, in 2003 PC party leader Peter MacKay negotiated with Stephen Harper, the leader of the Canadian Alliance, to dissolve the Progressive Conservatives and merge with the Alliance to form a new Conservative party.

The Reform Party and the Canadian Reform Conservative Alliance

Since the Diefenbaker era, many Western Canadians had supported the Progressive Conservatives, expecting that the Mulroney government would address their grievances. Although the PCs dismantled the hated National Energy Program, to many Westerners it seemed that the party was most concerned with pleasing Quebec nationalists (Flanagan, 2001). To give voice to these feelings of economic and political alienation from the traditional parties, Preston Manning, the son of a former Social Credit premier of Alberta, founded the Reform party in 1987.

Reform's populist program called for more public input into policymaking through citizen initiatives, referendums, recall, and free votes in the House. It also supported a "Triple-E Senate": elected, equal, and effective. The Reform pushed for a free market over government intervention, deficit reduction, and reduced spending on social programs. It also opposed collective or group

SOCIAL CONSERVATISM
An ideology based on a commitment to traditional ideas about the family and morality.

rights in favour of individual rights. The party rejected any kind of special status for Quebec. As well, it was critical of official bilingualism and multiculturalism, affirmative action and preferential programs for minorities, and Aboriginal self-government. The ideology of **social conservatism** was reflected in its position that family and marriage are for heterosexuals exclusively, that a referendum should be held on restricting abortion, and that capital punishment should be reinstated.

Reform achieved a breakthrough in 1993, becoming the third-largest party in the House of Commons. However, it remained a regional party, fielding no candidates in Quebec and electing just one member from Ontario and none in Atlantic Canada. The Reform's decision to dissolve itself and create the Canadian Conservative Reform Alliance in 2000 was part of its bid to unite Reformers and PCs under one party tent. Within a matter of days, however, the party changed its official name to the Canadian Reform Conservative Alliance after media covering the convention pointed out that if the word "party" was added to its name, it would be referred to as the Canadian Conservative Reform Alliance Party, or CCRAP. In the 2000 election, the Alliance increased its support, but managed to win just two seats in Ontario.

The Conservative Party

Conservative Party of Canada
www.conservative.ca

In 2004 the newly formed Conservative party campaigned on a platform of government accountability, lower taxes, increased funding for the military, and stiffer sentences for serious crimes. The absence of campaign themes related to abortion, euthanasia, family values, or multiculturalism showed that the party was trying to present a moderate image for centrist voters. The Conservatives did not win and remained marginal in Quebec, but they made gains in Ontario, winning 24 of the province's 106 seats.

In 2005, the Conservative party eliminated the populist and regionally oriented parts of its platform that had been popular with Reform–Alliance supporters: a Triple-E Senate, citizens' initiatives, recall, and opposition to "unaccountable judges and human rights bureaucrats." It also eliminated most of the social conservative positions on issues like abortion and reached out to Quebec voters by supporting official bilingualism, limiting federal spending powers, and resolving to address what the Conservatives considered a fiscal imbalance between the revenues of the Canadian government and those of provincial governments. The jettisoning of the populist and most of the social conservative elements of their old platform, lingering voter anger with the Liberals over the "sponsorship scandal,"[4] and a focus on governmental accountability, tax cuts, and modest spending initiatives helped the

---

[4]The sponsorship scandal involved Liberal-connected advertising firms paying lobbyists to seek contracts to promote Canadian unity for which little work was actually done. In return, substantial sums of money were given to those involved in the Quebec branch of the Liberal party.

Conservatives win three consecutive elections between 2006 and 2011, while making further inroads in urban Ontario.

While in office, the Conservatives maintained increases for health care transfers and implemented an economic stimulus plan to deal with the 2008–2009 recession that included bailouts for the Canadian auto sector and infrastructure spending, all financed by deficits. Other elements of the Conservative party's program—planning to balance the budget in 2015, reducing the GST and small business and corporate tax rates, introducing a tax-free savings account in 2008, and increasing the maximum annual contribution to $10 000 in 2015—reflected the principles of classical liberalism. The party also pursued generally many FTAs including multilateral agreements with European Union and the Trans-Pacific Partnership. On the social policy front, the Conservatives chose not to create new federal programs, instead giving direct payments to specific groups of individual Canadians. They increased the universal child care benefit that provides parents with $160 a month for each child under age 6, and $60 a month thereafter until age 17, and introduced an income-splitting plan that allows families with children under 18 to assign up to $50 000 of income to the lower earning spouse in order to reduce their tax burden.

The Conservative party's strong support for non-renewable energy projects and fast-tracking environmental assessment reviews pitted it against environmentalists seeking a slowdown or moratorium on the development of the Alberta oil sands and the proposed Northern Gateway, Keystone, and Energy East oil pipelines. The 2015 budget did not refer to climate change or new initiatives to reduce greenhouse gas emissions (Canadian Press, 2015, April 21). In the same budget, the Conservatives committed an additional $11.8 billion for the Canadian military over 10 years and $292 million to the RCMP, CSIS, and the Canada Border Services Agency over 5 years to fight terrorism and enforce the government's new anti-terrorism law. On the foreign policy front, the Conservatives wound down Canada's combat operations in Afghanistan in 2011, but extended and expanded the mission against the Islamic State in 2015. See Figure 8-1 for a summary of the Conservatives' position on select policy areas in the 2015 federal election campaign.

The Liberal Party

The Liberal Party has been portrayed as the country's "natural governing party" and as one of the most successful political parties in the democratic world. It has formed the government after 23 of 42 elections held since Confederation. Over the twentieth century, it was in office for about seven of every ten years (Carty, 2015). Its record was built on its shrewd adoption of pragmatic and flexible policy positions and skill in bridging social divides between French and English, Catholic and Protestant, and business and labour interests. The weakness of the opposition parties and an electoral system that favoured the Liberals by giving them a larger share of House seats than their

Liberal Party of Canada
www.liberal.ca

popular vote also contributed to the Liberal party's dominance. But its support was often geographically unbalanced, and in decline over the twentieth century. In the first decade of the twenty-first century, it failed to win a majority in four consecutive elections. Whether the party's majority victory in 2015 (albeit based on only 39 percent of the vote) represents a return to Liberal dominance and a revival of "big tent" politics may become clear with the benefit of historical hindsight.

As with their main rivals, the Liberals have shifted their stance on key issues over their long history. For example, the party was initially a strong proponent of provincial rights and free trade policies. By the 1940s, the war effort and the spread of Keynesian economic theory, which urged governments to help stabilize economic cycles of "boom and bust" by spending money during bad times and cutting back during good times, transformed the Liberals into proponents of a strong central government. In the 1988 election, the Liberals campaigned against free trade. After their defeat, they returned to their free trade roots and later endorsed the North American Free Trade Agreement with the United States and Mexico.

Alexander Mackenzie formed Canada's first Liberal administration following the downfall of Macdonald's Conservative government in late 1873, triggered by the Pacific railway scandal. Macdonald had been forced to resign after the Liberal opposition revealed that a lucrative contract to build a railway to the Pacific coast had been awarded to a firm headed by a major contributor to the Conservative election campaign in 1872. The Liberals prevailed in the 1874 election, but were ousted from office four years later. They returned to power in 1896 under the leadership of the francophone Roman Catholic Wilfrid Laurier.

Laurier went on to win the next three elections by taking a cue from Conservative leader Macdonald's formula for success—build a nationwide coalition of supporters, support an expansionary role for government, and accommodate French and English interests. Some of Laurier's major policy initiatives included backing an aggressive immigration policy and supporting the transcontinental railway—the very initiatives that the Liberals had opposed in the 1880s (Clarkson, 2001). The Laurier Liberals negotiated a reciprocity agreement with the United States that provided for the reduction, and in some cases, the removal of import tariffs on raw and processed goods, but were defeated in the 1911 election after the Conservatives accused them of being too close to the Americans. Their anti-conscription stance in the 1917 election, while popular in Quebec, cost them votes in English Canada, and they were reduced to a largely Quebec-based caucus.

When William Lyon Mackenzie King succeeded Laurier as leader in 1919, he inherited a party divided by race and language. Despite these obstacles, he went on to become the longest-serving prime minister, from 1921 to 1948, except for two brief periods in opposition. King's success has been credited to his legendary skills in reconciling different interests. He rebuilt the Liberals as an alliance of English and French and accommodated the interests of ideologically opposed groups such as the Western free trade farmers and protectionist manufacturers from central Canada. His governments straddled the ideological centre by combining responsiveness to business concerns with social welfare policies such as the Old Age Pensions Act (1927), the unemployment insurance program (1940), and the universal family allowance benefits program (1944).

Liberal prime minister Louis St. Laurent (1948–1957) maintained the King government's mix of social welfare policies and a commitment to close economic ties with the United States. After the Progressive Conservatives defeated the Liberals in 1957, the Liberals remained in opposition until 1963, when Lester Pearson defeated the increasingly unpopular Diefenbaker. During Pearson's time in office (1963–1968), the Liberal government passed legislation establishing the Canada Pension Plan (1965) and public medical insurance (1966), and negotiated the Auto Pact with the United States (1965).

After Pearson's retirement, Pierre Trudeau, who had served as minister of justice, won a hard-fought leadership contest in 1968 to become the new leader of the Liberal party. Educated at prestigious institutions in the United States, France, and England, Trudeau had backpacked and hitchhiked around the world as a young man. Suave and free-spirited, Trudeau seemed to capture the spirit of the 1960s, and he swept into office on a wave of "Trudeaumania" in the 1968 election.

Trudeau's approach to constitutional reform and French Canada's place in Confederation was inspired by the principles of liberal individualism and hostility toward the granting of special constitutional status to Quebec. His approach to governance was based on progressive social policies and interventionist economic policies, such as regional economic development programs, the National Energy Program, and the Foreign Investment Review Agency, as discussed in Chapter 4.

The Progressive Conservatives defeated the Liberals in 1979, and Trudeau subsequently announced his intention to resign. However, before another leadership convention could be held, Joe Clark's minority government was defeated on a non-confidence motion and Trudeau was asked to stay on and fight a new election in 1980. The Liberals were re-elected with a majority, but did not win a single seat west of Manitoba. The last Trudeau government helped defeat the separatist forces in the 1980 Quebec referendum on sovereignty association. It also negotiated an agreement with nine provincial premiers to patriate the Constitution with an entrenched amending formula and the Charter of Rights and Freedoms.

Following Trudeau's resignation in early 1984 and two consecutive election losses to the PCs in 1984 and 1988, the Liberal party chose Jean Chrétien, a former cabinet minister with a folksy, populist speaking style, to succeed John Turner in 1990. In the 1993 election, Chrétien campaigned on the "Red Book" platform, which balanced pro-business policies with concerns for Aboriginal peoples, women, and universal medicare. Widespread public dissatisfaction with the policies of the Mulroney government and the collapse of the New Democrats helped Chrétien win a strong majority of seats (with 41.3 percent of the vote) with representation from every province.

The Chrétien governments of the 1990s cut social spending, arguing that a large foreign debt and the need for deficit and debt reduction required fiscally conservative policies. The government also reversed its position on axing the goods and services tax and withdrawing from the North American Free Trade Agreement, and did not implement a promised national child care program. The policy reversals did not seem to hurt the party's electoral fortunes. An upbeat economic picture, budgetary surpluses, and a political opposition that was split among four parties helped the Liberals win majority governments in 1997 and 2000.

Before Chrétien finished his term, he was pressured to resign by his former finance minister, Paul Martin, and his supporters. Martin became Liberal leader in 2003, but his tenure was dogged by the sponsorship scandal. The Liberals were reduced to a minority government in 2004 and were replaced by the Conservatives in 2006. Following a failed attempt by a Liberal-led coalition to replace the minority Conservative government in December 2008, leader Stéphane Dion resigned and was replaced by Michael Ignatieff, a prominent author and former Harvard University professor.

In March 2011, Ignatieff introduced a non-confidence motion declaring the Conservative government to be in contempt of Parliament for refusing to reveal the true cost of various budget items. The motion was supported by Liberal, New Democrat, and Bloc Québécois MPs, resulting in the fall of Stephen Harper's Conservative minority government. The showdown between the Conservative party and the opposition parties marked the first time in the history of the Commonwealth that a government had been found in contempt of Parliament. When the election writ was dropped on March 26, few expected that the fourth election to be held in the last seven years would end so dramatically.

The Liberals' 2011 election platform combined a leftist approach to issues—assistance for lower-income students to attend post-secondary institutions, help to care for aging parents or ill family members, increased contributions to the Canada Pension Plan—with plans for reducing the deficit (Jeffrey, 2011). However, Ignatieff failed to inspire Canadians in the campaign and could not overcome the toll that the Conservatives' negative ad blitz, launched against him in 2009, had taken on his image. The "natural governing party" was reduced to a historic low of 34 seats. The Liberals lost seats in every region of Canada, ceding further ground to the Conservatives and the NDP in urban Ontario. Defeated in his own Toronto riding, Ignatieff resigned the day after the election.

Since 2013, the Liberal party has been led by Justin Trudeau, a former math and French teacher and the eldest son of former prime minister Pierre Trudeau. The Liberals pledged to give tax breaks to the middle class, to cancel income splitting for families with children, and to increase taxes for those who make more than $200 000 a year (LeBlanc & Curry, 2015). The Liberal party platform promised to invest in developing more affordable housing units and improving access to affordable child care spaces. The Liberals opposed the Northern Gateway Pipeline (but supported the proposed Keystone XL Pipeline that would deliver Alberta oil to American refineries), and promised to meet with the provinces to set national targets on carbon emissions and pricing. The party would legalize marijuana, restrict mandatory minimum sentences to serious and violent offences only, and establish a national inquiry on missing and murdered indigenous women. On the foreign policy front, it opposed the Conservative government's motion to extend Canada's combat role in Iraq and expand it into Syria (Liberal Party of Canada, 2015a).

The New Democratic Party

The NDP's roots can be traced to the struggle of farmers and labourers for better working conditions in the early twentieth century. Labour unrest following World War I gave impetus to the trade union movement and the development of smaller labour parties. Cooperation between more ideologically inclined members of the farmer-led Progressives and independent Labour MPs inspired the formation of the Co-operative Commonwealth Federation in 1932 under the leadership of J.S. Woodsworth. The Regina Manifesto of 1933, the most important statement of CCF principles, advocated government planning of the economy through the nationalization of railways, banks, insurance companies, and other industries of large-scale economic importance. As well, the CCF argued for universal pensions, universal health care, and unemployment insurance.

The CCF drew rural support in Saskatchewan and urban support in Vancouver and Winnipeg, while also winning substantial support in Ontario in some elections. Nationally, the CCF never attracted more than 16 percent of the popular vote. The Cold War and the Liberals' adoption of some of the more popular CCF policies led to a decline in CCF support after World War II. By the end of the 1950s, its vote share had dwindled to less than 10 percent.

In order to broaden the party's appeal to urban central Canada, franco-phone Quebec, and the labour movement, the CCF and the Canadian Labour Congress partnered to found the NDP in 1961. The NDP's first leader was Tommy Douglas (1961–1971), a former Baptist minister and CCF premier of Saskatchewan who launched medicare. Since its foundation, the NDP has pressed for a moderate form of social democracy through government regulation, some public ownership, more generous social programs, and redistributive taxation (Whitehorn, 2001, 2007). The NDP played a key role in the minority Parliament of 1972–1974, when it pressured the governing Liberals into passing election finance reforms and increasing old-age pensions and family allowances.

The 1990s proved to be a difficult decade for the party. After leader Ed Broadbent (1975–1989) resigned, he was replaced by Audrey McLaughlin, the

first female leader of a major federal party. In the 1993 election, in which
regional parties achieved a major breakthrough, the NDP elected only nine
MPs. The party's next leader, Alexa McDonough, moved the party closer to
the centre, improving the party's seat share in the 1997 and 2000 elections.
After McDonough's resignation, Jack Layton, who had served as a Toronto
city councillor and president of the Canadian Federation of Municipalities,
defeated five rivals to win the 2003 party leadership race. During his term as
leader, Layton positioned the NDP as a moderate social democratic party,
improving its popular support and legislative representation. NDP election
platforms combined fiscally conservative policies, such as balanced budgets
and no new taxes, with social democratic promises to set up a national prescription drug plan and child care program.

Until 2011, the NDP had formed the government in five Canadian provinces and the Yukon Territory, but had never finished higher than third place in
federal elections. Analysts had attributed the NDP's perennial standing as a
third party to several factors. One of them was its leftist principles, which fell
out of favour during the 1990s when an increasing number of Canadians
became concerned that government spending was a more pressing problem
than limiting the power of big business. The single-member plurality electoral
system, which penalizes parties with geographically dispersed geographic
support (see Chapter 9) was also blamed for the party's inability to translate
popular support into more seats. Another source of party weakness was its
failure to build a strong following in Quebec, in part due to its preference for a
strong federal government—a position that is not widely shared by many
Quebecers. The emergence of the Bloc as a protest party with a generally social
democratic platform also undercut potential support for the NDP in the
province (Whitehorn, 2001, 2007).

The conditions that frustrated NDP ambitions in the past were not factors
in the 2011 campaign. Its platform presented the party as a moderate centre-
left alternative to the Conservatives. Policy differences between the Liberal
and NDP platforms were slight; both favoured a cap and trade system of pollution credits for industry, balancing the budget, increasing corporate tax
rates, spending more on child care spaces, reducing the cost of post-secondary
education, and implementing rehabilitative criminal justice (McGrane, 2011).
The vagaries of the electoral system also worked in the NDP's favour, as its
surge in Quebec allowed it to elect 59 members there. Voters in Quebec were
drawn to Layton's personal appeal and strong campaigning. Meanwhile, the
declining prominence of the sovereignty issue questioned the need for a sovereignist party in Ottawa to defend Quebec's interests (Bélanger & Nadeau,
2011). The particular combination of these conditions allowed the NDP to
capitalize on its social democratic heritage in a province that has been more
receptive to state intervention in the economy since the early 1960s.

Following the death of Jack Layton just four months after the 2011 election, the party selected Quebec MP Thomas Mulcair as leader. Like the Conservatives, NDP policy supports balanced budgets, however, its approach to

economic policy and workers' rights is distinct. The party proposes encouraging Canadian ownership and control of major economic sectors, strengthening the Investment Canada Act to ensure that foreign investment creates and maintains jobs in Canada, creating skilled jobs by developing "Made in Canada" products through the secondary processing of the country's natural resources, and enforcing a fair minimum wage for employees under federal jurisdiction. With respect to taxation, it favours tax reductions to help the middle class, working families, and the poor.

The NDP also differs from the Liberals and Conservatives in its approach to environment and education policy. The party favours establishing binding targets and standards to cut greenhouse gas emissions, creating a carbon market to ensure industry reduces greenhouse gas emissions to targets set by government, and food labelling requirements, including whether the food is genetically modified. New Democrats also support reducing tuition fees and increasing post-secondary education transfer payments to the provinces. On justice and defence issues, the New Democrats opposed the Conservatives' Anti-Terrorism Act and the expanded mission in Iraq and Syria against the Islamic State (New Democratic Party of Canada, 2013).

New Democratic Party of Canada
www.ndp.ca

The Bloc Québécois

In 1990, former PC cabinet minister Lucien Bouchard and a handful of dissident Conservative and Liberal MPs founded the Bloc Québécois following the defeat of the Meech Lake Accord. The demise of Meech Lake persuaded Bouchard that attempts at constitutional reform were futile and that a new federal party should be established to achieve an independent Quebec. The Bloc stunned political observers in 1993 when it emerged with 54 of the province's 75 seats—enough to guarantee it the role of the Official Opposition. While in opposition in the 1990s, the Bloc had three goals: to protect Quebec's interests, to promote the idea of deficit reduction (without affecting social programs), and to oppose the reduction of benefits paid to the unemployed and others hurt by the recession (Crête & Lachapelle, 2001).

Bloc Québécois
www.blocquebecois.org

Following the 1995 referendum on Quebec sovereignty, Parti Québécois leader Jacques Parizeau resigned, and Bouchard left national politics in January 1996 to become the premier of Quebec. The party elite chose Michel Gauthier as Bouchard's successor, but he was replaced a year later by Gilles Duceppe. After a period of relative decline in the 1997 and 2000 elections, the party rebounded in 2004 to elect 54 MPs. The Bloc's comeback was linked to rising support for sovereignty after the disclosure of corruption in the federal sponsorship program the Liberal government had set up following the 1995 referendum. The Bloc maintained its status as the leading party in Quebec federal politics following the 2004, 2006, and 2008 elections, but was reduced to four seats in 2011. Political scientists Bélanger and Nadeau (2011) attributed the Bloc's resounding defeat in 2011 to weariness over the constitutional debate, an uninspired campaign, and the emergence of the NDP as an attractive alternative to the Bloc.

A week after the party's and his own personal defeat, Duceppe resigned. Duceppe's successor, Daniel Paillé, stepped down from the post in 2013 due to health reasons. Party members subsequently elected Mario Beaulieu, a long-time advocate for Quebec independence and strengthening the French language in Quebec, as their new leader. By May 2015, defections and expulsions of Bloc MPs had reduced the BQ caucus to just two MPs. In 2015, Duceppe took over as Bloc leader prior to the general election announcement. In the aftermath of the election—in which it won 10 seats based on 19.3 percent of the Quebec vote—the Bloc will face a difficult road to recovery as it searches to define its role and as its public funding disappeared with the ending of the per vote party subsidies.

The Green Party

Green Party of Canada
www.greenparty.ca

The Green Party of Canada is part of the global environmental movement. Founded in 1983, it has fielded candidates in all or nearly all federal ridings since 2004, and has won an average 4.7 percent of the popular vote in the four elections held between 2004 and 2015. Although Green parties in many democratic countries have elected representatives to their national legislatures, this did not happen in Canada until 2011, when party leader Elizabeth May—an American-born lawyer, writer, and activist—became the first Green MP to be elected to the House (and re-elected in 2015). The single member plurality electoral system has been one barrier to Green representation in the House. Its lingering image as a "fringe" party and relatively low profile in the national media are also factors (Harada, 2006).

The Green party has adapted its platform over time to demonstrate that it is more than a single issue party by broadening its platform beyond ecological issues to address human rights, poverty, health care, and globalization. The party's platform in 2015 presented a mix of environmental and socially progressive principles. It supported reducing global greenhouse gas emissions; introducing a carbon tax; investing in renewable energy like wind, solar, and hydro for sustainable economic development and job creation; and instituting "polluter pays" taxes to reduce the use of fossil fuels. Its leftist position on fiscal reform supports eliminating personal taxes on incomes below $20 000 and raising taxes on the profits of large corporations. The Greens also favour electoral and parliamentary reform—eliminating the single member plurality system and, like the NDP, replacing it with a form of proportional representation, and reducing the power of party leaders to whip votes in the House of Commons (Green Party of Canada, 2015).

PARTY ORGANIZATIONS AND THEIR MEMBERS

Historically, methods of selecting party leaders and candidates, along with procedures for accommodating regional demands, were a far cry from what we would now consider to be democratic. In the 1860s and 1870s, there were no extensive party organizations outside Parliament, and parliamentarians and local elites carried out most party business. Party leaders were selected by the parliamentary caucus or by the governor general in consultation with party leaders (Courtney, 1973). The cabinet or party leaders worked out broad accommodations of diverse regional demands. In the electoral districts, locally prominent individuals selected candidates and offered party supporters jobs and public works contracts (Carty, 1991). After World War I, parties gradually expanded their organizations beyond Parliament and a small number of local notables.

Today's party organizations are far more elaborate. They consist of a parliamentary wing composed of the party leader and caucus, and an extra-parliamentary wing, which consists of an executive and permanent office, the national convention, and local electoral district associations. **Party conventions** are held to elect party officials and debate policy and amendments to the party's constitution. Until fairly recently, parties also held a **leadership convention** at which selected delegates chose the party leader.

Although the vast majority of party members join a party because they believe in its policies (Cross & Young, 2006), party conventions have not evolved into forums where members can influence those policies. That role is jealously guarded by professional pollsters, advertising agencies, media consultants, and the leader's personal staff. The work of party members in debating and adopting policies at these conventions is often forgotten once they are over, and governing parties have traditionally been less open to providing grassroots members with a say. For example, the first Trudeau government (1968–1972) promised that policy positions adopted at the Liberal party convention would be included in the next election platform, but this did not happen (Clarkson, 1979). True to tradition, in 2008, Conservative party members had no say in Prime Minister Harper's campaign announcement about the withdrawal of Canadian troops from Afghanistan by 2011.

Party members have been more successful in influencing policy when their parties have been in opposition. The Liberal party used the period between 1958 and 1962, when it was in opposition, to develop a platform for its return to government. Much of the policy agenda the party pursued in the first years of the Pearson government originated with these consultations on social, economic, and foreign policy.

An **electoral district association** is the local organization of political party members. It recruits members and volunteers, raises campaign funds, elects convention delegates who will debate party policies, and nominates the candidates who will represent the party in the riding. Although party membership fees are low and non-citizens and people as young as 14 years old can join a party, only a tiny minority of Canadians belong to parties between elections. Furthermore, party members do not reflect the broader population. They are disproportionately male, university educated, over the age of 40, and Canadian-born individuals of European ancestry (Cross, 2004).

PARTY CONVENTIONS
Meetings of party members that are held to elect party officials and debate policy and amendments to the party's constitution.

LEADERSHIP CONVENTION
A meeting of party members to select a new leader.

ELECTORAL DISTRICT ASSOCIATION
An association of members of a political party in a territorial area that is represented by a member in the House of Commons.

Canada's federal system has influenced both the structure of party organizations and the parties that Canadians can support at election time. Some federal parties do not have provincial counterparts of the same name, and some provincial parties do not have federal counterparts. This is why some voters may belong to the same party at both levels, others may belong to a party at just one level, and others may belong to different parties at the provincial and federal levels (Carty, 2006). See Box 8-2: Worlds Apart: Federal and Provincial Party Politics.

How Do Parties Choose Their Leaders?

One of the most important powers held by party members is the right to select their leader. It is also one of the main reasons why members say they join a party in the first place (Cross & Young, 2006). For most of the first party system, party leaders were chosen by members of the parliamentary caucus and the retiring leader, usually with the agreement of the governor general. The parties' desire to broaden their support base, as well as membership demands for a greater say in party affairs, has gradually led to the adoption of more inclusive and democratic leadership selection processes. In the early twenty-first century, all party members have a direct say in choosing their leader, who might become prime minister.

Until 1919, party supporters outside Parliament did not have a direct say in leadership selection. The first major change to this process occurred in 1919, when the Liberals chose King to succeed Laurier at a convention attended by thousands of delegates from across the country. In 1927, the Conservatives followed the precedent set by the Liberals, electing R.B. Bennett at a national convention.

Between 1927 and 1956, leadership conventions expanded to include a larger number of delegates elected by party members in each district. While these delegate conventions allowed more party members to select their leaders, the delegates did not mirror the general population. In fact, convention delegates were mostly older males drawn from the middle and upper classes (Courtney, 1995). By the 1960s, party members began to demand more open and representative conventions that would give grassroots supporters a stronger voice in leadership selection and party decision making. The trend toward larger conventions with designated youth, female, and Aboriginal delegates continued through the 1970s and 1980s (Cross, 2004).

As conventions became more inclusive, leadership campaigns became increasingly expensive because the contenders needed to mobilize a larger number of supporters. This meant that fewer leadership candidates could afford to mount a competitive campaign. When the Liberals met in Calgary in 1990 to select a leader, only two candidates—Jean Chrétien and Paul Martin—had a realistic chance of winning. Chrétien spent more than $2.5 million on his campaign and emerged the victor.

BOX 8-2

Worlds Apart:
Federal and Provincial Party Politics

When federal elections are called, Canadians begin the process of weighing the pros and cons of all the parties before they decide how to vote. One of the factors that might affect their choice is their allegiance to a provincial political party. But how should they vote if their favourite provincial party does not exist at the federal level? This is the dilemma facing, for example, supporters of the Saskatchewan Party, the Wildrose Party, and the Coalition Avenir Québec.

The Liberals and New Democrats are the only two parliamentary parties that operate at both the federal and provincial levels. The federal Conservatives are organizationally separate from the provincial Progressive Conservative parties in Atlantic Canada, Ontario, Manitoba, Alberta, and Saskatchewan, and from the British Columbia Conservative Party. Furthermore, although the Bloc works closely with the provincial Parti Québécois to promote Quebec sovereignty, there are no formal links between them.

The distinctive nature of federal and provincial party systems is reinforced by the fact that parties with the same name often operate independently of one another in federal and provincial arenas. In the Atlantic provinces and Saskatchewan, people who join the provincial Liberal party automatically become members of the federal Liberal party, and vice versa. The same is not true in Ontario, British Columbia, Alberta, Quebec, or Manitoba, where the provincial Liberal parties are organizationally separate from the federal Liberals. The NDP is the sole party that is integrated across the federal–provincial divide. Members join the party only at the provincial level (except in Quebec where there is no provincial New Democratic Party), and in the process become federal party members.

While there can be considerable cooperation between national and provincial party activists and staff in election campaigns (Esselment, 2010), and a majority of party members in Ontario report belonging to parties of the same name at the provincial and federal levels (Pruysers, 2014), the structural divisions can make it easier for political leaders to cross partisan boundaries (Carty, 2006). During the 2008 federal election, the PC premier of Newfoundland and Labrador, Danny Williams, exhorted voters across Canada to vote "ABC"—"Anything But Conservative." On the other hand, Ontario Liberal premier Kathleen Wynne actively supported Justin Trudeau and the federal Liberal party in the 2015 Canadian election.

The Canada Elections Act does not set limits on the amount that leadership contestants can spend on their campaigns. However leadership contestants are required to report all contributions, other sources of funds, and campaign expenses to Elections Canada. Only citizens and permanent residents can make contributions to leadership contenders to a maximum total of $1500 (as of 2015). Both the NDP and Liberal party have voluntarily placed limits on leadership campaign expenses, but those limits are not enforceable through the Act. While competitors in recent leadership contests have spent less than in previous eras, the cost of running a competitive campaign remains high. In 2012, Thomas Mulcair spent more than $595 000 in his campaign to succeed Layton as NDP leader. In 2013, Justin Trudeau spent nearly $1.5 million to win the Liberal leadership (Elections Canada, 2015).

The Reform party and the Bloc were the first federal parties to use the "one member, one vote" method of leadership selection, which allows every party member to participate directly in the selection of the leader. In response to criticisms about problems with the selection of delegates and the inability of many ordinary party members to afford the fees to attend leadership conventions, the major parties have also adopted the "one member, one vote" system.

The Conservative party used a modified "one member, one vote" method for the 2004 leadership contest between former Ontario Progressive Conservative cabinet minister Tony Clement, Stephen Harper, and Belinda Stronach, a businessperson and philanthropist. Under this system, every party member could vote directly for the leader and rank the candidates in order of preference on the ballot. Leadership candidates were assigned a number of points based on the percentage of the popular vote they received from party members in each riding. However, each vote did not have the same value, because each electoral district was assigned 100 points, regardless of the number of members voting in that district. To win the leadership, a candidate had to obtain a majority of points from across the country. Members could vote in person or by fax, and the results of the vote were announced at a convention in which the three candidates delivered their final speeches. If no candidate won a majority of support on the first ballot, then the candidate with the lowest number of votes would be dropped from the competition and the second place preferences on those ballots would be redistributed among the remaining candidates. Because Harper obtained 56 percent support after the first count, no additional rounds of counting were needed. The "one member, one vote" system will be used to choose the successor to Harper, who resigned as party leader following the Conservatives' loss in the 2015 election.

When the Liberals chose Stéphane Dion as their leader at the 2006 leadership convention, they used a combination of "one member, one vote" and delegate convention methods. Following their defeat in 2008, the Liberals took several steps to make the party more open and inclusive. In 2009, delegates at the party's leadership and biennial convention voted to replace the hybrid leadership selection method with a process giving every party member a direct vote in electing the next party leader. Like the Conservative party had done, the Liberals adopted a weighted vote system with each district given the same number of points regardless of the number of members voting. Delegates at the party's 2012 biennial convention went further when they voted to create a new "supporter" class of Liberals who could vote for their next leader without having to buy a party membership. Instead, "supporters" simply completed an application form declaring that they supported the Liberal party and were not a member of another federal party in Canada (Liberal Party of Canada, 2012).

In April 2013, more than 104 000 Liberal party members and supporters cast their ballots by phone or online to choose Ignatieff's successor by preferential ballot. Each electoral district was allocated 100 points. Points were allocated in proportion to the number of first preference votes received by each candidate in each district. The first leadership contestant to receive more than 50 percent of the points allocated nationally would win the leadership. Quebec MP Justin Trudeau prevailed over five competitors, winning in the first round of the preferential ballot.

The seven-month contest to replace Layton as NDP leader culminated in the selection of Thomas Mulcair from a field of seven candidates at a leadership convention held in March 2012. Party members were able to vote online or by mail in advance, or, alternatively, online or in person on convention day. A "one member, one vote" system was used. If no candidate received 50 percent plus one on the first ballot, then subsequent rounds of voting were held.[5] Candidates with the fewest votes were dropped from the next ballot (New Democratic Party of Canada, 2011). It took four ballots before Mulcair prevailed over party strategist Brian Topp.

How Do Parties Replace Their Leaders?

Until the mid-1960s, party members were stuck with unpopular leaders. There were no formal rules allowing party members to oust them, and leaders were replaced only upon their retirement or their death. This changed when the Liberals and Progressive Conservatives adopted procedures that would allow the party convention to review their leaders' performance.

The formal procedures for removing a party leader are laid out in party constitutions. The Conservatives' **leadership review** process is set into motion at the first national party convention following an election loss. Delegates vote by secret ballot on whether they wish to set a leadership selection process in motion. If more than 50 percent agree, a leadership race is called. The NDP's constitution allows delegates at every biennial convention to determine whether a leadership election should be called (New Democratic Party of Canada, 2011). No incumbent NDP leader has ever been defeated. Since 1992, all Liberal party members have had a direct say in reviewing the leader's performance. This vote takes place in every electoral district at meetings to select delegates to attend the first biennial convention following an election loss. If the leader obtains less than a majority of support, then the leader is not endorsed (Liberal Party of Canada, 2012). No incumbent leader has ever been defeated in a leadership endorsement ballot.

The Reform Act (C-586) provides another possible way to remove a leader and choose a new one. The caucus of each party in the House of Commons can decide at its first meeting after a general election whether or not to adopt a process that would allow for leadership review. If they adopt this process, then a leadership review would begin at any time that a majority of the caucus votes by secret ballot to endorse or replace the leader. If they vote to replace their leader, a second ballot would be used to appoint an interim leader until a

LEADERSHIP REVIEW
The formal process that sets out the procedures for evaluating and possibly replacing a party leader.

---

[5]Those voting in advance of the convention could list the candidates in order of preference.

new leader has been "duly elected by the party." Presumably the procedure to choose a new leader would then follow the rules in the party's constitution.

In addition to these formal rules, members of the parliamentary wing can place informal pressure on a sitting leader to resign. In 2003, Liberal prime minister Jean Chrétien was pressured to resign by supporters of his rival, Paul Martin. Chrétien initially argued that his leadership could be challenged only by a vote of the party membership scheduled for late 2003. When it appeared that he might not win the leadership review, Chrétien announced his intention to resign five months before the scheduled vote. Such was also the fate of Liberal leader Stéphane Dion. The failure of the Liberal–NDP coalition arrangement to prevent the prorogation of Parliament in December 2008 increased caucus pressure on Dion to resign immediately.

How Do Parties Select Their Local Candidates?

The ability to select a local candidate is one of the most important reasons why Canadians join parties (Cross & Young, 2006). The majority of candidate nomination processes take place in each federal election district, often before the drop of the election writ. Nominations are open to citizens aged 18 and over, and candidates are not required to live in the electoral district they want to represent. Local electoral district associations are encouraged or required to establish candidate search committees, while the central party organization screens applications from nominees and has the power to veto any individual's candidacy (Patten, 2010). Would-be candidates try to convince the party's members and potential supporters to attend a nomination meeting and vote for them. During hotly contested nominations, a party's membership can increase immensely. On the day of the nomination meeting, local party members listen to the candidates' speeches and vote for their preferred candidate. The individual who wins a majority of support from those present is chosen as the party's candidate. There are almost no restrictions on who can vote in the nomination meeting, other than that voters must have purchased a membership before an established cut-off date.

Although local associations are relatively autonomous when it comes to selecting candidates (Carty, 2004), party leaders have had the final say in candidate selection since 1972. This is when the Canada Elections Act was amended to provide for the inclusion of party affiliation next to local candidates' names on the ballot. Thus, a candidate who wants to be listed on the ballot with the party affiliation must have his or her nomination papers signed by the party leader. In some circumstances, leaders have used their powers to reject candidates whom they perceive as undesirable or even to remove them after they have been nominated (as happened for at least 11 candidates in 2015). Party leaders have also bypassed local nominations and appointed "star" candidates to strengthen the party's chances of winning a district or to increase the number of candidates from underrepresented groups. At times, parties have also protected sitting MPs from challenges to their nomination (Patten, 2010).

DIVERSITY AND LOCAL CANDIDACIES   Females, visible minorities, and Aboriginal peoples, among other groups, have long been underrepresented in the ranks of candidates and MPs. While the 2015 election saw a dramatic change to Canada's political landscape and a record number of individuals from these groups elected, their representation in the House of Commons still falls below their share of the population. A record high 10 Aborginal MPs were elected in 2015, up three from the 2011 election. The incoming cohort of Aboriginal MPs constitutes about 3 percent of the House of Commons membership (Fontaine, 2015), slightly less than their 4.3 percent share of the population (Statistics Canada, 2015b).

Between 1980 and 2015, the representation of female MPs increased from 5 percent to 26 percent. However, the 26 percent figure remained virtually unchanged over 2011, when about 25 percent of elected MPs were female (Parliament of Canada, 2015). Equal Voice, an advocacy group dedicated to electing more women, noted that electing a higher proportion of women in 2015 proved to be difficult as only 33 percent of candidates for the major five parties were women. In 97 of the 338 federal ridings, none of the leading three parties had a woman on the ballot (Equal Voice, 2015). There is considerable variability among the parties when it comes to nominating females. The NDP tends to nominate more women than other national parties (see Table 8-2).

Similarly a record high 46 visible minority MPs were elected to the Forty-Second Parliament, including the first-ever MPs of Afghan, Iranian, and Somali heritage. That figure is about 14 percent of the total 338 seats, up 5 percent from the previous high of 9.1 percent, when 28 visible minority MPs were elected in 2011 (Chowdhry, 2015). Nevertheless, while the number of visible minority MPs has grown since 1993 when 13 were elected, their representation still lags their 19 percent share of the population (Figure 8-2). The 2015 election also saw a change in the partisan affiliation of the incoming cohort of visible minority MPs. In 2011, the NDP elected the most visible minority MPs of any party (13), followed by the Conservatives (12) (Black, 2013). In 2015, the vast majority (39) of visible minority MPs were Liberal (Fontaine, 2015). (see Figure 8-2).

	CANDIDATES (2011)	ELECTED (2011)	PERCENTAGE ELECTED	CANDIDATES (2015)	ELECTED (2015)	PERCENTAGE ELECTED
Total (all registered parties	451	76	16.9	533	88	16.5
NDP	124	40	32.3	145	18	12.4
Green party	99	1	1.0	135	1	0.74
Liberal party	90	6	6.7	105	50	47.6
Conservative party	68	28	41.2	65	17	26.2
BQ	24	1	4.2	21	2	9.5

TABLE 8-2
FEMALE CANDIDATES AND MPs IN 2011 AND 2015 FEDERAL ELECTIONS, BY PARTY AFFILIATION

SOURCE: *Women Candidates in General Elections—1921 to Date.* Parliament of Canada (2015)

FIGURE 8-2
VISIBLE MINORITY CANDIDATES AND MPs IN FEDERAL ELECTIONS, 2004–2015

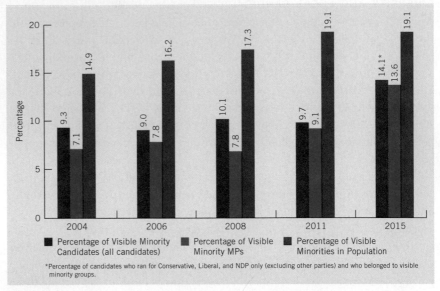

■ Percentage of Visible Minority Candidates (all candidates)   ■ Percentage of Visible Minority MPs   ■ Percentage of Visible Minorities in Population

*Percentage of candidates who ran for Conservative, Liberal, and NDP only (excluding other parties) and who belonged to visible minority groups.

SOURCE: Black, J. (2013). "Racial Diversity in the 2011 Federal Election: Visible minority candidates and MPs." *Canadian Parliamentary Review, 36*(3), 21–34.

The parties have responded in different ways to the question of whether they should implement special measures to encourage members of traditionally underrepresented groups to run for office (see Box 8-3: Electing a Diverse House of Commons). While the adoption of these initiatives is one of several factors that influence the diversity of a party's slate of candidates, parties that have adopted more proactive strategies to recruiting female candidates tend to nominate more of them. In 2015, the NDP (43 percent) and Liberals (31 percent) nominated proportionately more female candidates than the Conservatives (20 percent) (Equal Voice, 2015).

Maryam Monsef, MP for Peterborough-Kawartha, is one of the increased proportion of non-Caucasians elected to the House of Commons in 2015. Monsef, born in Afghanistan, came to Canada at age 11 as a refugee. She was appointed Minister for Democratic Institutions; at 30 years old the youngest member of the first Trudeau cabinet.

Electing a Diverse House of Commons

Of all the parties, the NDP has introduced the most clear-cut affirmative action measures. Since 1991, it has required that the party field female candidates in a minimum of 60 percent of ridings where it has a chance of winning. Moreover, in at least 15 percent of ridings where the NDP has a reasonable chance of winning, it must run candidates who reflect Canada's diversity. They include women, visible minorities, Aboriginals, gays, lesbians, bisexuals and transgendered individuals, people with disabilities, and Canadians under the age of 26 (Tossutti & Hilderman, 2014). The party also assigns established female politicians and party activists as mentors to women running for a nomination (McGrane, 2011).

Other parties have adopted less hands-on approaches to electing a more diverse House. Liberal strategies to improve female representation have involved identifying and encouraging promising candidates to run for office, as well as providing training sessions and financial assistance for campaigns (Erickson, 1998). In 1984, the Liberals set up the Judy LaMarsh Fund, which provides financial support to female candidates. In 1993, the Liberals changed party rules to allow the leader to bypass a nomination meeting and appoint a local candidate. Chrétien took advantage of this freedom to appoint female or visible minority candidates in certain ridings. In 2008 and 2011, Liberal party leaders established a 33 percent target for female candidacies.

In 2015, a group of women involved with the Liberal party launched a digital campaign inviting Canadians to nominate women they believed would make strong candidates. After receiving hundreds of nominations, the party followed up with about 200 women who expressed some interest. About a third of the party's candidates in 2015 were women. During the election, Liberal leader Justin Trudeau also pledged that women would make up 50 percent of his cabinet, a promise that was fulfilled on November 4, 2015. In contrast, the Conservative party does not make use of special initiatives to increase the number of candidates from underrepresented groups.

The different approaches raise questions about how to build a House that better reflects the Canadian population. Should party leaders use their power to appoint candidates from underrepresented groups, or should nomination decisions be left up to party members in the electoral district? So far, the more proactive strategies have failed to create a House of Commons that fully reflects Canada's diversity. If these initiatives don't work, what else might?

Source: Canadian Democracy from the Ground Up

Summary and Conclusion

Political parties perform vital electoral and non-electoral functions in a representative democracy. They have largely succeeded in organizing campaigns and recruiting candidates and leaders, albeit individuals who do not reflect Canada's social diversity. They have evolved into more inclusive and democratic organizations that provide their members with opportunities to select key officials and influence policies. However, falling rates of voter turnout and party identification, along with low rates of party membership, suggest that their power to engage Canadians in the political life of the country is limited. As well, how much parties offer their members meaningful opportunities to influence policies and the selection of key personnel is debatable. Party members have little influence over the policies and decisions that are adopted when their party is in government.

Party leaders and their advisers still wield the ultimate authority over campaign platforms and the suitability of local candidates.

Canadians have formed new parties when they have felt that established parties were neglecting their interests. This behaviour has contributed to the shift of party competition from a two-party to multiparty system. It is clear that Canadians have more party choices, if not more distinct options. It was proposed at the beginning of this chapter that party organizations are not static and that they resemble living organisms. There is no doubt that their ideas and internal practices have changed over time. Their continued survival will hinge on their ability to meet the expectations of a diverse population for democracy and good government.

Discussion Questions

1. How do political parties support Canadian democracy?

2. Why are many Canadians turning away from political parties? What can parties do to engage citizens in party and electoral politics?

3. Are the diverse interests of Canadians better-served when there are fewer or more parties competing for power?

4. Do political parties offer Canadians distinct policy choices?

5. Why have some political parties enjoyed more electoral success than others?

6. Who should have the final say in removing an unpopular party leader—the parliamentary caucus or party members?

7. Have political parties given their members enough influence over important decisions?

8. Should political parties strive to increase the presence of females and visible minorities in Parliament? If so, how should they go about it? If not, why not?

Further Reading

Carty, R.K. (2015). *Big tent politics: The Liberal Party's long mastery of Canada's public life.* Vancouver, BC: UBC Press.

Carty, R.K., Cross, W., & Young, L. (2000). *Rebuilding Canadian party politics.* Vancouver, BC: UBC Press.

Clarkson, S. (2005). *The big red machine: How the Liberal party dominates Canadian politics.* Vancouver, BC: UBC Press.

Cross, W. (2004). *Political parties.* Vancouver, BC: UBC Press.

Flanagan, T. (2009). *Harper's team: Behind the scenes in the Conservatives' rise to power* (2nd ed.). Montreal, QC: McGill-Queen's University Press.

Gagnon, A., & Tanguay, B.G. (Eds.) (2007). *Canadian parties in transition* (3rd ed.). Toronto, ON: Nelson Canada.

Gidengil, E., Nevitte, N., Blais, A., Everitt, J., & Fournier, P. (2012). *Dominance and decline: Making sense of recent Canadian elections.* Toronto, ON: University of Toronto Press.

Jeffrey, B. (2010). *Divided loyalties: The Liberal Party of Canada, 1984–2008.* Toronto, ON: University of Toronto Press.

Laycock, D., & Erickson, L. (Eds.). (2015) *Reviving social democracy: The near death and surprising rise of the federal NDP.* Vancouver, BC: UBC Press.

LeDuc, L., Pammett, J., McKenzie, J., & Turcotte, A. (2010). *Dynasties and interludes: Past and present in Canadian electoral politics.* Toronto, ON: Dundurn Press.

Martin, L. (2011). *Harperland: The politics of control.* Toronto, ON: Penguin Canada.

Tremblay, M., & Trimble, L. (Eds.). (2003). *Women and electoral politics in Canada.* Toronto, ON: Oxford University Press.

CHAPTER 9

Elections, the Electoral System, and Voting Behaviour

CHAPTER OBJECTIVES

After reading this chapter, you should be able to

1. Outline the rules and procedures for conducting elections.
2. Discuss the strengths and weaknesses of Canada's single-member plurality electoral system.
3. Evaluate whether election campaigns help to inform the electorate.
4. Discuss the financing of political parties and their election campaigns.
5. Examine the explanations of the choices made by voters.

For many Canadians, the very mention of jail conjures up images of barred windows, barbed wire, sullen inmates, and snarling German shepherds. Less common is the image of prisoners casting their (mail-in) ballots to elect Members of Parliament.

In the past, prisoners were stripped of the right to vote; however, in 1992, court rulings struck down this provision. Parliament afterward amended the Canada Elections Act to ban voting by prisoners who were serving a sentence of two or more years. Then in 2002, the Supreme Court of Canada struck down this provision in a narrow 5–4 vote. Some would argue that those who committed serious criminal offences have proven that they are not responsible citizens, and thus have forfeited their right to vote. In the opinion of the majority of Supreme Court justices, however, "to deny prisoners the right to vote is to lose an important means of teaching them democratic values and social responsibility. . . . Denial of the right to vote on the basis of attributed moral unworthiness is inconsistent with the respect for the dignity of every person that lies at the heart of Canadian democracy and the Charter" (*Sauvé v. Canada*, 2000, quoted in Courtney, 2004, p. 38). The Conservative party questioned the wisdom of the Supreme Court ruling. In the 2006 election, the Conservative platform included a promise that the party would "work for a constitutional amendment to forbid prisoners in federal institutions from voting." However, the Conservative government did not pursue this election promise.

At what age individuals deserve the right to vote is another hotly disputed topic. Canada, like most other countries, has adopted 18 as the minimum age to vote. However, there has been some discussion about lowering the voting age to 16. Advocates argue that this would help to encourage young people to get involved in the political process, that youth are affected by the decisions of government, and that many young people are interested in and knowledgeable about politics. After all, they point out, 14-year-olds can become members of political parties and vote for their party's leader, and 17-year-olds can join the Armed Forces. In contrast, critics claim that young people generally lack maturity and have a low level of interest in and knowledge about politics and government. In 2005, the House of Commons rejected a private member's bill that proposed lowering the voting age to 16.

The right of all citizens to vote is a fundamental principle of democracy. Nevertheless, as discussed in this chapter, changes to the Elections Act in 2014 made it more difficult or impossible for a substantial number of Canadian citizens to vote. Are any exceptions to this principle justified? Is a violent criminal who is politically aware more deserving of this right than a politically apathetic 16-year-old with a clean record?

INTRODUCTION

Elections are the cornerstone of Canadian democracy. When we cast our ballot, we are exercising a hard-won right: the ability to participate in the selection of an individual to represent our electoral district in the House of Commons. Since nearly all of those elected represent a political party, our vote also matters to the overall outcome of the election in terms of which party will take charge of governing the country and which party leader will assume the office of prime minister. Voters can play a role in shaping the future direction of the country by choosing the party whose ideological perspective, policy proposals, or election promises they view as most desirable. Elections also create an opportunity for a variety of parties to raise issues and present policy proposals, and for individuals and groups to try to influence those seeking to be elected. Furthermore, voters can hold the governing party accountable for its actions (or inactions). Finally, if an election is perceived as being fair, it will help to establish the legitimacy of government; even those voters who hoped for a different outcome will be more likely to accept the winning party and to respect its right to govern.

ELECTORAL SYSTEM
The system by which the votes that people cast are translated into the representation of political parties in the House of Commons.

In this chapter, we examine how elections are conducted and the **electoral system** that translates the votes we cast into the representation of political parties in the House of Commons. As well, we discuss the campaigns organized by parties and candidates as they try to sway voters. Finally, we summarize some of the research revealing why people vote the way they do. As you read this chapter, consider the extent to which Canadian elections are effective in implementing the democratic ideal of rule by the people.

ELECTION RULES AND PROCEDURES

Ideally, an election can be considered fair and fully democratic if a number of conditions are met:

- All adult citizens can vote and measures are taken to ensure that all citizens have a reasonable opportunity to cast their ballot.
- All adult citizens have the right to run for office with no financial or other obstacles limiting the effective exercise of this right.
- All political parties are free to nominate candidates and campaign on their behalf.
- Voting is done by a secret ballot so that voters cannot be bribed or intimidated.
- Each voter can cast only one vote and each vote counts equally.
- An impartial organization oversees the process of elections and the counting of votes.
- Candidates and parties are able to witness the casting of votes and the counting of ballots with the right to demand a recount.
- The electoral process is used to fill all of the seats in the legislative body.
- Parties and candidates have a reasonable opportunity to carry their message to voters.
- The information needed to make an intelligent choice is easily available to voters.
- Elections are required to be held every few years.

Voting

In the past, as discussed in Chapter 6, women; those who did not own a certain amount of property; Aboriginals; and various ethnic, racial, and religious minority groups were denied the right to vote and to seek public office. Almost all restrictions were removed by 1960, and in 1970 the minimum voting age was dropped from 21 to 18. The right to vote is guaranteed constitutionally through the Charter of Rights and Freedoms (1982), which provides that "every citizen of Canada has the right to vote in an election of members of the House of Commons or of a legislative assembly and to be qualified for membership therein" (Section 3). In practice, however, requirements for the identification needed to vote can create problems particularly for the homeless, Aboriginals, and students.

Most votes are cast at polling stations that are expected to be in accessible local venues. Voting is by secret ballot, which helps to prevent the selling of votes and intimidation of voters. People hired and trained by Elections Canada are responsible for the voting procedures, and representatives of each candidate are entitled to observe the process of casting and counting votes.

Civic participation is vital to democracy. By completing her ballot, this BC voter exercises her rights and duties as a citizen.

© Nathan Denette/Canadian Press Images

A National Register of Electors is maintained with updated information collected from such sources as income tax returns, postal change of address forms, and motor vehicle registrations. To vote (or to be registered at the polling station), an individual must present valid photo identification that includes the voter's residential address. The Fair Elections Act, 2014, eliminated the voter information card that could be used to prove one's address. Instead a person can sign an oath confirming his or her address, provided another valid voter who accompanies the person also signs an oath confirming the person's address; the confirming voter must (1) reside in the same polling district and (2) not have given an oath for another voter. Nevertheless, the Act can make it more difficult for students, homeless persons, Aboriginals, and the elderly in seniors' homes to vote. An Ontario Superior Court judge rejected a request from the Canadian Federation of Students and the Council of Canadians for an injunction to suspend the application of this new identification provision of the Act. Even though the judge stated that there was a risk of "irreparable harm" to the right to vote, a full hearing (that could not be held in time for the 2015 election) was needed (Nicol, 2015).

For those who will be away on Election Day, the option exists to vote through advance polls and mail-in ballots. Likewise, provisions are made for those who are ill, disabled, or in jail. Employers must ensure that voters in federal elections have three consecutive hours off during voting hours. For the 2015 election, a pilot project allowed students at 39 colleges and universities to vote on campus and Aboriginals to vote at 13 friendship centres (regardless of their permanent residence). This contributed to a large increase in voting by students and Aboriginals in the election.

The provision in the Fair Elections Act, 2014, that removed the right to vote for Canadian citizens (except for members and employees of the Armed Forces, public servants, those working for international organizations of which Canada is a member, or those living with someone in these categories) who had lived outside Canada for at least five consecutive years was upheld by the Ontario Court of Appeal. Even though they agreed that this law violated the Charter of Rights and Freedoms, two of the three judges ruled that the provision was justified because non-residents were not affected by the decisions of Parliament and their votes would "erode the social contract and undermine the legitimacy of the laws" (*Frank v. Canada* cited by Sarin, 2015).

Canadian elections are run by an independent, non-partisan agency of Parliament, Elections Canada. The chief electoral officer is appointed through a resolution of the House of Commons, holds office for a single 10-year term, and can be removed only for cause by the governor general after a joint address of the House of Commons and Senate.

Elections Canada
www.elections.ca

Running for Office

Any citizen who is at least 18 years old can be a candidate for elected office, even if that citizen does not live in the electoral district. For candidates seeking election to the House of Commons, several requirements exist:

- a minimum of 100 eligible electors must sign the nomination papers (50 in certain remote areas);
- an official agent and auditor must be appointed; and
- a deposit of $1000 must be paid (this is reimbursed after an audited statement of expenses is submitted).

However, unless a person is a candidate for one of the major political parties, the likelihood of being elected is very low. To have a party affiliation alongside the candidate's name on the ballot, a designated representative of the party must confirm that the candidate has been accepted as the party's nominee for that electoral district.

To become a registered political party, a party must meet several criteria:

- two hundred and fifty eligible voters must support the party's application;
- the party must run at least one candidate in each general election; and
- the party must have a leader, three officers, an auditor, and a chief agent.

Representation in the House of Commons

Canada uses a single-member plurality electoral system (SMP); however, as discussed below, this might change for the 2019 election. SMP involves electing one representative from each electoral district (also known as a constituency or riding). The candidate who attracts the most votes (regardless of whether or not the candidate has a majority of votes) is elected. Dividing the country into electoral districts is a complex and sometimes contentious process.

The House of Commons is based, in part, on the principle of representation by population. If fully applied, this principle would mean that each electoral district would have about the same number of people. The Constitution requires that readjustments of electoral districts occur after the comprehensive census that is conducted every 10 years to take account of population changes.

The number of seats allocated to each province is generally in proportion to its population. However, the Constitution modifies this principle by specifying that no province can have fewer seats in the House than its number of Senators. As a result, Prince Edward Island elects four members to the House, even though its population would only justify a single member. As well, the Representation Act (1985) guarantees that a province will have no fewer seats than it had in 1976, or in the period between 1984 and 1988, even if its population dwindles or does not grow as fast as that of the rest of the country. The three territories are guaranteed one seat each. Guarantees of minimum representation for certain provinces and each territory might be considered a violation of the principle of equal representation by population. However, it can be argued that in a federal system it is important that each province and territory receives adequate representation in Parliament (Courtney, 2004).

Legislation adopted in December 2011 moved closer to provincial representation by population by increasing the total number of representatives from 308 to 338. Using population figures from the 2011 census, Ontario gained 15 members in the House of Commons, Alberta and British Columbia 6 each, and Quebec 3. Quebec's representation is almost proportionate to its share of population, while Ontario, British Columbia, and Alberta continued to be slightly underrepresented. For example, Ontario, with 38.87 percent of Canada's population, has 36.45 percent of the seats in the House of Commons. The Liberal party was critical of the legislation, arguing that increasing the membership of the House of Commons was unnecessary and undesirable.

Until 1964, the design of electoral districts was the responsibility of Parliament. This frequently resulted in **gerrymandering**—the drawing of boundaries

GERRYMANDERING
The drawing of boundaries for partisan advantage, particularly for the advantage of the governing party.

for partisan advantage, particularly for the advantage of the governing party (Courtney, 2004). It is now carried out by a three-member independent boundary readjustment commission for each province, chaired by a judge with the other members chosen by the Speaker of the House of Commons. Both the public and Members of Parliament have an opportunity to voice their opinion about proposed changes to the electoral districts. However, the commission makes the final decision.

Each commission is expected to draw the boundaries of electoral districts so as to take into account existing communities and territorially based "communities of interest." They are also expected to draw the boundaries so that each electoral district in the province is as close as possible to having the same number of residents, with no electoral district being more than 25 percent above or below the average number of residents in that province, other than in exceptional circumstances. In practice, remote districts with low population density tend to have smaller numbers of residents than urban districts. Although this might be considered a violation of the principle of equal representation, the Supreme Court of Canada has ruled that the desirability of "effective representation" may justify some deviation from the absolute equal voting power of individuals (Courtney, 2004). For example, the very large electoral district of Labrador (which is separated geographically and in terms of cultural characteristics from the rest of the province) has a population of less than 26 000, about one-third of the average population of Newfoundland's six other electoral districts. In 2003, the Federal Court overturned a redistribution of federal seats in New Brunswick because the NB boundary readjustment commission did not protect the representation of the province's francophone communities (Thomas, Loewen, & MacKenzie, 2013).

The Timing of Elections

The Constitution requires that the House of Commons (and provincial and territorial legislatures) cannot continue for more than five years without holding a general election. An exception is allowed in times of real or apprehended war, invasion, or insurrection if no more than one-third of the members of the Commons (or legislature) oppose the extension. The prime minister recommends to the governor general when a Canadian election is to be called. When the governing party loses the confidence of a majority in the House of Commons (e.g., if the opposition parties pass a non-confidence motion, or if a major piece of government legislation such as a budget is defeated), the prime minister will ask the governor general to dissolve Parliament and call an election. A prime minister can also ask the governor general to call an election at a time that the prime minister chooses.[1]

---

[1]The governor general has the right to refuse the prime minister's request for an election and can call on another member of Parliament to form a government. (see Chapter 13).

Fixed Election Dates or a Fixed Election?

In the 2006 election campaign, the Conservative party promised that it would institute a system of fixed election dates. Harper criticized former Liberal prime minister Jean Chrétien for calling an early election in 2000 that caught the new leader of the Canadian Alliance, Stockwell Day, unprepared. Fixed election dates, Harper said, would stop leaders from trying to manipulate the election calendar and level the playing field for all parties (CTV News, 2006).

In 2007, Parliament passed an amendment to the Canada Elections Act requiring that elections be held on the third Monday in October every four years, with the first election to be held in October 2009. However, "the power of the governor general to dissolve Parliament at the governor general's discretion" was retained. On September 7, 2008, Prime Minister Stephen Harper asked Governor General Michaëlle Jean to dissolve Parliament and hold an election on October 14, even though his government had not been defeated in the House of Commons. Amid a storm of controversy over Harper's request, she granted him permission.

The opposition parties complained that Harper had ignored his government's own fixed-date election law in hopes of catching the other parties unprepared for the election campaign. In turn, Harper claimed that he asked for an early election because Parliament had become "dysfunctional." In particular, he argued that his 31-month-old minority government could no longer govern in a fractious Parliament. The opposition parties argued that the governing party itself had made Parliament dysfunctional and pointed out that Parliament had passed much of the legislation presented to it by the government.

The next election also occurred before the fixed four-year date. On March 25, 2011, the House of Commons passed a motion that the government was in contempt of Parliament and had lost the confidence of the House. Prime Minister Harper's request that Parliament be dissolved and an election called was granted by the governor general the next day. In this case, there was little controversy about the need for an election as a government cannot remain in office once it has lost the confidence of the House of Commons. The October 19, 2015, election was the first election held on the date established by the fixed-date election law.

While some flexibility is desirable in a parliamentary system, some argue that the governor general should not agree to call an early election unless other options (such as the willingness of other parties to form or support a different government) have been considered.

In 2007, the procedure for calling national elections was modified by legislation establishing that elections will be held on a specified date every four years. Similar legislation has been adopted by all provinces except Nova Scotia, and two territories: Yukon, and Nunavut. However, as discussed in Box 9-1: Fixed Election Dates or a Fixed Election?, the adoption of fixed election dates has not prevented elections from being held at an earlier date.

THE SINGLE-MEMBER PLURALITY ELECTORAL SYSTEM

SINGLE-MEMBER PLURALITY ELECTORAL SYSTEM (SMP)
An electoral system in which voters in each district elect a single representative. The candidate with the most votes is elected, regardless of whether that candidate received the majority of votes.

Canada's method of electing members to the House of Commons and provincial legislatures, the **single-member plurality electoral system (SMP)**, has provoked considerable criticism and many proposals for change.

SMP (also known as "first past the post") does not accurately translate the votes that are cast for each party into the representation each party receives in a legislative body. Typically, the party that receives the most votes ends up with a larger proportion of seats than the proportion of the vote it received. This can result in a **majority government** (i.e., one with a major- ity of seats) even when the majority of votes went to other parties. For example, in the 1993, 1997, and 2000 elections, the Liberal party led by Jean Chrétien only received about 40 percent of the votes cast, yet emerged with a comfortable majority of seats in the House of Commons. Likewise, the Conservative party won a majority of seats in the 2011 election based on 39.6 percent of the votes cast and the Liberal party won a majority of seats in the 2015 election based on 39.5 percent of the votes. In a few cases, the effect of overrepresenting the leading party can be so strong that the other parties receive few seats. Indeed, in the 1987 New Brunswick election, the Liberal party, with 60.4 percent of the vote, won all 58 seats.

Occasionally, the party that received the most votes does not win the most seats. This can occur when the second most popular party wins a substantial number of seats by a small margin, while the most popular party "wastes" votes by winning some seats by large margins. For exam- ple, in the 1979 Canadian election, the Progressive Conservative (PC) party won 136 seats with 35.9 percent of the vote, while the Liberals won only 114 seats with 40.1 percent of the vote. Despite receiving nearly 1 million votes fewer than the Liberals, the PCs became the governing party, just six seats short of a majority. This pattern has repeated itself several times in provincial politics. For example, in 1998 the Parti Québécois won a large majority of seats despite having slightly fewer votes than the Liberal party.

SMP discriminates against smaller parties, particularly those whose sup- port is spread relatively evenly across the country (see Table 9-1). For exam- ple, since its founding in 1961, the New Democratic Party received a smaller proportion of seats in the House of Commons than its proportion of the vote in every election except 2011. In the 2011 election, the third-place Liberal party was disadvantaged by the electoral system.

MAJORITY GOVERNMENT
A governing party that has a majority of seats in the House of Commons regardless of whether it received a majority of votes in an election.

PARTY	VOTE %	SEATS %
Liberal	39.5	54.4
Conservative	31.9	29.3
NDP	19.7	13.0
Bloc	4.7	3.0
Green	3.5	0.3
Other	0.8	0.0

SOURCE: Unofficial results reported in the media.

TABLE 9-1
THE IMPACT OF THE SMP ELECTORAL SYSTEM, 2015 CANADIAN ELECTION

The SMP electoral system also tends to exaggerate the regional character of political parties. For example, the Liberal party won every seat in Atlantic Canada in the 2015 election based on 51.6 percent of the vote in New Brunswick, 61.9 percent in Nova Scotia, 58.3 percent in PEI, and 64.5 percent in Newfoundland and Labrador. Similarly, 35.7 percent of the vote in Quebec for the Liberals resulted in 51.3 percent of the seats, and the Liberal party's 44.8 percent of the vote in Ontario yielded almost two-thirds of the seats in that province. These regionalizing effects can also leave national parties without an effective voice in their parliamentary caucus for certain regions of the country. For example, Conservative parties have often lacked significant representation from Quebec, while the Liberal party has often had very few representatives from Western Canada since 1957. People in certain regions may feel alienated from the Canadian government if their region lacks effective representation in the cabinet and believe that this results in policies that harm their region or province. As well, parties have a strong incentive to concentrate their efforts and appeals on those areas of the country where a small shift in support may yield a large number of seats. Areas where a party is weak may be "written off" (Cairns, 1968),[2] while areas where it is strong might be taken for granted.

Because SMP generally discriminates against political parties with lower levels of support across the country, it typically results in fewer parties being represented in legislative bodies. Although it does not necessarily produce a two-party system (Duverger, 1959), it tends to create a limited version of a multiparty system. For example, the near collapse of the PC party in 1993 enabled the Reform party (aided by the workings of the electoral system) to gain a high proportion of the seats in Western Canada with a platform that appealed strongly to many residents of that region. However, as it tried to gain support to become a serious challenger for national power, the party (and its successor, the Canadian Alliance) found that splitting the right-wing vote with the PC party in Ontario was a serious obstacle. Each party attracted about 20 percent of the votes, resulting in the Liberals winning almost every seat in the province. This set the stage for Liberal party dominance in Canadian elections for a decade, and led to pressure for the two right-wing parties to merge into the Conservative party in 2003. If Canada's electoral system more accurately translated the strength of each party into representation, these two parties, somewhat different in their perspectives, might not have united.

The supporters of Canada's SMP argue that it fosters stability by facilitating the creation of a majority government, which allows a party to carry out its election platform. It also may enhance the accountability of the

---

[2]An exception to this strategy occurred in the 1984 election, when the PC party led by Brian Mulroney successfully appealed to Quebecers (particularly Quebec nationalists) and greatly increased his party's Quebec representation, despite the party's traditional weakness in that province.

government as voters can assess the record of the governing party and decide whether to re-elect that party or choose an alternative party.

Critics argue that it is undemocratic for a party that did not gain the support of a majority of voters to determine the laws and policies of the country. As well, in a majority government, the diverse viewpoints of different parties are not taken into account and the domination of Parliament by the prime minister and cabinet is facilitated.

Electoral System Reform

Much discussion has been devoted to changing Canada's single-member plurality electoral system. Many of those advocating reform favour some version of a **proportional representation system**, particularly the mixed member proportional system. Unlike SMP, proportional representation (PR) systems feature a close relationship between the proportion of votes received by a party and the proportion of legislative seats it obtains. Voter turnout tends to be somewhat higher in countries with PR systems because every vote counts toward the number of representatives a party gains. As well, countries with PR systems are generally home to a number of significant parties representing different interests and viewpoints in their legislature, thus giving more choices to voters. Countries with this system often feature a higher proportion of women and minority group members in their legislative bodies. Because each party draws up a list of its candidates for election, each party will likely find it advantageous to ensure that its list presents a representative set of candidates.

Countries with PR systems (such as Sweden, the Netherlands, and Spain) almost always feature governments based on a coalition of parties. It is unusual for one party to win a majority of votes when a number of significant parties compete in an election.[3]

Without the distortion that can allow SMP to create an "artificial" majority for one party, parties in countries with PR systems have usually found that coalitions in which two or more parties share in governing are needed to provide stable and effective government. In some countries, this has resulted in instability; in others, parties have realized that they need to cooperate with other parties to form a stable coalition. Considerable bargaining among political parties is usually needed to decide on the composition and policies of the government.

In a **mixed member proportional system (MMP)**—used, for example, in Germany, New Zealand, and Scotland—voters cast two ballots: one for the candidate they prefer and one for the party they prefer. Candidates who get the most votes in their electoral district are elected, but others are selected

PROPORTIONAL REPRESENTATION SYSTEM
An electoral system in which the proportion of seats a party receives in the legislative body reflects the proportion of votes the party obtained.

MIXED MEMBER PROPORTIONAL SYSTEM
An electoral system in which voters cast one vote for the party they prefer and one vote for the candidate they prefer. Some legislators represent the district in which they received the most votes, while other legislators are selected based on the proportion of votes received by their party.

Fair Vote Canada
www.fairvote.ca

---

[3]Most countries with PR (or MMP) systems set a minimum percentage that a party must obtain to receive representation.

(based on their position on their party's list) so as to make the overall representation of the parties in the legislature reasonably proportional to the votes received by each party in the election.[4] In Canada, this system has been advocated by the New Democratic Party.

Preferential voting (also known as the alternative vote, instant run-off voting, and ranked ballots) involves voters ranking candidates in order of preference. If no candidate receives a majority of first preferences, the second preferences of those who voted for the candidate with the least votes are added to the votes received by the other candidates. The process continues until one candidate has a majority. This system is used by the Australian House of Representatives and most of its state governments, British Columbia in the 1952 and 1953 elections, and some U.S. cities. Voters in the United Kingdom rejected this system in a 2011 referendum. The Liberal Party of Canada adopted a resolution calling for preferential voting at its 2012 convention. In 2015, Prime Minister Justin Trudeau stated that the 2015 election would be the last one using the single member plurality system, and that an all party parliamentary committee would make recommendations to the House of Commons regarding reforms including proportional representation, ranked ballots, and online and mandatory voting (Benzie, 2015, October 21).

Other electoral systems include the **single transferable vote system** used by Ireland. Voters mark their preferences for a number of candidates in a multimember electoral district with a certain percentage (quota) of votes needed for a candidate to win. The second preferences that are surplus to what the winning candidates need are then transferred to candidates who have not reached the quota. This process continues until all the seats in the district are filled. This system was rejected by 60.9 percent of British Columbia voters in a 2009 referendum. The **runoff election** system (used by France) involves holding a second election (often with only the top two candidates) if no candidate wins a majority of votes in the first election. Generally, the single transferable vote system leads to representation of parties that is somewhat closer to proportional representation than the single-member plurality system. Preferential voting and runoff elections ensure that successful candidates can claim to have majority support, but discriminate against smaller parties.

ELECTION CAMPAIGNS

The official election campaign at the national level now lasts at least 37 days; the Canada Elections Act does not specify a maximum campaign length. The 2015 election officially started on August 2, resulting in the longest campaign since 1872, at 78 days (see Box 9-2: The 2015 Election Campaign). By having a long campaign, the spending limits for the parties increased for each

---

PREFERENTIAL VOTING
An electoral system in which voters rank candidates in order of preference. If no candidate receives a majority of first preferences, the second preferences of the candidate with the least votes are added to the votes of the other candidates. The process continues until one candidate has a majority.

SINGLE TRANSFERABLE VOTE SYSTEM
An electoral system in which voters mark their preferences for a number of candidates in a multimember district with a certain percentage (quota) of votes needed for a candidate to win. The second preferences that are surplus to what the winning candidates need are transferred to candidates who have not reached the quota. This process continues until all the seats in the district are filled.

RUNOFF ELECTION
A second election that is held (often with only the top two candidates) if no candidate in the first election wins a majority of votes.

---

[4]Voters in Ontario (2007) and Prince Edward Island (2006) rejected the adoption of MMP for their provincial elections in referenda.

BOX 9-2

The 2015 Election Campaign

The long and often acrimonious federal election campaign in 2015 gave voters an unprecedented opportunity to learn party stances on important issues and to evaluate the party leaders.

The opening weeks of the campaign did not begin auspiciously for the incumbent Conservatives, as the criminal trial of Conservative senator Mike Duffy (which implicated the Prime Minister's Office) dominated news coverage. By the end of August, the focus shifted to reports from Statistics Canada that the economy had contracted during the first two quarters of 2015. The heartbreaking story of Alan Kurdi, the three-year-old lying dead on a Turkish beach after his aunt had tried unsuccessfully to get permission for his family to come to British Columbia, made the Conservative government's limited willingness to accept Syrian refugees a significant issue. Subsequently, the niqab became an important "wedge" issue after Stephen Harper asserted that the niqab should not be worn when new Canadians take their citizenship oath, even though a court ruling had struck down the niqab ban. The NDP and the Liberals took the unpopular position that Muslim women should be allowed to wear the niqab at the citizenship ceremony.

Throughout the campaign, the Liberals emphasized their commitment to helping the middle class through such measures as cutting the tax rate on income between $44 701 and $89 401, while those earning $200 000 or more would face higher taxes. The Liberals also promised to stimulate the economy, particularly through major infrastructure projects. The Conservatives focused on attacking Justin Trudeau, calling him "just not ready" to govern. As well, they claimed that they had a good economic management record and emphasized their tough-on-crime agenda, anti-terrorism measures, and the combat mission against the Islamic State. The NDP leader tried to portray himself as prime ministerial and promised careful economic management to avoid the budgetary deficits that the Conservatives had run. Although the NDP promised higher corporate taxes, the Liberals were able to position themselves as the most "progressive" party while the NDP seemed closer to the Conservatives on economic policy.

Overall, Trudeau outperformed expectations during the campaign and his "sunny" disposition contrasted with that of his older opponents.

additional day after the minimum 37 days. Thus, each of the three major parties was allowed to spend a maximum of over $50 million, more than double what they could spend in a 37-day campaign. The maximum amount individual candidates could spend also increased substantially as a result of the longer campaign period. There are no limits on how much money parties and candidates can spend prior to the official beginning of an election campaign.

Modern political campaigning can be never-ending as parties regularly promote themselves or castigate their opponents with an eye to the eventual election. As described by a former Conservative campaign manager, a permanent campaign includes always being prepared for "political war" with the other parties, the appointment of a permanent campaign manager directly reporting to the party leader, a campaign platform developed by the leader's policy advisors, extensive "message management," and ensuring that the party's "MPs religiously follow official talking points" with cabinet ministers "carefully controlled by the Prime Minister's Office" (Flanagan, 2014, p. 127). In particular, the Conservatives with their superior financial resources were able to use extensive advertising to define the image and characteristics of new Liberal leaders for voters in a negative way prior to the 2008 and 2011elections that was difficult for those leaders to change (Flanagan, 2014).

The permanent campaign can also include the extensive use of government advertising that promotes the policies of the governing party. For example, the Harper government spent more than $100 million to advertise its "Economic Action Plan," with the advertising continuing for two years after the program ended (Curry, 2014, January 14). Unlike advertising that provides information about government programs and services, such ads are "really just to tout what the government is doing and draw attention to the governing party's platform" (Rose cited in Geddes, 2012).[5]

The governing party also has the ability to adopt popular measures just before an election. For example in 2015, the Universal Child Care Benefit was increased for parents of children under 6 years old and expanded to provide a new benefit for children aged 6 to 17. The first enhanced payment was issued on July 20, 2015, and included a retroactive payment for the previous six months. For example, parents with two children received a government cheque for about $1000 just before the start of the election campaign.

Election campaigns have become highly professionalized, with expert campaign managers, advertising agencies, and pollsters responsible for designing and running the campaigns of the major political parties. At the same time, campaigns have become highly centralized, with the national party campaign office trying to tightly control the message that the campaign seeks to deliver. Each party's candidates are expected to echo their party's message in their electoral district and to avoid straying from the message, which might be seized upon by the other parties or the media as evidence of disagreement within the party. However, due to language differences and the distinct political culture and interests of Quebec, the campaign themes and advertising strategies created to appeal to Quebecers often differ from those used in the rest of the country (McGrane, 2011).

Campaigns are highly leader-oriented, with a focus on the leader's tour. The leaders criss-cross the country, usually visiting every province accompanied by national reporters and a pooled camera crew supplied by the major television networks. From one day to another, the leaders can be spotted flipping burgers, kissing babies, or posing for "selfies" to provide a positive "photo op" for the media, but with limited meaningful interaction with voters. The leaders' speeches are tightly scripted to focus on their party's major campaign themes. In the 2011 and 2015 campaigns, Stephen

---

[5]The 2015 Liberal platform included a promise to appoint an advertising commissioner to help the auditor general oversee government advertising and ensure it is non-partisan.

Harper allowed only five questions from reporters per day (with no follow-up questions to the leader's response). At times, NDP leader Tom Mulcair also refused to take questions from reporters. All persons attending Conservative party rallies had to be vetted to ensure they were Conservative supporters, and other parties made sure that rallies were filled with party supporters.

At the local level, many candidates work hard to meet as many voters as possible, particularly by going door-to-door and attending small get-togethers arranged by their supporters. Volunteers are mobilized to assist in the campaign by erecting signs, distributing leaflets, and identifying supporters by phone or canvassing and encouraging them to vote. All-candidates meetings are held in many districts, and the local media often interview and profile the candidates. Candidates increasingly make use of social media to convey their message, as well as using advertisements in the traditional media. Generally, however, candidates stick closely to the "talking points" prepared by the national campaign organization. The national campaigns increasingly use call centres to reach voters, including targeting messages designed for voters with particular characteristics. Furthermore, the major parties have developed extensive national databases of the characteristics of potential supporters that are used in fundraising, canvassing, messaging, and getting out the vote on Election Day.

"Dirty tricks" such as defacing or removing the opponent's signs and circulating false rumours have been quite frequent occurrences (Marland, 2011). The Conservatives in the 2011 election were accused of using misleading "robocalls" (automated phone calls) to give supporters of other parties misleading information purporting to be from Elections Canada about the

Michelle Siu/Canadian Press Images

During an election campaign, "photo ops" allow party leaders to target the media and the public and share their message with party supporters in particular electoral districts or regions. Pictured here: NDP leader Thomas Mulcair during the 2015 election campaign.

location of their polling station. A Conservative campaign staffer in Guelph, Ontario, was convicted and sentenced to nine months in jail for arranging 6700 misleading calls in his district.

Campaign Debates

Nationally televised leaders' debates involving the leaders of parties represented in the House of Commons were organized by the major television networks in 1968 and 1979 and from 1984 to 2011 (with English and French debates on separate days). Some of the debates have involved dramatic clashes between leaders that have, on occasion, affected support for the parties. For example, in 2011, NDP leader Jack Layton's attack on Michael Ignatieff for a poor attendance record in the House of Commons contributed to the negative rating of the Liberal party leader (Clarke, Scotto, Reifler, & Kornberg, 2011).

In 2015, Prime Minister Harper indicated that he would not participate in debates organized by the television network consortium. NDP leader Thomas Mulcair responded by announcing that he would only participate in debates in which Harper was a participant. After the start of the 2015 campaign, *Maclean's* magazine hosted a debate in which the five party leaders participated, although it was only carried on a few television stations. A debate on economic issues hosted by the *Globe and Mail* only included the Conservative, Liberal, and NDP leaders. Likewise, a foreign policy debate hosted by the Munk School of Global Affairs involved only the three leaders of the largest parties.[6] The only debate organized by the network consortium was a French language debate (with English translation) in which the five leaders participated. The last debate (in French) was organized by Quebec broadcaster TVA and excluded the Green party leader. Overall, the 2015 debates (carried by CPAC and its cable partners[7]) were not viewed by large audiences, although the news and social media brought to public attention the highlights of some of the debates.[8]

Campaign Platforms and Promises

Read the political parties' 2015 platforms
www.cbc.ca/news/politics/
canada-election-2015-party-
platforms-1.3264887

Historically, political parties would issue a campaign platform that included a variety of promises, usually with specific commitments to appeal to each province or region and to various interests (Carrigan, 1968). The Liberal and PC parties largely abandoned this practice in the 1970s and 1980s, preferring

---

[6]Elizabeth May, the Green party leader, tweeted her comments during the three debates that excluded her.

[7]All of the 2015 debates are available at CPAC's Digital Archive: http://www.cpac.ca/en/digital-archives/?.

[8]A debate on women's issues was cancelled after Harper and Mulcair decided not to participate. Instead *Up for Debate* taped interviews with four of the party leaders; Harper refused to be interviewed.

instead to have their leaders announce promises day by day during the campaign to maximize the media impact. However, the Liberal party, as part of their rebuilding effort after their defeats in the 1984 and 1988 elections, devoted considerable attention to developing the Liberal platform. This was published and circulated as the 112-page "Red Book" at the start of the 1993 campaign. The PC party scrambled to produce a smaller "Blue Book" in response. With the development of the Internet, the parties have been able to make their platforms easily accessible to anyone who goes to their party's website. In 2015, as in previous elections, the major parties released their full platform shortly before Election Day, including the estimated costs of their promises and proposals.

Party platforms and the campaign speeches of the leaders often contain an array of promises. Some promises are vague, and thus it is hard to tell how successfully the governing party has fulfilled them. Although governing parties usually claim to have fulfilled most of their promises by the time of the next election, they frequently have ignored or only partially fulfilled some major promises. For example, on winning the 2006 election, Harper immediately violated a promise not to appoint anyone who was not elected to the Senate and the cabinet. Similarly Pierre Trudeau's major election promise in 1974 not to introduce wage and price controls and Jean Chrétien's promises in the 2003 election to repeal the goods and services tax and replace it with a different tax as well as renegotiating NAFTA were ignored after taking office. Undoubtedly some promises are made simply to gain votes and may not represent a real commitment. However, sometimes circumstances change so that acting on a promise may no longer be in the public interest.

In analyzing campaign promises, we need to keep in mind not only the specific promises made, but also the overall program that is being proposed. For example, voters need to consider whether it is realistic for a party to promise a variety of new government spending programs at the same time as promising to reduce taxes and avoid a government budgetary deficit.

Advertisements

The Canada Elections Act requires that each radio and television broadcaster provide parties with prime time at its lowest rates for campaign advertisements. This is allocated based primarily on each party's percentage of seats, votes, and candidates in the previous election. Representatives of the registered political parties meet to decide on the distribution of time, but if agreement cannot be reached the broadcasting arbitrator, an official appointed by the chief electoral officer, can decide on the allocation. In addition, some radio and television networks are required to provide free broadcasts to the parties, allocated in about the same proportion as the paid commercials. However, there is no requirement that these be aired in prime time. Unlike some other countries, Canada imposes no minimum length for campaign advertisements.

As a result, 30-second television advertisements have become the standard. Although short advertisements can catch the attention of viewers who might be unwilling to listen to a lengthy explanation of a party's views and positions, they provide scant information on which to base one's vote.

Campaign ads tend to focus on the party leaders and include attacks on opposing leaders. For example, in the 2015 campaign, Conservative ads focused on the Liberal leader: "Justin: He's just not ready." Liberal ads featured an energetic Trudeau and had a positive tone with an emphasis on the party slogans of "Real change now" and "Real change for the middle class."

Campaign ads can be misleading. Although the use of "negative" or "attack" advertising has often been criticized, a distinction should be made between critical advertising and advertising based on "dirty politics" that uses such techniques as deception, fear-mongering, and mudslinging (Jamieson, 1992). Advertisements that reveal how one party's position differs from another may help voters in deciding how to vote. Indeed, such advertisements may be more helpful than those that simply indicate that a party, if elected, will look after everyone, make the country strong, or protect the environment. Likewise, if voters are to hold the governing party accountable for its actions, it is useful for the opposition parties to point out the government's failures and broken promises. It would, however, be more helpful if an opposition party indicated how it would fix the problems or govern differently.

Negative ads have quite frequently gone beyond useful criticism to make unfair attacks on another party or its leader. In the 2008 campaign, for example, Conservative ads attacking the Liberal party's "green shift" (carbon tax proposal) were deceptive in their portrayal of the Liberal proposal. The Liberals engaged in fear-mongering in the 2004 election with an ad that quoted Stephen Harper out of context, saying, "When we're through with Canada, you won't recognize it," while the backdrop showed a Canadian flag disintegrating. Similarly, Liberal ads in the 2006 election claimed that Harper had a "hidden agenda" to dismantle the public health care system (Clarke, Kornberg, & Scotto, 2009). Some Conservative ads in the 2015 election were misleading in claimed that the Liberals would end income splitting for families and seniors and end monthly child care cheques. In fact, the Liberals said they would only end income splitting for families, and would establish a somewhat larger child benefit for households having an annual income of less than $200 000.

The Mass Media, the Internet, and Social Media

The mass media provide extensive coverage of the election campaign with a focus on the leaders of the major parties. Unless there appears to be a difference between the leader of a party and other notable party figures, the national media devote very little attention to the speeches and activities of cabinet ministers and prominent party candidates.

Media coverage of election campaigns has often been criticized. The media tend to highlight what is termed the "horse race" aspect of the campaign. That is, they are often fixated on who is leading or falling back in the race for electoral victory, rather than providing informed analysis of the issues in the campaign. Likewise, campaign debates are often discussed in terms of whether one leader scored a "knockout punch" on another leader. Moreover, considerable attention is paid to any gaffes made by the parties during the campaign. For example, during the 2006 campaign the Conservatives promised to give $1200 a year to parents with young children. Much was made of a critical comment by Scott Reid, the Liberal communications director: "Don't give people 25 bucks a week to blow on beer and popcorn."

In reaction to criticism of their campaign coverage, some media have included "reality checks" that involve a critical analysis of campaign statements. As well, a number of newspapers have provided useful comparisons of party positions. Nevertheless, campaign coverage tends to be dominated by the attacks and counterattacks that the leaders aim at each other. As Christopher Waddell (2009) pointed out in his analysis of the 2008 election, newspapers spent "vast amounts of column and news space endlessly chewing over strategy, analyzing poll results, and focusing on the party leaders. Issues, beyond the economy . . . were virtually ignored" as the media largely reported on what was given to them by the leaders' campaigns (Waddell, 2009, pp. 233–234). Likewise, in the 2011 campaign, the media devoted considerable attention to Harper's claim that a "stable majority" was needed to prevent government by a "power-hungry coalition" of the opposition parties. Television news largely ignored the looming crisis in financing health care, climate change, the decay of Canada's infrastructure, and the involvement of the Canadian military in Afghanistan and Libya (Francoli, Greenberg, & Waddell, 2011). Similarly, both the media and the parties in the 2015 election largely ignored important issues such as the state of Canada's health care system.

The Internet has become an important avenue for each party's efforts to influence voters. Unlike the broadcast media, the Internet has no restrictions on its use. Along with their campaign platforms, parties have included their advertisements (including some specially designed for the Internet), announcements, and other campaign materials such as their leader's speeches on their websites. In the 2008 election campaign, the Conservative party set up a separate website, NotaLeader.ca, specifically designed to criticize Liberal leader Stéphane Dion. A notorious video on the site featured a puffin flying around and pooping on Dion's shoulder.

Social media such as Facebook and Twitter have increasingly become part of election campaigns. Parties and their leaders have created Facebook profiles to convey messages to their "friends" and the leaders and many candidates regularly "tweet" brief campaign messages. However, social media have not been used to any significant degree by the parties to encourage discussion among their followers (Francoli, Greenberg, & Waddell, 2011). Instead, social media, YouTube, and blogs have become an important way for citizens to convey their views among themselves as well as a way for party supporters to post their views outside the confines of the official campaign. In effect, then, the Internet and social media have reduced the ability of politicians and the conventional media to define election issues.

ELECTION AND PARTY FINANCE

In the past, a very large proportion of the funds the Liberal and PC parties needed for their election campaigns (and the operations of their party organization) came from large corporations, as well as from those seeking to gain government contracts. This pattern of election and party finance often led to criticism that the leading political parties favoured the interests of large corporations. Fuelling this argument were various scandals concerning government favours to major donors. Not all parties relied on funding from corporate sources. The NDP raised the largest proportion of its funding from its members, although it received, in addition, a significant proportion of its funding from labour unions. The unregulated system of party and election finance also raised questions about whether those parties that were able to raise large sums of money for their campaigns enjoyed an unfair advantage.

Amendments to the Canada Elections Act have made party financing at the national level more transparent by requiring that donations of $200 or more to parties and candidates be publicly reported. Cash donations of over $20 cannot be accepted. To encourage small individual donations rather than large corporate ones, a generous system of tax credits for donations was established (a 75 percent tax credit for donations up to $400 with a lower credit for contributions in excess of $400).

The most radical change has been the ending of corporate donations and the placement of strict limits on individual contributions. Beginning in 2007, only individuals who are Canadian citizens or permanent residents have been allowed to contribute to political parties, leadership contenders, candidates in an electoral district, and those seeking nomination as candidates. As of 2015, these donations are limited to a maximum of $1 500 per year to each registered political party, to the various entities of each registered party (associations, nomination contestants, and election candidates), candidates for the leadership of a party, and independent candidates in an election.[9] Contributions by corporations, unions, and unincorporated associations are illegal.

At least until the 2015 election, the Conservative party has been the most successful in raising funds from a substantial number of individual donors, raising more money than the Liberals or NDP (see Table 9-2).

---

[9]These limits increase by $25 per year. Candidates can donate up to $5000 to their own election campaign and candidates for party leadership can donate up to $25 000 to their own campaign.

PARTY	CONTRIBUTIONS ($)	NUMBER OF CONTRIBUTORS
Conservative	20 113 303	91 736
Liberal	15 063 142	77 064
NDP	9 527 136	46 355
Bloc	425 661	4198
Green	3 002 189	23 726

SOURCE: *Registered Party Financial Transactions Returns, Contributions and Expenses Database.* Elections Canada. (2014). This is an adaptation of the version available at www.elections.ca. Reproduced with the permission of Elections Canada, but adaptation rests with the author.

TABLE 9-2
INDIVIDUAL CONTRIBUTIONS TO POLITICAL PARTIES, 2014

Note: Excludes transfers from registered associations, candidates, leadership contestants, and nomination contestants. It also excludes loans made to the parties.

In addition, individuals, groups, unions, and corporations (termed "third parties") other than candidates, registered political parties, and the district associations of registered parties could spend a maximum of $438 910 on their own 2015 election-related advertising, including a maximum of $8788 in any electoral district. (This was double what could be spent in a normal 39-day election campaign.) Although the National Citizens Coalition had challenged limits on spending as a violation of the Charter of Rights and Freedoms, the Supreme Court of Canada ruled that it was a "reasonable limit" on freedom of expression needed to ensure fairness in elections [*Harper v Canada* (AG), [2004]). This has helped Canada avoid the massive campaign-related spending by political action committees (PACs) characteristic of American elections.

Rebates of campaign expenditures are provided to parties and candidates who receive a significant proportion of votes. Specifically, candidates who receive at least 10 percent of the valid votes in their district can receive a reimbursement of 60 percent of their eligible campaign expenses. Political parties are reimbursed for 50 percent of their eligible campaign expenses if their party receives at least 2 percent of the valid votes nationally or 5 percent of the valid votes in those electoral districts in which the party ran a candidate.[10] Thus, parties that are able to spend the most money on their election campaign receive the largest rebate that can be used in the next election.

VOTING BEHAVIOUR

In this age of skepticism surrounding politicians, voters may struggle more than ever to find a candidate or party that expresses their point of view. What explains the choices voters make in casting their ballots in an election? Undoubtedly, the choice made by voters will reflect their thoughts about which party, party leader, and candidate are best. In turn these preferences will be shaped, to a considerable extent, by the long-term perceptions that voters have of the political parties, by the general political values that voters hold, and by the interests related to the groups to which voters belong or with which they identify.

Canadian Election Study
www.ces-eec.org

---

[10]An annual subsidy to registered parties based on the number of votes received in the previous election was phased out beginning in 2011 and ended April 1, 2015.

Long-Term Influences on Voting Behaviour

SOCIAL CHARACTERISTICS   Our social characteristics can have an impact on how we vote. People with the same social characteristics may have similar interests at stake in politics. For example, students may be inclined to vote for the political party that seems most favourable to reducing the cost of their education. Those who have similar social characteristics may also tend to have similar values that affect their choice of party. As well, we are more likely to come into contact with people of similar social characteristics, which may lead to having similar views about which party is best. If most of your friends or most of the people in your neighbourhood favour a particular party, that may influence your voting choice. Furthermore, our social characteristics are often associated with our sense of identity. Even if we as individuals do not stand to benefit materially by voting for a particular party, we may be inclined to vote for a party that we perceive as respecting and recognizing our identity as a member of a particular social group.

In national politics, there is a complex relationship between social characteristics and voting because of Canada's great diversity. A variety of social divisions are apparent, with no one division having a dominant influence on voting. Nevertheless, there are some persistent patterns in which people with certain social characteristics show a tendency to support a particular party. As discussed in Chapter 8, important provincial and regional differences affect the support for different political parties—differences that are highlighted and exaggerated by the nature of the Canadian electoral system. For example, support for the Liberal party has been weak in Western Canada since the mid-1950s. In most elections, Quebecers have provided relatively little support for Conservative parties.

The type of community people live in also affects their vote. The Conservatives have strong support in many rural areas and towns, but with the exception of the 2011 election have had difficulty winning many seats in Canada's largest cities.

There have also been long-standing and substantial differences in vote choice among those with different religious ties. In much of Canada, Catholics have been more likely than Protestants to support the Liberal party.[11] However, the Liberal lead among Catholic voters has dropped sharply since 2000 and disappeared in the 2011 election (Fournier, Cutler, Soroka, Stolle, & Bélanger, 2013). Fundamentalist and evangelical Christians have strongly supported the Conservative party in recent federal elections. The NDP tends to do better among secular than religious voters (Gidengil, Nevitte, Blais, Everitt, & Fournier, 2012).

Ethnic ancestry is also linked to voting patterns. Voters of non-European ancestry (as well as new immigrants from non-traditional locations) have

---

[11]The explanation of this aspect of voting behaviour has been a much examined puzzle (Blais, 2005; Stephenson, 2010).

shown a strong tendency to support the Liberal party (Bilodeau & Kanji, 2010; Blais, 2005). The Conservatives made major efforts to woo various ethnic groups and were successful in gaining many seats with large ethnic populations in 2008 and 2011. However, the return of much of the ethnic vote to the Liberal party in 2015 contributed to Liberal victories throughout the greater Toronto area. The Liberal party was the leading party of French Canadians for over a century. However, beginning with the 1984 election, many French Quebecers have shifted their votes to other parties: first to the Progressive Conservatives and then to the Bloc Québécois. In the 2011 election, the NDP, which had always been very weak in Quebec, won 59 of the province's 75 seats. In the 2015 election, the Quebec vote was divided among four parties, although the Liberals emerged as the leading party with 35.7 percent of the vote and 40 of the 78 seats.

Differences in voting among those of different social classes have never been strong at the national level, although class-based trends are evident in some provinces, such as British Columbia. The NDP does better among union members than non-members; nevertheless, a majority of union members have voted for the other parties.

To a limited extent there are also gender differences in voting choice, with the Conservatives (and particularly their Reform and Alliance predecessors) doing somewhat better among men than women. The NDP has attracted considerable support from younger women in some recent elections (Gidengil et al., 2012; Strategic Counsel, 2008). In the 2011 election, the overall "gender gap" between the voting patterns of men and women was quite small or insignificant (Soroka, Cutler, Stolle, & Fournier, 2011; LeDuc & Pammett, 2011). Public opinion polls conducted just before Election Day in 2015 found that men were slightly more likely than women to vote for the Conservative party; women were more likely to vote for the Green party than men. There was no gender difference in the proportion decided or leaning to vote Liberal or NDP (Ekospolitics.com, 2015).

The Green party and the NDP tend to draw more of their support from younger rather than older voters, while the Conservatives tend to draw their strongest support from older voters. The age difference was particularly evident in the 2011 election, with 50 percent of those 55 and older voting Conservative compared to 27 percent of those 18 to 34; 40 percent of younger voters supported the NDP (LeDuc & Pammett, 2011). This pattern was also found in the 2015 election to a lesser degree. Only 24.0 percent of those aged 18–34 favoured the Conservatives, compared to 34.1 percent for the Liberals, 24.4 percent for the NDP, 10.1 percent for the Green party, and 6.0 percent for the Bloc. In contrast, 37.1 percent of those aged 65 and older supported the Conservatives, 35.9 percent the Liberals, 18.2 percent the NDP, 3.0 percent the Green party, and 4.3 percent the Bloc (Ekospolitics.com, 2015). The switch of many young persons from the NDP to the Liberal party during the campaign likely made a significant contribution to the Liberal victory. As well, the Conservatives no longer had a substantial lead among seniors; a significant proportion switched from the Conservatives to the Liberals during the election campaign.

Education is also related to vote preference. In 2015, the Conservatives led among those who had a high school education or less, while the Liberals had a substantial lead among those with university education. Those with a university education were more likely to vote for the NDP than those with less education (Ekospolitics.com, 2015).

VALUES   The basic values and ideological perspectives held by Canadians help to shape their party preferences and voting choices. Those who support the values of the free enterprise system with limited government involvement in the economy are more likely to vote for the Conservative party and less likely to vote for the NDP. Those who hold socially conservative values (e.g., those who oppose same-sex marriage and have traditional views on the role of women) are more likely to vote Conservative and less likely to vote Liberal or NDP. Conservative voters are also more likely to favour, and NDP voters to oppose, closer relations with the United States. Conservative voters have also been less likely to favour accommodating Quebec than Liberal and NDP voters. The choices of Quebec voters (at least until the 2011 election) have been strongly affected by their views on Quebec sovereignty. Support for the Bloc and the NDP in Quebec is also associated with opposition to moral traditionalism, support for a substantial government role in the economy, and a belief that Quebec is not well treated by the Canadian government (Gidengil et al., 2012). Although Canadian politics is often described as non-ideological, basic political values and beliefs are related to the choices voters make.

PARTY IDENTIFICATION
A sense of attachment to a particular political party.

PARTY IDENTIFICATION   The majority of voters have a sense of attachment to a particular political party. That is, they will tend to view one party as "their party," even if they are not a member of that party and have never participated in any of its activities. For some people, this **party identification** starts at an early age and may be transmitted from parents to children. For others, it may develop over time as voters see a particular party as reflecting their preferred values, interests, and policy positions, or as having the best record when it forms the government.

Those who identify with a particular party will not only tend to vote for that party, but will also tend to evaluate their party's current leader, candidates, and issue positions in a favourable light. However, this does not mean that they will always vote for their party. An unpopular leader or candidate, the adoption of issue positions that the voter disagrees with, a poor performance by their party in government, or the attractiveness of another party may result in a party identifier voting for a different party in a particular election. This is especially the case for voters who do not have a strong party identification. Nevertheless, many voters retain their party identification even if they do not vote in line with that identification in each election.

Over one-third of the electorate can be considered non-partisan as they do not identify with any party or only report a weak party identification (Gidengil et al., 2012). This grouping can have an important effect on the outcome of an election.

A person's party identification tends to persist over time. However, a significant proportion of the electorate does change its party identification either in the sense of identifying with a different party or in changing to or from identifying with no political party.[12] At times, there have been major shifts in attachments to political parties. Because party identification in the Canadian electorate as a whole is not particularly strong and is subject to change, political campaigns and other political events can have important effects on voters and election outcomes.

Until fairly recently, the Liberal party had the lead compared to other parties in terms of party identification. However, the proportion of Canadians with a Conservative party identification rose steadily from 2004 to 2011, while the proportion of Liberal identifiers dropped sharply from 2006 to 2011. NDP identification also increased, particularly from 2008 to 2011 (Fournier et al., 2013). Shortly after the 2011 election, 30 percent of those surveyed indicated that they usually thought of themselves as Conservative in federal elections compared to 18 percent Liberal, 17 percent NDP, 6 percent Bloc Québécois, and 3 percent Green (Clarke et al., 2011).

A poll conducted before the 2015 election (October 5–8, 2015) found that 28 percent of persons outside Quebec identified with the Liberal party compared to 27 percent with the Conservatives, 14 percent with the NDP, 8 percent with the Green party or other party, and 23 percent were unaligned. In Quebec, 24 percent identified with the Bloc, 20 percent with the Liberal party, 16 percent with the NDP, 14 percent with the Conservative party, 4 percent with the Green or other party, and 22 percent were unaligned (Innovative Research Group, 2015). While it may be misleading to make comparisons between data from a sophisticated 2011 academic survey and a 2015 poll using a different (and less scientific) methodology and different wording, the decline in Liberal party identification likely has been reversed.

Short-Term Influences on Voting Behaviour

Increasingly voters say they make up their mind about whom to vote for during the election campaign. Thus, the leaders and candidates themselves, and the issues raised during a campaign, can be significant factors in the choices of the electorate. For example, support for the NDP in Quebec increased from 15 percent to 43 percent during the 2011 election campaign.

---

[12]Because the nature of party competition often differs between the national level and the provincial level, a substantial proportion of the electorate identifies with different political parties in the two political arenas.

This was largely a result of NDP leader Jack Layton's increased popularity and support for the party's advocacy of greater government spending on health care and the environment, and higher corporate taxes (Fournier et al., 2013). During the lengthy 2015 campaign, the NDP went from first place with 33.2 percent of the intended vote on August 2 to a third place 19.7 percent on Election Day. Conversely, the Liberal party began with 25.9 percent, but moved into first place in the last weeks of the campaign and then steadily increased its support to 39.5 percent, generally matching the NDP's decline. Conservative support was generally quite steady according to public opinion polls and ended up at nearly the same level of support as when they began (Grenier, 2015).

Many voters say that it is the issue positions of the parties, leaders, and candidates that matter most to their voting decisions (Pammett, 2008). However, since the leading parties often do not take markedly different positions on key issues in an election campaign and voters are often unclear about the differences in party positions, voters may have trouble expressing their views on important issues through their voting choice. A very unusual exception was the 1988 election, in which the Canada–United States Free Trade Agreement negotiated by the PC government dominated the campaign, with the Liberals and NDP opposing the agreement. Most voters had an opinion on the issue, knew where the parties stood, and voted for the party that took the position they preferred (Johnston, Blais, Brady, & Crête, 1992). Although more voters opposed than supported the agreement, the PCs were re-elected with 43 percent of the vote and passed the agreement. In other elections, voters are often affected by their perceptions of which party they feel is best able to handle various general problems, rather than the positions the competing parties take on controversial issues (Clarke et al., 2011). Issues linked to perceptions of the governing party's corruption can also affect voters. For example, the sponsorship scandal contributed to the substantial decline in Liberal party support in the 2004 and 2006 elections (Gidengil et al., 2012).

With the focus on the party leaders in an election campaign and in politics generally, it is not surprising that evaluations of the party leaders are generally the most important short-term influence on the vote (Bittner, 2010; Gidengil et al., 2012). This does not mean that the party with the most popular leader will necessarily win the election or even increase that party's vote. Overall, the average ratings of party leaders are more likely to be slightly negative rather than positive. Thus, they often do not provide a strong motivation to switch from the party that voters would otherwise support. Nevertheless, the comparative ratings of the party leaders can have a significant effect. For example, Jack Layton's positive rating in the 2011 election contributed to the NDP's increased vote, while the sharp drop in Liberal support reflected, in part, the strongly negative rating of the party's leader, Michael Ignatieff (Clarke et al., 2011). Undoubtedly, Justin Trudeau's positive image in the 2015 election contributed to the major increase in Liberal party support.

BOX 9-3

"Vegas Girl" and the "Orange Crush" in Quebec

Ruth Ellen Brosseau

On May 2, 2011, Ruth Ellen Brosseau, a single mother who worked at Carleton University's student pub, was shocked to learn that she had been elected as an NDP MP for Berthier-Maskinongé (Quebec), defeating the incumbent MP by a large margin. She received instant notoriety as the "Vegas girl" when the media discovered that she had vacationed in Las Vegas during the campaign. Indeed, she had never been in her district, had lived much of her life in Ontario, and was not very fluent in French.

With the NDP having only ever elected one MP from Quebec in a general election, the party concentrated its campaign efforts on a handful of Quebec districts. For most of the province, "placeholders" were recruited so that the party could claim to have a full slate of candidates. For Brosseau and a number of other successful candidates, there was no campaign office, no meetings with voters, no volunteers knocking on doors, no lawn signs or leaflets, and no media interviews. Brosseau's election expenses were $0, while her leading opponent spent over $50000. Voters in the district had no idea who she was. Clearly, Brosseau was elected because of the sudden rise in popularity of her party's leader and the willingness of Quebecers to switch from other parties to the NDP. Swept into office by the "Orange Crush" was a diverse group of Quebecers, including many young people, women, members of ethnic minorities, students, and "ordinary" persons.

Ruth Ellen Brosseau did not win the "jackpot" in Vegas, but as a sincere, hardworking MP she earned much more than she had working at a pub. Indeed, her efforts on behalf of her constituents paid off, as she was re-elected in the 2015 election despite the substantial decline of the NDP in Quebec.

Voters do not directly elect the party leader (and potential prime minister) they prefer, but rather have to choose among the candidates in their electoral district. Despite the considerable effort that goes into campaigning by most serious candidates, one study found that the local candidates scarcely affect the outcome of the election in their district (Clarke, LeDuc, Jenson, & Pammett, 1979). Another study found that preference for the local candidate was a decisive factor in the choice of 5 percent of Canadian voters, independent of the effects of their feelings about the parties and their leaders (Blais, Gidengil, Dobryznska, Nevitte, & Nadeau, 2003). In some unusual circumstances, an unknown candidate for a popular party who does not bother campaigning can get elected (see Box 9-3: "Vegas Girl" and the "Orange Crush" in Quebec). Likewise, when a party is suddenly unpopular, as was the case for the PCs in 1993, even very popular MPs and candidates cannot withstand their party's decline.

During the 2015 election campaign, much attention was given to strategic voting. For example, a person may decide to vote for his or her second choice if the candidate of the party the person favours is expected to lose. Despite about two-thirds of the electorate wanting to replace the Harper Conservative government, there were concerns that if votes were evenly split between the Liberals and the NDP, the Harper government could be re-elected. Groups such as Leadnow conducted substantial campaigns to encourage voters to vote for the NDP or Liberal candidate in their district that had the best chance of winning. Leadnow commissioned a number of polls to determine which candidate was most likely to defeat the Conservative candidate, particularly in 72 Conservative-held swing districts. Canvassers and the media carried the message to voters. Over 90 000 persons pledged to vote strategically.

However, their efforts were overshadowed by the success of the Liberal party which won many seats for which strategic voters had been encouraged to vote for the NDP candidate. As national polls documented, the sharp drop in NDP support was matched by the rise of the Liberals close to the end of the campaign; those who wanted to defeat the Conservatives may have decided to vote Liberal even if the NDP candidate in their district had seemed to have a better chance of defeating a Conservative candidate. At the time of writing, there was no available research to determine the extent and nature of strategic voting in the 2015 election.

Summary and Conclusion

All citizens residing in Canada who are at least 18 years old have the right to vote. There is, however, considerable controversy concerning Canada's single-member plurality electoral system. While the system has provided a simple voting mechanism and a connection between voters and their elected representative, it causes distortions in the translation of the votes for a party into the proportion of the seats that party obtains. This often results in the election of a government with a majority of seats that was supported by a minority of voters and, in some cases, in a government to which the majority of voters object. Questions have, therefore, been raised concerning whether the single-member plurality system is consistent with democratic principles. Furthermore, the electoral system tends to exaggerate regional differences and can prevent or discourage the representation of diverse minority perspectives and interests that are not geographically concentrated.

Supporters of the single-member plurality system argue that it is more likely than other electoral systems to result in good government because it increases the chances that a majority government will be formed. Others argue that the virtues of majority government are overrated: minority or coalition governments can also provide good government if politicians from different political parties are willing to negotiate with each other in good faith.

Concerns have been raised about whether campaign practices, such as negative advertising and robocalls, mislead voters and foster cynicism concerning politicians and government. As well, questions often arise as to whether the media coverage of election campaigns provides the information and analysis needed by the average voter to make an intelligent choice. Although elections are often considered to be the cornerstone of democracy, election campaigns might be viewed as involving the manipulation of voters by the contending parties rather than promoting a dialogue about the direction of the country.

The rules for financing election campaigns and political parties have changed considerably in recent times. In particular, donations by business and labour organizations have been banned, and strict limits have been placed on the amounts that individuals can donate. This can be viewed as a democratic advance, as it has reduced the dependence of political parties on a small number of corporations and wealthy donors. Nevertheless, some parties have a substantially better financial capability to appeal to voters than others.

Studies of voting behaviour have found that the long-term factors of social characteristics, basic political values, and party identification are associated with the choices that voters make. The regional, ethnocultural, and religious diversity of Canada is reflected, to some extent, in the patterns of support for each party. Differences based on class and gender generally have a weaker effect on voting choices. However, voting behaviour also reveals considerable flexibility. Short-term factors, including perceptions of which party leader is best, which party is most competent to deal with important issues, and which party is most in tune with the values and issue positions of voters are important. Strategic voting may also be significant in certain elections.

Discussion Questions

1. Should the voting age be lowered? Should prisoners have the right to vote? Should citizens living outside Canada have the right to vote?

2. Should every electoral district have about the same number of people?

3. Are fixed election dates desirable? Under what circumstances, if any, should an election be held after a period shorter than four years?

4. Should Canada change its single-member plurality electoral system? If so, what would be the best alternative?

5. Should donations to political parties be strictly limited? Should public funds be used to subsidize political parties?

6. How will you decide whom to vote for in the next election?

Further Reading

Anderson, C.D., & Stephenson, L.B. (Eds.). (2010). *Voting behaviour in Canada*. Vancouver, BC: UBC Press.

Clarke, H.D., Kornberg, A., & Scotto, T.S. (2009). *Making political choices: Canada and the United States*. Toronto, ON: University of Toronto Press.

Courtney, J.C. (2004). *Elections*. Vancouver, BC: UBC Press.

Flanagan, T. (2014). *Winning power: Canadian campaigning in the twenty-first century*. Montreal, QC: McGill-Queen's University Press.

Gidengil, E., Nevitte, N., Blais, A., Everitt, J., & Fournier, P. (2012). *Dominance and decline: Making sense of recent Canadian elections*. Toronto, ON: University of Toronto Press.

LeDuc, L., Pammett, J.H., McKenzie, J.I., & Turcotte, A. (2010). *Dynasties and interludes: Past and present in Canadian electoral politics*. Toronto, ON: Dundurn Press.

Milner, H. (Ed.). (2004). *Steps toward making every vote count: Electoral system reform in Canada and its provinces*. Peterborough, ON: Broadview Press.

Pammett, J.H., & Dornan, C. (Eds.). (2016). *The Canadian federal election of 2015*. Toronto, ON: Dundurn Press. (See also similarly titled books for other Canadian elections.)

Pilon, D. (2007). *The politics of voting: Reforming Canada's electoral system*. Toronto, ON: Edmond Montgomery.

Young, L., & Jansen, H.J. (2011). *Money, politics, and democracy: Canada's party finance reforms*. Vancouver, BC: UBC Press.

Elijah Harper, a member of the Manitoba legislature, holds an eagle feather for spiritual strength as he continues to delay the debate on the Meech Lake Accord, June 19, 1990.

© Library and Archives of Canada

CHAPTER 10

The Constitution, Constitutional Change, and the Protection of Rights and Freedoms

CHAPTER OBJECTIVES

After reading this chapter, you should be able to

1. Outline the basic elements of the Canadian Constitution and the procedures for changing the Constitution.
2. Examine the reasons that formal constitutional changes have been difficult to achieve.
3. Outline the major provisions of the Charter of Rights and Freedoms.
4. Discuss the significance of the "reasonable limits" and "notwithstanding" clauses in the Charter.

On June 12, 1990, Elijah Harper stood in the Manitoba legislature holding up an eagle feather to indicate his opposition to the Meech Lake Accord, an important package of constitutional changes that had been agreed to by the prime minister and premiers. While hundreds of Aboriginals beat their drums in support, Harper, a member of the Red Sucker Lake First Nation, prevented the legislature from voting on the accord by refusing to give the unanimous consent needed to bring it to an immediate vote. Frustrated that the accord did not address Aboriginal concerns, Harper raised the feather every day until the accord went down to defeat when it failed to be passed by the June 23 deadline.

The Meech Lake Accord was drafted in 1987 at a closed door, all-night meeting of Prime Minister Brian Mulroney and the 10 premiers. It was primarily a response to Quebec's demands for constitutional change and included a controversial clause recognizing Quebec as a "distinct society." Despite the unanimous agreement of the 11 leaders at the Meech Lake meeting, three provincial legislatures (Manitoba, New Brunswick, and Newfoundland) had not approved the accord a few weeks before the three-year deadline. On June 3, 1990, Mulroney invited the premiers to a dinner meeting in Ottawa to try to secure passage of the accord. They ended up staying for seven days and nights of intense meetings. An Ottawa clothing store donated clean shirts and underwear for the premiers, who had come unprepared.

The media badgered the prime minister and premiers as they entered and exited the closed-door meetings, and pundits claimed that this was "Canada's last chance"—the country would break up if no deal was reached. In the end, the prime minister and premiers left smiling from the meetings. An agreement had been struck: The accord would remain unchanged, but there would be another document outlining issues to be dealt with in future constitutional negotiations. Despite the apparent agreement, Newfoundland premier Clyde Wells added an asterisk to his signature, stating that he would submit the accord "for appropriate legislative or public consideration" prior to the deadline. Mulroney boasted that he had "rolled the dice" (by waiting until the last minute) and won.

With the deadline for passage just hours away, members of the Newfoundland House of Assembly stated their views in support of or in opposition to the accord. At the end, Premier Wells announced that he was cancelling the vote, thereby ensuring that the accord, which required the approval of all provincial legislatures, would fail. Wells was particularly annoyed that he was not informed about last-minute maneuvering by the Canadian government to ask the Supreme Court for a ruling about whether the deadline could be extended for three months to obtain Manitoba's agreement, provided that Newfoundland approved the accord by June 23 (Russell, 2004).

Constitutional issues have aroused intense controversy and at times raised doubts about the future of Canada. It was only after decades of constitutional negotiations that the Constitution (to which the Charter of Rights and Freedoms was added) was finally made a strictly Canadian document in 1982. The opposition by the Quebec government to the provisions of the Constitution Act, 1982, led to the Meech Lake and Charlottetown Accords, both of which failed to be passed. The difficulty in gaining approval for major constitutional changes and the conflicts that have accompanied attempts at important constitutional changes have made politicians reluctant to reopen the constitutional "can of worms."

INTRODUCTION

A **constitution** sets the fundamental rules by which a country is governed. In particular, a constitution provides the organizational framework within which various governing institutions operate, and the legitimate processes by which governments can act and laws can be passed. In addition, constitutions may limit the authority of governments by establishing various rights and freedoms for the population of the country. Finally, some constitutions state the general goals and values of the country (see Box 10-1: The Quest for Constitutional Values).

CONSTITUTION
The fundamental rules by which a country is governed.

THE CANADIAN CONSTITUTION

The word *constitution* may conjure up an image of a formal, legal document that establishes the rules for governing a country. However, there is no single document that contains all aspects of the Canadian constitution.

BOX 10-1

The Quest for Constitutional Values

The Constitution Act, 1867—the foundation in law of the new country—does not contain a statement of basic Canadian values. Indeed, the Act's preamble is more pragmatic than rousing: It simply states that the provinces "have expressed their Desire to be federally united into One Dominion under the Crown of the United Kingdom of Great Britain and Ireland with a Constitution similar in Principle to that of the United Kingdom." One phrase in the Act, however, stands out from the rest: "Peace, Order, and Good Government." Commentators have often cited this phrase in the Constitution Act, 1867, as representing Canadian values. Moreover, "Peace, Order, and Good Government" are often contrasted with the values of "life, liberty, and the pursuit of happiness" in the American Declaration of Independence. However, the "Peace, Order and Good Government" phrase falls under Section 91, which lists the legislative powers of the Canadian Parliament, and thus is not a general statement of values. Furthermore, the term "welfare" rather than "order" was commonly used in various pre-Confederation documents (such as the Constitutional Act, 1791). Indeed, the Quebec and London Resolutions that were the basis of the Constitution Act, 1867, used the phrase "peace, welfare, and good government" (Saul, 2008).

More than a century later, in negotiations between the Canadian government and provincial governments that eventually resulted in the Constitution Act, 1982, the authors attempted to draft a new preamble to the Constitution. However, no consensus could be reached. The Canadian government proposed that the preamble open with the words "We, the people of Canada . . ." echoing the preamble to the American Constitution. However, Quebec premier René Lévesque argued that the term "people" implied that Canada was a single nation and thus did not recognize the existence of the Quebec nation. Compromise proposals followed. The Canadian government suggested stating a commitment "to the distinct French-speaking society centred in though not confined to Quebec," whereas the Quebec government wanted to recognize the "distinctive character of Quebec society with its French-speaking majority." In the end, all of the proposals were unsuccessful (Romanow, Whyte, & Leeson, 1984, pp. 85–86).

Nevertheless, the preamble to the Charter of Rights and Freedoms (part of the Constitution Act, 1982) states that "Canada is founded upon principles that recognize the supremacy of God and the rule of law." The rule of law is an important constitutional principle. However, "the supremacy of God" is more problematic in a country of diverse beliefs. Some religions and belief systems held by Canadians (including Buddhism, varieties of Hinduism, and animist religions) do not believe in a single supreme god. In addition, nearly a quarter of Canadians (including 36 percent of those under 25) do not believe in any god (Angus Reid poll cited by CBC News, 2008a).

Instead, we can think of the constitution as consisting of four basic elements:

1. Formal constitutional documents
2. Ordinary acts of the Canadian Parliament and provincial legislatures that are of a constitutional nature
3. Constitutional conventions
4. Judicial decisions that interpret the constitution

Formal Constitutional Documents

A number of formal documents—including the Constitution Act, 1867; the Constitution Act, 1982; amendments to these acts; and sundry other documents—are listed in a schedule attached to the Constitution Act, 1982. Together, these documents are described as the Constitution of Canada.[1] The importance of the formal Constitution is indicated by the statement that it is "the supreme law of Canada, and any law that is inconsistent with the provisions of the Constitution is, to the extent of the inconsistency, of no force or effect" (Constitution Act, 1982, Section 52).

THE CONSTITUTION ACT, 1867   The British North America Act, 1867 (renamed in 1982 as the **Constitution Act, 1867**) is an act of the Parliament of the United Kingdom based on resolutions drafted by the leaders of the British North American colonies. Building on previous acts and practices, its particular importance was to establish Canada as a federal union of four provinces: Ontario, Quebec, Nova Scotia, and New Brunswick.

Following are some of the key provisions of the Constitution Act, 1867:

- establishing the Canadian Parliament, consisting of the House of Commons and the Senate, the legislatures of Ontario and Quebec, and the continuation of the legislatures of Nova Scotia and New Brunswick;
- dividing the authority to make laws between Parliament and provincial legislatures;
- making "property and civil rights" an exclusively provincial matter. This ensured that Quebec could maintain its system of civil law, which differs from the common law system of other provinces (discussed in Chapter 16);
- protecting the rights and privileges of denominational schools that were established by law at the time of Union; and
- allowing either English or French to be used in Parliament and the Quebec legislature, with both languages used in the records, journals, and the printed acts of those bodies. It also allows English or French to be used in Canadian and Quebec courts.

The Constitution Act, 1867, did not establish Canada as an independent country. The Act is a mundane legalistic document with almost no mention of individual rights and limited consideration of English–French relations. The position and rights of Aboriginal peoples were ignored, other than specifying that legislation concerning Indians and their lands falls under the jurisdiction of the Canadian Parliament (Gibbins, 2014).

CONSTITUTION ACT, 1867
An act of the Parliament of the United Kingdom that established Canada as a federal union of Ontario, Quebec, Nova Scotia, and New Brunswick.

---

[1]Throughout this textbook, we use Constitution with a capital "C" to refer to the formal Constitution and constitution with a small "c" to refer to the constitution as a whole.

The Constitution Act, 1867, remains Canada's basic formal constitutional document, although some provisions have been amended and new provisions added. The fundamental nature of the Canadian system of government is indicated by a statement in the preamble referring to "a Constitution similar in Principle to that of the United Kingdom." Thus, Canada would continue to have a system of responsible government in which the prime minister and cabinet are responsible to the elected House of Commons. However, by being "federally united" Canada differed from the basically unitary British system.

THE CONSTITUTION ACT, 1982   Although Canada became an independent country by the Statute of Westminster, 1931 (and, in practice, by 1926), Canada's Constitution was not fully a Canadian document until 1982. In particular, some aspects of the Constitution could only be amended (changed) by the Parliament of the United Kingdom, although in practice it only acted on the recommendation of the Canadian Parliament. In turn, beginning early in the twentieth century, the Canadian government would request an amendment directly affecting the legislative powers of the provinces only with the consent of all the provinces.

By adopting procedures to ensure that all aspects of the Constitution could only be amended in Canada, the Constitution was "patriated," that is, it became a wholly Canadian document, in 1982. In addition to establishing amending formulas, the **Constitution Act, 1982,**[2] added the Charter of Rights and Freedoms, recognition of the existing rights of Aboriginal peoples (discussed in Chapter 11), and a commitment to the principle of making equalization payments to the poorer provinces (see Chapter 12). As well, the Constitution Act, 1982, amended the Constitution Act, 1867, to give provinces greater legislative authority over non-renewable natural resources, forestry resources, and electrical energy.

CONSTITUTION ACT, 1982
This Act patriated the Constitution, established a formula for amending the Constitution, added the Charter of Rights and Freedoms, recognized the existing rights of Aboriginal peoples, and made a commitment to the principle of equalization payments.

OTHER FORMAL DOCUMENTS   The other formal documents that make up the Constitution include the Statute of Westminster (1931), an act of the Parliament of the United Kingdom that formalized the independence of Canada. In addition, the Constitution includes some other British statutes and orders-in-council, including those that added British Columbia (1871), Prince Edward Island (1873), Newfoundland (1949), and other territories to Canada. The acts of the Canadian Parliament establishing Manitoba (1870), Alberta (1905), and Saskatchewan (1905) are also part of the formal Constitution.

Acts of a Constitutional Nature

Various acts can be considered part of the constitution, even though they are not included in the list of documents that form the Constitution of Canada. Such

---

[2]Technically, the Constitution Act, 1982, is a schedule attached to the Canada Act, 1982, which was passed by the Parliament of the United Kingdom. The Canada Act simply terminated any power of the United Kingdom to legislate for Canada.

important laws as the Canada Elections Act and the Clarity Act (which sets up the provisions by which a province could separate from Canada) are of this nature. However, such acts (sometimes termed "quasi-constitutional") are not part of the supreme law, and thus do not have priority over other laws. No formal list of such acts exists, and they do not differ from other laws passed by Parliament or provincial legislatures in the method by which they are approved or changed.

Constitutional Conventions

Constitutional conventions are widely accepted informal constitutional rules. Some reflect the basic principles underlying Canada's system of responsible government, such as the convention that the prime minister and cabinet must maintain the confidence (support) of the House of Commons.

> **CONSTITUTIONAL CONVENTIONS**
> Widely accepted informal constitutional rules.

Canadian courts have recognized the existence of conventions and have provided opinions describing particular conventions (e.g., the *Patriation Reference* [1981] discussed later in this chapter). As well, the courts may consider conventions in cases involving interpretations of the Constitution (Heard, 1991). Conventions are deeply embedded in the ways that many people think about the governing system. A government that violated an important convention would likely be viewed as acting illegitimately by a significant part of the population. Nevertheless, despite their importance, conventions are not legally enforceable by the courts.

Constitutional conventions are important because the formal constitutional documents do not fully describe how government is to operate. Indeed, the prime minister and cabinet are absent from the Constitution acts—they receive no mention at all. Similarly, even though the Constitution appears to grant great authority to the monarch, there is an important convention that the governor general (acting in the name of the monarch) follows the advice of the prime minister and cabinet.

Judicial Decisions That Interpret the Constitution

Judicial decisions have played a major role in interpreting the provisions of the Constitution. In effect, important judicial interpretations of the Constitution have become an essential part of the constitution. To fully understand the provisions of the Constitution, it would be necessary to review the multitude of court decisions that have added to the very sparse wording of many provisions of the Constitution acts. The Supreme Court of Canada has drawn on its view of the "unwritten principles" of the constitution—such as democracy, federalism, minority protection, and judicial independence—to go beyond the "literal language" of the Constitution acts in its judgments (Hogg, 2006, p. 16).

> **JUDICIAL REVIEW**
> The authority of the courts to invalidate laws passed by Parliament or provincial legislatures that they deem to be in violation of the Constitution.

The Constitution Act, 1867, did not explicitly authorize the courts to overturn laws passed by Parliament or provincial legislatures that they deemed to be in violation of the Constitution (a power known as **judicial review**). However, because of Canada's colonial status, the United Kingdom's Colonial

Laws Validity Act meant that Canadian laws could be struck down as invalid if they conflicted with British laws (including the Constitution Act, 1867). The **Judicial Committee of the Privy Council**, a panel of judges primarily from the British House of Lords that acted as the highest court of appeal for Canada in constitutional and civil matters until 1949, used the power of judicial review to strike down a number of laws that it viewed as violating the division of powers between Parliament and provincial legislatures. Its judgments were important in clarifying the constitutional division of powers between the Canadian Parliament and provincial legislatures. In 1949, the **Supreme Court of Canada** took over as the country's highest judicial body in all matters. The adoption of the Charter of Rights and Freedoms in 1982 has considerably expanded the scope of judicial review.

CHANGING THE CONSTITUTION

Because a constitution sets the fundamental rules for governing a country, the provisions of a constitution are expected to be stable features of the political scene. However, some flexibility is needed in a constitution to take into account changes in the country and its values. Canada has expanded from 4 provinces to 10 provinces and 3 territories, and democratic values are much more important than they were at Canada's founding. Canada's population has become much more diverse, and governments have faced a variety of challenging issues that did not exist in the 1860s.

Constitutional conventions generally evolve gradually as new situations arise or different understandings of the conventions develop. Likewise, judicial interpretations of the provisions of the Constitution change as rulings in new cases sometimes modify interpretations in previous cases. Laws that are of a fundamental nature, but that are not in the formal Constitution, can be changed by a majority in Parliament or a provincial legislature. For example, election laws have changed so as to give women, those who do not own property, and Aboriginal peoples the right to vote. Changing many aspects of the formal Constitution is much more difficult.

Formal Amendments to the Constitution

The Constitution Act, 1982, sets out the requirement that one of the following four formulas, determined by the subject matter, has to be used to amend the formal Constitution:

1. *A majority in the House of Commons (and in the Senate) plus a majority in each provincial legislature.* This is needed for amendments that change:
   - the office of the Queen, the governor general, and the lieutenant governor;
   - the requirement that a province have at least as many seats in the House of Commons as it had in the Senate in 1982;
   - certain constitutional provisions concerning the use of English and French;

- the composition of the Supreme Court of Canada; and
- the amending formulas.

2. *A majority in the House of Commons (and in the Senate) and a majority in at least two-thirds of the provincial legislatures that represent at least one-half of the population of all the provinces.* This applies to many aspects of the Constitution acts, including:

   - the powers, the method of selection, and the number of senators for each province;
   - the establishment of new provinces; and
   - the division of legislative powers between Parliament and provincial legislatures. However, provincial legislatures can "opt out" of any constitutional changes that reduce their rights or powers. If the change is related to education and other cultural matters that are under provincial control, the provincial government that opted out is guaranteed "reasonable" financial compensation from the Canadian government so that the province can continue to run its own programs.

3. *A majority in the House of Commons (and in the Senate) as well as a majority in the legislature of the province or provinces that are affected by the change.* For example, a change in the boundaries of a province would require only the approval of Parliament plus the affected provinces.

4. *Parliament or provincial legislatures operating alone.* Except for matters covered in the first two formulas, Parliament or provincial legislatures can change the operating procedures and institutions of their own government.

The first formula, which requires Parliament and all provincial legislatures to agree on certain changes, safeguards some basic features of the governing system. The requirement of unanimity makes it difficult to change these features and, as discussed later in this chapter, has made it challenging to achieve a comprehensive package of major constitutional changes.

The second formula (often referred to as the "general formula") can be viewed as a compromise between the principle that each province should be treated the same regardless of its population and the reality that Canadian provinces vary dramatically in population and importance. However, if Quebec is viewed as a nation whose agreement is needed for changes that affect its powers, then it is not surprising that the formula is controversial. The possibility exists that Quebec could be forced to surrender some of its powers if most of the other provinces agreed to hand over specific provincial powers to Ottawa. To reduce the impact of that possibility, the second formula allows a province to "opt out" of any constitutional changes that reduce its own rights or powers. To ensure that opting out is not unrealistic given the costs involved in a province exercising a power, the formula guarantees "reasonable" financial compensation if related to education or other cultural matters. Although education and culture are highly prized in Quebec, Quebec governments have argued that compensation should not be limited to those areas.

Formal constitutional amendments normally need to be passed by majorities in both the House of Commons and the Senate. However, the House of Commons can override objections by the Senate for most provisions of the Constitution Act by passing a constitutional resolution a second time after a delay of 180 days. This provision ensures that the Senate cannot indefinitely prevent constitutional changes that would change the Senate itself—a major topic of constitutional reform discussions. Indeed, the Supreme Court of Canada has ruled that the abolition of the Senate would require the approval of Parliament and all provincial legislatures (*Reference re Senate Reform*, 2014).

The Constitution Act, 1982, does not require the use of a referendum to gain the approval of Canadian citizens for a constitutional amendment. Nevertheless, in 1992 the public voted on a major package of constitutional changes (the Charlottetown Accord) in a referendum.[3] It may well be that there is a political expectation that significant changes to the Constitution should have the approval of a majority of those voting in a referendum. British Columbia and Alberta have adopted laws requiring that a referendum be held before their legislatures will approve a constitutional amendment.

Since 1982, the Constitution has been amended to extend Aboriginal rights in 1983, to change representation in the House of Commons (1985 and 2011), to create the territory of Nunavut (1999), and to make several changes that only apply to specific provinces.

Finally, an act of Parliament, the **Constitutional Amendments Act, 1996**, requires that proposed constitutional changes cannot be presented to Parliament by the Canadian cabinet unless it has the support of the following:

- Quebec;
- Ontario;
- British Columbia;
- a majority of the Prairie provinces having at least one-half of the population of the Prairie provinces (in effect, Alberta plus either Saskatchewan or Manitoba); and
- at least two of the four Atlantic provinces containing a majority of the region's population.[4]

The Constitutional Amendments Act is not part of the formal Constitution and thus could be changed or eliminated by a simple act of Parliament.

CONSTITUTIONAL AMENDMENTS ACT, 1996
An act of Parliament that sets out the combination of provinces and regions whose support is needed before the Canadian cabinet presents proposed constitutional changes to Parliament.

Constitutional Amendments Act
www.constitutional-law.net/ conamact.html

---

[3]Newfoundland and Labrador held two referendums to gain public support for its proposal to change its constitutionally protected denominational school system. However, Quebec did not hold a referendum when it changed its denominational school system.

[4]The Constitutional Amendments Act does not specify whether the approval of provincial legislatures is needed or whether some other mechanism, such as a referendum, could be used to gain the necessary support.

THE POLITICS OF CONSTITUTIONAL CHANGE

Proposals to change various aspects of the Constitution have often been highly controversial. Key issues have included the amending formula, Quebec's place in Canada, Aboriginal rights, the powers of provincial governments, constitutional protection of rights and freedoms, and the Senate.

Quebec governments have long promoted the view that Canada is based on "two founding peoples"—English and French. Quebec governments have seen themselves as the principal custodian of the French "fact" in Canada, and thus have rebuffed attempts by the Canadian government to encroach upon the powers of the Quebec government.

As Quebec underwent major social and political changes in the early 1960s, the Quebec government sought more constitutional powers to lead the province's social and economic development. Quebec governments also argued for greater constitutional powers to protect and promote language and culture. As well, they demanded that Quebec retain what they consider Quebec's traditional right to veto any constitutional changes that could result in a loss of their province's powers. And finally, Quebec governments have fought for constitutional recognition of the province's distinctiveness. The growth of support for Quebec independence and the election of a Parti Québécois government in 1976 committed to pursuing Quebec sovereignty created a sense of urgency about constitutional change, but also presented obstacles to achieving it.

Western Canadian governments, particularly the government of Alberta, also began lobbying for major constitutional changes in the 1970s based on Western Canadian resentment of the domination of Canadian politics by Ontario and Quebec. Not long after, Canada's National Energy Policy (1980) was seen as robbing Alberta of the benefits of high oil prices to satisfy the industries of central Canada. Thus, the Alberta government, bolstered by other Western Canadian governments and by the Newfoundland government, pressed for constitutional changes to enhance provincial government control over natural resources and natural resource revenues. The Alberta government also sought to give the smaller provinces a stronger voice in Parliament by advocating a **"Triple-E Senate"**; that is, an elected and effective Senate based on equal representation from each province regardless of population.

TRIPLE-E SENATE
A proposal that the Senate be reformed to be elected and effective based on equal representation from each province regardless of population size.

Aboriginals have also demanded basic constitutional changes so as to recognize what they view as their inherent right to self-government, to establish Aboriginal governments with wide-ranging powers, and to have guaranteed representation in national political institutions. Aboriginal leaders have also sought to secure a place in constitutional negotiations for Aboriginal representatives.

Finally, the Canadian government, especially the government of Prime Minister Pierre Trudeau, has wanted to enhance the Canadian political community to counter the forces of Quebec nationalism and provincialism. In particular, a major goal of the Trudeau government was to entrench a Charter of

FIGURE 10-1
CONSTITUTIONAL TIMELINE

1867
British North America Act
(renamed Constitution
Act in 1982)

1931
Statute of Westminster

1949
Supreme Court of Canada
becomes final court of appeal

Rights and Freedoms that included expanded French- and English-language rights in the Constitution. Some provincial governments opposed a constitutional Charter, fearing that a uniform set of rights would undermine the diversity of Canada and erode the power of provincial governments. At times, the Canadian government has also wanted to safeguard its ability to establish national standards in social programs and to remove provincial barriers to trade and mobility within Canada.

THE CONSTITUTION ACT, 1982

Beginning in 1927, various attempts were made to find agreement between the Canadian and provincial governments on an amending formula so that the Constitution could become fully Canadian (see Figure 10-1).[5] Agreements reached by the Canadian and all provincial governments in 1965 (the Fulton-Favreau formula) and 1971 (the Victoria Charter) each failed when the Quebec premier withdrew his support. Only after an extremely difficult series of events was the Constitution Act, 1982, adopted.

Pierre Trudeau led the Liberal party to victory in the 1980 Canadian election, including winning 74 of Quebec's 75 seats. A few months later, the Parti Québécois government (elected in 1976) held a referendum, hoping to win a

---

[5]A 1949 amendment did give the Canadian Parliament the right to make amendments to most of the provisions of the Constitution that did not affect provincial powers, language rights, or denominational school provisions.

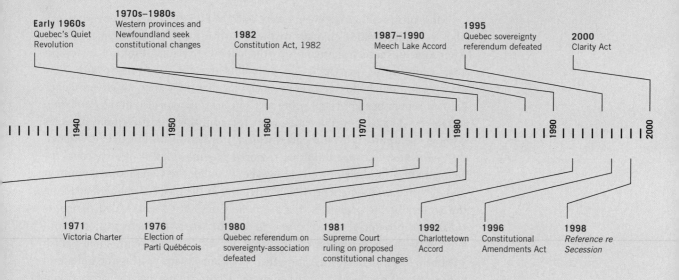

Early 1960s
Quebec's Quiet
Revolution

1970s–1980s
Western provinces and
Newfoundland seek
constitutional changes

1982
Constitution Act, 1982

1987–1990
Meech Lake Accord

1995
Quebec sovereignty
referendum defeated

2000
Clarity Act

1940   1950   1960   1970   1980   1990   2000

1971
Victoria Charter

1976
Election of
Parti Québécois

1980
Quebec referendum on
sovereignty-association
defeated

1981
Supreme Court
ruling on proposed
constitutional changes

1992
Charlottetown
Accord

1996
Constitutional
Amendments Act

1998
*Reference re
Secession*

mandate from Quebecers to negotiate sovereignty–association—that is, political sovereignty (independence) for Quebec while retaining an economic association with the rest of Canada. In urging Quebecers to reject this proposal, Prime Minister Trudeau and other political leaders promised Quebecers that a "no" vote would lead to a "renewed federalism." Although Trudeau's promise of "renewed federalism" was vague, the Quebec Liberal party presented a detailed proposal that would have given the Quebec government substantially greater powers.

The referendum battle concluded with Quebecers rejecting sovereignty–association. With a second chance to unify the country, Trudeau was determined to reassert the leadership role of the Canadian government and achieve his goals of patriating the constitution and entrenching a Charter of Rights and Freedoms in the Constitution. However, three months of negotiations failed, and a lengthy list of proposals for constitutional changes, presented by the premiers to Trudeau, was rejected. Trudeau felt that the proposals transferred massive powers to the provinces. Instead, he presented a proposal to Parliament that included a Charter, a commitment to the principle of equalization payments to the poorer provinces, and an amending formula that would have allowed Parliament to bypass provincial government opposition to constitutional changes through the use of a referendum. By presenting the plan before the Canadian Parliament with the intention of sending it to the Parliament of the United Kingdom for final approval, Trudeau avoided the established practice that included provincial government approval of constitutional changes that affect provincial powers.

Most provincial governments were outraged by the Trudeau government's plan to request major changes to the Constitution without their approval. After some unsuccessful attempts by the federal government to find an acceptable compromise, provincial governments (except for Ontario and New Brunswick) launched reference[6] cases challenging the Canadian government's plan. In September 1981, the Supreme Court of Canada ruled in the *Patriation Reference* (1981) that Trudeau's plan for adopting constitutional changes without the approval of provincial legislatures was *legal,* but that it violated the *constitutional convention* that required provincial legislative approval for changes affecting their powers. However, although the Canadian government had obtained *unanimous* provincial approval in the past for changes affecting the powers of the provinces, the Supreme Court of Canada ruled that only *substantial* provincial approval was needed to satisfy the constitutional convention (with the definition of "substantial" left unclear). With some British Members of Parliament indicating their uneasiness with passing the unilateral constitutional proposal, and the Supreme Court ruling that the process violated constitution convention, the prime minister and the premiers met to try to reach an agreement. With little progress over several days, an informal night-time meeting in a hotel kitchen worked out a compromise agreement while Premier Lévesque and the Quebec delegation slept. The following morning, the prime minister and nine premiers signed the agreement. Lévesque angrily denounced the "betrayal" by the other premiers (see Chapter 3 for his specific objections).

The compromise agreed to on November 5, 1981 (with Premier Lévesque refusing to sign), involved two basic elements: (1) the amending formula proposed by the dissenting provinces was accepted, and (2) the Charter of Rights and Freedoms proposed by the Trudeau government was also accepted, but a "notwithstanding clause" was added to allow a legislative body to override some provisions of the Charter. The women's movement successfully mounted pressure to prevent the male–female equality clause in the Charter from being subject to the notwithstanding override.

Aboriginals were not represented in the constitutional discussions. Nevertheless "existing aboriginal rights and treaty rights" were "recognized and affirmed" in Section 35.[7] A constitutional amendment in 1983 clarified that the rights acquired by land claims agreements or new treaties are recognized in the Constitution.

A challenge to the Constitution Act, 1982, by the Quebec government claimed that amendments to the Constitution without Quebec's consent

---

[6]*References* are questions posed by the federal or a provincial government asking a supreme court for an advisory opinion.

[7]A proposal to include a general constitutional right to Aboriginal self-government failed to gain the agreement of four provincial governments in 1987 after a series of three constitutional conferences on Aboriginal issues.

© Lane, Mark

In 1983, Peter Greyson entered Ottawa's National Archives (known today as Library and Archives Canada) and poured red paint over the Constitution. The Toronto artist was displeased with U.S. missile testing in Canada and wanted to "graphically illustrate" how wrong he thought this was. Specialists opted to leave most of the paint stain intact, fearing attempts at removing it would only do further damage.

violated constitutional convention. This was, however, rejected unanimously by the Supreme Court of Canada (*Quebec Veto Reference, 1982*). A challenge by three provincial Indian groups to the Constitution Act, 1982, was rejected by the British Court of Appeal (McWhinney, 1982).

The Canada Act (which included the Constitution Act, 1982) was passed by the Parliament of the United Kingdom. While Queen Elizabeth II signed the official documents making the Constitution fully Canadian at a ceremony in Ottawa, Premier Lévesque ordered flags in Quebec to fly at half-mast.

The Meech Lake Accord

The Progressive Conservative party led by Brian Mulroney won the 1984 Canadian election on a platform that included a promise to bring Quebec back into the Constitution "with honour."[8] Likewise, the death of Parti Québécois premier Lévesque and the subsequent election victory of the Quebec Liberal Party led by Robert Bourassa provided an opportunity to reach a settlement. However, the Mulroney government's attempts to make major changes to the Constitution ended in failure.

At a private meeting in April 1987, the prime minister and the 10 premiers reached a unanimous agreement known as the **Meech Lake Accord**. The accord

MEECH LAKE ACCORD
An agreement on constitutional change reached by the prime minister and premiers in 1987 that failed to be ratified by all provincial legislatures. The accord satisfied the conditions laid out by Quebec for signing the Constitution Act, 1982, while extending the powers granted to Quebec to all provinces.

---

[8]Although the Quebec government did not agree to the Constitution Act, 1982, it is nevertheless bound by it. "Bringing Quebec back in" refers to gaining the support of Quebec for the Constitution.

included the controversial **distinct society clause**—that the constitution should be interpreted in a manner consistent with "the recognition that Quebec constitutes within Canada a distinct society."[9] Quebec's role in preserving and promoting its distinct identity would be affirmed, but no specific new powers were attached to this role. Other provisions would have enhanced the powers of all provincial governments by giving them a role in nominating senators and Supreme Court justices, establishing their right to opt out of national social programs while receiving reasonable financial compensation to set up their own programs, and increasing their role in immigration. As well, the Meech Lake Accord proposed changing the general amending formula for the Constitution so as to require the agreement of every provincial legislature (as well as Parliament) for changes to the Constitution.

Strong opposition developed to the accord. Many English-speaking Canadians complained about the recognition of Quebec as a distinct society. Former prime minister Pierre Trudeau bitterly denounced the accord, which he argued would "render the Canadian state totally impotent" (Trudeau, 1987). Aboriginal groups were upset that recognition of their inherent right to self-government had not been considered. Those in the Territories objected to provisions that would make it difficult to eventually gain provincial status. As well, many Western Canadians were upset that Senate reform to create a Triple-E Senate was not included. Women's groups outside Quebec campaigned strongly against the accord, claiming that recognizing Quebec as distinct could allow that province to undermine the male–female equality that was guaranteed in the Charter of Rights and Freedoms. Multicultural groups were concerned the accord only recognized French- and English-speaking Canadians as "a fundamental characteristic of Canada." And finally, there was considerable criticism of the process of constitutional change by those who felt that deal-making by 11 heads of government (all white males) in closed meetings hardly made for a model of democracy at work.

Because the package of constitutional proposals in the Meech Lake Accord included changes to the amending formula and the Supreme Court, the accord required the approval of Parliament and all provincial legislatures. Despite the support of the prime minister and all the premiers for the Meech Lake Accord and the ratification of the agreement by Parliament and the legislatures of most provinces (including Quebec), elections brought new governments to power in Newfoundland and New Brunswick that were critical of the accord. In particular, although the Newfoundland House of Assembly had ratified the accord, this was reversed when the Liberal party, led by Clyde Wells, was elected in 1989. Wells campaigned vigorously across the country against the

---

[9]The clause also recognized "that the existence of French-speaking Canadians, centered in Quebec but also present elsewhere in Canada, and English-speaking Canadians, concentrated outside Quebec but also present in Quebec, constitutes a fundamental characteristic of Canada."

Robert Bourassa, premier of Quebec during 1970–1976 and 1985–1994, tried hard to achieve constitutional changes that would increase support for the Canadian federal system in his province, but he was ultimately unsuccessful.

accord, which he viewed as undermining the equality of the provinces. As discussed in the opening vignette, a last-minute effort to win the approval of all provincial legislatures failed.

Many Quebecers were deeply troubled by the defeat of the accord, which they viewed as the minimum set of changes that their province could accept. Support for independence rose sharply. To step up the pressure for change, Quebec premier Robert Bourassa arranged for a referendum on Quebec sovereignty to be held in 1992 if the rest of Canada had not put forward an acceptable binding constitutional proposal. As political scientist Léon Dion graphically put it, Quebec was holding "a knife at the throat" of English Canada quoted in (Bothwell, 1998, p. 219).

The Charlottetown Accord

Faced with the threat of a referendum on Quebec independence, politicians resumed efforts to develop a package of constitutional changes acceptable to all the diverse elements of Canadian society. Unprecedented and lengthy efforts were made to involve Canadians in the public discussion of constitutional issues before formal negotiations began. About 400 000 people participated in the Citizens' Forum that travelled across the country (Russell, 2004).

Formal negotiations on constitutional change involving representation of the Canadian government, provincial and territorial governments, and four national Aboriginal organizations began in March 1992 with the Quebec government joining the talks in July. An agreement was reached at a meeting in Charlottetown, PEI, on August 28, 1992.

CHARLOTTETOWN ACCORD

An agreement in 1992 on a broad package of constitutional changes, including Aboriginal self-government, Senate reform, and a statement of the characteristics of Canada. The agreement, which had the support of the prime minister, all premiers and territorial leaders, and four national Aboriginal leaders, was defeated in a referendum.

Consensus Report on the Constitution
**www.solon.org/Constitutions/
Canada/English/Proposals/
CharlottetownConsensus.html**

The **Charlottetown Accord** reached beyond the more limited provisions of the Meech Lake Accord. Its provisions included the following:

- recognition in the Constitution of the inherent right of Aboriginals to self-government within Canada;
- an elected Senate with six senators from each province, one from each territory, and representation of Aboriginals to be determined at a later date;
- a guarantee that Quebec would have at least one-quarter of the seats in the House of Commons;
- a "Canada clause" that the Constitution be "interpreted in a manner consistent with a number of fundamental characteristics," including: democracy, a parliamentary and federal system of government, the rule of law, Aboriginal rights, Quebec's distinct society, official language minority communities, racial and ethnic equality, individual and collective rights and freedoms, equality of female and male persons, and equality of the provinces;
- a commitment to establish a social and economic union that would include such objectives as reasonable access of all people to housing, food, and other basic necessities, as well as access to post-secondary education, protection of the rights of workers to organize and bargain collectively, protection of the integrity of the environment, the goal of full employment, and the free movement of people, goods, services, and capital;
- greater powers for provincial governments in a number of fields of jurisdiction, including the right to opt out of new national shared-cost programs in areas of provincial jurisdiction and receive full financial compensation; and
- appointment of Supreme Court of Canada justices by the Canadian government from lists of nominees prepared by the provinces and territories.

Although the accord was supported by all premiers, groups representing gays, lesbians, and persons with disabilities were upset that they were not recognized in the Canada clause. Women's groups argued that male–female equality was not given the same priority in the Canada clause as the rights of other groups. The Native Women's Association claimed that too much power would be placed in the hands of male Aboriginal leaders, while First Nations chiefs feared that the right to Aboriginal self-government would be unduly limited by the Charter of Rights and Freedoms.

More generally, many English-speaking Canadians felt the accord went too far in appeasing Quebec, while many Quebecers felt the accord provided less for Quebec than the Meech Lake Accord. There was also uncertainty about the provisions of the Charlottetown Accord because the legal text of the accord was not prepared until shortly before the referendum date. Even so, the legal text left many provisions open to further negotiations.

Because British Columbia and Alberta had adopted requirements that constitutional changes had to be approved by a referendum, it was decided to hold a national referendum. In Quebec, a referendum on the Charlottetown

	YES	NO	TURNOUT
Newfoundland	63.2	36.8	53.3
Prince Edward Island	73.9	26.1	70.5
Nova Scotia	48.8	51.2	67.8
New Brunswick	61.8	38.2	72.2
Quebec	43.3	56.7	82.7
Ontario	50.1	49.9	71.9
Manitoba	38.4	61.6	70.6
Saskatchewan	44.7	55.3	68.7
Alberta	39.8	60.2	72.6
British Columbia	31.7	68.3	76.7
Northwest Territories	61.3	38.7	70.4
Yukon	43.7	56.3	70.0
Canada	45.0	55.0	74.7

TABLE 10-1
RESULTS OF THE REFERENDUM ON THE CHARLOTTETOWN ACCORD, 1992, BY PROVINCE AND TERRITORY (PERCENTAGE)

Referendum question: "Do you agree that the constitution of Canada should be renewed on the basis of the agreement reached on August 28th, 1992?"

SOURCE: McRoberts & Monahan, 1993, Appendix 3. Elections Canada. This is an adaptation of the version available at www.elections.ca. Reproduced with the permission of Elections Canada, but adaptation rests with the author.

Accord replaced the planned referendum on Quebec sovereignty. Fifty-five percent of voters rejected the accord, including majorities of Quebecers, non-Quebecers, and Aboriginals living on reserves (see Table 10-1). Like the Meech Lake Accord before it, the Charlottetown Accord had to be scrapped.

The failure of the Charlottetown Accord shut down the process of seeking major changes to the Constitution. The Progressive Conservative party that held power while both the accords were negotiated was reduced to just two seats in the House of Commons. Instead, the Liberal party, led by Jean Chrétien, promised that constitutional issues should not be reopened for "a long, long time," and won the 1993 Canadian election.

The Liberal plan to avoid constitutional issues was, however, upended by political events in Quebec. The Parti Québécois was elected in 1994 and wasted no time in holding a referendum in 1995 on whether or not "Quebec should become sovereign after making an offer of economic and political partnership to Canada." When it appeared that a majority might vote yes, Prime Minister Chrétien made a last-minute television appeal to Quebecers. He vowed to recognize Quebec as a distinct society, to ensure that constitutional changes that affect the powers of Quebec should only be made with the consent of Quebecers, and to work toward greater decentralization of power from the Canadian government to provincial governments. Quebecers responded to Chrétien's promises—but just barely. The referendum result was extremely close: 49.4 percent voted yes, and 50.6 percent voted no.[10]

Finding too little support from provincial governments for a constitutional amendment to recognize Quebec as a distinct society, Chrétien encouraged the

---

[10]In two separate referenda, 96 percent of the Cree and Inuit of northern Quebec voted against the separation of Quebec from Canada.

House of Commons to pass a symbolic resolution recognizing Quebec as a distinct society. The Constitutional Amendments Act (discussed earlier in this chapter) in effect gave Quebec and other provinces and groups of provinces a veto over constitutional changes.

FUTURE CONSTITUTIONAL CHANGE?

Given the great difficulty involved in obtaining agreement on formal amendments to the Constitution and the intense conflicts that have surrounded constitutional negotiations, it is unlikely that further attempts to make substantial changes to the Constitution will occur in the foreseeable future. Instead, changes to the governing system will probably continue to occur in a gradual fashion through specific laws, agreements between the federal and provincial governments, judicial interpretations of the constitution, and evolving constitutional conventions (Russell, 2010).

Quebec Liberal premier Phillip Couillard stated that he would like Quebec to sign the Constitution by 2017, the 150th anniversary of Confederation (Canadian Press, 2014, September 6). However, the next day he said that his comments had been misunderstood: he wasn't referring to the Constitution; rather, he had said that Quebec's ties to Canada should be "reaffirmed." Instead of signing the Constitution, his priority is the economy (Canadian Press, 2014a, September 7). In response a spokesperson for Prime Minister Harper stated that the Canadian government had no intention to re-open the Constitution (Canadian Press, 2014b, September 7).

THE PROTECTION OF RIGHTS AND FREEDOMS

Historical Development

PARLIAMENTARY SUPREMACY
The principle that Parliament is the supreme law-making body whose ability to legislate has not been restricted by a superior constitutional document.

The British political system is based on the principle of **parliamentary supremacy**. Their Parliament is the supreme law-making body whose ability to legislate has not been restricted by a superior constitutional document. Unlike the United States, where rights and freedoms are protected by the constitutional Bill of Rights, which can be used by the courts to invalidate legislation, British courts cannot overturn an act of Parliament. Nevertheless, the protection of individual freedom is an important part of the British political culture.

Canada inherited many aspects of the British system of law and governing. However, unlike the United Kingdom, Canada has had a written constitution since 1867 that places some limits on the supremacy of Parliament, particularly by dividing legislative authority between Parliament and provincial legislatures. This has given judicial bodies the power of judicial review—that is, the power to declare a law invalid because it violates the Constitution.

The Constitution Act, 1867, outlined only a narrow set of rights. The right to use either English or French in the Canadian Parliament, in the Quebec legislature, and in federal and Quebec courts was protected, along with the existing rights and privileges of denominational schools. However, by including in the preamble to the Constitution Act, 1867, that Canada would have a "constitution similar in principle to that of the United Kingdom," it was assumed that traditional British liberties would continue to be respected in Canada.

The record of protecting rights and freedoms before the adoption of the Charter of Rights and Freedoms was far from exemplary. Although many traditional rights based on the English common-law system were respected, at times various minorities were stripped of their rights (including the right to vote) by the federal or provincial governments. As well, Aboriginals living on reserves were denied basic human rights, and Japanese Canadians were arrested, interned, and deprived of their property during World War II.[11]

Canadian courts and the Judicial Committee of the Privy Council (JCPC)—the final court of appeal until 1949—did, on occasion, invalidate laws that interfered with rights and freedoms on the grounds that the legislative body that passed the law did not have the authority to do so under the Constitution Act, 1867. Less frequently, some justices used the concept of an **implied bill of rights** in the Constitution. For example, in 1937 the Alberta legislature passed a law designed to stifle newspaper criticism of the Social Credit government. The Supreme Court of Canada struck down the law as ultra vires—that is, beyond the legislative authority of the provincial legislature because criminal law was the responsibility of the Canadian Parliament. Chief Justice Lyman Duff (supported by two of the six judges) stated that suppressing debate would be "repugnant to the provisions of the British North America Act" (quoted in Russell et al., 2008, p. 163). Some Supreme Court justices also used the concept of an implied bill of rights to strike down a series of Quebec laws in the 1950s that interfered with political and religious freedoms (Gibson, 2005). This included Quebec's Act to Protect the Province Against Communistic Propaganda (the "Padlock Law"). However, in *Canada v. City of Montreal et al.* (1978), the majority of Supreme Court justices rejected the notion that there was an implied bill of rights that protected freedoms from legislation that is within the constitutional competence of a legislative body.

IMPLIED BILL OF RIGHTS
The judicial theory that rights are implied by the preamble to the Constitution Act, 1867, and therefore could not be infringed upon by ordinary legislation.

The Canadian Bill of Rights

In 1960, Parliament passed the **Canadian Bill of Rights**. The Bill of Rights is quite limited in its significance. It is an ordinary statute (law), and does not clearly specify that the courts have the power to invalidate legislation that violates rights and freedoms. Nor does it fully challenge the traditional

CANADIAN BILL OF RIGHTS
An act of Parliament passed in 1960 establishing various rights and freedoms that only applies to matters under federal jurisdiction.

---

[11]The existence of a constitutional Bill of Rights did not prevent similar violations of rights in the United States.

principle of the supremacy of Parliament. Rather, it contains a clause that allowed Parliament to pass a law infringing upon rights and freedoms provided that the law made an express declaration to that effect. As well, the War Measures Act was excluded from the provisions of the Bill of Rights. This allowed the Canadian cabinet, after the kidnappings of the British trade commissioner and Quebec's minister of labour by the Front de libération du Québec in 1970, to declare a state of apprehended insurrection and jail people without explanation and without bail. In addition, the Canadian Bill of Rights only applies to matters within the legislative authority of the Canadian Parliament, although most provincial governments adopted their own bills of rights (beginning with Saskatchewan in 1947).

The courts were very reluctant to use the Bill of Rights to invalidate federal legislation. In only one case (*R. v Drybones*, 1970) did the Supreme Court rule a provision of a law invalid (because it contained a more severe penalty for an Indian than a non-Indian). In contrast, in *Lavell* and *Bédard* the Supreme Court ruled that the Bill of Rights should not render "Parliament powerless" even though the Indian Act discriminated against women (but not men) who lost their Indian status for marrying non-Indians (quoted in Russell et al., 2008, p. 183).[12]

The Charter of Rights and Freedoms

CHARTER OF RIGHTS AND FREEDOMS
As part of the Constitution Act, 1982, the Charter is superior to ordinary legislation, allows the courts to invalidate legislation, and applies to the actions of all governments and organizations under the control of government.

Liberal prime minister Pierre Trudeau passionately advocated the adoption of the **Charter of Rights and Freedoms**. Trudeau viewed constitutional protection of rights and freedoms as necessary to prevent government from tampering arbitrarily with the rights and freedoms of individuals. In the face of growing nationalism and separatism in Quebec, he also saw the protection of French- and English-language rights of people throughout Canada as being crucial to promoting national unity. Accordingly, he pushed hard for the entrenchment of the Charter in the Constitution despite the opposition of some premiers. In particular, the premiers of Manitoba and Saskatchewan were concerned that the Charter would undermine the principle of parliamentary supremacy—the foundation of much of the Canadian governing system. René Lévesque, the premier of Quebec, was also critical of the Charter, viewing it as imposing a centralist, uniform view of Canada.

When televised Parliamentary hearings on the proposed Charter were held, many groups supported the idea of the Charter while lobbying for various additions to it. In particular, women's groups and various ethnic groups mobilized supporters to successfully press for the adoption of provisions for strong protections of women's rights and the recognition of the multicultural nature of Canada. In the end, all the premiers except Lévesque agreed to the inclusion

---

[12]This discriminatory provision in the Indian Act was changed in 1985.

of the Charter in the Constitution Act (modified to keep an element of parliamentary supremacy, the "notwithstanding clause" discussed below).

The Charter is a much more powerful tool for protecting rights and freedoms than the Canadian Bill of Rights. For example, the Supreme Court of Canada used the Charter to strike down the federal Lord's Day Act as a violation of freedom of religion,[13] unlike its earlier decision to uphold the Act despite the Canadian Bill of Rights. The Supreme Court's judgment stated that, "the Charter is intended to set a standard upon which present as well as future legislation is to be tested" (*R. v. Big Drug Mart Ltd.*, 1985).

The Constitution Act, 1982, of which the Charter is an important part, states that the Constitution is "the supreme law of Canada, and any law that is inconsistent with the provisions of the Constitution is, to the extent of the inconsistency, of no force or effect" (Section 52). Thus, the Charter is clearly superior to ordinary legislation. Furthermore, Section 24 of the Charter provides that anyone whose Charter rights or freedoms "have been infringed or denied may apply to a court of competent jurisdiction to obtain such remedy as the court considers appropriate and just in the circumstances."

Thus, unlike the Bill of Rights, the Charter clearly empowers the courts to invalidate legislation that is inconsistent with the Charter. Furthermore, the Charter does not only apply to legislation passed by the Canadian Parliament and provincial legislatures, but also to the actions and policies of the Canadian, provincial, territorial, and municipal governments, as well as to agencies under the control of government or carrying out government policies. The Charter does not apply to businesses, private organizations, or the relations among individuals. Instead, human rights codes adopted by the Canadian and provincial governments apply to situations where, for example, a business or a landlord discriminated against a person based on such characteristics as age, gender, or race. Such codes are expected to be consistent with the provisions of the Charter.

Provisions of the Charter

The Charter is more comprehensive than the Canadian Bill of Rights in establishing rights and freedoms. Indeed, its scope is wider than the U.S. Bill of Rights to which it is often compared (e.g., by including language rights and equality rights). The Charter establishes seven basic categories of rights and freedoms:

The Canadian Charter of Rights and Freedoms
http://laws.justice.gc.ca/en/charter

1. Fundamental freedoms, consisting of "freedom of conscience and religion; freedom of thought, belief, opinion and expression, including

---

[13]Striking down the Lord's Day Act did not necessarily make provincial Sunday closing laws invalid. In *R. v. Edwards Books and Art Ltd.* (1986), Ontario's Retail Business Holiday Act was upheld because it was framed in secular rather than religious terms and because it had an exemption for those small business owners who have a religious duty to close on Saturdays.

freedom of the press and other media of communication; freedom of peaceful assembly; and freedom of association" (Section 2).

2. Democratic freedoms, including the right of all citizens to vote and hold elected office as well as limiting the maximum term of the House of Commons and provincial legislatures to five years. (Through ordinary legislation, Parliament and most provincial legislatures have reduced their maximum term to four years.)

3. Mobility rights, including the right to move and to pursue a livelihood in any province.

4. Legal rights, including the right to life, liberty, and security of the person, the right to a trial within a reasonable period of time if charged with an offence, the right to be secure against unreasonable search or seizure, and the right to be presumed innocent until proven guilty by an independent and impartial tribunal.

5. Equality rights, including the provision that every person is equal under the law and has the right to the equal protection and equal benefit of the law without discrimination on such grounds as race, national or ethnic origin, colour, religion, sex, age, or disability. This does not preclude laws, programs, or activities designed to improve the conditions of disadvantaged individuals or groups. The equality rights clause was at the centre of the issue of same-sex marriage (as discussed in Box 10-2: Same-Sex Marriage: Kevin and Joe, Elaine and Anne, and the Charter of Rights and Freedoms).

6. Language rights, including the right to communicate with and receive services in English or French from Canadian government offices where there is sufficient demand. New Brunswick is the only province that has entrenched these language rights in the Charter.

7. Minority language education rights, including the right of Canadian citizens whose mother tongue is either English or French to have their children educated in that language where numbers warrant. In Quebec, this right only applies to parents who received their primary schooling in English in Canada.

Other provisions of the Charter require that "the Charter shall be interpreted in a manner consistent with the preservation and enhancement of the multicultural heritage of Canada," and that the rights and freedoms in the Charter "are guaranteed equally to male and female persons." In addition, the rights and freedoms specified in the Charter do not affect any treaty or other rights or freedoms of Aboriginal peoples.

The Charter does not contain provisions for all of the rights and freedoms that some people would like. Some were disappointed that **social rights** such as the right to education, housing, or employment are not mentioned. Such rights (which are included in some of the international treaties Canada has signed) need government action, including government spending, to provide the rights. Nevertheless, Section 15 of the Charter provides that "every individual . . . has the right to the equal protection and equal benefit of the law." Likewise, Section 36 of the Constitution Act, 1982, includes commitments to

SOCIAL RIGHTS
Rights that require government action, such as the right to education, housing, or employment.

BOX 10-2

Same-Sex Marriage:
Kevin and Joe, Elaine and Anne, and the
Charter of Rights and Freedoms

On January 14, 2001, two couples—Kevin Bourassa and Joe Varnell, and Elaine and Anne Vautour—exchanged wedding vows in Toronto's Metropolitan Community Church. They were in love and ready to commit, but the Ontario government refused to register the wedding licences of the two same-sex couples. The couples undertook legal actions challenging the 1866 common-law definition of marriage: "as understood in Christendom . . . the voluntary union for life of one man and one woman, to the exclusion of all others" (quoted in Russell et al., 2008, p. 364). The definition was, argued the challengers, a violation of equality rights provisions of the Charter. Courts in a number of provinces ruled that the prohibition on same-sex marriage was unconstitutional, and

Recognition of same-sex equality rights in Canada came after much struggle. Couples Kevin Bourassa (left, glasses) and Joe Varnell and Anne Vautour and Elaine Vautour (right) may have exchanged wedding vows in front of Reverend Brent Hawkes in January 2001, but their marriages were not officially registered until 2003.

the Ontario government registered the marriages in 2003.

The Canadian government did not appeal the rulings of the provincial courts of appeal, but instead drafted its own legislation: "Marriage, for civil purposes, is the lawful union of two persons to the exclusion of all others." The Liberal government anticipated stormy opposition to the legalization of same-sex marriage and therefore asked the Supreme Court of Canada for a reference opinion on four questions related to the proposed legislation. The Supreme Court confirmed that Parliament has the legislative authority to decide who may marry, that extending the capacity to marry to persons of the same sex is consistent with the Charter, and that the Charter's guarantee of freedom of religion protects religious officials from being forced to perform same-sex marriages contrary to their religious beliefs. The Supreme Court refused to answer the fourth question—whether an opposite-sex requirement for marriage is consistent with the Charter—since the government had not pursued an appeal to the ruling of the lower courts on this issue. Already, thousands of same-sex couples had been legally married as a result of the lower court decisions.

To the cheers of the gay and lesbian community and the jeers of Catholic bishops, Canada became one of the world's first countries to officially recognize same-sex marriages.

"promoting equal opportunities for the well-being of Canadians" and "providing essential public services of reasonable quality to all Canadians." Despite these provisions, governments have generally resisted efforts to pursue social rights and only occasionally have the courts used these provisions to advance the provision of social rights (Porter & Jackman, 2014).

Although considered in the development of the Charter, property rights were not explicitly protected. In addition, the Charter does not provide any rights to a clean and healthy environment, unlike the more than 110 countries that have added environmental rights to their constitutions (Boyd, 2014).

The rights and freedoms listed in the Charter are quite broadly written and can even be considered somewhat vague. The courts have to interpret these rights as they apply to the particular cases that come before them. Judges are expected to examine precedents—that is, how the courts have interpreted a particular clause in similar cases. The lower courts are expected to follow the interpretations of the Supreme Court of Canada. However, the Supreme Court has not always felt bound by its previous rulings. For example, in 2002, the BC government passed legislation that changed provisions of a collective agreement between health care workers and their employer allowing such measures as layoffs and contracting out services without discussion with the workers' union. In *Health Services and Support* (2007), the Supreme Court stated that its earlier decision that "the Charter did not guarantee the collective bargaining rights of public employees" did not "withstand principled scrutiny," and ruled that the Charter's freedom of association provision protected the process of collective bargaining (quoted in Russell et al., 2008, p. 396).

Limitations on Rights and Freedoms

The Charter does not provide absolute guarantees of listed rights and freedoms. In particular, the Charter allows "reasonable limits" on rights and freedoms. As well, through the "notwithstanding" clause, Parliament and provincial legislatures can pass laws that contradict some of the Charter's provisions.

THE "REASONABLE LIMITS" CLAUSE   Clause 1 of the Charter guarantees that the rights and freedoms in the Charter are "subject only to such reasonable limits prescribed by law as can be demonstrably justified in a free and democratic society." If, in ruling on a particular case, a court decides that a particular law or government action violates the Charter, the **reasonable limits clause** places the onus on the government to provide evidence to demonstrate that the law or action is a reasonable limit on rights and freedoms. It is, however, a matter of judgment as to what reasonable limit is justified in a free and democratic society. How much and what kind of evidence is needed to "demonstrably" justify the limit on rights and freedoms is also often hotly debated.

In developing the **Oakes test,** the Supreme Court of Canada laid out the basic principles to apply in determining whether a limit on rights and freedoms is justified in a particular case (see Box 10-3: Innocent Until Proven Guilty? David Oakes and the Narcotics Control Act).

THE "NOTWITHSTANDING" CLAUSE   The Charter allows Parliament or provincial legislatures to explicitly declare that a particular law shall operate notwithstanding certain provisions of the Charter. Such a declaration is effective

REASONABLE LIMITS CLAUSE
A clause of the Charter of Rights and Freedoms that allows for reasonable limits on rights and freedoms, provided the limits can be demonstrably justified in a free and democratic society.

OAKES TEST
A Supreme Court of Canada ruling setting out basic principles in applying the reasonable limits clause.

BOX 10-3

Innocent Until Proven Guilty? David Oakes and the Narcotics Control Act

David Edwin Oakes was arrested outside an Ontario tavern in 1981 and was found to be in possession of $619.45 and eight, one-gram vials of hashish oil. He was charged with trafficking under the Narcotics Control Act, which carries a much more severe penalty (potentially life imprisonment) than for simple possession. The Act required that the accused had to prove he or she was not engaged in trafficking when claiming only possession.

The lawyer for Mr. Oakes challenged the Narcotics Control Act, arguing that it violated the right to be considered innocent until proven guilty that is guaranteed in the Charter—it was therefore up to the Crown prosecutor to prove that Oakes was guilty of trafficking, not up to the defendant to prove his innocence. After the court hearing the case struck down the provision in the act concerning trafficking, the Supreme Court of Canada was eventually called upon to decide if the Act's provision was a reasonable limit on a guaranteed legal right.

In their ruling, the Supreme Court judges laid out two criteria that together could help determine when "reasonable limits" could be used to uphold a law that interfered with the rights and freedoms in the Charter:

1. The objective of the law "must be sufficiently important to warrant overriding a constitutionally protected right or freedom." That is, the objective must at least "relate to societal concerns which are pressing and substantial in a free and democratic society."
2. The interests of society must be balanced against the rights and freedoms of individuals and groups. Specifically,
   - the measures contained in the law "must be carefully designed to achieve the objective in question" and "rationally connected to the objective,"
   - the measures "should impair as little as possible* the right or freedom in question," and
   - the more harmful the effects of the measures are in limiting rights and freedoms, the more important the objective must be.

Applying these criteria to the Oakes case, the judges agreed that drug trafficking was a "substantial and pressing" concern, thus meeting the first criterion. However, the second criterion was not fulfilled, since there was "no rational connection" between the possession of a small amount of hashish oil and the presumption that the possession was for the purpose of trafficking. Therefore, the judges concluded that Section 8 of the Narcotics Control Act was of "no force and effect," and the appeal of the acquittal of Oakes was dismissed (*R. v. Oakes*, 1986).

The "Oakes test" has been used in many cases since 1986, although not always resulting in an acquittal of the accused. For example, in *R. v. Keegstra* (1990), the Supreme Court of Canada upheld the conviction of a high school teacher under the "hate speech" provision of the Criminal Code for his willful promotion of hatred against Jews in his classes. The judges found that the "hate speech" provision infringed upon the Charter's guarantee of freedom of speech. However, the majority of judges upheld the provision, finding that hate propaganda was a "pressing and substantial concern," that there was a rational connection between the law and the objective of the law, that freedom of expression was impaired as little as possible, and that the limitation of hate speech is "only tenuously connected with the values underlying the guarantee of freedom of speech" (quoted in Russell et al., 2008, p. 282).

---

*However, in *Edwards Books* (1986), this was interpreted as meaning "as little as *reasonably* possible" (Hausegger, Hennigar, & Riddell, 2015, p. 357).

for only five years, although it can be re-enacted by the legislative body as often as is desired.

The **notwithstanding clause** applies to the rights and freedoms listed in Sections 2 and 7–15 of the Charter:

1. fundamental freedoms,
2. legal rights, and
3. equality rights.

Democratic, mobility, and language rights and other provisions of the Charter cannot be overridden. As well, rights and freedoms "guaranteed equally to male and female persons" cannot be overridden by the notwithstanding clause (Section 28).

The requirement that legislation has to explicitly state that a law or provision operates notwithstanding a provision of the Charter makes it politically risky for a government to use the clause, as the government may be accused of trampling on individual rights. For example, in 1998, the Alberta government invoked the notwithstanding clause in proposed legislation to limit compensation to those who had been sexually sterilized without their consent by an act of the legislature. After the *Edmonton Journal* ran the front-page headline, "Province Revokes Rights," the public outcry resulted in the government withdrawing the proposed legislation within 24 hours (McLachlin, 2005).

The most widely publicized use of the clause was by the Quebec government in 1988. As discussed in Chapter 3, the Quebec National Assembly passed a law banning languages other than French on signs outside businesses and invoked the notwithstanding clause to protect the law from being challenged as a violation of the right to freedom of expression. However, the Quebec government did not seek to renew its use of the notwithstanding clause when the five-year limit ran out and instead passed less restrictive legislation. The Quebec government also included the clause in all legislation between 1982 and 1985 as a protest against the passage of the Constitution Act, 1982.

There have been only a very small number of other uses, none of which have been significant. For example, in 1990, the Alberta legislature invoked the notwithstanding clause when amending the Marriage Act to define marriage as involving only opposite-sex couples. This turned out to be irrelevant when the Supreme Court of Canada ruled that defining marriage is a Canadian government responsibility.

The notwithstanding clause is highly controversial. For some, the clause is inconsistent with the Charter's protection of rights and freedoms. Pierre Trudeau viewed his reluctant acceptance of the clause as "the greatest regret of his political life" (quoted in Whyte, 2011). Progressive Conservative prime minister Brian Mulroney claimed that, "any constitution that does not protect . . . the rights of individual Canadians is not worth the paper it is written on" (quoted in Manfredi, 2003). Others argue that the clause is an integral part of the Charter that allows the ultimate responsibility to rest with elected

---

NOTWITHSTANDING CLAUSE
A provision in the Charter of Rights and Freedoms that allows Parliament or a provincial legislature to explicitly declare that a particular law (related to some sections of the Charter) shall operate notwithstanding the provisions of the Charter.

When the Quebec National Assembly banned languages other than French from signs outside businesses in 1988, it invoked the notwithstanding clause to protect the law from a Charter challenge. Although French must still dominate, the language restrictions have loosened since 2003, as seen in this sign outside the venerable Schwartz's deli in Montreal.

representatives of the people rather than unelected and unaccountable judges. Indeed, in introducing the Charter to the House of Commons, justice minister Jean Chrétien argued that the clause would be "an infrequently used safety valve to ensure that legislatures rather than judges would have the final say on important matters of public policy" (quoted in Manfredi, 2001, p. 22).

During the 2004 Canadian election campaign, Conservative leader Stephen Harper said that he would use the clause to strengthen child pornography laws and perhaps to deny same-sex couples the right to marry. Liberal leader Paul Martin strongly criticized Harper, saying that a Liberal government would never use the clause.[14] The issue surfaced again in the 2006 election. Martin accused Harper of wanting to use the clause to take away the rights of minorities and women. Instead, Martin promised to amend the constitution to remove the ability of Parliament to use the clause. Harper countered the criticism by promising not to use the clause to overturn the law allowing same-sex marriages. Overall, the notwithstanding clause has never been used by the Canadian Parliament and has rarely been used by provincial legislatures.[15] Saskatchewan premier Brad Wall said he was considering using the notwithstanding clause after the Supreme Court struck down Saskatchewan's Public Service Essential Services Act, which limited unionized public workers' right to strike (Charlton, 2015). However, in October 2015, the Saskatchewan government modified the Essential Services Act to comply with the Supreme Court ruling rather than using the notwithstanding clause.

---

[14]Earlier, however, Martin had said he might use the clause if needed to protect churches that refused to perform same-sex marriages (MacIvor, 2006).

[15]During her unsuccessful Quebec election campaign in 2014, Premier Pauline Marois said that her government would use the notwithstanding clause if the Supreme Court of Canada struck down proposed the Secular Charter proposed by the Parti Québécois.

Effects on the Political Process

The Charter has increased the political significance of the courts. By striking down legislation and policies deemed to be violations of the Charter, the courts have become an important part of the political process. This, some argue, have made the courts too powerful.

Given the potential importance of court decisions, many groups and individuals find it useful or necessary to use the courts to advance or defend their interests. The courts have encouraged this development by allowing a variety of groups and individuals to have intervener status so that they can present their positions in court. The Charter has thus provided another avenue for groups and individuals to engage in the political process. This is particularly helpful for groups that have trouble making their voices heard by government, legislators, and political parties.

Conservative critics of the courts have argued that feminists, civil liberties groups, those seeking greater social equality, and other "special interests" have succeeded in advancing causes that would not garner support from a majority of the public (Morton & Knopff, 2000). However, while groups seeking social change have gained considerable attention through their Charter cases, business interests have also made extensive use of the Charter (Hein, 2000).

Using the courts to advance political interests is very expensive. Taking a case to the Supreme Court of Canada can cost hundreds of thousands of dollars in legal fees. It can also be a very slow process, as it often takes many years before a case makes it to the Supreme Court. Furthermore, it diverts the energies of advocacy groups away from the political struggle for change (Mandel, 1994). It has also been argued that the Charter has contributed to the "legalization" or "judicialization" of politics. In part, this involves "the ever-accelerating reliance on courts for addressing core moral predicaments, public policy questions, and political controversies" (Herschel, 2008, p. 94). More generally, there has been a shifting of political discussion to legal abstractions which "obscures. . . . the political nature of the choices being made" (Mandel, 1994, p. 4). Similarly it has been argued that the legalization of politics "has contributed to an impoverishment of Canadian democracy" (Petter 2010, p. 226).

Does the Charter Help to Foster National Unity?

The Charter defines a set of national values and may help to create a common sense of being Canadian based on our common possession of rights and freedoms. The Charter focuses attention on the rights of Canada-wide groups (including women, ethnic minorities, and people with disabilities) and on national issues (such as abortion and same-sex marriage) rather than on the concerns and grievances of particular provinces or regions (Cairns, 1992). And a national institution (the Supreme Court of Canada) has gained in power and visibility as a result of the Charter. In fact, despite the opposition of the Quebec government to the Constitution Act, 1982, Quebecers, like persons in the rest of Canada, overwhelmingly support the inclusion of the Charter in the Constitution (Séguin, 2012; Simpson, 2011).

However, the Charter may also be responsible for creating an atmosphere in which individuals and groups aggressively assert and demand their rights. In making decisions that support the rights of one group, the courts may stir up conflicts between groups. Rather than trying to make decisions that balance the views or interests of different groups, judges may tend to make their decisions based on principles that distinguish winners and losers. In this respect, the ability of the Charter to foster national unity may be limited.

Summary and Conclusion

Canada's constitution is not to be found in a single document, but rather consists of a variety of elements. The Constitution acts that form the cornerstone of the constitution are the supreme law of the country and can be used by the courts to invalidate laws that are inconsistent with the Constitution. Ordinary laws of a constitutional nature, constitutional conventions, and judicial interpretations of the Constitution are also key components of the constitution.

Canada's Constitution acts are difficult to change. Nevertheless, governments have been able to work around the provisions of the Constitution to adjust to changing circumstances. As well, the evolution of constitutional conventions and changing patterns of judicial interpretation of the Constitution have allowed for flexibility in Canada's constitution.

Disagreements about major changes to the Constitution have created severe political crises on several occasions. Developing a consensus about major changes in the Constitution is difficult because of different views about Canada. Should Canada be considered primarily as a country of equal provinces, two founding peoples, a partnership between Aboriginals and settlers, a diverse collection of ethnocultural groups, or a citizenry with equal individual rights? Although government leaders have been able at times to reach agreements on major constitutional changes, these agreements proved unacceptable to a variety of groups and to the public. The expectation has developed that major constitutional changes require citizen engagement and approval by a referendum.

The Charter of Rights and Freedoms, part of the Constitution Act, 1982, has become an important feature of the Canadian political system. It has increased the power of the courts by providing them with extensive grounds on which to overturn laws and government actions. Although the notwithstanding clause is a partial reaffirmation of the principle of parliamentary supremacy, governments have been reluctant to use this clause. Instead, the "reasonable limits" clause provides an opportunity for government to defend legislation that places limits on rights and freedoms provided it can convince the courts that such limits are demonstrably justified in a free and democratic society.

The ability and willingness of unelected and unaccountable judges to invalidate legislation is sometimes viewed as undemocratic. However, even though some court decisions do not reflect the views of the majority of citizens, the ability of the courts to strike down legislation that infringes on rights and freedoms is consistent with liberal democratic values. Indeed the courts have used the Charter to expand the scope of rights and freedoms on controversial topics such as gay and lesbian rights, which politicians have often hesitated to address.

Overall, the Charter has contributed to good government by providing protection against arbitrary government actions, entrenching rights and freedoms, and ensuring that Canadian diversity is maintained. However, legalistic interpretation of Charter provisions may inhibit democratic discussion and action about controversial political issues.

Discussion Questions

1. Should Canada's formal Constitution include a statement of Canadian values? If so, what values are important?

2. Why is it difficult to change Canada's formal Constitution? Should there be another effort to reform some elements of the Constitution?

3. Should the notwithstanding clause be removed from the Charter of Rights and Freedoms?

4. Should additional rights, such as the right to an education, health care, housing, a clean environment, and property rights, be added to the Charter of Rights and Freedoms?

5. Should parts of the Charter of Rights and Freedoms be suspended when there is a threat of terrorism?

Further Reading

Bateman, M.J., Hebert, J., Kopf, R., & Russell, P. (2008). *The court and the Charter: Leading cases.* Toronto, ON: Emend Montgomery.

Graham, R. (2012). *The last act: Pierre Trudeau, the Gang of Eight, and the fight for Canada.* Toronto, ON: Penguin Canada.

Greene, I. (2014). *The Charter of Rights and Freedoms: 30+ years of decisions that shape Canadian life* (2nd ed.). Toronto, ON: Lorimer.

Harder, L., & Patten, S. (Eds.). (2015). *Patriation and its consequences. Constitution making in Canada.* Vancouver, BC: UBC Press.

Jackman, M., & Porter, B. (Eds.). (2014). *Advancing human rights in Canada.* Toronto, ON: Irwin Law.

James, P. (2010). *Constitutional politics in Canada after the Charter: Liberalism, communitarianism, and systemism.* Vancouver, BC: UBC Press.

Russell, P. (2004). *Constitutional odyssey* (3rd ed.). Toronto, ON: University of Toronto Press.

Strayer, B.L. (2013). *Canada's constitutional revolution.* Edmonton, AB: University of Alberta Press.

Webber, J. (2015). *The constitution of Canada: A contextual analysis.* Oxford, UK: Hart Publishing.

CHAPTER 11

Aboriginal Rights and Governance

CHAPTER OBJECTIVES

After reading this chapter, you should be able to

1. Outline the historical background of the relations between Aboriginal peoples and the Canadian government.

2. Explain the significance of constitutional changes and court rulings in establishing Aboriginal rights.

3. Examine the key features of recent land claims settlements.

4. Describe the changes to government policy concerning Aboriginal peoples.

5. Discuss what is needed to improve the relationship between Aboriginal and non-Aboriginal peoples.

Under the gaze of Assembly of First Nations Chief Phil Fontaine (right, wearing headdress), Prime Minister Stephen Harper stands in the House of Commons on June 11, 2008, to apologize officially on behalf of all Canadians to former students of Aboriginal residential schools for more than a century of abuse and cultural loss involving the schools and their programs.

© Kevin Frayer/Canadian Press Images

Phil Fontaine, then head of the Assembly of Manitoba Chiefs, shocked Canadians in 1990 when he revealed in a national television interview that he had been subjected to 10 years of physical and sexual abuse at the Fort Alexander Indian Residential School. Although he was reluctant to provide the details of the abuse that the children at his school had experienced, he did say that his aunt had been stripped and whipped by a priest in front of a class (Fontaine, 1990). In the following years, other Aboriginals from across Canada came forward with similar stories of abuse in residential schools.

The residential schools funded by the Canadian government and run primarily by the Catholic, Anglican, United, and Presbyterian churches reflected the persistent view that Aboriginals were primitive, should give up their native customs, and needed to be taught European values. The first residential school was established in 1883, and in 1920 education was made mandatory for Aboriginal children aged 7 to 15. From 1883 until the last school was closed in 1998, about 160 000 First Nations, Inuit, and Métis children were enrolled in the residential school system.

Children were forcibly removed from their parents to attend schools that were often distant from their homes. They were not allowed to speak their native languages during or outside class hours, and many were beaten for violating this rule. They were taught that their culture was inferior and were required to adopt the Christian religion. Physical and sexual abuse by those in authority was common, and there was a high death rate as a result of malnutrition and tuberculosis in the more crowded schools. Many students tried to run away, and some committed suicide to escape their horrific treatment. The residential school experience had the effect of making many Aboriginals ashamed of their ancestry and heritage, and disrupted the transmission of language and culture from parents and other family and community members to children.

While some who went through the residential school system turned to alcohol, drugs, and prostitution, Phil Fontaine pursued his education, receiving a degree in political studies at the University of Manitoba. As National Chief of the Assembly of First Nations during 1997–2000 and 2003–2009, he worked to achieve reconciliation by seeking an apology for past injustices at the residential schools and compensation for the victims of abuse.

Faced with the threat of lawsuits on behalf of thousands of victims, the Canadian government eventually accepted responsibility and paid about $1.9 billion in compensation for the victims of residential schools. The religious denominations that ran most of the schools apologized to the victims. Finally, in June 2008, in the presence of Fontaine and other Aboriginal leaders, Prime Minister Harper issued a formal apology in the House of Commons and asked the forgiveness of Aboriginal peoples for the great harm caused by the policy of assimilation and the abuse of helpless children who were separated from their "powerless families and communities" (Harper, 2008). Nevertheless, the Canadian government claimed that 7000 pages of documented evidence of sexual abuse did not exist until the Ontario Superior Court ordered the government to release the documents in 2014 (Saul, 2014).

Despite the formal apology, the Canadian government was reluctant to take meaningful actions to rectify the many injustices suffered by Aboriginal peoples, including the very poor social and economic conditions they continue to face. As well, the Conservative government rejected requests to hold an inquiry into the 1122 women and girls murdered or declared missing from 1980 to 2012 according to an RCMP report. In December 2015, the Liberal government announced that it hold a national public inquiry regarding the murdered and missing indigenous women.

INTRODUCTION

About 1.4 million Canadians (4.3 percent of Canada's total population) consider themselves as having an Aboriginal identity, according to the 2011 National Household Survey (see Table 11-1). Moreover, the Aboriginal population (First Nation, Inuit, and Métis) is growing more rapidly than the non-Aboriginal population. In addition to a higher birth rate, a greater number of those with Aboriginal ancestry are now willing to describe themselves as having an Aboriginal identity. Indeed, when the Qalipu Mi'kmaq First Nation was established on the island portion of Newfoundland as a landless band in 2011, over 101 000 persons applied for membership, greatly exceeding the

Canada	TOTAL ABORIGINAL IDENTITY POPULATION*
Canada	**4.3%**
Newfoundland and Labrador	7.1
Prince Edward Island	1.6
Nova Scotia	3.7
New Brunswick	3.1
Quebec	1.8
Ontario	2.4
Manitoba	16.7
Saskatchewan	15.6
Alberta	6.2
British Columbia	5.4
Yukon Territory	23.1
Northwest Territories	51.9
Nunavut	86.3

TABLE 11-1
ABORIGINAL IDENTITY POPULATION (PERCENTAGE)

Note: The statistics are derived from the voluntary 2011 National Household Survey, which is less accurate than earlier mandatory censuses. As well, the survey was not conducted on all reserves for various reasons.
*The total Aboriginal identity population includes the Aboriginal groups (North American Indian, Métis, and Inuit), multiple Aboriginal responses, and Aboriginal responses not included elsewhere.

SOURCE: *Statistics Canada. (2013).* Table 2. Number and distribution of the population reporting an Aboriginal identity and percentage of Aboriginal people in the population: Canada, provinces and territories, 2011. Retrieved from: www12.statcan.ca/nhs-enm/2011/as-sa/99-011-x/2011001/tbl/tbl02-eng.cfn. This does not constitute an endorsement by Statistics Canada of this product.

10 000 expected members.[1] After a bungled enrollment process, about 23 000 members were approved and thus became Registered (Status) Indians with benefits under the Indian Act.

Of those who reported an Aboriginal identity, 60.8 percent were First Nations (North American Indian), 32.3 percent were Métis, and 4.2 percent were Inuit.[2] Canada's First Nations population includes 637 660 Registered First Nations members (**Status Indians**), of whom 49.3 percent live on reserves. A further 213 900 identified themselves as First Nations or North American Indian but did not have official Indian status. Most of the registered First Nations are a member of one of the 617 recognized "bands" that have an average membership of 1338 (Aboriginal Affairs and Northern Development Canada, 2010b).

Status Indians are exempt from taxes on income earned on a reserve and from GST or HST on goods and services bought on reserve.[3] The Registered population has increased greatly from 341 968 in 1983, in part because of legislation (required as a result of the Charter of Rights and Freedoms) ending

STATUS INDIANS
Those of Indian ancestry who are listed in the official government registry and are entitled to certain benefits, including exemption from taxation on property and income earned on the reserve.

[1] Membership involved proving Canadian Indian ancestry descended from a Newfoundland Mi'kmaq community pre-Confederation [1949], self-identified prior to the formation of Qalipu, and accepted by the Mi'kmaq group based on a current and substantial connection. In April 2015, an agreement was reached between the Qalipu chief and the Canadian government to review 94 000 additional applications.

[2] Calculation excludes those with multiple identities.

[3] In Ontario and Quebec, registered Indians are exempt from the province's portion of the HST on goods and services anywhere in the province.

the discrimination against Indian women who lost their Indian status if they married a non-Indian man. Likewise the passage of the Gender Equity in Indian Regulations Act, 2011, increased the Indian population as the grandchildren of those who lost status as a result of marrying non-Indian men can now be registered.

As discussed in Chapter 4, Aboriginals are much worse off than other Canadians in terms of lifespan, income, housing, employment, poverty, and education.[4] As well, they have a much higher rate of suicide, alcohol and drug abuse, and incarceration.

Congress of Aboriginal Peoples
www.abo-peoples.org

Many Aboriginal communities lack the basic necessities of life, such as safe drinking water and proper sewage facilities. Moreover, natural resource developments—such as mining, petroleum extraction, forestry, and dam construction—often harm the environment of Aboriginal communities; the health of their inhabitants; and the sustainability of their hunting, fishing, and trapping activities. The lack of progress in improving public services provided to Aboriginals is particularly evident on First Nations reserves that are the responsibility of the Canadian government (Office of the Auditor General of Canada, 2011).

The relationship of Aboriginal peoples to the Canadian state and its governing structures often poses difficult but important challenges. While many Canadians believe that all Canadians should be treated as equal citizens with the same rights, many Aboriginals argue that they have special rights because of their prior occupancy of land that was often taken away from them illegally or improperly. First Nations typically expect to relate to Canadian governments on a "nation to nation" basis. Indeed, some First Nations claim that they never gave up their sovereignty and thus argue that they should not be subject to Canadian law without their approval.

In this chapter, we examine the constitutional status of Aboriginals, the variety of court cases that have increasingly recognized Aboriginal rights, the slow process of settling Aboriginal land claims, and the movement toward self-government for Aboriginal peoples.

HISTORICAL BACKGROUND

Unlike many other indigenous peoples in the Americas, Canada's indigenous peoples were never conquered by the European powers. Instead, many First Nations signed treaties with the French, British, and Canadian governments. These included the Great Peace (1701) between the Iroquois Confederacy and

---

[4]The Kelowna Accord reached by the Canadian government, provincial and territorial leaders, and the leaders of national Aboriginal organizations in 2005 would have brought Aboriginal education, health services, and housing closer to Canadian standards at a cost of $5 billion spread over five years. However, it was not implemented by the Conservative government that was elected shortly afterward.

New France, peace and friendship treaties with the British in the Maritimes (1725–1779), and the Upper Canada treaties (1764–1836) ceding various parcels of land in Ontario for a cash payment. As well, Douglas treaties in the colony of Vancouver Island (1850–1854) were signed with 14 First Nations. After Confederation, the Canadian government sought to expand the new country and open it up to large-scale immigration. Eleven numbered treaties (1871–1906) in the Prairies, the North, and parts of what is now northern Ontario and northeastern British Columbia involved First Nations ceding ownership of large areas of land in return for small remote reserves, annual cash payments, and other benefits (such as clothing, ammunition, and hunting and fishing rights). In many cases, the written text of the treaties differed substantially from the oral agreements and promises made to the First Nations. From the perspectives of First Nations, the treaties were permanent agreements to share the land in a peaceful manner that did not interfere with their way of life (Royal Commission on Aboriginal Peoples, 1996).

The Royal Proclamation of 1763 that formalized British control over the former French colonies in Canada declared that "the several Nations or Tribes of Indians with whom we are connected and who live under our protection shall not be molested or disturbed in the possession of such parts of our dominions and territories as, not having been ceded or purchased by Us, are reserved to them, or any of them, as their hunting grounds." To protect against exploitation from non-Aboriginal settlers, private individuals were prohibited from buying land reserved for Indians. Although the Royal Proclamation indicated that Indians would continue to be self-governing in their internal affairs, the implication of the phrase "our dominions and territories" was that the British claimed "sovereign title" over the entire territory (Royal Commission on Aboriginal Peoples, 1996, vol. 1, p. 124).

The Constitution Act, 1867, gave exclusive jurisdiction to the Parliament of Canada to make laws concerning "Indians, and Lands reserved for the Indians" (Section 91 [24]).[5] However the Canadian government has inconsistently and improperly decided who is an "Indian" (particularly "Status Indians" living on a reserve) and thus subject to federal jurisdiction. In 2013, the Federal Court ruled that Métis and non-Status Indians were "Indians" under the Constitution Act, 1867 (Peach & Mintz, 2013).[6] However, the Federal Court of Appeal in 2014 ruled that the Métis, but not non-Status Indians, were covered by the

---

[5]This provision is usually viewed by the Canadian government as applying primarily to the members of the 617 First Nations bands living on reserves. Provincial laws and programs can also apply to First Nations, but the federal Indian Act is considered superior to provincial legislation. Generally, the Canadian government has provided services such as education, health care, and housing to those living on reserves while provincial governments have provided services to other Aboriginals.

[6]The Inuit were provided federal government services as a result of a 1939 Supreme Court decision that rejected the federal government's assertion that Quebec's Inuit were a provincial responsibility. Since 1951 the Inuit have been exempted from the Indian Act.

Constitution Act, 1867. An appeal of this decision was heard by the Supreme Court of Canada in October 2015, but their judgment had not been reached at the time of writing.

The Constitution Act, 1867, did not include any provisions concerning the rights of "Indians." Instead, Canadian governments adopted a policy of trying to assimilate indigenous peoples. As Prime Minister Macdonald told Parliament: Canada's goal is "to do away with the tribal system and assimilate the Indian people in all respects with the inhabitants of the Dominion" (quoted by the Royal Commission on Aboriginal Peoples, p. 165).

Indian Acts

Under the Indian Acts passed by Parliament beginning in 1876, the Canadian government tried to strictly control the lives of First Nations people and their communities. The Canadian government placed an official (the "Indian agent") in charge of each reservation. The people of First Nations were considered "wards" of the state rather than citizens. Efforts were made to destroy First Nations cultures. For example, some First Nations cultural practices were declared illegal, including the potlatch, a feasting ceremony of the peoples of northwestern North America in which the host gains prestige by giving gifts or, sometimes, by destroying personal wealth. As well, many bands were required to elect band councils in keeping with Canadian models of governance rather than the traditional First Nations models of governance that relied on the wisdom of tribal elders.

In effect, the Canadian government acted like the imperialist powers whose racist belief in the superiority of Europeans was used to try to justify the subjection of indigenous peoples around the world. Because they were deemed to be incapable of governing themselves, it was thought that Aboriginals needed to remain under the tutelage of the Canadian government and had to be encouraged to adopt the values and practices of the more "advanced" or "superior" civilization. The overall effect of control by the Canadian government, according to a 1983 House of Commons committee report (the Penner Report), was to turn "previously free self-sustaining First Nations communities" into a state of "dependency and social disorganization" (quoted in Prince & Abele, 2005, p. 243).

The system of reserves tended to isolate the First Nations from the Canadian mainstream and thus was inconsistent with the goal of assimilation. However, the Canadian government tried to encourage Status Indians to give up their Indian status and assimilate into the general population (a process termed "enfranchisement"). As Duncan Campbell Scott, deputy superintendent general of Indian Affairs, stated in 1920, "I want to get rid of the Indian problem. Our object is to continue until there is not a single Indian in Canada that has not been absorbed into the body politic and there is no Indian question, and no Indian Department" (quoted in Cairns, 2004, p. 351). Very few Indians voluntarily gave up their status. However, those who accepted a government offer of money and land, voted, owned property, or served in the Armed Forces were often required to give up their Indian status.

PROPOSALS FOR CHANGE

The Hawthorn Report

In 1963, the Canadian government commissioned a major study of the condition of Indians under the direction of anthropologist Henry Hawthorn. The **Hawthorn Report** was critical of the Canadian government's policy of treating Indians as wards rather than as citizens and recommended that Indians be regarded as "**citizens plus**" (Cairns, 2000). That is, "in addition to the normal rights and duties of citizenship, Indians possess certain additional rights as charter members of the Canadian community" (quoted in Cairns, 2000, pp. 161–162). The Hawthorn Report was also critical of the long-standing government policy of assimilation and recommended that Indians should not be forced to acquire the values of the majority society (Dickason, 2009).

The White Paper on Indians

Prime Minister Pierre Trudeau rejected the Hawthorn Report's key recommendation. Trudeau's view (consistent with his rejection of a "special status" for Quebec) was that all Canadians should be treated as individual citizens, with each person having exactly the same rights. Trudeau's view was reflected in the Canadian government's **White Paper on Indians** (1969), which argued that "the separate legal status of Indians and the policies which have flowed from it have kept the Indian people apart from and behind other Canadians." Instead, Indian people should have the fundamental right "to full and equal participation in the cultural, social, economic and political life of Canada" (Indian and Northern Affairs Canada, 1969). To achieve this, the White Paper proposed ending the different legal status of Indians and the separate provision of services to them. Specifically, the special responsibility of the Canadian Parliament to legislate for Indians would be ended, the federal Indian Affairs Department would be phased out, and provincial governments would be responsible for providing the same services (such as health, education, and welfare) as provided to other provincial residents. Control of Indian lands would be transferred from the government to Indian bands, with each band deciding whether to manage the lands itself or to transfer title to individuals. Although "lawful obligations" would be recognized, the White Paper viewed treaties as providing minimal benefits to Indians, and thus called for a review to see how the treaties could be "equitably ended."

The White Paper held out the promise that Aboriginal identities could be strengthened and their distinctive cultures preserved while Aboriginals would play a full role in Canadian society. However, in a bestselling book, *The Unjust Society*, Alberta Cree leader Harold Cardinal (1969) condemned the

HAWTHORN REPORT
A Canadian government report that recommended that Indians should have rights in addition to those of other citizens and not be forced to assimilate into the majority society.

CITIZENS PLUS
The idea that Indians possess certain rights in addition to the normal rights and duties of citizens.

WHITE PAPER ON INDIANS
A 1969 Canadian government discussion paper that proposed to end the different legal status of Indians.

White Paper as "a thinly disguised programme of extermination through assimilation" (p. 1). Many First Nations leaders mobilized strong opposition to the proposals in the White Paper (which was withdrawn in 1971) because they wanted to maintain their distinctive status and collective rights. This mobilization fuelled the development of politically active Aboriginal organizations and the willingness and determination of Aboriginal peoples to take political actions to pursue their rights.

Initially some First Nations leaders who opposed the White Paper advocated the "citizens plus" concept of the Hawthorn Report. However, within a short time, the developing First Nations movement turned to gaining recognition of what they viewed as their **inherent right of self-government**—that is, the right to govern themselves based on their independence before European colonization. They view this right as *inherent* in that it was not ceded by First Nations and thus does not depend on the Canadian Constitution or Canadian law (McNeil, 2007).

The Royal Commission on Aboriginal Peoples

In 1991, the Canadian government established the **Royal Commission on Aboriginal Peoples** headed by four Aboriginal and three non-Aboriginal commissioners. Its 4000-page report published in 1996 detailed the ill treatment and injustices suffered by Aboriginals and called for a fundamental restructuring of the relationship between Aboriginal and settler societies based on the recognition of Aboriginal nationhood. Canada should be viewed as a partnership of Aboriginal and non-Aboriginal nations, with the details of the relationship worked out on a nation-to-nation basis. The hundreds of specific recommendations of the Royal Commission included the following:

- A new Royal Proclamation should acknowledge past injustices and recognize the inherent right of Aboriginals to self-government.
- A Lands and Treaties Tribunal should be instituted to speed up the process of settling land claims, with the authority to impose binding orders if negotiations fail.
- The more than 600 Indian bands should be consolidated into 60 to 80 self-governing nations with an average population of 5000 to 7000 people and an enlarged land base.
- Aboriginal governments should be recognized as a "third order" of government in Canada (federal, provincial/territorial, and Aboriginal), each autonomous with its own spheres of jurisdiction and sharing the sovereignty of Canada as a whole. Aboriginal governments would be subject to the Charter of Rights and Freedoms.
- An Aboriginal House of First Peoples should be established to provide advice to the House of Commons and Senate and should eventually be empowered to initiate and pass legislation crucial to Aboriginal peoples.

INHERENT RIGHT OF SELF-GOVERNMENT
The perspective that First Nations have the right to govern themselves based on their independence before European colonization, a right that was never ceded.

ROYAL COMMISSION ON ABORIGINAL PEOPLES
A Royal Commission established by the Canadian government that recommended a fundamental restructuring of the relationship between Aboriginal and settler societies based on the recognition of Aboriginal nationhood.

Highlights From the Report of the Royal Commission on Aboriginal Peoples
www.aadnc-aandc.gc.ca/ eng/1100100014597

- There should be a very substantial increase in funding by the Canadian government to deal with Aboriginal problems, and an equalization formula should ensure that Aboriginal governments have the financial capacity to provide services to their people equivalent to the services provided by other governments.
- Aboriginals would be citizens of the First Nation community to which they belong as well as citizens of Canada.

Aboriginal leaders generally responded positively to the report and demanded the implementation of its recommendations. Some Inuit leaders, however, felt that the report did not give sufficient attention to the problems faced by their people.

CONSTITUTIONAL PROPOSALS AND CHANGES

The Constitution Act, 1982 recognized "the existing aboriginal and treaty rights" of Indian, Inuit, and Métis peoples. A constitutional amendment in 1983 clarified that rights established by current and future land claims agreements are constitutionally protected. A proposal to entrench the right to self-government in the Constitution failed to gain sufficient provincial government approval in 1987. The Charlottetown Accord (1992), which included a proposal to recognize the inherent right of Aboriginal self-government, was defeated in a national referendum. The accord would have set the framework for Aboriginal governments as a "third order" of government with the authority "to safeguard and develop their languages, cultures, economies, identities, institutions, and traditions and to develop, maintain and strengthen their relationship with their lands, waters and environment, so as to determine and control their development as peoples according to their own values and priorities and to ensure the integrity of their societies" (*Consensus Report on the Constitution*, 1992, pp. 37–38).

Land Claims and Modern Treaties

In most of British Columbia, Quebec, Newfoundland and Labrador, and the three territories, governments took control of the land without signing treaties with Aboriginals. In the Maritimes, the peace and friendship treaties did not involve Aboriginals giving up their right to their land and its resources. In British Columbia, the provincial government did not see the need for treaties to extinguish Aboriginal land rights as it didn't recognize Aboriginal title to the land (BC Treaty Commission, 2008). In other parts of the country, First Nations argue that the Canadian government did not fulfill the promises made when they signed treaties. As various groups started to pursue land claims in the courts, an amendment to the Indian Act in 1927 made it illegal to raise funds to pursue land claims (a restriction that was ended in 1951).

In recent decades, Aboriginal groups have launched legal actions as they energetically pursue recognition of their communal rights[7] and title to traditional lands. In several important decisions, the Supreme Court of Canada has recognized Aboriginal rights and, since 1982, expanded upon the meaning of the recognition and affirmation of "existing aboriginal and treaty rights" in the Constitution Act, 1982.

The Supreme Court of Canada decision in 1973 regarding the claim by the Nisga'a Tribal Council in British Columbia that "their aboriginal title to their ancient tribal territory . . . has never been lawfully extinguished" opened the door to recognition of land claims (*Calder v. Attorney General of British Columbia*, 1973). The Nisga'a claim was dismissed by four of the seven judges on the technicality that the tribal council had not received the required permission to sue the government. Three of the judges who voted for dismissal went on to say that the governor of British Columbia, when the province was a colony of the United Kingdom, had acted within his powers to take possession of all lands in the colony and that the Royal Proclamation of 1763 did not apply to British Columbia. The "right of occupancy" that the Nisga'a "might have had" was ended when "the sovereign authority elected to exercise complete dominion over the lands in question."

The three judges who dissented argued that the claim should have been upheld because the actions of the BC governor to remove the Nisga'a's Aboriginal title were beyond the scope of his powers. The Nisga'a had a legal right that could only be extinguished "by surrender to the Crown or by competent legislative authority, and then only by specific legislation"[8] (*Calder v. Attorney General of British Columbia*, 1973). Significantly, then, the court recognized that Aboriginal title to land could exist through occupancy before European settlement, although the court was divided on whether that right had been extinguished in this particular case. A Supreme Court of Canada decision in 1984 (*Guerin v. The Queen*) recognized Aboriginal title as "a legal right derived from the Indians' historic occupation and possession of their tribal lands" (quoted in Hogg, 2006, p. 634). These decisions helped persuade the Canadian government to negotiate treaties (using the term "land claims agreements") in areas of the country where none existed. In the *Guerin* case, the Supreme Court also ruled that the Crown has a fiduciary (trust-like) obligation to act in the best interests of the band with land that had been surrendered to the Crown.

In *Delgamuukw v. British Columbia* (1997), the Supreme Court ruled that oral histories can be admissible as evidence concerning Aboriginal

---

[7]Communal rights are "grounded in the existence of a historic and present community, and exercisable by virtue of an individual's ancestrally based membership in the present community" (*R. v. Powley*, 2003).

[8]The power of Parliament to extinguish Aboriginal and treaty rights through legislation no longer exists as a result of the Constitution Act, 1982.

traditional occupancy of lands where written records do not exist, and that the Aboriginal perspective on their practices, customs, and traditions, and on their relationship with the land, should be given due weight by the courts. Chief Justice Lamer concluded: "Ultimately, it is through negotiated settlements, with good faith and give-and-take on all sides, reinforced by the judgments of this Court, that the reconciliation of the pre-existence of aboriginal societies with the sovereignty of the Crown [will occur]. Let us face it, we are all here to stay."

The Supreme Court also ruled in *Delgamuukw* that Aboriginal title to land (determined by occupation at the time of the Crown's assertion of sovereignty) is not just a right to activities such as hunting and fishing. Aboriginal title to land is distinct from other forms of property ownership in that it can only be sold to the federal Crown, is held collectively by the band members, and cannot be held by individuals. It also grants the right to engage in a variety of activities on the land as long as they do not impair traditional use of the land by future generations. The title can only be infringed by the Canadian or provincial governments "in furtherance of a legislative objective that is compelling and substantial" to the broader Canadian community (of which Aboriginal communities are a part) and ordinarily requires fair compensation for the infringement.

Further elaboration of the rights of First Nations who did not cede the land they used through a treaty was provided by the Supreme Court of Canada in 2014 (*Tsilhqot'in Nation v. British Columbia*). The case arose when the First Nation objected when the British Columbia government in 1983 granted a company a logging licence on land used by the Tsilhqot'in people. In the unanimous judgement, "Aboriginal title . . . confers on the group that holds it the exclusive right to decide how the land is used and the right to benefit from those uses, subject to the restriction that the uses must be consistent with the group nature of the interest and the enjoyment of the land by future generations." Any action by government that limits this benefit requires "demonstrating both a compelling and substantial governmental objective . . . consistent with the fiduciary duty owed by the Crown to the Aboriginal group."[9]

Since Aboriginal claims to title to their traditional lands often take decades to be adjudicated, the Supreme Court has ruled that the "Honour of the Crown" imposes a duty to consult and, if necessary, to accommodate the interests of Aboriginal peoples before authorizing actions that could diminish the value of the land they are claiming. This obligation "from the assertion of sovereignty to the resolution of claims and the implementation of treaties" (*Haida Nation v. British Columbia*, 2004) affects many major natural resource developments on lands that are subject to treaty negotiations (see Box 11-1: Big Oil Versus Aboriginal Rights: The Northern Gateway Pipelines).

---

[9]The ruling established Aboriginal title to 17 000 square kilometres of land which the semi-nomadic bands had traditionally used.

BOX 11-1

Big Oil Versus Aboriginal Rights: The Northern Gateway Pipelines

In 2012, hearings began on the proposal by Enbridge Corporation to build a 525 000 barrel per day dual pipeline from northern Alberta's oil sands to Kitimat, British Columbia. With the proposed Keystone XL pipeline (which would carry Alberta oil to refineries in the United States) in doubt, the major oil companies were anxious to quickly gain approval for the Northern Gateway twin pipelines that would deliver crude oil and diluted bitumen from Alberta's oil sands to energy-hungry Asian markets, particularly China. Following the controversial hearings that recommended approval of the pipelines (subject to a large number of conditions), the Harper government approved the $7.9 billion pipelines in 2014.

However, the pipelines would pass through territory claimed by a number of First Nations communities who fear that an oil spill would cause immense damage to their ancestral lands and important salmon fisheries. Large oil tankers leaving Kitimat would have to navigate treacherous waters. With promises of community benefits to the area's First Nations and a 10 percent share in the pipelines, some First Nations along the route have supported the pipelines project. Other First Nations along the proposed route have initiated legal action to stop the pipelines because they were not properly consulted. Many environmental groups along with other First Nations strongly oppose the pipelines. A majority of Kitimat voters rejected the pipelines in a plebiscite. The British Columbia government, at the time of writing, had not accepted the proposed pipelines in part because it felt the benefits to the province were insufficient. A moratorium on crude oil tanker traffic on B.C.'s north coast announced by the Trudeau government in November 2015 could end the Northern Gateway project.

Enbridge asserted that the pipelines would add $270 billion to Canada's gross domestic product over a period of 30 years and would create 1150 long-term jobs. Despite the anticipated economic benefits from the pipelines, the potential for long-lasting damage to one of the last intact temperate rainforests as well as the land's great importance to First Nations made the project highly controversial.

Fishing and Hunting Rights

The extent to which Aboriginal rights to fish and hunt are constitutionally protected has been at the heart of a number of cases. In particular, the *Sparrow* case (1990) involved a member of British Columbia's Musqueam Band charged with fishing with a larger net than allowed by the band's food fishery licence issued under the federal Fisheries Act regulations. The Supreme Court found that the right of the members of the band to fish was an existing Aboriginal right, and thus guaranteed by the Constitution.

The government's argument that Fisheries Act regulations had extinguished the right to fish was rejected. The court ruled that the regulations controlled the fisheries but did not extinguish underlying rights. Furthermore, the Supreme Court judgment stated that the phrase "existing aboriginal rights" in the Constitution Act, 1982 "must be interpreted flexibly so as to permit their evolution over time" (*R. v. Sparrow*, 1990). In other words, the traditional rights of Aboriginals to fish and hunt were not limited to the use of spears and bows and arrows that were used by their ancestors.

BOX 11-2

Standoff at Burnt Church:
The *Marshall* Rulings

On October 3, 1999, violence occurred at Burnt Church, New Brunswick, after non-Aboriginal fishers destroyed Mi'kmaq lobster traps. The traps had been set out during the closed season by Mi'kmaq fishers who maintained that a Supreme Court ruling based on a treaty dating back to 1760 authorized them to fish out of season. In the middle of allegations and retaliatory actions, one thing was not disputed—the direct origins of the incident at Burnt Church began with the case of Donald Marshall, Jr.

The *Marshall* case involved a Mi'kmaq who had been charged with fishing and selling eels without a licence, and fishing during the closed season with illegal nets. Lawyers for Marshall claimed that he had a right to catch and sell fish under the 1760 Mi'kmaq peace and friendship treaty with the British governor of Nova Scotia. During the negotiations for the 1760 treaty, the Aboriginal leaders asked for "truckhouses" (trading posts) "for the furnishing them with necessaries, in Exchange for their Peltry." However, the treaty itself did not contain any provisions linked to this request. Nevertheless, the Supreme Court of Canada in September 1999 ruled that the minutes of the negotiations over the treaty should not be excluded as evidence given "the difficulties of proof confronted by aboriginal people" (*R. v. Marshall,* 1999). The court defined "necessaries" as the right to a "moderate livelihood," which could be obtained through fishing and hunting, and trading such products subject to "justifiable" regulations by the government. Since the prosecution had not provided justification for the regulations, Marshall was acquitted.

The Supreme Court ruling provoked an uproar. Non-Aboriginal fishers complained that Aboriginals would have "unlimited and unregulated access" to the Atlantic fishery, depriving them of their livelihood (quoted in Russell et al., 2008, p. 453). Aboriginal statements that the ruling would allow them rights to the region's timber and mineral resources caused further concern. The Supreme Court of Canada refused a request for a re-hearing of the *Marshall* case. However, in a very unusual move, the Supreme Court decided to elaborate on its ruling.

In their second judgment on November 17, 2007, the Supreme Court justices reaffirmed that the treaty rights involved the right to a "moderate livelihood" by hunting, fishing, and berry picking, but did "not extend to the open-ended accumulation of wealth." The Canadian and provincial governments could regulate Aboriginal fishing for conservation or "other compelling and substantial public objectives," including fishing by non-Aboriginal groups, provided there was consultation with Aboriginals about limitations on their rights (quoted in Russell et al., 2008, pp. 458–459).

The Supreme Court's clarification of its first ruling did not end the tension between Aboriginal and non-Aboriginal fishers and between Aboriginals and the Department of Fisheries and Oceans. Eventually, however, all First Nations in the area gave up their right to fish for a "moderate livelihood" in return for the boats, equipment, training, licences, and quotas needed for a commercial fishery, subject to the same regulations as non-Aboriginal fishers. Thus, the *Marshall* decision did not result in the restoration of a traditional way of life (Bedford, 2010).

Fishing rights were also at issue in the *Marshall* case (*R. v. Marshall,* 1999). This case involved the interpretation of a historic treaty signed by a people that relied on their understanding of oral negotiations rather than a document they were unable to read (as discussed in Box 11-2: Standoff at Burnt Church: The *Marshall* Rulings).

Métis Hunting Rights

In 2003, Steve and Roddy Powley, members of the Métis community in the Sault Ste. Marie area, were charged with unlawfully hunting a moose without a licence. The Supreme Court of Canada (*R. v. Powley*, 2003) ruled that the Métis community had a traditional Aboriginal right to hunt for food under Section 35(1) of the Constitution Act, 1982, because it had existed before "the time of effective European control" (quoted in Hogg, 2006, p. 638).[10] The case is particularly important because it established that members of a Métis community had Aboriginal rights. Specifically, the Métis were defined as "distinctive peoples who, in addition to their mixed ancestry, developed their own customs and recognizable group identity separate from their Indian or Inuit and European forebears."

The Supreme Court's Interpretation of Aboriginal Rights

Overall, as the cases in the preceding pages illustrate, the Supreme Court of Canada has played a significant role in determining Aboriginal and treaty rights by taking into account the history and circumstances of Aboriginal peoples rather than applying a narrow legal interpretation of those rights. Nevertheless, the Supreme Court has indicated that these rights are not absolute, but rather can be subject to some limitations. For example, government regulations for the conservation of resources may be justified, and Aboriginal rights to fish and hunt for food do not necessarily give Aboriginals an exclusive right to commercial use of these resources. Likewise, the Supreme Court has asserted that "distinctive aboriginal societies exist within, and are a part of, a broader social, political and economic community, over which the Crown is sovereign" (*Delgamuukw v. British Columbia*, 1997).

The Supreme Court has generally avoided ruling on the right to self-government, arguing that this is best achieved through negotiations between First Nations and the federal and provincial governments. When rejecting an Aboriginal gambling law that conflicted with the Canadian Criminal Code, the Supreme Court stated that, "Aboriginal rights, including any asserted right to self-government, must be looked at in light of the specific circumstances of each case and, in particular, in light of the specific history and culture of the aboriginal group claiming the right" (*R. v. Pamajewon*, 1996).

Negotiating Comprehensive Land Claims Agreements

As a result of the *Calder* ruling (discussed above), the Canadian government in 1973 began to negotiate comprehensive land claims with First Nations that

---

[10]This differed from an earlier Supreme Court decision (*Van der Peet*) which only upheld rights that existed before the time of European arrival in North America.

had not signed treaties in the past. In negotiating **comprehensive land claims agreements** (which are also referred to as modern treaties), the Canadian government has insisted that the settlement of land claims provide a full and final settlement of Aboriginal rights. Most Aboriginal groups have made the establishment of the right to self-government an essential component of any settlement. The process of reaching land claims settlements has been drawn out and fraught with difficulties. For example, negotiations with the Nisga'a (whose chiefs had canoed to Victoria in 1887 to demand a treaty) began in 1976; an agreement was not reached until 1999. In 2014, the Nisga'a finally paid off the $84 million debt that they had incurred to pursue their treaty (discussed below).

The agreements that have been reached generally involve removing the group from the provisions and benefits of the Indian Act. In return, Aboriginal groups have been awarded specific rights and benefits (such as a cash settlement) and provisions for self-government (Papillon, 2008). Modern treaties generally recognize the right of Aboriginal governments to provide many public services, manage their natural resources, and determine who are citizens of their First Nation. The treaties specify that Aboriginal governments are subject to the Canadian Charter of Rights and Freedoms. The powers of Aboriginal governments set out in recent agreements are constitutionally protected and therefore cannot be changed without the approval of the Aboriginal government.[11]

Overall, since 1973, 26 land claims agreements (of which 18 included self-government agreements) and 4 self-government agreements have been reached. As of 2015, about 100 comprehensive land claims and self-government agreements were at various stages of the very lengthy process of negotiations (Aboriginal Affairs and Northern Development Canada, 2015).

The first agreements in the James Bay area and northern and northeastern Quebec (1975 and 1978) were negotiated to avoid the possibility that the Supreme Court of Canada might grant the Cree and Inuit an injunction to block the development of a large hydroelectric project that would flood lands claimed by these groups. An agreement between the Canadian government and the Yukon First Nations in 1993 provided the basis for modern treaties with 11 of Yukon's 14 First Nations bands. Other modern treaties have been ratified in the Northwest Territories, Nunavut, northern Quebec, and Labrador.

In British Columbia, treaty negotiations with the Nisga'a began in 1973. After intense controversy, agreement was reached in 1998 (ratified in 2000) establishing self-government for the Nisga'a in northwest British Columbia (see Box 11-3: Nisga'a Self-Government Sparks a Public Outcry). The treaty provides the Nisga'a Lisims government with the authority to make laws

COMPREHENSIVE LAND CLAIMS AGREEMENTS
Agreements involving First Nations that had not signed treaties giving up their land.

BC Treaty Commission
www.bctreaty.net

---

[11]This constitutional protection does not require a formal constitutional amendment, since Section 35 of the Constitution Act, 1982, provides for recognition of rights that may be acquired through land claims agreements.

BOX 11-3

Nisga'a Self-Government Sparks a Public Outcry

In 1998, the final agreement on the Nisga'a comprehensive land claims caused a public outcry in British Columbia. Open-line radio shows and letters to the editor were filled with scathing comments. Critics argued that the treaty discriminated against non-Aboriginals, and fears were raised that claims by various Aboriginal groups could result in all the land in British Columbia being returned to Aboriginals.

Opponents of the agreement demanded political action. They lobbied for a province-wide referendum on the treaty, and BC Liberal opposition leader Gordon Campbell mounted a 30-day filibuster in the BC legislature. Similarly, the Reform Party of Canada proposed 471 amendments to the treaty in the House of Commons to try to delay its passage. The BC Liberals challenged the treaty in court, arguing that it was unconstitutional because it infringed upon federal and provincial legislative powers. However, the BC Supreme Court ruled that the distribution of legislative powers between Parliament and provincial legislatures in the Constitution Act, 1867, did not preclude the right of the Nisga'a government to exercise legislative powers and that the treaty was compatible with the sovereignty of the Canadian state (*Campbell et al. v. Nisga'a*, 2000).

Campbell's BC Liberals gained power in a landslide victory in the 2001 election because of general dissatisfaction with the previous government. They decided not to appeal the loss of their legal challenge to the Nisga'a treaty. Instead, the BC government held a non-binding referendum in 2002 to address the controversy (although the treaty was already in effect). Voters were asked whether they agreed with eight statements that criticized various elements of the treaty, such as "private property should not be expropriated for treaty settlements." Voters agreed with such statements by large margins, but only 35 percent of the electorate bothered to fill out the mail-in ballot (Lochead, 2004).

Although votes of the members of First Nations have been held in British Columbia and elsewhere to approve modern treaties, governments have shied away from referendums to win the approval of the broader population.

concerning such matters as culture and language, public works, regulation of traffic and transportation, land use, solemnization of marriages, health, child welfare, and education services. The authority of the Nisga'a government is not exclusive in these areas, but on some subjects Nisga'a law prevails if in conflict with federal or provincial law, while on other subjects federal or provincial law prevails. The Nisga'a received the authority to levy income and sales taxes and collect royalties on their land's resources. They were also given ownership of 2019 square kilometres of land, with the authority to manage forest resources provided they meet or exceed provincial forest standards. In addition, the agreement included a phasing out of the exemption from paying income tax for those on the reserve. The Nisga'a also have to pay provincial and federal sales taxes. The Nisga'a government received a payment of $190 million spread over 15 years, along with fiscal arrangements that would allow the Nisga'a government to provide health, education, and other social services equivalent to those enjoyed by other people in the region. They were also given a share of the total allowable salmon catch in the region. Although some Nisga'a argued that their negotiators had given up too much to reach

Nisga'a Treaty
**www.gov.bc.ca/arr/firstnation/nisgaa/
default.html**

The 19 independent members of the Nunavut legislative assembly govern using the consensus model, a system inherited from the Northwest Territories. Without the need for a division between government and opposition benches, the legislature chambers in Iqaluit were designed in the round, and members of the legislative assembly meet in a circle.

agreement (e.g., by gaining less than 10 percent of traditional lands), 61.2 percent of Nisga'a voters approved the treaty (Lochead, 2004).

In 1992, British Columbian First Nations and the Canadian and BC governments agreed to establish an independent BC Treaty Commission. As of October 2015, only 4 treaties (covering eight First Nations) had been ratified in British Columbia (in addition to the Nisga'a treaty that involved a different process) while about 60 potential treaties (covering about one-half of BC's First Nations) were at various stages of negotiations.

Nunavut

In 1993, a comprehensive land claims agreement was signed with the Inuit in the eastern Arctic, giving the Inuit ownership of 18 percent of the land (including subsurface mineral rights in 2 percent of the vast territory), $1.173 billion over 14 years, co-management of land and resources, natural resource royalties on Crown land, and hunting and fishing rights (Henderson, 2007). It also involved an agreement to establish the new territory of Nunavut, which would take over wildlife and natural resource management, land use planning, and property taxation. The Nunavut government is a public government representing all persons in the territory (rather than being based on ancestry).[12] The benefits of the land claims agreement are administered for the social, cultural, and economic well-being of Inuit by Nunavut Tunngavik Inc., of which all Nunavut Inuit are members.

Inuit Tapirit Kanatami
www.itk.ca

A Plain Language Guide to Nunavut Land Claims
www.tunngavik.com/documents/ publications/2004-00-00-A-Plain-Language-Guide-to-the-Nunavut-Land-Claims-Agreement-English.pdf

---

[12]Similarly, the Kativik regional government in the far north of Quebec (established in 1978) is elected by and provides services to both Inuit and non-Inuit people, while the Makivik Corporation administers the benefits of the land claims agreement for the Inuit people of the region.

Specific Claims

Comprehensive land claims agreements in areas where no treaties were signed are not the only category of claims that need negotiating. A large number of **specific claims** exist based on allegations that treaties and other legal obligations of the Canadian government have not been fulfilled, or that the Canadian government has not properly administered Aboriginal lands and other assets. The negotiation process established in 1973 to settle specific claims was extremely slow, with claims taking an average of 13 years to be settled. A more streamlined process created in 2008 allows Aboriginal First Nations to use the independent Specific Claims Tribunal, consisting of superior court judges, if their claim has not been resolved within a specified period of time or has not been accepted for negotiation. The tribunal has the power to make binding decisions and provide monetary compensation of up to $150 million. The specific claims process does not establish rights to self-government.

ABORIGINAL SELF-GOVERNMENT

In 1995, the Canadian government announced its **Inherent Right of Self-Government Policy**. Specifically, Aboriginal peoples would "have the right to govern themselves in relation to matters that are internal to their communities, integral to their unique cultures, identities, traditions, languages and institutions and with respect to their special relationship to their land and their resources" (quoted in Abele & Prince, 2007, p. 178). This right would be exercised under the existing Constitution, with the Charter of Rights and Freedoms applying to Aboriginal governments. Laws of overriding federal and provincial importance would prevail over laws passed by Aboriginal governments. The Canadian government would maintain its exclusive authority in areas such as defence and external relations, management of the national economy, maintenance of national law and order and criminal law, and protection of the health and safety of Canadians.

A proposed first step toward self-government was the First Nations Governance Act (2002), which would give greater independence to bands to manage their own affairs. However, among the specific provisions to provide for "effective governance" were the setting of minimum standards for leadership selection and the administration of band governments including publicly available audited financial statements. The Assembly of First Nations strongly objected to the Act, arguing that it violated the inherent right of self-government, imposed more bureaucratic controls on their governments, and added to the cost of governing First Nations (Hurley, 2003). As well, several chiefs argued that they had not been consulted about the proposed Act. In 2004, the government decided not to pursue passage of the Act.

Nevertheless, band councils are now largely responsible for administering most programs and services, and generally have some flexibility in shaping programs to suit the particular circumstances of their community. However, delivery of services does not create full self-government. Band councils still have only delegated power that is limited to specified local matters and can have their bylaws overturned by the minister responsible federal government (Bakvis, Baier, & Brown, 2009). Furthermore, with a very high proportion of band revenues coming from the Canadian government, often with conditions attached, band councils still depend heavily on government support (Prince & Abele, 2005). Band councils are accountable to the Canadian government for the funds allocated for the programs, and the Canadian government can also unilaterally change or cancel most programs (Papillon, 2008).

In its 2011 Throne Speech, the Harper government announced that it was committed to making First Nations governments democratic, transparent, and accountable. The First Nations Financial Transparency Act (2014) requires that the salaries and expenses of chiefs and councillors as well as the audited consolidated financial statements of each band council be disclosed to the general public through a website.[13] The Assembly of First Nations was critical of the Act, arguing that their accountability should be to their own people rather than to the government. As well, they pointed out that the large number of reports (averaging 160 each year) that are required to be submitted to the Canadian government places a huge burden on each band council (Land, 2011). Furthermore, they argued that the government failed to consult with First Nations leaders, that the bill represented a continuation of "colonialism and paternalism," and that it did not deal with the real issues facing First Nations (Simeone & Troniak, 2011). In addition, their financial statements could be misleading to the public since they could include revenues from the business operations of the band. Financial statements could also create problems in reaching business agreements with non-Aboriginal corporations (e.g., for resource developments) that want to keep the information confidential for competitive reasons.

Assembly of First Nations
www.afn.ca

The First Nations Elections Act, 2014, increased the term of office of chiefs and councillors from two years to four years, provided penalties for questionable activities, and established a procedure for recalling elected officials. As well, appeals of election results go to the courts rather than to the Aboriginal Affairs minister and the cabinet could set aside an election if there were corrupt practices. The Act only applies to the 238 bands that hold elections under the provisions of the Indian Act[14] if they decide to opt in. However, if there were protracted leadership disputes in a First Nation, the minister could require that the band come under the First Nations Elections Act. Critics pointed out that there had been inadequate consultation with First Nations in preparing the Act.

The Budget Implementation Act passed by Parliament in December 2012 reduced the environmental protection of nearly all of Canada's lakes and rivers, reduced the number of projects requiring environmental protection, and

[13]First Nations were already required to provide this information to the Aboriginal Affairs Department.

[14]As of 2015, 343 bands use community-designed or customary systems to choose leaders, while 36 use provisions in the constitution of their self-government agreement.

allowed the surrender of band lands without the approval of the band council. These changes were made without consultation with First Nations and helped to spark the grassroots Idle No More movement of Aboriginals and their supporters who held rallies, demonstrations, and blockades across Canada.

SELF-GOVERNMENT ISSUES AND CHALLENGES

Aboriginal governments face many challenges. Most First Nations are small, with the majority having only a few hundred people. Establishing a substantial government responsible for developing and administering various programs and services equivalent, in some cases, to those provided by provincial governments is a daunting task. A sizable expert staff is also needed to coordinate the laws, regulations, and programs of Aboriginal governments with those of the federal and provincial governments. Although there has been a substantial increase in the number of Aboriginal people with university educations and professional degrees, still only about 40 percent of on-reserve First Nations youth aged 20–24 have completed high school (Richards, 2014). Part of the problem is that schools on reserves are poorly equipped, since the federal government funding of these schools is much less per student than schools that are provincially funded (White, 2015).

The Royal Commission on Aboriginal Peoples pointed out that the division of Indians into numerous small bands was primarily the result of past federal government policy designed to weaken and assimilate Indians. It recommended that Indian bands be consolidated into 60 to 80 nations based on similarities in language and culture. However, merging existing First Nations bands might not be acceptable because these bands have developed separate identities and governing structures. And even with consolidation, most First Nations would still have small populations.

Self-government agreements generally require that Aboriginal governments operate democratically with a constitution that Aboriginal laws and governing procedures must follow (as well as being subject to the Charter of Rights and Freedoms and other provisions of the Canadian Constitution). However, putting a meaningful democracy into practice can be challenging. First Nations communities can face governing problems resulting from factionalism, nepotism, and corruption. With high levels of poverty and unemployment, and an inadequate supply of housing, it is not surprising that politics in some Aboriginal communities is very contentious. Some chiefs and band councils have been accused of rewarding their family, clan, and supporters with scarce resources such as jobs and housing and a few chiefs have obtained very high incomes.

Good governing requires that Aboriginal citizens be able and willing to hold their government accountable for its actions. This can be difficult in small communities, particularly where a high proportion of people depend on the chief and band council for employment, housing, and other benefits (Bedford, 2010).

Creating institutions such as an Aboriginal auditor general and ombudsman rather than relying on the Aboriginal Affairs bureaucracy that has often been criticized for its paternalism and ineffectiveness might help to create good self-government. The development of independent Aboriginal media with the capability to investigate and publicize Aboriginal issues and problems may also help to make Aboriginal governments more accountable to the people they serve.

Most First Nations have a limited economic base. Inevitably, they depend heavily on federal government funding, which, in effect, limits their autonomy. A few exceptions are bands that are wealthy because they occupy valuable land, have precious resources, or operate successful businesses. Generally, however, the lack of opportunities in remote and isolated areas has meant that an increasing proportion of the Aboriginal population has migrated to cities. According to the 2011 National Household Survey, 56 percent of Aboriginals lived in urban areas (Aboriginal Affairs and Northern Development Canada, 2014).

Some have argued that the communal ownership of land with the legal title held by the Canadian government is a major factor in hindering the economic development of Aboriginal communities (Flanagan, Alcantara, & Le Dressay, 2010). Without private ownership of property, it is difficult to borrow money to start businesses or for individuals to obtain mortgages to build their own home. Most First Nations chiefs are opposed to the idea of private landowning on reserves, arguing that it would threaten First Nations control of land for future generations.[15] Instead, the Assembly of First Nations favours looking at ways to combine communal ownership with private property, such as allowing non-band members to lease reserve property (Curry, 2011).

Although Aboriginal governance faces an array of problems and challenges, there is a positive side to self-government, namely that establishing effective self-government can help change attitudes of despair and dependence. Some Aboriginal communities that have gained self-government have become active in economic and community development. For example, the Inuit of Nunavik (Quebec) used some of the money provided by their land claims agreement to establish the Makivik Corporation, owned by all members of the Inuit community. The corporation operates various businesses, including the major northern airline, First Air.

ABORIGINAL SOVEREIGNTY AND THE RIGHT TO SELF-DETERMINATION

Some First Nations have refused to enter into negotiations to establish self-government arrangements, with some asserting that they are sovereign nations. In their view, the early treaties that were signed with the British

---

[15]As part of their comprehensive land claims agreement, the Nisga'a became the first First Nation to allow private ownership of reserve land including the right of individuals to sell their land to non-Aboriginals.

BOX 11-4

Sovereign Powers:
The Two-Row Wampum Belt

The Haudenosaunee (Six Nations Confederacy) in northeastern North America had developed a democratic political system long before European colonization. In their treaties with the European powers, they used the traditional symbolism of two rows of beads (wampum) to describe and document a relationship of peace and friendship with Europeans. The beads represented the relationship in terms of a canoe and a ship travelling side by side down a river. Each vessel avoided interference with the other and neither crew tried to steer the other's vessel.

In the eyes of the Confederacy, the concept of the two vessels was the basis for the early treaties signed by the Six Nations with other nations, including Holland, France and Britain. From this perspective, the goal to be pursued by First Nations should not consist of self-government under the conditions set by the Canadian government within the Canadian Constitution. Rather, in keeping with the two-row wampum belt tradition, First Nations should reassert their sovereignty and share territory with the Canadian government, which they view as the representative of non-Aboriginal peoples. Instead of viewing Aboriginal self-government as enhancing participation in the Canadian governing system, the two-row wampum tradition looks to the parallel, but separate, development of sovereign Aboriginal and non-Aboriginal peoples. In this perspective, the decolonization of Canada requires the full recognition of the sovereignty of indigenous people and separate systems of laws, government, and constitutions for Aboriginal nations and a nation-to-nation relationship between Aboriginal nations and the Canadian nation.

Crown involved an agreement between independent nations to share territory, with First Nations retaining their sovereignty while delegating some specific powers to the Crown. The Six Nations Confederacy, for example, has a long history of asserting its independence[16] (see Box 11-4: Sovereign Powers: The Two-Row Wampum Belt). However, Tom Flanagan (2000) has challenged the assertion that First Nations have retained their sovereignty. His argument is that Canadian sovereignty has been acquired, in keeping with international law, by long-term continued possession and effective control of the whole country.

A somewhat different approach is suggested by the United Nations Declaration on the Rights of Indigenous Peoples (2009). This declaration focuses on the right of Aboriginal peoples to self-determination; that is, "freely determining their political status and freely pursuing their economic, social, and cultural development." This includes the "right to autonomy or self-government in matters relating to their internal and local affairs as well as ways and means of financing their autonomous society." In addition, it includes "the right to

---

[16]The Six Nations Confederacy has never accepted Canadian sovereignty. Indeed, in 1923 they unsuccessfully applied for membership in the League of Nations, the predecessor of the United Nations (Woo, 2003).

maintain and strengthen their distinct political, legal, economic, social, and cultural institutions while retaining their right to participation, if they so choose, in the political, economic, social, and cultural life of the state" (Articles 3–5). However, the declaration does not justify "any action that would dismember or impair, totally or in part, the territorial integrity or political unity of sovereign and independent states" (Article 46).

Although the declaration was passed by the General Assembly of the United Nations in 2007, Canada voted against the declaration.[17] Nevertheless, Canada endorsed the declaration in 2010, although noting that it is not legally binding and is "an aspiration document" (Aboriginal Affairs and Northern Development Canada, 2010a). However, in 2014, Canada was the only country that objected to a reaffirmation of the declaration's commitment to obtain from indigenous peoples their "free, prior and informed consent, before adopting and implementing legislation or administrative measures that may affect them" (Lum, 2014).

Summary and Conclusion

Aboriginal peoples played a major role in Canada's early development. However, as settlement by those of European ancestry increased, First Nations were pushed to the margins of society and treaty promises were often ignored. In recent decades, Aboriginal peoples have actively pursued their rights and sought to change their relationship with Canadian governments through legal and political action. Nevertheless, many Aboriginal communities continue to suffer from poor housing, inadequate services, poverty, and serious social and health problems. Aboriginals are less likely than non-Aboriginals to participate in Canada's democratic processes, in part because of their historic exclusion and marginalization from the political process and because of the inequalities they continue to face.

Aboriginal and treaty rights were recognized and affirmed by the Constitution Act, 1982. Although attempts to add the inherent right of self-government to the Constitution have not succeeded, the Canadian government has declared its commitment to the "inherent right of self-government" principle.

Nevertheless, Aboriginal nations have had to undertake extremely lengthy and costly legal battles in the courts to secure their rights and have faced various legislative obstacles to full self-government.

In those areas of the country where First Nations did not sign treaties, a few recent comprehensive land claims agreements have included self-government provisions and have removed First Nations from the provisions of the Indian Act. For most First Nations, powers have been delegated from the Canadian government to band councils. However, these communities are still subject to the Indian Act and generally lack the financial resources to be truly self-governing. Furthermore, the small and impoverished populations of most First Nations raise questions about the capacity of the more than 600 First Nations to exercise a wide range of governing responsibilities. Developing good government is a difficult challenge.

The circumstances of the Métis and non-Status Indians often receive much less attention than those of

---

[17]The three other countries that voted against the declaration—the United States, Australia, and New Zealand—have also reversed their opposition.

Status Indians. Nevertheless, these diverse groups represent a substantial proportion of the Aboriginal population and can claim constitutional rights, even though who qualifies as a Métis or a non-Status Indian is often unclear and their rights are largely undefined. Likewise, inadequate attention has been paid to the majority of Aboriginals who now live in urban areas.

Overall, the treatment of Aboriginal peoples is a serious blot on Canada's human rights record. However, beyond apologies for past injustices (such as the residential schools) and rectifying the "Third World" conditions of many Aboriginal communities, a fundamental rethinking of the nature of Canada may be necessary. As the former grand chief of the Assembly of First Nations stated, "We want to reset the relationship between First Nations and Canada on its original foundation of mutual recognition, mutual respect and partnership" (Atleo, 2011).

Discussion Questions

1. Should Aboriginals have special rights because of their occupancy of the land before European control? Should these rights be limited to activities engaged in prior to European contact?

2. Is the Nisga'a agreement a suitable model for other First Nations?

3. Should Aboriginals be encouraged to integrate into Canadian society?

4. Should Canada be viewed as an equal partnership between sovereign Aboriginal nations and the Canadian government?

5. Should Aboriginal governments be constituted as a third order of government?

Further Reading

Alfred, T. (2005). *Wasáse: Indigenous pathways of action and freedom*. Peterborough, ON: Broadview Press.

Asch, M. (2014). *On being here to stay: Treaties and Aboriginal rights in Canada*. Toronto, ON: University of Toronto Press.

Belanger, Y. (Ed.). (2008) *Aboriginal self-government in Canada: Current trends and issues* (3rd ed.). Saskatoon, SK: Purich.

Borrows, J. (2010). *Canada's indigenous constitution*. Toronto, ON: University of Toronto Press.

Cairns, A.C. (2000). *Citizens plus: Aboriginal peoples and the Canadian state*. Vancouver, BC: UBC Press.

Flanagan, T. (2008). *First nations? Second thoughts* (2nd ed.). Montreal, QC: McGill-Queen's University Press.

Flanagan, T., Alcantara, C., & Le Dressay, A. (2010). *Beyond the Indian Act: Restoring Aboriginal property rights*. Montreal, QC: McGill-Queen's University Press.

Frideres, J.S., & Gadacz, R.R. (2011). *Aboriginal peoples in Canada* (9th ed.). Toronto, ON: Pearson Prentice Hall.

Miller, J.R. (2009). *Compact, contract, covenant: Aboriginal treaty-making in Canada*. Toronto, ON: University of Toronto Press.

Murphy, M. (Ed.). (2005). *Canada: The state of the federation 2003: Reconfiguring aboriginal-state relations*. Kingston, ON: Institute of Intergovernmental Relations, Queen's University.

Newman, D.G. (2009). *The duty to consult: New relationships with Aboriginal people*. Saskatoon, SK: Purich.

Saul, J.R. (2014). *The comeback*. Toronto, ON: Penguin Canada.

Schouls, T. (2003). *Shifting boundaries: Aboriginal identity, pluralist theory, and the politics of self-government*. Vancouver, BC: UBC Press.

Timpson, A.M. (Ed.). (2010). *First nations, first thoughts: The impact of indigenous thought in Canada*. Vancouver, BC: UBC Press.

Woo, G.L.X. (2011). *Ghost dancing with colonialism: Decolonization and indigenous rights at the Supreme Court of Canada*. Vancouver, BC: UBC Press.

CHAPTER 12

The Federal System

CHAPTER OBJECTIVES

After reading this chapter, you should be able to

1. Define a federal system and explain its significance for politics and government in Canada.
2. Discuss the constitutional provisions concerning the federal system and how they have been affected by judicial interpretations.
3. Outline how the federal system has evolved in terms of centralization and decentralization and the level of interaction between the Canadian and provincial governments.
4. Explain how post-secondary education, health care, and welfare are funded.
5. Describe the system of equalization payments and discuss why it has been controversial.
6. Evaluate the contemporary Canadian federal system.

Danny Williams, premier of Newfoundland and Labrador, demonstrated his ire when he ordered Canadian flags struck from provincial buildings in 2004—but he also guaranteed federal government attention for his issues. Balancing national and provincial interests is an ongoing challenge of the federal system.

© Office of the PMO Canada Press

On December 23, 2004, the premier of Newfoundland and Labrador, Danny Williams, ordered the Canadian flag removed from all provincial buildings. Williams was upset that Prime Minister Paul Martin had reneged on a written promise made during the 2004 election campaign. This promise guaranteed that the Newfoundland and Labrador government would receive 100 percent of the royalties from its offshore oil resources without a reduction in the equalization payments the provincial government received as a "have not" province. In Williams's view, a federal offer to solve the dispute was a "slap in the face" that would leave the province $1 billion short of what was promised. The Canadian government, he argued, "was not treating us as a proper partner in Confederation."

A month later, a deal was reached that allowed the provincial government to continue to receive all of its offshore resource revenues. The Canadian government would give an "offset payment" for a number of years to fully compensate for the cuts in equalization payments resulting from those revenues. The deal satisfied Williams, and the Canadian flag was hoisted once again in Newfoundland and Labrador.

Premier Williams's satisfaction was short lived. During the 2006 election campaign, Stephen Harper promised that non-renewable natural resource revenues would not be included in the calculation of a new equalization formula and that there would be no cap on equalization payments. However, the formula adopted by the Harper government in 2007 included 50 percent of natural resource revenues and placed a cap on equalization payments. The result: the end of equalization payments to the government of Newfoundland and Labrador. Economics professor Wade Locke presented an analysis estimating that the broken promise would mean a total of about $11 billion less for the provincial government over the following 13 years than it would have received if the promise had been kept (CBC News, 2007).

Danny Williams was livid: "Yesterday, Prime Minister Harper told the people of Newfoundland and Labrador and essentially the people of Canada that his promises do not matter. His promises do not count, and they most certainly cannot be relied upon" (Newfoundland and Labrador Executive Council, 2007). This time, he did not order the flags lowered. Instead Williams, a Progressive Conservative, announced that he would actively campaign to elect "anything but Conservatives" in the next federal election. In addition to speeches denouncing Harper, a popular website (anythingbutconservative.ca) was set up, and a large billboard carrying the message greeted motorists on the Gardiner Expressway in Toronto. Support for the Conservative party plummeted in Newfoundland and Labrador, and no Conservatives were elected in that province in the 2008 federal election. Williams claimed, "We've sent a very strong message to the Harper Conservatives." However, with no representatives from the province in Harper's cabinet or in the Conservative caucus to promote the message, the equalization formula was not changed to meet the demands of the premier.

Ensuring that all Canadians can receive an equitable level of services from their governments while each province feels that it is being treated fairly is one of the challenges facing the Canadian federal system. Another important challenge is finding a balance between having a robust national government able to look after the interests of the country as a whole and strong provincial governments able to respond to the diverse interests of different areas of the country.

INTRODUCTION

FEDERAL SYSTEM

A system of governing in which authority is divided and shared between the central government and provincial governments, with each deriving its authority from the constitution.

A **federal system** is a system of governing in which authority is divided and shared between the central (federal) government and provincial governments, with each deriving its authority from the constitution. Provincial governments are not legally subordinate to the Canadian government. Provincial legislatures do not need the approval of the Canadian government to act on matters within the exclusive law-making authority that the constitution has granted them. Neither does the Canadian Parliament need the approval of provincial governments for matters under its constitutional authority.

UNITARY SYSTEM

A system of governing in which authority rests with the central government; regional and local governments are subordinate to the central government.

The Canadian federal system differs from a **unitary system**, in which authority rests with the central government and regional and local governments are subordinate to the central government. Canada's governing system thus differs substantially from that of the United Kingdom, which basically has a unitary system, although significant legislative powers have been devolved to the Scottish Parliament in recent times. A federal system also differs from a *confederal system,* in which sovereign countries have agreed to delegate some of their authority to a joint government that has limited authority while retaining their sovereignty.[1]

In practice, as discussed in this chapter, the contemporary federal system involves quite a high level of interaction between the federal and provincial governments in the development, funding, and implementation of many policies. The Canadian federal system is not only a matter of divided legislative powers, but also requires close cooperation in making and implementing the decisions that affect our lives.

The adoption of a federal system in 1867 was necessary to unite the British North American colonies. Uniting in one country with a central government made it easier to develop the economy and provide for military defence. By adopting a federal system, provincial governments could maintain and nurture their distinctive cultures, traditions, and identities. In other words, the federal system embraces the challenging goal of bringing together unity and diversity (Bakvis & Skogstad, 2008).

THE CONSTITUTION AND THE FEDERAL SYSTEM

Sir John A. Macdonald, a leading proponent of the union of the British North American colonies, wanted a strong central government with the capability to build and unite the new country. The United States, whose constitution greatly limited the scope of the American government, had just gone through a devastating civil war. Macdonald's idea of a vigorous central government was reflected, to a considerable extent, in the Constitution Act, 1867.

The Constitution Act, 1867

The Constitution Act, 1867, divides most government activities into two categories of exclusive legislative authority: that of the Canadian Parliament and that of provincial legislatures.

In particular, this document lists many areas of government activity where the Canadian Parliament has exclusive legislative jurisdiction and somewhat fewer areas of exclusive provincial jurisdiction (see Table 12-1). In two policy areas—agriculture and immigration—both Parliament and provincial legislatures received legislative authority,[2] although Canadian laws take precedence if Canadian and provincial laws in these areas conflict.

---

[1] Confederal systems are rare; the Haudenosaunee (Iroquois) Confederacy is an early example, while the European Union is often depicted as a combination of federal and confederal systems. Although the formation of Canada in 1867 is often described as "Confederation," Canada has never had a confederal system.

[2] In the case of criminal law, Parliament makes the laws while provincial governments are responsible for enforcing them (Bakvis & Skogstad, 2008).

TABLE 12-1
THE DIVISION OF LEGISLATIVE POWERS IN THE CONSTITUTION ACT, 1867

Note: See the Constitution Act, 1867 (Sections 91–95, 109, and 132), for the complete list and the precise wording.

EXCLUSIVE POWERS OF PARLIAMENT	EXCLUSIVE POWERS OF PROVINCIAL LEGISLATURES	POWERS OF BOTH
Regulation of trade and commerce	Direct taxation for provincial purposes	Agriculture
Raising money by any mode of taxation	Management and sale of public lands	Immigration
Postal service	Hospitals and asylums	
Census and statistics	Municipal institutions	
Military and defence	Shop, saloon, and other licences	
Navigation and shipping	Local works and undertakings	
Fisheries	Incorporation of provincial companies	
Currency and coinage	Solemnization of marriage	
Banking and incorporation of banks	Property and civil rights	
Weights and measures	Administration of justice	
Bankruptcy and insolvency	Education	
Patents and copyrights	Lands, mines, minerals, and royalties	
Indians and lands reserved for Indians		
Marriage and divorce		
Criminal law		

The Constitution Act, 1867, gave Parliament legislative authority over many, but not all, of the important areas of governing in the nineteenth century. However, the provinces retained legislative authority in areas such as education, health, and welfare, which in the nineteenth century were often the responsibility of religious and charitable organizations as well as municipal governments. These responsibilities entrusted to the provinces have evolved into major governmental activities in modern times.

A constitutional document cannot anticipate all matters about which governments might want to legislate. The **residual power** (the power over matters not listed in the Constitution Act) was basically given to the national level of governing, as Section 91 of Constitution Act provides that Parliament can make laws for the "peace, order and good government of Canada" in relation to all matters not assigned exclusively to the provincial legislatures. Some residual power was also handed to provincial legislatures, which have the authority to legislate on "property and civil rights" and "generally all matters of a merely local or private nature in the province" (Section 92).

RESIDUAL POWER
Legislative power over matters not listed in the Constitution.

Constitutional Amendments

The provisions of the Constitution Act, 1867, concerning the division of legislative powers have not changed much. Constitutional amendments have given the Canadian Parliament the authority to pass laws concerning unemployment insurance (1940). As well, Parliament received the authority to pass legislation regarding old-age pensions (1951) and disability benefits (1964), provided those laws do not conflict with provincial laws. Constitutional amendments in 1982 gave the provinces some extra authority related to the control and taxation of natural resources.

Judicial Interpretations

Judicial interpretations of the Constitution have significantly affected the division of legislative powers between the federal and provincial governments. Until 1949, the Judicial Committee of the Privy Council (JCPC) in Britain was the final court of appeal, except for criminal cases. Its decisions frequently overturned the rulings of the Supreme Court of Canada and other Canadian courts. Appeals to the Judicial Committee were abolished in 1949, making the Supreme Court of Canada the country's highest court.

THE JUDICIAL COMMITTEE OF THE PRIVY COUNCIL   In a number of important rulings (particularly from about the mid-1890s), the Judicial Committee declared various laws passed by Parliament invalid because they overstepped the authority granted to the Canadian Parliament. This helped to shift Canada away from a highly centralized federal system.

Of particular importance has been the interpretation of the "peace, order, and good government" clause. This clause might be interpreted as giving Parliament very broad powers to override the specified provincial powers. An early case involved the Temperance Act, passed by Parliament in 1878, which allowed local governments to ban the sale of alcohol if voters supported the ban in a plebiscite. With his livelihood at stake, pub owner Charles Russell challenged his conviction for selling alcohol in the "dry" city of Fredericton, New Brunswick. In *Russell v. The Queen* (1882), the Judicial Committee upheld the constitutionality of the Temperance Act on the basis that provincial jurisdiction over property and civil rights did not prevent Parliament from passing laws "designed for the promotion of public order, safety, or morals, and which subject those who contravene them to criminal procedure and punishment" (quoted in Russell, Knopff, Bateman, & Hiebert, 2008, p. 41).

In later decisions, the Judicial Committee proved less inclined to support a general power for the Canadian Parliament. In the *Local Prohibition* case (1896), the JCPC was asked whether a province could set up its own system of local prohibition. In the JCPC's opinion, the peace, order, and good government clause did not exclude provinces from enacting their own prohibition laws. To safeguard provincial autonomy, the peace, order, and good government clause could not be used to overrule the powers of the provinces enumerated in the Constitution: "Parliament has not the authority to encroach upon any class of subjects which is exclusively assigned to provincial legislatures" (quoted in Russell et al., 2008, p. 49).

The Judicial Committee, particularly after Viscount Haldane became a member in 1911, generally viewed the peace, order, and good government clause as applying only to temporary emergencies (Hogg, 2006). For example, in the *Fort Frances* case (1923), the JCPC upheld the system of price controls that was created during World War I. The "sufficiently great emergency" of the war justified federal action, even though the regulations fell within the normal competence of the provinces (quoted in Hogg, 2006, p. 475). In the *Board of Commerce* case (1922), the JCPC struck down laws passed by the Canadian Parliament after World War I to deal with the serious problems of profiteering, monopolies, and hoarding. In their ruling, the JCPC argued that the emergency power could only be used in "highly exceptional circumstances" to override the exclusive provincial power over property and civil rights. Similarly, the JCPC struck down several Canadian laws to tackle the problems of the Great Depression of the 1930s (including unemployment insurance), arguing that only an emergency would justify the use of the peace, order, and good government clause. In the eyes of the JCPC, the Great Depression did not rate as an emergency. The possibility that these measures might become permanent rather than temporary may also have influenced the JCPC decision (Hogg, 2006).

In addition to viewing the peace, order, and good government clause as providing an "emergency" power to Parliament, the Judicial Committee saw the clause as granting residual legislative power to Parliament to deal with subjects not included in the lists of enumerated powers. For example, the Constitution Act, 1867, gave Parliament "all powers necessary or proper for performing the obligations of Canada or of any province thereof, as part of the British Empire, towards foreign countries, arising under treaties between the Empire and such foreign countries" (Section 132). In 1935, the Canadian Parliament ratified the draft conventions of the International Labour Organization and passed three acts dealing with hours of work, minimum wages, and weekly rest to fulfill the obligations of the conventions. The Canadian cabinet subsequently requested a judicial reference concerning the validity of these acts. In the *Labour Conventions* case (1937), the JCPC upheld the power of the Canadian government to sign the conventions (an international treaty), because Canadian treaty-making power was not specifically included in the list of enumerated powers. However, because the labour conventions dealt with the class of subjects under provincial jurisdiction, the legislative power to implement the conventions rested with provincial legislatures rather than Parliament.[3] In the view of the JCPC, "While the ship of state now sails on larger ventures and into foreign waters she still retains the water-tight compartments

---

[3]In the *Radio Reference* case (1932), the JCPC ruled that Canada could regulate radio transmission in accordance with international agreements Canada had signed because radio was a new matter not mentioned in the Constitution Act, 1867.

which are an essential part of her original structure" (quoted in Russell et al., 2008, p. 74). In other words, the JCPC thought the federal system should be based on autonomous federal and provincial governments, each with its own specific areas of responsibility—a view often described as **classical federalism**.

When there was a "national dimension" or a "national concern" involved, the Judicial Committee, at times, used the peace, order, and good government clause to uphold legislation passed by Parliament that might be viewed as infringing on provincial powers. For example, in the *Canada Temperance Federation* case (1946), the JCPC gave the opinion that if the subject matter of the legislation "goes beyond local or provincial concern or interests and must from its inherent nature be the concern of the Dominion as a whole . . . then it will fall within the competence of the Dominion Parliament as a matter affecting the peace, order and good government of Canada, though it may in another aspect touch on matters specially reserved to the provincial legislatures" (quoted in Hogg, 2006, p. 462).

The national government's authority over the regulation of trade and commerce was interpreted narrowly by the Judicial Committee as legislative authority only over international and interprovincial trade. Trade and commerce within a province has been deemed a matter for provincial legislatures because of their "property and civil rights" power. For example, in the *Insurance Reference* case (1916), the JCPC ruled that the federal Insurance Act establishing a licensing system for insurance companies operating across Canada was not justified by the trade and commerce power. Likewise, a federal prohibition on the manufacture, sale, or possession of margarine (designed to assist dairy farmers) was struck down on the grounds that the trade and commerce power could not be used to prohibit transactions within a province (Hogg, 2006).

THE SUPREME COURT OF CANADA The Supreme Court of Canada has taken a somewhat different approach from the Judicial Committee, showing itself less inclined to limit the Canadian government's powers. For example, the Anti-Inflation Act passed by Parliament in 1975 instituted controls on wages, prices, and profits for up to three years (with the possibility of an extension). The Supreme Court, in a 7–2 decision, upheld the Act using the emergency powers interpretation of the peace, order, and good government clause, even though the Anti-Inflation Act involved legislating on provincial matters (e.g., by limiting wages of provincial government employees). Indeed, the majority ruled that the government did not need to prove there was an emergency; the burden of proof that an emergency did not exist rested with the opponents of the legislation (Hogg, 2006).

The Supreme Court of Canada has been divided on the use of the "national concern" interpretation of the peace, order, and good government clause to uphold national environmental laws. In 1980, Crown Zellerbach, a forest

CLASSICAL FEDERALISM
The view that a federal system should be based on autonomous federal and provincial governments, each with its own specific areas of responsibility.

products company, dredged logging debris including bark and wood from its shoreline water lot, and dumped it in deeper water off Vancouver Island. The company was charged with an offence under the federal Ocean Dumping Control Act, which prohibits dumping at sea, including dumping substances without a permit in provincial territorial waters (other than freshwater). In a 4–3 judgment, the Supreme Court upheld the provision, arguing, "marine pollution, because of its predominantly extra-provincial as well as international character and implications, is clearly a matter of concern to Canada as a whole." In particular, the majority noted that in deciding what distinguishes a matter of national concern, "it is relevant to consider what would be the effect on extra-provincial interests of a provincial failure to deal effectively with control or regulation of the intra-provincial aspects of the matter" (quoted in Russell et al., 2008, pp. 132–133).

In 1990, Hydro-Québec was charged with dumping polychlorinated biphenyls (PCBs)—a highly toxic substance that carries serious health risks to both animals and humans—into the St. Maurice River in violation of the Canadian Environmental Protection Act, 1985. The Supreme Court of Canada pointed out that the environment is a broad subject that the Constitution Act, 1867, did not assign exclusively to either level of government. Both national and provincial governments have legislative authority in this area and should cooperate to safeguard the environment. The Supreme Court unanimously agreed that the Environmental Protection Act was too broad to meet the peace, order, and good government criteria of "national concern" used in the *Crown Zellerbach* case. However in a 5–4 decision, the Supreme Court ruled that "Parliament may validly enact prohibitions under its criminal law power against specific acts for the purpose of preventing pollution . . ." (quoted in Russell et al., 2008, p. 152).

Overall, even though its justices are appointed on the recommendation of the prime minister, the Supreme Court of Canada has not drastically altered the interpretations of the division of powers developed in the JCPC decisions. In particular, the Supreme Court of Canada has indicated that it does not view the "peace, order and good government" clause as a sweeping power that can be used to undermine provincial jurisdiction (Kennett, 2000; Lucas & Shawitt, 2000). The Supreme Court of Canada has also hesitated to interpret the federal trade and commerce power as giving the Canadian government a general power to regulate trade by, for example, introducing legislation for national business practices or consumer protection (see Box 12-1: Is "Lite Beer" Light? The Supreme Court Verdict). Likewise, the Supreme Court unanimously provided an opinion that the federal government's proposal to establish a single national securities regulator was unconstitutional. A complete takeover of the regulation of the securities industry (which deals with the sale of stocks, bonds, and other instruments used by companies to raise money) from the provinces could not be justified by the federal trade and commerce power. The protection of investors is within the

BOX 12-1

Is "Lite Beer" Light?
The Supreme Court Verdict

In 1977, Labatt introduced Special Lite (now known as Labatt Lite). With many Canadians becoming diet conscious, this first low-calorie beer was an instant success. However, Labatt came into conflict with the Canadian government, which has a long history of regulating brewing.

Regulations under Canada's Food and Drugs Act, 1970, provide that light beer has to meet certain standards, including an alcohol content of between 1.2 percent and 2.5 percent. Federal inspectors seized Special Lite, which has an alcohol content of 4 percent. Labatt sought a court declaration that "Special Lite is not likely to be mistaken for a light beer" (quoted in Russell et al., 2008, p. 121).

The Supreme Court of Canada ruled that Special Lite could be mistaken for "light beer," even though the 4 percent alcohol content was on the beer's label. However, in a 6–3 decision, the Supreme Court struck down the standards for the composition of light beer, arguing that the federal trade and commerce power did not apply to the brewing process, even though the sale of beer involved interprovincial trade.

Like the Judicial Committee, the Supreme Court has been reluctant to accept a broad interpretation of the federal government's constitutional powers over trade and commerce. Nevertheless, federal laws concerning "false, misleading or deceptive" packaging and labelling do allow for the indirect enforcement of national standards for consumer products (Russell et al., 2008).

---

provincial legislative power over property and civil rights (*Reference re. Securities Act*, 2011).[4]

Disallowance, Reservation, and the Declaratory Power

Some political scientists have questioned whether the Constitution Act, 1867, established a purely federal system in part because the Act authorized the Canadian government to override the decisions of provincial governments. Specifically, the **disallowance power** gave the governor general in council (meaning the Canadian cabinet) the right to disallow provincial legislation within one year of its passage. In turn, the **reservation power** gave provincial lieutenant governors (who are appointed on the recommendation of the prime minister) the authority to reserve the passage of provincial legislation until the Canadian cabinet had approved it. In addition, with the **declaratory power** the Canadian Parliament could declare any "local works or undertakings" within a province to be "for the general Advantage of Canada or for the Advantage of Two or more of the Provinces" and then legislate on that matter.

DISALLOWANCE POWER
The right of the Canadian cabinet to disallow provincial legislation within one year of its passage.

RESERVATION POWER
The right of a lieutenant governor to reserve the passage of provincial legislation until that legislation is approved by the Canadian cabinet.

DECLARATORY POWER
The right of the Canadian Parliament to declare any "local works or undertakings" within a province to be "for the general Advantage of Canada or for the Advantage of Two or more of the Provinces" and then legislate on that matter.

---

[4]The Supreme Court did indicate that a national securities regulator might deal with some matters, such as national standards, systemic risk, and data collection. It also suggested that a cooperative approach to securities regulation between Ottawa and the provinces might meet the constitutional test.

The Canadian government quite frequently used the disallowance power and the reservation power until World War II. However, these powers have not been used since 1943.[5] Likewise, the Canadian Parliament often took advantage of the declaratory power to legislate on such matters as railways, grain elevators, telephones, and atomic energy, but that power has not been used since 1961. Generally, these powers are viewed as obsolete, and various constitutional reform packages have proposed getting rid of them.

THE CHANGING FEDERAL SYSTEM

Federal systems are often analyzed in terms of whether power tends to be concentrated in the central government or dispersed among provincial governments—that is, whether it is a basically centralized or decentralized federal system. Federal systems can also be analyzed in terms of the extent to which policies are developed and implemented through collaboration between national and provincial governments. Furthermore, a distinction can be made between basically symmetrical federal systems, in which each province has the same powers, and asymmetrical federalism, in which some provincial governments have greater powers than others.

Quasi-Federalism

The Constitution Act, 1867, with its substantial list of central government powers and the ability of the central government to override provincial laws, is often viewed as basically establishing a centralized federal system. In the first decades after Confederation, the Canadian government used its powers to carry out the vision of expanding Canada by opening up the west and constructing railway links to build a national economy. Scholars often refer to this period as one of "**quasi-federalism**" because of the dominance of the federal government, particularly through its use of the powers of reservation and disallowance to invalidate provincial legislation (Wheare, 1967).

QUASI-FEDERALISM
A system in which the federal government dominates provincial governments, particularly through its use of the powers of reservation and disallowance to invalidate provincial legislation.

Classical Federalism

As discussed above, the decisions of the Judicial Committee were important in moving Canada away from a centralized version of federalism. In addition, some assertive provincial governments challenged the dominance of the Canadian government. During his lengthy time in office (1872–1896), Ontario Liberal premier Oliver Mowat fiercely defended the interests of Ontario and

---

[5]One hundred and twelve provincial laws were vetoed from 1867 to 1943 and 69 bills were reserved until 1937. In 1961 the lieutenant governor of Saskatchewan reserved a bill, even though the prime minister did not want it reserved. The bill was quickly approved (Heard, 1991).

promoted the idea of "provincial rights," which clashed with the centralist views of Conservative prime minister Macdonald. In the 1880s, Mowat found an ally in Quebec nationalist premier Honoré Mercier. Ever since, most Quebec governments have energetically defended provincial autonomy based on the view that the Quebec government represents one of Canada's two "founding peoples" or "nations."

From about 1896 until 1939, Canada's federal system was quite decentralized and featured little interaction between national and provincial governments. However, during and shortly after World War I, the Canadian government assumed greater powers in order to mobilize the country for the war effort and to deal with problems in its aftermath. Similarly, the Canadian government took the dominant role during World War II. This time, however, the federal system did not revert to classical federalism afterward.

Cooperative Federalism

The inability of the classical federal system to deal with the problems of the Great Depression of the 1930s and growing support for a more active role for government resulted in important changes in the federal system after World War II. In addition to becoming more active in managing the economy (influenced by Keynesian economics), the Canadian government increasingly became involved in developing and funding various social programs (the "welfare state") as well as the construction of the Trans-Canada Highway. Provincial governments were responsible for administering these programs according to national guidelines and conditions. These **shared-cost programs** generally involved the Canadian government paying one-half of the cost. Since the federal and provincial governments generally cooperated in developing these programs and shared in their funding, the period from about 1945 to the early 1960s is typically referred to as featuring **cooperative federalism**. In particular, the Canadian government used its **spending power** to be involved in matters that are constitutionally under provincial legislative jurisdiction (see Box 12-2: The Federal Spending Power).

The era of cooperative federalism was, to a considerable extent, one of centralized federalism combined with a substantial level of federal–provincial interaction. The Canadian government often took a leadership role in the era of cooperative federalism, although some of the programs were initiated by a provincial government (such as Saskatchewan's hospital insurance) and later turned into a national shared-cost program. Cooperation was facilitated by good working relationships between federal and provincial public servants in particular policy areas. As well, provincial governments (other than the Quebec government, which favoured classical federalism and opposed federal social programs) were generally willing to work with the Canadian government on the development of the welfare state programs that were a key feature of this era (Simeon, 2006).

SHARED-COST PROGRAMS
Provincial programs in which the Canadian government generally paid half the costs.

COOPERATIVE FEDERALISM
The feature of Canadian federalism following World War II in which federal and provincial governments generally cooperated under federal leadership in developing the welfare state.

SPENDING POWER
The ability of the Canadian government to spend money as it sees fit, even on matters under provincial jurisdiction.

BOX 12-2

The Federal Spending Power

The Canadian government has asserted its right to spend the money it raises as it sees fit, even on matters under provincial jurisdiction. This includes money transferred to provincial or local governments for particular purposes as well as payments to individuals (including income tax credits for children's sports, textbooks, and transit passes) and organizations for objectives established by the Canadian government.

The spending power of the Canadian government is not explicitly provided for in the Constitution. The Judicial Committee of the Privy Council indicated that legislation is invalid if it encroaches on provincial jurisdiction and rejected the notion that money raised by taxation could be disposed of by Parliament in any manner that it sees fit (Petter, 1989). However, in commenting on a community job creation program supported by a federal contribution, the Supreme Court of Canada cited the view that "the federal spending power can be exercised so long as it is not, in substance, legislation on a provincial matter" (Petter, 1989). Although some judicial decisions have indicated that the Canadian government can grant or withhold money to provincial governments and attach conditions to its use, there has not been a definitive statement by the Supreme Court about the constitutionality of the spending power and its limits (Richer, 2007).

The federal spending power has been controversial. Its supporters have viewed it as a way to achieve important national social and economic goals, such as ensuring equal opportunity, the equality of public services across Canada, and effective management of the national economy. Critics argue that it undermines the federal system by allowing the Canadian government to strongly influence provincial policy priorities and decisions by attaching conditions to money transferred to provincial governments. The use of the spending power also reduces the accountability of governments, as voters find it difficult to determine which level of government is responsible if programs are not adequately funded (Petter, 1989). Furthermore, while many Canadians outside Quebec see national social programs as the right of every Canadian, Quebec governments have consistently argued that their ability to develop their own social programs is an essential component of maintaining and developing Quebec's distinct society and culture.

Competitive Federalism

Although considerable intergovernmental cooperation continues to be an important part of the Canadian federal system, provincial governments have become more reluctant to accept the leadership of the Canadian government, and the federal government has replaced most shared-cost programs with block funding (discussed later in this chapter). The development of a dynamic and assertive form of nationalism in Quebec, the growing capabilities of provincial governments, the disagreements between the resource-rich provinces and the Canadian government over energy policy, and the highly charged controversies over constitutional change made conflict a key aspect of federal–provincial relations beginning in the early 1960s. In particular, Prime Minister Pierre Trudeau frequently clashed with various premiers as he sought to maintain a strong central government and avoid any special status for Quebec. Serious conflicts also developed between the Canadian and Alberta governments over the National Energy Program. This resulted in what some term **competitive federalism,** in which "provincial and national governments inevitably butt heads as each seeks to maximize its autonomy, jurisdiction, and standing with the voters" (Bakvis & Skogstad, 2008, pp. 7–8).

Collaborative Federalism

Controversies related to the Constitution were a major feature of federal–provincial relations from the early 1960s until the defeat of the Charlottetown Accord in 1992 (and the unsuccessful Quebec sovereignty referendum in 1995). This led to efforts to develop a more collaborative relationship between the federal and provincial governments through negotiated agreements rather than constitutional changes. In what has been termed **collaborative federalism,** both levels of government work together as equals in deciding some major national goals (Cameron & Simeon, 2002).

Collaborative agreements include the Agreement on Internal Trade (1994), the Canada-wide Accord on Environmental Harmonization (1998), and the 2003 and 2004 Health Accords. However, these agreements are not legally enforceable and have typically been limited in their scope and effectiveness.

The Social Union Framework Agreement (1999) was based on the idea that the Canadian government would work collaboratively with provincial and territorial governments to identify Canada-wide priorities and objectives for new federal–provincial social programs. New federal–provincial social programs would need to have the support of a majority of provincial governments. Provincial governments could design their own programs and receive funding provided they met "agreed Canada-wide objectives." The Quebec government did not sign most of the collaborative agreements, instead reaching agreements with the federal government about somewhat equivalent provisions for Quebec. Despite considerable controversy between its supporters and critics, the Social Union Framework Agreement has only had a minimal effect on the federal system (Fortin, 2009) and on the making of social policy (Inwood, Johns, & O'Reilly, 2011).

Overall, it is not clear that federalism from the early 1990s until 2006 was truly collaborative (Simmons & Graefe, 2013).

Open Federalism

Stephen Harper, a strong advocate of decentralized federalism and provincial autonomy, proclaimed during the 2006 election campaign a commitment to what he termed **open federalism.** As defined by Harper, this involved a new relationship with provincial governments, including the following:

- fixing the "fiscal imbalance" (the view that provincial governments do not have a proper share of government revenue) by transferring more money unconditionally to provincial governments.
- respecting the constitutional division of powers and provincial autonomy.

COMPETITIVE FEDERALISM
A feature of Canadian federalism, beginning in the early 1960s in which provincial and national governments competed to maximize their autonomy, power, and popularity with voters.

COLLABORATIVE FEDERALISM
A trend in contemporary federalism in which both levels of government try to work together as equals in deciding some major policies.

OPEN FEDERALISM
The Harper government's approach to federalism involving such measures as transferring more money to provincial governments, respecting the constitutional division of powers and provincial autonomy, and limiting the use of the federal spending power.

- placing formal limits on the use of the federal spending power.
- allowing provincial and territorial governments to opt out of new shared-cost programs with "reasonable compensation if they offer compatible programs" (Government of Canada, 2007).
- giving the Quebec government a role in international affairs related to its constitutional responsibilities through a seat at the United Nations Educational, Scientific and Cultural Organization (UNESCO).

Despite its label, "open federalism" did not meant that federal–provincial relations became more open to public scrutiny or more open to participation by non-governmental groups (Bakvis, Baier, & Brown, 2009). Instead, Harper's "open federalism" could be viewed as reflecting his basic ideology of free market conservatism and a reduced role for government as well as his desire to move Canada in the direction of classical federalism. Specifically, the Harper government viewed the proper role of the Canadian government primarily in terms of military actions, taking tough measures to punish criminals, and strengthening the "economic union" (i.e., ensuring the free movement of goods, services, labour, and capital). By reducing direct federal involvement in establishing national standards in such areas as social programs, health care, and environmental protection, provincial governments would be freer to compete with each other to attract business (Harmes, 2007).

For example, the Harper government cancelled the bilateral agreements with each province negotiated by the previous Liberal government in 2005 to help finance quality, regulated child care, and instead implemented a taxable benefit to parents. Thus, the widely varying but generally inadequate provincial provision of child care for working parents remained in place.

However, the tendency toward greater decentralization should not be attributed solely to Harper's "open federalism." Both the Liberal governments of Jean Chrétien and Paul Martin generally also moved in this direction (DiGiacomo, 2010). In the area of environmental policy, for example, much of the responsibility for environmental regulations has been delegated to the provinces in recent decades with few national standards established or enforced (Weibust, 2010). The trend accelerated under Harper's Conservative government with further substantial cuts to Environment Canada, refusal to take meaningful national action on climate change, and in 2012 withdrawal from most environmental impact assessments and the protection of most fish habitats. Although the Trudeau goverment has proclaimed its commitment to greater environmental protection and substantial reductions in greenhouse gas emissions, Trudeau has promised to work with the provincial governments on these important issues.

CANADA: A DECENTRALIZED FEDERAL SYSTEM

Canada today has a basically decentralized federal system. Indeed, in terms of the low proportion of public spending by the federal government as compared to provincial governments, Canada can be considered one of most decentralized

BOX 12-3

Centralization Versus Decentralization

The movement in contemporary federalism in a basically decentralized direction has received considerable criticism. Advocates of better health care, child care, and poverty reduction often look to action by the Canadian government to ensure that all Canadians, regardless of where they reside, can enjoy equal treatment (DiGiacomo & Flumian, 2010). This may involve programs established by the federal government or provincial programs funded by the Canadian government that are required to follow conditions established by the Canadian government. Such programs are more likely to ensure equality among Canadians and promote a sense of Canadian identity. For example, Canada's public health care system (provided in comparable ways by provincial and territorial governments) is often viewed as a source of Canadian pride based on the shared values of most Canadians even though substantial improvements in the health care system are needed. Federal conditions established by the Canada Health Act have helped to ensure that public health care is free for all Canadians (although unlike many European countries this does not include pharmaceutical drugs).

On the other hand, a decentralized federal system can be viewed as an essential counterpart to the diversity and multinational character of Canada. Provincial programs may be more efficient than national ones because their governments can respond to the particular needs of their province. Different provinces have different characteristics and interests, and provincial governments are more likely to be in tune with the people they represent. Innovations are also more likely to be developed at the provincial level. For example, policies to deal with global climate change (such as carbon taxes and cap and trade systems) have been adopted by several provinces. Decentralization may also be more democratic, as citizens can more easily hold their provincial government accountable and can more easily engage in political action and political dialogue with their government at the provincial level.

Underlying many of the arguments regarding the desirability of centralization or decentralization is the challenge of finding an appropriate balance between diversity and unity for Canada's federal system.

federal systems in the world (Watts, 2008). Nevertheless, the federal government continues to involve itself, to some extent, in matters that are constitutionally provincial legislative responsibilities, such as health care. Questions about the desirability of centralized and decentralized federalism (discussed in Box 12-3: Centralization Versus Decentralization) have been an enduring feature of Canadian politics.

The diversity of Canada helps to explain the development of Canada's decentralized federal system. Provincial governments have sought to defend and promote the particular interests, values, cultures, and identities of those they represent. The concentration of the French minority in Quebec and the determination of Quebec governments to protect their language and culture have been key to ensuring that the federal system does not become highly centralized. To varying degrees, other provincial governments have sought to maintain or expand provincial powers, fearful that their interests would not be looked after in a more centralized system. As provincial governments increased their capabilities to develop, assess, and administer policies and programs, they have been better able to pursue the specific interests of their province (Cairns, 1977).

Provincial electorates have often supported efforts by their provincial government to take on "Ottawa" and advance their province's interests. Voters often elect different parties at the national and provincial levels. Even when the same political party is in office provincially and nationally, the provincial government will not necessarily follow the national government's lead. Furthermore, the careers of provincial and federal politicians tend to follow separate paths. Relatively few politicians use provincial political experience as a stepping stone to national politics. Thus, there is not a strong incentive for provincial politicians to be concerned about the national interest or their national image to advance their careers.

EXECUTIVE FEDERALISM

The basic nature of federal–provincial interaction since the 1940s is often described as **executive federalism**; that is, the interaction of the executives (prime minister and premiers, cabinet ministers, and government officials) of the federal and provincial levels of government determines many of the policies that affect our lives.

At the peak of executive federalism are the prime minister and premiers (termed "First Ministers").[6] Only three formal meetings of the First Ministers were held before the 1930s. To deal with problems stemming from the Great Depression, four Dominion–Provincial Conferences took place in the 1930s. From 1945 to 1992, 80 **First Ministers conferences** were held. Since then, the First Ministers conferences have given way to more informal, private, and less frequent **First Ministers meetings**. Proposals in the Victoria Charter and Charlottetown Accord that regular annual meetings of First Ministers be held have not been adopted. Instead, First Ministers meetings are called when desired by the prime minister, who chairs the meetings. In fact, in the twenty-first century, the federal government has increasingly preferred the flexibility provided by dealing with individual provincial governments (Wallner, 2014). From 2006 to 2015, Prime Minister Harper only called First Ministers meetings four times (2006, 2008 twice, and 2009); instead he preferred to meet privately with some individual premiers and to act unilaterally when provincial agreement was not needed. Prime Minister Justin Trudeau held a meeting with premiers shortly after his government was elected and planned to hold another meeting a few months later.

Meetings of ministers responsible for particular policy areas are typically held regularly, often with support from a full-time secretariat. Some of the Councils of Ministers invite non-governmental groups with an interest in the policy area to participate (Bakvis, Baier, & Brown, 2009).

EXECUTIVE FEDERALISM
The basic nature of federal–provincial interaction since the 1940s, involving the interaction of the executives of the federal and provincial governments.

FIRST MINISTERS CONFERENCES
Formal meetings of the prime minister and premiers, along with large supporting delegations of ministers, aides, and officials.

FIRST MINISTERS MEETINGS
Informal private meetings of the prime minister and premiers.

[6]Territorial premiers have been regular participants since 1992.

Prime Minister Harper and the 13 provincial and territorial premiers were deep in discussion at their First Ministers meeting on November 10, 2008, in Ottawa.

© Montreal Gazette Group Inc

Furthermore, national and provincial government officials hold numerous meetings (as well as having informal contacts). In part, such meetings, particularly among deputy ministers, lay the groundwork for ministerial meetings. Officials who implement and administer programs find it useful to meet with others who have similar responsibilities. Generally, relationships among officials of different governments and, to a considerable extent, ministers, are friendlier and more cooperative than relationships among First Ministers. However, intergovernmental agreements are usually finalized by the First Ministers.

Canadian Intergovernmental Conference Secretariat **www.scics.gc.ca**

Not surprisingly, critics have pointed out that executive federalism is undemocratic. The negotiations between the executives of the two levels of government are often secretive and not open to scrutiny by Parliament, provincial legislatures, and the public. Many agreements reached at intergovernmental meetings either do not need legislative approval or are considered a "done deal" and not subject to much scrutiny and debate before legislative passage (Smith, 2004).

Executive federalism has also been criticized for its tendency to lead to confrontation and conflict between federal and provincial governments. In particular, the departments or branches within governments specifically devoted to intergovernmental affairs are often focused on maintaining or enlarging the power of their government. As well, prime ministers and premiers have usually taken a "hands-on" approach to intergovernmental relations, making the relations highly politicized. Thus, although federal and provincial departmental officials dealing with particular issues are often able to work cooperatively, they may be overruled by those more concerned about the power and autonomy of their government.

Alternatively, executive federalism could be viewed as a practical response that has developed out of a need to coordinate federal and provincial policies. Because of Canada's great regional and cultural diversity, the Canadian government is "unable to forge a national consensus unilaterally" (Hueglin, 2008., p. 153). Instead, through bargaining and negotiations, flexible compromises can be worked out. Furthermore, it has been argued that a quiet process of working out compromises among national and provincial cabinet ministers and leaders (termed "elite accommodation") is more likely to succeed than processes that involve public debate and legislative scrutiny. In particular, some argue that political elites are more likely to grasp the need for the differential treatment of Quebec than the majority of Canadians (Bakvis, Baier, & Brown, 2009).

Interstate and Intrastate Federalism

INTERSTATE FEDERALISM
A federal system in which provincial interests are represented primarily by provincial governments.

INTRASTATE FEDERALISM
A federal system in which provincial interests are represented in national political institutions.

Executive federalism reflects a basic characteristic of Canadian federalism often described as **interstate federalism**, that is, a federal system in which provincial interests are represented primarily by provincial governments. In contrast, some countries can be characterized primarily in terms of **intrastate federalism**. In such federal systems, the subnational units are effectively represented in national political institutions where their interests are taken into account. For example, in the German federal system, the approval of the *Bundesrat* (federal council) composed of the head of government and several cabinet ministers from each *Land* (equivalent to a province) is required (along with approval by the *Bundestag* chosen in a national election) for a substantial proportion of national legislation. Canada's upper chamber of Parliament, the Senate, does not represent provincial interests to any significant degree because the appointment of its members is on the recommendation of the prime minister. Although Canadian cabinets have included members from all, or almost all, provinces, the conventions of cabinet solidarity and secrecy, along with the concentration of power in the hands of the prime minister, limit the effectiveness of cabinet in representing provincial interests. Furthermore, because Parliament features tight party discipline, members of Parliament are expected to vote along party lines even if this conflicts with the interests of their province. Thus, provincial interests may not be effectively taken into account within national-level institutions. Instead, provincial governments often have been able to gain support from voters for challenging the initiatives of the Canadian government and advocating the particular interests of their province.

Interprovincial Cooperation

Provincial governments have tried to develop a united front to be in a better position to bargain with or make demands on the Canadian government.

This strategy can be traced back to 1887 when some premiers met to demand a reduction in the powers of the Canadian government based on the view that Canada was a compact (agreement) among provinces. As well, the premiers aired a variety of provincial grievances. However, it was not until 1960 that annual meetings of the premiers were established. Interprovincial cooperation was institutionalized in 2003 with the creation of the **Council of the Federation**, which consists of the 13 provincial and territorial premiers who meet twice a year along with a small permanent secretariat. Despite its name and its commitment to developing greater collaboration with the Canadian government, prime ministers are not part of the Council of the Federation and the federal government "has demonstrated little willingness to engage with the Council" (Wallner, 2014).

COUNCIL OF THE FEDERATION
An organization established by the premiers to enable cooperation among the provinces and territories.

The premiers hoped that the council would give them a stronger, more united voice as well as facilitating interprovincial cooperation. However, reaching a consensus on some key issues has proven challenging. For example, at the July 2012 council meeting, Premier Christy Clark of British Columbia rejected the national energy strategy accepted by the other premiers because it did not address the issue of the Northern Gateway pipeline that would transport Alberta's bitumen across the province and down British Columbia's coastline.

Council of the Federation
www.canadaspremiers.ca

In addition to the Council of the Federation, there is also a Council of Atlantic Premiers that promotes regional cooperation and a less formalized Western Premiers' Conference that includes four provincial premiers and the three territorial premiers. There have also been significant intergovernmental agreements among particular provinces, such as the New West Partnership established in 2010 between B.C., Alberta, and Saskatchewan and the Ontario–Quebec Trade and Cooperation Agreement, 2009. These agreements seek to remove inter-provincial barriers to trade, investment, and labour mobility.

Council of Atlantic Premiers
www.cap-cpma.ca

ASYMMETRICAL FEDERALISM

Some countries can be described as having an **asymmetrical federal system**—that is, some subnational governments have a different relationship with the national government, including different powers, than other subnational governments. Canada's federal system has been largely symmetrical but with some asymmetrical elements. The Constitution Act, 1867, allowed Quebec to retain its system of civil law while the other provinces retained their common law systems. As well, Quebec was the only province that was required to use both English and French in its legislature and courts. The Charter of Rights and Freedoms provided more limited minority-language education rights in Quebec than in other provinces. It also established New Brunswick as the only province that is officially bilingual and recognized the equality of English and

ASYMMETRICAL FEDERAL SYSTEM
A federal system in which some subnational governments have a different relationship with the national government, including different powers, than other subnational governments.

French linguistic groups in that province. The "notwithstanding clause" within the Charter can be used to limit certain rights and freedoms in a particular province. The Constitution Act, 1982, also allows any province to opt out of any constitutional changes that reduce its rights or powers and be guaranteed reasonable financial compensation if the change relates to education and other cultural matters. However, this provision has not been used thus far. Nevertheless, there are several joint federal–provincial policy areas in which asymmetry exists including the Canada/Quebec Pension Plan, immigration agreements, manpower training, environmental harmonization, and the 2004 Health Accord (Gagnon, 2009).

The idea of asymmetrical federalism has been controversial. Notions that Quebec should have a "special status" and that Quebec should be recognized in the constitution as a "distinct society" aroused considerable opposition. For many in "English Canada," asymmetrical federalism is viewed as undermining the equality of the provinces and national unity. Nevertheless, the recognition by the House of Commons that Quebec is a "distinct society" and that "the Québécois constitute a nation within a united Canada" provides a rationale for asymmetrical federalism with regards to Quebec. Asymmetry can also be viewed as promoting greater flexibility in the federal system by allowing for different arrangements to suit the circumstances and wishes of the different provinces.

FEDERAL–PROVINCIAL FINANCIAL ARRANGEMENTS

The power and reach of any government depends not only on the authority granted to it by the Constitution, but also on its financial capabilities. A government with inadequate revenues may be unable to exercise its full constitutional powers. In contrast, a government that has more revenues than it needs to carry out its own constitutional powers may use its extra resources to pursue matters that are within the legislative authority of the other level of government. In other words, a government with abundant revenues may find ways to promote its interests that exceed its legislative powers.

Taxes

As Table 12-2 indicates, the Canadian and provincial governments raise their revenues from some of the same sources. Facing criticisms of the centralized income tax rental system established in 1941, tax collection agreements in 1962 allowed each provincial government to determine its own provincial income tax rate as a percentage of the federal tax rate. The current tax system adopted in 2008 allows more flexibility as provincial governments determine their own tax on income. The Canada Revenue Agency collects personal

	FEDERAL	PROVINCIAL	MUNICIPAL
Personal income tax	Yes	Yes	
Corporate income tax	Yes	Yes	
Sales tax	Yes	Yes	
Natural resource revenues		Yes	
Property tax			Yes
Payroll taxes	Yes	Yes	
Customs and excise duties	Yes		
Lotteries and gaming		Yes	
Alcohol sales		Yes	

TABLE 12-2

FEDERAL, PROVINCIAL, AND MUNICIPAL TAX REVENUES

Note: The federal government has the constitutional authority to raise money by any mode.

SOURCE: Based on Bakvis, Baier & Brown, *Contested federalism.* Oxford University Press, 2009, p. 141.

income taxes on behalf of both levels of government (except in Quebec, which has had its own provincial tax collection system since 1954). The Canada Revenue Agency also collects corporate income taxes for all provinces except Quebec and Alberta.

Another major source of revenue for both levels of government, the sales tax, features federal–provincial coordination in some provinces but not in others. Newfoundland and Labrador, Nova Scotia, New Brunswick, Ontario, and Quebec use the harmonized sales tax (HST), a value-added tax on a common tax base.[7] The other provinces levy and collect their own retail sales tax (except Alberta and the three territories, which have avoided using this tax), while the Canadian government collects the goods and services tax (GST) in provinces and territories that don't use the HST.

Transfer Payments

Looking at government revenues in total, the Canadian government has more revenue than it needs to carry out its own activities. Although provincial governments collectively raise more money than the Canadian government, they have legislative responsibility for some of the most expensive government activities, including health, education, and social services. To try to ensure that provincial governments have the financial resources to carry out their responsibilities, the Canadian government transfers to provincial governments considerable amounts of money that it has raised itself. In the 2015–2016 fiscal year, for example, the Canadian government planned to transfer about $68 billion to provincial governments (as detailed in Table 12-3). Overall, provincial governments receive on average about one-fifth of their revenue from the federal government, although the poorer provinces receive a higher proportion

[7]The harmonized sales tax (HST), which combines the federal and provincial retail sales tax, is collected by the Canada Revenue Agency except in Quebec. British Columbia adopted the HST in 2010, but withdrew from the HST in 2013 as a result of a provincial referendum.

	($ MILLIONS)
Major transfers	
Canada Health Transfer	34 026
Canada Social Transfer	12 959
Equalization	17 341
Offshore accords	116
Territorial formula financing	3 561
Total federal support	68 004

SOURCE: Data extracted from Department of Finance Canada. *Federal Support to Provinces and Territories.* Retrieved March 16, 2015, from http://www.fin.gc.ca/fedprov/mtp-eng.asp.

of their revenues from the Canadian government than the richer provinces (see Figure 12-1).

The Constitution Act, 1867, required that the Canadian government provide a grant in aid of each provincial government. However, these small sums were inadequate to help provincial governments deal with the problems caused by massive unemployment during the Great Depression of the 1930s. After World War II, governments greatly expanded their role in providing services such as health care, social welfare, and post-secondary education. However, provincial governments that have the legislative authority for many of

FIGURE 12-1
FEDERAL CASH TRANSFERS TO PROVINCIAL GOVERNMENTS AS A PERCENT OF TOTAL PROVINCIAL GOVERNMENT REVENUE, BY PROVINCE, 2013–2014

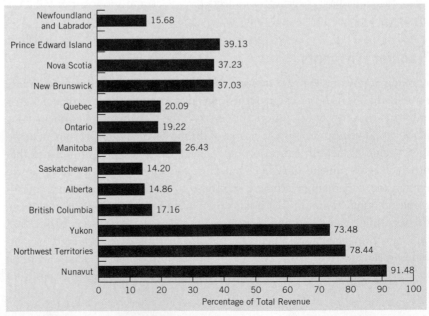

SOURCE: Compiled and calculated from Department of Finance Canada, Fiscal Reference Tables 2014, Tables 28 to 30. Retrieved on March 19, 2015, from http://www.fin.gc.ca/frt-trf/2014/frt-trf1404-eng.asp#PTGPA.

these services did not have the deep pockets to fund them—their responsibilities outstripped their financial resources.

CONDITIONAL GRANTS   To establish national programs in areas in which the provinces have legislative authority, the Canadian government made use of **conditional grants**. Provincial governments administered the programs that were often developed at the initiative of the Canadian government and had to meet conditions set by the Canadian government to receive money for the programs. By taking the lead in developing national social programs, the Canadian government could ensure that everyone was able to receive a similar basic set of social services wherever they lived. Generally, the Canadian government paid half of the costs of the program, so these are often called shared-cost programs.

The Quebec government and, at times, the governments of some other provinces objected to conditional grants, arguing that health, post-secondary education, and welfare fall exclusively within provincial jurisdiction according to the Constitution. As well, some provincial governments (notably Ontario) argued that the conditional grant programs distorted provincial government priorities by encouraging provincial governments to spend their money on these programs (because they had to pay only half the cost) instead of on other provincial government priorities.

BLOCK GRANTS   In 1977, the Canadian government changed its cash transfers for health care and post-secondary education from a shared-cost basis to a single **block grant**—that is, a basically unconditional grant of a block of money to provincial governments. In 1996, the Canada Assistance Plan, which provides welfare and some other social programs, was added to the block grant. In 2004, the grant was divided into two blocks: the **Canada Health Transfer** (for medicare and hospital insurance) and the **Canada Social Transfer** (for post-secondary education, social assistance, early childhood education, and child care programs). The Canadian government notionally divides the Social Transfer into funding for three categories: social programs, post-secondary education, and child-related programs. However, each provincial government is free to decide how the Social Transfer is to be used.

Block grants are calculated for each province on what is essentially a per capita basis and flow into the general revenues of a provincial government. Unlike shared-cost grants, they are not based on the costs of provincial programs. Since the Canadian government is no longer committed to providing 50 percent of the costs of the programs, it has managed to unilaterally reduce its share of the costs. In particular, the Canadian government slashed the transfer for health, welfare, and post-secondary education by about one-third in its 1996–1997 budget to deal with a serious deficit problem. Provincial governments now pay a substantial majority of the costs for these programs.

CONDITIONAL GRANTS
Federal grants to provincial governments for specific programs that have to meet conditions set by the Canadian government.

BLOCK GRANT
The unconditional transfer of a block of money from the federal government to a provincial government.

CANADA HEALTH TRANSFER
A block grant intended to fund medicare and hospital insurance, although some conditions are involved.

CANADA SOCIAL TRANSFER
A block grant intended to fund post-secondary education, social assistance, early childhood education, and childcare programs.

Although the Health and Social Transfers are described as block grants, there are some strings attached. The Canada Health Act (1984) allows the Canadian government to cut back on payments to any province that does not respect the principles of public administration, comprehensiveness, universality, portability, and accessibility in its public health care system. The Canadian government has used this Act at times to withhold some money from provincial governments that allowed extra billing of patients and user charges for basic (core) health care services. The only condition attached to the Canada Social Transfer is that provincial governments cannot impose a residency requirement for recipients of social assistance.

Because of the soaring costs of providing health care, provincial governments have lobbied for greater funding from the Canadian government and guarantees that block funding not be subject to unilateral cuts by the federal government. In turn, the Canadian government has wanted some accountability for the funds it transfers to the provinces for health care, as well as kudos from the public for helping to address the problems facing the health care system. As a result of the federal–provincial Health Accord in 2004, the Canadian government committed to increasing the Canada Health Transfer by 6 percent per year for 10 years. After 2016–2017, there is a commitment to increase the Health Transfer by at least 3 percent per year.[8] In addition, federal–provincial Health Accords in 2003 and 2004 provided special funds for provincial governments that were earmarked for specific purposes, such as reducing waiting times for certain operations and purchasing medical equipment. To improve accountability to the public, the Health Council of Canada was set up to monitor and report on the performance of the health care systems. However, the Health Council and some other provisions of the federal–provincial Health Accord were cancelled by the Harper government in 2014.

EQUALIZATION PAYMENTS   Because provinces differ widely in their economic resources and their ability to raise funds through taxation, some provincial governments are better equipped to provide services to their populations than others. Since 1957, the Canadian government has directed equalization payments to the governments of the poorer provinces. A commitment to the principle of equalization, defined as ensuring that "provincial governments have sufficient resources to provide reasonably comparable levels of public services at reasonably comparable levels of taxation," was included in the Constitution Act, 1982.

Basically, **equalization payments** are unconditional grants by the Canadian government to the governments of the poorer provinces to bring their revenue-raising capabilities up to a national standard. The total amount of equalization payments is limited to a three-year moving average of gross domestic product

EQUALIZATION PAYMENTS
Unconditional grants from the Canadian government to the governments of the poorer provinces to bring their revenue-raising capabilities up to a national standard.

---

[8]There is also a commitment to increase the Canada Social Transfer by 3 percent per year. The Liberal party promised to negotiate a new Health Accord (including long-term funding) with the provinces in the 2015 election campaign.

"It's going to be a long wait." Health care services and funding are perpetual concerns for voters, which makes them a perennial issue for federal–provincial discussion as well.

(GDP) growth. For the 2015–2016 fiscal year, six provinces received about $17.3 billion (see Table 12-4). Equalization does not involve taking money from the governments of the richer provinces, but rather comes out of the general revenues of the Canadian government. Unlike equalization in the Australian federal system, the Canadian equalization method does not take into account the costs of providing services in different provinces or the contrasting needs of the provinces. Although the federal government receives more tax revenue per capita from persons and businesses in the richer provinces than the poorer provinces, equalization does not create total equality among provinces.

The method for calculating equalization payments has varied over time. The system adopted in 2007 and modified in 2009 involves setting the national standard as the average revenue-raising (fiscal) capacity of all 10 provinces in

PEI	361
Nova Scotia	1690
New Brunswick	1669
Quebec	9521
Ontario	2363
Manitoba	1738

TABLE 12-4
EQUALIZATION PAYMENTS, 2015–2016 ($ MILLIONS)

SOURCE: Compiled from Federal Support to Provinces and Territories. Retrieved from www.fin.gc.ca/fedprov/mtp-eng.asp.

terms of how much each province can raise from its personal income tax, corporate income tax, sales tax, property tax, and 50 percent of its natural resource revenues. Increases in the federal government's total equalization payments are limited to the nominal growth in Canada's gross domestic product. There is also a cap on the amount a province receiving equalization can obtain based on the average fiscal capacity of the equalization-receiving provinces (including equalization payments and 100 percent of their resource revenues) (Smart, 2009).

As noted in the introductory vignette, the equalization formula adopted in 2007 was strongly condemned by the government of Newfoundland and Labrador. From its perspective, royalties from the province's offshore oil are only a temporary source of wealth, allowing this traditionally poor province a chance to pay down its large provincial debt and to work on developing its economy. On the other hand, former Ontario premier Dalton McGuinty called upon Ontario residents to fight to change the equalization system that transfers billions of federal tax dollars paid by Ontarians to other provinces (CBC News, 2008c). However, because of a nosedive in its economy, Ontario began receiving equalization payments in the 2009–2010 fiscal year. Alberta's former finance minister Ron Liepert was critical of the unconditional nature of equalization payments, arguing that recipient provinces should have to prove that the money is being used wisely (Walton, 2012).

Territorial Governments

In the past, the northern territories were largely under the control of the Canadian government. Beginning in the 1970s, the Canadian government gradually transferred responsibility for major services such as health, education, and social services to the territorial governments. Each territorial commissioner now holds a position quite similar to that of provincial lieutenant governors. The process of devolution (transferring authority to the territories through acts of the Canadian Parliament rather than a constitutional change) was largely completed in Yukon in 2003 and the Northwest Territories in 2014 with the transfer of land and resource management responsibilities to the territorial government. In 2014, negotiations to devolve these responsibilities to the Nunavut government began. Indigenous peoples have been participants in devolution negotiations in the three territories and have obtained a share of resource revenues on their lands.

Despite devolution and the adoption of responsible government generally equivalent to that of provincial governments, the territories depend on federal government transfer payments (the Territorial Formula Financing, an unconditional grant) for a substantial majority of their revenues. Issues concerning the share of resource revenues that flows to the federal government and federal control of offshore resources (and related environmental concerns) are also important.

LOCAL GOVERNMENTS

Local (municipal) governments are very important in providing essential services such as drinking water, garbage disposal, fire protection, building and maintaining roads, and snow clearing. They also make an important contribution to the quality of our lives through parks, playgrounds, recreational and cultural activities, public transportation, and zoning bylaws.

Canada's Constitution makes local government the exclusive legislative responsibility of provincial governments. However, while Canada's federal system has become quite decentralized, with provincial governments having substantial independence, provincial governments have generally been reluctant to reduce their controls over local governments. Even the very existence of local governments can be changed by provincial governments. For example, the Ontario government amalgamated the six municipalities of Metropolitan Toronto in 1998 despite opposition from the local governments and local citizens (as expressed in a referendum). In addition, municipal governments are subject to various rules and regulations set down by their provincial government.

A basic problem for municipal governments is that they have limited financial capabilities. Property taxes are their primary source of revenue, with some funds derived from various licence fees. These sources of revenue are insufficient and thus local governments depend to a considerable extent on financing from their provincial government. At times, the federal government has provided some funds for municipalities. This has been formalized in commitments to refund the money that local governments pay in federal tax for goods and services. As well, the Canadian government's Gas Tax Fund provides $2 billion per year (increasing by 2 percent per year) to provincial and territorial governments for a variety of local infrastructure projects.[9]

Overall, however, municipal governments are underfunded, resulting in aging infrastructure (such as roads, bridges, and water and sewage treatment) that needs to be replaced at a cost estimated to be $171.8 billion (Federation of Canadian Municipalities, 2012). In addition, many cities and towns face serious problems such as insufficient affordable housing and the need for better public transit systems. Furthermore, given the size and importance of Canada's major cities, greater self-government and a stronger voice in Canadian issues would seem to be desirable.

Finding ways to include city governments in the processes of federalism is an important challenge for the future of Canadian federalism. Efforts in the 1980s and early 1990s to constitutionalize a role for local governments in the federal system failed. There has been a "developing relationship" between

Federation of Canadian Municipalities
www.fcm.ca

---

[9]The 2013 Canadian budget incorporated these two sources of municipal revenue into the Community Improvement Fund (part of the Building Canada Plan that promised $47 billion over 10 years in support of local and economic infrastructure projects).

municipalities and the federal government most notably in the provision of infrastructure financing. However, in the view of the Federation of Canadian Municipalities (2012), "we are no closer to FCM's goal of a true collaborative intergovernmental partnership to deal with the issues in our cities and communities" (p. 14).

Summary and Conclusion

Canada's contemporary federal system is quite decentralized, with provincial governments responsible for many of the programs and services that affect our lives. Equalization payments have allowed the poorer provinces to maintain a reasonably comparable level of services to that of the richer provinces. The conditions attached to federal health transfers have maintained a degree of uniformity in the basic public health services provided by each province and territory.

The modern federal system usually also involves a high level of interaction between national and provincial governments. However, despite considerable cooperation and collaboration between national and provincial governments in some policy areas, conflicts are often a major feature of intergovernmental relations.

The tendency toward decentralization could be viewed as consistent with the diversity of the country. However, it may weaken the ability of the country to achieve national goals and maintain national unity along with a sense of national identity.

In some ways, the distinctiveness of Quebec has been recognized in the functioning of the federal system. However, there has been considerable opposition outside Quebec to moving further toward an asymmetrical federalism in which the powers of Quebec would differ substantially from those of the other provinces.

The complexity of the modern federal system and the closed door nature of executive federalism make it difficult for citizens to effectively participate in trying to influence public policy and in holding their governments accountable. In addition, governments are often not held accountable to their elected legislative bodies concerning important intergovernmental agreements.

The bargaining and negotiating characteristic of executive federalism has allowed governments to overcome the rigidity of the Constitution and the hurdle of achieving formal constitutional change. At times, though, a tug-of-war between the Canadian government and various provincial governments has endangered national unity and made it difficult to deal with national problems. Some tension in the federal system is inevitable as Canadian federal governments pursue national objectives and address the concerns of the population as a whole, while each provincial government has its eye on the interests of its own province.

Overall, a discussion of Canadian federalism raises important questions about how national unity can be maintained and efficient and effective government programs and services provided in a country with substantial territorial and cultural diversity. Can the tensions in the Canadian federal system be reduced through greater provincial autonomy, with Quebec in particular having substantially greater powers than other provinces would like? Or is a strong central government needed to promote Canada-wide interests and values? Is it more democratic to have provincial governments that may be closer to the people responsible for most areas of public policy? Or is a central government with strong financial resources and legislative powers needed to ensure the equality of services that most Canadians expect? In addition, should the federal system be modified to constitutionally recognize territorial and municipal governments? And where do Aboriginal governments (a potential third order of government) fit in the federal system?

Discussion Questions

1. What are the advantages and disadvantages of Canada's federal system?

2. Is Canada's federal system a help or a hindrance to democracy?

3. Is the Canadian federal system too centralized or decentralized?

4. Is an asymmetrical federal system a threat to national unity?

5. Should there be greater provincial representation within national governing institutions?

6. Does Canada's equalization system need to be changed?

7. Does the Canadian federal system provide an appropriate balance between unity and diversity?

Further Reading

Bakvis, H., Baier, G., & Brown, D.M. (2009). *Contested federalism: Certainty and ambiguity in the Canadian federation*. Toronto, ON: Oxford University Press.

Bakvis, H., & Skogstad, G. (Eds.). (2012). *Canadian federalism: Performance, effectiveness, and legitimacy* (3rd ed.). Toronto, ON: Oxford University Press.

Chaudry, S., Gaudreault-Desbiens, J.-F., & Sossin, L. (Eds.). (2006). *Dilemmas of solidarity: Rethinking redistribution in the Canadian federation*. Toronto, ON: University of Toronto Press.

DiGiacomo, G., & Flumian, M. (Eds.). (2010). *The case for centralized federalism*. Ottawa, ON: University of Ottawa Press.

Gagnon, A.-G. (Ed.). (2009). *Contemporary Canadian federalism: Foundations, traditions, institutions*. Toronto, ON: University of Toronto Press.

Harrison, K. (Ed.) (2006). *Racing to the bottom? Provincial interdependence in the Canadian federation*. Vancouver, BC: UBC Press.

Horak, M., & Young, R. (Eds.). (2012). *Sites of governance: Multilevel governance and policy making in Canada's big cities*. Montreal, QC: McGill-Queen's University Press.

Hubbard, R., & Paquet, G. (Eds.). (2010). *The case for decentralized federalism*. Ottawa, ON: University of Ottawa Press.

Inwood, G.J. (2013). *Understanding Canadian federalism: An introduction to theory and practice*. Toronto, ON; Pearson Canada.

Rocher, F., & Smith, M. (Eds.). (2003). *New trends in Canadian federalism* (2nd ed.). Peterborough, ON: Broadview Press.

Sancton, A., & Young, R.A. (Eds.) (2009). *Foundations of governance: Municipal government in Canada's provinces*. Toronto, ON: University of Toronto Press.

Smith, D.E. (2010). *Federalism and the constitution of Canada*. Toronto, ON: University of Toronto Press.

Smith, J. (2004). *Federalism*. Vancouver, BC: UBC Press.

Stevenson, G. (2009). *Unfulfilled union: Canadian federalism and national unity* (5th ed.). Montreal, QC: McGill-Queen's University Press.

Tindal, C.R., & Tindal, S.N. (2012). *Local government in Canada* (8th ed.). Toronto, ON: Nelson Canada

Watts, R.L. (2008). *Comparing federal systems* (3rd ed.). Kingston, ON: Institute of Intergovernmental Relations.

CHAPTER 13

The Executive

The decision that Canada would not participate in the United States–led attack on Iraq in 2003 was made by Prime Minister Jean Chrétien. Eddie Goldenberg (right), then senior policy adviser in the Prime Minister's Office, briefed the prime minister on the issue.

© Fred Chartrand/Canadian Press Images

CHAPTER OBJECTIVES

After reading this chapter, you should be able to

1. Explain what it means to have a "constitutional monarchy."
2. Examine the powers of the governor general.
3. Outline the bases of prime ministerial and cabinet power.
4. Discuss whether the prime minister is too powerful.
5. Examine how the policy process works.

It was 9:15 a.m. on March 17, 2003, and Eddie Goldenberg had no way of knowing what was coming next.* As senior policy adviser to Prime Minister Jean Chrétien, he had been preparing in his Wellington Street Langevin Block office for a meeting on Chrétien's landmark legislation prohibiting corporate and union financing of political parties. Instead, Chrétien phoned him and said something far more urgent had come up. Indeed it had.

Chrétien told Goldenberg that the British government had contacted the Canadian Foreign Affairs Department and asked for an urgent response to four questions: Would Canada politically support military action against the regime of Saddam Hussein in Iraq? What military capabilities would it bring to the venture? Would it make its position public? What

---

* This vignette is based on Edward Goldenberg, *The way it works: Inside Ottawa*. Toronto, ON: McClelland & Stewart, 2006, pp. 1–3 and 8–9.

humanitarian assistance and reconstruction aid could it provide? Furthermore, the Blair government in Britain and the Bush administration in the United States wanted a response to these questions by noon that day!

Chrétien instructed Goldenberg to work on the file right away and draft a set of recommendations. Goldenberg headed to the office of Claude Laverdure, head of the Foreign Policy and Defence Secretariat in the Privy Council Office and the point man on this issue. Before meeting with Chrétien, they reviewed the recent history of military intervention in Iraq: Chrétien had said several times that Canada would not engage Iraq militarily without the United Nations' approval. Canada's ambassador to the UN, Paul Heinbecker, told Goldenberg and Laverdure that the UN Security Council was not going to authorize force. Moreover, Parliament was in session, and although "the prime minister would have to make the final decision," and "there is no constitutional requirement to inform Parliament first," Chrétien agreed that the Commons should be the forum for an announcement at 2:15 that afternoon. Goldenberg drafted a statement for question period, which would undoubtedly home in on the issue.

Sure enough, Iraq was the first matter to come up. Chrétien was ready with his reply: If the Security Council did not approve military action against Iraq, Canada would not participate in it. All parties but the Opposition Canadian Alliance cheered.

Here was the Canadian executive in a nutshell. As Goldenberg would put it later in his book, *The Way It Works,* there were several factors affecting major public policy decisions and several participants, but some decisions have to be funnelled and made quickly. "That," he said, "is what heads of government are elected to do." The incident also highlighted aspects other than the prime minister's dominance: the important policy role played by central executive agencies (notably the Privy Council Office), the executive's primary role in international affairs and conflicts, and the ambiguous role of Parliament in the decisions about wars and conflicts. But this just touches the surface of what the executive can do in this country.

ORIGINS AND POWERS

Before there were legislatures and courts of justice, there were kings and their advisers. Of all the branches of government, the executive is the oldest. Executives carry with them a long historical memory of pre-eminence and dominance—and they act accordingly. Yet legislatures and courts have the will of the people and the rule of law to challenge this pre-eminence. Modern history is one of attempting to bind political executives to democratic impulses, as mediated by parliaments, and to various refinements of the rule of law.

As with any entity that has grown over centuries, the executive has taken on differences in form that follow from specializations in function. Where once the monarch and his advisers were unchallenged, later came the prime minister whose job it was to manage a parliament for the monarch, his cabinet (who in the British tradition doubled as advisers to the monarch and the prime minister), and a burgeoning bureaucracy. In the British tradition, the evolution happened particularly slowly and peacefully for the most part, creating a wealth of precedent, convention, and common law. We still refer to these today as *Westminster systems*, that is, those fashioned after the **Westminster Model.**

In this model, named after the area of London where the Houses of Parliament are situated, voters cast votes for party candidates, and the leader of the party with the largest number of candidates elected to the House of Commons

WESTMINSTER MODEL
The model of representative and responsible government used in the United Kingdom and in other countries that emulate it.

PRIME MINISTER
The head of government, meaning the person chosen by the governor general to form a government able to retain the confidence of a majority of the elected house of Parliament, the House of Commons.

is usually called upon to form the government. The leader, the **prime minister**, nominates the cabinet and therefore the government. There is a fusion of legislative and executive power in the cabinet. That is, the political executive (the prime minister and cabinet) is responsible for the day-to-day functioning of government ("executing" the laws) and can usually expect to have its legislative and budgetary proposals successfully passed because the majority in the House will support its initiatives. Normally, the prime minister and almost all of the members of cabinet are members of the House of Commons and are expected to answer for the actions of the government in the House.

One result of the evolutionary aspect of executive growth is the existence of formal and informal parts of the executive. The *formal executive* is expected to be non-partisan and avoid political controversies. By "informal" we refer to the *political executive* (prime minister and cabinet), whose far-reaching powers derive largely from custom and convention, but also from their political resources.

THE FORMAL EXECUTIVE

The Queen, the Governor General, and the Privy Council

FORMAL EXECUTIVE
That part of the executive consisting of the Queen, the governor general, and the Queen's Privy Council for Canada, which possesses formal constitutional authority and by convention acts on the advice of the political executive.

Sections 9 to 11 of the Constitution Act, 1867, outline the **formal executive** and aspects of their authority. Executive government and authority is "vested in the Queen."[1] However, as established by the Letters Patent, 1947, the governor general permanently exercises virtually all of the monarch's powers and authorities. Thus the Queen performs only ceremonial duties for Canada.

The governor general, appointed by the Queen on the recommendation of the prime minister, is entrusted with "carrying on the Government of Canada on behalf of and in the name of the Queen," in other words representing the Crown. Provincial lieutenant governors represent the Crown for provincial purposes.[2] Thus, the Queen remains Canada's formal head of state, even though some governors general have occasionally referred to themselves as such.

The formal duties of the governor general include summoning people to membership in the Senate, appointing judges, summoning Parliament, dissolving Parliament (which results in an election), and giving royal assent to legislation. By convention, the governor general normally performs these duties on the advice of the cabinet or, in some cases, the prime minister alone. The governor general also has the duty of choosing a new prime minister upon the resignation or death of a prime minister. However, because the prime minister is normally the leader of the party that has the most seats in the House of Commons, the choice of prime minister is usually obvious.

---

[1] If a king takes the throne, the wording changes accordingly.

[2] The lieutenant governor of each province, appointed by the governor general on the recommendation of the prime minister, is the counterpart of the governor general. See *Liquidators of the Maritime Bank of Canada v. Receiver-General of New Brunswick*, 1982.

The mandate of the Queen's Privy Council for Canada is "to aid and advise in the Government of Canada." It is the governor general who appoints, and also may remove, members of the Privy Council. The Privy Council consists of all those who have ever been federal cabinet ministers, plus a limited number of honorific appointments. The Constitution Act, 1867, establishes that the Privy Council is the main source of advice to the governor general (Section 13). Nevertheless, the Privy Council seldom meets, let alone offers advice to the governor general. By convention, the **cabinet** is the only active part of the Council. However, when acting officially, the cabinet will rely on the formal authority of the Council.

Overall, then, the formal executive is the legal mask for the informal executive. By adopting a "Constitution similar in Principle to that of the United Kingdom" (wording found in the Preamble to the Constitution Act, 1867), Canada took on the relevant customs and conventions that had developed in the United Kingdom. Specifically, the monarch's representatives only act upon the legally and constitutionally tendered advice of the government of the day. Thus, the prime minister and cabinet direct the business of government in the name of the Crown. Canada, like the United Kingdom, can thus be described as a constitutional monarchy or as a parliamentary democracy.

> **CABINET**
> The active part of the Queen's Privy Council for Canada. Composed of the prime minister and ministers, it controls most of the executive and legislative powers of government.

The Crown, Monarchy, and Prerogative

The best way to discuss the formal executive is to differentiate among the Crown, monarchy, and prerogative. In turn, the best way to investigate the Crown is to review its many meanings and the various sources of its powers.

The Crown is most generally understood to be the repository of all of the executive powers of the state. Government is carried on in the name of the monarch—the Queen—but the Crown remains the supreme authority. The authority of government thus comes not from Parliament but from the Crown. "The Crown" is also a term that is used in a looser sense in many circumstances: as a symbol of what belongs to the Canadian public (e.g., Crown corporations), as the body that prosecutes in criminal cases, and as government acting as a trustee in specific instances (e.g., regarding the interests of some of the Aboriginal peoples of Canada).

> **THE CROWN**
> The repository of all of the executive powers of the state and the supreme authority for government.

The powers of the Crown come from statute (legislation) and common law (the accumulation of judicial decisions). Parliament grants the Crown statutory powers, which give the Crown both executive power (the power to implement the laws) and legislative power (the power to make law of a delegated or subordinate nature in the form of regulations or orders-in-council). In the ancient past, the common law allowed the monarch to legislate and act as well. These powers were called the prerogative power. A **prerogative power**, as Dicey (1965) says, is "the residue of discretionary authority, which at any given time is left in the hands of the Crown." (p. 424). This means that the ancient powers the monarch once uniquely possessed that have not been taken

> **PREROGATIVE POWER**
> The powers the monarch once uniquely possessed that have not been taken away by Parliament.

away by Parliament are still intact. Two types have evolved: discretionary prerogative powers and prerogative powers devolved to ministers.

DISCRETIONARY PREROGATIVE POWERS   There are a few **discretionary prerogative powers** (also known as *personal prerogatives* or *reserve powers*)—those that the monarch's representative "may exercise upon his or her own personal discretion" (Hogg, 2006, p. 284). These include the appointment and dismissal of the prime minister and the dissolution of Parliament. The governor general may also use personal discretion if the government is violating the constitution or does not have the confidence of the House of Commons.

The governor general has used discretionary prerogative powers in only a few instances. In 1896, Conservative prime minister Charles Tupper recommended the appointment of a number of his party's supporters to the Senate and the courts after his party was defeated in a general election. Governor General Lord Aberdeen rejected the recommendations. Since the prime minister did not have the confidence of the Commons (and the electorate) and the appointments would have been irrevocable, few would question the use of the discretionary power in this situation. In 1926, however, the use of the discretionary power to refuse the prime minister's request to grant the dissolution of Parliament and call an election was highly controversial (see Box 13-1: A Governor General Stirs Up Controversy: The King–Byng Affair). In more recent times, Governor General Edward Schreyer later revealed that he had been prepared on his own to call an election if Prime Minister Pierre Trudeau had pressed on with the unilateral amendment of the Constitution after the Supreme Court in 1981 declared this action a violation of constitutional convention (as discussed in Chapter 10). Governor General Adrienne Clarkson stated that she would not have granted Prime Minister Paul Martin a request for dissolution and an election if he had requested it within the first six months after the 2004 election that resulted in a minority government (Levy, 2009).

Finally, Governor General Michaëlle Jean generated considerable controversy when, on December 4, 2008, she granted Prime Minister Stephen Harper his request to prorogue (end the session of) Parliament. In this case, Parliament had sat for only 13 days since the October 14 election that had returned a minority Conservative government. In addition, a vote on the budget, which the government was certain to lose, was imminent, and the Liberal and New Democratic parties had signed a formal agreement to form a coalition government, which the Bloc Québécois had pledged to support for at least a year and a half.

Critics of the prime minister's request to prorogue Parliament argued that the situation was comparable to Prime Minister Mackenzie King's request for dissolution in 1926 when his government was facing censure in the Commons. Proroguing Parliament, like dissolving Parliament, would prevent the House of Commons from expressing its will. Furthermore, it is a primary responsibility of

BOX 13-1

A Governor General Stirs Up Controversy: The King–Byng Affair

Prime Minister William Lyon Mackenzie King, whose grandfather led the Upper Canada Rebellion in 1837, had a great interest in the occult and regularly communicated with the spirits of his dead mother (whom he consulted for advice) and his beloved dog. Politically, he is still remembered for his challenge to the discretionary power of the governor general in 1926.

King earned a doctorate in political economy at Harvard, served as Canada's first deputy minister of labour, and headed up the Rockefeller Foundation's industrial research department. In 1919, King won the Liberal party's first leadership convention. Two years later, he became prime minister as head of a minority government that relied on the support of the Progressive party.

The next election, in 1925, returned 101 Liberals, 116 Conservatives, 24 Progressives, 2 Labour, and 2 Independents. Despite the second-place finish, King did not resign and governed for a year with the support of the Progressives, Labour, and Independents. In June 1926, facing a vote of censure over a customs bribery scandal and with his support in the minor parties deserting him, he asked Governor General Lord Byng to dissolve the House and call an election. Byng refused, noting that the Progressives were now ready to support Arthur Meighen's Conservatives, less than a year had passed since the last general election, and the motives of King—to avoid the will of the House to express censure—were evident.

King resigned, and Meighen accepted the governor general's request to form a government. However, three days later the government was defeated by a single vote. This time, the governor general had no alternative but to grant dissolution. King used the situation to his advantage. As he fought the 1926 election, he argued that the governor general should not have used the prerogative power to deny his request for an election, and was treating Canada like a British colony (Beck, 1968). King's Liberals won a majority government in the 1926 election and he went on to become Canada's longest-serving prime minister.

the governor general to ensure that there is a government in place that has the support of the majority in the House of Commons. In this case, an alternative government that clearly would have the support of the majority of the House was ready to assume office. Thus, the governor general should have rejected the request for prorogation.

Those who supported the governor general's decision to prorogue Parliament argued that a change of government without an election would be undemocratic and tantamount to a "coup." Furthermore, they claimed that the reliance of the proposed coalition on the support of the Bloc Québécois posed a threat to Canadian unity because of that party's advocacy of Quebec's independence. They also pointed out that the Liberals had promised during the election campaign that they would not form a coalition government (Flanagan, 2009). Furthermore, they were critical of the coalition agreement that would see Stéphane Dion (who had led the Liberals to one of their worst defeats) as prime minister and "socialists" (the New Democratic Party) given 6 of the 18 cabinet positions.

Byng's use of the discretionary power and Jean's decision to accept the request of the prime minister both generated controversy. However, in both cases it was the prime minister who put the governor general in a difficult spot by trying to avoid the will of the majority in the House of Commons.[3]

PREROGATIVE POWERS DEVOLVED TO MINISTERS Other prerogative powers have devolved from the monarch to ministers who act in the name of the Crown. For example, the large field of foreign policy—including making treaties and trade agreements, declaring war, deploying the armed services in international conflicts, appointing ambassadors, recognizing states, and accrediting diplomats—is largely governed by prerogative power. In the more humdrum areas like issuing passports, granting honours, appointing Queen's Counsel, and clemency, ministers enjoy the exercise of all these powers without necessarily having to involve Parliament. In fact, throughout history, Parliament was bypassed in the decisions to grant this ministerial "prerogative power." Some would argue that in a democracy, the democratically elected representatives ought to be the ones who have the right to declare war, end a war, and determine how a war should be conducted.

THE POLITICAL EXECUTIVE

The Prime Minister, Cabinet, and Ministers of State

POLITICAL EXECUTIVE
The prime minister, cabinet, and ministers of state.

The **political executive** is made up of the prime minister, cabinet ministers, and ministers of state. The prime minister is sometimes referred to as the "first minister" to indicate his or her leadership role in the cabinet.

The political executive is the most powerful part of the political system, but surprisingly, the formal Constitution is silent on its existence and operation. It operates mostly under the cloak of custom and constitutional convention (politically but not legally binding practices), and occasionally under usages of the constitution (non-binding practices). Silence opens the way for flexibility, and the executive has made full use of flexibility to extend its reach. Thus, the political executive takes much of its direction from convention rather than statute.

GOVERNOR IN COUNCIL
The formal name given to cabinet in order to cloak its decisions with constitutional authority. The phrase means that the governor general is acting on the advice of the Queen's Privy Council for Canada, the active part of which is the cabinet.

In particular, convention dictates that only the active part of the Privy Council—the "Government," or cabinet of the day—can exercise governmental power. Nevertheless, the cabinet adopts the garb of the Privy Council. This is reflected in the language of government decision making. For example, the *Governor General in Council* (usually referred to as the **Governor in Council**)

---

[3]Harper's successful request to prorogue Parliament in December 2009 was also controversial. While the opposition parties claimed it was designed to muzzle criticism related to an inquiry into Canada's role in the torture of Afghan detainees, the government used the upcoming Winter Olympics in Vancouver as its rationale for suspending Parliament for two months.

is the formal name of cabinet, a *minute of council* is a decision of cabinet, and an *order-in-council* is a decision taken by virtue of power delegated to the cabinet. The term *Governor in Council* does not imply that the governor general actually presides over the cabinet—a practice that ended in the nineteenth century—or even attends cabinet meetings, but that the governor general acts on the advice of the cabinet.

Many of the executive functions of the cabinet are undertaken in the name of the governor general or the Governor in Council. These include some aspects of the prerogative power delegated to the cabinet collectively: the appointment of privy councillors, judges, and senators; involvement in international affairs; and the power of clemency, or pardon, given to federal offenders.

THE FLEXIBILITY OF THE WESTMINSTER SYSTEM   Canadians sometimes take their form of government, and especially cabinet government, for granted, thinking that only one variety exists. This is not the case; parliamentary systems come in a surprising number of guises. The legislatures of Nunavut and the Northwest Territories make for fascinating examples. They do not have political parties, candidates run as independents, all members of the legislative assembly elect the premier and cabinet in a secret ballot, and the cabinet as permanent minority[4] often sees its policy and budget decisions subject to change by the legislature. The major similarities to other legislatures in Canada are that the premier chooses the portfolios that cabinet members hold, and certain Westminster principles such as confidence votes and cabinet solidarity apply (White, 2006).

Interesting examples of the variety of the Westminster system can be gleaned from outside Canada as well. For instance, the parliamentary caucuses of the U.K. Conservative party and of the Australian Labour party can choose and remove the prime minister. In Australia and New Zealand, the parliamentary caucuses of the Labour parties select members of the ministry. Also, in the United Kingdom, the "Government," which can number as many as 100 members, encompasses many different types of ministers: the 20 to 25 or so senior cabinet ministers who run Whitehall departments (sometimes called the "inner cabinet"), and junior ministers and Parliamentary private secretaries.

The Canadian ministry follows few of these characteristics, and furthermore has not varied much over the years. The governing party's caucus does not choose the prime minister. Instead, the prime minister is the leader of a political party who is normally chosen, in recent times, by a direct vote of all party members (see Chapter 8). The prime minister advises the governor general on the appointment of all ministers, and the caucus has

---

[4]It is a permanent minority because it cannot depend on a party to marshal a majority in the legislature to support its program.

little role to play other than that of a sounding board for the prime minister and cabinet. The government does not swell to the size of that of the United Kingdom, and with the exception of an experiment with the short-lived Clark government (1979–1980), recourse to an inner cabinet is unknown.[5]

Categories of Office in the Ministry   Canadian practice also differentiates between categories of office in the ministry, but not in ways identical to the United Kingdom. The following are the most common categories.[6]

The first category is the *prime minister*. The prime minister is the most powerful of the ministers by virtue of method of appointment, electoral base, and various prerogatives.

Second are the *ministers* who head departments of government. Specific departmental acts and the Interpretation Act set out the responsibilities of most ministers. However, in special cases comprehensive statutes such as the Financial Administration Act create certain ministerial portfolios and departments. Some ministers—termed line ministers—head departments that are primarily involved in providing services to the public or a segment of society (such as the ministers of agriculture and health). Others are responsible for departments that are more concerned with policy coordination (such as the ministers of international trade and finance).

Third are *ministers of state* (also termed *secretaries of state*). Many of these people have been assigned to assist ministers in specific areas of their portfolios. The Martin government (2003–2006) created a distinction between the cabinet and the ministry; in the former were the traditional cabinet ministers and in the latter were secretaries of state, who were members of the Privy Council but not of the cabinet. Like cabinet ministers, secretaries of state were bound by the convention of collective responsibility (discussed below). They earned three-quarters of the salary of cabinet ministers. Secretaries of state were able to attend cabinet on a rotational basis in the Chrétien years, and in Martin's interlude they were expected to attend all cabinet meetings. *Ministers without portfolio* were the forerunners to this post in the last century and have very occasionally been appointed in more recent times; they were valuable to the setting of collective policy in cabinet but were not given a department to manage.

Stephen Harper maintained the distinction between "ministry" and "cabinet" but called the officials "ministers of state." Ministers of state can attend the

---

[5]The term "inner cabinet" has a variety of meanings, most of them referring to an elite committee within cabinet that is the most influential or sets broad policy directions for the rest of cabinet. However, the sense in which we use the term here is that of the Clark government (1979). Clark had an inner committee of ministers with final decision-making power, and the full cabinet was simply a forum for discussion and coordination.

[6]Occasionally there are deviations from the pattern, particularly in the occasional appointment of an associate minister of defence—a practice that goes back to the 1940s Cabinet War Committee.

The 2012 Canadian cabinet with Governor General David Johnston.

cabinet committee meetings relevant to their areas of responsibility. Ministers of state represent ministers at events, stakeholder meetings, parliamentary committees, and question period, and demonstrate policy leadership in areas specified by the prime minister or minister. Unlike ministers, however, they do not oversee any area of the public service. In his cabinet appointed in 2015, Justin Trudeau termed all the members of his cabinet as Ministers regardless of whether they headed a department of government.

Parliamentary secretaries are government party members chosen by the prime minister to assist a minister, or occasionally more than one minister. Their major function is to act as intermediaries or liaisons among the minister, the Commons and its committees, the caucus, and the general public. However, parliamentary secretaries are not considered to be part of the ministry and do not have access to cabinet documents. Their status may vary according to the prime minister in question. Paul Martin had his parliamentary secretaries sworn in as members of the Privy Council, and they were thus bound by the requirements of cabinet solidarity and secrecy. No matter which government they serve, parliamentary secretaries are subject to the Conflict of Interest Act and to the Conflict of Interest Code for Members of the House of Commons.

The Political Executive in Action

Whereas conventions govern the relationship between the formal and political executive, other conventions are intended to guide the operation of the political executive itself. The most important ones involve recognizing responsible government and ministerial responsibility.

RESPONSIBLE GOVERNMENT   Responsible government is the central convention of the Canadian constitution. It maintains that the cabinet needs the continued support of the majority of the elected House to stay in office. This is also known as "collective responsibility." Responsible government is a British heritage, because Britain was the model for our struggles for democracy in Canada.

Responsible government still matters, and involves two related aspects: **individual ministerial responsibility** and the **collective responsibility** of the whole cabinet.

Individual Ministerial Responsibility   Individual responsibility is essentially the duty to submit, to defend, and to resign, if necessary. A minister has to submit his or her department's budgets and plans to the House, to defend them there, and to answer questions about these and related aspects of the department's operations. The minister may be expected to resign if guilty of improper behaviour or of failure to offer correctives to problems in running the department. Members of the House may direct questions to a minister about official duties relating to the minister's present portfolio. According to parliamentary rules, the minister does not have to answer questions directed at him or her, but public opinion creates pressure for the minister to complete this ring of ministerial responsibility.

In addition, individual ministerial responsibility includes political culpability or blame that may taint a minister's reputation and reflect badly on the government as a whole. The classic approach holds that the minister is responsible (culpable) for every action that takes place in the department, whether or not the minister knew of it. This approach seems to have had currency up until the mid-twentieth century. However, the enormous job of monitoring increasingly large and complex bureaucracies has led to questioning of the doctrine, although parliamentary opposition members still occasionally refer to it in the hope of making a minister resign for some bureaucratic indiscretion.

The modern realist version of the doctrine recognizes a distinction between official acts of which the minister can reasonably be expected to be aware and those incompetent or illegal actions the minister could not have known about. To be sure, once having become aware of such incompetence or illegality, the minister may be held culpable before Parliament for failing to take remedial administrative measures or appropriate corrective action. In the House, a minister may be called upon to resign in certain other obvious cases: misleading Parliament, authorizing unreasonable use of executive power, or engaging in immoral conduct or conduct unbecoming a minister of the Crown. "Conduct unbecoming" has been the undoing of several ministers in recent decades. For example, Solicitor General Francis Fox resigned in 1978 after forging the signature of his mistress's husband so she could get an abortion; he returned to cabinet two years later. Defence minister Maxime Bernier was forced to resign in 2008 because he broke rules regarding government classified documents;

INDIVIDUAL MINISTERIAL RESPONSIBILITY
The responsibility of individual cabinet ministers to the House of Commons for the decisions and actions of the department they administer.

COLLECTIVE RESPONSIBILITY
The convention that the cabinet as a group is responsible to the House of Commons for the decisions and actions of the government.

specifically, he left NATO documents for five weeks at the apartment of his girlfriend, who had connections to biker gangs. In February of 2013, Aboriginal affairs and northern development minister John Duncan resigned from the Harper cabinet after it was revealed that he had contacted a Tax Court judge on behalf of a constituent over a Canada Revenue Agency matter, writing a character reference letter to a judge (and thus implicitly violating the principle of judicial independence) (CBC News, 2013, February 15). A month later, the minister of intergovernmental affairs/president of the Privy Council, Peter Penashue, resigned over the issue of "ineligible contributions" to his 2011 election campaign in Labrador to run (unsuccessfully, as it turned out) in the ensuing by-election. So, conduct unbecoming can take many forms; there are many roads to resignation.

Ultimately, the prime minister determines the fate of a minister under attack in the Commons. The calculus that the prime minister considers when deciding whether or not the minister is to go is complex. It can include such considerations as whether the minister is only trying to administer a policy that cabinet decided on collectively, whether the fate of the whole ministry is at stake if the minister does not go, whether the government will appear weak if the prime minister bows to demands from the opposition for the minister's resignation, and, of course, whether public opinion is a threat to the government. Ordering a minister to resign is one of the most painful decisions a prime minister has to take.

Collective Responsibility   Collective responsibility is the second major part of the doctrine of responsible government. As Heard (1991) notes, there are three interrelated aspects of collective responsibility: the responsibility of the cabinet to the monarch, the responsibility of the cabinet to itself, and the responsibility of the cabinet to the House. The first gives rise to the oaths that new members of the Privy Council take, the second to the doctrines of cabinet solidarity and cabinet secrecy, and the third to the confidence convention (the requirement that the cabinet retain the confidence of the majority in the House of Commons).

The responsibility of the minister to the monarch is reflected in the oaths new privy councillors take after they receive a commission from the governor general summoning them to the Privy Council. The oath carries with it the duty to honour the right of the monarch's representative to be consulted, to encourage, and to warn—that is, to be kept up to date on government business and to be consulted on it—and the duty to resign upon refusal of dissolution if the governor general decides to use the reserve power. Conventional wisdom holds that these monarchical consultation, encouragement, and warning rights are more meaningfully exercised in the United Kingdom than they are in Canada, but Canada's new governor general, David Johnston, hinted when appointed that he expected they would indeed be guiding principles during his tenure (Chase, 2010).

CABINET SOLIDARITY
The basic principle that ministers must avoid public disagreements over policy once cabinet decides on it, and that they must vote in unison in the House on government business.

Cabinet is responsible to itself in a number of ways. **Cabinet solidarity** is an important fact of life for Westminster-type governments. Basically, it means that ministers must avoid public disagreements over policy, even if they have already clashed in their opinions in the cabinet room, and that they must vote in unison in the House on government business. In a frequently quoted section of their work on responsible government, Forsey and Eglington (1985) noted the range of consequences that flow from cabinet solidarity:

1. Government advice to the Crown must be unanimous, even if arrived at after considerations of strongly held but opposed views.

2. A minister (i) must loyally support and defend any cabinet decisions and not quaver by suggestion he was compromised or was reluctantly persuaded; (ii) must be prepared not only to refrain from publicly criticizing other ministers but also to defend them publicly; (iii) must not announce a new policy or change in policy without prior cabinet consent—if he does so cabinet may adopt the policy and save him from resignation, but if it does not, he must resign; (iv) must not express private views on government policies; (v) must not speak about or otherwise become involved in a colleague's portfolio without first consulting him and gaining his approval and probably that of the prime minister; (vi) must not make speeches or do acts which may appear to implicate the government, and must not express personal opinions about future policy except after consultation; (vii) must carry out the policy decided upon by cabinet so far as it affects his own portfolio; (viii) must vote with the government, whether it is in danger or not; (ix) must speak in defence of the government and any of its policies if the prime minister insists. (pp. 147–148)

Cabinet solidarity is important not just because it is a historical practice, but because of its strategic value. The opposition and the media will take advantage of division in the cabinet, potentially leading to the defeat of the government in the House of Commons, especially if a revolt in the caucus is a factor. Prime Minister Harper adopted a strict version of cabinet solidarity, directing the Privy Council Office to vet public appearances and interviews by cabinet ministers, providing them with talking notes, as well as approving departmental information sent out to journalists.

As in the case of ministerial resignations, the prime minister decides the degree to which the words or actions of ministers count as a breach of cabinet solidarity and a threat to the stability of the government. However, occasionally the first minister does not have to judge a minister who resists discipline; instead, the minister may decide that the disagreement with the cabinet is so fundamental that it is necessary to withdraw from the government. For example, Lucien Bouchard withdrew from Brian Mulroney's cabinet in 1990 because he was unable to accept changes to the Meech Lake Accord. Michael Chong resigned from Stephen Harper's cabinet in 2006 because he did not support the government's motion recognizing the "Québécois as a nation within a united Canada." Joe Comuzzi resigned in 2005 because he disagreed with the government's same-sex marriage bill. However, resignations from cabinet on matters of principled disagreement are few and far between. Ministers tend to leave cabinet because the prime minister has judged their behaviour to be a detriment to the government's image (Maxime Bernier, 2008; Helena Guergis, 2010) or because they have better career opportunities (John Baird, February 2015). Ministerial exits are not rare; there were 20, for various reasons, from 1993 (Chrétien) to 2015 (Harper).

There may also be instances when the prime minister does not enforce solidarity over issues of conscience. Such was the case with several votes over capital punishment. By a free vote in 1976, Parliament abolished the death penalty, except for certain offences under the National Defence Act. Another free vote in 1987 kept the abolition in place. In 1998, Parliament removed the last exceptions under the National Defence Act.

Cabinet Secrecy   Cabinet secrecy protects the expression of views by ministers in the setting of cabinet and cabinet committee discussions to encourage frankness. All ministers take an oath committing them to secrecy in their cabinet deliberations. D'Ombrain (2007) notes that "cabinet secrecy is widely assumed to be akin to executive privilege, shielding all that is internal to the cabinet. The cabinet secrecy convention does not protect the substantive secrets of the cabinet; rather it protects the processes whereby ministers arrive at decisions. That is all it protects" (pp. 334–335). Cabinet secrecy is the reason that cabinet ministers will go to great lengths not to divulge to the incoming administration (of a different party) the cabinet minutes of the previous administration. They will, however, pass along to the new administration the records of decision, which are necessary for the functioning of the state.

Cabinet secrecy also safeguards cabinet ministers from having their opinions made public and having to defend them in the public realm. It complements cabinet solidarity, which is a linchpin of the cabinet–parliamentary system. It protects the anonymity of public servants: their advice to ministers is made in confidence and intended to stay that way. Otherwise the public would identify public servants with a certain course of action when they are duty bound to serve the will of the government in office. Cabinet secrecy also provides the forum in which brokerage of regional interests can take place. Canadians have come to expect that the political executive is the venue for bargaining between regions rather than the legislative arena, as is the case in the United States.

CABINET SECRECY
A convention that forbids the disclosure of the views expressed by particular ministers during cabinet (and cabinet committee) discussions, in order to encourage frankness.

EXECUTIVE DOMINANCE

Canadians live in a system marked by executive dominance. This means that the prime minister and cabinet dominate the legislative branch—they direct its business and are the main originators of policy change and innovation. Some would say that this fact is due to cultural traits that predispose Canadians to "deference to authority" (Friedenberg, 1980). Others have noted a tendency for the executive to gather power around itself over time, especially through the prime minister (Savoie, 2008). Still others will see in executive dominance a holdover of British practices of government inherited from colonial times.

Whatever the broad reasons, the power structure itself contributes to the executive being the pre-eminent body in the political system. The power structure promotes executive dominance through constitutional authority and organizational factors. As we have seen, the Constitution is heavily biased toward the formal executive. In fact, the informal executive is the beneficiary of this constitutional windfall, and expresses its will through legislation that refers to the governor general, the Governor in Council, or individual ministers. As well, only about 4000 staff work for the Canadian Parliament compared with approximately 240 000 departmental positions in the federal public service (Axworthy, 2008). Accordingly, the ability of Parliament to scrutinize the executive and hold it accountable is very limited.

However, executive dominance is sometimes weakened. Occasionally the tables turn and Parliament is able, in a limited way, to set the agenda for the government. This is particularly the case in minority government situations. In some cases, the minority government has been toppled by a vote on a matter of confidence, while in other cases (such as in 2008) the prime minister has requested an election in hopes of gaining a majority. Nevertheless, the threat of defeat by vote of non-confidence is often enough to convince the government of the day to adopt some policies promoted by the opposition. The minority Pearson government in the 1960s was coaxed into developing medicare by its dependence on NDP support. The minority Trudeau government of 1972–1974 took on many initiatives that the NDP had promoted, such as the creation of Petro-Canada and electoral funding legislation. Somewhat similarly, the threat of a Liberal–NDP coalition government replacing the Conservative minority government in 2008 spurred the government to action. In November 2008, the government's economic statement had done little to respond to the severe worldwide recession, despite calls for economic stimulus from the opposition parties. After the coalition emerged, the Conservative government quickly changed its tune to announce a major economic stimulus package.

The Prime Minister

Both the prime minister and cabinet have special powers and functions in the Canadian version of the Westminster Model. First of all, the prime minister in the Canadian system enjoys the "five Ps of power": parliamentary leader, party leader, patronage, policymaker, and public face. The prime minister leads the cabinet, which sets the priorities for Parliament, and is influential in allocating Parliament's time along with the government House leader. The prime minister is a party leader elected by the broad membership of the party. The prime minister also holds the power of rewarding or thwarting ambition, because of the office's control over the levers of patronage. There are thousands of non-public-service-related positions in the public sector to be handed out. As well, the prime minister is the chief policymaker for government, overshadowing in recent years the plenary (full) cabinet and inviting a kind of "court government," an undemocratic, almost aristocratic approach to governing (Savoie, 2008). Finally, the prime minister is the public face of government; when the prime minister is popular, the governing party is popular and the prime minister needs to expend relatively little political capital to maintain support within the party.

The prime minister is also powerful as a result of being the principal communicator with the Crown. Instruments of Advice are one mechanism the prime minister can use to intercede in, or affect, matters of governance. These are letters informing the governor general of the prime minister's views on matters involving the Royal Prerogative; since 1953, the principal ones have been the summoning of Parliament, recommending the dissolution of Parliament and requesting an election, nominating the cabinet, summoning qualified people to the Senate, and changing the Crown's prerogative. Other uses of Instruments of Advice are to designate a cabinet minister as deputy prime minister,[7] to accept resignations of ministers, and to change the Table of Precedence for Canada (the list of seniority and rank of government officials). Appointment of the governor general of Canada is done by an Instrument of Advice submitted to the Queen.

The prime minister's powers include the ability to intercede in most procedural and policy areas of government. These run the gamut of public policy but usually apply to foreign affairs, national unity strategy, and intergovernmental affairs—some of the highest-profile issues that can affect a government. In fact, in recent years the foreign affairs and intergovernmental affairs ministers have understood that the policy direction in these areas ultimately comes from the prime minister. Sometimes reminders of the prime minister's dominance take the form of surprise announcements that enable the prime minister to assert authority over cabinet, knowing that members will seldom raise their voices in objection, at least not publicly. For example, Pierre Trudeau's announcement of a major financial restraint program in the mid-1970s surprised even his own finance minister.

Power also originates in the prime minister's role as the principal architect of government. The prime minister can shift the attention of ministers and officials by simply focusing attention on organizational matters. Early in the twentieth century, the prime minister chose personnel for a cabinet that stayed relatively stable in size and configuration. In the intervening years, it became this and more: now added was a general responsibility for the design of government. The first minister can thwart the ambition of both ministers and

---

[7]Although many prime ministers have chosen a deputy prime minister, prime ministers Joe Clark, Stephen Harper, and (upon announcing his first cabinet) Justin Trudeau did not do so.

bureaucrats by forming small cabinets; can control ministers by having a large and powerful planning and policy-oriented central agency; and can position certain ministers above others by assigning the most important departments to them, such as finance. In addition, the prime minister can turn to the Royal Commissions and commissions of inquiry to energize or change the basic direction of government, as was the case with the reports of the Rowell-Sirois Commission (1940), the Gordon Commission (1957), the Macdonald Royal Commission (1985), Royal Commission on Aboriginal Peoples (RCAP) (1996), and the Royal Commission on the Future of Health Care in Canada (Romanow Commission, 2002). Rowell-Sirois changed intergovernmental fiscal relations in the country and led to federal jurisdiction over employment insurance; Gordon resulted in economic nationalist policies; Macdonald paved the way for the adoption of free trade agreements; RCAP led to recognition of the inherent right of Aboriginal self-government and a higher profile for Aboriginal issues; and Romanow led to the creation of a 10-year federal–provincial health accord in 2004 and the creation of the Health Council of Canada (closed down by the government in 2014).

The appointment power is significant, as the prime minister is able to choose the personnel of crucial institutions and agencies of the Canadian state. These include the following:

- Senate vacancies
- the governor general and all the provincial lieutenant governors
- the justices of the Supreme Court of Canada
- the chief justices and associate chief justices of the superior courts of the provinces
- all of the deputy ministers in the government of Canada
- most of the deputy minister equivalents in agencies, boards, and commissions at the federal level (see Chapter 15)
- all ambassadors who represent the country abroad
- all appointees to international organizations, including the United Nations and the International Monetary Fund
- the head of the RCMP
- the governor of the Bank of Canada and its board
- several of the officers of Parliament

An additional aspect of prime ministerial power is that elected representatives do not carry out meaningful reviews of these appointments. In this respect, the Canadian system differs considerably from that of the United States. Although the Harper government established the Canadian Public Appointments Commission in 2006 to oversee various public sector appointments, with a secretariat to support it, the commission was never appointed, and the secretariat was finally disbanded in 2012. Apparently the inaction on appointment was in retaliation for opposition parties blocking the appointment of Alberta businessman and prominent Conservative Gwyn Morgan as its first commissioner.

© Brian Milne

Stephen Harper exercised his prime ministerial power to appoint ambassadors in August 2009 when he named former Manitoba premier Gary Doer as the next Canadian ambassador to the United States.

In many ways, the prime minister has power because he is a leader and has leadership qualities. Leadership power comes through the official roles that the prime minister is expected to play: symbolic leader, cabinet leader, parliamentary leader, and national leader. Beyond these roles, the prime minister is sometimes seen as the embodiment of the country, reflected in the utterances he or she is called upon to make in the appropriate context, like a natural disaster, the deaths of soldiers in conflicts abroad, or in international contexts. Indeed, like American presidents, prime ministers, along with their families, have in modern times been treated as celebrities by the media.

The job of leader of cabinet involves a number of tasks that enhance the authority of the first minister. The prime minister determines the agenda of cabinet meetings. The leader voices the consensus of cabinet, which can range from a true consensus to a consensus of one—the prime minister—in unusual cases. Of course, if this minority consensus style becomes the rule rather than the exception, cabinet discord can arise, but this style may often be necessary to move the cabinet along. Moreover, the prime minister is the only member of the cabinet who is focused on the overall direction of the government, whereas other ministers tend to develop what is called "portfolio loyalties," which limit their ability to see more broadly. The prime minister also determines the way that cabinet business is handled; for example, whether or not cabinet committees will have effective sign-off on some policy matters. Another leadership power is to determine the relative balance between cabinet material generated by departmental staff on the one hand and central agencies (notably the Privy Council Office, which is under the direction of the prime minister, as discussed in Chapter 15) on the other. In the early days of cabinet operation, there was only a vertical orientation to policy advice, with departments as the main source of information to cabinet. In modern cabinets this vertical axis remains, but there is also a horizontal axis: the provision of policy and financial management counsel by central agencies and central departments (including the Department of Finance Canada and the Treasury Board Secretariat). To the extent that the centre grows stronger, the departments grow weaker.

Parliamentary leadership is another in the list of seemingly endless aspects of power of the first minister. Prime ministers choose a special member of cabinet called the government House leader, and therefore directly affect many aspects of parliamentary operations, as discussed in Chapter 14. The prime minister is usually the focus of the daily question period in the House of Commons, and therefore is in a position to influence public opinion. (The timetable contrasts sharply with that of the UK prime minister, who appears for questions only once a week and for a mere half-hour.) As well, the prime minister, acting through the House leader and others, is able to allocate the time of Parliament to government bills, which typically take up a substantial majority of the time of the lower house.

LIMITS ON THE PRIME MINISTER'S POWER   Although journalist Jeffrey Simpson (2001) once described Canada as a "friendly dictatorship" because of the great power of the prime minister, there are some limits to the power of those who hold this position. It is the nature of power to be met, ultimately, with power. In Canada, the federal system provides an important limit to what a prime minister can do. Federal politicians have to tread lightly when it comes to matters that fall within provincial jurisdiction, such as resource taxation, social programs, and education.

Public opinion can sometimes act as a potent counter to the prime minister. The Mulroney government shelved its plans for partial de-indexation of the old-age pension in 1984 after an old-age pensioner predicted it would be "Goodbye Charlie Brown" to the prime minister in a TV scrum on Parliament Hill, stirring up public opinion (Savoie, 1999). Circumstances await an unwary prime minister; as former prime minister Harold Macmillan of Britain allegedly replied when asked what he thought was the greatest threat a statesperson might face, "Events, dear boy, events." For example, Prime Minister Pearson faced a blizzard of scandals in his first term: individual cabinet ministers were accused of helping the escape from prison of a notorious drug dealer, buying furniture on favourable terms, and accepting a bribe. Prime Minister Paul Martin's short term in office was disrupted by the "sponsorship scandal," which involved a number of government contracts that had been improperly awarded to advertising agencies that produced little or no work on the contracts, with some of the money ending up as donations to Liberal party officials. A series of unexpected travel and housing scandals began to surface in 2012 involving Harper appointees to the Senate and damaged the prime minister's political capital.

Finally, the cabinet can provide an important limitation to prime ministerial power. Even with the support of the Privy Council Office and the Prime

Minister's Office, the prime minister necessarily relies on cabinet ministers for advice. Inevitably, the prime minister cannot know about and participate in all of the deliberations and decisions of modern governments. As noted above, prime ministers tend to focus their attention on selected important policy areas and on setting the overall direction and political strategy of the government. For other matters, ministers, supported by the expertise of their department, usually wield considerable influence. Furthermore, the minister of finance with responsibility for the budget will typically have a strong impact on what the government can or cannot do. In addition, some cabinet ministers are powerful political figures in their own right because of their support within a particular region of the country or among powerful interests, or because of their following within the caucus or the party as a whole. For example, Paul Martin had considerable power through most of the years that Jean Chrétien was prime minister not only because of Martin's position as finance minister, but also because of his support within the Liberal party.

Cabinet

The cabinet carries out a variety of legislative and executive functions. Cabinet introduces most of the legislation that Parliament deals with, not only because Canadians expect this, but also because the government party arranges the timetable to accommodate this. By virtue of Section 54 of the Constitution Act, 1867, cabinet introduces all financial legislation, including ways and means bills, which affect taxation; appropriation bills, which authorize the withdrawal of funds from the Consolidated Revenue Fund; and borrowing authority bills, which seek authority to borrow money. It is therefore unconstitutional for the legislature to introduce financial measures as Congress, its counterpart in the United States, can do in the United States.[8]

Traditionally parliaments have recognized the limitations of their legislative role and have chosen to share this role with the executive. The executive is better placed to address the specifics of policy areas than is the legislature, and regular legislation involves an extensive planning cycle that is not always convenient, quick, and efficient. Parliament often delegates to the executive the power to pass secondary legislation and regulations to flesh out the details of primary legislation passed by Parliament. This power to pass **subordinate (delegated) legislation** is held either by the full cabinet (and expressed as being passed by the Governor in Council), by a minister of the Crown, or by an administrative agency vested with delegated legislative authority. It takes a variety of forms: orders-in-council, regulations, and other statutory instruments, such as rules, warrants, and proclamations. The reach of delegated legislation is extensive.

SUBORDINATE (DELEGATED) LEGISLATION
Authority for subordinate legislation that comes from a primary piece of legislation passed by Parliament and takes the form of orders-in-council or regulations made by a minister or agency.

---

[8]The Commons can affect expenditures by moving for the reduction in a vote, but this is a rare occurrence.

CABINET'S EXECUTIVE FUNCTIONS   The cabinet is responsible for several executive functions. First, it plays a leadership role for the whole political system. Individual ministers have responsibility for the management and direction of their department. Second, the cabinet is expected to be the main source of policy generation in the political system. Third, it performs certain measures collectively in the name of the governor general and usually upon the initiative of the prime minister, as discussed earlier in this chapter. Finally, the cabinet as a great crossroads of information and strategy setting has to provide coordination for all the activities and decisions of government. This places a heavy burden on the prime minister.

CONSIDERATIONS IN CABINET CONSTRUCTION   The prime minister chooses cabinet ministers from among the governing party's members of Parliament. Almost all cabinet ministers are selected from the House of Commons. In the past, the leader of the government in the Senate was appointed to the cabinet in order to defend government policies in that chamber. Occasionally other Senators have been appointed to the cabinet particularly to provide representation for provinces that did not elect an MP from the governing party. Justin Trudeau's cabinet reflected a commitment not only to provincial representation but also to gender equality (see Box 13-2: Justin Trudeau Appoints a Cabinet).

In constructing the cabinet, the prime minister is aware of precedent. In particular, a very strong norm dictates that the prime minister should choose at least one minister from each province. Sometimes Prince Edward Island has had no cabinet representation, and Newfoundland and Labrador lost cabinet representation after the 2008 election. These exceptions aside, every province has been represented in every cabinet. Not surprisingly, the provinces with larger populations expect to have more representatives in the cabinet. In those provinces, there are expectations that certain regions (e.g., northern Ontario) and cities (particularly Toronto, Montreal, and Vancouver) be represented if at all possible.

Because governing parties have sometimes lacked elected representatives from certain provinces or regions, prime ministers have occasionally drawn cabinet ministers from the Senate to provide provincial representation. Prime Minister Pierre Trudeau chose senators from the Prairie provinces when very few Liberals were elected from that region; Joe Clark selected three senators from Quebec; and Stephen Harper appointed Michel Fortier to the Senate in his 2006 cabinet so that he could have representation from Montreal in his first cabinet. Reversing himself and past practice, however, he later downplayed the Senate–cabinet link. In July 2013, stung by the effect that Senate scandals were having on the government's popularity, Harper sought to distance himself from the institution by stating that the leader of the government in the Senate would no longer be a cabinet position.

BOX 13-2

Justin Trudeau Appoints a Cabinet

During the 2015 election campaign, Justin Trudeau promised that 50 percent of his cabinet would be female. As well, he would have a smaller cabinet of around 25 ministers, in contrast to Stephen Harper's 39 member cabinet (Crawford, 2015, October 20). Trudeau lived up to his gender equality promise by appointing 15 women and 15 men to his cabinet. The cabinet also represented Canada's ethnic diversity to a considerable degree with, for example, four Sikh and two Aboriginal members. Thus, Trudeau claimed, he put together a cabinet that "looks like Canada."

Trudeau's cabinet also reflected the long-standing practice that there would be at least one cabinet minister from each province. Unlike some prime ministers, Trudeau did not have to appoint senators to the cabinet to represent provinces that did not elect any governing party members, as the Liberals won seats in every province. (As well, Trudeau had removed all Liberal senators from the Liberal caucus.) Trudeau's cabinet was somewhat larger than planned, having 30 members plus the prime minister. Eleven cabinet ministers were chosen from Ontario (of whom seven were from the greater Toronto area), six (plus the prime minister) were from Quebec, three were from British Columbia, two were from Alberta, two were from Manitoba, and there was one from each of the other provinces and one from Nunavut. With the Liberals out of power since 2006 and reduced to 34 seats in 2011, the majority of cabinet ministers were inexperienced in governing. Eighteen had never sat in the House of Commons and only six had previous experience as federal cabinet ministers.

Change was also evident in the titles of those appointed to the cabinet. For example, instead of *environment minister*, Catherine McKenna became *minister of the environment and climate change*, thus signalling that the new government planned to make climate change an important priority. Likewise there were two ministers who had "science" in their title. Trudeau himself took on responsibility as minister of intergovernmental affairs and minister of youth. The names of several departments were changed as well. For example, the Department of Foreign Affairs, Trade and Development became the Department of Global Affairs.

Although Trudeau claimed that he was instituting "government by cabinet" (rather than "prime ministerial government," a term that was often used to describe the Harper government), he established nine cabinet committees and one cabinet subcommittee. Gender equality was not entirely evident in the committees as 7 of the 10 committees were chaired by men. Instead of the Planning and Priorities Committee that had been at the centre of cabinet decision-making in previous governments, Trudeau appointed an Agenda and Results Committee with himself as chair. Trudeau also decided to chair the Intelligence and Emergency Management Committee.

At the start, then, Trudeau put a different face on the cabinet. At the time of writing it was too early to tell if the cabinet would be fundamentally different from previous cabinets in its decision-making processes.

Historically, prime ministers also paid attention to ensuring that the cabinet had the appropriate proportion of Catholics and various Protestant denominations. While religion no longer appears to be a consideration in cabinet construction, language is of continuing importance. Prime ministers normally include an English-speaking minister from Quebec in their cabinet and, at least in modern times, a French-speaking minister from outside Quebec. In recent times, prime ministers have attempted to increase diversity in their ministries with increased representation of women and ethnic and visible minorities.

There has also been a tendency to assign certain types of portfolios to ministers from certain regions. With some exceptions, fisheries and oceans is often headed by a minister from Atlantic Canada, public works and justice frequently go to Quebec, Ontario cabinet ministers are typically appointed to the finance and industry departments, and the West often gets agriculture and various other natural resources portfolios. Justin Trudeau's first cabinet only partly reflected this characteristic, particularly with the finance minister from Ontario.

STAGES OF CABINET DEVELOPMENT   The cabinet has taken several forms since Confederation. In analyzing the development of the cabinet, J. Stefan Dupré (1985) described three different models.

The Traditional, Departmentalized, and Institutionalized Cabinets   The traditional cabinet (1867 to the 1920s) was at work before the rise of the administrative state, that is, when government's role was modest. The federal cabinet was primarily a mechanism for federal–provincial adjustment, assembling and voicing regional concerns, and awarding patronage. The **departmentalized cabinet** (1920s to 1960s) arose when the administrative state began to grow and government departments and ministers directed public-sector expansion. Ministers had decision-making autonomy and relied on departmental experts for policy formulation and implementation. "Portfolio loyalty"—or ministers' primary commitment to their departments—was a distinguishing characteristic of this period. The cabinet was simple in structure, had few standing committees, and displayed limited collegial or collective decision making over departmental matters. The prime minister was the dominant politician and accepted cabinet-making as his main task (Dunn, 1995).

From the 1960s to the 1990s, the **institutionalized cabinet** became the common pattern. This cabinet features "various combinations of formal committee structures, established central agencies and budgeting and management techniques [combined] . . . to emphasize shared knowledge, collegial decision making, and the formulation of government-wide priorities and objectives" (Dupré, 1985, p. 4).

The institutionalized cabinet has a complex structure, many standing committees, and a significant degree of collective decision making in matters of departmental policy (Dunn, 1995). The prime minister becomes the designer of government. Both central departments and central agencies now exist. Central agencies (the Prime Minister's Office for partisan input, and the Privy Council Office for non-partisan policy input) perform government-wide coordination with the prime minister as responsible minister. Budgeting features wider aims than mere financial control, and planning is far more common and comprehensive. Cabinet receives policy advice from central agencies and central departments (particularly finance and the Treasury Board) and not only

DEPARTMENTALIZED CABINET
A form of cabinet organization that emphasizes ministerial autonomy and relies on the prime minister and full cabinet to achieve coordination.

INSTITUTIONALIZED CABINET
A form of cabinet organization that emphasizes collective decision making and seeks to achieve it by a highly structured system of cabinet committees and central agencies.

from the responsible minister and his or her deputy. Decision making is more centralized: Cabinet makes a wider range of decisions, and central departments and central agencies monitor departments to a greater extent.

Prime Minister–Centred Cabinet   Some writers have contended, implicitly or explicitly, that the days of the institutionalized cabinet have ended, replaced by a new pattern of a **prime minister–centred cabinet** (or prime ministerial government). Donald Savoie's *Governing from the Centre* (1999) argued that the cabinet decision-making process (i.e., the institutionalized cabinet process), which was premised on collective decision making, now primarily "belonged" to the prime minister. Power had shifted from ministers and departments to the centre (cabinet and cabinet committees), and from the cabinet and cabinet ministers to the prime minister and central advisers. Central agencies had gone from facilitating the collective will of the cabinet to extending the prime minister's will. Whereas once there had been comprehensive policy agendas, now there were "bolts of electricity"—a few key personal objectives hand-picked by the prime minister and pressed into effect by trusted lieutenants. One set of rules applied to the prime minister, the finance minister, and the president of the Treasury Board, formerly the "guardians" of government finances, and another to the "spenders," or line departments (departments primarily concerned with providing services). The guardians' programs would pass approval with little difficulty. Line department ministers would go through the regular cabinet committee process, where their proposals seldom emerged unscathed, unlike those of the guardians.

The situation was worse nearly a decade later, Savoie reported. Cabinet government in both Canada and the United Kingdom has been steadily weakened and "all but destroyed" (Savoie, 2008, p. 229). A kind of (presumably medieval) "court government" reigned. "Individuals now rule, starting with the prime minister and his most trusted courtiers, carefully selected ministers, and senior civil servants, and they have more power in a court-style government than they do when formal policy and decision making processes tied to cabinet decision making are respected" (Savoie, 2008, p. 230). There is differentiation of status within cabinet. "Ministers now have to learn to work with the prime minister's court more than they have to learn to work with cabinet and cabinet colleagues" (Savoie, 2008, p. 238).

Recent literature has tempered the characterization of cabinet governance as mainly prime minister–centred. In particular, David A. Good (2007) presents a more nuanced perception. He notes that the so-called spender–guardian dichotomy is outmoded, and that four sets of actors actually affect federal government spending. The first, spenders, are generally spending ministers (and occasionally the prime minister and finance minister); the second are guardians, the finance department and the Treasury Board; the third are priority setters, the prime minister, Prime Minister's Office, and Privy Council Office; and as for the fourth, watchdogs, the main one is the Office of the

PRIME MINISTER–CENTRED CABINET
A form of cabinet organization in which the first minister is so powerful that the nominal mechanisms for collective decision making, such as cabinet committees and central agencies, serve the prime minister's personal agenda.

Auditor General (OAG). The Harper government created even more watchdogs—the parliamentary budget officer, the chief audit executive in each department, accounting officers in each department, an independent procurement officer, and a public sector integrity commissioner.

Despite their different interests, guardians and priority setters have combined to control the effects of spenders and watchdogs (Good, 2007). However, departments can indeed have some wins and convince the prime minister to adopt their concerns if they do their "homework," develop a clientele, think like guardians, and develop ties to key sectoral and regional ministers. Both Savoie and Good, however, agree that cabinet and its committees no longer affect budget priority setting, and that only a limited set of centrally determined priorities are created annually (Good, 2007).

HOW THE CABINET POLICY PROCESS WORKS

Whatever debate surrounds changes in the policy process of the federal government, the outlines of the process itself have remained in place for decades, and most ministers must adhere to them. The decision process is organized around process and purpose. Broadly speaking, there are two processes: the cabinet decision-making process and the budget process.

The Cabinet Decision-Making Process

The cabinet decision-making process deals with policymaking in the broad sense. It is about setting priorities, deciding modes of implementation, establishing expected results, and fine-tuning the aspects of policy, by regulation and related matters, that cannot be dealt with by legislatures themselves.

Two levels typify cabinet decision making: full cabinet and cabinet committees. The full cabinet deals with priority setting, approval of new programs and major expenditures, and sensitive political problems. It is the end of the line in the policy process. Cabinet makes choices that may have stumped lower levels like committees of cabinet or the bureaucracy. The prime minister, acting as the chair of cabinet, leads the process. It is the prime minister who determines the consensus of cabinet, a task that may occasionally amount to the first minister imposing the decision on the rest of the cabinet. The prime minister is, however, mindful of the nature of "political capital" or acceptable leeway, and tends to impose decisions only reluctantly, knowing that the essence of effective leadership is building teamwork.

As in many other large organizations, work in the cabinet relies on the division of labour. Such division takes the form of creating cabinet committees and endowing them with specific tasks. Some tasks relate to policy and some to financial management. Policy matters are dealt with by policy committees of cabinet, and financial matters by the Treasury Board of cabinet, a specialized committee with its own cabinet minister as head (president of the

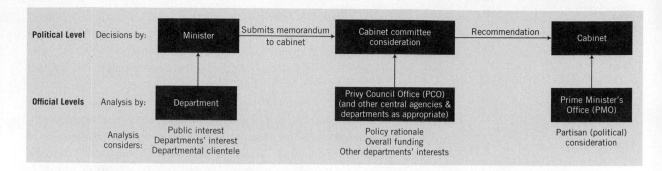

FIGURE 13-1
THE ROUTING OF
MEMORANDA TO CABINET

Treasury Board) and its own secretariat (department), which dates back to the founding of the country in 1867.

Cabinet receives three main types of policy submission: the memorandum to cabinet (MC), the Treasury Board submission, and the Governor in Council (GIC) submission. The first typically works its way through the cabinet committee system, whereas the Treasury Board handles Treasury Board and GIC submissions in a more abbreviated and less linear process. MCs are needed for a new program or policy direction, whereas the Treasury Board submission covers the subsequent parts of the policy process, including program design, program implementation, and program evaluation. GIC items deal with delegated legislation.

There is a standard process for the routing of memoranda to cabinet. The diagram in Figure 13-1 shows the origins and outcomes of memoranda to cabinet.

Analysis by the Privy Council Office, a central agency, is meant to introduce a significant element of horizontality into the cabinet process. This means that the Privy Council Office ensures that other ministers, departments, and agencies that are affected by the department's policy are consulted, that room is left in the agenda for the input of affected parties, and that the measure makes for good public policy. Of course, not only the cabinet and its committees are briefed, but also the prime minister, who orchestrates the policy process. As the minister responsible for both the Privy Council Office and the Prime Minister's Office, the prime minister has the advantage of both policy and partisan political input.

Cabinet Committees

Cabinet committees are relatively recent but important actors in the Ottawa policy scene. They were sparsely used before the 1960s for a number of reasons, one being a perception that collective responsibility would be weakened if cabinet decision making was subdivided. Another was that some prime ministers, such as Mackenzie King, felt that they could not adequately exercise power over other ministers if the ministers were out of sight of the

CABINET COMMITTEES
Groups of cabinet ministers who examine policy proposals from related policy fields and recommend to the plenary (full) cabinet what action should be taken. Their recommendations generally are accepted.

prime minister. Others, like John Diefenbaker, the self-proclaimed outsider to the federal scene, distrusted their fellow ministers and felt more comfortable in a full cabinet situation. One important consideration was that government was still relatively small and its business manageable by full cabinet.

Later on, committees became progressively more central to the cabinet decision-making process. Lester B. Pearson made use of cabinet committees, but they had modest mandates and could not make final decisions. Pierre Trudeau formalized the committee process and allowed committees to make more decisions by themselves. With the Policy and Expenditure Management System (PEMS), which spanned three prime ministers—Clark, Trudeau, and Mulroney (1979–1989)—committees even began to make budgetary decisions to dovetail with their policy recommendations. This system ended with the 1980s. Yet after this, it was still a cabinet committee—the Expenditure Review Committee chaired by Don Mazankowski—that made most of the important budgetary decisions. However, the Harper government budget of 2010–2011, which set out a policy of returning to balanced budgets by 2014–2015, eschewed cabinet committees as the operative mechanism. Instead, a strategic and operating review was established to review $80 billion of direct program spending led by the president of the Treasury Board and a specially constituted committee of the Treasury Board. Generally, the committees make many final decisions in government but, in keeping with the convention of collective responsibility, ministers have a right—not often exercised—to challenge the committee recommendation before cabinet reaches its final decision.

One of the powers of the prime minister is to design the decision-making apparatus. In doing so, the prime minister personally assesses what will work most efficiently and what will most effectively use that rarest of things—ministerial time. The net effect is that the design of government at the centre changes from prime minister to prime minister. Some have numerous cabinet committees, others fewer; some have more ministers and portfolios, others fewer. As well, over time, the prime minister's apparatus tends to become larger and more detailed. The Harper government, for example, had a ministry of 31 in 2006 (25 ministers and 6 ministers of state) but then grew to 38 in 2009 (27 ministers and 11 ministers of state) and 39 in 2011 (the same number of ministers and ministers of state as 2009, but with an associate minister of defence added). It had seven cabinet committees in 2006, eight in 2009 (one added on Afghanistan), and seven in 2011 (plus one subcommittee). Before Harper, Prime Minister Martin had had a sizable cabinet at 39 ministers, including 8 ministers of state, and 9 cabinet committees. These both contrast significantly with the 4 cabinet committees Prime Minister Chrétien relied on for most of his tenure (although his initially small cabinet swelled to 28 ministers and 11 ministers of state). Prime Minister Justin Trudeau started with 30 ministers and 9 cabinet committees (plus 1 subcommittee). Whether the size of the cabinet would later increase was not known at the time of writing.

Yet, in some ways, the first ministers show consensus on the nature of the central executive. Since Chrétien, they have usually distinguished between the ministry—the collection of ministers who are sworn in as members of the Queen's Privy Council for Canada—and the cabinet—those privy councillors who have received departmental portfolios or the equivalent. They have seen fit to distinguish between senior and junior ministers, with ministers of state forming the latter although Justin Trudeau's first cabinet did not make this distinction among ministers. The majority of prime ministers in the last half-century—excluding Chrétien but including Harper—have seen the need for a priorities and planning committee. This amounts to a kind of "inner cabinet"— a group of the more influential ministers who set priorities for government and coordinate the work of the other committees. The prime minister chairs this important cabinet committee, which can be considered another basis of the prime minister's power. Justin Trudeau's Agenda and Results Committee may have a similar function and significance as the former Priorities and Planning Committee.

The Budgetary Process

Each winter, the president of the Treasury Board tables in the House of Commons the government's Main Estimates. Parts I and II provide the government's expenditure plan and detailed spending for the coming fiscal year. Part III of the Estimates tabled in the fall is composed of two parts: Canada's performance and departmental performance reports (DPRs). Normally three supplementary estimates are tabled at various times of the year. The minister of finance presents the budget to Parliament normally in the first three months of the year. Timing of budgets can be changed under extraordinary circumstances; in January 2015 finance minister Joe Oliver announced that the federal budget would not be tabled before the end of the current fiscal year (March 31) due to "current market instability." (It was presented on April 21.)

This crucial document outlines the government's spending priorities for the coming year and often beyond, and explains how the government will collect and spend the taxes of Canadians. The budget often contains new initiatives, such as the major expenditure cuts in the 2012 budget. These changes can affect the Supplementary Estimates. The budgeting process is outlined in Figure 13-2.

The minister of finance, the president of the Treasury Board, and the prime minister are the major players for most of the process, and the full cabinet is brought in only at the end of the budget cycle, shortly before the budget is presented. However, individual ministers are involved in presenting wish lists of new programs earlier in the process, and the cabinet will have made its general approach known in cabinet retreats that generally take place the summer before the process starts.

FIGURE 13-2
THE BUDGETARY PROCESS

SOURCE: Based on Treasury Board of Canada. (2010). The reporting cycle for government expenditures. *Tools and Resources for Parliamentarians.* Retrieved from www.tbs-sct.gc.ca/ems-sgd/rc-cr-eng.asp.

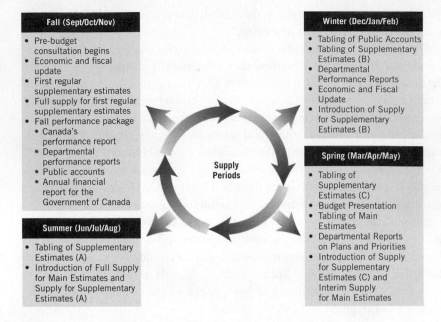

Fall (Sept/Oct/Nov)
- Pre-budget consultation begins
- Economic and fiscal update
- First regular supplementary estimates
- Full supply for first regular supplementary estimates
- Fall performance package
  - Canada's performance report
  - Departmental performance reports
  - Public accounts
  - Annual financial report for the Government of Canada

Summer (Jun/Jul/Aug)
- Tabling of Supplementary Estimates (A)
- Introduction of Full Supply for Main Estimates and Supply for Supplementary Estimates (A)

Supply Periods

Winter (Dec/Jan/Feb)
- Tabling of Public Accounts
- Tabling of Supplementary Estimates (B)
- Departmental Performance Reports
- Economic and Fiscal Update
- Introduction of Supply for Supplementary Estimates (B)

Spring (Mar/Apr/May)
- Tabling of Supplementary Estimates (C)
- Budget Presentation
- Tabling of Main Estimates
- Departmental Reports on Plans and Priorities
- Introduction of Supply for Supplementary Estimates (C) and Interim Supply for Main Estimates

REFORM AND THE PRIME MINISTER AND CABINET

No political system is immutable. Changes can always be brought to the decision-making structure. Over time, reforms have been suggested that would whittle away some of the prerogatives and powers of both the prime minister and cabinet.

With regard to the prime minister, many ideas have been advanced. Aucoin, Smith, and Dinsdale (2004) analyze some in their report on responsible government in Canada. One idea is to lessen the prime minister's appointment power by reducing the number of appointments that the prime minister can make. Another is to enable the parliamentary party caucuses to remove party leaders, regardless of whether their party leader is currently the prime minister.[9] Yet another is to have members of the governing party's caucus select the members of the ministry. Other analysts have suggested that the way to control the overwhelming power of the prime minister and the cabinet is to put into statute what are now prerogative powers and to subject their decisions to democratic debate. This might include, for example, a law requiring that Parliament approve any foreign combat mission. It would also be possible to put into statute the right of the ordinary public servant to resist political directives that are improper or indicate bad management practices (Savoie, 2008).

---

[9]The Reform Act passed in 2015 now provides a possible method by which a party caucus can choose to conduct a leadership review and appoint an interim leader. See Chapter 14.

As well, many of the standard reforms suggested by critics in the eras of constitutional and non-constitutional reform hold the possibility of reduced dominance by the central executive. These include the Senate reform, electoral system reform that would tilt the system toward more minority or coalition government scenarios, and provincial input into judicial appointments.

Of course, the context is important. Canadians now live in a world where the reigning idea is not government as such, but **governance** (the sharing by government of the process of governing with societal partners such as private sector organizations and non-governmental organizations). More and more, public, private, and non-governmental organizations (NGOs) are sharing power to effect change for public purposes. To some extent, the drifting away of the centralized power of the executive is a natural event and does not have to be planned. Cultural context is also important. A better-educated Canadian public is going to insist on more dialogue surrounding public policy to take place in more venues.

GOVERNANCE

The sharing by government of the process of governing with societal partners such as private sector organizations and non-governmental organizations; governing changes from the "command and control" model to the "partnership" model.

Summary and Conclusion

The executive has many faces to it and involves many issues. It has a formal face, which is presented to us in the Constitution Act—that of the Queen, governor general, and Queen's Privy Council for Canada. It has its informal but powerful face—the prime minister, cabinet, and bureaucracy. The formal face carries with it the still-powerful elements of the distant past: Prerogative and convention mark it even today and regulate its relations with the informal executive. Although issues arise from the formal side—the validity of monarchy in Canada and the pros and cons of having an elected head of state—by far the most pressing issues are in the political executive's ballpark. The reach of the prime minister's power seems to become more extensive with every new administration, and the recommendation for reforms more urgent.

The concentration of power in the hands of the prime minister and some influential advisers, particularly in the Privy Council Office and the Prime Minister's Office, raises important questions about the quality of democracy in Canada. Nevertheless, cabinet and cabinet committees continue to be an important part of the policymaking process, while the finance minister and department play the key role in the budgetary process.

Furthermore, particularly in a majority government situation, the ability of the House of Commons to provide an effective check on the power of the prime minister and cabinet is limited. The concentration of power could be viewed as resulting in effective government that is able to pursue a particular course of action. On the other hand, if good government is judged in terms of responsiveness, accountability, and transparency, then the concentration of power has to be viewed negatively.

In terms of representativeness, contemporary cabinets do not always fully represent the diversity of Canadian society. Nevertheless, they are much more diverse than cabinets before 1957, which included no women, ethnic or visible minorities, Aboriginals, or non-Christians. At the apex of power, only one woman, Kim Campbell, has held the office of prime minister; her prime ministership lasted for only a few months in 1993 before her Progressive Conservative party suffered a catastrophic election defeat. As well, with the exception of John Diefenbaker, all prime ministers have been of British or French ancestry.

Discussion Questions

1. Should Canada retain the monarchy?

2. Should the governor general always act on the advice of cabinet?

3. Did the governor general make the right decision in proroguing Parliament in 2008?

4. Is the prime minister too powerful?

5. Is it important to have a representative cabinet?

Further Readings

Aucoin, P., Smith, J., & Dinsdale, G. (2004). *Responsible government: Clarifying essentials, dispelling myths and exploring change.* Ottawa, ON: Canadian Centre for Management Development.

D'Ombrain, N. (2007). Cabinet secrecy. *Canadian Public Administration, 47,* 332–359.

Dunn, C. (2010). The central executive in Canadian government: Searching for the Holy Grail. In C. Dunn (Ed.). *The handbook of Canadian public administration* (2nd ed.). Toronto, ON: Oxford University Press.

Goldenberg, E. (2006). *The way it works: Inside Ottawa.* Toronto, ON: McClelland & Stewart.

Good, D.A. (2007). *The politics of public money: Spenders, guardians, priority setters, and financial watchdogs in the Canadian government.* Toronto, ON: University of Toronto Press.

Harris, M. (2014). *Party of One: Stephen Harper and Canada's Radical Makeover.* Toronto: Viking Canada.

Mallory, J.R. (1984). *The structure of Canadian government.* Toronto, ON: Gage.

Savoie, D. (1999). *Governing from the centre: The concentration of power in Canadian politics.* Toronto, ON: University of Toronto Press.

Savoie, D. (2008). *Court government and the collapse of accountability in Canada and the United Kingdom.* Toronto, ON: University of Toronto Press.

Simpson, G. (2001). *The friendly dictatorship.* Toronto, ON: McClelland & Stewart.

Ward, N. (1987). *Dawson's The Government of Canada.* Toronto, ON: University of Toronto Press.

Wells, P. (2013). *The longer I'm prime minister: Stephen Harper and Canada, 2006–.* Toronto: Random House Canada.

White, G. (2005). *Cabinets and first ministers.* Vancouver, BC: UBC Press.

Parliament

CHAPTER OBJECTIVES

After reading this chapter, you should be able to

1. Explain the origins and evolution of parliaments in Britain and Canada.
2. Describe the general functions of parliaments, as well as the specific functions of the House of Commons and the Senate of Canada.
3. Explain the functions of parliamentary committees and what forms they take.
4. Assess the effectiveness of the House of Commons.
5. Evaluate possible reforms to the Senate.

Although he was never childish about his duties, Pierre Trudeau was as capable of parliamentary antics as the next member of Parliament (MP). Here he is as a first-term MP, sliding down a banister at Ottawa's Château Laurier in 1968, a week before he became leader of the federal Liberal party.

© Courtesy Senator Wallin

Pierre Trudeau once said that Liberal backbenchers were "trained seals" who did the bidding of the government without thinking for themselves, and later described opposition MPs as "nobodies once they found themselves fifty yards from Parliament Hill." Although Canadians often look to the House of Commons as the centre of representative democracy, many observers point out that political power has shifted from Parliament to the executive. Does this mean the House of Commons is an irrelevant sideshow that only provides the illusion of democracy? Can the power of the representatives we elect be increased?

Ideas for shifting powers from the party leader to backbench MPs came from a surprising source: Conservative MP Michael Chong (who had gone against party policy to support the Kyoto Accord and to oppose a resolution recognizing Quebec as a nation) tabled a private member's bill (PMB), the Reform Act (Bill C-586), in December 2013 (Mas, 2013).

Having taken on the power structure around two of the most controversial issues in Canada—national unity and climate change—he challenged the very nature of the power structure itself. He was bothered by disempowered local party organizations and party caucuses, and party leaders who punished MPs for speaking out and who could stay in power interminably. He proposed that party caucuses be given the power to initiate a leadership review; that electoral district associations (EDAs), rather than the party leader, would have power to approve the party candidate; that there would be caucus votes for the election of caucus chairs and the expulsion and re-admission of caucus members; and that MPs could vote against a bill if constituents so desired.

Cross-party support for Bill C-586 encouraged Chong to continue his quest. Deconcentrating power is hard to achieve, however. The bill was softened in many ways to achieve support within and across the parties. Incorporating feedback he had received, Chong introduced an amended version of the bill the next spring (Chong, 2014). Rare for a PMB that did not have support of the prime minister, Chong's bill proceeded through the entire legislative process. A variety of amendments made the bill more acceptable to the prime minister.

In its final version, Bill C-586 removed the requirement in the Canada Elections Act that the party leader (or a representative) sign nomination papers of electoral candidates for the party. However, it did not specify who would sign; instead, a person or persons authorized by the party would be responsible for endorsing candidates. Thus a party could choose to give this power to the leader (Canadian Press, 2014, December 11). Bill C-586 also amended the Parliament of Canada Act to allow each party's caucus, at its first meeting after a general election, to vote on whether to adopt processes to expel and readmit members to the caucus, to elect or remove the caucus chair, and to conduct a leadership review and elect an interim leader.

With the passage of Bill C-586, it is up to each party's backbench MPs to rise to the challenge of empowering themselves so that they can no longer be labelled "nobodies."

THE GENERAL FUNCTIONS OF PARLIAMENTS

Parliaments are expected to carry out a variety of functions, many of which are of great importance in a democracy:

- *Representation.* Members of Parliament can voice the concerns and promote the interests of their constituents.
- *Conferring legitimacy.* Legitimation means that we feel obligated to obey laws that are fairly considered and duly passed. To ensure that laws are widely accepted as legitimate, they must be passed properly: widely accepted rules and procedures must be followed, a majority of each house votes for the act, and the laws should reflect the basic values of society.
- *Scrutiny.* Members of Parliament examine the proposals and actions of the executive.
- *Recruitment.* The prime minister chooses the cabinet from among the governing party's members of Parliament (almost all from the House of Commons).[1]

---

[1]Very occasionally, a Canadian prime minister has chosen a cabinet minister who does not hold a seat in Parliament, but this has been quickly followed by the person being elected to the Commons or appointed to the Senate. The appointment of Judy Manning to the Newfoundland cabinet in 2014 without seeking to be elected in a by-election received considerable criticism.

- *Law making.* Although the government presents most legislative proposals to Parliament, members of Parliament can play a role in law making by carefully examining legislative proposals and developing modifications to improve the proposals.
- *Financing government.* All bills for the raising and spending of public monies (which have to be recommended by the cabinet) must originate in the House of Commons and must be approved in both houses. An officer of Parliament, the auditor general, verifies the accuracy of public financial statements and the legitimacy of expenditures.
- *Political education.* Parliament raises and debates issues, and informs the public, using such instruments as question period, committee hearings and reports, and budget debates.
- *Accountability.* The government is obligated to submit its program to Parliament, defend it, and resign if the House of Commons lacks confidence in it.

This is not to suggest that the Canadian Parliament does a satisfactory job in tackling all of these functions. In this chapter, we will consider how successfully Parliament fulfills these functions. As well, we will examine the organization and operations of Parliament.

THE CANADIAN PARLIAMENT

Canada's Parliament consists of three elements: the House of Commons, the Senate, and the Queen. The citizens of each electoral district elect the members of the House of Commons (often referred to as members of Parliament, or MPs). In contrast, senators are appointed on the recommendation of the prime minister and hold office until their retirement at age 75. The governor general (representing the Queen) follows the advice of the prime minister and cabinet in granting royal assent to legislation passed by Parliament. The governor general does not participate in the deliberations of the two houses of Parliament. The governor general is expected to be non-partisan and not involved in politics, but does have the right to advise, encourage, and warn the prime minister and cabinet.

Parliament of Canada
www.parl.gc.ca/parlinfo

Parliament can be described as a **bicameral legislature**. That is, it has two chambers, each of which meets separately.[2] Both the House of Commons and the Senate must adopt legislation in identical form before it can be submitted to the governor general for royal assent. Each chamber has the authority to initiate most legislation; however, financial legislation has to be introduced by the government in the House of Commons.

BICAMERAL LEGISLATURE
A legislature with two chambers or houses.

---

[2]Although some provinces once had bicameral legislatures, all provincial legislatures are now unicameral.

British Roots

The British Parliament is called the "Mother of Parliaments" because of its age, having started in the thirteenth century, although some attribute this honour to proto-legislatures earlier in history. In 930, the first legislature, a one-house arrangement called the *Althing,* met in Iceland. There was also the example of the *Witan,* or *Witangemot* ("the assembly of the wise"), the council of the Anglo-Saxon kings. However, the British parliamentary model has proven to be the most exportable and flexible of the early models, so much so that it serves as the primary example in the literature of "parliamentary government."

There are three parts to Parliament, because over time three great estates—the Crown, the nobility, and the common people—vied for power. The evolution of Parliament can be traced to the rise and fall of each estate. In British history, effective power has passed from the Crown, to the Lords, to the Commons, and from the Commons to the executive.

The authority of the Commons was aided by the expansion of the franchise in the nineteenth century and the so-called Golden Age of Parliament, characterized by the ability of the Commons to defeat legislation and dismiss ministers on the floor of the House. In the twentieth century, the legislative and financial power of the Lords was curtailed further by the Parliament Acts of 1911 and 1949, which reduced to a month the Lords' delaying power for financial bills and, in 1949, one year for other bills. Most of those who held hereditary positions in the House of Lords were removed in 1999. However, by the twentieth century, the executive government had become dominant, so the Commons had won against the Crown and the Lords but faced an even more formidable rival.

The Evolution of Parliament in Canada

Canada's Parliament has evolved as well, but in a more compressed time frame. In 1840, the Act of Union established an elected Legislative Assembly for the United Province of Canada, but the increase in parliamentary influence did not come until 1848 after the adoption of the system of responsible government. At least nine ministries (governments) after 1848 had to resign, advise dissolution, or change their leadership and other personnel when they faced the possible loss of support of the Assembly. No ministry in the Province of Canada survived for what would now be called the government's normal life. Despite the existence of some firm factions and alignments, the ministries were overwhelmed by the more politically fickle "loose fish" and "ministerialists," who were faithful only to whichever government could supply them and their ridings with favours.

This pattern continued for about a decade in the new country of Canada, at which time the growth of disciplined parliamentary parties began to change the political dynamics considerably. Gradually parliamentary influence became

BOX 14-1

Canadian and American Legislatures: A Study in Contrast

Canadians are sometimes baffled by the workings of Parliament because so much of our news and popular entertainment highlights the U.S. Congress. Despite some similarities, there are fundamental differences between the two.

Both Canada and the United States share the tradition of bicameral legislatures. In both countries the upper house is called the Senate, although the American Senate is elected (with two senators from each state) while the Canadian Senate is appointed on the recommendation of the prime minister. In practice, the U.S. Senate is much more powerful than the Canadian Senate. The elected lower house is the House of Representatives in the United States and the House of Commons in Canada. Both legislatures have elaborate committee systems, although the committees are more influential and independent in the American system. Both Parliament and Congress have faced charges of losing influence in the face of encroaching executive power: in the United States, in the context of "the imperial presidency," and in Canada, in relation to "prime ministerial government."

One marked difference between the two systems is that the executive and legislature are constitutionally separate in the United States, whereas in Canada the executive and the legislature are connected. The American president is elected by the people and holds office for four years whether or not Congress supports the president's policies. Neither the president nor cabinet can be members of Congress, nor do they participate in congressional discussion.

The Canadian prime minister and cabinet are members of Parliament and must hold the continued support of the majority of the elected House. Furthermore, since the U.S. executive does not exercise rigid control over the legislative branch, individual members of Congress (with the support of a sizable staff) actively develop and propose policy, including budgetary measures. In Canada, Parliament's policy role is primarily to ratify policy and budgetary initiatives that come from the executive. Finally, although Congress is organized along party lines, like Parliament, party discipline is not as tight in Congress. Individual members of Congress do not usually rely heavily on financial support from their party to be elected, and often some members of the Democratic and Republican parties work together to promote or oppose particular policies. Overall, legislation is easier to pass in Parliament than in Congress.

more restricted. It amounted only to the right of the opposition to demand answers from the government and significant time allowed by the rules of the House for the opposition to criticize the government. Over the post-Confederation history of Parliament, only one government (that of Mackenzie King in 1926) has changed hands without an election held.

Overall, there are some differences between the contemporary Canadian and British Parliaments (including important differences between the House of Lords and the Senate and in the practice of party discipline). However, the U.S. Congress (and its governing system in general) differs much more dramatically from the Canadian Parliament and the parliamentary system (see Box 14-1: Canadian and American Legislatures: A Study in Contrast).

THE HOUSE OF COMMONS

Although the House of Commons is often termed the "lower house" and the Senate the "upper house," the House of Commons is clearly the more important of the two houses:

- The House of Commons is a **confidence chamber**, meaning that the life of the government of the day rests on the continued support of a majority of the members of the Commons. Defeat of government measures in the Senate is of no consequence for the cabinet's continuance.
- The Commons, whose members are elected, offers representative government. Unelected senators have trouble claiming that they represent the people of Canada.
- It is primarily the House that holds the government accountable for its actions. It is in the House that the government is expected to answer questions and respond to the criticism of the opposition parties, which have opportunities to scrutinize government management and expenditures.
- The House is where grievances and problems are usually raised and brought to the attention of the public and the media.

CONFIDENCE CHAMBER
A legislative body (in Canada, the House of Commons) whose continued majority support is necessary for the government to remain in office.

Representation in the House of Commons

The House of Commons hinges primarily on the concept of representation by population. Each province is entitled to a share of the seats in the House of Commons that is nearly proportionate to its share of the population. As discussed in Chapter 9, there are some qualifications to this principle, however, particularly to protect the representation of the smaller provinces. Nevertheless, the central Canadian provinces still dominate numerically. After the 2015 election, Ontario and Quebec together, with 62 percent of the population of Canada, comprise 58.9 percent of the Commons membership, with Ontario itself amounting to 35.8 percent of the Commons. Although representation by population is usually considered a key democratic principle, it means that the regional diversity of Canada is not fully reflected in the House of Commons, given the small number of members from some of the remote areas of the country.

STYLES OF REPRESENTATION   Political scientists have often analyzed three different styles of representation that an elected member might adopt. Members who view themselves as *delegates* will try to act according to the wishes of their constituents. *Trustees* will use their own judgment in acting in what they view as the best interests of their constituents and the country. *Politicos* combine these delegate and trustee roles (Docherty, 2005; Eulau, 1978). However, this analysis of representation is of limited usefulness in understanding the House of Commons.

Individual members of the House of Commons do spend considerable time putting forward the interests of the people of their electoral district. Opposition members, in particular, may raise concerns of their constituents in question period (Soroka, Penner, & Blidook, 2009). As well, MPs and their small staffs try to help constituents with the problems they face with government—such as getting a passport in a hurry, determining eligibility for an old-age pension, or helping family members immigrate to Canada. Furthermore, in the closed-door meetings of their party's **caucus**, MPs may alert their colleagues to the interests and viewpoints of people in their district and try to persuade their caucus to adopt certain policies and positions. To achieve this objective, they may meet regularly with other members of their own party from their province or with their party's members who have similar interests to make a stronger case. However, in the governing party, caucus often receives the legislative proposals of the government with little notice, which may not lead to much discussion before the legislation is presented to Parliament.

CAUCUS
Parliamentary members who belong to a particular party.

PARTY DISCIPLINE   Party discipline is usually very strict in the House of Commons. Once a party has decided on its position on a particular issue, its MPs are expected to vote in keeping with that position even if it clashes with the views and interests of their constituents. Therefore, all of the members of the governing party have almost always supported legislation proposed by the cabinet. Those who vote against government legislation that is considered a matter of confidence may find themselves ousted from their party's caucus and denied their party's nomination for the next election. Breaking party discipline can also have consequences for members of the opposition parties. With the exception of the very few "free votes" (where MPs are freed from party discipline) that have been held on matters of conscience, such as abortion and capital punishment, MPs rarely vote against the position taken by their party caucus. It is also rare for members of different parties from the same province or region to work together to advance the common interests of those they represent.

PARTY DISCIPLINE
The expectation that parliamentary members will vote in keeping with the position that their party has adopted in caucus.

The 2015 election platform of the Liberal party promised to "make free votes in the House of Commons standard practice. For members of the Liberal Caucus, all votes will be free votes with the exception of: those that implement the Liberal electoral platform; traditional confidence matters, like the budget; and those that address our shared values and the protections guaranteed by the Charter of Rights and Freedoms" (Liberal Party of Canada, 2015b, www.liberal.ca/realchange/freevotes).

Although the individual MP is not irrelevant, representation is primarily by political parties rather than by individuals acting as delegates or trustees of their constituents. Not surprisingly, this can create problems for MPs, who may be accused of acting against the interests or wishes of their constituents. However, party discipline does have advantages: The positions of each party are clearer, individual MPs are not pressured to act according to the wishes of powerful special interests, and each national party can try to develop a position on what it views as being in the interests of the country as a whole.

DIVERSITY AND REPRESENTATION   Representation can also be viewed in terms of the personal characteristics of the members of the House of Commons. With the proportion of women, Aboriginals, and visible minorities in the House being much smaller than their proportion of the population, observers often note that the House is unrepresentative of the diversity of the country. In addition, lawyers and businesspeople have been prominent among the MPs. Only a small proportion of MPs can be considered to be members of the working class, although farmers have made up a significant proportion of MPs.

Executive Domination

Executive domination is a fact of life for most legislatures in the world. Legislatures often do not have significant influence in policy and budget making, and parties and members of the legislature may not have enough funding to perform their roles effectively. In addition, legislative committees may lack independence and support staff, and opposition parties often have a limited ability to hold the government to account.

A significant degree of executive domination characterizes the Canadian Parliament. Four factors encourage executive domination.

1. *High rate of turnover in the national legislature* (see Table 14-1). Some elections result in new members making up more than a third of the Commons, which means that the executive may be able to exploit the inexperience of many members.
2. *Workload.* Relatively short sessions are the hallmark of the House of Commons, with one result being that part-time legislators confront full-time governments.
3. *Selectivity of the parliamentary press gallery.* The focus of media coverage tends to be on governments rather than on oppositions and on government policy announcements rather than on debates—tendencies that are enhanced by the shortness of legislative sessions.
4. *Tendency toward "executive federalism"* (discussed in Chapter 12). Decisions reached by executives at federal–provincial conferences cannot easily be modified and often cannot be retracted without considerable embarrassment.

Executive dominance is often seen as a challenge to representative and responsible government. Citizens elect members to *represent* them in the legislature, and the executive (cabinet) is directly *responsible* to the legislature (and thus indirectly responsible to the public). If the House loses confidence in the executive, so the theory goes, the legislature can support a new ministry or a general election can be imposed, as decided by the governor general. Generally, however, responsible government makes itself evident in less dramatic

GENERAL ELECTION DATE	NEW MEMBERS OF PARLIAMENT	PERCENTAGE OF TOTAL
1968	97 of 264	37
1972	95 of 282	34
1974	50 of 282	18
1979	98 of 282	35
1980	43 of 282	15
1984	133 of 295	45
1988	116 of 295	39
1993	199 of 301	66
1997	84 of 301	28
2000	45 of 301	15
2004	101 of 308	33
2006	65 of 308	21
2008	65 of 308	21
2011	111 of 308	36
2015	200 of 338	59

TABLE 14-1

TURNOVER IN PARLIAMENT: NUMBER AND PERCENTAGE OF NEW ELECTED MEMBERS IN THE HOUSE OF COMMONS, BY GENERAL ELECTION 1968–2015

SOURCE: Data from the Library of Parliament, Canada. http://www2.parl.gc.ca/parlinfo/default.aspx?Menu=Hom. Unofficial results from CBC News, "The New House of Commons," October 20, 2015, http://www.cbc.ca/news/politics/multimedia/the-new-house-of-commons-more-women-and-aboriginal-mps-1.3280256.

ways such as the necessity for the government to allow enough legislative opportunities for scrutiny and debate, to respond to criticism, and to disclose enough information to keep legislators and the public informed about the actions and decisions of government. When the government tries to thwart the will of the House by proroguing it (ending a session) in the face of a sure defeat in the Commons (as occurred in 2008), or when it avoids scrutiny and disclosure, the responsible government system is undermined.

However, executive dominance offers some positive features. Many of the policies that are today regarded as central to Canadian life came not from parliamentary initiative but from the executive—and more often than not from a prime minister willing to drive an initiative through over the objections of parliamentarians and even cabinets. This was the case with the maple leaf flag, the Constitution Act of 1982, free trade, and many others. The fact that so much power is concentrated in the hands of a few individuals makes for decisive, purposeful action on pressing policy issues. It also allows for relatively swift action and quick responses to emergencies. As well, it should be noted that the Constitution mandates a certain kind of executive domination in taxation and spending matters, placing fiscal initiative and direction plainly in the hands of the federal cabinet. Having fiscal planning in the hands of both the legislature and the executive might promote irresponsibility and lack of accountability. Governments would not have to take responsibility for finances, since Parliament would be involved in deciding them, and consequently there would be no clear set of individuals to accept praise or blame.

Furthermore, it can be argued that in a diverse country with distinct cultures and a limited sense of national identity, executive dominance at the federal and provincial level can bolster national unity. Prime ministers and premiers or other federal and provincial executives may be able to reach agreements or understandings through elite accommodation—that is, a process of bargaining and compromise—that allows the country to function. In the more public and adversarial environment of legislatures, it may be more difficult to gain acceptance for unpopular compromises. Nevertheless, as discussed in Chapter 12, the process of elite accommodation has been challenged as being undemocratic, and meetings of the prime minister and the 13 premiers have often been infrequent and unproductive.

"JUDICIAL SUPREMACY" AND PARLIAMENT   The threat to parliaments may come not only from the executive, but from the judiciary as well. There is a school of thought that sees "judicial supremacy" as the rising reality. The courts dictate what the other two branches can do since the Constitution is what they say it is. This view has its supporters and its detractors as discussed in Chapters 10 and 16.

MINORITY AND MAJORITY GOVERNMENT   Executive dominance is particularly strong when one party holds a majority of seats in the House of Commons—that is, a *majority government*. By imposing party discipline on its members, the prime minister and cabinet can be almost certain that the House will pass the legislation and financial measures they propose. In addition, the government does not have to worry about losing the confidence of the House, and thus can govern for a full four-year term without an election.

If the governing party does not hold a majority of seats in the House and forms a *minority government*, the ability of the prime minister and cabinet to dominate Parliament is more limited. In this case, the prime minister normally has to bargain and negotiate with one (or more) of the other parties in the House for support or risk losing power on a vote of non-confidence (see Box 14-2: A Minority Government Hangs in the Balance). Alternatively, the cabinet could introduce proposals that opposition parties are unwilling to defeat. If opposition parties are reluctant to force an election, the cabinet may be able to pass its key proposals with one or more opposition parties abstaining from those votes, as occurred during the Harper Conservative minority governments.

Just as is the case with executive dominance, there is division among political scientists with regard to governmental and parliamentary performance under conditions of minority (and coalition) government. Some tend to see them as unwelcome aberrations in governance and welcome their demise. Professor C.E.S. Franks (1987) noted that majority governments tended to be more efficient and that minority governments tended to compromise responsibility and accountability. There is also the notion that minority governments are not appropriate instruments to deal with the complexities of governance in

BOX 14-2

A Minority Government Hangs in the Balance

It was the afternoon of Thursday, May 19, 2005, and the atmosphere in the House of Commons was electric. The fate of the minority government of Paul Martin, in office only a year, hung in the balance.

To prevent being defeated on its budget, the Liberal government had agreed to a demand by the New Democratic Party for an amendment that added an additional $4.6 billion in the budget for social programs. Even with the support of the NDP, the Liberals needed additional votes to stave off defeat by the combined forces of the Conservative party and the Bloc Québécois.

Conservative star Belinda Stronach had recently crossed the floor of the House to join the Liberals and was rewarded with a cabinet position. Independent MP Carolyn Parrish (who had been expelled from the Liberal caucus after a TV appearance in which she stomped on a doll representing American president George W. Bush) decided to support the Liberals. Likewise, independent MP David Kilgour opted to vote with the Liberals. With the government still having one vote fewer than those determined to bring it down, attention became focused on another independent MP, Chuck Cadman.

Cadman was first elected as a Reform party MP in 1987, and represented Surrey North (BC) as an independent after losing the Conservative party nomination in 2004. The independent MP, whose decision could topple the government, did not make up his mind until a half hour before the vote. To add to the drama, Cadman had malignant melanoma and did not have long to live. He literally raised himself up from his sickbed to attend the vote. Suffering was etched in Cadman's face, but he knew his vote was important. When Cadman voted for the amendment, he said the deciding factor was a poll he had taken in his district, where a sizable majority made it clear that they did not want an election. His vote created a tie: 152 to 152. Citing convention, the speaker, Peter Milliken, voted for the amendment, which passed by one vote.

Chuck Cadman died on July 9, 2005. His widow, Dona Cadman (elected as a Conservative in the 2008 election), said her husband told her that he had turned down an offer from two Conservative party officials of a $1 million life insurance policy in exchange for his vote. However, the RCMP claimed they found no evidence to support a charge of bribing an MP. When Cadman died, the story of the bribe was buried with him, and the minority government of Paul Martin survived for another eight months. Then the NDP, influenced by the intensifying Liberal sponsorship scandal, decided to vote with the Conservatives and the Bloc to defeat the government and force an election, which resulted in a Conservative minority government.

the twenty-first century. Decisive action rather than delay is necessary in the face of economic recession, military missions, and diplomatic initiatives. There is also the danger that minority governments may be forced into compromises with the third parties that force public expenditures to increase unduly. Lastly, they tend to be unstable, argue the detractors, and may encourage indecision and endless compromises. The sense of citizen efficacy may decline, with politicians listening more to each other than to the public.

In recent decades, Canadians have learned to live with minority governments and often find value in them. As Table 14-2 demonstrates, there have been nine minority governments since the mid-1950s, and some of them have

TABLE 14-2
FEDERAL MINORITY GOVERNMENTS IN CANADA, 1921–2011

MINISTRY	GENERAL ELECTION	TERM OF PARLIAMENT	HOUSE OF COMMONS SITTING DAYS	MINORITY*
William Lyon Mackenzie King	June 12, 1921	March 8, 1922, to June 27, 1925	366	Government—116 Opposition—119 Minority—3
William Lyon Mackenzie King (to June 28, 1926) Arthur Meighen (June 29, 1926 to September 24, 1926)	October 29, 1925	January 7, 1926, to July 2, 1926	111 (Meighen met the House for three of those days)	Government—99 Opposition—146 Minority—47
John George Diefenbaker	June 10, 1957	October 14, 1957, to February 1, 1958	78	Government—112 Opposition—153 Minority—41
John George Diefenbaker	June 18, 1962	September 27, 1962, to February 6, 1963	72	Government—116 Opposition—149 Minority—33
Lester Bowles Pearson	April 8, 1963	May 16, 1963, to September 8, 1965	418	Government—129 Opposition—136 Minority—7
Lester Bowles Pearson	November 8, 1965	January 18, 1966, to April 23, 1968	405	Government—131 Opposition—134 Minority—3
Pierre Elliott Trudeau	October 30, 1972	January 4, 1973, to May 9, 1974	256	Government—109 Opposition—155 Minority—46
Charles Joseph (Joe) Clark	May 22, 1979	October 9, 1979, to December 14, 1979	49	Government—136 Opposition—146 Minority—10
Paul Martin	June 28, 2004	October 4, 2004, to November 29, 2005	160	Government—135 Opposition—173 Minority—38
Stephen Harper	January 23, 2006	April 3, 2006, to September 7, 2008	292	Government—124 Opposition—184 Minority—60
Stephen Harper	October 14, 2008	October 29, 2008, to March 26, 2011	262	Government—143 Opposition—165 Minority—22

*As at the general election.

SOURCE: Based on O'Neal, B., & Bedard, M. (2011, April 11). *Government of Canada's 41st Parliament: Questions and Answers.* Parliamentary information and research service, Library of Parliament. Table prepared by the authors using data from *Sitting Days of the House of Commons by Calendar Year: 1968 to Date*, Parliament of Canada.

been of long duration. Political science professor Peter Russell says that there may be more to come, but that Canadians should not fear but welcome them in view of their significant advantages. One is that minority governments are a way of mitigating executive dominance, and especially "prime ministerial government." The charge of chronic instability is not borne out internationally or even nationally. As Table 14-2 shows, more than half of the minority governments since 1921 have lasted more than 150 sitting days, and of these, six lasted more than 250. (Sitting days are not always the same as calendar days.) As Russell (2008) points out, a few adept reforms to Parliament—fixed election dates, regulating the role of the governor general by formal rules, formal written agreements between parties, and electoral reform—could all bring a measure of stability to minority government situations. Alternatively, many democracies regularly feature coalition government in which two or more parties share in governing with cabinet positions divided among the coalition partners (as, for example, the United Kingdom's coalition government from 2011 to 2015).

The Organization and Operations of the House

PRESIDING OFFICERS OF THE HOUSE   A variety of members and officials are necessary to keep the House of Commons working (see Figure 14-1). The **speaker** acts as the presiding officer for the Commons, which means applying

SPEAKER
The presiding officer of the House of Commons, who is responsible for applying the rules and procedures, maintaining order in debate, and overseeing the administration of the Commons.

FIGURE 14-1
THE HOUSE OF COMMONS

1 Speaker
2 Pages
3 Government Members*
4 Opposition Members*
5 Prime Minister
6 Leader of the Official Opposition
7 Leader of the Second Largest Party in Opposition
8 Clerk and Table Officers
9 Mace
10 Hansard Reporters
11 Sergeant-at-Arms
12 The Bar
13 Interpreters
14 Press Gallery
15 Public Gallery
16 Official Gallery
*Depending on the number of MPs elected from each political party, some government members may be seated on the opposite side of the chamber with opposition members (or vice versa).

SOURCE: *Report to Canadians*, 2008. URL: http://www.parl.gc.ca/About/House/ReportToCanadians/2008/rtc2008_3e.html. House of Commons, 2008. Reproduced with the permission of the House of Commons.

the rules and procedures that have been devised by the chamber itself. The speaker also has the responsibility to see that parliamentary privilege is protected, that the rights and prerogatives of both the majority and the minority are recognized and upheld, and that order in debate is maintained. He or she is expected to be impartial in the exercise of the position's duties. As well, the speaker is responsible for overseeing the administration of the House of Commons, although the clerk of the House of Commons, a permanent official, looks after the day-to-day administration of the House and advises the speaker. The Board of Internal Economy, which approves the expenditures of the House, is chaired by the speaker.

As we saw in Box 14-2, by convention the speaker (who is an elected MP usually representing a particular party) does not cast a vote unless it is to break a tie, and that is usually done to maintain the status quo. In the past, the prime minister chose this key parliamentary presiding officer, usually from the governing party and alternating between English- and French-speaking speakers. Since 1986, however, the speaker has been chosen by a secret ballot of the members of the House of Commons. This reform was designed to try to ensure that the speaker would enjoy the respect of the House and not be viewed as a representative of the prime minister and the governing party. Peter Milliken, Liberal MP for Kingston and the Islands, was elected speaker four times; he served while both Liberals and Conservatives have been the governing party. Upon Milliken's retirement in 2011, Conservative MP Andrew Scheer became the new speaker, chosen from a field of eight after six rounds of voting by members in the Forty-First Parliament. In 2015, Liberal Geoff Regan was elected speaker by a preferential ballot.

The **leader of Her Majesty's Loyal Opposition** is more than a consolation prize—it is a key position in Canada's parliamentary system. This is usually the person who leads the second-largest party in the House and who would normally be considered the most likely to be prime minister in the event of a change in government. Thus, it is the duty of the leader of the opposition to be familiar with the actions and policies of the government, to appoint opposition party members as critics to "shadow" all government portfolios (sometimes referred to as the "shadow cabinet"), and to go about preparing an alternative program by which to govern. The leaders of the other opposition parties also appoint their members as critics to scrutinize the activities of particular ministers and their departments and to develop their party's policy positions.

The **House leaders** are members of each party in the Commons who are tasked by their party leaders (in the case of the government House leader, the prime minister) to be the chief strategists for their party. This means negotiating with the other House leaders on a parliamentary timetable and seeking out broad plans for getting the message of the party onto the floor of the House and in committees. The **party whips** are similarly members of each parliamentary party whose job is to maintain party discipline; make sure that members attend for crucial votes; and hand out crucial favours such as good offices, parliamentary trips, and placement on the list of speakers in question period.

LEADER OF HER MAJESTY'S LOYAL OPPOSITION
The person who usually leads the second-largest party in the House and who would normally be considered the most likely to be prime minister in the event of a change in government.

HOUSE LEADERS
Members of each party who are responsible for their party's strategy in the House of Commons, including negotiating the parliamentary timetable with other House leaders.

PARTY WHIPS
Members of each party who maintain party discipline and ensure that members attend votes.

THE PARLIAMENTARY SCHEDULE   "A parliament" is the term used to denote the life of the legislature between elections. For example, the Thirty-Ninth Parliament was elected in 2006 and continued until it was dissolved and an election was called in 2008. A parliament begins with its summoning and calling together by the governor general and ends with its dissolution (or termination) by proclamation of the governor general. The life of a parliament is subdivided into smaller periods: sessions, sittings, adjournments, and prorogations. *Sessions* are the periods into which parliaments are split; they do not necessarily correspond to calendar years and can be of any length, and there is no set number per parliament. A session is composed of many *sittings*. Sittings are meetings of the House, as directed by the Standing Orders of the House, and do not necessarily have to correspond to days. Sittings are ended by *adjournments,* which are the periods, generally short (a few hours or weeks), between sittings. A session of parliament is ended by a *prorogation,* and the period of time between sessions is referred to as a *recess.* Prorogations have the effect of ending the work of committees and official duties of individual members. If the next session should see fit, these may be resumed at the will of the House, but this is not guaranteed.

The first session of a new parliament sees some events that are not repeated in subsequent sessions: the summoning of the parliament, the swearing in of new members, and the election of the speaker. Each session opens with the governor general reading the **Speech from the Throne**. The Speech from the Throne (written under the direction of the prime minister) is the government's indication of what it considers to be the state of the country, together with a general outline of the kinds of legislation that it has planned for the session. Speeches from the Throne are generally regarded as lacking in any meaningful detail, sometimes derisively referred to as containing nothing but "governor generalities." However, during the minority governments of 2004–2011, the speech took on greater strategic importance with more pointed appeals designed to prevent a defeat on a confidence vote. The January 2009 Throne Speech, for example, adopted a conciliatory tone because a proposed Liberal–NDP coalition government had been set in motion by the Conservatives' combative economic statement. The Throne Speech is followed by six days allotted for the Throne Speech Debate—a wide-ranging opportunity for all parties to score political points. The Standing Orders provide for a vote of confidence at the end of the Throne Speech Debate.

The **budget** (often scheduled for February) is one of the highlights of the session. The budget's main task is to deliver news of tax increases or decreases as well as other revenue and borrowing measures, and to outline the state of the economy and government finances in general. The budget speech is always delivered by the minister of finance and is the government's major policy statement of the session. In recent years, the finance minister has even begun to monopolize the announcement of new programs in budget speeches and economic statements. The budget is followed by a four-day debate, at the end of

SPEECH FROM THE THRONE
Government's indication of what it considers to be the state of the country, together with a general outline of the kinds of legislation that it has planned for the parliamentary session the speech introduces.

BUDGET
Government statement that proposes tax increases or decreases as well as other revenue and borrowing measures, outlines the state of the economy and government finances in general, and often includes announcements of major new programs.

Each parliamentary session opens with the reading of the Speech from the Throne, in which the government describes the state of the country and provides a general outline of the kinds of legislation planned for the session.

© Adrian Wyld/Fred Chartrand/CP

ESTIMATES
The money the government says is needed by government departments and agencies for the next fiscal year.

A Typical Day in the House
**www.parl.gc.ca/About/House/
compendium/web-content/c_g_
typicalsittingday-e.htm**

which is the next scheduled opportunity for the opposition parties to introduce a vote of non-confidence. Although the budget occurs only once during a session, governments often provide economic and fiscal updates or statements in the fall to adjust the projections made in the budget and, sometimes, to announce new taxing and spending proposals.

The tabling of the **estimates** usually follows very closely on the budget and is the next major matter of business for the House for a very good reason. Financial matters were historically the major power that the Commons had to assert its will versus the executive, and there are still elements of that authority today. The House asserts its control not only by insisting on its right to determine how the government may raise money, but also what the government can spend it on. The government must submit all of its expenditures to the House for approval, and it does not have the right to spend money that has not been approved by Parliament and, more importantly, by the House. Parliament does not offer extra revenue or extra expenditure to the government on its own because this would provide the executive with extra room to manoeuvre and defeat the purpose for which Parliament came into being centuries ago.

The degree to which the House can still perform its function of controlling government expenditures is a matter of debate. In 1965 experimentally, and again in 1968 permanently, the House decided to leave the detailed examination of departmental estimates to standing committees and to have them report back by a strict deadline. If they do not finish estimates review by the deadline, they are considered to have reported back anyway and the estimates proceed to the House for approval. The common consensus among academics and parliamentarians alike is that the committees have not done a particularly good job at estimates review. The committees do not take the job seriously and are overly partisan in their work. They also lack the mechanisms that could force the government's hand, particularly the ability to delay the passage of spending programs.

THE PASSAGE OF BILLS   The rest of the session of the House of Commons is devoted primarily to the consideration of bills (proposed laws). **Public bills** have an impact on the whole of society or are designed to promote the general welfare. Most of the bills passed are government public bills that a minister introduces on behalf of the cabinet. **Private members' bills** are public bills put forward by a member of Parliament who is not a cabinet minister. Private members' bills cannot involve the imposition of taxes or the spending of public money for a new and distinct purpose without the approval of cabinet. Although a large number of private members' bills are put forward every session, traditionally only a very small number are passed, unless the government supports them. There is, for example, a perception that the Harper government often lent support to some bills put forward by Conservative party backbenchers to act as its "stalking horse" on controversial issues. To allow the possibility of a private member's bill to be passed in the limited time available for private members' business, a lottery system is used to select and rank 30 bills, from which a House of Commons committee chooses five to be debated and voted on. **Private bills** are those of concern to a limited group, such as an individual, a corporation, or a charity. For example, the incorporation of a chartered bank requires approval by a private bill. Private bills are generally introduced first in the Senate and examined most closely by that chamber. Government public bills can also be introduced in the Senate, although this is much less common than introduction in the House.

The Canadian Parliament (like other legislatures that follow the British model) requires that bills be approved on three separate occasions, or "readings," in the House of Commons and three times in the Senate, as well as being subject to a detailed committee examination (see Figure 14-2). The first reading in the House is basically a formality to introduce the bill. The second reading typically features considerable debate in the House and can result in the approval of the bill in principle. The bill then normally goes to one of the standing committees of the House for detailed "clause-by-clause" analysis. Amendments to the proposed legislation are often made at the committee stage. These amendments cannot, however, change the basic principles of the bill. The bill and the amendments agreed to by the committee are then reported back to the Commons ("report stage"). Any member of the House can also propose amendments at this stage, although the speaker decides which amendments are debatable. The Commons votes to accept or reject the amendments. The bill then proceeds to third reading for final approval by the House. If, as is usually the case, the bill was first introduced in the House of Commons, the bill then proceeds to the Senate, where it undergoes a similar process. If the Senate passes the bill in identical wording, the bill can proceed to royal assent (approval by the governor general on the advice of the prime minister and

PUBLIC BILLS
Proposed laws that have an impact on the whole of society or are designed to promote the general welfare.

PRIVATE MEMBERS' BILLS
Public bills put forward by a member of Parliament who is not in the cabinet.

PRIVATE BILLS
Proposed laws that are of concern to a limited group.

FIGURE 14-2
STAGES IN THE PASSAGE OF BILLS, PARLIAMENT OF CANADA

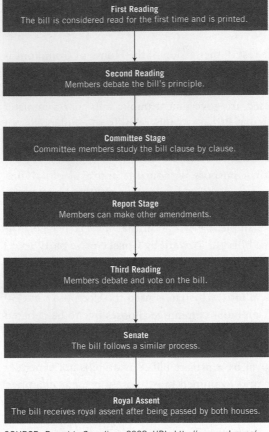

First Reading
The bill is considered read for the first time and is printed.

Second Reading
Members debate the bill's principle.

Committee Stage
Committee members study the bill clause by clause.

Report Stage
Members can make other amendments.

Third Reading
Members debate and vote on the bill.

Senate
The bill follows a similar process.

Royal Assent
The bill receives royal assent after being passed by both houses.

SOURCE: *Report to Canadians*, 2008. URL: http://www.parl.gc.ca/ About/House/ReportToCanadians/2008/rtc2008_3e.html. House of Commons, 2008. Reproduced with the permission of the House of Commons.

cabinet). If the Senate has amended or rejected the bill, it goes back to the House and cannot be passed until both Houses of Parliament are in agreement. Finally, the government can decide when (or if) the new law (an act of Parliament, also known as a statute) is proclaimed (i.e., comes into effect).

Reforms designed to enhance the importance of the House of Commons have created the possibility for bills to be sent to a special legislative committee after first reading rather than the normal second reading to allow for review of the proposed legislation without being limited by the bill's approval in principle. A special legislative committee can, therefore, propose substantial changes to bills. To date, however, only a few bills have followed this procedure.

The passage of legislation is time-consuming. Since the government typically has many bills it would like to be passed during a parliamentary session, the allocation of time to debating government public bills is often contentious. While the government would prefer to rush legislation through

Parliament, the opposition parties want to voice their criticism of legislation, often in the hope that public pressure will lead the government to back down and withdraw the bill, or at least to modify the proposal by accepting amendments proposed by the opposition.

However, the Standing Orders (SO) of the House allow for three aggressive time management motions that allow government to speed passage of legislation in a fashion which curtails debate. **Closure (SO 57)** can be invoked to prevent further adjournment of debate on any matter and to require that the question be put (i.e., a vote be taken) before the end of the sitting to which a motion of closure is adopted. From 1913 (when it originated to help government pass the controversial Naval Bill) to 1999, it was applied only to the stage of debate being debated; after 1999, it could be applied to all stages. Closure has been used to cut off debate on some important issues, such as the free trade agreements and the goods and services tax. Historically, this has been considered an extreme, undemocratic measure as it means that individual MPs may be prevented from discussing the proposed legislation. However, in recent decades closure has been used more often. More frequently, a second technique, **time allocation** adopted in 1968, is used to set the amount of time provided for debate on a bill. If House leaders cannot agree on time allocation, a minister by SO 78(3) may introduce a motion allocating the time for the stage of the bill that is being debated, provided that at least one day is allocated. A *routine motion by a minister* can also be used as a time management technique. SO 56(1) allows a minister during routine proceedings to request that the speaker "put the motion forthwith, without debate or amendment" if, previous to this, unanimous consent has been requested and denied for presentation of a routine motion. Introduced in 1991, and intended to be used for routine procedural matters and not to limit debate on bills at various stages, it has nevertheless sometimes been used to the latter effect (Plante, 2013).

Determining the appropriateness of using time management involves a value judgement about the balance between the government's need to expedite public business and the opposition's right to debate extensively and, if necessary, oppose legislation. It is obvious, however, that governments are getting progressively more intolerant of opposition prerogatives. Figures researched by Francois Plante tell a tale of an increased tempo of debate curtailment. Only 2.8 percent of the 5278 government bills introduced since the Twelfth Parliament began in 1912 have been the subject of the time management techniques outlined. From 1912 to June 2012, closure was used 56 times, 23 of which were applied to various motions and 33 of which were to curtail debate on a total of 24 bills. Time allocation under SO 78(3) was imposed 168 times. This was aimed at 118 bills and 241 stages of bills. Routine motions by ministers were used 24 times, most in the 10 year period after its introduction (Plante, 2013: 29–31). However, in the first year of the Harper majority government (2011–2012), Plante found that closure and time allocations

CLOSURE
A motion in the House of Commons to limit debate on a bill.

TIME ALLOCATION
A motion in the House of Commons that allocates the time that can be spent debating a bill.

limited debate on one-third of the government bills, "an abnormally high proportion" (Plante, 2013)

Governments have frequently resorted to another more unorthodox method of expediting their legislative programs. **Omnibus bills**, so named because they are large amalgams of many sorts of unrelated legislation, have become increasingly common. When they were used in the past, they stood out by their rarity and unusual nature. Liberal Pierre Trudeau instigated three (1968, 1971, and 1982), and Conservative Brian Mulroney one (in 1988, implementing free trade) (**Bédard, 2012**).

The Harper Conservative government came to depend on omnibus budget bills:

> [B]etween 1994 and 2005, the 12 budget implementation bills passed with the Liberals in power averaged just under 74 pages. Under the Conservatives, such bills have swollen exponentially. In 2006, the Conservatives tabled two budget bills totalling more than 300 pages. In 2007, the two bills combined for more than 500 pages. In 2009, more than 600 pages. In 2010, more than a thousand pages—including a single bill, C-9, that numbered 904 pages. While efforts were made to split up C-9, they languished. With the government in a minority position at the time, any effort to amend or defeat a budget bill could have been considered a confidence measure, and may have triggered yet another election. (Wherry, 2013)

By 2010, omnibus bills had become commonplace, as Table 14-3 shows.

Bill C-38 exemplified the flaws and benefits of omnibus legislation. Critics noted that many of the matters it dealt with—such as downloading federal environmental responsibilities to provincial governments, eventually raising the age of eligibility for Old Age Security from 65 to 67, and changing the nature of the employment insurance program—were not budget measures but matters of policy, unannounced in the 2011 Conservative election manifesto and deserving of separate and detailed debate in the interests of democracy and respect for Parliament (*Globe and Mail*, 2012). Defenders of the approach said that doing otherwise would have meant that the government's program would have been delayed, possibly until late in the government's mandate. Some bills are omnibus in nature by necessity, in fact. This is the case for laws that involve updating statutes or bringing legislation into line with the Charter, or court decisions. The question is one of balance, and respect for Parliament. Speaker of the House Lucien Lamoureux, reluctantly ruling on the admissibility of the Government Organization Act in 1971, posed the basic issue: "However, where do we stop? Where is the point of no return? . . . [W]e might reach the point where we would have only one bill, a bill at the start of the session for the improvement of the quality of life in Canada which would include every single proposed piece of legislation for the session" (House of Commons Journals, 1971, January 26,

YEAR INTRODUCED	BILL	DESCRIPTION
2010	Bill C-10, the Safe Streets and Communities Act	An omnibus crime bill, comprising nine separate measures
2012	Bill C-38, the Jobs, Growth and Long-term Prosperity Act	A 425-page budget implementation bill, the 753 clauses of which modified or amended 69 acts
2012	Bill C-45, the Jobs and Growth Act	An omnibus budget implementation bill (consisting of 450 pages of changes to 60 pieces of legislation)
2014	Bill C-31, the Economic Action Plan 2014 Act, No. 1	A 359-page bill that changed 40 different pieces of legislation
2014	Bill C-43, the Economic Action Plan 2014 Act, No. 2	A 443-page bill including changes to 64 pieces of legislation, that was later split
2015	Bill C-51, the Anti-Terrorism Act	An omnibus public safety bill amending several acts and granting sweeping new powers to CSIS

TABLE 14-3
OMNIBUS BILLS, FEDERAL PARLIAMENT, 2010-2015

SOURCE: Author calculations.

pp. 284–285). The 2015 Liberal election platform promised to change the House of Commons Standing Orders to bring an end to the undemocratic practice of omnibus bills.

The opposition parties have some ability to slow down the process of passing government bills. Limits apply to the length of time that an individual member can speak, but if each member uses the full allotment of time, this can slow down the passage of legislation. Similarly, proposing numerous amendments, requesting recorded votes at each reading, raising points of order, and using other techniques can sometimes result in the government bargaining with the opposition to modify the legislation or occasionally to withdraw controversial legislation that the government does not view as a high priority.

One additional opposition tactic can be to "filibuster" or, technically, to generate debate on a "hoist motion." The filibustering party or parties can move to "hoist"—that is, defer debate—on a bill for a specified period, say three or six months. This is useful for the opposition, since it suspends debate on the main item as long as the party can present MPs to speak to the motion for their allotted amount of time. Most filibusters are of limited effect, mostly used to attract public attention to certain bills, like the 2011 back-to-work legislation which the NDP filibustered for 58 hours before the legislation was passed.

ACCOUNTABILITY Although the House devotes much of its time to the passage of legislation and other government business, it also sets aside time for the opposition parties to try to hold the government accountable for its actions. Of particular importance is the daily 45-minute oral question period in which members, particularly from the opposition, can question the ministers and the ministers can respond. Question period is the highlight of the day in the House of Commons—it receives almost all of the media attention as the opposition raises criticisms of the government on hot-button issues and the ministers defend the government, often by launching a counterattack on the opposition. Four days a week, a half-hour debate on adjournment (known as the "late show") also provides an opportunity for a few members to discuss further an issue raised in question period. In addition, although most of the session of the House is devoted primarily to government's business, 20 "opposition days" are provided (in addition to the days allotted to debate on the Throne Speech and the budget), in which motions by the opposition (including motions of non-confidence) receive priority.[3]

House of Commons Committees
www.parl.gc.ca/CommitteeBusiness/
Default.aspx

HOUSE OF COMMONS COMMITTEES   Visitors to the House of Commons or those who watch the parliamentary channel are often surprised when, except during question period, they see only a small number of MPs in the House. What they may not realize is that much of the work of the Commons is done in committee, and thus members are often busy with committee meetings that typically run simultaneously with meetings of the House. Committees are very useful because they can examine witnesses, question leading bureaucrats, hold public hearings (including hearings in different parts of the country), engage in detailed consideration of legislation and estimates, and provide oversight of government. Ordinary members of Parliament often view their work in committees as the most satisfying part of their job, as committees are often less partisan than the strongly adversarial nature of the House. This can provide an opportunity for MPs to work with committee members from other parties to help shape laws and policies.

There are five different types of committees: standing committees, legislative committees, special committees, Committees of the Whole, and joint committees.

STANDING COMMITTEES
Permanent committees of the House whose responsibilities include detailed examination of proposed legislation and review of departmental estimates.

Standing committees are permanent committees whose terms of reference are established by the Standing Orders of the House. Many of the standing committees parallel equivalent departments of government, such as the committees on fisheries and oceans, health, and national defence. Others deal with special topics such as access to information, privacy, and ethics; procedure and house affairs; and public accounts. Most bills go to the appropriate standing committee after second reading in the House. Likewise, a standing committee will review the estimates of the particular department that it parallels. In addition, committees can review relevant department-specific statute law, policy objectives, program effectiveness, and regulations. They also are able to

---

[3]However, the government determines when these days will be held and thus can delay a non-confidence motion that might result in the defeat of the government.

launch independent investigations as they see fit on the mandate, management, organization, and operation of the department(s) assigned to them by the House.

Committees are no longer as large as they once were; instead of having 20 to 30 members, as was the case before 1984, all of the 24 standing committees as of February 2015 had 10 members. As a result, committees have tended to become more businesslike, and a degree of cooperation can develop that softens rigid loyalty to party. However, partisan political considerations still influence the workings of committees (as was the case in the first two Harper Parliaments in the last decade). The members of each committee are chosen so as to approximately reflect the proportion of each party's members in the House. The committee members elect the committee chairs and vice-chairs.[4] Members of the governing party chair most committees, with the vice-chairs representing the opposition parties. However, members of the Official Opposition party chair five committees, including the Public Accounts Committee, which deals with the Auditor General's Report. There are as well two standing joint committees of the House and Senate, one dealing with the Library of Parliament, the other with the Scrutiny of Regulations (also known as delegated or subordinate legislation). One permanent (but not standing) committee, the seven-member Liaison Committee, decides on resources for all standing committees.

Legislative committees are appointed by the House to review specific bills or, occasionally, to prepare and bring in a bill. They cease to exist with the submission of their report. The Speaker appoints the chair of a legislative committee. For example, legislative committees were used to review the Copyright Act in 2011 and the Canadian Wheat Board Act in 2012.

Special committees are chosen to study an issue, with their existence limited to the duration of the study or to the end of the session. Their terms of reference end with prorogation, but they may be continued into a new session with the agreement of the Commons. In 2015 there was one such committee, the Special Committee on Violence Against Indigenous Women.

Committees of the Whole are composed of the membership of the entire House and were once used extensively for consideration of financial bills and legislation. Supply (spending) motions are the only bills regularly referred to Committees of the Whole, although the House may go into the Whole on other matters if it wishes. The incentive for moving to such a committee is informality. The speaker is not in the chair and the rules of debate and procedure are relaxed. "Take notice" proceedings, where the government gauges the will of the Commons on a non-binding vote, are also conducted in the Committee of the Whole.

LEGISLATIVE COMMITTEES
Temporary committees of the House established primarily to review a specific bill.

SPECIAL COMMITTEES
Committees of the House established to study a particular issue.

COMMITTEES OF THE WHOLE
Committees composed of all members of the House using relaxed rules of debate and procedure to deal with supply motions or other topics.

---

[4]In 2002, 56 Liberals broke ranks with their party to support a motion by the opposition parties for a secret ballot to elect committee chairs. This reduced the ability of the government to control committees (Docherty, 2005).

Joint committees are standing committees composed of members of both the House of Commons and the Senate. One deals with issues related to the Library of Parliament, the other with the scrutiny of regulations.

House of Commons Effectiveness

Many observers have commented on the "decline of legislatures" around the world. Some Canadian observers have advanced similar arguments about the decline of the House of Commons:

- The growth of power in the hands of the prime minister and central agencies means less power in the hands of legislators.
- The growing disparity between the research capabilities available to the Commons and those available to the executive results in an increasingly weaker Commons.
- The high turnover of MPs between some elections has often made for a repetitive pattern of a group of amateur legislators facing a more experienced government.
- The growth of subordinate legislation has exploded in recent decades, leaving effective power to flesh out skeleton legislative proposals in the hands of ministers and departmental officials. Those who are supposed to be implementing laws are increasingly making them.
- Despite the growth of technologies that theoretically make transparency and openness more possible, the executive is becoming more and more reluctant to share information with legislators. Information is the mother's milk of politics, and without it legislatures suffer.
- Committees are not very effective in their oversight of the executive.
- Parliamentary reforms have taken away some elements of parliamentary influence, such as the ability to delay supply and to speak at length in the House.

These are serious allegations. However, there are some ways in which the House of Commons has also grown in importance, including the five outlined below.

STANDING COMMITTEE INDEPENDENCE   A measure of independence for standing committees is desirable if legislatures are to be stronger and more accountable. Indices of committee independence include the degree of flexibility in the committees' terms of reference and the resources allowed to fulfill these terms of reference.

The 1986 alterations to the federal House of Commons Standing Orders significantly aided committee independence. As noted above, standing committees can now begin independent investigations regarding the mandate, management, organization, or operation of the department(s) assigned to them by the House. The government must table a comprehensive response to the report of a standing or special committee within 120 days. To further aid independence, committee members have a degree of tenure, with membership to continue from session to session within a Parliament during a given year (but ending in the last sitting day of the year). Standing, special, and legislative committees may obtain expert staff as deemed necessary, and the Board of Internal Economy will approve budgets for committee expenses. The 2015 election platform of the Liberal party included a promise to strengthen the role of parliamentary committee chairs, including their selection by secret ballot.

ECONOMIC AND FISCAL OVERVIEW   A legislative focus for review of broad economic and fiscal matters is also useful in modifying executive dominance. Despite the importance of such matters, little opportunity exists for legislators to tap public input and both governmental and non-governmental expert opinion on economic and fiscal issues. Two major federal reports—the Lambert Report of 1979 and the Macdonald Commission of 1989—called for committees of the House of Commons to be set up to conduct pre-budget consultations and broad investigations of economic policy. Ultimately a Commons Committee on Finance was established, which follows this general purpose. The Office of the Parliamentary Budget Officer took over another purpose for the proposed committee: the assessment of the accuracy of the government's revenue and expenditure projections.

COMMITTEE SCRUTINY OF APPOINTMENTS   The Standing Orders of the House of Commons [SO 32(6) and SO 110] now require that order-in-council appointments (other than appointment of judges) and, at the discretion of the government a nominee for appointment, be referred to a standing committee of the House for its consideration during a period not exceeding 30 sitting days. The committee can examine the individual's qualifications and competence for the position and can call the individual to appear before the committee. However, the appointment or nomination cannot be vetoed by the committee.

INCREASING THE NUMBER OF OFFICERS OF THE LEGISLATURE AND THEIR STRUCTURAL INDEPENDENCE   Officers of the legislature are neutral officials who fulfill roles central to the operation of the legislature as a collective body in a way that is above politics. In recent years, their number and independence of status have increased. These officers are discussed in Chapter 15.

RECOGNITION OF PARTIES IN PARLIAMENT[5]   Some resources are provided for Commons party organization and research purposes, and this strengthens the role of Parliament, giving its driving forces some influence. However, the research capacity of parliamentary parties could be increased so that parties could be more effective in holding the government accountable and better able to analyze and develop legislative proposals.

---

[5]Parties are officially recognized only if they have at least 12 members in the House of Commons.

In a high profile 2015 trial, prominent Conservative senator Mike Duffy was charged with fraud, breach of trust, and bribery related to allegations related to his Senate expenses.

© Sean Kilpatrick/Canadian Press Images

Despite some moves to increase the independence of the House of Commons and enhance its effectiveness, party discipline has been tight, thereby limiting the independence of the Commons. For decades, party leaders have promised to loosen party discipline, but those promises have rarely been carried out. Prime Minister Paul Martin did introduce a system of reduced party discipline in February 2004 as part of a plan for democratic reforms. Specifically, he adopted the modern British system of one-, two-, and three-line votes. A three-line vote would impose party discipline on all members but would apply only to votes of confidence in the government and a limited number of matters of fundamental importance to the government. Two-line votes would bind cabinet ministers and relevant parliamentary secretaries to support the government position; other members would be encouraged, but not required, to vote in the way preferred by the government. Finally, one-line votes would leave all MPs free to vote as they saw fit. Many votes during Martin's brief term of office were designated as two-line votes, and a small number of government bills were defeated. The system was not continued when Stephen Harper became prime minister despite Conservative commitments to greatly diminish party discipline. Instead, most votes were declared to be matters of confidence, so that a failure to pass a bill would trigger an election. Prior to the 2015 election, Justin Trudeau stated his view that party discipline should be less rigid. Specifically, party discipline would only apply to promises in the Liberal election platform, the budget and significant financial matters, and values related to the Charter of Rights and Freedoms.

THE SENATE

Parliament's upper house, the Senate, has attracted criticism and ridicule for over a century. It has been described as composed of "greedy, greying, old geezers," or as the late senator Ernest Manning once said, "It runs on protocol, Geritol, and alcohol" (quoted in Hermanson, 1995). "Greedy" certainly pertained to some senators, as was revealed in the "Senate Expenses Scandal" that began in 2012. In 2015, prominent Conservative senator Mike Duffy was charged with fraud, breach of trust, and bribery (and his highly publicized trial revealed the involvement of the Prime Minister's Office in the affair). The Senate has also earned itself a reputation as a sinecure for retired (or retiring) party figures.

The Senate has attracted the attention of a host of institutional reformers who see it as a potentially valuable reflection the federal principle and Canadian diversity. Indeed, proposals for reform abounded in the first two decades of this century. The Harper government presented a package of "non-constitutional" reforms calling for consultative elections and senatorial term limits. In December 2015, prime minister Trudeau announced that, after provincial government consultation, he would appoint an independent advisory board that would create based on wide consultation a short-list of 5 merit-based, non-partisan candidates for a Senate vacancy. The prime minister would choose from among those recommended who would sit as independent Senators.

On the other hand, some critics, including the federal NDP and former Ontario premier Dalton McGuinty, call for the outright abolition of the upper house. The current premier of Ontario, Kathleen Wynne, and her Quebec counterpart, Philippe Couillard, want it retained, with the former noting it should serve as a chamber of sober second thought, and the latter seeing the issue as a bargaining chip for reopening constitutional discussions on Quebec's place in the federation (Wynne, 2014; Hébert, 2014). Other premiers such as Saskatchewan's Brad Wall have said that the issue is way down on the list of priorities for the country and that the institution should be allowed to die by atrophy: just do not appoint any more senators (CBC News, 2014, July 12). In July 2015, Prime Minister Harper announced that he would not make any more Senate appointments although there were 22 vacant seats at the time (and he had not made any Senate appointment since March 2013). He stated that this decision was designed to persuade premiers to agree to reforming or abolishing the Senate. Death of the Senate by atrophy rather than by a constitutional amendment would eventually prevent Parliament from passing any legislation. However, the Constitution Act, 1867 (Section 32), requires that Senate vacancies must be filled.

Reasons for Establishment

The Senate was established (along with the House of Commons) by the Constitution Act, 1867, at a time when upper houses were meant to serve as bulwarks against unfettered democracy. John A. Macdonald viewed the Senate as a body that would provide "sober second thought" and thus a check on possible rash decisions by the Commons. His Quebec partner in the Confederation project, George-Étienne Cartier, made it clear that second-guessing the Commons would balance democracy and protect private property. In the Confederation Debates (1865), Cartier noted it was important to "give the country a Constitution which might reconcile the conservative with the democratic element; for the weak point in democratic institutions is the leaving of all the power in the hands of the democratic element" (Parliamentary Debates on the Subject of the Confederation of the British North American Provinces, 1865, p. 571). In order to represent propertied interests, the Constitution Act, 1867, required all senators to own lands or tenements worth at least $4000 within the province for which they were appointed, and required them to have a personal net worth of at least $4000 over and above their debts and liabilities. By establishing a body to represent the interests of the propertied elite, Canadians were trying to copy the House of Lords in the United Kingdom, which had long served such a purpose. Indeed, in the past, the Senate—especially its Banking, Trade and Commerce Committee—often acted as a lobby for the interests of big business (Campbell, 1978). However, this role has become less important, as business interests find it more useful to focus on the policymakers in government, and fewer senators come from a big-business background.

The Senate was also established to protect regional and provincial interests. French Canadians viewed this protection as the most important part of the whole Confederation agreement, which provided equality in the Senate between Ontario and Quebec. New Brunswick and Nova Scotia saw the Senate as protection against domination by central Canada. To achieve these goals, the Senate was established with equal regional ("division") representation. The provinces of Ontario and Quebec qualified as divisions, with 24 senators each, and the two Maritime provinces formed the third division, with 24 senators between them. The expansion of Canada led to the establishment of a fourth division, Western Canada, as well as representation for Prince Edward Island (within the Maritime division), Newfoundland and Labrador, and the Territories (see Table 14-4).

Appointments to the Senate

The governor general appoints senators on the recommendation of the prime minister, and with some notable exceptions, prime ministers have filled the Senate with loyal party members. Senators have to be at least 30 years old and can serve only until age 75.[6] They can be removed from their secure positions only if they fail to attend two consecutive sessions of Parliament; become bankrupt; or are convicted of treason, a felony, or other "infamous" crime. Because senators are not elected, the Senate has a legitimacy problem, meaning that public acceptance of its right to affect public policy is limited. It also has an

---

[6]Until 1965, senators were appointed for life.

DIVISION/PROVINCE/TERRITORY	NUMBER OF REPRESENTATIVES
Ontario	24
Quebec	24
Maritimes, consisting of	24
Nova Scotia	10
New Brunswick	10
Prince Edward Island	4
Western Canada, consisting of	24
Manitoba	6
Saskatchewan	6
Alberta	6
British Columbia	6
Newfoundland and Labrador	6
Yukon	1
Northwest Territories	1
Nunavut	1
Total	105

TABLE 14-4

PROVINCIAL AND TERRITORIAL REPRESENTATION IN THE SENATE

SOURCE: Based on the Constitution Act, 1867 (as amended). Retrieved from www.laws.justice.gc.ca/en/const/index.html.

accountability problem, which stems from the fact that there is no real audience to whom senators can relate and be held accountable.

The method of appointment and lengthy tenure of senators greatly undermine their claim to represent regional and provincial interests. Since the recommendation for their appointment comes solely from the prime minister unless Trudeau's reforms are adopted, neither the people nor the provincial government has had a say in who is chosen. Although there is a requirement that they normally reside in their province, some senators have only a tenuous connection to the province they "represent." Likewise, since they are secure in their position, they do not have to worry about maintaining the support of people in their province. Unlike other federal systems, therefore, the upper chamber is not relevant in representing provincial interests in the national legislative body.

In a limited way, the Senate is more representative of the characteristics of Canadians than the House of Commons. For example, as of October 2015, nearly two-fifths of senators were female, compared with about a quarter of Commons members. To some extent, the Senate also reflects Canada's ethnic and racial diversity.

The Significance of the Senate

The House of Commons and the Senate are nearly equal in their legislative powers. All legislation must be passed in exactly the same words by both bodies. Financial bills involving government spending and taxing must be introduced first in the House of Commons and approved by the Senate, although governments typically view Senate amendments to or rejection of financial bills as exceeding the Senate's authority. In effect, the Senate can potentially check the power of the government by rejecting government bills that the House of Commons has passed. Indeed, before 1943, the Senate vetoed 143 government bills, including a bill to establish an old-age pension in 1927 (Schneiderman, 1991). In modern times, the Senate has generally been reluctant to reject government bills outright, preferring to propose amendments for the House (and government) to consider. For example, senators proposed 150 amendments to the Harper government's important Accountability Act, 90 of which were incorporated in the final version of the Act.

Nevertheless, when a new party comes to power it will typically confront a Senate dominated by the party it defeated. Indeed, if an NDP government were elected, it would likely have no party members in the Senate. Until the new party can fill enough vacancies with its own supporters to give it a majority, it may find that its legislative proposals face obstacles in the Senate. This occurred particularly in the 1980s, when the Progressive Conservative government led by Brian Mulroney engaged in a number of confrontations with a dynamic Liberal majority in the Senate. The Senate rejected important legislative proposals, including the government's spending plans, drug patent legislation, and changes to unemployment insurance, although the Senate eventually gave in after the House re-passed the bills for a second or third time. While Liberal senators generally accepted that they did not have the legitimacy needed to kill legislation approved by the House, they were effective in informing the public about their criticisms of the legislation. However, when Liberal senators stalled the passage of the unpopular goods and services tax, the government took highly controversial action (see Box 14-3: Pandemonium in the Senate).

More common than the occasional dramatic confrontations between the Senate and the government is the Senate's important contribution to the "technical review" of legislative proposals. Some senators are very diligent in their review of legislation that has been passed by the House of Commons. Senators have often caught technical errors that the House did not notice and have suggested many improvements in the details of legislation. Senators have also been active members of the Joint Standing Committee on Regulations, which reviews subordinate or delegated legislation.

The Senate has been especially good at policy work. With its more relaxed, less partisan atmosphere, the Senate can engage in the more long-term investigatory work that is usually within the scope of royal commissions. In the past few decades, Senate committees have produced important reports on such topics as poverty, the mass media, aging, unemployment, science policy, Canadian–American relations, security, and national defence. Despite the "establishment" image of the institution, some Senate committee reports have been surprisingly critical of the government. The Senate has

Senate Committees
**www.parl.gc.ca/
SenCommitteeBusiness**

BOX 14-3

Pandemonium in the Senate

Cartoonists typically depict the Senate as a quiet, sedate chamber compared to the Commons. However, events in 1990 contradicted this image. Liberal senators had prevented a major piece of government legislation, the imposition of the goods and services tax (GST), from coming to a vote. Prime Minister Mulroney asserted that unelected senators were undermining democracy and challenging the supremacy of the House of Commons. To overcome the opposition of the Liberals, who had the majority in the Senate, the Mulroney government drew upon an obscure, never-before-used provision of the Constitution Act, 1867 (Section 26), that allowed the Queen to expand the Senate by either four or eight members on the recommendation of the governor general (in effect, the prime minister). Not surprisingly, the prime minister recommended eight people committed to supporting the GST for appointment to the Senate.

The Liberals were incensed. They broke protocol by inviting the media onto the floor of the Senate. Then, blowing kazoos, they approached the speaker to demand more time to debate the GST. A hasty compromise was reached to allow the Liberals some additional time to voice their criticisms of the proposed tax. With the support of the eight additional senators, the Senate passed the unpopular GST legislation.

also been effective in serving as an early warning mechanism for some national issues. For example, the Senate Standing Committee on National Security and Defence was sounding the alarm about the decline of defence preparedness of the Canadian Forces and airport security a decade before they became issues.

Despite some positive achievements, the Senate has often disappointed Canadians. Some senators simply do not devote much time to their job. Attendance is generally far lower than it is in the Commons, although the Senate workweek is less taxing. The Senate's role as defender of regional and provincial interests, one of the original aims of the Confederation settlement, is virtually non-existent. Another role, defender of minorities, which some have said was implied in the Constitution, has met a similar fate.

The elite nature of the Senate has often been criticized. One should not be surprised that the intent of the drafters of the Constitution to have propertied and/or economic elite in the upper house has indeed appeared to be realized. A review of the occupations of senators shows a remarkably consistent pattern of businesspeople, lawyers, and other upper middle class professions dominating Senate appointments. Nevertheless, many senators are dedicated to improving the lives of Canadians, whatever their background.

Senate Reform

While some believe that the Senate should be scrapped as a relic of the undemocratic past, many see promise in a reformed upper house and have suggested a whole variety of possible functions for it, some old (and modified) and some new.

REGIONAL AND PROVINCIAL REPRESENTATION There have been many proposals that reflect the need to counterbalance the power of the more populous areas of Canada by creating a new Senate with more meaningful regional or provincial representation. With the growth of the West, the six seats allotted to each of the provinces in this region are often viewed as inadequate. As well, representation in the Senate does not reflect the principle of the equality of the provinces that many people hold. However, reducing Quebec from nearly one-quarter of the seats in the Senate to slightly less than one-tenth would not go over well in that province. Likewise, people often have criticized the notion that Prince Edward Island should have the same number of representatives as Ontario in a reformed Senate.

Meaningful representation of regions or provinces requires that the power to recommend appointments to the Senate be removed from the hands of the prime minister. In the 1970s, those seeking reform of the Senate often looked to provincial governments or provincial legislatures to nominate senators. Since then, many reformers adopted the more democratic idea that the population of the province should elect senators to represent their province, with senators required to seek re-election at regular intervals.

LEGISLATIVE REVIEW Reformers sometimes stress the idea that review of proposed legislation should continue to be an important role for the Senate, but that it must be a review with a clearly subordinate and supportive role. In this perspective, the Senate would exist not to challenge the principle of the legislation but to make it better. This subordinate role would be highlighted by including a suspensive veto (the ability to suspend the passage of legislation for a specified period of time), rather than an absolute veto over legislation passed by the Commons.

Redefining the powers of the Senate would be particularly important if it were to become an elected body. An elected Senate would likely result in a more active and more partisan upper house that was more willing to challenge legislation passed by the Commons. If the Senate were elected on the basis of equal provincial representation, this would likely often result in different parties controlling the Senate and the Commons. A suspensive veto would help to ensure that a deadlock did not occur between the House and the Senate.

INTERGOVERNMENTAL RELATIONS A reformed Senate could serve as a chamber for the coordination of federal–provincial relations. It could also provide protection against federal policies that might hurt provincial interests by, for example, requiring that provincial government representatives approve federal legislation that affects the interests of the provinces (as is the case for Germany's Bundesrat). Alternatively, it could act as an intermediary between the federal and provincial governments and thus help to reduce federal–provincial conflict.

REPRESENTATION OF MINORITIES The original Constitution Act, 1867, gave limited recognition to the minority protector role of the Senate Act, 1867. Representation for Quebec is divided into 24 districts, thereby providing representation for the English-speaking enclaves in the Eastern Townships of the province. Some suggest that the diversity of Canada should be more fully recognized in the Senate by, for example, providing guaranteed representation for Aboriginal peoples, women, and various minorities. The Charlottetown Accord proposed that both a majority of francophone senators and a majority of the Senate as a whole should have to pass bills affecting the French language and culture.

PROTECTION OF DEMOCRACY AND REPRESENTATIVENESS One common theme of many Senate reformers is that Canada has too many centralizing elements and not enough countervailing or counterbalancing elements. One way the power of the prime minister could be held in check is by giving the Senate a role in ratifying appointments to the Supreme Court and various agencies, boards, and commissions. As well, enhancing the legitimacy of the Senate by electing its members would allow it a more equal say in Parliament's policy role, thereby limiting the ability of the prime minister and those at the centre of government to dominate Parliament.

ATTEMPTS TO REFORM THE SENATE As discussed in Chapter 10, Senate reform has been one important part of the discussions of comprehensive changes to the Canadian Constitution. Reflecting the development of a movement for a "Triple-E" Senate (one that is equal, elected, and effective) in Western Canada, former Alberta premier Don Getty, supported by several other premiers, pushed hard for major Senate reforms that require constitutional amendments. The Meech Lake Accord proposed that senators be chosen from a list of nominees put forward by the government of the province for which there was a vacancy. The Charlottetown Accord proposed that the Senate consist of six persons from each province and one from each territory. Senators would be elected either by the population or by the legislature of the provinces and territories. Although these accords failed, Alberta has held elections to choose "senators-in-waiting" since 1989. Saskatchewan passed a law in 2009 providing for elections to choose nominees for the consideration of the prime minister, but no election ever took place, and in 2013 the legislature repealed the act and passed a motion calling for the abolition of the upper chamber (CTV News, 2013, November 6). Although Prime Minister Martin refused to recommend the appointment of elected senators, Prime Minister Harper recommended the appointment of Bert Brown, a leader of the Triple-E Senate movement who had won two Alberta senatorial nominee elections to the Senate in 2007, Betty Unger (who finished second to Brown in the 2004 election) in 2012, and Scott Tannas (the second place finisher in the 2012 Alberta senatorial election).

Stephen Harper, an advocate of an elected Senate, promised in the 2006 election campaign to recommend for appointment to the Senate only those who had been elected. Within days of becoming prime minister, however, Harper recommended the appointment to the Senate of Michel Fortier, who had failed to win a seat in the Commons. Part of Harper's motivation was that he wanted to have a cabinet minister from the Montreal area. Nevertheless, Harper tried to bring some changes to the Senate. From its first term in office in 2006, the Harper government presented a series of (unsuccessful) bills to Parliament concerning Senate reform. In 2006, Bill S-4 would have limited senators to renewable eight-year terms of office. In 2007, Bill C-20 would have provided for consultative elections for nominees for Senate posts: the winners' names were to be submitted to the prime minister, who would consider them for Senate recommendations to the governor general.

On June 21, 2011, the government presented yet another effort. The Senate Reform Act (Bill C-7) proposed to allow a province or territory (if they so chose) to hold an election to select nominees for the Senate, nominees the prime minister must consider when recommending Senate appointments to the governor general. It also proposed that senators appointed after the October 2008 general election would be subject to a nine-year limit after the bill came into effect. Elected senators would be prevented from seeking re-election. A Senate election could be held at the same time as the provincial general election or during municipal elections provided there was a common election day for all, or at a date determined by the provincial cabinet.

The Supreme Court of Canada in *Reference re: Senate Reform* (2014)[7] ruled that Parliament alone could not provide for senatorial term limits, or consultative exercises—the general amending procedure[8] was necessary to achieve both these ends. As well, abolishing the Senate could only take place with the unanimity procedure Measures that maintain or change the Senate without altering its fundamental nature and role—like changing property qualifications or the net worth requirement for senators—could be changed by Parliament (or, for Quebec senators, Parliament and the Quebec legislature).

For the time being, the Senate faces the daunting mixture of lack of legitimacy and a perceived but frustrated need for change.

---

[7]This was in response to a series of questions prepared by the Canadian government based on various reform proposals. Earlier, the Quebec government had sought an opinion from the Quebec Court of Appeal on the constitutionality of Bill C-7.

[8]The general amending formula requires the agreement of Parliament and the legislatures of at least two-thirds of the provinces containing at least one-half of the population of all the provinces. The unanimity formula requires the agreement of Parliament and all the provincial legislatures. In the view of the Supreme Court, abolishing the Senate would be a fundamental change in the Constitution and thus requires unanimous agreement.

Summary and Conclusion

The House of Commons is at the centre of Canada's system of representative democracy and responsible government. The prime minister and cabinet can only govern as long as they retain the support of the majority of our elected representatives. Not only can the Commons make or unmake governments, but it is also the key institution for scrutinizing the activities of the government and holding it accountable for its actions.

The House of Commons and the Senate do not usually play a major role in developing new laws and policies, but they are not altogether ineffectual. Their detailed examination of proposed legislation can result in significant modifications and improvements in government's legislative proposals. As well, debate in the House helps to inform the public.

The tight party discipline that characterizes the Commons limits the representational capabilities of individual MPs. However, party discipline helps to clarify the positions taken by the opposing parties, thus making it easier for the public to know where each party stands. It also makes individual MPs less likely to be pressured by powerful lobbyists. When one party has a majority in the House, party discipline ensures that the government will have its way and be able to enact the policies in its election platform, and also to pass unpopular measures that the government believes are necessary or desirable.

In a minority government situation, the House of Commons assumes greater importance, as opposition parties determine the fate of the government. Sometimes this leads to a degree of cooperation between the governing party and one or more of the opposition parties. Other times it results in a dysfunctional House, in which party competition is especially intense and the constant threat of an election overshadows all of the activities of the members. Unlike many European countries, Canada has seen little support for coalition governments, which could allow for a more cooperative power-sharing arrangement between parties and avoid the instability that tends to be associated with minority governments.

The Senate, as currently constituted, is often criticized as being an undemocratic institution. Even though the Senate performs some useful tasks, most observers agree that Senate reform is long overdue. However, changes to the powers of the Senate, the method of selecting senators, and the number of senators for each province require a constitutional amendment.

Making the Senate an elected body would increase its legitimacy, and thus would make it more likely to use its powers to reject the government's legislative proposals that have been passed by the Commons. The distribution of seats in the Senate would become an issue. Not only are there strong advocates for equal representation for each province, but also demands for guarantees of representation for women, Aboriginals, and various minority groups. A Senate that represented the diversity of Canada would likely have a different view of legislative proposals than the House of Commons. More generally, Senate reform has to address questions about what functions the upper house should perform and how deadlocks between the House and the Senate should be resolved. Achieving agreement to amend the Constitution to institute major reforms of the Senate would not be easy.

Discussion Questions

1. How well do the House of Commons and the Senate perform their functions?

2. How do the national legislatures of the United States and Canada differ? Can they learn anything from each other?

3. Are reforms of the House of Commons and the Senate needed?

4. Should party discipline in the House of Commons be loosened?

5. Should the Senate be abolished?

Further Reading

Axworthy, T.S. (2008). *Everything old is new again: Observations on parliamentary reform.* Kingston, ON: Centre for the Study of Democracy, Queen's University.

Campbell, C. (1978). *The Canadian Senate: A lobby from within.* Toronto, ON: Macmillan.

Canada, Library of Parliament. (2003). *The Parliament we want: Parliamentarians' views on parliamentary reform.* Ottawa, ON: Author.

Docherty, D.C. (2005). *Legislatures.* Vancouver, BC: UBC Press.

Franks, C.E.S. (1987). *The Parliament of Canada.* Toronto, ON: University of Toronto Press.

Joyal, S. (Ed.). (2005). *Protecting Canadian democracy: The Senate you never knew.* Ottawa, ON: Canadian Centre for Management Development.

Russell, P.H., & Sossin, L. (Eds.). (2009). *Parliamentary democracy in crisis.* Toronto, ON: University of Toronto Press.

Smith, D.E. (2007). *The people's House of Commons: Theories of democracy in contention.* Toronto, ON: University of Toronto Press.

Smith, J. (Ed.). 2009. *The democratic dilemma: Reforming the Canadian Senate.* Montreal, QC: McGill-Queen's University Press.

Thomas, P.G. (2010). Parliament and the public service. In C. Dunn (Ed.), *The handbook of Canadian public administration* (2nd ed.). Toronto, ON: Oxford University Press.

Canada's first census was conducted in New France by intendant Jean Talon, the leading bureaucrat who served under the colony's Governor.

© Library and Archives Canada/Lawrence R. Batchelor collection/C-011925

CHAPTER 15

The Public Bureaucracy

CHAPTER OBJECTIVES

After reading this chapter, you should be able to

1. Outline the characteristics of the public, private, and third sectors.
2. Discuss the origins of the public bureaucracy in Canada.
3. Provide a general overview of the staff who work for the three branches of government.
4. Describe the three types of executive department.
5. Discuss the adoption of businesslike approaches in providing public services.

In late July 2010, official Ottawa was stunned by the resignation of Statistics Canada chief statistician Munir Sheikh (one of their own—he had been a senior executive in finance, Privy Council Office, health, human resources, and Social Development Canada). What is more, he had done so in apparent protest against having his name and his institution associated with the comments of the industry minister, Tony Clement, a week earlier in the *Globe and Mail* (Chase, 2010). Clement had said that the government's decision to replace StatsCan's long-form census for 2011 with a voluntary National Household Survey had been based on advice from StatsCan—implicitly from Sheikh—and that steps were being taken to make up for the absence of the mandatory long-form census and that "the quality of the census is maintained." Sheikh wrote in a public resignation letter, responding to "the question of whether a voluntary survey can become a substitute for a mandatory census. It can not" (Chase & Grant, 2010). Here was a clear denial. He felt that his integrity, the integrity of the statistical agency, and that of the deputy minister function left him no option.

The long-form census sent to 20 percent of households had additional and more detailed questions than the short formcensus sent to 80 percent of households. Both were legal requirements, with penalties attached ranging from fines to jail time for non-compliance. The practice had begun with the 1971 decennial census—a century after the first national census and three centuries after intendant Jean Talon's first New France census (1666)—and was meant to elicit information about an increasingly complex and diverse population undergoing significant growth. The Harper Conservative government stopped the practice in the 2011 decennial census, citing privacy and government intrusiveness issues.

It was an important issue for expert and layperson alike. The long-form census was the benchmark used for a host of other Statistics Canada surveys, which suffered as a result (Sheikh, 2010). The response rate was inferior for the voluntary National Household Survey—68.6 percent compared with 93.5 percent for the 2006 long-form census (Ditchburn, 2015). The development of good public policy fields often depended on the detail provided by the long-form census. Ivan Fellegi, chief statistician from 1985 to 2008, said that the long-form census was the only way to track many social trends and policies, like the integration of new immigrants, young adults' role in the labour market, the status of official languages by province, and the state of Aboriginal people. He called knowing if social conditions were getting better or worse "almost an existential question" (Proudfoot, 2010). In the 2015 Canadian election campaign, the Liberal party (and the NDP) promised to restore the mandatory long-form census.

The controversy concerning the long-form census can be related to some classic public administration conundrums:

- the correct roles of minister and deputy minister, in what is called the classical bargain (minister takes responsibility, public servants retain anonymity and are identified with certain policy advice);
- accountability to ministers and governments versus adherence to the basic norms of one's profession;
- the duty to speak truth to power (the classic guardian role) versus the need to be sensitive to the government's political direction (Bourgault & Dunn, 2014);
- the view that public servants needed close control by their political masters versus the need of the people to hear the experts' views publicly (what came to be known as the Friedrich–Finer debate in public administration literature).

BUREAUCRACY

BUREAUCRACY
Rule by offices and officials.

The word **bureaucracy** was first used in 1764 by the French philosopher Baron de Grimm to describe what he considered to be a new and undesirable form of government: rule by offices and officials (Albrow, 1991). In the classic view of German sociologist Max Weber, the development of bureaucracy reflected the focus of modern society on rationality and efficiency. For Weber, a bureaucratic organization featured a hierarchical chain of command; work that is organized in terms of specialized positions; detailed, impersonal rules; and a system of hiring and promotion based on qualifications and merit. Although Weber thought that the bureaucratization of society was inevitable, he worried that powerful bureaucratic organizations controlled by senior officials would dominate government and sabotage the democratic ideal (Heywood, 2002).

PUBLIC BUREAUCRACY
The staffs of a variety of governing institutions.

Although the terms *bureaucracy* and *bureaucrat* indeed conjure up very negative images, we prefer to use the terms more neutrally. In this chapter, the term **public bureaucracy** is used to refer to the staffs of a variety of governing institutions. Governing institutions require sizable staffs to be effective.

Although bureaucracies are important and influential, the claim that bureaucracies "rule" is an exaggeration. The prime minister and cabinet play a leading role in the Canadian governing system, although top public servants help them in setting the direction of government. The negative perception of bureaucrats is also misleading. Although many public servants carry out their tasks using well-worn routines, rules, and regulations, crusading public officials have spearheaded many of the advances in social progress in Canada.

A New Way to Understand Bureaucracy

The organization of the large number of public servants who work primarily in the departments of government could be viewed, to a considerable extent, as matching Weber's model of bureaucratic organization. Yet, even here the image of employees carrying out routine, detailed administrative tasks can be misleading. Some public servants are heavily involved in developing policy proposals that are eventually decided upon by cabinet and passed by Parliament. Putting laws and policies into effect can involve a substantial degree of creativity and thought in designing effective programs and dealing with changing circumstances.

Beyond the public service, a wide variety of organizations can be found whose staffs also support the workings of the political executive (prime minister and cabinet). In addition, legislative and judicial institutions receive support from their own bureaucratic organizations and officials. In other words, bureaucracies take on many differing forms.

Since understanding the rather labyrinthine federal public service is a challenge, even for public servants themselves, we take a different tack, and arrange the public service according to a "rule of threes." The way to understand the shape of the service is to see it as a series of influences and bodies arranged in sets of three. In other words, there are:

- three sectors of Canadian society;
- three national influences on the bureaucracy in Canada;
- three bureaucracies (executive, legislative, and judicial);
- three categories of executive institutions;
- three categories of executive departments;
- three levels of bureaucratic elite in departments;
- three kinds of officials in parliamentary institutions; and
- three kinds of officials in judicial institutions.

This is a unique and simpler way to present complex information.

THE THREE SECTORS OF CANADIAN SOCIETY

Public bureaucracies exist in a specific context, namely a tripartite division of Canadian society. It is common to talk of the private (or market) sector, the public (or governmental) sector, and the third (or voluntary non-profit) sector. The **private sector** exists in a competitive environment and strives to maximize profit for private owners, be they corporations, family-owned businesses, or self-employed individuals. The **public sector**, which consists of the institutions and agencies of the state, is ideally concerned with acting in the public interest. The **third sector** consists of voluntary non-profit organizations that contribute to the general good of the public. This sector includes charitable organizations, religious and cultural institutions, and non-profit child care facilities and nursing homes (Evans & Shields, 2002).

Those in the private sector frequently argue that the public sector has grown too large and is crowding out the private sector, jeopardizing its resources and mission. Those in the public sector may feel that they provide services more fairly and equitably than does the private sector. Nevertheless, those in the public sector may also justify many of their actions by arguing that their role is to promote the health of the market. As former U.S. president Calvin Coolidge once said, "The business of government is business." Canadian politicians have often offered much the same rationale for their actions. For example, in announcing a $4 billion bailout for the Canadian subsidiaries of U.S. automotive manufacturers Chrysler and General Motors in December 2008, Prime Minister Harper stipulated that "Canadian taxpayers expect their money will be used to restructure and renew the automotive industry in this country" (CBC News, 2008b).

There is also a tendency for one sector to influence another sector's administrative practices. In the last quarter century, the public sector has been deeply influenced by something called New Public Management, a school of public administration that modelled itself on private sector precepts. The financial practices of the public sector (such as the accounting systems and planning and budgeting tools) more and more resemble approaches in the private sector.

For its part, the third sector depends increasingly on the public sector for funding. One implication of this trend is that non-profit organizations have begun spending more of their time and resources on meeting the reporting and accountability requirements that come with such dependence on public financing. Some non-profit organizations even complain that such efforts sidetrack them from their core missions. As well, the third sector tends to mimic the private sector in its financial management practices: "Many voluntary organizations operate as if they were profit-and-loss entities, with cash flows (from fundraising, endowments, or fees charged for services) that dictate the scope of their activities in a similar way to [private sector] firms that are fully revenue-dependent. While their objectives are public in a broad sense, they can act like private organizations from a money-management perspective" (Graham, 2007, p. 8).

THE COMPOSITION OF THE PUBLIC BUREAUCRACY

The federal bureaucracy is just one among many in this country. As Table 15-1 indicates, over 3.6 million Canadians are employed in the many different public organizations. Indeed, the federal government bureaucracy accounts for only a small proportion of total public sector employment.

Some Canadians think of government as a collection of minister-directed departments, but this is only part of the picture. Andrew Graham (2007) insists it is necessary to define government expansively, given the extensive reach of the public sector in modern times. For example, he points out that there is a "shadow government": people working for the private sector under government grants or grants to non-profit organizations. As well, government

TABLE 15-1
PUBLIC SECTOR EMPLOYMENT, CANADA, 2007–2011

	EMPLOYMENT (NUMBER OF PERSONS)				
	2007	2008	2009	2010	2011
PUBLIC SECTOR	3 383 821	3 493 580	3 563 406	3 609 274	3 631 837
Government	3 090 234	3 183 310	3 248 253	3 294 159	3 313 320
Federal general government	387 121	400 196	415 397	420 685	427 093
Provincial and territorial general government	352 931	361 988	358 461	358 237	356 709
Health and social service institutions, provincial and territorial	783 142	800 200	822 904	844 762	859 350
Universities, colleges, vocational and trade institutions, provincial and territorial	358 138	365 137	374 745	387 056	382 245
Local general government	548 298	581 221	596 144	605 562	608 094
Local school boards	660 603	674 568	680 603	677 857	679 828
Government business enterprises	293 587	310 270	315 154	315 114	318 519
Federal government business enterprises	99 121	104 864	104 692	104 042	102 319
Provincial and territorial government business enterprises	135 876	144 779	147 616	145 616	147 914
Local government business enterprises	58 589	60 627	62 845	65 456	68 286

Notes:
• Employment data are not in full-time equivalent and does not distinguish between full-time and part-time employees. Includes employees both in and outside of Canada.
• As of December 31 of each year. More recent data is not available.
• Federal general government data includes reservists and full-time military personnel.

SOURCE: Statistics Canada. (2012). *Public sector employment, wages and salaries.* Retrieved from www.statcan.gc.ca/tables-tableaux/sum-som/l01/cst/govt54a-eng.htm. This does not constitute an endorsement by Statistics Canada of this product.

often achieves its aims by using a variety of "governing instruments," some of which are practices that depend on the private sector for their implementation, such as regulations, inducements, and persuasion designed to change private sector behaviour.

The Origins of the Public Bureaucracy in Canada

There have been three national influences on the bureaucracy in Canada. The public bureaucracy, especially the public service bureaucracy, owes its origins to British and American sources and to the Canadian nation-building ethos, which carried with it some aura of patronage and doing what was necessary.

BRITISH INFLUENCE The traditional British style of public administration, modified by Canadian practice and convention, came to be known as the **Whitehall Model**. It would consist of a number of interrelated principles (see Table 15-2).

The British model was a subject of both pride and consternation to Canadians. It offered a familiar and relatively workable set of principles that could be passed from generation to generation, but it also resisted easy change.

AMERICAN INFLUENCE American influences have also left a lasting mark in Canada. In the late nineteenth century, the **Progressive movement**, spearheaded by individuals like Woodrow Wilson, sought to break the "spoils system" (in which the winning political party gave government jobs to its supporters) by making the public sector at all levels more businesslike and shielding it from the political realm. The Progressive movement had its strongest effect at the local and state levels, where the patronage-ridden political "machines," the target of the Progressives, had their greatest hold.

In Canada's first half century, government jobs were given to political supporters; public contracts went to friends of the government; political figures enriched themselves at public expense, often by padding construction projects; and recent immigrant communities received special "favours" in exchange for

WHITEHALL MODEL
The traditional British style of public administration with such features as ministerial responsibility, public service anonymity and neutrality, secrecy, and the merit principle.

PROGRESSIVE MOVEMENT
A late nineteenth-century movement that sought to break the "spoils system" in government by making the public sector at all levels more businesslike and shielding it from the political realm.

TABLE 15-2
THE TRADITIONAL WHITEHALL MODEL AND ITS CANADIAN APPLICATION

TRADITIONAL WHITEHALL MODEL	MODIFICATIONS BY CANADIAN PRACTICE AND CONVENTION
Parliamentary supremacy	Subordinate (delegated) legislation
Ministerial responsibility	Answerability and accountability
Public service anonymity	Accounting officers Boards of Crown corporations and commissions Media access to public servants
Public service neutrality	Rights to engage in various forms of political activity
The secrecy norm	Access to information or freedom of information
The rule of law	Canadian Charter of Rights and Freedoms
The merit principle	Employment equity
	Representative bureaucracy

voting support at the polls. Among the Progressive movement's effects in Canada were the creation of city managers for urban governance, the foundation of special purpose bodies to manage some politically sensitive services, and reforms in public budgeting.

Around the turn of the century, the second American influence, the **scientific management** school first set in motion by Frederick Taylor (1856–1915), gained in popularity.[1] Frederick Taylor was a member of the New England upper class who was accepted to Harvard but instead chose to become immersed in the burgeoning American manufacturing sector, first as an ordinary worker, then as an engineer, then as what would today be called a management consultant. Tireless study of the nature of work and management led him to publish his immensely popular work *The Principles of Scientific Management* in 1911.

Taylor's ideas on the organization of work found many expressions throughout his career, and practitioners have tended to seize on discrete elements of his thought and use them as they see fit. He reckoned that the job of managers was to acquire the knowledge of work that traditionally belonged to workers and to organize it so as to make it available to current and future managers. He rather optimistically referred to this as "scientific management," by which he simply meant the organization and quantification of such knowledge as well as finding "the one best way" to perform tasks.

Scientific management principles influenced the federal public administration for the better part of the twentieth century. In particular, the Civil Service Commission (established in 1908) adopted an extensive employee classification system based on a report by American consultants (Dawson, 1929).

NEW PUBLIC MANAGEMENT   In the final decades of the twentieth century, ideas and practices from Britain, the United States, and New Zealand influenced thinking about public administration. **New Public Management (NPM)**, the adaptation of the practices of private business to the administrative activities of government (see Table 15-3), emerged as the result of two overlapping influences: rational choice theory and principal–agent theory. As discussed in Chapter 7, rational choice theory (also known as public choice theory) assumes that all individuals, including bureaucrats, are self-interested. **Principal–agent theory** is based on the idea that the bureaucrat (the nominal agent, or "servant") who is supposed to follow the will of the principal (the minister or the legislature) often uses specialized knowledge to thwart this arrangement. The emphasis of NPM was on establishing institutional and behavioural counters to these two alleged tendencies.

Other factors were at play as well. Ideologues such as British Conservative prime minister Margaret Thatcher and U.S. Republican president Ronald

SCIENTIFIC MANAGEMENT
A complex system of management of the production process, often popularly associated with time and motion studies, which maintains that there is one best way to increase output.

NEW PUBLIC MANAGEMENT (NPM)
The adoption of the practices of private business in the administrative activities of government.

PRINCIPAL–AGENT THEORY
A theory based on the idea that the bureaucrat, who is supposed to follow the will of the minister or the legislature, often uses specialized knowledge to thwart this arrangement.

---

[1]The term *scientific management* was coined by lawyer Louis D. Brandeis in hearings before the Interstate Commerce Commission.

TABLE 15-3
**PRINCIPLES OF NPM
VERSUS BUREAUCRATIC
GOVERNMENT**

PRINCIPLES OF NEW PUBLIC MANAGEMENT (NPM)	TRADITIONAL BUREAUCRATIC GOVERNMENT
Entrepreneurial government	Emphasis on spending
Steering rather than rowing	Concentration on one or a few governing instruments (or means)
Competition	Monopoly
Performance measurement	Rule-driven
Customer-driven government	Ministerial responsibility
Decentralization	Centralization
Market orientation	Command and control
Empowerment	Service

Reagan convinced many people that behind poorly performing governments were self-serving bureaucrats who in some areas had scaled the heights of power and needed to be checked. The book *Reinventing Government* by David Osborne and Ted Gaebler (1992) was key to popularizing entrepreneurial government in Canada. In particular, Osborne and Gaebler argued that governing should involve "steering"—setting the policy direction—rather than "rowing"—delivering services that should be contracted out to private business as much as possible. NPM was seen as the opposite of the traditional bureaucratic form of government. In fact, it was hailed as an antidote to bureaucratic ills, which, it was claimed, resulted in inefficient governing.

CANADIAN DEVELOPMENT   Although influenced by British and American ideas, the Canadian public bureaucracy has developed, to some extent, in its own way. Until 1917, there was only nominal attention to the merit principle

Michael Ferguson, appointed auditor general in 2011, and his staff are responsible for providing Parliament with the information and analysis needed to hold the government accountable for its use of public funds.

(the right person for a specific job) and more to patronage (a public service job seen as a political favour to be bestowed on those who supported the governing party). For the next 50 years (1918–1967), the merit system-focussed Whitehall Model largely dominated. Since 1967, collective bargaining by public service unions and the adoption of the Charter of Rights and Freedoms have modified the Whitehall Model. For example, strict restrictions on the political activities of public servants to maintain their political neutrality were struck down by the Supreme Court as a violation of the freedoms protected by the Charter. New Public Management also had an effect—although not to the same extent as in some other countries. The long-term effect of these developments is the current blend of rights-based, bargaining-based, and entrepreneurial-based management.

EXECUTIVE INSTITUTIONS

People often think of bureaucracy as involving the standard public service, with the employees in each department answering to a cabinet minister. However, there are many kinds of bureaucracies, and only one kind answers to ministers. The three powers or branches of government—Parliament, the executive (prime minister and cabinet), and the judiciary—each have their own bureaucracies with a variety of specific aspects.

Executive institutions fall into three categories:

1. Executive departments headed by cabinet ministers
2. Semi-independent public agencies: Crown corporations and assorted agencies, boards, and commissions
3. Alternative service delivery (ASD), a variety of different methods for delivering public services

Executive Departments Headed by Cabinet Ministers

Ministers preside over **executive departments**. Executive departments are those listed in Schedule I of the Financial Administration Act (FAA), a list that may only be amended by Parliament and not at the discretion of the minister or cabinet. Departments are financed through parliamentary appropriations. As of February 2015, there were 19 departments. Ministers, in the language of most of the acts creating departments, have "direction and management" of the department. According to convention, ministers are individually responsible to Parliament for implementing the mandate that is conferred upon them in the act.

A minister may have personal responsibility to Parliament for personnel management, staffing, and finances of the department, but does not in fact exercise direct responsibility over the employees or finances of the department. The Public Service Commission is given exclusive responsibility for the staffing of departments under the Public Service Employment Act, which came into

EXECUTIVE DEPARTMENTS
Organizations headed by cabinet ministers.

effect in 2005. This power is often delegated, but it is delegated to the deputy minister, not to the minister of the department. Personnel management other than staffing is the responsibility of the Treasury Board and the department's deputy minister, not the minister. Similarly, control over financial administration is shared between the Treasury Board and the department's deputy minister under the Financial Administration Act, and the minister is excluded. The reason for these exclusions is historical: In the past, ministers enjoyed much greater powers, but they abused them, aggrandizing the power of their departments, their parties, and themselves.

Semi-Independent Public Agencies

SEMI-INDEPENDENT PUBLIC AGENCY
A government organization that has a degree of independence from executive controls and parliamentary scrutiny.

The **semi-independent public agency,** the second type of executive institution, differs from its departmental counterpart in important ways. Although both have a designated minister, Parliament does not usually scrutinize the agency's affairs to the same extent. Ministers will generally submit less readily to questioning in the House of Commons on matters related to boards, commissions, or Crown corporations. These agencies generally have more freedom from central controls in their budgeting and staffing practices. Some are advisory agencies, some perform regulatory functions, and some engage in commercial or business activities—all activities that are rare for departments to perform.

CROWN CORPORATIONS   Crown corporations are legal entities set up by the government to pursue commercial or other public policy objectives. The type of Crown corporation most Canadians are familiar with is called a parent Crown corporation (see Table 15-4). Some of these affect Canadians directly every day, like the Canadian Broadcasting Corporation (CBC), Marine Atlantic, or the Bank of Canada, whereas others have a more indirect impact, like the Business Development Bank of Canada, Atomic Energy of Canada, and the International Development Research Centre (IRDC). A parent Crown corporation is a legally distinct entity wholly owned by the Crown and managed by a board of directors. The mandate, powers, and objectives of the corporation are set out in one of two ways: (1) There is special legislation constituting the parent Crown corporation, or (2) the mandate, powers, and objectives are set out in the "articles of incorporation" under the Canada Business Corporations Act. As of December 31, 2014, there were 45 parent Crown corporations, excluding subsidiaries (Treasury Board of Canada Secretariat, 2014b). (See Table 15-4.) As of December 2012, they employed close to 88 000 people and managed more $400 billion.

Crown corporations report through specific ministers to Parliament, but the relationship between corporation and minister is not as close or direct as is the case with ministers and departments. The reason the Crown corporations came into existence in the first place was to free them from the rules and political control that are evident in the regular bureaucracy. However, the arm's-length relationship raises difficulties for those used to thinking in terms of the orthodox doctrine of ministerial responsibility, where the minister is responsible for all matters administrative and political.

Parliament has dealt with this problem in various reform efforts over the past several decades. There have been three major versions of accountability frameworks for Crown corporations, namely, the amendments to the Financial Administration Acts of 1951, 1984, and 2006. They outline other mechanisms for oversight and accountability for the Crown corporations. All Crown corporations have to prepare financial statements, and most of them are

TABLE 15-4
PARENT CROWN CORPORATIONS GROUPED BY MINISTERIAL PORTFOLIO (AS OF AT DECEMBER 31, 2014)

*Public–Private Partnerships Canada, a wholly owned subsidiary of the Canada Development Investment Corporation, has been directed by Order-in-Council (P.C. 2008-0855) to report as if it were a parent Crown corporation.

Agriculture and Agri-Food
- Canadian Dairy Commission
- Farm Credit Canada

Canadian Heritage and Official Languages
- Canada Council for the Arts
- Canadian Broadcasting Corporation
- Canadian Museum for Human Rights
- Canadian Museum of History
- Canadian Museum of Immigration at Pier 21
- Canadian Museum of Nature
- National Arts Centre Corporation
- National Gallery of Canada
- National Museum of Science and Technology
- Telefilm Canada

Citizenship, Immigration and Multiculturalism
- Canadian Race Relations Foundation

Employment and Social Development
- Canada Mortgage and Housing Corporation

Finance
- Bank of Canada
- Canada Deposit Insurance Corporation
- Canada Development Investment Corporation
- Canada Pension Plan Investment Board
- PPP Canada Inc.*
- Royal Canadian Mint

Fisheries and Oceans
- Freshwater Fish Marketing Corporation

Foreign Affairs, Trade and Development
- Canadian Commercial Corporation
- Export Development Canada
- International Development Research Centre
- National Capital Commission

Industry
- Business Development Bank of Canada
- Canadian Tourism Commission
- Standards Council of Canada

Infrastructure and Communities
- The Jacques-Cartier and Champlain Bridges Inc.

Natural Resources
- Atomic Energy of Canada Limited

Public Works and Government Services
- Canada Lands Company Limited
- Defence Construction (1951) Limited

Transport
- Atlantic Pilotage Authority
- Blue Water Bridge Authority
- Canada Post Corporation
- Canadian Air Transport Security Authority
- Federal Bridge Corporation Limited, The
- Great Lakes Pilotage Authority
- Laurentian Pilotage Authority
- Marine Atlantic Inc.
- Pacific Pilotage Authority
- Ridley Terminals Inc.
- VIA Rail Canada Inc.
- Windsor-Detroit Bridge Authority

Treasury Board
- Public Sector Pension Investment Board

SOURCE: Parent Crown Corporations Grouped by Ministerial Portfolio https://www.tbs-sct.gc.ca/reports-rapports/cc-se/crown-etat/ccmp-smpm-eng.asp. Treasury Board Secretariat. (2014). Reproduced with the permission of the Minister of Public Works and Government Services Canada. 2015.

subject to annual audits of their financial statements by the auditor general of Canada. Since 1984, most have been required to submit to value-for-money audits known as "special examinations" at least once every five years.

The Federal Accountability Act of 2006 anticipated the establishment of a Public Appointments Commission to assure merit-based appointments to government boards, commissions, and agencies. However, this commission never functioned and was eliminated in 2012. Thus, the Harper government continued to make a number of appointments on a patronage basis. The Act also extended the Access to Information Act to cover all Crown corporations, officers of Parliament, and foundations. However, some Crown corporations, such as the Canadian Broadcasting Corporation, have been reluctant to comply fully with the Access to Information Act. The Act also removed the government's power to exempt Crown corporations from the Public Servants Disclosure Protection Act, its "whistleblower" legislation. As well, it split the position of CEO and chair of the board for Crown corporations, making the former the only representative of management to the board; it also restricted public servants from participating on Crown corporation boards.

In 2013, the Harper Conservative government altered the arm's-length relationship between government and the CBC and three other Crown corporations (the Canada Council for the Arts, the National Arts Centre, and International Development Research Centre) by giving cabinet control over their collective bargaining. The Financial Administration Act was amended, by means of a budget implementation bill, to require the Treasury Board to approve the corporations' collective bargaining approach and collective agreements reached through such bargaining (Naumetz, 2013).

ABCS   A wide variety of agencies, boards, and commissions (ABCs) serve a number of functions, which may overlap to a large extent. They may have *adjudicative* roles, such as the role played by the Canadian Human Rights Tribunal, which decides cases arising from the Canadian Human Rights Act. Some *regulate* particular industries (see Box 15-1: Dodging the Financial Crisis: The Regulation of Canada's Financial Institutions). For example, the Canadian Radio-television and Telecommunications Commission (CRTC) determines which companies can have broadcasting licences and sets requirements for Canadian content in the broadcast media. Some of the CRTC's decisions have been controversial, such as refusing to renew the licence of Quebec City's popular CHOI-FM in 2004 over failure to comply with radio regulations governing offensive language. Also controversial was the licensing in 2005 of two satellite radio services, Canadian Satellite Radio and Sirius Canada, without the normal Canadian content controls. Other agencies have *operating* responsibilities, like those undertaken by the Canadian Food Inspection Agency, whose mandate is to safeguard food, animals, and plants and to provide overall consumer protection. Some federal agencies have *research responsibilities*. For example, the National Research Council (NRC) conducts

BOX 15-1

Dodging the Financial Crisis: The Regulation of Canada's Financial Institutions

In 2008, the world was hit hard by a financial crisis that began in the United States with the bankruptcy of Lehman Brothers, one the world's leading financial institutions. Within weeks, longstanding major banks and other financial institutions around the world faced bankruptcy and either failed or had to be bailed out by government. In many countries, the wave of deregulation of the financial industry in the 1980s and 1990s allowed major financial institutions to make complex, highly speculative investments that collapsed like a house of cards in 2008.

Fortunately, Canadian banks came out of the 2008–2009 financial crisis intact. Indeed, Canada has not had a bank failure since 1985. Although Canada also engaged in deregulation, Canadian banks have been encouraged to be cautious by maintaining substantial capital reserves.

The primary agent for regulating financial institutions is the Office of the Superintendent of Financial Institutions (OSFI), created in 1987 and led from 2007 to 2014 by Julie Dickson. She was replaced by Jeremy Rudin, an ex-academic economist and most recently the assistant deputy minister of the financial sector branch of the department of finance. The OSFI, an independent agency of the Canadian government that reports to Parliament through the minister of finance, regulates federally chartered financial institutions. This means all banks and federally incorporated or registered trust and loan companies, cooperative credit associations, and insurance companies fall under its purview. The agency also regulates federally administered pension plans. Its mandate is to protect the policyholders, depositors, and pension plan members from financial loss.

The OSFI often takes a tough-love approach. Dickson discussed best practices with the banks, and they usually took the hint. However, the OSFI can discipline a bank by requiring it to change its business plan or acquire more capital, or by taking control of its assets.

The OSFI does not act in a vacuum. Its mandate is financial institutions, but the management of the larger financial sector falls to a group composed of the finance minister, an associate deputy minister in finance, the chief executive officers of Canada's largest financial institutions, and the superintendent of financial institutions. Each of these members represents different facets of financial policy. But much of the credit for the strong financial reserves that allowed the banks to weather the crisis of 2008–2009 goes to Dickson, according to *Report on Business* magazine (Perkins, 2009). Charged with overseeing the Canada Mortgage and Housing Corporation, the OSFI pays special attention to monitoring the housing market, which the Bank of Canada has singled out as the largest current risk to the Canadian economy and financial system (Perkins & Carmichael, 2014).

Others, however, see the situation differently. Although Canada avoided the collapse of banks experienced by other countries, the Canadian government assisted the banks by purchasing about $75 billion of the mortgage loans they held. As Russell Williams (2009) points out, there is a huge gap in the regulatory framework for activities of Canadian financial institutions engaged in securities trading. No regulations are in place to prevent Canadian banks from investing heavily, as did American financial institutions, in highly risky investments. It was "simply lucky they did not," as monitoring of the banks' holdings is insufficient (p. 50). Unless securities regulations are tightened, Canada's financial institutions might face serious trouble in a future financial crisis.

scientific research and development. Others combine *research and funding responsibilities*. For example, the Canada Council for the Arts, the federal government's arm's-length arts funding agency, provides funding to artists, endowments, and arts organizations and performs research, communications, and arts promotion activities.

Various rationales have been offered for the use of the agencies, boards, and commissions that generally operate at arm's length from government. One common rationale for the non-departmental form has been the alleged inability of departments to undertake business functions or similar activities, and the need for the organizational flexibility that these independent agencies provide. Some agencies have been set up in part to allow for freedom in personnel and wage policy that supposedly would not have been possible with directions by the Public Service Commission or the Treasury Board. As well, businesspeople and certain researchers may feel uneasy in highly organized departmental structures and prefer to join organizations that are less foreign to their experience and more open to expressions of opinion.

A second reason cited is the need to take away some functions from the controversial political arena. Some functions might be inefficient if too much political interference were allowed. It is argued that pricing policies, monetary policy, capital installation locations, and extension of services should be decided in a non-partisan environment.

A third related justification is to remove quasi-judicial functions from the political realm so that a specialized impartial body with no particular interest in the outcome can make the decisions after holding hearings in a court-like manner.

Other reasons for adopting the non-departmental form include the desire to have an "umbrella organization" to deliver services that involve different government departments or different levels of government. For example, the Canada Revenue Agency was transformed from a department (Revenue Canada) to agency status in 1999. This agency administers federal, provincial, and territorial tax programs and other services. It is managed by a board of management with 15 members appointed by the cabinet, 11 of which are nominated by the provinces and territories.

Alternative Service Delivery (ASD)

ALTERNATIVE SERVICE DELIVERY
Methods of delivering government services apart from the use of traditional departments and agencies, with the goal of making government more businesslike and responsive to the needs of the recipients of services.

The third kind of executive organization, **alternative service delivery** (ASD), is aimed particularly at improving the delivery of government services, reducing the role of government, increasing flexibility, improving coordination among government departments and programs, and generally making government more businesslike and responsive to the needs of the recipients of services. This approach may include establishing new organizational forms within departments or outside traditional departmental structures, termed special operating agencies (such as the self-financing Passport Canada). Alternative service delivery may also involve setting up partnerships with business and voluntary non-governmental organizations, commercializing the provision of services, or contracting out services to private business or to former government employees (Inwood, 2009). Overall, ASD can mean turning to unusual organizational forms and instruments that do not fit the traditional view of government instruments.

THE THREE TYPES OF EXECUTIVE DEPARTMENTS

Three types of executive government departments exist:

1. Central agencies and central departments
2. Central coordinating departments
3. Line departments

Central Agencies and Central Departments

CENTRAL AGENCIES   Central **agencies,** the Privy Council Office (PCO) and the Prime Minister's Office (PMO), are headed by the prime minister and perform service-wide policy, facilitative, and control functions. Their authority comes from the statutory and conventional authority of cabinet itself, and their roles are to assist the prime minister directly and to help with the setting of objectives by cabinet. They have a formal or informal right to intervene in or otherwise influence the activities of departments. The **central departments** (Department of Finance and the Treasury Board Secretariat) also perform these service-wide functions, but they are headed by ministers rather than by the prime minister, their authority comes from statute, and their objectives are usually collectively set or influenced by cabinet. They also have the right to intervene in or otherwise influence the activities of other departments. The term *central agency* is often used to refer to both types of structures. However, differentiating between the two can be useful, since one type, central agencies, provides a venue for direct prime ministerial power and the other, central departments, does not. In fact, one of the central departments, Finance, occasionally jockeys with the prime minister and the central agencies for relative influence.

In contrast, **line departments** are charged with delivering the basic services of government, such as health and defence. Line departments do not normally have a mandate to intervene in the affairs of other departments. Although the central agencies and central departments exert great influence over government policies and actions, they do not have as large a staff or budget as most government departments do. Despite their importance, the central agencies and central departments are the organs of government that parliamentarians (and most Canadians) know least about and whose workings are the least transparent, compared with the others.

CENTRAL AGENCIES
The Prime Minister's Office and the Privy Council Office, which provide direct assistance to the prime minister and facilitate the setting of objectives by cabinet.

CENTRAL DEPARTMENTS
The Department of Finance and the Treasury Board Secretariat, which, along with the central agencies, advise cabinet and its committees and influence the direction and policies of the government.

LINE DEPARTMENTS
Departments that deliver the basic programs and services of government.

PRIME MINISTER'S OFFICE
Provides partisan political advice to the prime minister and is staffed by supporters of the party in power.

Prime Minister's Office
www.pm.gc.ca

The Prime Minister's Office   The **Prime Minister's Office** (PMO) gives partisan political advice to the prime minister and is staffed by supporters of the party in power, although they are hired under the Public Service Employment Act (PSEA). They are classified as "exempt staff" or "ministerial staff" in order to free them from normal public service hiring practices.[2] The reasoning behind this is that the prime minister's government was elected to set a certain political direction for the country. The prime minister thus needs a loyal group to monitor conformity to the program. The PMO has the following functions, among others:

1. Advising on political strategy and the political implications of new policy initiatives
2. Advising on the prime minister's senior appointments
3. Organizing the prime minister's correspondence, media relations, speeches, and timetable
4. Liaising with ministers, members of caucus, and national party officials

PRIVY COUNCIL OFFICE
The central agency that provides non-partisan policy advice to the prime minister and cabinet.

The Privy Council Office   The **Privy Council Office** (PCO) is the central agency that provides non-partisan policy advice to the prime minister and cabinet.[3] It serves as the secretariat for the cabinet and its committees and provides specialized public policy advice to the prime minister. It is responsible for ensuring that the cabinet decision-making process runs smoothly and that the government's agenda is implemented. It is also the main designer and adviser for machinery-of-government issues (meaning the design of major structures like departments and agencies) and tries to "foster a high-performing and accountable Public Service" (Privy Council Office, 2007). The head of the PCO advises the prime minister on the appointment of each **deputy minister**, who functions as the administrative head of a department and provides the link between the minister who is politically responsible for the department and the non-partisan public servants in the department. Finally, the PCO coordinates the federal government's strategy in federal–provincial and territorial relations.

DEPUTY MINISTER
The administrative head of a department and the link between the minister who is politically responsible for the department and the non-partisan public servants in the department.

The Privy Council Office
www.pco-bcp.gc.ca

The head of the Privy Council is the clerk of the Privy Council, who serves as the prime minister's deputy minister, the secretary to the cabinet, and the head of the public service (see Box 15-2: Master Multi-Tasker: The Duties of the Clerk of the Privy Council). The designation "head of the public service" has been in place since the early 1990s to provide leadership for the public service of Canada. As head of the public service, the clerk is responsible for matters relating to public service renewal, for representing the public service to the politicians and to the public, and for issuing an

---

[2]Each cabinet minister also has a small political staff separate from the public servants in the department.
[3]The PCO's name comes from the Queen's Privy Council for Canada, which is discussed in Chapter 13.

BOX 15-2

Master Multi-Tasker:
The Duties of the Clerk of the Privy Council

The clerk of the Privy Council is arguably the most important public servant in the government of Canada. It falls to the clerk to set the "tone at the top" for the public service and to rally it behind the efforts of the current government.

Kevin G. Lynch is a good example of what an individual clerk is relied upon to do. He was appointed in February 2006 in the new Harper government. Even though new prime ministers often appoint new clerks when they come to office, the latter are expected to be non-partisan and to "speak truth to power." This was the case with Kevin Lynch, say Ottawa insiders. He, as most good clerks have to do, balanced the wants of the government with the needs of the public administration that served it.

Few clerks have had to operate in such a turbulent public policy environment. As the world reeled from an international financial crisis in 2008, the worst since the Depression of the 1930s, Lynch worked with the prime minister and the finance department, where he had previously been deputy minister, to design and implement a wide-ranging stimulus package. The year before, he had worked with the same people to manage a crisis in asset-backed commercial paper and to help design the tax reductions that had played a key role in the new government's program.

Lynch also took responsibility for overseeing Canada's involvement in the Afghanistan war, the most intense military conflict the country had seen in a half century. In addition, he is often identified with changing the "foreign affairs focus from Africa and Europe to the Americas . . . pushing strengthened ties to the US and [focusing] on rebuilding Canada's Arctic infrastructure" (Laghi, 2009).

One area closely monitored by clerks of the Privy Council Office is the health of the nation's public service. Lynch was no exception. He launched a public service renewal exercise, convinced his political masters to boost federal recruitment efforts, and reorganized the human resources function with the help of outside advisers.

If this seems like an exercise in multi-tasking, that's exactly what it is. Clerks know that the longest they will be in their position is about three or four years, the average length of service for the office. Like his forerunners, Lynch worked tirelessly to make a difference. When he retired in 2009, after 33 years in the public service, his legacy was secure. Although the media speculated about possible causes for his stepping down as head of the Privy Council Office, Kevin Lynch said simply that "the time was ripe" and "he wanted to go out on a high" (Laghi, 2009).

Wayne G. Wouters replaced Lynch. A consensus-building official with over 30 years of experience in the federal public service, he faced a different set of challenges. Early on, he committed himself to dealing with the demographic renewal of the service as many public servants retire, but faces challenges stemming from the Harper government's deficit reduction program. Wouters in turn was followed by Janice Charette, the former deputy clerk for the Privy Council and associate secretary to the cabinet, and deputy minister of intergovernmental affairs. The point is that for all the similarities in their mandates, the challenges and contributions of each clerk are unique.

annual report on the status of the public service. The "public service" means the core public administration—the employees of the departments as well as some agencies such as the Canada Revenue Agency, the Parks Canada Agency, the Canadian Food Inspection Agency, and the National Research Council Canada.

CENTRAL DEPARTMENTS

Treasury Board Secretariat   The Treasury Board Secretariat (TBS) is a central department that serves the central management board for the public service, the Treasury Board. The Treasury Board establishment and mandate is outlined in the Financial Administration Act, which gives the department responsibility for general administrative policy, financial management, human resources management, internal audit, and public service pensions and benefit programs. It also has responsibilities under a number of other acts, such as the Public Service Employment Act, the Official Languages Act, the Access to Information Act, and the Employment Equity Act. In general, the responsibilities of the TBS include the following:

1. Setting management policies and monitoring performance
2. Directing expenditure management and performance information systems
3. Serving as principal employer of the public service

However, in recent years the Treasury Board Secretariat has had a more difficult time carving out a distinct role for itself in the central executive. David Good (2007) reveals that of all the central bodies, the TBS has struggled most for a meaningful role after having decentralized most of its management roles to departments in the last few decades.

The establishment in 2009 of the Office of the Chief Human Resources Officer (OCHRO) within the Treasury Board Secretariat centralizes human resources policy (hiring and managing people in the public service), which had been scattered across different organizations for several decades. The OCHRO represents the Canadian government as the "employer" in relations with public service employees and deals with all aspects of salaries and benefits. It also develops broad performance indicator framework policies, analyzes basic data on the public service, and provides leadership in human resources management. Within the policy framework of legislation and the OCHRO, the deputy ministers take responsibility for human resources management in their own departments (see Figure 15-1).

The Department of Finance   Finance is often considered the most influential department in the government. It directly and indirectly affects everything that happens in government. It helps prepare the annual federal budget, which dictates whether government expenditure in general will be expansionary, stay-the-course, or restrictive. Finance is also instrumental in

- developing taxes and tariffs;
- arranging federal borrowing;
- advising on and managing transfer payments to provincial and territorial governments;
- representing Canada within international financial institutions such as the International Monetary Fund, the World Trade Organization, and the World Bank; and
- acting as the government's analytic think tank with regard to major economic issues.

Treasury Board Secretariat
www.tbs-sct.gc.ca

FIGURE 15-1
**NEW HUMAN RESOURCES
GOVERNANCE STRUCTURE**

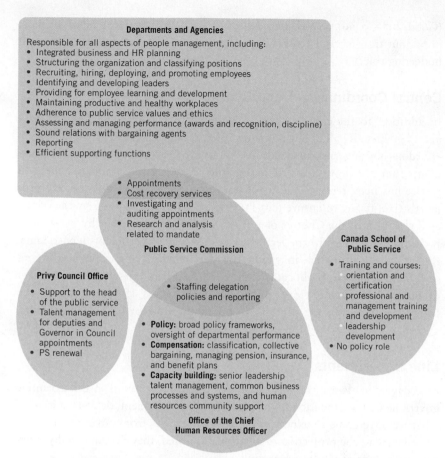

Departments and Agencies
Responsible for all aspects of people management, including:
• Integrated business and HR planning
• Structuring the organization and classifying positions
• Recruiting, hiring, deploying, and promoting employees
• Identifying and developing leaders
• Providing for employee learning and development
• Maintaining productive and healthy workplaces
• Adherence to public service values and ethics
• Assessing and managing performance (awards and recognition, discipline)
• Sound relations with bargaining agents
• Reporting
• Efficient supporting functions

• Appointments
• Cost recovery services
• Investigating and auditing appointments
• Research and analysis related to mandate

Public Service Commission

Canada School of Public Service
• Training and courses:
  orientation and certification
  professional and management training and development
  leadership development
• No policy role

Privy Council Office
• Support to the head of the public service
• Talent management for deputies and Governor in Council appointments
• PS renewal

• Staffing delegation policies and reporting

• **Policy:** broad policy frameworks, oversight of departmental performance
• **Compensation:** classification, collective bargaining, managing pension, insurance, and benefit plans
• **Capacity building:** senior leadership talent management, common business processes and systems, and human resources community support

Office of the Chief Human Resources Officer

SOURCE: *Sixteenth Annual Report to the Prime Minister on the Public Service of Canada.* URL: http://www.clerk.qc.ca/eng/feature.asp?featureId=19&pageId=225. Privy Council Office, 2009. Reproduced with the permission of the Minister of Public Works and Government Services Canada, 2012.

The finance minister has responsibilities that touch many areas. Although each of these responsibilities is of great significance, the annual federal budget is undoubtedly the one that matters most to the majority of ordinary Canadians. The pre-eminent role of finance is evident in the construction of the budget. David Good says that outsiders view the budget as one item, but federal insiders view it as comprising five separate parts, four of which are the direct responsibility of finance: major transfer payments to individuals (e.g., benefits to the elderly and employment insurance); major transfer payments to provincial and territorial governments (the Canada Health Transfer, the Canada Social Transfer, and equalization payments); public debt charges; and tax expenditures (tax breaks, such as the Registered Education Savings Plan, designed to achieve a policy objective). The Treasury Board Secretariat oversees operating and other expenditures, but "in the words of a senior official, these operating and other expenditures are 'really a residual category' and are what officials refer to as the 'small p' programs of government"

(Good, 2007, p. 46). So it is finance that has the major share of some of the most important transfer and economic programs, as well as playing an important budgeting role.

Central Coordinating Departments

In addition to the central agencies and central departments that are key actors in virtually all policy decisions (Smith, 2009) and play a major role in coordinating government decisions, there are central coordinating departments that also have a coordinating role. For example, the department of justice has been responsible for "Charter-proofing" federal legislative proposals (i.e., trying to ensure that they will not be struck down by the courts as a violation of the Charter of Rights and Freedoms), either by itself or by providing guidelines to the legal services units in government departments. Likewise, the minister (in effect, the department) of public works and government services is allocated exclusive jurisdiction under the Department of Public Works and Government Services Act of 1996 and under the Defence Production Act of 1985 to procure goods for other departments, as well as for the armed forces.

Line Departments

Line departments are the third type of organization found in the executive government. They function as the backbone of government, delivering most of what we have come to expect in the way of services from government, from the military to the protection of aviation. As noted, they do not usually intervene in the affairs of other departments.

Line departments have often been portrayed as the drab, unexciting area of government. They are said to be the most driven by bureaucratic rules, the most dominated by politicians—their own ministers and the prime minister—and the most in need of, but at the same time the most deeply resistant to, basic reform. A.W. Johnson (1992) noted that between the 1960s and the early 1990s there was at least "one new major push for reform every three to five years" (p. 7). Even the Privy Council felt compelled to note, in an internal paper, that a few perennial themes seem to have dominated the public administration landscape since the early 1960s. From a human resources (HR) management perspective, frustrations over cumbersome and inflexible staffing mechanisms or the lack of integrated HR and business planning echo across the generations. At a broader level, there has been an almost constant tension between the need for rigorous accountability on one hand and the desire for creative and flexible management on the other (Privy Council Office, 2007).

Some academics have contributed to this view of the federal line bureaucracy as being overwhelmed with paperwork and rules. Savoie (2008) describes it thus:

Reports of one kind or another, performance measurement schemes, management targets, horizontal government, oversight bodies, major developments in IT (information technology), political crises (often caused by information obtained through access to information legislation), a much more aggressive media, whistle-blowing legislation, an emphasis on managing publicly not privately, constantly changing priorities, collective bargaining, and unionized workers operating in a world with no bottom line. . . . [no wonder] Front-line managers and workers firmly believe that getting things done is much more difficult today than it was forty years ago. (p. 223)

However, others consider the line bureaucracy as a more independent and a more challenging place to work. Some theorists of the rational choice school, or those who are attracted by the principal–agent theory, see the average bureaucrat as a significant power-seeking agent, one whose nominal superiors do not under normal circumstances have enough information or resources to control their employees. The move to the New Public Management approach to public sector organization and management is a sign of just how much politicians fear the power of the bureaucracy in Canada and Britain (Aucoin, 1995).

Recent writing about the federal bureaucracy views some federal deputy ministers as having great success in achieving the departmentally driven agendas. As noted in Chapter 13, David Good (2007) says that departments can be effective if they follow three elemental rules: (1) link the department's proposals to the priorities of government, (2) do your homework, and (3) have a constituency. Linking to government priorities means cultivating close ties with finance, the PMO, and the PCO and convincing the prime minister that it is "the prime minister's issue," not cabinet's, and that the prime minister will garner personal credit for the issue and be able to resolve any division in cabinet on the side of the department. Doing one's homework means doing the policy work surrounding the issue and knowing the issue better than finance; linking to the concerns of finance; and thinking like a "guardian," that is, like finance or the Treasury Board would. Having a constituency means developing support both inside and outside of government, including regional ministers, key sectoral ministers, and important interest groups; and distributing benefits and pain equitably across the whole range of provinces (Good, 2007).

The Three Levels of Bureaucratic Elite in Departments

Three levels of bureaucratic elite characterize departments:

1. The deputy minister (DM) level (and in some departments, associate deputy ministers)
2. The assistant deputy minister (ADM) appointments
3. Director-level appointments

Deputy and associate deputy ministers are called Governor in Council (GIC) appointments because they are made by the governor general upon the advice of the cabinet (acting in the name of the Privy Council). In practice, it is the prerogative of the prime minister, not the minister of the department, to appoint these individuals. In doing so, the prime minister takes into account the need to ensure that the appointees can be trusted to carry out his or her will and see to the needs of the government of the day. The clerk of the Privy Council provides advice to the prime minister on these appointments.

Despite being chosen by the prime minister and closely associated with the policies of the government, most deputy ministers are retained even when a new government is elected. The deputy minister is expected to be politically neutral and impartial—neither for the government nor against it, but rather the guardian of the administrative order. The task at hand is to advise, to speak truth to power, and to supply the government with the best and most cautious information in spite of how unpalatable this may be politically. The deputy minister controls the management of the department. Although traditionally it is the minister, rather than the deputy minister, who is responsible to Parliament for the actions of the department, the Financial Administration Act (2007) has modified this tradition. Specifically, the deputy minister is the accounting officer for the department and, as such, is legally obliged to appear before parliamentary committees to report on conformity to that Act (Inwood, 2009).

More generally, the thinking about the role of the deputy minister has evolved in recent years. The public sector has lost its image both as an employer for life and as protector of the public interest. Many young entrants to the public service have an "in and out" mentality; government is only one alternative in the menu of career opportunities. This changed image has meant that the role of deputy minister has to take on added hues. Now the deputy minister needs to pay great attention to succession planning, corporate human resources planning, and employee engagement levels, and generally needs to be sensitive to the issue of government as "employer of choice" (Dunn & Bierling, 2009).

Assistant deputy ministers generally manage branches within a department. They are merit-based positions competitively chosen in recent years by the Office of the Chief Human Resources Officer.

Directors general and directors are the third level of the administrative elite. These are also merit-based appointments and are often considered to be the "middle management" level of the federal service. Several hundred individuals operate at this level. For example, reporting to the assistant deputy minister for science and technology at Environment Canada are five directors general (water, atmospheric, wildlife and landscape, science and risk assessment, and strategies) as well as a director of the Environmental Science and Technology Centre.

PUBLIC SECTOR RENEWAL IN PERSPECTIVE

One matter has not been dealt with yet in this chapter and can only be mentioned in passing: public sector renewal. Canada has been engaged in an almost constant search for an optimal design for public administration.

Consistency has not been a notable characteristic of the process. The Glassco Commission (Royal Commission on Government Organization) in the early 1960s introduced the notion of decentralization with its "let the managers manage" slogan. In contrast, the Lambert Commission of 1979 (Royal Commission on Financial Management and Accountability) reintroduced centralization as an option for the public service. Then in the 1990s, the *PS 2000 Report* emphasized the importance of managers in the federal administration.

Public service renewal has faced challenges over the years in figuring out how best to balance the market, government, and non-governmental sectors. Observers of the executive have seen the government struggling to loosen the rigidity of traditional administration by having it bolstered first by Crown corporations, ABCs, and then the wide menu of alternative service delivery arrangements, all the time questioning whether such measures are tenable in the long term. Even within government, the role of the central agencies and the departments remains an issue. The patterns outlined in this chapter suggest that these tensions will be around for a long time to come.

DIVERSITY AND A REPRESENTATIVE BUREAUCRACY

To develop a competent, professional public service based on permanent employees, the hiring of public servants since the early twentieth century has been guided by the merit principle. That is, instead of hiring the supporters of the governing party, the public service focuses on the qualifications of candidates and uses competitive examinations in its hiring practices. However, appointments made strictly on merit do not necessarily result in a public service that represents the diversity of society. In fact, the public service until the 1970s consisted largely of English-speaking males of British ancestry. Since the late 1960s, efforts have been made to create a more bilingual public service able to provide government services in both English and French. As well, supporters of national unity hoped the greater presence of French speakers in the Canadian government would help to offset the growing separatist movement in Quebec. Today, about 31.6 percent of public servants speak French as their first language (Treasury Board of Canada Secretariat, 2011–2012, p. 4) and about two-fifths of positions in the public service require knowledge of both official languages (Treasury Board of Canada Secretariat, 2007).

In recent decades, efforts have continued to develop a *representative bureaucracy* that reflects the diversity of various aspects of Canadian society.

EMPLOYMENT EQUITY GROUP	2005–2006	2006–2007	2007–2008	2008–2009	2009–2010	2010–2011	2011–2012	2012–2013	WFA*
Women	54.0%	54.5%	54.9%	55.1%	55.1%	55.3%	55.3%	55.0%	52.8%
Aboriginal Peoples	3.8%	3.9%	4.0%	4.2%	4.2%	4.3%	4.5%	4.6%	2.9%
Persons with Disabilities	5.5%	5.5%	5.7%	5.6%	5.6%	5.6%	5.7%	5.8%	4.0%
Visible Minorities	9.6%	9.8%	10.3%	11.1%	11.6%	12.6%	13.3%	14.0%	13.0%

Population: Indeterminate population and term population of three months or more, excluding employees on leave without pay, in the **Core Public Administration (CPA)** and employees of **separate agencies**. Some small separate agencies were not included because of missing information.

SOURCE: Office of the Chief Human Resources Officer, Treasury Board Secretariat. http://www.tbs-sct.gc.ca/res/stats/images/demo13-03-eng.html, Treasury Board of Canada Secretariat, 2013. Reproduced with the permission of the Minister of Public Works and Government Services Canada, 2015.

Employment equity targets and timetables have been set up to increase the proportion of women, people with disabilities, Aboriginal peoples, and visible minorities in the public service, particularly in the higher ranks. Some people have raised concerns that efforts to develop a representative bureaucracy will weaken the merit principle. However, those hired and promoted still have to meet the appropriate criteria of competence for their positions. Nevertheless, the requirement to hire the person "best qualified" for a position no longer exists. Instead, managers have to justify their hiring decisions in terms of the "right fit" for the job among applicants meeting the essential merit criteria. Furthermore, a deputy minister of a department has the authority to restrict the selection of hiring for a position to the members of a designated group and to include employment equity objectives as a criterion of merit (Public Service Commission, 2007).

As Table 15-5 indicates, the public service as a whole is quite representative of the available workforce. Women are still underrepresented in some positions. Nevertheless, the public service bureaucracy has become much more representative than in the past.

PARLIAMENTARY INSTITUTIONS

In the Canadian Parliament, three sets of institutional players keep the institution running: political officers, officers of Parliament, and procedural officers.

Political Officers

Political officers are not bureaucratic officers in the normal sense, but because they do some routine administrative work—administering rules, scheduling, monitoring, rendering accountability, and so forth—they might be considered part of the bureaucracy of Parliament. The political officers of the House of

Commons—including parliamentary party officials such as the speaker, the deputy speaker, the party House leaders, and the party whips—have come to be known as **House officers**. These individuals are at once politicians and administrators, in the sense of making the routine machinery of Parliament work. It should also be added that many of them have individuals working for them as well. The speakers, for example, have legal and financial officers attached to their offices, who assist in deciding on matters of parliamentary law and in administering the precincts of Parliament.

HOUSE OFFICERS
Political officers of the House of Commons.

Officers of Parliament

Officers of Parliament, along with the offices they head, have sometimes been called "servants of Parliament," "parliamentary watchdogs," or the "parliamentary control bureaucracy." Paul Thomas (2002) has described them as "independent accountability agencies created first to assist Parliament in holding ministers and the bureaucracy accountable and, second, to protect various kinds of rights of individual Canadians" (p. 288). As "servants of Parliament," these are offices that serve and are responsible to the legislative branch rather than the executive, and to that end they have been freed from the normal constraints that bind the executive government.

OFFICERS OF PARLIAMENT
Independent officials who assist Parliament in holding government accountable and protecting various rights of Canadians.

One of the most pre-eminent of the officers of Parliament—and certainly the oldest, established in 1878—is the auditor general (AG) of Canada. The AG audits departments and agencies, most Crown corporations, and other federal organizations as well as the three territories, and his or her reports are presented directly to Parliament. Since 1977, when the Auditor General Act was broadened to include "triple-E reporting"—commenting on whether government is implementing policies economically, efficiently, and with adequate means for judging their effectiveness (also referred to as "value for money [VFM] auditing")—the auditor's reports have become central to Canadian political life. For example, the auditor general's strong criticism of the spiralling cost of a proposed purchase of F-35 stealth fighter jets and the inaccurate reporting of these costs to Parliament became a controversial political issue in 2012.

Over time, the category of officers has tended to expand, as have some of their powers. The present list of officers is presented in Table 15-6. Although the federal level has no exact equivalent to the post of ombudsman,[4] a post found in many provinces and other jurisdictions, some of the federal officers have quasi-ombudsman roles. In other words, they take complaints from citizens and public servants regarding the failure of government to perform duties it has taken on itself. Such analogies can be made with regard to the commissioner of official languages, the information commissioner, the privacy commissioner, and the public sector integrity commissioner.

---

[4]There is, however, an Office of the Ombudsman for the Department of National Defence and the Canadian Forces.

TABLE 15-6

OFFICERS OF PARLIAMENT AND THEIR MANDATES

NAME OF OFFICER	DATE ESTABLISHED	RELEVANT LEGISLATION	MANDATE
Auditor General of Canada	1878	Financial Administration Act, 1985; Auditor General Act, 1985	Prepares a statement for the public accounts on whether the latter represent stated federal accounting practices Prepares reports regarding VFM and whether spending fits with the purposes for which it was appropriated
Chief Electoral Officer	1920	Canada Elections Act, 2000; Fair Elections Act, 2014	Conducts federal elections Registers eligible voters Appoints election officers Supports independent boundaries commissions Pursues studies of voting methods Supervises party registration, party leadership races, political financing, and political broadcasts
Commissioner of Official Languages	1970	Official Languages Act, 1985	Ensures recognition of equality of status, rights, and privileges for English and French in federal institutions Supports the advancement of linguistic minority communities
Information Commissioner	1982	Access to Information Act, 1985	Maintains the purposes of the Act, which are to ensure availability of government information, that access exceptions are limited, and disclosure decisions are reviewed independently Investigates complaints from citizens regarding access to government information Launches independent complaints
Privacy Commissioner	1982	Privacy Act, 1985, which applies to government's handling of personal information, and the Personal Information Protection and Electronic Documents Act, 2000, which is privacy law applying to Canada's private sector	Oversees compliance with both the Privacy Act and the Personal Information Protection and Electronic Documents Act (PIPEDA) Investigates complaints regarding illegal use or disclosure, or denial of access to personal information by government Monitors various privacy issues
Conflict of Interest and Ethics Commissioner	2007	Conflict of Interest Act, 2006; Parliament of Canada Act, 1985; Lobbyists Registration Act, 1985; An Act to Amend the Lobbyists Registration Act, 1993; Conflict of Interest Code for Members of the House of Commons	Administers the conflict of interest code applying to Members of the House of Commons Advises, investigates, and issues compliance orders and imposes administrative monetary penalties on public office holders under the terms of the Act

TABLE 15-6 *(continued)*

NAME OF OFFICER	DATE ESTABLISHED	RELEVANT LEGISLATION	MANDATE
Public Sector Integrity Commissioner	2007	Public Servants Disclosure Protection Act, 2005; FAA; Federal Accountability Act, 2006	Investigates wrongdoing by public servants, recommends corrective action regarding such, and refers complaints about reprisals arising from reporting of wrongdoing to adjudication
Commissioner of Lobbying	2008	Lobbying Act, 1985, as amended 2008; Federal Accountability Act, 2006	Maintains a registry of lobbyists who register themselves under the Lobbying Act and makes such registration information public Develops a lobbyists' code of conduct Conducts investigations and ensures compliance with the code and the Act

The Harper government also created another official, who is like an officer of Parliament but not designated as such, called the parliamentary budget officer (PBO). The PBO is an independent officer of the Library of Parliament who reports to the parliamentary librarian who, in turn, reports to speakers of both chambers. The Office of the Parliamentary Budget Officer provides non-partisan financial and economic analysis to support Parliament's oversight role and to provide budget transparency. For example, Kevin Page, the parliamentary budget officer appointed for a five-year term in 2008, issued a report in 2009 detailing the high cost of Canada's involvement in Afghanistan. As well, his office's estimate of the government's likely deficit was far greater than the official government estimate.

However, issues have been raised concerning the independence of this officer, the budget of this office has been cut back, and there are rumours about the weakening of the position. Unlike officers of Parliament, such as the auditor general or the chief electoral officer, whose mandate explicitly includes independence from the government of the day, there have been concerns that the parliamentary budget officer may be constrained by the parliamentary library's desire to avoid political controversy.

Page complained about the lack of information provided to his office by the Harper government on its spending cuts and their impact on the provision of government services. In November 2012, he asked the Federal Court for a ruling on this matter. The Court dismissed his case on the basis of justiciability—saying he had not actually asked departments for the information he said was denied to him—but the decision was a kind of victory nevertheless. Government and the speakers of both houses of Parliament had maintained that the Court had no jurisdiction in this question because of parliamentary privilege, but the decision was clear that indeed the Court did. The subtext of the decision included broad hints affirming the independence of the PBO and the officer's right to seek a broad range of economic and financial information (*Page v. Mulcair*, 2013).

Jean-Denis Frechette, the former senior director of the economics, resources and international affairs division of the Library of Parliament's information and research service, replaced Page in 2013, with the question of independence unresolved (CBC News, 2013, August 30).

Procedural Officers of Parliament

Procedural officers of Parliament are essentially the public servants of Parliament, providing the equivalent of department-like services to the House of Commons and the Senate. The key figures in the House who furnish these services are the clerk of the House, the deputy clerk, the clerk assistant, the law clerk and parliamentary counsel, and the sergeant-at-arms. In the Senate there are similar procedural officers.

The clerk of the House is the senior permanent official responsible for advice on the procedural aspects of the plenary (whole) House and looks after the ongoing administration of the House of Commons. The clerk of the Senate performs the same role for the Senate. The clerks' role is comparable to the role of deputy ministers in the executive departments. In the Commons, the clerk is the permanent head responsible for the management of staff and daily operational affairs. The clerk takes direction from the speaker in relation to policy matters. In turn, the speaker takes overall direction in management from the Internal Economy Commission (IEC), an all-party committee statutorily charged with administering the House. In parliamentary matters, within

As they accompany the speaker during the ceremonial walk to start the daily session, the procedural officers and staff of the House of Commons—the sergeant-at-arms, the clerk, the law clerk, and even the page—represent the bureaucracy that supports the speaker and the House.

© Geoff Howe/Canadian Press Images

the House itself, the speaker is supreme and takes direction from no one in particular, except the will of the House.

JUDICIAL INSTITUTIONS

The Supreme Court of Canada, the Federal Court, the Federal Court of Appeal, the Tax Court, and the Court Martial Appeal Court are administered federally. Reflecting the principle of judicial independence, the administration of these courts operates at arm's length from the executive government.

The staff of the Supreme Court of Canada is headed by the registrar who is responsible to the chief justice of the court. The registrar and deputy registrar are Governor-in-Council appointees who oversee a staff of nearly 200 public servants who manage cases and hearings; provide legal support to the judges; edit, translate, and publish judgments; manage the flow of documents; and perform a variety of other essential tasks.

Support for the four other federally administered courts is provided by the Courts Administrative Service. The chief administrator, a Governor-in-Council appointee, is responsible for the overall operations of these four courts and their staff of about 600 public servants. The chief justice of any of the four courts may issue binding directives to the chief administrator. There is also a kind of third administrative option. In addition to the above, each chief justice has authority over such matters as determining workloads and court sittings and assigning cases to judges, and may appoint a judicial administrator from among the employees of the service for such duties as establishing the time and place of court hearings.

THE PUBLIC BUREAUCRACY AS A LOCUS OF CONTROVERSY

The preceding may lead one to conclude that the public bureaucracy is a mechanical and straightforward topic, but in fact the state apparatus is as much a place of controversy as is any other. In fact, public service issues were often raised in press coverage of the Harper government. Space does not permit an extensive coverage of this topic, but there is no lack of material in public administration literature on such matters. Here are some issues to mull over as we leave this area of investigation:

What is the role of the public servant in public policy discussions? In 1940, two social scientists engaged in a debate about this topic. Herman Finer (1940) maintained that the public servant should be just that, exercising no independent judgment on issues of the day and following as closely as possible the will of the legislature and political masters. Carl Friedrich (1940) held the opposite view, stating that the public official owed it to the polity to share his or her specialized knowledge in the public dialogue on issues, and thereby enrich it. Such a debate still resonates. For example, sources as wide-ranging as the

Canadian Science Writers' Association and Climate Action Network Canada charged that the Harper Conservative government muzzled public comments of climate and fisheries scientists and weakened the research capacity of Canada's science community.

How open should government be? There have been a variety of official and academic reports (see, for example, Access to Information Review Task Force, 2002) on the need to make government more open and transparent, and some action has indeed been forthcoming. The issue is the degree of response, with reformers calling for more powers for the information commissioner and relaxing of the bar for access. Information commissioner Suzanne Legault noted as well in an appearance before the Standing Committee on Access to Information, Privacy and Ethics on September 22, 2011, that "As reflected in Treasury Board statistics, over the past ten years there has been a steady decline in the timeliness and disclosure of information by federal institutions." For its part, the Harper government emphasized its wide-ranging response to demands for transparency, which it called "open government." Stephen Harper announced in March 2011 that open government has three windows: open data, open information, and open dialogue. The first promises that government data sets will be released in reader-friendly formats; the second is about the proactive release of government information on its activities—for example, summaries of completed access to information requests; and the latter aims to expand the citizen voice in policymaking and broaden citizen engagement through Web 2.0 technologies.

These are just two of the contemporary questions that have given rise to the spirited debate in Canada about public bureaucracy; there are several others. They concern such matters as whether the federal spending power should be limited, whether pay and employment equity measures need to be restrained, whether the institutions of Parliament and the judiciary need strengthening, whether government is too big and too intrusive, plus others. We encourage the reader to pursue such avenues; they are of immense importance, as the coming years will prove.

Summary and Conclusion

Public officials work in a multiplicity of organizational forms. The majority of government employees work in departments under the political direction of a cabinet minister and the administrative direction of the deputy minister. However, central agencies and central departments have developed a considerable influence over the direction of government departments. Furthermore, a variety of Crown corporations and semi-independent agencies, boards, and commissions do not operate according to the traditional departmental model of public administration. When we think of the staff of the various governing institutions, we often ignore those who work for Parliament and the courts. Of particular importance has been the establishment of various officers of Parliament who, with their staffs, help Parliament in trying to hold the executive accountable for its actions and assist people who have complaints about government.

Bureaucratic organizations are necessary for the achievement of good government. A large, professional staff is required to administer the multitude of government programs. Many government officials play a major role in developing new policies and in evaluating existing policies and programs. Career public servants may be more likely than politicians to take a long-term perspective on what is in the public interest. They are able to be an important source of non-partisan advice for cabinet ministers. Through their interactions with interest groups and diverse backgrounds, public servants can make government more responsive to societal concerns. Moreover, by speaking "truth to power," public servants can play a vital role in the pursuit of good government.

The public service bureaucracy in the executive departments has been the subject of considerable criticism. Some argue that the bureaucracy is too rule-bound and inflexible and not oriented to providing good service to people and businesses. Those who use the rational choice theory view bureaucrats as self-interested individuals seeking to expand government so that they can gain more status, privileges, and power. Indeed, some critics argue that senior bureaucrats wield excessive undemocratic power by influencing cabinet ministers who rely on them for advice.

However, there are limits to the power of bureaucrats. The prime minister and cabinet, working with the central agencies and central departments, are able to set the direction of government policy. As well, the prime minister and cabinet increasingly rely on alternative sources of advice from partisan political advisers, consultants, and think tanks. Furthermore, the various officers of Parliament, such as the auditor general, information commissioner, and privacy commissioner, provide some checks on the power of the executive bureaucracy. Although the convention of ministerial responsibility for the actions of government can shield the bureaucracy from public scrutiny, access to information legislation (even though imperfect in its application) and other reforms have brought some transparency and accountability to the activities of the bureaucracy.

Discussion Questions

1. Is bureaucracy a threat to democracy?

2. Is it important to have a non-partisan bureaucracy, or would it be better to have senior officials committed to carrying out the political direction of the government?

3. If you were to envisage yourself as a future public servant, what branch of government and what level strikes you as being the most interesting? The most challenging?

4. If you were to lead a program of public service reform in the government of Canada, on what would it focus?

5. Is it important to have a representative bureaucracy?

Further Reading

Aucoin, P. (1995). *The new public management: Canada in comparative perspective.* Montreal, QC: Institute for Research on Public Policy.

Dunn, C. (2010). *The handbook of Canadian public administration* (2nd ed.). Toronto, ON: Oxford University Press.

Bourgault, J., & Dunn, C. Eds. (2014). *Deputy Ministers in Canada: Comparative and Jurisdictional Perspectives.* Toronto: University of Toronto Press.

Evans, B., & Shields, J. (2002). The third sector: Neo-liberal restructuring, governance, and the remaking of state-civil society relationships. In C. Dunn (Ed.), *The handbook of Canadian public administration.* Toronto, ON: Oxford University Press.

Good, D.A. (2007). *The politics of public money: Spenders, guardians, priority setters and financial watchdogs inside the Canadian government.* Toronto, ON: University of Toronto Press.

Graham, A. (2014). *Canadian public sector financial management* (2nd ed.). Montreal, QC: McGill-Queen's University Press.

Inwood, G.J. (2011). *Understanding Canadian public administration: An introduction to theory and practice* (4th ed.). Toronto, ON: Pearson Education Canada.

Savoie, D.J. (2003). *Breaking the bargain: Public servants, ministers and Parliament.* Toronto, ON: University of Toronto Press.

CHAPTER 16

The Judicial System: Law and the Courts

CHAPTER OBJECTIVES

After reading this chapter, you should be able to

1. Examine the significance of the rule of law and the independence of the judiciary.
2. Explain how the legal system in Quebec differs from that of other provinces.
3. Outline the structure of the court system.
4. Discuss the procedures for appointing judges.
5. Examine the importance of judicial review of legislation

The statue of the "Famous Five" on Parliament Hill depicts the reactions of Emily Murphy, Irene Parlby, Nellie McClung, Louise McKinney, and Henrietta Edwards on hearing the news of the 1929 judgment of the Judicial Committee of the Privy Council in Great Britain declaring women "persons" and eligible to sit in the Senate.

© Supreme Court of Canada

Emily Murphy was born in 1868 into a family of prominent lawyers and politicians. After moving with her husband and three daughters to Alberta, she became a prominent campaigner for women's rights, as well as a popular writer using the pen name "Janey Canuck."

In 1916, Emily Murphy was appointed as the first female magistrate in the British Empire. Earlier that year, women had won the right to vote in Alberta and were soon elected to the provincial legislature. Murphy had greater ambitions: She wanted to be appointed to the Canadian Senate. Unfortunately, she had to confront a formidable legal obstacle before she could enter this male bastion of privilege. The British North America Act, 1867, specified that "persons" with certain qualifications were eligible to be appointed to the Senate. Although Murphy met these qualifications, under the common law women were not considered "persons" with rights and privileges. She was hostage to her gender.

Murphy decided to challenge this interpretation. Murphy and four other women's rights advocates (Henrietta Edwards, Louise McKinney, Irene Parlby, and Nellie McClung)—known as the "Famous Five"—submitted a petition to the Supreme Court of Canada in 1927 asking for an advisory opinion as to whether "persons" included women.

In their judgment, the majority of judges cited English common law rulings, including one that claimed, "chiefly out of respect to women, and a sense of decorum, and not from their want of intellect, or their being for any other such reason unfit to take part in the government of the country," women have "been excused" from taking part in public affairs. Given this legal context, if Parliament had intended to allow women to be appointed to the Senate, it should have expressly written that in the British North America Act (*Edwards v. A.G. of Canada,* 1928).

Prime Minister Mackenzie King agreed to ask the Judicial Committee of the Privy Council in Great Britain, which was at the time the highest appeal body, for its opinion on the issue. In a unanimous ruling in 1929, the Judicial Committee concluded that women were eligible to be appointed to the Senate as "persons." Excluding women from public office was a "relic of days more barbarous than ours."

In explaining their ruling, the Judicial Committee argued that the Constitution should not be interpreted in a "narrow and technical" manner, but rather as a "living tree capable of growth and expansion within its natural limits" (*Edwards v. A.G. of Canada,* 1930). The law should evolve in response to the changing values and circumstances of society. By applying the "living tree" concept, the courts can have an important political role in affecting the course of public policy rather than, as some would prefer, sticking to the precise wording of the law, the express intention of those who wrote the laws, and past precedents of interpreting the law.

The Persons case (as it has come to be known) is celebrated as a major victory for the rights of women. In 1930, Cairine Reay Wilson was the first woman to be appointed to the Senate. As for Emily Murphy, she died in 1933 without receiving the Senate appointment she so cherished. Her role in the Famous Five assures her place in history, but she also finally has a place in the upper chamber: In October 2009, the Senate voted for Murphy and the other members of the Famous Five to be named honorary senators.

INTRODUCTION

The United States is often described as having three branches of government: the executive (led by the president), the legislative (Congress), and the judicial (headed by the Supreme Court). Each separate branch is expected to check and balance the power of the other branches. Canada's Constitution Act, 1867, also makes a distinction among the executive, legislative, and judicial. However, as discussed in Chapters 13 and 14, the practice of executive dominance and party discipline has greatly limited the independence of Parliament and its ability to check the power of the prime minister and cabinet. Nevertheless, the judiciary as the "third branch" of government continues to have an important role in checking the power of the executive and ensuring that the rule of law is followed. As well, the constitutional Charter of Rights and Freedoms has increased the importance of the courts in determining the validity of laws and government actions. In this chapter, we examine Canada's legal systems, the structure of the court system, the procedures for appointing judges, their decision-making processes, and some issues concerning the judicial system.

THE RULE OF LAW AND THE JUDICIARY

A basic feature of the Canadian political system is the **rule of law**—the principle that individuals should be subject only to known, predictable, and impartial rules, rather than to the arbitrary orders of those in governing positions. This does not only mean that we are expected to abide by the many thousands of laws that control our behaviour and our relationships with others; crucially, it also means that those people with authority, including those responsible for making, implementing, and enforcing laws, are expected to act in keeping with the law, including the legal and constitutional procedures for passing and changing laws. In particular, the rule of law protects the people against arbitrary actions by government and those empowered to act for the state, including police and security services.

The rule of law is a key feature of liberal democratic government, distinguishing it from various forms of dictatorial rule. The rule of law includes the principle that all individuals are equal before and under the law, regardless of their wealth, social status, or political position. The rule of law also requires that the courts be independent, so that judges can be impartial in settling disputes without interference from government.

The judiciary is important in the governing process. Not only do judges administer justice by applying laws and penalizing those who break the law, but they are also essential in interpreting the law and the constitution. As well, the courts have the authority to review laws to determine their validity (i.e., the power of judicial review).

RULE OF LAW
The principle that individuals should be subject only to known, predictable, and impartial rules, rather than to the arbitrary orders of those in governing positions.

LAWS

Laws can be thought of as rules of behaviour concerning the relationships and disputes involving individuals, businesses, groups, and the state (Hausegger, Hennigar, & Riddell, 2015). Laws fall primarily into two basic categories: public and private, each of which involves various specific areas of law (see Table 16-1). Laws concerning the relationship of the state to individuals and laws concerning the authority and operations of the state are referred to as **public law**. There are four major types of public law:

1. *Criminal law* deals with behaviour that is an offence against the public of sufficient importance that the state (the Crown) is responsible for prosecuting the alleged offender.
2. *Constitutional law* deals with the rules concerning those aspects of governing that are set out in the Constitution, including the division of authority between the national and provincial governments and the rights and freedoms of individuals.
3. *Administrative law* concerns the standards that government and its agencies are required to follow in their administrative and regulatory activities.
4. *Tax law* refers to the rules for the collection of revenue from individuals and businesses.

PUBLIC LAW
Laws concerning the relationship of the state to individuals and laws concerning the authority and operations of the state.

TABLE 16-1
TYPES OF LAWS

PUBLIC LAW	PRIVATE LAW
Criminal law	Contract law
Constitutional law	Property law
Administrative law	Family law
Tax law	Torts
	Various others (e.g., intellectual property rights, wills and trusts, business organization, real estate, and consumer rights)

SOURCE: Adapted from Hausegger, Hennigar, & Riddell, 2015, p. 9.

PRIVATE LAW
Areas of law dealing with the relationships among individuals, groups, and businesses that are primarily of private interest rather than general public interest.

TORT
Harmful actions, negligence, or words that allow the injured party to sue for damages.

STATUTORY LAW
A law that has been passed by an act of Parliament or a provincial legislature.

Private law (often termed civil law) deals with issues in the relationships among individuals, groups, and businesses that are primarily of private interest rather than general public interest. Various types of private law exist. For instance, contract law establishes rules for enforceable agreements; property law concerns the rights linked to owning and possessing property; family law deals with domestic relations, including rules related to the consequences of the break-up of a marriage; and **tort** law establishes rules for the remedies available to an injured party as a result of the actions, negligence, or words of another party. Other areas of private law relate to such topics as intellectual property rights, wills and trusts, business organization, real estate transactions, and the rights of consumers. Disputes in the area of private law involve one side (the plaintiff) initiating action against the other side (the defendant).[1]

The Sources of Law

The Canadian Constitution divides the authority to pass laws between Parliament and provincial legislatures, with only a small number of areas in which both Parliament and provincial legislatures have legislative power. For example, the Canadian Parliament is responsible for criminal law, while provincial legislatures are responsible for many subjects related to private law. However, some areas of private law—such as marriage and divorce, and patents and copyrights—fall under the legislative authority of the Canadian Parliament.

A law that has been passed by an act of Parliament or a provincial legislature is known as a **statutory law**. Legislative bodies often delegate the ability to pass subordinate legislation to other institutions. For example, Parliament can delegate to the cabinet the authority to make regulations in keeping with the general principles of an act of Parliament. Provincial governments delegate authority to municipal governments to make bylaws, provided the bylaws are consistent with provincial legislation.

---

[1]Some legal actions can involve both public and private law. For example, if one person attacks another causing injury, criminal proceedings on the charge of assault may be launched by the Crown, while the injured person may sue the attacker for damages under the law of torts.

Many laws are not set out in statutes, but rather are based on common law and codified civil law. Public law throughout Canada, along with private law in all provinces except Quebec, is based on the English system of **common law**. This system started in the twelfth century as the increasingly powerful king's courts began to use the "common customs" of the entire country as the basis for their decisions rather than the traditions of different localities used by the courts of various nobles (Hausegger et al., 2015, p. 11). The practice that developed was for judges to use precedents (i.e., examine decisions in previous similar cases) to guide their decisions.[2] Common law thus consists of court judgments from many centuries of cases, first in England and then in Canada, that have never been brought together in a single document. In court, lawyers present a variety of precedent cases that they consider relevant to the case being decided. The judge has to decide which precedents are most relevant, keeping in mind that precedents set in cases before superior courts are binding on lower courts.

COMMON LAW

A body of law developed through the accumulation of court decisions that become binding precedents for similar future cases.

The common law system is used in most of the English-speaking Commonwealth and in the United States (other than Louisiana). It has sometimes been criticized for preserving rules that are outdated and no longer reflect the changing values of society. However, the common law can evolve over time as judges find features in the cases before them that differ from precedent cases, and thus interpret the principles underlying common law somewhat differently. As well, legislatures have been active in passing laws that, in effect, replace the provisions of common law.

Quebec uses the **Quebec Civil Code** as the basis of its private law. This system of **codified civil law** traces its origins back to the sixth century, when the Byzantine emperor Justinian I created a code of laws out of the laws of the Roman Empire, along with the commentaries of legal scholars (Hausegger et al., 2015). The French emperor Napoleon commissioned a codified system of law in 1804 (that become known as the Napoleonic Code) based on Roman and French sources. This code has become the foundation of the private law systems of many continental European and Latin American countries. In 1866, Quebec established a system of codified civil law based, in part, on the Napoleonic Code. This was replaced by the Quebec Civil Code, which came into effect in 1994. Because civil code systems provide a full set of legal principles for resolving disputes, judges can apply these principles to reach their decisions in particular cases (Hausegger et al., 2015).[3]

QUEBEC CIVIL CODE

A codified system of law that is the basis of private law in Quebec.

CODIFIED CIVIL LAW

A system of private law used in Quebec based on a comprehensive set of legal principles.

Common law and Quebec's civil code continue to be important sources of law, resulting in differences in the private law between Quebec and the rest of Canada.[4] (For an example, see Box 16-1: Lola and Eric: The Civil

---

[2]This is known as the doctrine of *stare decisis*, a Latin term meaning "to stand by decided matters."

[3]Quebec judges also increasingly use precedents to help in applying laws (Hausegger et al., 2015).

[4]Because of these differences, most lawyers are educated and can practise in only one of the two legal systems. However, a few universities offer law students the opportunity to qualify in both systems.

BOX 16-1

Lola and Eric: The Civil Code and the Common Law

In 1992, 32-year-old Quebecer "Eric" saw 17-year-old "Lola"* on a Brazilian beach. Despite his inability to speak Portuguese, Eric persistently wooed her. Lola's father didn't approve of their relationship, but Eric promised to take care of Lola. However, he rejected requests by Lola to get married. After living together in Quebec for seven years and having three children (without getting married), they separated. Eric, who had become a billionaire, provided Lola with $34 260 a month for child support as well as a house, a car, and money for their children's tuition and travel (Patriquin, 2009).

Lola sued Eric in Quebec Superior Court seeking a $50 million payment and $56 000 a month. The court dismissed the case, noting that Quebec's Civil Code only provided a right to spousal support in a legal marriage or a civil union. However, the Quebec Court of Appeal struck down this provision in the code on the basis that it violated the equality rights provision of the Charter of Rights and Freedoms (Section 15). The nature of the relationship should not be grounds for refusing to claim support for basic needs and thus would constitute discrimination based on marital status. Nevertheless, the court of appeal ruled that the sharing of property was a contractual relationship because the couple had freely decided not to marry. Thus, in its view, there was no requirement for an equal sharing of property (Feldman Family Law Group, 2012). The Quebec attorney general appealed the ruling to the Supreme Court of Canada.

In England, common-law marriages (those not formalized by civil or religious authority) were recognized based on a voluntary agreement between a man and a woman provided they had the legal capacity to marry, were cohabiting, had sexually consummated their relationship, and had public recognition of their relationship. Although the Marriage Act, 1753, abolished common-law marriages in England, they continued in Canada and some other common-law jurisdictions (Kronby, 2010).

Today, "common-law" relationships are recognized as equivalent to marriages by the federal and provincial governments for some purposes such as taxation, pensions, and custody, support, and access to children. Laws in Manitoba and Saskatchewan require that, after a specified period of time or if the couple has children, the property and debts of the couple have to be shared (Makin, 2012a). In other provinces, the common-law principle of "unjust enrichment" may allow a partner to claim monetary compensation for their contribution (such as domestic duties) to the relationship. The Supreme Court of Canada has interpreted this principle to indicate that in a "joint family venture" each common-law partner is entitled to a share of assets proportionate to their contribution (*Kerr v. Baranow*, 2011).

On January 25, 2013, the Supreme Court of Canada in a 5–4 decision ruled that Quebec's Civil Code exclusion of spousal support for unmarried couples violates the equality rights provision of the Charter. However, it was deemed a justifiable infringement particularly because the Code enhances freedom of choice and autonomy. Thus, the rights of those in non-marital relationships in Quebec continue to differ from rights in other provinces.

*Names have been changed to protect the privacy of their children.

Code and the Common Law.) However, the doctrine of parliamentary supremacy that Canada inherited from Britain means that statutory law has modified or replaced a considerable proportion of common law or the civil code provisions.

Judicial Review

In the traditional British system of government, Parliament is the supreme law-making authority, and thus the courts cannot review or invalidate legislation to decide its validity or desirability. They can, however, play a role in interpreting vague or ambiguous provisions in laws based on established principles of interpretation.

In Canada, in contrast, the door has always been left open for judicial review of legislation. That is, the courts have the authority to invalidate laws or government actions that they consider to be in violation of the Constitution. Because the Constitution divides legislative authority between the national Parliament and provincial legislatures, the courts can be called upon (by a government, individuals, groups, or businesses) to determine whether a piece of legislation passed by Parliament or a provincial legislature is within the constitutional authority of that legislative body. The constitutional Charter of Rights and Freedoms (discussed in Chapter 10) has greatly increased the political significance of the courts, as legislation and government actions can be struck down if they are deemed by the courts to have violated the Charter. In addition, the courts have occasionally "read in" additional words to make a law more inclusive, chosen a narrow interpretation to make a law conform to the Charter, or granted an exemption to individuals or groups from legislation that would violate the Charter (Hogg, 2006). For example, in 1991 an instructor was fired from King's College, Edmonton, after disclosing that he was gay. Alberta's Individual Rights Protection Act did not prohibit discrimination on the basis of sexual orientation. However, the Supreme Court of Canada viewed the discrimination as a violation of the equality rights clause of the Charter and read sexual orientation into the Act (*Vriend v. Alberta,* 1998). Similarly the courts can cut out a part of a law that is deemed to violate the Charter or provide a remedy if an individual's rights and freedom have been infringed or denied (Hausegger et al., 2015). Although governments could use the notwithstanding clause to maintain laws that violate some aspects of the Charter, this clause has rarely been used.

The Importance of the Courts in Governing and Policy-Making

The Charter of Rights and Freedoms has increased the importance of the courts. Many public policies have been affected or determined by Supreme Court and Federal Court decisions based on judicial interpretation of the Charter.

Although the power of the courts to strike down legislation using the Charter might be viewed as undemocratic, Peter Hogg and Allison Thornton (1997, 1999) have argued that the Charter has created a "dialogue" between the Supreme Court of Canada and legislative bodies. They point out that striking down legislation seldom stops a legislative body from pursuing a particular objective. A legislative body can use the notwithstanding clause to override a Charter-based decision it does not want to accept (for some aspects of the Charter). It also can modify the legislation so that it satisfies the "reasonable limits" provision, particularly by ensuring that it does not damage the right or freedom in question more than necessary. For example, when some of the provisions of the Anti-Combines Act were struck down by the Supreme Court on the grounds that they violated "the right to be secure from unreasonable search and seizure" of Section 8 of the Charter, Parliament changed the provision to require a warrant issued by a judge to authorize these actions (Hogg & Thornton, 1999, pp. 21–22).

CHARTER DIALOGUE
The view that the Charter has created a dialogue between the courts and legislatures.

The term "**Charter dialogue**" is somewhat misleading. It refers not to any discussion between the courts and legislatures, but rather to the responses of legislatures to court rulings (Macklem, 2001; Hogg, Thornton, & Wright, 2007). F.L. Morton (1999) contends that what is described "as a dialogue is usually a monologue, with judges doing most of the talking and legislatures most of the listening" (p. 26). Changes in a law in response to a Supreme Court decision often reflect the guidelines provided in the court's ruling. The notwithstanding clause has rarely been used and only applies to some sections of the Charter. Although the "reasonable limits" clause can be used by a legislative body to try to justify a limit on rights and freedoms, ultimately the courts can decide what is "reasonable."

The risk that legislation proposed by the government will be struck down by the courts can be reduced by "Charter proofing"—examining proposed legislation by justice department lawyers to determine if it is consistent with the Charter of Rights and Freedoms. Indeed, the justice minister has a legal obligation to notify Parliament if proposed legislation or regulations are likely to be inconsistent with the Charter. However, in 2012 a senior lawyer in the justice department testified that the department "does not identify and report on legislation that the department itself considers to be almost certainly illegal and unconstitutional" (Voices-voix.ca, 2014). This practice apparently goes back as far as 1993 (Curry, 2013).

The Supreme Court rejected a number of laws put forward by the Harper government. For example, in 2014 the Supreme Court struck down a law that established a mandatory minimum three-year imprisonment for gun crimes.[5] Likewise, in 2011 the Supreme Court overturned the federal government's decision to close Insite, a supervised drug injection site in Vancouver, because the denial of that service would increase the risk of death and disease. In addition, a variety of laws proposed by the Harper government and passed by Parliament are likely be found unconstitutional by the courts. These include C-24 (Strengthening Canadian Citizenship

[5]The court ruled this to be "cruel and unusual punishment," citing the example of a person who inherits a weapon but does not immediately report it. Some other aspects of the government's "tough on crime" agenda (such as ending early parole) have also been struck down.

Act) which creates a different class of citizenship for dual citizens and immigrants, C-13 (Protecting Canadians from Online Crime Act), S-4 (Digital Privacy Act) which gives police greater access to Internet subscriber information,[6] and C-51 (Anti-Terrorism Act) which limits free expression and gives extensive powers to the Canadian Security Intelligence Service (CSIS) with little oversight of that agency. While it often takes several years before controversial legislation reaches the Supreme Court, Prime Minister Justin Trudeau promised to introduce legislation to repeal C-24 and make some changes to the Anti-Terrorism Act.

Overall, the Charter has, to a considerable extent, moved Canada away from a system of parliamentary supremacy. With the notwithstanding clause used very infrequently, the courts often end up with the final say in interpreting Charter rights and freedoms. This is particularly controversial when social policy issues rather than questions of procedural fairness are at stake. For example, in *Eldridge*, the Supreme Court upheld a claim that deaf persons in British Columbia hospitals needed to be provided with sign language interpreters, while in *Auton*, the claim that the BC government was required to fund intensive treatment for children with autism was rejected (Macfarlane, 2013). In *Chaoulli*, a challenge to Quebec's law prohibiting private health insurance (viewed by some as a challenge to Canada's health care system) was successful in a 4–3 decision. In this case (as with some other cases dealing with controversial issues such as prostitution and doctor assisted suicide), the Supreme Court gave the government a specified length of time to pass legislation more consistent with the court's interpretation of the Charter.[7]

While the Supreme Court has used the Charter on a number of cases to invalidate or change legislation, the Supreme Court has been more deferential to legislative bodies when large government expenditures would be needed to address an issue (Macfarlane, 2013). For example, in 2004 the Supreme Court of Canada rejected a challenge by the Newfoundland Association of Public Employees to a provincial law that cancelled a 1988 pay equity agreement to increase the wages of health care employees in female-dominated occupations. The Supreme Court ruled that the law violated the equality clause of the Charter, but accepted the provincial government's argument that it was a "reasonable limit" given a severe financial crisis the province was facing.[8]

Although the courts now have a significant role in affecting public policy, questions have been raised about their capabilities to carry out this

---

[6]In this case, the government proceeded with the legislative process even though the Supreme Court had already ruled that a warrant was needed if Internet service providers were requested to disclose information about their customers to law enforcement officers.

[7]The Quebec government subsequently created and funded targets for various medical services; allowed the purchase of private health care insurance for hip, knee, and other surgeries if provided by doctors who did not participate in the public system; and allowed hospitals to contract some private services to meet wait time targets (Hausegger et al., 2015).

[8]In 2006, the provincial government agreed to give $24 million in back pay to those who had been deprived of the pay increase from 1988 to 1991.

responsibility. While Supreme Court judges are skilled at carefully analyzing the wording of legislation and constitutional provisions, the courts are not well equipped to deal with complex matters of public policy. The training and legalistic orientation of judges does not necessarily prepare them to consider the impact of their judgments on society and the economy. Judges do not have the staff needed to analyze the possible consequences and costs of their rulings. As well, because judges rarely oversee the implementation of their rulings, they do not have the opportunity to observe how well their rulings work in practice.

COURTS

The Structure of the Court System

Unlike the United States, which has separate federal and state court systems, Canada basically has a unified court system that hears most cases involving both national and provincial laws (see Figure 16-1). The Supreme Court of Canada, whose members are appointed on the recommendation of the prime minister, sits atop the hierarchy of the court system. Judges in provincial **superior courts** (which include trial and appeal divisions) are also appointed and paid by the Canadian government.[9]

SUPERIOR COURTS
Courts in each province whose judges are appointed and paid by the Canadian government.

FIGURE 16-1
OUTLINE OF CANADA'S COURT SYSTEM

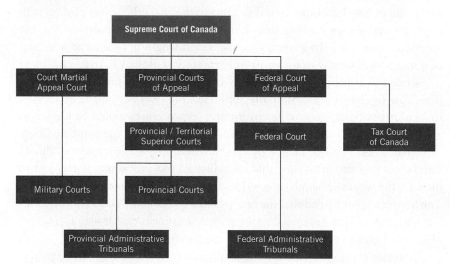

SOURCE: *Canada's Court System,* www.justice.gc.ca/eng/dept-min/pub/ccs-ajc/page3.html, Department of Justice Canada, 2005. Reproduced with the permission of the Minister of Public Works and Government Services Canada, 2012.

---

[9]In addition, in certain areas of seven provinces, unified family courts deal with both federal and provincial family law matters and may make available related social services (Boyd, 2014). In British Columbia, Prince Edward Island, Nova Scotia, Newfoundland and Labrador, Yukon, and the Northwest Territories the superior court is labelled the Supreme Court of the province or territory, while in Alberta, Manitoba, New Brunswick, and Saskatchewan it is known as the Court of Queen's Bench. Ontario and Quebec use the term Superior Court. Nunavut has a single Court of Justice combining the superior and territorial courts.

At the bottom of the hierarchy are provincial (or territorial) courts, whose judges are appointed and paid by each provincial government. **Provincial courts** are exclusively trial courts, with appeals from judgments going to superior courts. Some provinces have established specialized provincial courts, such as traffic, youth, and small claims courts. Until the 1960s, provincial courts dealt primarily with minor cases with most local magistrates having little or no legal training. Now, most criminal cases and many civil cases are heard in provincial court before judges with legal training equivalent to that of superior court judges (Russell, 2009). This has led to proposals for a unified rather than a two-tier court system.

Although the Canadian government appoints provincial superior court judges, provincial governments are responsible for setting up and administering the court system in their province. A superior court judge must hear certain serious criminal offences, such as murder, treason, and piracy. For other indictable offences[10] (serious offences such as arson and robbery), the person accused can choose to be tried in a superior or a provincial court. Petitions for divorce and a variety of private law cases are heard in superior court. Most offences against federal and provincial laws (including all summary offences—that is, less serious offences such as causing a disturbance) are heard in a provincial court.

An exception to the two-tier court system that deals with both provincial and federal laws is the **Federal Court of Canada**, which tries cases related to certain acts of Parliament (including laws concerning copyright and patents, citizenship and immigration, access to information, and privacy). It also hears appeals against the rulings of national administrative tribunals (e.g., appeals by those denied benefits by the Canada Employment Insurance Commission). Likewise, the Tax Court of Canada and military courts deal only with cases related to Canadian government responsibilities.

The Supreme Court of Canada was created by an act of Parliament in 1875. Although intended primarily to have a nationalizing effect on Canadian laws, the Supreme Court was unable to fulfill this purpose because appeals from provincial superior courts could go directly to the Judicial Committee of the Privy Council in the United Kingdom. Since 1949 the Supreme Court of Canada has acted as the final court of appeal for all cases. The court consists of nine judges appointed on the recommendation of the prime minister, three of whom must come from Quebec so as to be familiar with Quebec's distinctive legal system. Informally, there is a longstanding tradition that three Supreme Court judges are from Ontario, two are from Western Canada, and one is from Atlantic Canada. Appeals are often heard by panels of seven

PROVINCIAL COURTS
Trial courts whose judges are appointed and paid by the provincial government.

FEDERAL COURT OF CANADA
A court that hears cases related to certain acts of Parliament, such as laws concerning copyright and patents, citizenship and immigration, and access to information and privacy. As well it hears appeals against the rulings of national administrative tribunals.

---

[10]Many offences in the Criminal Code, such as impaired driving, are "hybrid offences" for which the Crown attorney may charge the accused with either an indictable or a summary offence. The penalties when convicted of a summary offence are less severe (a maximum of a $5000 fine and six months in jail) than when convicted of an indictable offence.

judges selected by the chief justice of the Supreme Court. Appeals from Quebec are normally heard by a five-member panel that includes the three judges from Quebec.

Since 1985, the right to appeal to the Supreme Court of Canada has been limited to a few specific circumstances (such as when a provincial court of appeal has overturned an acquittal). Instead the Supreme Court grants "leave" to hear appeals only in a small proportion of cases that it considers to raise issues of public importance.[11] These cases include those involving constitutional issues, the interpretation of important laws, the definition of Aboriginal rights, and the possible unfair conviction of a defendant (Hausegger et al., 2015). The Supreme Court of Canada can also hear **references**, questions asked by the Canadian government seeking an opinion on matters of law or constitutional interpretation, as well as appeals of references requested by a provincial government that are normally first heard in a provincial court of appeal.

REFERENCES
Opinions of the courts on questions asked by the federal or provincial government.

Characteristics of the Court System

The court system is by nature adversarial. That is, both the Crown prosecutor and the lawyer for the accused (or the lawyers for the plaintiff and the defendant in private law cases) make as strong a case as possible by providing evidence and arguments that support their position. Witnesses do not only give evidence for one side, but are also cross-examined by the other side to try to pinpoint flaws in their testimony. The trial judge is expected to uphold the rules governing proceedings, but generally leaves it up to the opposing sides to present their case without involvement in the questioning of witnesses.

Trial courts, presided over by a single judge, deal primarily with ascertaining the facts of the case, particularly by assessing the credibility of witnesses. Appellate (appeal) courts usually involve a panel of three judges. Generally, they take the facts presented at the trial as given, and focus instead on questions concerning the trial judge's interpretation of the law.

The Charter of Rights and Freedoms provides the right to choose trial by jury for offences where the maximum punishment is at least five years' imprisonment (except for offences under military law). In addition, the right to trial by jury is allowed for many other indictable offences. Juries are also occasionally used, at the discretion of the judge, in certain types of private law cases if requested by the parties to the dispute.[12]

JURY DUTY   Most people will from time to time receive a summons to report for jury duty. Jury duty is considered an important obligation for all citizens. A refusal to report can result in a fine or even imprisonment.

[11]A panel of three Supreme Court justices decides whether to grant leave to appeal.
[12]Juries are not used for private law cases in Quebec or in cases heard in federal courts.

To ensure that a jury represents a cross-section of the community, potential jurors are randomly selected from among adult citizens in a given area. Some people are shut out of jury duty because of their occupation (including lawyers, police officers, and employees of government agencies related to the justice system) or other characteristics (such as being elderly or physically weak, mentally incompetent, or unfamiliar with the language of the trial). Also, people can be excused from jury duty if serving on a jury would cause extreme hardship. In some provinces, full-time students are automatically exempted.[13]

Being summoned for jury duty involves being part of a group from which a jury is selected. A few questions are asked of each potential juror to gauge whether that person would be able to consider the case fairly. The judge has the right to dismiss a potential juror for cause (such as potential bias). As well, lawyers for the prosecution and the defendant are entitled to a certain number of pre-emptory challenges (the number depends upon the offence), which can be used to dismiss a potential juror without explanation.

After the prosecution and the defence present their case, the judge instructs the jury about the legal issues involved in the case. In particular, in a criminal case, the jury will be reminded that a guilty verdict has to be proven "beyond a reasonable doubt." In a private law dispute, the defendant is liable "on a balance of probabilities"—a lower level of proof. The jury then meets in private to discuss the case and reach a verdict. For criminal cases, the verdict has to be unanimous. In private law cases, in most provinces five of the six jurors have to agree on the verdict. In spite of the temptation many jurors may feel to share details of a case with friends or family, they are strictly forbidden to tell anyone what occurred in the jury room.

The jury system is not without critics. Some people argue that jurors generally lack the expertise to assess the often complicated issues that arise in a trial. In high-profile cases, the jury may be influenced by public opinion and media coverage despite instructions from the judge to consider the case only as it was presented in court. In the *Morgentaler* case, juries acquitted Dr. Morgentaler even though he admitted that he had broken the law by performing illegal abortions. Although the judge instructed the jury that they could not ignore the law, the jury likely concluded that they should not convict a person who felt the need to challenge a law that many considered unjust and harmful.

JUDICIAL INDEPENDENCE AND THE APPOINTMENT OF JUDGES

An important principle of liberal democracy is that of **judicial independence**. To ensure that all people receive a fair trial, the courts are expected to be independent of government and its agencies, legislative bodies, and other

JUDICIAL INDEPENDENCE
The principle that the courts are expected to be independent of government and its agencies, legislative bodies, and other influences.

---

[13]Employers are required to give time off for jury duty, although in some provinces they do not have to pay their employees for the time spent away. Some provinces provide daily payment for serving on a jury.

influences. Without an independent judicial system, governments, police, and security services could use their power to intimidate individuals with impunity. The independence of the judiciary thus serves as an important tool in helping to protect the rule of law.

To protect judicial independence, federally appointed judges hold office, assuming "good behaviour," until age 75 and can only be removed by a joint resolution passed by both the House of Commons and the Senate. The **Canadian Judicial Council**, composed of provincial chief and associate chief justices, reviews complaints about federally appointed judges. Although the council cannot dismiss a judge, it can hold an inquiry to decide whether to recommend dismissal, and it can also issue a statement expressing disapproval of a judge's behaviour. For example, in 1981 BC Supreme Court judge Tom Berger publicly supported the effort to have Aboriginal rights included in the Constitution. Although the Canadian Judicial Council ruled that he had been "indiscreet" in criticizing the government, they did not recommend his removal (Greene, 2006). Nevertheless, Berger resigned. In commenting on the case, Chief Justice Bora Laskin stated, "A judge has no freedom of speech to address political issues which have nothing to do with his judicial duties. His abstention from political involvement is one of the guarantees of his impartiality, his integrity, his independence" (quoted in Van Loon & Whittington, 1987, p. 218).

No superior court or Supreme Court of Canada judge has ever been removed for misconduct by a parliamentary resolution,[14] although several judges facing dismissal resigned when removal was recommended. Provincial judicial councils can reprimand, suspend, or recommend the dismissal of provincially appointed judges. In most provinces, the provincial attorney general and cabinet can choose to remove a judge based on the judicial council's recommendation.[15] Only Ontario requires a vote by the provincial legislature to remove a judge (Hausegger et al., 2015). Overall, the principle of judicial independence now applies to provincial court judges as well as federally appointed judges (Russell, 2009).

The independence of the judiciary is also maintained by the convention that cabinet ministers, elected representatives, and government officials should not contact judges about particular cases. As well, independent processes that recommend compensation for judges have been set up to ensure that the government cannot try to intimidate judges through control of their salaries.

The Appointment of Supreme Court of Canada Judges

The Supreme Court of Canada Act places the authority to appoint Supreme Court judges in the hands of the "Governor in Council"—in effect, the

CANADIAN JUDICIAL COUNCIL
A body of senior judges established to review complaints about federally appointed judges.

---

[14]Four federally appointed county or district court judges were removed by joint resolutions (Greene, 2006). County and district courts no longer exist.
[15]In Manitoba and British Columbia, the council's recommendation is binding on the government.

Controversy over a Supreme Court Appointment

In 2013, the appointment of semi-retired Federal Court of Appeal judge Mark Nadon to a vacant Quebec Supreme Court seat caused a serious controversy. Section 5 of the Supreme Court Act states that "any person may be appointed . . . who is or has been a judge of a superior court of a province or a member of the bar for at least 10 years." However Section 6 provides an additional stricter requirement that the appointment of Supreme Court judges for Quebec must be "from among" the Court of Appeal or Superior Court of Quebec or "from among" members of the Quebec bar.

Chief Justice Beverley McLachlin confidentially raised the question as to whether Nadon met the required qualifications as he was not currently a Quebec judge or member of the Quebec bar although he had been a member of the Quebec bar prior to his appointment to the Federal Court in 1993. Faced with a lawsuit initiated by a Toronto lawyer, the Canadian government in an omnibus budget bill included a change to the required qualifications in the Supreme Court Act to legitimize Nadon's appointment. However, in the *Reference re Supreme Court Act* launched by the Canadian government, the Supreme Court ruled that Nadon was not qualified under the Act, and could not be appointed to the Supreme Court.

The Supreme Court also ruled that the proposed change to the Supreme Court Act was unconstitutional and could only be changed by a constitutional amendment using the unanimous formula. In effect, this ruling added to the protection of the Supreme Court of Canada in the Constitution and confirmed that "the provinces have a role in the process of altering fundamental aspects" of the Supreme Court (Peach, 2014).

Canadian prime minister. Those appointed to the Supreme Court have to be or have been a judge of a superior court or a lawyer of a province for at least 10 years. Appointees from Quebec must also have a current Quebec Court of Appeal or superior court position or bar membership (see Box 16-2: Controversy Over a Supreme Court Appointment).

In the past, the prime minister recommended appointments after the minister of justice consulted informally with provincial attorneys general, chief justices, and leading members of the legal community. The Paul Martin government added an advisory committee that provided the minister of justice with a confidential unranked short list of three candidates (Hogg, 2009). The minister of justice appeared before the Standing Committee on Justice in the House of Commons to answer questions about the search process and the qualifications of the candidate selected for the Supreme Court position.

The Harper government added a small element of public transparency to this procedure in 2006. In a three-hour televised hearing, the selected candidate, Marshall Rothstein, answered questions before an ad hoc parliamentary committee chaired by the justice minister and a former law school dean. The members of the parliamentary committee were asked to be civil and respectful and to avoid questions about controversial issues, cases that might come before the court, and the rationale for his decisions in past cases. The committee did not have the power to confirm or reject the nominee and did not prepare a report or make a recommendation. After the hearing, the prime minister recommended the appointment of Rothstein.

In 2008 the Harper government established a selection committee consisting of five Members of Parliament, including one from each of the opposition political parties and two cabinet ministers from the governing party. From the justice minister's list of qualified candidates, the selection committee would choose three unranked candidates. The prime minister then selected one of these candidates and held a public parliamentary hearing. When the opposition parties argued that the presence of the two cabinet ministers compromised the independence of the committee, Prime Minister Harper cancelled the work of the selection committee and recommended the appointment of Thomas Cromwell without holding a public hearing. Subsequent appointments in 2011 and 2012 involved selection committees consisting of three Conservative MPs, one NDP MP, and one Liberal MP and public hearings.

In 2014, Prime Minister Harper appointed Clément Gascon and Suzanne Côté (who had never been a judge) to the Supreme Court, and in 2015 appointed Russell Brown without using a selection committee and without a public hearing.[16] The process used to appoint these Supreme Court judges has been described as "an utter regression to the kind of closed, unaccountable, unrepresentative, and enigmatic approach that, ten years ago, all parties agreed must change" (Cotler, 2014).

Because the choice of Supreme Court of Canada judges ultimately rests in the hands of the prime minister, some argue that the court system does not provide a fully independent check on the power of the prime minister (Russell, 2008). Although most people appointed to the Supreme Court have been well qualified and independent-minded, there is a risk that a prime minister could, over time, try to stack the Supreme Court and superior courts with judges likely to promote the prime minister's ideological perspective through their judgments. It could also be argued that the largely secretive process for choosing Supreme Court judges does not reflect democratic principles.

Others argue that Canada should avoid adopting the more open U.S. system, where the powerful Senate can veto the president's selection of Supreme Court judges. Public hearings conducted by the American Senate's Judiciary Committee have sometimes involved detailed, aggressive, and partisan questioning of nominees about their views on contentious issues that might come before the court, their past judgments, and their personal lives. The politicization of the process of selecting judges can undermine the principle of judicial independence and reduce public respect for the fairness of the judges and their decisions. However, there is no guarantee that political, patronage, or ideological considerations will not feature in a prime minister's selection of Canadian Supreme Court judges.

---

[16]Brown, a former law professor with strongly conservative opinions, had served only two years as a judge before his appointment (Fine, 2015, July 31).

The appointment of judges to the Supreme Court of Canada on the recommendation of the prime minister also raises questions of whether the Supreme Court of Canada, as currently appointed, is an appropriate body to rule on constitutional issues that often involve disputes between national and provincial governments. Both the Meech Lake and Charlottetown Accords proposed that Supreme Court judges be nominated by provincial governments and selected from among the nominees by the Canadian government. Critics of the Accords argued that this would further politicize the appointment procedure.[17]

There have also been questions about whether Supreme Court justices should be fluently bilingual. The NDP was critical of the 2011 appointment of Michael Moldaver, who could not speak French although he promised to become more proficient in French. In their 2015 election platform the Liberal party promised that all Supreme Court appointees would be "functionally bilingual". As well, the appointment process would be "transparent, inclusive and accountable to Canadians".

The Appointment of Superior Court Judges

In addition to recommending the appointment of Supreme Court of Canada judges, the prime minister is responsible for recommending the appointment of the chief justices and associate chief justices of each of the provincial superior courts. The federal minister of justice makes recommendations to the Canadian cabinet for other federally appointed judges. In turn, the attorney general of a province makes recommendations to the provincial cabinet for appointments to the provincial courts.

All federally appointed judges (and, in most cases, provincially appointed judges) have to be members of their provincial bar association and have at least 10 years of experience as a lawyer or a judge. Unlike the practice in a number of continental European countries, judges are not given extensive training and do not follow a separate career path from other lawyers. However, the National Judicial Institute and the Canadian Institute for the Administration of Justice put on a wide variety of courses and seminars for lawyers, including two six-day courses for new judges.

An eight-member **Judicial Advisory Committee** in each province makes a recommendation to the federal minister of justice concerning lawyers who apply to become a superior court judge. Each committee is composed of three people selected by the federal minister of justice, a judicial representative chosen by the chief justice of the province or territory, and one person from those nominated by each of the following groups and individuals:

- the provincial or territorial law society;
- the provincial or territorial branch of the Canadian Bar Association;

JUDICIAL ADVISORY COMMITTEE
A committee that assesses candidates for appointment as superior court judges.

---

[17]One suggestion is to have two courts: one court would deal with constitutional issues, while the Supreme Court of Canada would continue its role as the final court of appeal in criminal and civil cases (McCormick, 2013).

- the law enforcement community; and
- the provincial attorney general or territorial minister of justice.

Upon taking office, Prime Minister Harper stated that he wanted judges who supported his crackdown on crime and thus a police representative was added to the composition of the Committee. Generally the judges appointed from 2006 to 2015 tended to be more ideologically conservative and less supportive of judicial activism than previously appointed judges (Fine, 2015, July 25; Myers, 2015; Hausegger et al., 2015).

The advisory committee provides an assessment of applicants as "recommended" or "unable to recommend."[18] The federal minister of justice (or the prime minister, for the appointment of provincial chief justices and associate chief justices) can engage in further consultations before making a recommendation to the federal cabinet. The entire process is strictly confidential, and applicants do not have to be interviewed by the committee.

Diversity and the Selection of Judges

There have been some efforts to make the courts more representative of the diversity of Canada. As of August 2015, 34.4 percent of the 1140 federal judges were female (Office of the Commissioner for Federal Judicial Affairs, 2015) and 4 of the 9 Supreme Court of Canada judges were female (including the chief justice). Likewise about one-third of provincially appointed judges are female (Hausegger et al., 2015). However, there are very few non-white judges, with only 3 non-white judges out of nearly 200 federally appointed judges in recent years (Fine, 2014, April 10). To date, no Aboriginals have been appointed to the Supreme Court of Canada. The Canadian Association of Law Teachers has recommended that there should be at least four female judges and at least one Aboriginal judge on the nine-member Supreme Court of Canada (Sossin, 2013).

JUDICIAL DECISION MAKING

LEGAL MODEL OF JUDICIAL DECISION MAKING
The view that judges base their decisions on a careful reading of the relevant law.

STRATEGIC MODEL OF JUDICIAL DECISION MAKING
The view that a bargaining process among the judges takes place for them to reach a majority or a unanimous decision.

How do judges decide on the cases before them? In the **legal model of judicial decision making**, it is assumed that judges base their decisions on a careful reading of the relevant law using precedents, or in the case of Quebec the principles of the Civil Code, to aid them in applying the law to particular cases. If a statutory law is ambiguous, judges turn to the discussion of the law by those who developed it; for example, they can examine legislative debates. But do legal factors fully explain the decisions made by judges, particularly those at the highest level of the judicial system? The **strategic model of judicial decision making** assumes that a bargaining process among the judges takes place

---

[18]For provincial or territorial judges who are seeking to be appointed to a superior court, comments are provided rather than recommendations.

for them to reach a majority or a unanimous decision. Thus, the wording of decisions often reflects compromises among judges with differing opinions. Finally, the **attitudinal model of judicial decision making** postulates that judges pursue their own policy preferences in interpreting the law, as well as being influenced by their attitudes toward the facts of the case (Ostberg & Wetstein, 2007).

The attitudinal and strategic models were developed in studies of the Supreme Court of the United States, where individual judges are quite consistent in taking liberal or conservative ideological positions on many cases before the court. A study of the decisions taken by the Supreme Court of Canada between 1984 and 2003 on criminal, economic, and fundamental freedom cases found that ideological differences among the judges along liberal–conservative lines were significant. Even so, the attitudinal model was less applicable in Canada; that is, it "is less definitive and more subtle in the Canadian context than in the U.S. Supreme Court" (Ostberg & Wetstein, 2007, p. 11). For equality and civil rights cases, gender rather than liberal or conservative ideological orientation was particularly important. Female judges "speak in distinctively different voices," particularly to protect women and vulnerable minorities (Ostberg & Wetstein, 2007, p. 152). Similarly, a study of the Ontario Court of Appeal found that female judges were somewhat more likely than male judges to vote to convict the accused in criminal cases that did not involve Charter rights, to take the side of the female litigant in family law cases, and to favour the rights claimant in human rights cases (Hausegger, Riddell, & Hennigar, 2013).

Overall, many of the Supreme Court of Canada judges tend to be ideologically consistent in how they vote. However, this does not mean that they take consistent liberal or conservative positions. Chief Justice McLachlin, for example, has tended to take a "hard line" on the criminal cases (a conservative

ATTITUDINAL MODEL OF JUDICIAL DECISION MAKING
The view that judges pursue their own policy preferences in interpreting the law, as well as being influenced by their attitudes toward the facts of the case.

Canada's Supreme Court judges prior to the retirement of Marshall Rothstein and the appointment of Russell Brown, August 31, 2015.

© Adrian Wyld/Canadian Press Images

position) while taking a liberal approach favourable to civil liberties when ruling on other cases (Ostberg & Wetstein, 2007). A study of Ontario Court of Appeal judges found that judges who had an affiliation with the Liberal party before being appointed were more likely to favour the accused in criminal cases than those with a Progressive Conservative affiliation (Hausegger et al., 2013).[19]

The attitudinal model struggles to explain why a fairly high proportion of Supreme Court of Canada cases result in unanimous decisions. Research on unanimous decisions suggests that judges are sometimes willing to compromise to reach a unanimous decision, that they are open to persuasion by their colleagues on the court, and that the law and precedents may lead the judges to a common position. However, unanimity is less likely in cases where the most important political issues are at stake, particularly if the issue has a high public profile (Songer & Siripurapu, 2009).

Even if the Canadian Supreme Court judges do not fit the attitudinal model as consistently as U.S. Supreme Court judges, Canadian Supreme Court judges have indicated that they do not strictly follow the legal model of decision making. Most of them have made it clear that, in interpreting the Constitution, they will not be bound by the original wording. Rather, they will adjust the interpretation in response to changes in society and social values. Furthermore, in interpreting statutes, Supreme Court of Canada judges do not rely heavily on the record of legislative discussion to determine the intent of those who developed the legislation (Gall, 2004).

Supreme Court judges can also be viewed as being concerned about maintaining the legitimacy of their institution in the eyes of the public and key political actors. On highly visible and contentious cases they may try to avoid making a controversial decision. For example in the *Secession Reference*, the Supreme Court of Canada avoided clarifying what constituted a "clear majority" on a "clear question" that would be needed for Quebec to become independent. Instead, the judgment emphasized the "duty to negotiate" even though that wasn't raised in the hearings on the reference. This allowed the judgment largely to evade criticism by both federalists and separatists (Radmilovic, 2010).

PROBLEMS OF THE JUDICIAL SYSTEM

There are several problems in ensuring that justice is provided by the judicial system. First, it can take a long time for a case to go to trial. Most courts have a lengthy backlog of cases due, in part, to a shortage of judges. As well,

---

[19]However, there was no significant difference on family or human rights cases. Because this study examined judges appointed before the formation of the Conservative party in 2003, we can only speculate as to whether Conservative-affiliated judges appointed by the Harper government are more consistently conservative in their judgments.

lawyers will frequently engage in delaying tactics or are too busy to prepare their cases in a reasonable time. It may take years for an innocent person to clear his or her name. As well, the backlog of cases also encourages plea bargaining—that is, accepting a guilty plea to a lesser charge.

A Supreme Court of Canada decision (*Ashov*) found that a delay of nearly three years between a criminal charge and trial, caused by the underfunding of the Ontario court system, violated the Charter right "to be tried in a reasonable time." This led to 50 000 criminal charges being stayed or withdrawn (MacIvor, 2006).

Second, the costs of using courts can be prohibitive. It can take lawyers a long time to adequately prepare for a court case, and can involve many days if not weeks or even months of court time. Going to court can be a severe financial hardship for the average person. For example, a teacher in Richmond, British Columbia, who was charged with the sexual abuse of two students in 1992, spent over $500 000 in legal fees before being found not guilty in 1997 (Matas, 1998). It is hardly surprising that a growing number of people are turning up in court without a lawyer—a practice that creates problems for judges, who have to explain the rules of procedure to those without that expert knowledge.

Legal aid is available to low-income people with limited assets. However, legal aid programs have been chronically underfunded. Although the government of Canada pays one-half of the costs of provincial legal aid systems, it has capped the amount that it will share with provincial governments. It can also be challenging to find lawyers willing to take legal aid

David Milgaard and Solange Tremblay (seated), wife of wrongfully convicted Quebecer Michel Dumont, wait in Saskatoon for a 2005 news conference to begin detailing Milgaard's support of the wrongfully convicted. The table banner quotes William Gladstone: "Justice delayed is justice denied."

Sham Justice: Wrongful Convictions

In 1984, Guy Paul Morin was convicted in the first-degree murder of his nine-year-old next-door neighbour. Christine Jessop had been found 56 kilometres from her home with multiple stab wounds. A police dog given a scent of her clothing pawed at the window of Morin's car.

Although Morin had been acquitted in his first trial in 1986, the Ontario Court of Appeal ordered a new trial because of an error by the judge. Six years later, Morin was convicted in his second trial. Already lengthy, his experience with the legal system did not end there. Eventually Morin underwent DNA testing that proved his innocence, and in 1995—a full 11 years after he was first convicted—he was acquitted on appeal.

A commission of inquiry into the Morin affair found evidence of misconduct by the police and the prosecution, and a misrepresentation of evidence by the Ontario Centre for Forensic Sciences. The problems were many: A forensic analyst did not adequately communicate the limitations of hair analysis to the police and prosecution. Information about the contamination of the fibre evidence at the centre was withheld. In addition, the jailhouse informant who claimed to have overheard a confession had lied in the past and had been diagnosed as a pathological liar. Furthermore, the police had conducted a flawed and inadequate investigation, including failure to preserve evidence.

Similarly, a commission of inquiry into three wrongful murder convictions in Newfoundland and Labrador, headed by retired Supreme Court of Canada chief justice Antonio Lamer, found that the police were overly impressed by "junk" evidence and that the Crown prosecutors were overaggressive in pursuit of legal victories, had tunnel vision, lacked objectivity, and were wedded to police theories (Makin, 2006).

Fortunately for Guy Paul Morin, capital punishment for murder had been abolished in 1976. Christine Jessop's murderer has never been found.

cases, as the hourly rates paid by the system are substantially lower than the normal rates charged by lawyers and payment is only provided weeks after a case is concluded. In addition, legal aid often does not provide enough hours for adequate representation in complex cases. Legal aid generally covers criminal cases, serious family disputes, and immigration problems. Legal aid coverage for other private law cases varies from province to province, but tends to be spotty. Unlike other countries, legal insurance is not widely available in Canada, and thus only a small proportion of Canadians have purchased coverage. Some legal assistance is available through law clinics and the pro bono services of law students and some lawyers.

Third, a number of cases have come to light in which those accused of serious crimes have been wrongfully convicted (see Box 16-3: Sham Justice: Wrongful Convictions). In particular, the development of DNA testing has resulted in the overturning of a number of convictions after innocent people have spent many years behind bars. For example, 16-year-old David Milgaard was convicted of rape and murder and spent 23 years in prison until determined efforts by his mother led to an overturning of his conviction by the Supreme Court. Several years later, he was exonerated by DNA evidence and received $10 million in compensation for his ordeal. Although we cannot expect the courts to be right all of the time, some of the cases of wrongful conviction have resulted from serious and avoidable mistakes by the police and Crown prosecutors. In particular, those wrongly convicted have often been people of lower class status, which suggests that the judicial system may suffer from social class bias.

ABORIGINALS AND THE CANADIAN JUDICIAL SYSTEM

Compared with non-Aboriginals, a highly disproportionate number of Aboriginal persons find themselves in prison, not least because of the serious social problems plaguing their communities, including high levels of poverty, violence, and substance abuse. Moreover, Aboriginals have endured a long history of insensitivity and injustices by the Canadian legal system, and they have faced problems in dealing with a judicial system that is based on the culture of the non-Aboriginal majority. A growing awareness of these inequities has led to proposals that an Aboriginal justice system be established. For example, the Royal Commission on Aboriginal Peoples, noting what it viewed as the fundamentally different worldviews of Aboriginal and non-Aboriginal peoples, recommended that the inherent right of Aboriginals to self-government should include the right to establish and administer their own justice system.

It is often argued that the adversarial judicial system that Canada inherited from Britain does not mesh with Aboriginal traditions that focus on conflict resolution. The Canadian legal system emphasizes the punishment of offenders. Efforts to rehabilitate those in prison and reintegrate offenders into society have often been inadequate. In contrast, Aboriginal traditions focus on **restorative justice**—that is, taking responsibility for one's actions; repairing the harm that has been caused; and reconciling the offender, the victim, and the community. The concept of restorative justice has been applied in some cases through the use of **sentencing circles**. These circles may include the guilty individual, the victim, the families, elders, and other interested members of the Aboriginal community, along with the prosecutor, defence lawyer, and police officers. The goal is to reach a consensus about what measures are needed to reintegrate the offender as a responsible member of the community and to assist the victim. Measures may involve addiction treatment, counselling, community service, and reparations to the victim. Sentencing circles occasionally have also recommended the traditional Aboriginal penalty of banishment from the community for a length of time, as well as the conventional penalties of jail and probation. Normally, provincial courts use sentencing circles only for offences for which the maximum penalty is less than two years in jail. The use of sentencing circles in some cases is supported by a provision in the Criminal Code (Section 718.2) stating that one of the

RESTORATIVE JUSTICE
The perspective that justice should focus on offenders taking responsibility for their actions; repairing the harm that has been caused; and reconciling the offender, the victim, and the community.

SENTENCING CIRCLES
A group that may include the guilty individual, the victim, their families, elders, and other interested members of the community, along with the prosecutor, defence lawyer, and police officers. The goal is to reach a consensus about what measures are needed to reintegrate the offender as a responsible member of the community and to assist the victim.

principles a court should take into consideration when imposing a sentence is that "all available sanctions other than imprisonment that are reasonable in the circumstances should be considered for all offenders, with particular attention to the circumstances of aboriginal offenders."

In the *Gladue* case (1999), the Supreme Court of Canada ruled that cultural oppression, poverty, and abuse in residential schools must factor heavily in sentencing Aboriginal offenders. However, in 2012 the Supreme Court stated that the *Gladue* principles were not being met. Although the history and circumstances of Aboriginal peoples "do not necessarily justify a different sentence for Aboriginal offenders, they provide the necessary context for understanding and evaluating case-specific information . . ." (quoted by Sebesta, 2012). Nevertheless, the adoption of mandatory minimum jail sentences for a variety of offences in 2012 reduced the ability of judges to take into account the circumstances of Aboriginal (and other) offenders.

ALTERNATIVE DISPUTE RESOLUTION AND COLLABORATIVE FAMILY LAW

ALTERNATIVE DISPUTE RESOLUTION

A process where disputing parties choose a third party (rather than a judge) to try to resolve the dispute.

Alternative dispute resolution involves the disputing parties choosing a third party (rather than a judge) to try to resolve the dispute. There are two basic types of alternative dispute resolution. The first, mediation, involves a mediator actively working with the parties, most often informally, to try to find a solution to the problems that led to the dispute. The second, arbitration, is a more formal process in which the arbitrator listens to the positions put forward by the two parties and makes a binding decision (if the parties have already agreed to accept whatever decision the arbitrator makes). In some cases, arbitration is chosen after attempts at mediation have failed. Mediation and arbitration are commonly used in collective (union) bargaining and in some disputes between businesses and between businesses and consumers. Alternative dispute resolution is gaining popularity as a way of settling family disputes, such as those linked to divorce.

COLLABORATIVE FAMILY LAW

A process in which each party hires their own lawyer (or other professionals) who helps the parties reach an acceptable settlement without going to court.

Another alternative to using the courts to settle disputes (particularly related to divorce and child custody and support) is **collaborative family law**. Rather than using a neutral mediator or an arbitrator, each party hires their own lawyer (or other professionals) with training in this process to help reach a settlement that is acceptable to both parties.

Alternative dispute resolution and collaborative family law may allow some common ground to be found between the parties to a dispute, and thus lead to a more amicable solution than is likely in the adversarial format of a court. With Canadian courts often facing a severe backlog of cases, these approaches allow for a faster (and less expensive) outcome. Furthermore, they are often preferred by the individuals involved because of their private nature.

Summary and Conclusion

The rule of law is a fundamental principle of Canada's liberal democracy. Although there are instances when agencies of the state have not acted in accordance with the rule of law, for the most part Canadians have been protected from arbitrary orders by those in positions of authority.

Canada's legal system reflects, to some extent, the diversity of the country. Quebec's system of codified civil law is an important element in the maintenance of Quebec's distinctiveness. Other provinces and territories have maintained the common-law system inherited from England. Both Parliament and provincial or territorial legislatures can pass laws (consistent with their constitutional authority) that supersede the provisions of common law or Quebec's civil code. First Nations are likely to continue to look for the development of a system of justice to better reflect their culture and worldview.

Despite the federal nature of government in Canada, there is a basically unified court system that (with certain exceptions) is responsible for hearing cases involving both national and provincial laws. The courts are expected to be independent of governments, legislatures, and public officials in order to uphold the rule of law and ensure that those accused of violating the law receive a fair and impartial trial.

The courts are involved not only in applying laws but also in interpreting them and deciding on their validity. Not only can the courts strike down legislation deemed to be in violation of the Constitution, but also some judicial decisions have, in effect, established new policies.

The importance of judicial decisions for the good government of Canada makes the selection of judges of great significance. At present, the prime minister and the federal minister of justice have the primary responsibility for the appointment of Supreme Court and superior court judges, although some processes of consultation are often involved. Nevertheless, there has been considerable criticism of the lack of transparency in the process for appointing Supreme Court judges. Furthermore, although the courts have become somewhat more representative in terms of gender, appointments to the courts have not reflected other aspects of Canadian diversity.

Overall, the interpretation and application of laws by the courts is not simply a technical task of applying established rules. As noted in the introductory vignette, the law can be thought of as a "living tree" that is modified not only by new laws passed by legislatures, but also by changing interpretations by the courts that reflect changing circumstances, new challenges, and new ideas. The principle of judicial independence is very important to maintaining public respect for the courts. However, by applying their values and the changing values of society to particular cases, Supreme Court judges are, in effect, making important political decisions that can have profound effects on the governing of Canada and people's lives.

Discussion Questions

1. Should Parliament and provincial legislatures be involved in the selection and appointment of Supreme Court of Canada judges? Should the processes for appointing judges be more transparent?

2. Should judges be selected so as to reflect the diversity of Canada, with the Supreme Court required to have at least four female judges and one Aboriginal judge?

3. Should all Supreme Court of Canada justices be bilingual?

4. Should the use of juries be eliminated?

5. Would it be desirable to establish an Aboriginal system of justice for Aboriginal peoples?

Further Reading

Hausegger, L., Hennigar, M., & Riddell, T. (2015). *Canadian courts: Law, politics, and process* (2nd ed.). Toronto, ON: Oxford University Press.

MacFarlane, E. (2013). *Governing from the bench. The Supreme Court of Canada and the judicial role.* Vancouver, BC: UBC Press.

Manfredi, C., & Rush, M. (2008). *Judging democracy.* Peterborough, ON: Broadview Press.

McCormick, P.J. (2015). *The end of the Charter revolution: Looking back from the new normal.* Toronto, ON: University of Toronto Press.

Russell, P. (2001). *Judicial power and Canadian democracy.* Montreal, QC: McGill-Queen's University Press.

Sharpe, R.J., & McMahon, P.I. (2008). *The Persons case: The origins and legacy of the fight for legal personhood.* Toronto, ON: University of Toronto Press.

Songer, D.R., Johnson, S., Ostberg, C.L., & Wetstein, M. (2012). *Law, ideology, and collegiality: Judicial behaviour in the Supreme Court of Canada.* Montreal, QC: McGill-Queen's University Press.

Verrelli, N. (Ed.). (2013). *The democratic dilemma. Reforming Canada's Supreme Court.* Montreal, QC: McGill-Queen's University Press.

CHAPTER 17

Domestic Policy

In anticipation of the 2015 election, government spending increased to provide benefits to various groups of voters.

© Artizans Entertainment Inc.

CHAPTER OBJECTIVES

After reading this chapter, you should be able to

1. Outline the general, intermediate, and proximate factors affecting public policy.
2. Explain the rational, public choice, and stages models of public policy.
3. Discuss how globalization and pluralization affect social policy.
4. Describe how party politics has affected health policy.
5. Explain how neoliberalism has affected environmental policy.
6. Describe how macroeconomic policy differs from microeconomic policy.

It was April 21, 2015, budget day in Ottawa, and finance minister Joe Oliver was about to make a policy announcement that had been foreshadowed by other statements on the subject stretching back over the last four years. It was an important part of the narrative that had been established for the Harper government since it had taken office nearly a decade before. Sure enough, the budget included the expected news: The ceiling on annual contributions to each person's tax-free savings account (TFSA) was to be raised 82 percent to $10 000.

The tax-free savings account is a tax shelter that allows individuals at least 18 years old to protect a certain amount of savings and investments from taxation, and on a cumulative basis. The motivation for adopting the TFSA, finance minister Jim Flaherty said, was to promote savings among Canadians. The TFSA was announced in the 2008 budget and went into effect in 2009. When begun, it allowed individuals to deposit up to $5000 a year into a TFSA, an amount that was indexed to inflation but moved up only in $500 increments. The maximum amount was $5000 until 2012, then it became $5500 in 2013. However, amounts up to the accumulated contribution room could be contributed without penalty. The TFSA had to be opened at a financial institution, but within that could be self-managed. It could be used for savings accounts, GICs, stocks, mutual funds, and bonds.

Initially, many people had difficulty distinguishing the TFSA from a registered retirement savings plan (RRSP), but there were important differences. With a TFSA, one withdraws money from it tax-free, and the amount deducted can be added to the contribution limit the following year. RRSP contributions provide an income tax deduction; however, when money is taken out of the plan, it is fully taxed. Viewing the increase of the TFSA to $10 000 as primarily benefiting the wealthy, the Liberal party and the NDP indicated that they would roll back the maximum TFSA contribution to $5500 per year indexed to inflation, if elected.

The announcement had to be seen in context of its many facets; it was, simultaneously, an ideology, a public policy approach, a reading of electoral cycle dynamics, an attempt to hem in future governments' efforts to build back "big government," and lastly, plain old partisan warfare. The ideological underpinnings of the Harper government included neoliberalism—which places central emphasis on the free market, minimal government, individual self-reliance, low taxes, and free trade. The analogue of this in public policy terms is the public choice model, which sees individuals' actions in public life as being driven primarily by self-interest, a drive that results in parties accommodating the self-interest of key pockets of voters.

In addition, Stephen Harper's 2014 announcement that couples with children could split their income to reduce their combined income tax (to a maximum benefit of $2000) appealed to traditional families where the husband was the major or sole income-earner. Likewise, the expansion of the age range and aid level in the Universal Child Care Benefit (UCCB) blunted opposition calls for subsidized state-delivered child care by chewing up any future surpluses to pay for Conservative promises. The first six months of this benefit was delivered to parents in one lump-sum payment in July, three months before the 2015 general election.

So, ideology, theory, and partisan advantage overlapped with the TFSA, income splitting, and the UCCB. As with much public policy, evidence-based decision making is ideal, but policy ideals must be balanced with political realities.

INTRODUCTION

Public policy is an integral part of Canada's politics, but few Canadians know exactly what it is, how it is made, and why it changes. This chapter addresses those concerns and provides a basic introduction to policy concepts and major Canadian policy areas. It also reveals some paradoxes at work: Disagreements abound on what public policy means; there are many ways of examining it, but few guides on how to choose among them; and the outputs and outcomes are often hard to determine and to judge. Small wonder then, that the public policy field is typically viewed as mysterious and impenetrable.

PUBLIC POLICY
What government does or does not do, purposefully, or what it compels or encourages others in society to do, or not to do.

There are many definitions of **public policy**. There is the classic definition by Thomas Dye: "Whatever governments choose to do or not to do" (Dye, 1988, p. 2). Kraft and Furlong say it is "a course of government action or inaction in response to public problems . . . associated with formally approved policy goals and means, as well as the regulations and practices of agencies that implement programs" (Kraft & Furlong, 2015, p. 4). This chapter defines public policy as what government does or does not do, purposefully, or what it compels or encourages others in society to do, or not to do.

Public policy differs between political societies because of the **policy context**, a multilayered, interactive, and changeable environment that is composed of many elements. Depending on the circumstances, the elements may be constraints (bounding the freedom of choice of policy actors), or determinants (which compel certain options to be chosen), or aspects of agenda-setting (which establish what matters are under active consideration by political societies or political actors).

FACTORS AFFECTING THE CONTEXT OF PUBLIC POLICY

This chapter adopts the idea of "nested" or cascading sets of variables affecting public policy ranging from the general to the intermediate to the proximate, a notion that became popular in some public policy literature (Simeon, 1976; King, 1973; Hofferbert, 1974; Miljan, 2012). Figure 17-1 outlines the many factors setting the context of public policy. Nested factors interact with one another, but the diagram does not indicate how. It is the job of the policy analyst to examine what sorts of connections exist, and to add perspectives on the differences that temporal circumstances can make. In the space of three decades, for example, the ideological state of the world changed. In the 1980s, it was still the battle of communism and capitalism; in the 1990s, Francis Fukuyama (1992) heralded the "end of history" (or triumph of liberalism); and by the dawn of the 2000s, it was the era of radical Islamists versus the West (Huntington, 2011).

In the context of Canada's politics, the diagram provides a useful schema for explaining the factors that guide policy in the country. We shall

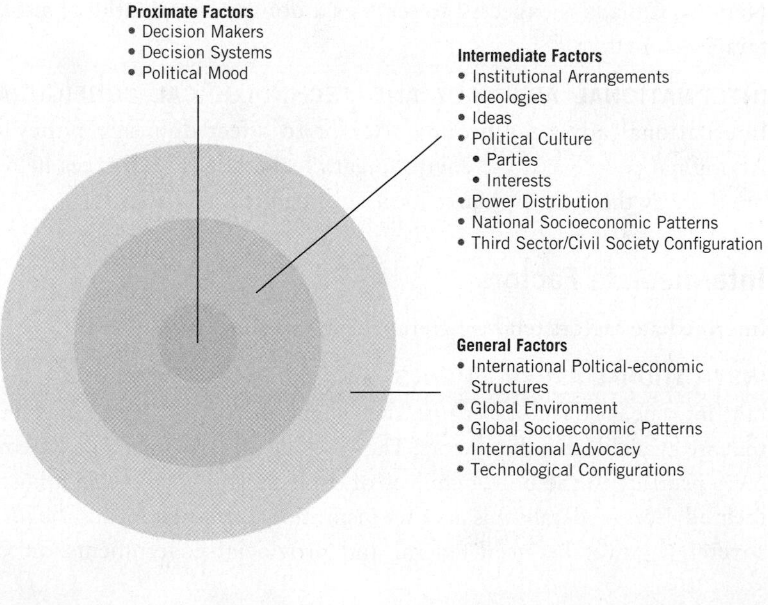

POLICY CONTEXT
Those multilayered, interactive, and changeable elements connected with the policy process which bound the freedom of choice of policy actors, or compel certain options to be chosen, or establish what matters are under active consideration by political societies or political actors.

Proximate Factors
• Decision Makers
• Decision Systems
• Political Mood

Intermediate Factors
• Institutional Arrangements
• Ideologies
• Ideas
• Political Culture
  • Parties
  • Interests
• Power Distribution
• National Socioeconomic Patterns
• Third Sector/Civil Society Configuration

General Factors
• International Poltical-economic Structures
• Global Environment
• Global Socioeconomic Patterns
• International Advocacy
• Technological Configurations

FIGURE 17-1
FACTORS SETTING THE CONTEXT OF PUBLIC POLICY

concentrate on some of the more striking general, intermediate, and proxi-mate factors.

General Factors

Several general factors set parameters within which Canadian policy-makers work.

INTERNATIONAL POLITICAL–ECONOMIC STRUCTURES   Canada is a member of NATO (the North Atlantic Treaty Organization, which is founded on the principle of "collective security"), and of several more informal alliances loosely based on the developing doctrine of "the responsibility to protect" (discussed in Chapter 18) that was used as a justification for Canadian partici-pation in air wars in Libya, Iraq, and Syria.

GLOBAL ENVIRONMENT   The global environment is a concern to most Canadians, in part because of the dramatic effects on our northern lands. Con-cerns about climate change have sparked a number of initiatives at the provin-cial and regional levels: cap and trade arrangements in Quebec and Ontario, energy exchanges in Alberta, and a carbon tax in British Columbia. Each of these has implications for industrial policy.

GLOBAL SOCIOECONOMIC PATTERNS   Global socioeconomic circumstances are such that Canada has worked its way into the club of the more developed nations of the world, and this has certain implications for public policy. Canadian citizens judge our domestic policy against other nations with similar levels of development (e.g., ranking education scores with the Programme for International Student Assessment [PISA], or economic policy with the Organ-isation for Economic Co-operation and Development [OECD]). As a member of elite global summit groups like the G7, G8, and G20 as well as the United Nations, Canada is expected to serve as a donor of international aid at a cer-tain level of effort.

INTERNATIONAL ADVOCACY AND TECHNOLOGICAL CONFIGURATIONS
International advocacy groups attempt to affect domestic policy toward Aboriginal people and the environment. Technological advances help config-ure the way the state organizes itself and regulates its citizens.

Intermediate Factors

Intermediate factors tend to operate at the national level.

INSTITUTIONAL ARRANGEMENTS   Institutional arrangements are an impor-tant intermediate factor because they shape the opportunities and incentives that are available to policy actors. They include the parliamentary system, which gives primacy to the policy choices of cabinets and responsible ministers and their advisors. Federalism is another institutional factor. It means the division of sovereign power between federal and provincial governments. In Canada, executive federalism has meant that the development of many policies has involved negotiations between the leading ministers of the two levels of government. However, the Harper government bequeathed much of its role in some policy areas, such as health and the environment, to provincial governments.

IDEOLOGIES   Ideologies are also important in the public policy field because they tend to preclude certain policy options and privilege others. Centre-left governments tend to choose collectivist alternatives like Crown corporations and regulation, whereas centre-right governments tend toward privatization, deregulation, and provision of social services by the voluntary sector. Business-oriented liberalism is seen by policy observers like Gad Horowitz (1966) and Ronald Manzer (1985) as the dominant idea set. Manzer calls the "dialectic of economic and ethical liberalism" (p. 190) Canada's ruling policy paradigm, although Horowitz qualifies his statement by noting that tory (traditional conservative) and socialist "streaks," or options, are also seen as valid culturally, although they have less effect relative to liberalism.

POLITICAL CULTURE   Political parties have been important in setting the policy agenda for the country, sometimes for extended periods of time. Prime Minister John A. Macdonald's National Policy established relatively protectionist trade and industrial policy for the better part of a century; his Conservative counterpart Brian Mulroney inaugurated a free trade era that is still in place; and Pierre Trudeau instituted a rights regime that constrains both orders of government. Chapter 7 showed that interest groups can influence public policy by direct influence and indirect methods. Interests can have direct influence by getting in "on the ground floor" in the early stages of policy development in their target department; by becoming part of a relevant "policy community"; by providing input to advisory councils and think tanks; by influencing parliamentarians, candidates, and the public; and, when necessary, by instigating legal action.

POWER DISTRIBUTION   The distribution of power in society can be interpreted in many ways. For example, government policy has had to decide whether to encourage or discourage the growing corporate concentration that is taking place, as well as the increasing role of foreign capital in Canadian businesses. As well, governments are coming to recognize the importance of civil society, seeing it as a delivery mechanism for certain policies, thus encouraging the growth of what some have called "the shadow government" (Light, 1999; Graham, 2014, pp. 11–12).

NATIONAL SOCIOECONOMIC PATTERNS   The national socioeconomic profile also has important effects on policy. Canada is an aging society, which has implications for health expenses (the elderly get more). It is concentrated in central Canada with pockets of growth in the West, which means large urban electorates get more—as with urban transit expenditures for Toronto, Ottawa, and Vancouver in the 2015 federal budget (Ivison, 2015) and commitments by the Liberal party. Diversity in immigration sources also has important impli-cations for various policies.

Proximate Factors

Proximate aspects of the policy context mean those that impact on the person or persons involved in making the decision; these factors are proximate, or near, to the actual decision.

DECISION MAKERS   The preferences of the decision maker(s) count here: the life experience, policy orientation, and state of knowledge of the prime minister/premier and cabinet, for example.

DECISION SYSTEMS   The decision system in place may count: whether there is a dispersal of decision making across several cabinet committees or centralization in a prime minister's office makes a difference, as observers of the Harper years have observed (Wells, 2013; Harris, 2014; Ibbitson, 2015; Martin, 2011).

POLITICAL MOOD   The political mood at the time decisions are made makes a difference as well. It was easier to get stricter national security legislation under way after the terrorist attack on the World Trade Center in the United States in 2001 and the killing of Canadian soldiers and the attack on Parlia-ment by domestic Canadian terrorists in 2014.

POLICY PARADIGMS

POLICY PARADIGMS
The generally accepted norms for how the policymaking process takes place and what relevant questions and evidence are acceptable.

Public policymaking may differ between eras because of the importance of **policy paradigms**. Policy paradigms have been described in different ways, but here we understand them to be the generally accepted norms for how the policymaking process takes place and what relevant questions and evidence are "acceptable" (Kuhn, 1962, 2012).

The standard paradigm for many years was the standard command and control approach. This maintained that government departments and cabi-nets, or agencies and corporations under their influence, were the major actors in policymaking, and that research should focus on what influences them and how they use the instruments that are available to them.

Another paradigm states that governments are no longer in control of the process, as before, and that they have given way to networks of policy actors in government, business, and civil society. The job of achieving public aims is parceled out to actors who are best able to do the job, or who manage to con-vince the other partners that this is the case.

Still another policy paradigm gives the forces of globalization a significant role in policymaking. According to this view, the internationalization of capi-tal markets, culture, and market sourcing means that most governments will have to be attentive to market forces as interpreted by international trade regimes and international economic bodies.

POLICY DISCIPLINES

Context and paradigmatic considerations affect how policy is conceived and carried out, and so do policy disciplines. There is a tendency for political scientists to imagine that their discipline is the major one in the public policy area; however, policy analysis is actually a multidisciplinary enterprise. Conceiving the field otherwise is to take the richness out of public policy and to ignore vast areas of useful scholarship.

This text seeks to address that problem by suggesting a schema (Figure 17-2) whereby the major contributions of the policy-relevant disciplines are highlighted. Students of public policy need to judge from the context of the policy

FIGURE 17-2
MULTIDISCIPLINARY CONTRIBUTIONS TO PUBLIC POLICY THEORY

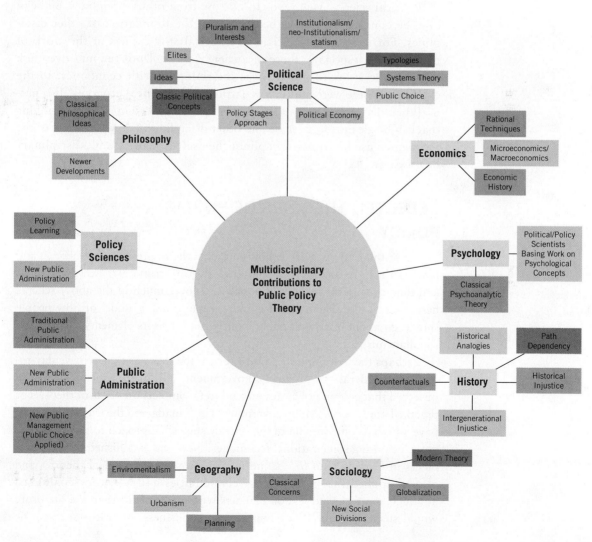

problem in question which disciplines and subsets should be appropriated for which problem.

Take, for example, the question of what sorts of services the federal Department of Indigenous and Northern Development Canada should be undertaking. A conscientious policy analyst would have to have a good basis in history (understanding the breadth of European/Aboriginal relations in Canada), philosophy (comprehending the nature of colonialism and Aboriginal political theory), public administration (understanding the role of the department in relation to others), law (understanding the concepts involved in Aboriginal rights cases), and economics (grasping the implications of land claims for national economic development). We could list other policy areas, but most would have multidisciplinary implications.

Political science itself tends to borrow from other disciplines, and can even be considered to have been built on the foundation of other disciplines. For example, the origin of political studies was in the work of philosophers, especially those of ancient Greece. Until the mid-twentieth century, the study of politics was intermingled with economics, to the extent that there were multiple departments of political economy. It is natural then that policy specialists in political science are open to the insights that can be gleaned from these and other disciplines. Likewise, many of the techniques used in other disciplines themselves feature multidisciplinary borrowings.

SELECTED THEORIES OF PUBLIC POLICY

The next thing to consider is how to tackle the multiplicity of theories and models that are available to the analyst. Unfortunately, however, space and time constraints make it impossible to cover much in the above schema here. Indeed, the schema itself is more a map than a model of how people should go about analyzing public policy; not all of its elements can be used simultaneously.

Perhaps the best thing to do is to review the theories that achieve day-to-day use in federal and provincial governments and in civil society. We have observed that certain policy actors tend to favour certain kinds of theories or practical approaches. Many governments in Canada and the Commonwealth have adopted some version of the "policy stages" approach to public policy, as well as using some rational techniques. New and established social movements in Canada tend to operate on the basis of sociological theories and also of applied theories of policy communities and advocacy coalitions, although some depend less on contacts with government than the literature would suggest. Umbrella organizations for business interests—such as the

C.D. Howe Institute, the Conference Board of Canada, the Atlantic Institute for Market Studies, the Fraser Institute, and the Frontier Centre for Public Policy—tend to use a mixture of welfare economics and public choice analysis. Let us examine some of these policy approaches in a little more detail.

Bearing in mind, then, that not every theoretical area can be covered here, we can nonetheless consider some of the more common and utilitarian ones. These include the rational model, public choice, and stages (or policy cycle) approach to the policy process.

The Rational Model

The **rational model** of the policy process presumes that decision makers are oriented toward achieving objectives and influenced by a desire to be as complete as possible with regard to examination of options to reach those objectives. More often than not, the rational model is presented as a series of steps that are advisable. Catherine F. Smith, although not calling it the rational approach, presents a series of steps that are compatible with it: "Public policy making in a democracy is an institutional process of solving problems that affect society or its environment . . . . [and] includes the following activities: defining the problem, developing knowledge including knowledge of prior action or inaction on the problem, proposing policy alternatives, deliberating the alternatives, adopting policy, administering and implementing policy, [and] changing policy" (Smith, 2013, p. xxi). Basically the model is this: You say what you want, and examine what is the best way to get it, and choose it. Many techniques in public policy are based on this simple theme: cost–benefit analysis, planning theory, budgeting analysis, and evidence-based decision making.

RATIONAL MODEL
A model of the policy process that maintains decision makers are oriented toward achieving objectives and influenced by a desire to be as complete as possible with regard to examination of options to reach those objectives.

Public Choice

Public choice is another influential model of public policy. It has become the de facto basis for many decisions in the public sphere in the last quarter-century in Canada, and even longer in other countries like the United Kingdom and United States. It is the work of theorists such as Gordon Tullock, William Niskanen, Elinor Ostrom, James M. Buchanan, Douglas Hartle, and Michael Trebilcock. Its basic assumption (or axiom) is that all actors in the public sphere are driven by self-interest and public policy reflects this, although it may not be readily apparent to many, again because self-interested actors attempt to hide this fact. The actors are diverse; they include politicians, government officials, interest groups, media outlets, and voters. Public choice reformers seek to change the shape of public services so that they reflect the best aspects of the private sector: competition, innovation, consumer sovereignty, and efficiency.

PUBLIC CHOICE
The model of the policy process whose basic assumption is that all actors in the public sphere are driven by self-interest and public policy reflects this.

Stages (or Policy Cycle) Approach

STAGES (OR POLICY CYCLE)
APPROACH
Sees the policy process as
including a number of separate
elements, or stages, that
altogether add up to a sequence
of events that unfold in logical
succession in a more or less
cyclical fashion.

The **stages (or policy cycle) approach** sees the policy process as including a number of separate elements, or stages, that altogether add up to a sequence of events that unfold in logical succession in a more or less cyclical fashion, leading to the name "policy cycle." Authors disagree on the exact nature of the stages of the policy cycle. Lasswell (1935, 1951, 1971) was at the lengthy end of the spectrum with his seven stages. So was Charles Jones, who is generally credited with popularizing the notion of stages of policy (1997), and Hoggwood and Gunn (1984): they had 10 each! The more common approach is to list five or six. Such is case with Brewer and deLeon who had six (initiation, estimation, selection, implementation, evaluation, and termination) (Brewer & DeLeon, 1983), and Howlett, Ramesh, and Perl (2009), who have five (agenda setting, policy formulation, decision making, policy implementation, and policy evaluation).

The "stages heuristic" as it has sometimes been called (since it is a guide to further examination or research) has been both praised and criticized. Its critics decry the tendency of the model to suggest tidiness and predictability in the way that the policy process unfolds, whereas the process is often chaotic and unpredictable. It can miss whole steps or steps can even happen in reverse at times. It is said not to be a theory in the sense that analysts cannot use it to predict policy development. Still, the model is popular among analysts and governments all around the world because of its strongly utilitarian nature. It allows one to disaggregate a very complex set of phenomena and study each in considerable detail. It also corresponds closely to the way in which noted policy academics structure their work; for every stage, one can name one or more outstanding scholars offering the definitive take on it (Brewer & DeLeon, 1983).

The model can also serve as an organizing tool. One can, for example, examine a specific policy or policy area and have a ready-made research plan at hand. This is in fact what Hessing, Howlett, and Summerville (2005) do in their examination of Canadian resource policy and environmental policy. The authors assemble their data so as to reflect both political economy and stages ("policy cycle") approaches. They also do what is discussed earlier in this chapter and take an interdisciplinary approach.

Stagist approaches can also serve as a tool for organizing the vast body of policy literature. Howlett, Ramesh, and Perl (2009) use the stages model to categorize a massive amount of policy-theoretic literature in a way that is unique in policy textbooks, making an untidy field finally manageable. It is also the text that introduces most Canadian policy students to their field. Table 17-1 gives a highly abbreviated summary of their stages categorization of policy literature.

POLICY STAGES
Agenda-setting: recognition by government or the public that a problem exists and needs attention
Policy formulation: policy actors explore the relative merits of options and alternatives to solve policy problems and narrow down the list for the decision stage
Decision making: an option considered at an earlier stage is adopted as a course of action
Implementation: putting decisions into practice by devoting personnel, budgets, and rule making to effect them
Policy evaluation: the assessment of how appropriate the aims and implementation of a policy have been in practice

TABLE 17-1
STAGES SCHEMA FOR ORGANIZING POLICY LITERATURE: HOWLETT, RAMESH, AND PERL (2009)

THEORY AND PRACTICE

So much for theory and process. But how does it relate to the "real world?" Putting aside qualms about critics who make such a distinction—theory is supposed to be an abstraction of the way the real world operates, after all—this is a valid concern. Students of Canadian politics are justified in wanting to see the application of theory to distinct areas of public policy design and operation. In subsequent sections, we will show how public policy theory affects the design of government processes and government policies.

Cabinet Policy and Budgetary Processes: The Rational Model by Design?

Policy theory has been of immense importance in the design of government in Canada at both the federal and provincial levels. One theory in particular has shown itself in organization of cabinet policy and budgetary processes. Christopher Dunn has demonstrated that the institutionalized cabinet—the structured or highly complex version of modern cabinets which got its start roughly 50 years ago—was in part a result of the impact of "social science rationalism," or the rational decision-making model. "The social science of the day," he said, "held that governing was just as much a matter of designating correct procedures as it was of political will. It promoted a so-called rationalism which involved establishing primary objectives, then designing structures and processes to move the system towards achieving them, and finally providing for feedback and evaluation. Government was rational inasmuch as it was purposeful and self-correcting" (Dunn, 1995, p. 284).

The rational model can be seen to be inherent in the way that the cabinet and central agencies specialize in their functions. The system attempts to achieve a kind of sector rationality by having cabinet committees structured along policy sector lines. Cabinet committees tend to engage in priority setting within their discrete sectors or areas and become expert at ranking policy options therein—a kind of "horizontal decision making" or system of tradeoffs. Then the full cabinet is free to engage in the tradeoffs *between sectors*, both in policy and in budgetary matters.

Cabinet receives three main types of policy submission: the Memorandum to Cabinet (MC), the Treasury Board submission, and the Governor in Council (GIC) submission. The first typically works its way through the cabinet committee system, whereas the Treasury Board handles Treasury Board and GIC submissions in a more abbreviated and less linear process. MCs are needed for a new program or policy direction, whereas the Treasury Board submission covers the subsequent parts of the policy process, including program design, program implementation, and program evaluation. GIC items deal with delegated legislation.

There is a standard process for the routing of Memoranda to Cabinet. The diagram in Figure 17-3 shows the origins and outcomes of Memoranda to Cabinet.

Analysis by the Privy Council Office, a central agency, is also meant to introduce a significant element of horizontality into the cabinet process. This means that the Privy Council Office ensures that other ministers, departments, and agencies that are affected by the department's policy are consulted, that room is left in the agenda for the input of affected parties, and that the measure makes for good public policy. Of course, not only the cabinet and its committees are briefed, but also the prime minister, who orchestrates the policy process. As the minister responsible for both the Privy Council Office and the Prime Minister's Office, the prime minister has the advantage of both policy and partisan political input.

The first major budget reform in the 1960s, the Planning–Programming–Budgeting System (PPBS), was explicitly based on rationalist assumptions. Its specific purpose was to overcome the deficiencies of the incrementalist model of budgeting, which involved only slight modifications from what previous budgets had been. Other budgeting programs that followed—Zero-Base Budgeting (ZBB), the Envelope System, and others—also used rationalist concepts.

FIGURE 17-3
THE ROUTING OF MEMORANDA TO CABINET

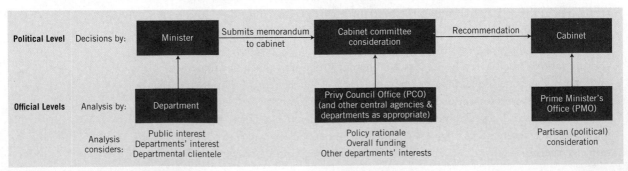

Public Policy Areas

Another way we can relate theory to practice is to analyze what shapes actual policies and affects their implementation. We have therefore identified four high-profile areas of public policy: social policy, health policy, economic policy, and environmental policy. For each of them, we will identify the general, intermediate, and proximate variables (factors) that affect policy development in that area, and also consider selected aspects of theories of public policy (see Table 17-2).

Social Policy

Social policy is difficult to define succinctly. Observers have tried to do justice to its many facets. Richard Titmuss's "iceberg" explanation is a common reference point. He refers to *social welfare* (the top, or only seemingly visible, aspect of welfare state spending as redistribution from the rich to the poor); *occupational welfare* (benefits delivered as a component of being employed, such as work-related pensions, health plans, education and training, and subsidies);

SOCIAL POLICY
Commonly understood to include public policies that knit communities together in a sense of fraternity and mutual aid, such as income redistribution, work-related benefits, and fiscal transfers.

TABLE 17-2
VARIABLES AFFECTING CANADIAN SOCIAL, HEALTH, ECONOMIC, AND ENVIRONMENTAL POLICY

CLASS OF VARIABLE	SOCIAL POLICY	HEALTH POLICY	ECONOMIC POLICY	ENVIRONMENTAL POLICY
General	Globalization Pluralization	International health indicators International health regulations	G7, G8, G20 Multinational corporations	Global environmental degradation Statements by international bodies and scientists
Intermediate	Welfare state paradigm Neoliberal paradigm Provincial social philosophies	Moral imperatives Party politics New public management (neoliberal management theory)	Orthodox economic analysts Liberalism dominant cultural element Liberal interventionism Liberal internationalism Current policy instruments	Demographic change Environmental movements
Proximate	Federal–provincial–territorial relations	Federal finance minister/officials Federal–provincial–territorial ministers	National economic institutional actors	The role of prime ministers Human agency

and *fiscal welfare* (benefits delivered through the tax-system like targeted tax breaks and allowances) (Titmuss, 1956). The first tends to favour the least well-off, the last two the better-off.

Ernie Lightman suggests that social policy means different things to different people. To many, it is values and programs that bring citizens together as a community. To social justice advocates, it comprises a series of programs meant to free the poor and vulnerable from lives of dependency. To practitioners, it is simply a list of programs that have "social" attached as the umbrella term (Lightman, 2003).

Michael Prince outlines what might be called the practitioner's list of 12 social policy areas and representative programs. There are what the literature commonly refers to as social policy—health care, education, income security, and social services. As well, provincial governments (who are mainly responsible for social policy) often refer to social policy as including housing; employment and labour; justice and public safety; arts, culture, and heritage; disability and inclusion; tax expenditures; immigration and multiculturalism; and recreation and tourism. Jurisdictions may have different items on their social policy lists, because "like all other domains of public policy, social policy is a political construction" (Prince, 2015). The first four are what the literature tends to cover in depth and call "social welfare policy"[1] (see Table 17-3 for the traditional 4 of the 12 fields).

FEDERAL–PROVINCIAL ASPECTS OF SOCIAL POLICY   There are both federal and provincial aspects of social policy. The Parliament of Canada may make laws in relation to old age pensions and supplementary benefits, including survivors' and disability benefits irrespective of age, according to Section 94A of the Constitution Act, 1867 (as amended 1964). However, provincial legislatures have paramountcy in these areas, meaning no federal law may overturn the provincial legislation of a similar nature in cases where the two conflict. Section 93 gives provinces exclusive jurisdiction over education (subject to federal remedial actions for certain denominational minorities), but Parliament has pockets of education responsibilities (for Aboriginals and the military) and some ancillary official language education responsibilities. Fiscal welfare can be (and frequently is) delivered by both levels of government by their taxation powers, with the federal one being wider ("any mode or system of taxation," Section 91(3)) than the provincial ("direct taxation within the province," Section 92(2)). Both health and social policy is implied in the provincial responsibility for Section 92(6), the establishment and maintenance of hospitals, asylums, and charities in the province. Miscellaneous social aspects are caught in "property and civil rights" (Section 92(13)) or "generally all matters of a merely local or private nature" (Section 92(16)).

---

[1]Health policy is discussed later in this chapter.

TABLE 17-3
**MICHAEL PRINCE: SCHEMA
OF TRADITIONAL SOCIAL
POLICY FIELDS**

HEALTH CARE	EDUCATION	INCOME SUPPORT	COMMUNITY SERVICES
• Hospital, nursing, and physician services • Aboriginal health • Mental health • Public health • Addictions and substance use • Prescription drugs	• Primary and secondary schools • Colleges, technical institutes, and universities • Public libraries • School districts • Student financial aid • Anti-bullying programs	• Canada/Quebec Pension Plans • Social assistance • Workers' compensation • Child and family benefits • Elderly supplements • Disability benefits • Shelter allowances	• Adoption services, foster homes, and child and family welfare • Early learning and child care • Adult and elderly care services • Family violence prevention
HOUSING	**EMPLOYMENT AND LABOUR**	**JUSTICE AND PUBLIC SAFETY**	**ARTS, CULTURE, AND HERITAGE**
• Cooperatives and non-profits • Homeless initiatives • Seniors' housing • Landlord–tenant relations	• Employment standards • Labour market and job programs • Minimum wage rates • Job subsidies • Workfare programs	• Legal aid • Courts, probation and parole services • Victim services • Provincial and municipal policing • Correctional services	• Community arts • Galleries • Historic sites • Museums
DISABILITY AND INCLUSION	**TAX POLICY EXPENDITURES**	**IMMIGRATION AND MULTICULTURALISM**	**SPORTS, RECREATION, AND TOURISM**
• Personal supports • Accessibility in built structures • Transit services • Employment programs	• Exemptions for basic groceries, children's clothing • Refundable tax credits for sale • Non-refundable credits for tuition and education	• Refugee/immigrant settlement services • Language training • Citizenship instruction • Grants to ethno-racial community groups	• Provincial and regional parks • Recreation and wellness programs • Community centres

SOURCE: Michael Prince, "The provinces and social policy: Canada's multiple welfare states," in Dunn (2015). ed. in *Provinces: Canadian Provincial Politics* (3rd Ed.). Toronto: University of Toronto Press. Used with permission.

VARIABLES AFFECTING SOCIAL PROGRAMS   Many of the social programs that now exist in Canada were initially introduced under the aegis of the federal spending power (the power of Parliament to spend in any area it wants, even if such spending involves matters within provincial jurisdiction, provided such spending does not amount to federal regulation of a provincial head of power). Table 17-4 lists some of the social policy spending power programs that Ottawa introduced in the postwar period.

There were several reasons for the proliferation of such programs. We have earlier outlined the variables that affect public policy in Canada. Here we make reference to those policy variables we mentioned that affect social policy.

TABLE 17-4
EVOLUTION OF SPENDING POWER PROGRAMS IN CANADA

HEALTH PROGRAMS	SOCIAL WELFARE PROGRAMS	TECHNICAL AND VOCATIONAL EDUCATION PROGRAMS	INCOME SUPPORT PROGRAMS
1948 Hospital Construction	1937/51 Blind Persons' Allowances	1937 Student Aid	1927 Old Age Pensions Act
1948 General Public Health	1952 Old Age Assistance	1944 Apprenticeship Training	1945 Family Allowances
1948 Tuberculosis Control	1954 Disabled Persons' Allowances	1945 Technical and Vocational Training-Capital Cost Allowance	1966 Canada Assistance Program
1948 Public Health Research	1956 Unemployment Insurance	1946 Training in Co-operation with Industry	1966 Guaranteed Income Supplement
1948 Cancer Control	1966 Canada Assistance Plan	1948 Training of Unemployed	1998 National Child Benefit
1948 Professional Training-Health		1950 Training of Disabled	2006 Universal Child Care Benefit
1948 Mental Health		1950 Vocational High-School Training	
1948/53 Medical Rehabilitation and Crippled Children		1953 Rehabilitation of Disabled Persons	
1953 Children and Maternal Health		1960 Teacher Technical Training	
1957 Hospital Insurance and Diagnostic Services (HIDSA)		1960 Technician Training	
1966 Health Resources Fund		1960 Trade and Occupational Training	
1968 Medical Insurance ("Medicare")		1964 Student Loans (Interest)	

One was the Keynesian consensus (see Chapter 4) that dominated Canadian policymaking for decades after World War II and whose policy implications pointed to concepts of interventionist government committed to a common national interest. Another was asymmetry in federal and provincial power; Ottawa collected the great majority of all tax revenue and provincial public services were underdeveloped and basically infrastructural concerns. Another reason was that shared cost programs were flexible; the federal government did not administer its side with a heavy degree of supervision. Alternative governing instruments, such as amendments to the division of powers and the use of the declaratory power, often faced provincial government opposition. A final and important factor was that both orders of government tended to agree on the goals of the programs, which in some cases the provinces had pioneered themselves.

FEDERAL–PROVINCIAL–TERRITORIAL (FPT) RELATIONS The story of how the spending power ceased to be a policy instrument after the 1960s is an interesting one, and stereotypically Canadian. Canadian federalism features a see-saw effect, with the relative strength of federal and provincial partners shifting back and forth over time. Indeed, what followed from the 1960s to the 1990s was the era of "province building." This had the effect of putting the brakes on the use of the spending power instrument, and with this, the overwhelming predominance of Ottawa in social policy questions. Factors opposite those which had promoted the earlier prominence of the spending power were now in play. Keynesian economic prominence faded. Provincial power, especially Quebec's power, accelerated as politicians sponsored programs to compete for citizen loyalties. Policy-makers now considered alternative instruments like equalization and change in the division of powers, Senate reform, and federal–provincial partnerships. Recourse to the institutionalized cabinet (Dunn, 1995) reshaped the policymaking world for federal and provincial governments; central actors discouraged cross-governmental departmental allegiances. These factors came together to promote a new phenomenon: A formidable constitutional industry advocated a grand megaconstitutional reform effort involving a comprehensive renegotiation of the federal bargain struck a century before (Dunn, 2010). Many of these renegotiations featured demands for severe limitation of the spending power, or even its negation, damaging its viability as an instrument. The Social Union Framework Agreement (SUFA) of 1999 was an example of limitation; Prime Minister Harper's "Open Federalism" amounted in some respects to a negation of the federal use of the spending power.

PROVINCIAL SOCIAL PHILOSOPHIES AFFECTING SOCIAL PROGRAMS   After the sidelining of the spending power instrument, social policy became more provincial in delivery, but there were still some federal aspects. What we found was Ottawa and the provinces using social policy as a component of a larger social vision the sponsoring party had in mind. Before the turn of the twenty-first century, with a tendency for several provinces to elect NDP governments, many social programs were in line with party ideology married to provincial sensibilities. In Manitoba, for example, the NDP government's main planning documents, *Guidelines for the Seventies* and *The Northern Plan*, enunciated some central ideas: dual labour market theory to help the unorganized, poorly paid or underemployed enter the organized, well-paid sector from which they were historically excluded; the "stay option" that offered social and economic incentives to stop northern and rural depopulation; and self-sufficiency for northern communities. Western provinces tended to have relatively more generous social assistance programs than Eastern Canada, due mainly to their level of financial well-being.

All provincial governments signed the $5 billion comprehensive public child care plan proposed by the Liberal government of Paul Martin. However, after the Liberal defeat in the 2006 election, the plan was cancelled by the incoming Harper government, which introduced a program focused on monetary transfers to parents instead of subsidized public child care.

Some provinces, such as Quebec and Newfoundland and Labrador, have introduced Poverty Reduction Strategies involving multifaceted social policy initiatives. The Strategy in Quebec was a matter of social consensus, being the product of two successive parties in government, the Parti Québécois and the Liberal Party of Quebec, with two five-year plans, established in 2004 and 2010. The plan took a longitudinal (lifetime) perspective, and stressed the importance of employment as the bedrock concept, accompanied by a commitment to reducing social exclusion and enhancing empowerment. It committed the government to reducing disincentives to employment in the provincial "Employment Assistance" (welfare) program, which featured raises indexed to the provincial income tax. There were investments in social housing, regional food security projects, dental care, and subsidized child care in addition to the Canada Child Tax Benefit, specialized services for youth returning to school and for teenage parents and their children, and involvement of the larger society in projects like microlending (Torjman, 2010). This was in contrast to some other provinces in the neoliberal era that had rejected such models and initiated punitive social welfare strategies. The Harris PC government in the 1990s cut social assistance rates by over one-fifth, and instituted "Ontario Works" (dubbed "Workfare" by some) for able welfare recipients.

Globalization and Pluralization   James J. Rice and Michael Prince (2013) have observed that recent social policy in Canada is heavily influenced by globalization and pluralization. Globalization is the latest adaptation in market liberalism and means (among other things) the internationalization of markets, communications, and products. **Pluralization** is their term for the increasing social divisions based on gender, ethnicity, sexual orientation, family form, age, or relation to the labour market. Economic globalization means that corporations can easily transfer resources and technology between countries, and that there is increasing concentration of economic power in multinational companies and decreasing of trade barriers, thereby opening domestic markets. Globalization lessens workers' employment security and polarizes the employment market between high and low job security and benefits. Globalization lessens the state's role in society, especially that of protecting the social fabric of the community. Pluralization is engendered, in part, by globalization, and social policy has to adapt. Social policy was partially based on idealizing the nuclear family, but now the "politics of inclusion" is more the aim as various groups seek influence in the public space. There are multiple versions of families, diverse identities are to be promoted, the notion of a general public interest is put into question, and social movements increasingly demand roles in social policy-making (Rice & Prince, 2013).

PLURALIZATION

A new term to describe the increasing social divisions based on gender, ethnicity, sexual orientation, family form, age, or relation to the labour market.

The first issue is which **design factors** to use, and in what combination. There are a variety of criteria for income redistribution programs, for example: means or need tests, contingency, contribution, and demography (Manzer, 1985). Means tests establish an income ceiling below which benefits follow; needs tests involve a judgment of what individuals or families need. Assistance in contingency programs flows when disasters or misfortunes of various types occur, such as unemployment. Contributory programs are those in which there is a right to benefits based on previous payments one has made, and demographic benefits depend on factors such as age (child benefits) or population characteristics, like Aboriginality. One also has to figure out to what extent funding comes from general taxation or contributions, to what extent the program will be targeted or universal, what the relationship between benefits and contributions will be (how much of the benefit is covered by contributions, and with what degree of progressivity), and whether the benefits will be delivered by the tax system or by governments themselves (McGilly, 1998).

Another issue is to what extent the programs should have a **federal role**. Stephen Harper's Open Federalism was premised on the notion of restricted use of the spending power and strict attention to the "original" division of powers, so the traditional federal role of introducing new shared cost social programs was not on. A corollary to this is that the federal enforcement of national standards, which used to be one of the main rationales for federal involvement in shared cost social programs, has apparently been eschewed by the federal government in recent years. There is a middle ground—collaborative standard setting, which the Social Union Framework Agreement of 1999 established—which could avoid the stark choices of no federal role and an overwhelming federal role.

Fiscal sustainability of social programs is yet another issue. For example, the long-term fiscal viability of Old Age Security (OAS), the largest spending program of the federal government, was an issue that sparked a row between the finance minister and the parliamentary budget officer (PBO) in 2012 and was a forerunner to changes in the 2012 federal budget. The minister maintained that the long-term viability of OAS was in danger, with 4.7 million receiving it in 2010 and 9.3 million in 2030. The PBO said that it was indeed sustainable, the federal fiscal structure being able to accommodate a variety of seniors' benefits programs in spite of significant population aging (CBC News, 2012b). Ultimately, the minister prevailed, and the age of eligibility for the OAS was raised from 65 to 67 starting in 2023. However, during the 2015 election campaign, Justin Trudeau pledged to make 65 the age of eligibility.

As one might expect from such a complex area, there are a number of issues surrounding social policy (see Box 17-1: Social Policy Issues). A few of the outstanding ones are what design criteria to choose, what federal role there should be, and the fiscal sustainability of existing social programs.

Health Policy

BACKGROUND **Health policy** is a special type of social policy concerned with curative and preventive measures; that is, it is meant both to alleviate illness and to establish a state of well-being that includes measures that will

HEALTH POLICY
A special type of social policy concerned with curative and preventive measures.

ward off illness in the future. This is not just a semantic exercise, but has implications for the way in which health services are organized and delivered.

There are many facets to health policy. The World Health Organization (WHO) lists the key components of a well-functioning health system (World Health Organization, 2010). They include:

- leadership and governance (defining and steering and regulating health policies in all sectors, public and private);
- establishing health information systems on matters like financing, human health resources, access and service quality;
- a finance system to alleviate inequalities (raising, pooling, and auditing the use of financial resources);
- a health human resources strategy featuring methods of achieving the right mix of health personnel, appropriate pay and incentives, work norms and stakeholder cooperation;
- medical products and technologies, including diagnostic and treatment protocols, and universal access monitoring; and
- service delivery consisting of networks of primary care, backed up with other specialized delivery mechanisms.

The national and provincial governments share roles in many of these.

FEDERAL–PROVINCIAL ASPECTS OF THE POLICY   Some aspects of health policy are federal, some are provincial, and some overlap between the two levels of government. The constitution restricts the federal role, allocating to Parliament only "Quarantine and the Establishment and Maintenance of Marine Hospitals" in Section 91(11) of the Constitution Act, 1867. It also has ancillary responsibilities for health delivery arising from personnel covered under certain other heads of jurisdiction: Section 91(11) for the military, Section 91(24) for Indians (Aboriginals), and Section 91(28) for inmates in penitentiaries. The provincial responsibilities are captured under Section 92(6), for the establishment and maintenance of hospitals, asylums, and charities in the province, which in practice includes most of the WHO health system characteristics. Both levels of government are involved in health information systems on various aspects of health delivery—for example, the general reporting of matters like wait times for certain procedures. Areas of overlap usually occur because of the federal spending power that has been the rationale for federal conditional and block grants to the provinces for several decades. The spending power rationale for federal health involvement has lost its edge however, since in 2011 the Harper government began not only to diminish the rate of growth of transfers for health, but also to withdraw from enunciating a federal vision for the field.

EVOLUTION OF HEALTH PROGRAMS   The evolution of health financing and organization can be linked to the Hospital Insurance and Diagnostic Services Act (HIDSA, 1957), Medicare (1966), Federal-Provincial Fiscal Arrangements and Established Programs Financing Act (EPF, 1977), the Canada Health Act (CHA, 1984), Canada Health and Social Transfer (CHST, 1996), and Canada Health Transfer (CHT, 2004). Before the 1950s, there were a series of spotty local and provincial services, with some general services provided by religious and charitable organizations. Saskatchewan (under Premier Tommy Douglas's CCF government) instituted universal access to hospital services in 1947 with the Saskatchewan Hospital Services Plan, and universal access to physician services in 1961. These were the models for later federal legislation.

The Hospital Insurance and Diagnostic Services Act [or HIDSA], 1957, introduced universal, portable, and publicly administered national hospital insurance, based on a conditional grant to provinces, with costs shared evenly between Ottawa and provinces. The Medical Care Act, 1966, provided a 50–50 shared open-ended conditional grant for medical services not delivered in hospital. In 1977, a de-coupling of federal grants and program costs took place; hereafter, federal contributions were tied to economic growth.

The Federal–Provincial Fiscal Arrangements and Established Programs Financing Act, 1977 (or EPF), repealed the first two acts. It was now not a conditional grant, but a block grant (meaning allocated for general, rather than specific purposes), and featured a combination of cash transfers and tax points tied to growth in the GNP. This format was the direct result of federal concerns with the largely open-ended nature of the two previous grant programs and the larger federal finance picture of growing government deficits. There was an understanding that the EPF monies were to be spent by provinces on a "two-thirds health, one-third social programs" basis, but this proved more a wish than an enforceable policy. This matter was to be clarified in later transfer programs.

Thereafter came a series of acts that shaped the current configuration of health insurance arrangements. The Canada Health Act, 1984 (CHA), established five criteria, or national principles, for provincial governments to fulfill in order to receive full federal cash transfers. These were *public administration* (administration by an accountable public authority); *comprehensiveness* (provinces to insure all "medically necessary" services, meaning services that they categorize as such); *universality* (all residents of a province or territory to have access to health insurance and insured services); *portability* (all Canadians are covered when they move to another province and when they travel in Canada or abroad); and *accessibility* (uniform access meaning avoiding financial barriers, and health services provided without discrimination by reason of income, or health). Two provisions prohibiting user charges and extra billing, meant to elaborate on the accessibility principle, were added as well.

The Canada Health and Social Transfer (CHST) replaced the EPF in 1996 and combined it with transfers to provincial governments under the Canada Assistance Plan (CAP), which funded a variety of welfare programs. It continued the federal insistence that its transfer was a combination of cash transfers and tax points, and it tied federal cash transfers to continued provincial adherence to the national principles of the CHA. In 2004, the CHST was split into the Canada Health Transfer (CHT) and the Canada Social Transfer (CST), because federal authorities wanted more accountability for their transfers. It was also a combination of cash and tax, and tied to provinces meeting the CHA criteria, at least in theory.For further discussion, see Chapter 12.

VARIABLES AFFECTING HEALTH POLICY   It is difficult to disentangle reasons why health services evolved the way they did, but various general, intermediate, and proximate variables can suggest avenues researchers can further explore.

INTERNATIONAL INDICATORS AND REGULATIONS   International indicators and indicative standards have long had an effect on domestic Canadian health policy. For instance, the Canadian Institute for Health Information (CIHI), an institution that collects and reports on provincial health performance indicators, uses a variety of international health indicators, such as the Commonwealth Fund's International Health Policy surveys and the OECD's quality of care indicators. It finds that "policy-makers, practitioners and the public can use international comparisons to establish priorities for improvement, set goals and motivate stakeholders to act" (Canadian Institute for Health Information, 2015).

International regulations are a long-standing and more intrusive—for good reason—influence on health policy. Katherine Fierlbeck notes, in terms of public health regimes, that "The WHO . . . requires governments to meet certain requirements as part of its International Health Regulations system. The response to mass infection must be carefully coordinated, as a single weak link can compromise the coordinated efforts of other jurisdictions. Thus all governments have, at the national level, implemented strategies for dealing not only with infectious diseases, but also chemical, biological, and radiological disasters" (Fierlbeck, 2013). The level of response is politically and financially driven in each country because governments do not get credit for disasters that do not happen.

MORAL IMPERATIVES   Gregory Marchildon argues convincingly that the roots of the modern health system—in other words, how it got on the public and governmental agenda and displaced other options in policy formulation—lie in Tommy Douglas's evangelical Christianity (particularly, the final ascendancy of the Baptist modernism combined with Fabian socialism to emphasize collective responsibility) over contemporary Alberta premier Ernest Manning's Baptist fundamentalism and insistence on individual responsibility (Marchildon, 2015).

The moral foundations of policy in Canada might go even farther back, to the debates over Confederation and especially to the sentiments of George-Étienne Cartier, one of the federation's principal founders. Canada, for

Cartier, had three purposes: (1) a commercial union, (2) the continuation of the French race, and most interestingly, (3) different races joining together for the general welfare—a kind of "fraternal" sentiment (LaSelva, 1996). Canadians in general do manifest a kind of fraternal sentiment toward each other in health matters. That is why they have been relatively comfortable with the concept of national standards—Quebec aside—in matters of health.

PARTY POLITICS   The postwar federal Liberal partisan political urge to out-manoeuvre the CCF/NDP party also no doubt played a role. The mention of a national health program by the Liberals in the 1945 campaign—the CCF had been very popular in 1944—and its inclusion in the 1963 Liberal platform were not coincidences. "The successful but very difficult creation of such a program in Saskatchewan by its socialist government in 1961 had set a standard that Liberal leader Lester Pearson knew his party must match, especially since the Saskatchewan premier, Tommy Douglas, had become leader of the federal New Democratic Party that year" (English, 2015).

THEORY   Public administration-based theory has also affected agenda setting and policy formulation in modern health policy. Katherine Fierlbeck (2011) has argued that "new public management" (NPM)—an approach which argues that public sector organization and operation should closely follow the lead of private sector models—was the key driver of provincial health reorganizations from the 1990s onward.

PROXIMATE DECISION MAKERS   Federal finance ministers can, if they are alarmed by the shape of federal finances and cost drivers in health, have a marked effect on the shape of health policy. Finance ministers Paul Martin (1995) and Jim Flaherty (2011) both announced drastic reductions in health expenditure growth rates, with important effects in many areas (e.g., physician supply). As well, the health field is a poster child for the decision accretion theory, which we mentioned in the 'stages' section of this chapter. Generation after generation of provincial health ministers and federal and provincial health reports have left their mark on health policy in ways that make it hard to disentangle who did what and when.

Overall, a host of issues face health care in Canada's future. They range from financial sustainability, to appropriate roles for the federal and provincial governments, to privatization (see Box 17-2: Issues in Health Care in Canada's Future).

Economic Policy

Economic policy affects all other areas of public policy and is the prime concern of governments. It is usually conceived of as occurring at two levels as macroeconomic policy and microeconomic policy. This is essentially the

BOX 17-2

Issues in Health Care in Canada's Future

FINANCIAL SUSTAINABILITY

In December 2011, the federal government announced that it was going to change the annual growth rate for Canada Health Transfers (CHT) from 6 percent, which it had maintained during 2004–2014, to a formula tied to a three-year moving average of nominal GDP growth with a minimum annual growth rate of 3 percent, starting in 2017–2018. The difficulty is that this rate does not reflect projected increases in the health costs paid by provinces, who cover most of the costs. In 2012, the parliamentary budget officer projected the CHT to grow at 3.9 percent annually from 2017–2018 to 2024–2025 and the provincial/territorial health spending to increase 5.1 percent over the same period. From 2025–2026 to 2040–2041, with the same formula, the CHT growth would average 3.8 percent annually and provincial/territorial expenditures would increase 5.3 percent. This spread will be of concern to Canadians in the future.

APPROPRIATE ROLES FOR THE FEDERAL AND PROVINCIAL GOVERNMENTS

For many years, federal involvement in health and in other areas has been based in large part on the "spending power" of Parliament, presumably because provincial governments would find it very difficult to raise the revenues needed. This enabled Ottawa to have a role in policy areas over which it lacked jurisdiction, simply by offering transfers to provincial governments. The Harper government demonstrated on many occasions a reluctance to emulate past governments' use of the federal spending power.

In fact, Finance Minister Joe Flaherty's announcement in 2011 of the forthcoming CHT transfer arrangements featured no explicit expectations of provinces—national standards, in other words—even though it did not formally renounce the CHA principles (CBC News, 2012a). Canadians are divided on which model is preferable. In addition, some have suggested that there are new roles that Ottawa should be fulfilling. Steven Lewis (2015) has suggested that the greatest unmet need Ottawa can serve is intelligence—or meaningful information for clinicians, patients, and governments—to overcome the design flaws in current systems like the Canadian Institute for Health Information (CIHI), the Canadian Health Infoway, and the Canadian Foundation for Healthcare Improvement.

PRIVATIZATION

Provinces vary widely as to what qualifies as "medically necessary" services and may even "de-insure" services it previously paid to deliver; de-insuring effectively privatizes the service to the citizen level, and is a concern to the one paying, especially if it is expensive. Two-tier health care—private payment for either quicker service (queue jumping) or the expansion of private for-profit health entities that may threaten the principle of public administration if pushed too far—is of constant concern for health care decision makers. Things are never unidirectional in Canadian public policy, however; at the same time as there was movement toward privatization, there was evidence of a popular desire for movement in the opposite direction toward universal pharmacare.

MACROECONOMIC POLICY
Deals with the general health of the economy, in particular with monetary policy, economic stability, employment, the level of inflation, and with the overall level of spending, taxation, and deficits.

difference between large aggregates and smaller economic actors. **Macroeconomic policy** deals with the general health of the economy and, in specific terms, with monetary policy, economic stability, employment, and the level of inflation. It also deals with fiscal policy, which concerns itself with the overall level of spending, taxation, and deficits. **Microeconomic policy** focuses on the behaviour of individual or smaller sets of actors like consumers, firms, unions, and local governments. The levels interact with eacher other and must to a greater or lesser extent be coordinated.

FEDERAL–PROVINCIAL ASPECTS OF ECONOMIC POLICY   Economic policy in Canada is decentralized, as is the political system; both federal and provincial governments have responsibilities in economic policy. The Constitution Act, 1867, established that the major economic levers went to the national government, including:

- Section 91(1A) Public Debt and Property;
- Section 91(2) The Regulation of Trade and Commerce;
- Section 91(3) The Raising of Money by Any Mode or System of Taxation;
- Section 91(4) The borrowing of Money on the Public Money on the Public Credit;
- Section 91(10) Navigation and Shipping;
- Section 91(12) Sea Coast and Inland Fisheries;
- Section 91(14) Currency and Coinage;
- Section 91(15) Banking, Incorporation of Banking and Issue of Paper Money;
- Section 91(16) Savings Banks;
- Section 91(18) Bills of Exchange and Promissory Notes; and
- Section 95 Concurrent Powers of Legislation respecting Agriculture [but with the laws of Parliament paramount]

In addition, the national government's residual power in Section 91 and the declaratory power in Section 92(10)(c) had economic implications. In fact, the striking thing about the federal heads of power is that most of them were economic in nature. All of these impressive powers flowed from the intention of the new union, which was to engage in nation building and economic expansion.

Yet the provinces came to exercise economic powers on a par with the federal authority. Fiscal policy is in effect a shared jurisdiction with spending, taxation, and deficits policy of the provinces just as important in the aggregate as that of the federal government (Soucy & Wrobel, 2000). Important provincial sources of revenue for provinces are direct taxation [Section 92(2)] and resource ownership and taxation [Section 109]. Howlett and Wilder (2015) have noted that, despite swings in centralization between the national and provincial capitals, and shifts toward cooperative federal–provincial–municipal governance, there is a sustained and increasing role of provincial governments in matters of economic policy-making—in other words, a kind of "province-building." The provincial role in subsidies to private sector production overwhelms that of the national government, there are more people working in provincial state-owned enterprises than federal and local ones, and provincial transfers to local governments far outstrip federal transfers to local governments.

MICROECONOMIC POLICY
Focuses on the behaviour of individual or smaller sets of actors like consumers, firms, unions, and local governments.

The aims of orthodox macroeconomic policy are substantial; the challenge is to strike the right balance between them, according to the various publics that are served. There are also economic policy aims that may change according to the spirit of the times. Examples of standard economic aims, ones that remain relatively constant regardless of the times, are economic stability and economic growth, low inflation, full employment, underemployment, and a positive trade balance. Examples of time-bound economic aims (i.e., aims that may change according to the times) are low levels of taxation, market provision of most goods and services, low debt and deficit levels, and free trade. It is interesting that the main web page for the 2015 budget highlights several from both lists: balancing the budget, training a highly skilled workforce, protecting jobs and economic growth, and keeping taxes low for families (Canada, Budget, 2015).

Economic stability and growth mean the increase in the gross domestic product year over year and the avoidance of recessions and depressions. Low inflation means keeping inflation to a manageable level—usually considered around 1–3 percent—that does not threaten those with low or fixed wages, or program and benefit plans that are indexed to the cost of living. Full employment is having a socially acceptable level of unemployment—something around 6–7 percent in today's world. Avoiding underemployment means having an appropriate match between the needs of employers and the human capital qualifications of the workforce. A positive trade balance is having more exports than imports.

As noted, some objectives are more particular to certain periods of time. Modern Canadian federal and provincial governments have been loath both to raise taxes and to run deficits because these activities make them look like poor economic managers. Yet, for a period of time in the post-war period, there had been a certain amount of tolerance for both of these economic phenomena. Likewise in the 2015 election campaign, the Liberal party platform called for higher taxes on those earning more than $200 000 and running a deficit to stimulate the economy. Provision of public services by the private sector has become more commonplace; the Harper government mentioned this theme in many budgets and even set up a "P3 Canada Fund" and "PPP Canada Inc.," a federal Crown corporation specializing in private–public partnerships (P3s). As of July 2015, 12 free trade agreements had been put into effect by both Liberal and Conservative governments in the previous few decades (with many more at some stage of negotiation and finalizationas discussed in Chapter 4)—a development that a quarter-century ago would have been highly controversial.

The tools of economic policy are fiscal policy, monetary policy, regulation, subsidies, and taxation policy. The major circumstance for the exercise of fiscal policy is the government's budgetary process, which has two parts: (1) the finance minister's budget, which is traditionally concerned with the raising of revenue and is normally followed in a few weeks by (2) the expenditure budget, also known as the Estimates of Expenditure.[2] Monetary policy is concerned with the money supply (the amount of money in circulation) and also with interest rates and exchange rates. Regulation is aimed at a wide variety of purposes, but can often take on an economic hue when it seeks to correct market failures such as monopolies, destructive competition, imperfect information, and negative externalities (where producers or consumers do not bear the costs to society of decisions taken by them, for example in relation to pollution). Subsidies are incentives to the private sector to encourage it to engage in certain types of activity. Taxation policy may include indirect taxes (featuring a variety of customs and excise measures, as well as corporation and sales taxes that are usually passed on to a third party), and direct taxes (levied on income and property taxes). A special form of tax measure is the tax expenditure, which is a deviation from a generally levied tax measure in favour of certain classes of potential taxpayer, again meant to foster some economic or social policy objective. The income tax credit for tuition and textbooks is just one example of the many tax expenditures that exist.[3]

VARIABLES AFFECTING ECONOMIC POLICY. There are so many actors involved in making economic policy (see Table 17-5), and so many aspects to it, as we have described, that it is difficult to be specific about the variables affecting it. (For a description of the general budgetary process, see Chapter 13.)

The budget begins with international economic variables. These include global economic developments and outlook, with particular attention to the United States, Europe, Japan, and emerging economies. World commodity prices and financial market developments also figure in budget making. The impact of lower oil prices on the Canadian economy is weighed. International trade expansion is encouraged.

Domestic economic variables come into consideration as well. The manufacturing and small business sectors, the needs for a highly qualified workforce, and the state of Canada's infrastructure are all important. Those sectors considered particularly important in manufacturing are automotive, aerospace, and defence procurement.

Domestic social and political variables round off the budget. One can intuit from the 2015 budget that the winners were seniors, middle-class families, and police and security establishments. Those with less influence were public servants, tax evaders, and Employment Insurance contributors.

---

[2]There are exceptions. For example, the main estimates were tabled first, in February 2015, followed by the budget in April of that year.

[3]Occasionally government will publish "tax expenditure accounts" which make the system more transparent. See, for example, "Government of Canada Tax Expenditures" published by the federal Department of Finance. http://www.fin.gc.ca/purl/taxexp-eng.asp

TABLE 17-5
INSTITUTIONS AND ACTORS IN CANADIAN ECONOMIC POLICY

MONETARY POLICY	
INSTITUTIONS	**DECISION MAKERS/ACTORS**
Bank of Canada	The bank's governing council (governor, senior deputy governor, four deputy governors), the Monetary Policy Review Committee (MPRC), and the four economics departments at the bank
International markets	
FISCAL POLICY	
INSTITUTIONS	**DECISION MAKERS/ACTORS**
Department of finance	Minister of finance
	Tax policy division
Prime minister and cabinet	Prime minister
Parliament	Treasury Board Secretariat
Treasury Board (cabinet committee)	PAC chair
Public Accounts Committee (PAC)	
House of Commons Standing Committee on Finance (FINA)	FINA chair
Office of the Parliamentary Budget Officer	Parliamentary budget office
Provincial versions of the above	
MICROECONOMIC POLICIES	
INSTITUTIONS	**DECISION MAKERS/ACTORS**
Plenary cabinet	
Cabinet committees	
Ministers of economic departments	Ministers of departments overseeing labour, regional, competition, environment, health and safety matters:
	Agriculture and Agri-Foods Canada
	Competition Bureau Canada; plus
	Competition Tribunal
	Employment and Social Development Canada
	Environment Canada
	Labour Program
	Natural Resources Canada
	Superintendent of Financial Institutions Canada
	Transport Canada
Specialized economic agencies	Business Development Bank of Canada
	Regional development agencies

EVOLUTION OF ECONOMIC POLICY   There are countless issues in contemporary economic policy; here, we will cover a few that have made their way to the public policy "agenda" in recent years: oil prices, innovation, and inequality (see Box 17-3: Issues in Contemporary Economic Policy).

BOX 17-3

Issues in Contemporary Economic Policy

The Impact of Falling Oil Prices After several years in the $100-plus range per barrel, oil prices began a precipitous fall from June 2014 to early 2015. The market price of West Texas Intermediate crude fell to its lowest level in six years—US$47.47 on March 12, 2015 (Isfield, 2015). The effects have been mixed. Consumers' disposable incomes have increased and there have been benefits for certain sectors such as transportation and manufacturing, which have seen some of their input costs decline. However, the Bank of Canada forecasted a negative overall impact for Canada, with lower incomes in the oil patch, spillover effects on the supply chain to the rest of the economy (30 percent of the goods and services to the Alberta oil sands come from the rest of Canada), a decline in Canada's terms of trade, declining investment and exploration, and a decline in the dollar (Bank of Canada, 2015). The policy implications that flow from this are challenging.

Lagging Innovation The Science, Technology and Innovation Council of Canada (STIC) in its *State of the Nation 2008* report defined innovation as "the process by which individuals, companies and organizations develop, master and use new products, designs, processes and business methods. These can be new to them, if not to their sector, their nation or to the world. The components of innovation include research and development, invention, capital investment and training and development" (Science, Technology and Innovation Council of Canada, 2008, 2010). It noted that Canada held its own in the world in some building blocks of innovation, like education, but that business research and development was low by international standards, and that two vital productivity drivers—investments in machinery and equipment, and investments in information and communications technologies—lacked notably in comparison to the United States.

The innovation lags have been attributed to several matters, including policy set elsewhere by parent multinationals of local firms, small markets, and a timid business culture. A Mowat Centre report attributed the underperforming innovation record to misplaced government involvement. It argued that the mainly federal and framework tax-based approach should be increasingly balanced by more provincial direct support such as technology transfer, mentoring, target procurement, and subsidies (Creutzberg, 2011).

Income Inequality Concern over income inequality has become more generalized in Canada. In the past, redistributive policy was aimed at reducing poverty, but then later became focused on social insurance, or security for the general population. Over the past several decades, social insurance has been de-emphasized and income inequality has increased.

According to the Organisation for Economic Co-operation and Development (OECD), in the 1980s and early 1990s, government taxes and transfers reduced the gap the most between rich and poor in Canada, Denmark, Finland, and Sweden (Organisation for Economic Co-operation and Development, 2011). By the late 1990s and early 2000s, Canada had joined Switzerland and the United States as the countries with the smallest redistributive impact. The redistributive fade in Canada between the mid-1990s and the mid-2000s was among the most dramatic in the OECD world. Moreover, Canada is on the leading edge of the 99/1 phenomenon, with the OECD estimating that the top 1 percent of Canada's income earners have captured 37 percent of total income growth over the past three decades (Organisation for Economic Co-operation and Development, 2014b; Banting & Myles, 2015).

Environmental and Climate Change Policy

Environmental policy concerns a wide variety of matters touching on the biophysical environment. Environmental laws seek protection of species and of natural areas of the globe and beyond; the furtherance of biodiversity; and the control of pollution of the air, land, water, and food that would negate the preceding aims.

Environmental policy is so wide ranging that it is difficult to know where its boundaries are. We can get a sense of what some governments see as the boundaries by listing some of the federal acts and those of a province with a varied environmental picture, Newfoundland and Labrador (see Table 17-6). They suggest that matters that qualify as environmental policy are protection of the environment, prevention of pollution, protection of biodiversity and conservation, sustainable development, and environmental assessment and enforcement.

FEDERAL–PROVINCIAL ASPECTS OF THE POLICY   Just as there are many aspects to environmental policy, there are many constitutional aspects to it as well, although "environment" is not a subject that appears in the division of powers. First of all, we have the sections of the Constitution that have obvious connections to the environment. Federal powers that involve obvious environmental matters are Section 91(10) Navigation and Shipping, and Section 91(12) Seacoast and Inland Fisheries. Those obvious provincial environmentally related sections are Section 92(5) Management and Sale of the Public Lands Belonging to the Province and the Timber and Wood Thereon, Section 92(13) Property and Civil Rights in the Province, and Section 109 All Lands, Mines, Minerals and Royalties Belonging to the Provinces (and not the Federal Government). There are also sections that supplement federal and provincial explicit environmental roles. Such federal powers are the "general power" in the preamble to Section 91, Section 91(24) Indians and Lands Reserved for Indians, and Section 91(27) Criminal Law. The provinces have supplementary environmental powers as Section 92(A), the natural resources amendment, gives increased powers to provinces to manage and capture resource revenues from non-renewable natural resources, forestry, and electrical energy generation. Section 92(8) Municipal Institutions and Section 92(16) relate to matters of a merely local or provincial nature.

Judicial interpretation has added some clarity to the law in terms of environmental responsibilities of the two levels of government. Muldoon lists examples of the status of jurisdictional decisions to date:

> Pollution "deleterious" to fish, marine pollutions, regulation of highly toxic substances such as polychlorinated biphenyls (PCBs), and environmental assessment of actions related to subjects on the federal list have all been held to be within the federal constitutional powers. The control of water pollution (even where fish are present) that results from debris from logging operations in provinces, and the environmental regulations of (otherwise federally regulated) railways in provinces were ruled to lie within the exclusive powers of the provinces (Muldoon et al., 2015 p. 41).

TABLE 17-6
EXAMPLES OF FEDERAL AND PROVINCIAL ENVIRONMENTAL ACTS

	FEDERAL ACTS	PROVINCIAL ACTS (NEWFOUNDLAND AND LABRADOR)
Environmental Protection	• The Department of the Environment Act • Water Governance and Legislation • Lake of the Woods Control Board Act • Weather Modification Information Act	• Environmental Protection Act • Occupational Health and Safety (OHS) Act and Regulations • Dangerous Goods Transportation Act • Waste Management Act
Pollution Prevention	• Canadian Environmental Protection Act, 1999 (CEPA 1999) • Fisheries Act • Antarctic Environmental Protection Act (AEPA) • Arctic Waters Pollution Prevention Act • Pest Control Products Act • Transportation of Dangerous Goods Act • Food and Drug Act	• Water Resources Act
Biodiversity and Conservation	• Species at Risk Act (SARA) • Migratory Birds Convention Act, 1994 (MBCA) • Wild Animal and Plant Protection and Regulation of International and Interprovincial Trade Act (WAPPRIITA) • Canada Wildlife Act	• Wildlife Act • Endangered Species Act • Wilderness and Ecological Reserves Act • Provincial Parks Act • Lands Act
Sustainable Development	• Federal Sustainable Development Act • Canada Foundation for Sustainable Development Technology Act	
Environmental Assessment and Enforcement,	• Canadian Environmental Assessment Act, 2012 • Environmental Enforcement Act • Canadian Environment Week Act • National Wildlife Week Act	• Environmental Assessment Act, 2000

Rather than using the general power to allocate a blanket environmental power to the federal authority, courts have tended to allocate powers to one or the other level, and sometimes both. The result is that both levels of government have important aspects of the environment under their nominal protection, necessitating a series of intergovernmental agreements under the framework of acts like the Canadian Environmental Protection Act, 1999, and the Canada-Wide Accord on Environmental Harmonization (Muldoon et al., 2015).

VARIABLES AFFECTING ENVIRONMENTAL POLICY With humanity collectively considering its future on the planet, there is no lack of variables that affect environmental policy. The general factors include global environmental degradation, and statements by international bodies and scientists. Intermediate factors include environmental movements and demographic change. An important proximate factor is the role of prime ministers, premiers, and Aboriginal groups.

Global climate change can be viewed as the most important challenge facing humanity. The enormity of the issue has become apparent even to non-experts from the signs of global environmental degradation. Rising sea levels have threatened the future of countries like the Maldives. Biodiversity has significantly declined. Global warming has increased, bringing with it health problems, catastrophic weather events, and other negative effects. Fresh water supplies are becoming imperiled in places like the Southern United States, and where it is readily available, it is often put to uses that are wasteful and/or harmful, such as bottled water.

International bodies and scientists have spoken forcefully about the global threats faced by environmental degradation. Three of the most impactful have been the Brundtland Commission (1987), the Earth Summit (2007), and the International Panel on Climate Change (2014). The World Commission on Environment and Development (the Brundtland Commission) introduced the concept of sustainable development to the international dialogue. It recommended that economic and environmental policy be considered in tandem and that they meet present needs without posing threats to future needs. The United Nations Conference on Environment and Development (the "Earth Summit") formally approved this notion of sustainable development and led to the Kyoto Protocol which included commitments to reduce greenhouse gas emissions. Urgent pleas were made to the international community to consider the dangers of continuing present patterns of unimpeded economic development. The International Panel on Climate Change (2014) issued a similarly dramatic and engaging message: "Continuing emission of greenhouse gases will cause further warming and long lasting changes in all components of the climate system, increasing the likelihood of severe, pervasive and irrevocable impacts for people and ecosystems" (International Panel on Climate Change, 2014, p. 18).

With continual increases in the global burning of coal, oil, and natural gas, atmospheric carbon dioxide (a leading greenhouse gas that can remain in the atmosphere for centuries) reached 400 parts per million (ppm) in 2014. According to some scientists, a safe level of carbon dioxide is 350 ppm (Hansen et al., 2013). Others view limiting emissions to a maximum of 450 ppm as having a reasonable chance of keeping temperatures from rising more than 2°C from pre-Industrial Revolution levels. Going beyond this level risks a runaway, unstoppable increase in temperature by releasing large amounts of carbon dioxide and methane (a highly potent greenhouse gas) that are sequestered in oceans, Arctic tundra, vegetation, and forests.

Demographic change has been a factor in making the environment an outstanding issue. Since 1867, Canada's population has grown from 3.7 million to 35.7 million people and its rate of population growth is considerable. Hessing et al. (2005) note the effects of this:

> *Acceleration in rates of population growth and the economic activity puts pressure on the amount and quality of resources upon which these activities are based. Today's economy is almost seven times larger than that of fifty years ago, and it places additional demands on the environment, especially in regard to industrial processes, resource use, energy consumption, and transportation (p. 6).*

Prime ministers can be important in environmental policy, as they tend to set the tone for the government and the country by being responsive or recalcitrant on the issue. Pierre Trudeau's government, for example, introduced nine environmental acts, among which were the Clean Air Act, the Ocean Dumping Control Act, and the Canada Water Act, and it also created a Department of the Environment in 1971 (McKenzie, 2002, p. 118). Boyd (2012) notes that Prime Minister Brian Mulroney built

> *. . . a relatively strong record on the environmental file, leading to his surprising selection as Canada's Greenest Prime Minister by a panel of environmental experts in 2003. He oversaw the creation of six new national parks, the passage of Canada's first comprehensive pollution law (the Canadian Environmental Protection Act) and the creation of an ambitious multi-billion-dollar Green Plan that the head of the UN Environment Programme called a model for the world. . . . Under his leadership, Canada was the first industrialized nation to ratify the UN Convention on Biological Diversity and the UN Framework Convention on Climate Change in 2002. (Boyd, 2012, p. 50)*

Prime Minister Harper, on the other hand, said his lack of definitive action on the greenhouse gas file was due to his assessment that "under current conditions it would be . . . crazy economic policy to penalize the oil and gas sector. . . . We are clearly not going to do it" (quoted by McCarthy, 2014).

EVOLUTION OF ENVIRONMENTAL REGIMES   Judith McKenzie (2002) provides a review of the evolution of environmental regimes, meaning an emphasis on what policy instruments were popular at what points in history. Decentralized *bipartite bargaining* took place during 1968–1972 and featured traditional "command and control" instruments, largely government regulations conducted under the authority of several new acts. Most actual policy was made by provinces, however, and policy was made by in-camera *bipartite bargaining* negotiations between government and powerful industry groups.

The second period involved *multipartite bargaining* and occurred from the mid-1980s to the mid-1990s. This featured a bargaining process expanded beyond the previous bipartite partners to include a number of environmental and other groups, who tended to emphasize legal challenges before the courts to force policy changes, not always successfully. One success was to force the government to introduce the Environmental Assessment Act, which toughened the assessment review process, and the Environmental Protection Act, which identified a list of prohibited toxic substances and regulated the transport of hazardous waste.

A third stage took place from the mid-1990s on: *deregulation, destaffing, defunding, and voluntary compliance*. This was the time of the ascendancy of neoliberalism in Canada, with its emphasis on government as facilitator of private sector development and the diminution of its server and protector role. Environmental policy instruments were now less intrusive: "right to know" pollutant information disclosure, and less regulation and more voluntary compliance by industry (McKenzie, 2002).

On the other hand, some observers note that command and control policy instruments have never gone away. Muldoon maintains that "almost all environmental protection regimes that have been established in Canada over the past 30 years generally follow this command and control structure" (Muldoon et al., 2015, p. 145). Instruments of this type set standards and implement compliance mechanisms. Standards are set in the form of statutes, regulations, environmental approvals, performance standards, and pollution control arrangements. Control mechanisms typically include financial incentives, licences and approvals, administrative orders, and prosecutions.

Most experts, however, agree that government efforts in the environmental protection field have been scaled back. For instance, in 2012 there was a provision in an omnibus finance bill that greatly reduced the protection of fish habitats, limited the number of projects requiring federal environmental assessment, weakened the protection of endangered species, and placed restrictions on public consultation for proposed projects such as new pipelines.

One of the most pressing issues in environmental policy has been *global climate change* related to the use of fossil fuels. The failure to take meaningful actions to reduce carbon emissions has detracted from Canada's global image (see Box 17-4: Global Climate Change).

BOX 17-4

Global Climate Change

Canada has been ranked the worst climate change performer of the 58 industrialized countries (Burck, Marten, & Bals, 2014). In the past, Canada played a leading role in promoting action on various environmental issues including acid rain, sustainable development, ozone depletion, and climate change. In 1997, Canada signed the Kyoto Protocol (ratified by Parliament in 2002) which included binding international commitments to reduce greenhouse gas (GHG) emissions. Specifically, the Canadian government undertook to reduce GHG emissions so that they would be 6 percent lower by 2012 than in 1990. However, in 2011, Canada became the only country to withdraw from the international agreement and, in fact, increased GHG emissions by 18 percent in the 1990–2012 period. Although the Canadian government has generally played a negative role in annual international conferences on global climate change negotiations in recent years, Canada did sign the non-binding Copenhagen Accord (2009) with a pledge to reduce GHG emissions by 17 percent from their 2005 level by 2020. However, in 2014, Environment Canada noted that without new actions Canada would miss fulfilling the pledge by a large margin.

Plans to greatly increase oil sands production (along with the production of natural gas to convert to liquid natural gas for export, hydraulic fracturing of natural gas to produce liquefied natural gas for export, and highly risky exploitation of large reservoirs of oil in Arctic waters) suggested that Canada would continue to increase its share of GHG emissions while many other countries are reducing theirs. Although Canada's proposed projects could be worth hundreds of billions of dollars over several decades, opposition to pipelines to bring diluted bitumen and other products to foreign markets could interfere with the Harper government's goal of making Canada an energy superpower. However, after being elected, the Trudeau government took an active role at the 2015 UN Climate Change Conference (seeking a global target of keeping the increase in temperature to 1.5°C), and committed to take action on reducing Canada's carbon emissions in collaboration with provincial governments. At the time of writing, it appeared that the change in government would lead to a major change in environmental policy.

Summary and Conclusion

Public policy is what government does or does not do, purposefully, or what it compels or encourages others in society to do, or not to do. Domestic policy is simply all policy made internal to the country. Public policy differs between Canada and other political societies because of the policy context, those multilayered, interactive, and changeable elements connected with the policy process which bound the freedom of choice of policy actors, or compel certain options to be chosen, or establish what matters are under active consideration by political societies or political actors. We have adopted a layered, or nested, approach used by some analysts to describe how proximate decision makers are actually affected by several intermediate regional and national variables or factors, which are in turn affected by general/global/universal factors.

Specific areas of policy in Canada are affected by different sets of nested variables, as one might expect, but they also share some common determinants as well. Social policy is affected by globalization and pluralization in the most general sense, but also by more national influences like the federal spending power, the post-war Keynesian consensus, federal–provincial–territorial relations and provincial social philosophies. Health policy, for its part, is affected by international standards and protocols, moral imperatives, party politics, and the role of first ministers. Economic variables are harder to pin down, but not to be ignored are the major international economic variables like world commodity prices, financial market developments, and oil prices, as well as such domestic economic variables as the needs of the manufacturing and small business sectors and the state of the automotive, aerospace, and defence procurement sectors. The general factors affecting environmental policy include global environmental degradation, and statements by international bodies and scientists. Intermediate factors include environmental movements and demographic change. The roles of prime ministers, premiers, and Aboriginal groups are important proximate factors. How decision makers tackle the myriad issues besetting each of these sectors will be driven in large part by these factors.

Discussion Questions

1. Should public policy be made more removed from politics?

2. What factors—general, intermediate, or proximate— seem to be most important in the making of Canadian public policy?

3. Thinking of a specific policy made in Canada, what general, intermediate, and proximate factors have interacted to produce it?

4. What issues need to be considered by the Canadian public in social policy? Health policy? Economic policy? Environmental policy?

5. Is Canada advancing or retreating in environmental protection?

6. Examine the latest budget of the federal government, or your provincial government. Describe the policy context that affected that budget.

Further Reading

Banting, K. (1982). *The welfare state and Canadian federalism.* Montreal: McGill-Queen's University Press.

Dunn, C. (2010). The federal spending power. In C. Dunn (Ed.) *The handbook of Canadian public administration.* Don Mills, ON: Oxford University Press.

Fierlbeck, K. (2011). *Health care in Canada,* Toronto: University of Toronto Press.

Green, D.A., Riddell, W.C., & St-Hilaire, F. (Eds.). (2015). *Income inequality: The Canadian story.* Montreal, QC: Institute for Research on Public Policy.

Hoggwood, B.W., & Gunn, L.A. (1984). *Policy analysis for the real world.* New York: Oxford University Press.

Howlett, M., Ramesh, R., & Perl, A. (2009). *Studying public policy.* Don Mills, ON: Oxford University Press.

Jones, C.O. (1997). *An introduction to the study of public policy.* (3rd Ed.) Monterey, Calif.: Brooks/Cole Publishing Company.

Muldoon, P., Lucas, A., Gibson, R.P., Pickfield, P., & Williams, J. (2015). *An introduction to environmental law and policy in Canada* (2nd Ed.). Toronto: Edmond Montgomery.

Prince, M. (2015). The provinces and social policy: Canada's multiple welfare states. In C. Dunn (Ed.) *Provinces: Canadian provincial politics* (3rd Ed.). Toronto: University of Toronto Press.

CHAPTER 18

Foreign Policy

CHAPTER OBJECTIVES

After reading this chapter, you should be able to

1. Discuss the general perspectives on Canadian foreign policy.
2. Outline the history of Canadian foreign policy.
3. Discuss Canada's involvement in peacekeeping, peace operations, and combat missions and issues concerning national security.
4. Examine and evaluate Canada's role in promoting human security and humanitarian intervention.
5. Evaluate Canada's role in providing development assistance and its involvement in international organizations

Prime Minister Lester B. Pearson continues to watch over Parliament Hill through this statue that honours his lifetime accomplishments, nationally and internationally.

© Tom Hanson/Canadian Press Images

Canada's peacekeeping activities have been a source of pride for many Canadians. In fact, Lester B. Pearson was responsible for creating the United Nations' first peacekeeping force when he was Canada's external affairs minister in 1956. For this remarkable accomplishment, Pearson was awarded the Nobel Peace Prize in 1957.

Pearson was born in 1897 in Newtonbrook, Ontario, the son of a Methodist minister. He experienced first-hand the horrors of war as a stretcher-bearer and a fighter pilot in World War I. After receiving his master's of arts degree at Oxford, he taught modern history at the University of Toronto. When recruited for the fledgling Canadian Foreign Service in 1928, Pearson eagerly took up the challenge of pursuing his vision of Canada's foreign policy.

Pearson participated in the founding of the United Nations (UN) and in 1946 became the top official in the Department of External Affairs. Two years later, he began a political career as external affairs minister in the Liberal government of Louis St. Laurent. He played a major role in the formation of the North Atlantic Treaty Organization and served for a term as president of the General Assembly of the United Nations. He was prime minister of Canada from 1963 to 1968. Pearson believed that Canada as a "middle power" could play a key role in the world by mediating disputes, helping to forge peaceful compromises, and encouraging the establishment of international institutions to foster cooperative relationships. The Suez Canal Crisis presented him with an opportunity to put his ideas into practice.

On July 26, 1956, the government of Egypt nationalized the Suez Canal Company owned by British and French investors, including the British government. The canal, which runs through Egypt, provides a strategically and economically important shipping link between Europe and Asia. As part of a secret plan to allow Britain and France to seize control of the Canal Zone, Israel (which had been prevented from using the canal) invaded Egypt on October 29. As Israeli troops fought their way toward the canal, the British Royal Air Force started bombing Egypt and, on November 6, British and French troops invaded Egypt and quickly captured the canal. The U.S. government opposed the invasion and called for a ceasefire and the withdrawal of British and French troops.

At the beginning of November, Pearson went to the UN with a proposal that the UN set up its first peacekeeping force to resolve the conflict. Previously, the UN had only sent observers to oversee ceasefire agreements. The UN General Assembly voted to accept the proposal for a UN Emergency Force and, on November 15, the first UN contingent, including Canadian troops, arrived in Egypt to set up a buffer zone in the canal area between Egyptian and Israeli troops. As part of the agreement, Israel withdrew from the Sinai Peninsula and UN peacekeepers were stationed on the Egyptian side of the country's border with Israel.

Pearson's peacekeeping efforts came in for considerable criticism at home, particularly by the Progressive Conservatives, who denounced Pearson and St. Laurent for betraying Britain by criticizing its invasion of Egypt. Nonetheless, Pearson's efforts helped to ensure that the sharp disagreement between the United States and Britain did not threaten the unity of the Western allies during the Cold War. It also helped to save the Commonwealth, as many former British colonies were enraged by the imperialist action of Britain in Egypt.

Canada is no longer a major contributor to UN–led peacekeeping forces. Nevertheless, in a world of continuing conflict and serious global problems, the Canadian government is faced with important but often controversial foreign policy decisions.

INTRODUCTION

Canadian politics often focuses on what are seen as basically domestic issues, such as management of the economy, health care, taxes, and national unity. Nevertheless, with Canada's heavy dependence on exports, the wealth and employment opportunities of Canadians are strongly affected by the economies of our major trading partners and the functioning of the global economic system. Many Canadians are concerned about their foreign homeland or the homeland of their ancestors. Some issues—such as conflicts in the Middle East, uprisings against dictatorial regimes, and extreme poverty in a number of African countries—have captured the interest of many people without a direct connection to those areas. In addition, important political issues such as climate change, terrorism, and the depletion of fish stocks are global in nature. Many young people have a deep interest in helping people and communities in the world's least developed countries. Finally, Canada's identity has been shaped, to a considerable extent, by this country's participation in wars, peace-building efforts, and its generally positive international image.

Foreign affairs, military action, and national security are one of the few policy areas where the Canadian government is the key actor, with provincial governments generally having little role.

GENERAL PERSPECTIVES ON CANADA'S FOREIGN POLICY

In the 1920s and 1930s, Canada tended toward isolationism (a desire to steer clear of foreign involvements), but subsequently became an active participant both in military alliances and a variety of international organizations including the United Nations. Canada's foreign policy since World War II has often been described as **internationalism**, which includes the idea that each country should take "a constructive role in managing global conflicts" by working with other countries rather than acting unilaterally. This involves actively supporting international institutions and promoting international law (Nossal, 2013, p. 23).

More specifically, Canada's foreign policy as it developed particularly during the governments of St. Laurent and Pearson can be termed **liberal internationalism**. This involves the idea that the application of liberal values—including rights and freedoms, democracy, the rule of law, and justice, combined with the growing interaction and interdependence among the peoples, economies, and countries of the world—can make a peaceful world possible, particularly through the development of international institutions (Nossal, Roussel, & Paquin, 2011).

Liberal internationalism differs from the **realist perspective**, which contends that because the world has no central authority able to impose order, each country is concerned primarily with security, survival, and promotion of its own national interests.

Liberal internationalism has often been viewed as an appropriate foreign policy for Canada. As a "middle power," Canada can try to constrain the great powers by encouraging (particularly in cooperation with other middle powers) the development of international law that all countries are expected to follow. Likewise, establishing multilateral organizations like the United Nations gives all member countries a voice and a vote (even though the five great powers on the Security Council of the UN each hold a veto on important decisions). At times, Canada as a middle power has used quiet diplomacy to try to resolve international conflicts or, particularly during the Cold War, to try to persuade its ally, the United States, to avoid actions that might lead to a world war (Nossal, Roussel, & Paquin, 2011). Nevertheless, despite the emphasis on promoting peaceful cooperation, advocates of the liberal

INTERNATIONALISM
The idea that each country should take a constructive role in managing global disputes by working with other countries rather than acting unilaterally. This involves actively supporting international institutions and promoting international law.

LIBERAL INTERNATIONALISM
The idea that the application of liberal values—including rights and freedoms, democracy, the rule of law, and justice, combined with the growing interaction and interdependence among the peoples, economies, and countries of the world—can make a peaceful world possible, particularly through the development of international institutions.

REALIST PERSPECTIVE
The view that in a world without a central authority able to impose order, each country is concerned primarily with survival, security, and promotion of its own national interests.

NORTH ATLANTIC TREATY ORGANIZATION
An alliance of the United States, Canada, and many European countries formed during the Cold War.

NATO
www.nato.int

internationalist approach like Pearson saw the Soviet Union as a threat to world peace and supported building the military strength of the **North Atlantic Treaty Organization** (NATO), including the stationing of a substantial number of Canadian troops in Europe, to contain the Soviet Union.

Liberal internationalism has tended to be a declining characteristic of Canadian foreign policy in recent decades. Certainly the Conservative government of Stephen Harper displayed little interest in liberal internationalism, perhaps because of its perceived connection to the Liberal party. Although it is difficult to characterize the changes in the general approach to foreign policy,[1] the middle power idea of "helpful fixer" seems to have disappeared. Instead there tended to be a more "hard-line" approach that characterizes international affairs in terms of good versus evil (although the characteristization of which countries are "good" and worthy of Canada's support is often controversial[2]). Instead of seeking to mediate Middle East conflicts, the Harper government became an extremely strong supporter of Israel and the government of Benjamin Netanyahu. The government's view of the United Nations was highly negative, and the role of Canada's diplomatic corps diminished under much tighter control from the government. As well, Canada closed its embassy in Iran and expelled Iranian diplomats from Canada in 2012. Although Iran's regime is repressive, cutting ties greatly limits Canada's ability to try to influence a major regional power.

To some extent, domestic partisan considerations have become an important influence on foreign policy (Nossal, 2013). For example, the strong position taken against the Russian attacks on Ukraine in 2015 might be explained, in part, by the importance of Canada's large population of Ukrainian ancestry. Economic considerations also have an important effect on foreign policy positions. For example, Stephen Harper viewed China's communist government very negatively before and after becoming prime minister. However, with the growth of China's economy, Harper realized the need to develop good relations with China's leaders in order to increase Canadian exports to that country.

Some analysts assert that Canada's foreign policy does not really reflect liberal internationalist principles. The **peripheral dependence perspective** describes Canada as economically, politically, culturally, and militarily dependent on the United States (Kirton, 2007). Thus, Canada has often been unable or unwilling to develop independent foreign policies because of constraints imposed by the United States—the dominant partner in Canada–U.S. relations. However, there have been exceptions such as the

PERIPHERAL DEPENDENCE PERSPECTIVE
The view that Canada is unable or unwilling to develop independent foreign policies because of constraints imposed by the United States.

---

[1]Unlike previous governments, the Harper government did not undertake a general review of Canadian foreign and defence policy after taking office.
[2]For example, in 2014 the Canadian government approved the sale of armoured fighting vehicles to Saudi Arabia for $15 billion despite that country's having one of the worst human rights records and having used military force to suppress protests in neighbouring countries.

Canadian government's decision not to join the U.S.–led invasion of Iraq in 2003. Nevertheless, Canada continues to be a close international ally of the United States, but an ally usually with little influence on American policy.

Very different is the **principal power perspective**. Changes in the international system, notably the end of the **Cold War** and the decline of the United States as the dominant international power, mean that power capability has become more diffused, creating a number of "rising powers." Canada is one of the countries in this "new, expanded top tier of principal powers" (Kirton, 2010, p. 71). As a principal power, Canada is able to independently assert its national values and interests in its foreign policy and help to shape the world order.

Clearly Canada does not have the military power of the United States, China, Russia, or various other countries including Britain, and France. However, Kirton argues that, through its active involvement in important international organizations, Canada has been able to effectively pursue its interests and affect the positions adopted by these organizations. In addition, Canada's abundant natural resources, large territory, livable cities, multiculturalism, and distinctive national values give Canada important bases of power (Kirton, 2011). Nevertheless, Canada's once substantial influence at the United Nations has declined. Likewise, although Canada once had a leading role in promoting various international environmental goals, it was widely condemned for its failure to take meaningful action on global climate change.

Hard Power and Soft Power

"Hard power" involves using coercion to get another country to act in a certain way. Hard power includes the use or threat of military force as well as the use of economic sanctions. For example, Canada convinced a number of other countries to join in imposing economic sanctions on South Africa to pressure that country to end its racist policy of apartheid. Joseph Nye (2004) asserts that a country's success in world politics can come from its "soft power": the attractiveness of its culture, its political values (provided it acts consistently with them), and its foreign policies ("when they are seen as legitimate and having moral authority" (quoted by Clark, 2013, p. 18)).

Canada's hard power is limited and can only be used effectively in conjunction with other countries. In fact, despite the emphasis of Prime Minister Harper on Canada's past wars, Canadian armed forces continued to decline in personnel numbers and military equipment purchases since 2006.

Canada's soft power can be significant. Canada's democratic, politically stable federal system in a multicultural society with a prosperous economy and protection of human rights has created a positive image in many countries. However, this image is sometimes marred by the condition of Aboriginal peoples and, for some countries, our close connection to the United States.

PRINCIPAL POWER PERSPECTIVE
The view that changes in the international system have resulted in Canada's becoming a principal power able to independently assert its national values and interests in international politics.

COLD WAR
The severe tensions between the Western countries (led by the United States) and communist countries (led by the Soviet Union) that developed after the end of World War II and ended with the collapse of the Soviet Union in 1991.

As well, Canada's unwillingness to take strong action on climate change resulted in a negative international image on this important issue. In the past decade, Canada's once highly respected diplomatic corps has been weakened, Canada reduced its involvement with the United Nations, and its strong, unqualified defence of Israel has been at odds with the view of a large majority of UN members. Furthermore, Canada's mining industry (which has a large presence in many parts of the world) sometimes has a negative image for exploiting workers, damaging the environment, and bringing few long-term benefits to developing countries.

Soft power is not always successful, and hard power may be necessary to achieve important objectives. However, as discussed later in this chapter, the use of military force even with the best of intentions can have negative consequences.

HISTORICAL BACKGROUND

Confederation and the Early Years

At its founding in 1867, Canada was part of the British Empire. Although Canada was basically self-governing in domestic matters, Britain directed the country's external relations. Only gradually was Canada able to take control of its foreign policy.

In 1871, Canada's prime minister, Sir John A. Macdonald, was part of the British delegation that negotiated the Treaty of Washington, which laid the groundwork for friendly relations between Britain and the United States and dealt with a variety of issues affecting Canada–U.S. relations. As it turned out, Macdonald was unhappy with the concessions made by Britain at Canada's expense. In 1880, Canada took a step toward representing itself by appointing a high commissioner to London to voice Canadian interests

Participation in international institutions is important to Canada's place in the contemporary world. Here, the heads of state and government are shown at the G20 Summit in Los Cabos, Mexico, June 2012.

© Edgard Garrido/Reuters/Landov

related to immigration and trade. In 1893, Canada negotiated a tariff agreement with France, although the British ambassador in Paris had to sign the treaty on behalf of Britain, as the Canadian government did not have treaty-making power. In 1909, a tiny Department of External Affairs was set up (housed above an Ottawa barbershop), although foreign policy remained a British responsibility.

World War I and Its Aftermath

Canada's contribution of over 600 000 soldiers to the British Empire's forces in World War I, along with its heavy casualties, earned the country a place at the negotiating table that set the terms of peace. In 1920, Canada became a founding member of the League of Nations, an organization created after the war to try to prevent future conflicts. In 1922, the Canadian government refused a request for military assistance to protect British and French troops that were threatened by Turkish forces in the demilitarized Dardanelles.[3] In 1923, despite British objections, Canada negotiated and signed a treaty with the United States to protect Pacific halibut.

A resolution at the 1926 Imperial Conference (confirmed by the British Statute of Westminster (1931)) made it clear that Canada and the other dominions were not subordinate to Britain in domestic and external affairs. To reflect its new control over its own foreign policy, Canada appointed ambassadors to the United States (1927), France (1928), and Japan (1929).

World War II

Canada entered World War II after a vote in the Parliament. Overall, about 1.1 million Canadians served in the armed forces during World War II—a high proportion of Canada's population of about 11.5 million.

World War II marked the beginning of a close military relationship with the United States. With the real possibility that most of Canada's armed forces would be lost if Nazi Germany successfully invaded Britain, President Roosevelt promised to defend Canada. The Ogdensburg Agreement in 1940 included the creation of a Permanent Joint Board on Defense to plan for the defence of North America. This was followed by the Hyde Park agreement in 1941, in which the United States (still officially neutral in the war) provided Canada with components for the production of munitions to be sent to Britain, and increased its purchase of Canadian goods to offset the large trade deficit that Canada was experiencing because of the war.

---

[3]Liberal prime minister Mackenzie King had not been consulted about the issue and responded that the Canadian Parliament would decide on Canada's course of action. Although Conservative party leader Arthur Meighen stated that Canada should have replied "ready, aye, ready" to the British request, the incident established the principle that Canada would not automatically take part in British wars.

The Cold War

The end of World War II brought a major change to the international system. With the other major powers devastated by the war, the United States and the Soviet Union emerged as the "superpowers." This created a "bipolar system" in which two superpowers competed with one another, and most other countries became either allies or satellites of one or the other of the superpowers.

The establishment of the United Nations in 1945 led to hopes that this body would prove more effective than the League of Nations in encouraging the development of a more peaceful world. In addition to promoting human rights, decolonization, and development, the United Nations provided the basis for the collective security of countries by empowering the **Security Council** to take action, including military action if necessary, "to maintain or restore international peace and security" (Charter of the United Nations, Chapter VII). Although Canada emerged from World War II with a powerful military and a vigorous economy, the country was not included among the five permanent members of the Security Council (the United States, Soviet Union, Britain, France, and China), each of which continues to have a veto over the actions of the council. Canada has been elected six times by the UN General Assembly to serve a two-year term on the 15-member council. However, Canada lost its bid for a seat in 2010.

The hopes for world peace in the aftermath of World War II were dashed by the Cold War. A communist coup in Czechoslovakia in 1948 and the blockade of Berlin by Soviet forces from 1948 to 1949 encouraged Canada and the United States to form a military alliance, the North Atlantic Treaty Organization (NATO), with a number of European countries. This collective security agreement included the provision that an armed attack against any of the member countries in Europe or North America would be considered an attack against all of them. Each member would be required to take "such action that it deems necessary, including the use of armed force" in such circumstances.

The Cold War resulted in large numbers of NATO troops and weaponry being stationed in central Europe in order to respond to a possible attack by the Soviet army. Canada sent about 10 000 troops, stationed mainly in Germany. However, it was in other parts of the world that Cold War hostilities led to warfare. The invasion of South Korea by communist North Korea in 1950 was countered by forces from a number of countries (including Canada) led by the United States and authorized by a resolution of the Security Council of the United Nations.[4]

United Nations
www.un.org/en

SECURITY COUNCIL
A key body of the United Nations responsible for maintaining international peace and security. It consists of 5 permanent members who each has a veto and 10 members elected by the UN General Assembly for two-year terms.

---

[4]The Soviet Union did not exercise its veto because it was boycotting the Security Council at the time to protest that the government of the Republic of China (Taiwan) rather than the communist People's Republic of China was holding China's permanent seat on the council.

"You Pissed on My Rug!"

In a speech delivered at Temple University in Philadelphia on April 2, 1965, Prime Minister Lester B. Pearson criticized Democratic president Lyndon Johnson's decision to begin bombing North Vietnam. The next day at a luncheon meeting, Johnson berated Pearson for more than an hour. Then, according to journalist Lawrence Martin, "He moved beyond the realm of words. Having pinned the much smaller Pearson against the rail, the president of the United States grabbed him by the shirt collar, twisted it and lifted the shaken prime minister by the neck. The verbal abuse continued in a venomous torrent. 'You pissed on my rug!' he thundered." At a later meeting with the press, Johnson reported that it had been a friendly discussion and

Pearson said, "It has been a very pleasant couple of hours" (quoted in Martin, 1982, p. 2).

Whether or not Martin's depiction is entirely accurate, relations between prime ministers and presidents have varied from the coziness between Brian Mulroney and Ronald Reagan to the frostiness between Stephen Harper and Barack Obama. Indeed, because of the close ties between the two countries, Pearson may have felt free to mildly criticize American policy while in the United States, and Johnson felt justified in indicating his displeasure in private. Regardless of the personal relationships between prime ministers and presidents, the governments of the two countries will have differences based on their separate interests, values, and power positions.

Despite the relatively cozy relationship between Canada and the United States that developed during the Cold War, Canada avoided direct participation in the U.S.–led Vietnam War (1964–1973). Not only was there limited public support for the war, but Canada also represented Western democracies on the International Commission for Supervision and Control in Vietnam, set up by the Geneva Accords that ended the French Indochina War in 1954.[5] However, Prime Minister Lester Pearson, in a striking departure from "quiet diplomacy," publicly criticized the American bombing of North Vietnam (as discussed in Box 18-1: "You Pissed on My Rug!").

The Cold War, along with innovations in military technology, also ended Canada's isolation from the potential theatres of war. In the 1950s, the Soviet Union deployed long-range bombers carrying nuclear weapons that could strike targets in the United States and Canada. Canada's position between the Soviet Union and the United States thus became of strategic importance. In the 1950s, Canada and the United States cooperated in building three radar systems across Canada—the Pinetree Line, the Mid-Canada Line, and the Distant Early Warning System (the DEW Line)—to detect, warn about, and potentially intercept Soviet bombers. Each quickly became out of date, particularly with the development of intercontinental and submarine-launched ballistic missiles.

---

[5]Nevertheless, Canadian companies produced some of the armaments used by the United States, including the notorious Agent Orange (a jungle defoliant), which was tested at Camp Gagetown, New Brunswick.

In 1957, the desire for the coordinated air defence of North America led to the establishment of the North American Air Defense Command (NORAD), based in Colorado with an American commander who reports to the president of the United States and a Canadian deputy commander who reports to the Canadian prime minister. As part of Canada's participation in NORAD and NATO, the Canadian government in the 1950s committed to using fighter aircraft, bombers, and anti-aircraft missiles designed to carry nuclear warheads. However, when Progressive Conservative prime minister John Diefenbaker postponed the acceptance of nuclear weapons, he was criticized by the American government. After the defence minister and two other ministers resigned from the cabinet over the issue, the minority government was defeated on a motion of nonconfidence in 1963. The Liberals, headed by Lester B. Pearson, won the subsequent election. Despite his earlier opposition to acquiring tactical nuclear weapons, Pearson proceeded to allow nuclear warheads to be located in Canada and supplied to Canadian forces in Germany.[6]

NORAD was renamed the **North American Aerospace Defense Command** in 1981 to reflect its role in securing the North American airspace through an integrated system including satellites, ground and airborne radar, and fighter aircraft. In 1985, some of the DEW Line stations located mainly in the high Arctic were converted into the North Warning System, which provides aerospace surveillance of the polar region with the ability to detect supersonic bombers and long-range cruise missiles.

NORTH AMERICAN AEROSPACE DEFENSE COMMAND
A joint American–Canadian organization that provides for the detection of and response to an attack on North America, particularly by aircraft and missiles.
NORAD
www.norad.mil

THE CONTEMPORARY WORLD

With the ending of communist rule in Eastern European countries in the late 1980s and the dissolution of the Soviet Union in 1991, the Cold War drew to a close. The end of the Cold War fundamentally transformed the international system, making it unipolar rather than bipolar. The United States became the lone superpower, whose military capabilities far exceeded those of any other country and, indeed, surpassed those of almost any combination of countries. This has given the United States the capability to launch unilateral actions nearly anywhere in the world. Nevertheless, there are limits to the military and financial capabilities of the United States. Therefore, the United States has persuaded other countries to join in various military actions, both to reduce its personnel and financial burdens and to try to enhance the legitimacy of its actions. Furthermore, while the United States can wield its military might globally, several regional powers (including Russia, China, India, Iran, and South Africa) are influential in their own parts of the world.

---

[6]Pierre Trudeau, who had bitterly attacked the Liberals for their pro-nuclear position, gradually phased out the deployment of nuclear weapons during his time as Liberal prime minister.

The collapse of the Soviet Union in 1991 led to the expansion of NATO to 28 members, including many Eastern European countries that were members of the Soviet–led Warsaw Pact, as well as the Baltic states that were once part of the Soviet Union. Although the Russian Federation is smaller and weaker than the Soviet Union, it is still an important international actor. Not only is it a leading nuclear power, but it also has important energy resources needed by many European countries. Further under authoritian president Vladimir Putin, it took the Crimean peninsula from Ukraine, supported rebels in eastern and southern Ukraine[7] who seek to rejoin Russia, fought a brief war with Georgia, and occupied two of its regions. Russia has also led the establishment of the Eurasian Union as a counterpart to the European Union, has supported the governments of Syria and Iran, and has been developing closer relations with Venezuela and Brazil and, to some extent, India and China. Although some of these ties are economic, they do point to Putin's desire for Russia to have increased influence in the world.

NATO's activities have moved beyond the collective security of its members and beyond the borders of Europe. In particular, NATO has played an active role in various conflicts arising from the breakup of Yugoslavia as well as combating the insurgency in Afghanistan and supporting rebel forces in Libya.

The end of the Cold War has not resulted in a peaceful world. For example, a war in the Democratic Republic of the Congo during 1998–2003 (sometimes referred to as "Africa's world war") involved eight African countries and a variety of armed groups. It resulted in millions of deaths, and conflict has continued in the eastern Congo. Ethnic tensions underlying the breakup of the multinational Federal Republic of Yugoslavia led to war between Serbs, Croats, and Muslims in Bosnia between 1992 and 1995. Some conflicts have involved massive human rights violations, such as the genocide in Rwanda (1994), where Hutu militias massacred as many as a million people, mostly members of the Tutsi minority as well as Hutu moderates. Sudan, Somalia, Yemen, Syria, Sierra Leone, and a number of other countries have also suffered devastating civil wars, some of which have lasted for many years. As well, many countries have been affected by terrorism.

Although Canadians and Americans have often taken pride in having the world's longest undefended border, the fear of terrorist attacks led the U.S. government to tighten its border with Canada. With Canada heavily reliant on exports to the United States, long delays at border points can seriously harm Canadian businesses. Business interests have therefore pressured the Canadian government to coordinate, collaborate, and share information with

---

[7]Ukraine, a former Soviet republic, is not a member of NATO. Since the breakup of the Soviet Union, it has experienced serious tensions between its eastern regions that have a large Russian-speaking population and Western regions that seek close ties with the European Union.

the United States on a variety of matters relating to security. Furthermore, concerns about access to American markets have led some associated with the business community to lobby for a close integration of Canada and the United States, including a North American security perimeter and closer military ties (Tomlin, Hillmer, & Hampson, 2008). For some, Canada's national interest should be pursued by developing a close partnership with the United States rather than promoting internationalist values (Hart, 2008; Rempel, 2006).

In December 2011, Prime Minister Harper and President Obama announced an agreement to establish a North American Security and Trade Perimeter. However, concerns have been raised that the agreement could reduce Canadian sovereignty, and increased sharing of information about individuals could undermine Canadian privacy protections.

United States Northern Command
www.northcom.mil

Intense anxiety about terrorism led the United States in 2002 to establish the Northern Command (NORTHCOM) to provide a unified American military command that would coordinate the defence of North America in the event of an attack. Because NORTHCOM's jurisdiction includes all of Canada and Mexico, as well as up to 800 kilometres of adjoining ocean, both Canada and Mexico have voiced concern about the potential threat to their countries' sovereignty.

Because of concern about terrorism (as well as concern about the flow of illegal drugs into the United States), the role of NORAD has grown to include a maritime warning system. Although the government of Paul Martin resisted American pressure to participate in the U.S. ballistic missile defence system, the Canadian government agreed that NORAD's radar and surveillance system could contribute to the operation of such a system (Tomlin et al., 2008).

Peacekeeping and Peace Operations

As discussed in the introductory vignette, the Canadian government played a leading part in the development of a substantial peacekeeping role for the United Nations and participated in many of the UN-authorized peacekeeping missions. The nature of peacekeeping has changed over the years, however. In what Stephen Holloway (2006) describes as **classic peacekeeping**, the goal is generally to support a ceasefire between countries in conflict or to supervise the implementation of a peace agreement. This might involve positioning observers to monitor the actions of the conflicting countries or placing peacekeepers in a neutral zone between the combatants to uphold a ceasefire agreement. If the "blue helmeted" UN forces are armed, they are expected to use their weapons only in self-defence. Finally, classic peacekeeping is carried out with the agreement of the countries involved, respects the sovereignty of those states, and is under the control of the United Nations (Holloway, 2006).

CLASSIC PEACEKEEPING
Activities carried out under the United Nations' banner to support a ceasefire between countries in conflict or to supervise the implementation of a peace agreement.

Classic peacekeeping has proven useful in some situations, but it is not always successful. For example, in the case of the UN Emergency Force that was deployed in 1956 as a result of the Suez Canal crisis, the peacekeeping mission did not prevent further warfare. In 1967 the Egyptian president, Gamal Abdel Nasser, ordered the UN Emergency Force out of the country and amassed large numbers of troops and tanks on the Israeli border. Shortly afterward, Israel launched a pre-emptive strike on Egypt, beginning the Six Day War in the Middle East.

Although classic peacekeeping is still important, most of the use of international forces under the banner of the United Nations in recent decades has involved conflicts within a state rather than between states (Pelz & Lehmann, 2007). In failing or failed states (such as Somalia), where the governing authorities are unable to exercise effective control, outside intervention is often needed to ensure that humanitarian relief is delivered, human rights are protected, law and order are established, and help is provided to set up effective governing institutions and to monitor elections. To recognize the spectrum of activities that aim to build and enforce peace, the term **peace operations** is often used instead of *peace-keeping*; however, these terms can be misleading when operations by foreign troops (often not directly under the UN banner) primarily involve combat.

Peace operations often involve not only troops under UN command but also police and civilians, as well as non-governmental organizations offering development assistance. Furthermore, organizations other than the United Nations, such as NATO and the African Union, have increasingly carried out these operations.

Canada has participated in 48 UN peacekeeping missions since 1948, with Canadians suffering 114 fatalities. However, Canada's contribution to UN peacekeeping operations has shrunk drastically since 1995 as Canada has turned down requests to take an active role in some major UN peacekeeping operations, such as the mission in the Democratic Republic of Congo. As of September 2015, Canada had 115 peacekeepers (88 police, 9 military experts, and 18 troops) out of a total of 105 480 UN peacekeepers (United Nations Peacekeeping, 2015).

Combat Missions

Canada is often thought to be a peace-loving country, although it has participated in wars and other military missions (see Table 18-1). From the end of the Korean War in 1953 to the end of the Cold War in 1981, Canada did not directly engage in active combat. Since then, Canada has taken an active role in several conflicts.

In 1991 Canada, along with 33 other countries, participated in the U.S.-led Gulf War against Iraq. This combat mission was authorized by the

PEACE OPERATIONS

A wide range of activities with the aim of building and enforcing peace, including peacekeeping, peace building, and peace enforcement.

Pearson Centre
www.peaceoperations.org

TABLE 18-1
CANADIAN COMBAT MISSIONS

Notes: Figures for World War II refer to troops sent overseas. Deaths include disease and accidents as well as those that are combat related, but do not include deaths that occurred after the end of the war related to injuries suffered during the war. Different sources provide different figures for the number involved and number of deaths. Two aid workers, one diplomat, and a journalist were also killed in Afghanistan. The only casualty in the war against ISIS (as of October 2015) was by friendly fire.

MISSION	DATE	NUMBER INVOLVED	DEATHS
Nile Expedition (Sudan)	1884	386	16
South Africa (Boer War)	1899–1902	8 300	242
World War I	1914–1918	Over 600 000	60 661
Siberian Expedition	1918–1919	4 197	19
World War II	1930–1945	About 1.1 million	42 042
Korean War	1950–1953	About 26 000	516
Gulf War (Iraq)	1990–1991	Over 4 000	0
Yugoslavia	1999	300	0
Afghanistan	2002–2011	2 500	158
Libya	2011	630	0
Islamic State	2014–	About 600	1

SOURCES: Isitt, 2006; Morton, 2007; Veterans Affairs Canada, n.d.: Department of National Defence, 2011.

UN Security Council after Iraq invaded and annexed Kuwait. Canada's participation in this short war included the use of fighter aircraft to protect American bombing missions, naval vessels to enforce a blockade of Iraq, and a mobile military hospital to treat the wounded. Canada refused to take part in the American–led invasion of Iraq in 2003, which lacked specific UN authorization. From 2001 to 2011, Canada participated in ground combat missions in Afghanistan (see Box 18-2: Canada's Longest Combat Mission: Afghanistan).

Libya

Beginning in Tunisia in late 2010, youthful protests and demonstrations against dictatorial governments in many Arab countries (termed the "Arab Spring") seemed poised to bring democracy to this troubled region. While successful in ousting dictators in Tunisia and, for a time, in Egypt with a minimum of violence, the situation in Libya (which borders those two countries) was different. Libya's long-time brutal dictator, Muammar Gaddafi, would not resign without a fight.

Rebel forces including many defectors from Libya's army took control of Benghazi, Libya's second largest city, and a civil war erupted as Gaddafi's army bombed the rebels. The United Nations Security Council agreed to establish a "no fly zone" over Libya to protect civilians and placed the Libyan government under an arms embargo. NATO (along with four non-member countries) took further action by initiating airstrikes against Gaddafi's forces. Canada participated in the bombing and the naval blockade of Libya. This aided rebel forces who were able to capture the capital of Tripoli and much of the country. The war ended on October 31, 2011, when Gaddafi was killed in his home town.

Canada's Longest Combat Mission: Afghanistan

On September 11, 2001, al-Qaeda, which had its base in Taliban-controlled Afghanistan, launched a terrorist attack on the United States. NATO quickly invoked its Article 5, which obliged member states to come to the defence of the United States. Shortly afterward, Canada sent military vessels to the region, secretly deployed its elite Joint Task Force 2, and early in 2002 deployed regular troops to fight alongside the Americans in Kandahar for six months. In 2003, Canada took leadership of the International Security Assistance Force (ISAF), a NATO force authorized by the UN Security Council. The ISAF provided security around the capital, Kabul, to support the establishment of a transitional governing authority, as well as to provide security for humanitarian relief.

In 2005, Canada sent a provincial reconstruction team (PRT) combining military and civilian personnel to Kandahar to develop good governance, build relationships with local and provincial leaders, and undertake various reconstruction projects including repairing a dam and building schools. The following year, as the Taliban insurgency grew, Canadian forces took responsibility for the dangerous southern region based in Kandahar. This was primarily a combat mission that included killing insurgents rather than a peacekeeping mission. The initial two-year mission was extended to 2009, confirmed by a close vote (149–145) in the House of Commons. After a further extension, Canadian troops returned home in 2011, although military and police trainers remained in Afghanistan until 2014. Overall, Canada played a larger role in Afghanistan than most other NATO countries.

Canadian governments justified participation in this lengthy conflict in terms of promoting such values as democracy and the rights of women and girls that would be attacked if the Taliban returned to power. However, the Afghan government, plagued with incompetence and corruption, has had difficulty exercising effective control over much of the country where tribal loyalties and regional "warlords" are strong.

Was the more than $18 billion Canadian mission in Afghanistan a costly and wasted effort? As the United States found in Vietnam and Iraq, and the Soviet Union learned in Afghanistan, foreign military might cannot ensure a meaningful, lasting peace. Whether some improvements in education, human rights, and democratic governance will have a lasting effect remains to be seen.

Rebel victory did not bring peace to Libya, however, as different rebel forces fought for control of the country. Islamic extremists gained importance and were responsible for killing the U.S. ambassador and three other American officers at the U.S. mission in Benghazi in 2012. As of 2015, Libya was still in the throes of a devastating civil war. However, much of the world's attention had turned to the rise of ISIS,[8] which posed an even more serious threat to peace (see Box 18-3: ISIS, the Islamic State).

---

[8]Also known as as the Islamic State of Iraq and the Levant (ISIL). Beginning in 2014 they referred to themselves as the Islamic State.

BOX 18-3

ISIS, the Islamic State

In 2014, the Islamic State of Iraq and Syria (ISIS) swiftly gained control of large portions of Iraq and Syria. ISIS is an extremist Sunni Muslim group committed to following all the practices of Mohammed and the Qu'ran, including the killing of apostates and perhaps preparing for the battle that will mark the end of times (Wood, 2015).

In Iraq, ISIS took advantage of Sunni opposition to the Shiite dominated government. The Iraq army left large amounts of American-supplied military equipment behind as it fled from the small but determined ISIS forces. In Syria, the brutal suppression of protesters in 2011 by the authoritarian Assad government based on the Alawite (basically Shiite) minority led to a horrific civil war with at least 250 000 people killed, 7.6 million people forced from their homes, and 4 million people fleeing from the country as of October 2015. The various opposition forces (including the Free Syrian Army, the al-Qaeda connected al-Nusra Front, ISIS, and the Kurdish People's Protection Units) often fight each other as well as fighting Assad's forces (which are supported by Iran, Hezbollah, and Russia).

In June 2014, ISIS declared the establishment of an Islamic caliphate which claims to lead a single international Islamic state headed by a successor to the Prophet Mohammed to which all Muslims are required to pledge allegiance. While most Islamic scholars criticized this declaration, tens of thousands of male and female foreigners (including a number of Canadians) left their homelands to fight for the Islamic State. Furthermore, some extremist groups in other countries pledged allegiance to the Islamic State, and in 2015, 21 Coptic Christians on a beach in Libya were beheaded by a group claiming to be affiliated with ISIS. Although ISIS may not be directly involved in other countries, its message and methods have captured the attention of other extreme Islamic groups and individuals in various countries.

In October 2014, the Canadian House of Commons approved a government motion to conduct a six-month aerial bombing campaign against ISIS in Iraq and to send some soldiers to help train Kurdish Iraqis fighting ISIS. In March 2015, the House of Common approved a one-year extension as well as expanded the bombing of ISIS to Syria. NDP, Liberal, and Green parties opposed the mission, arguing that humanitarian assistance to those displaced by the fighting would be more useful. Most Western countries along with Arab countries have joined the United States in airstrikes against ISIS in Iraq. In December 2015, the new Liberal government announced that it would end the bombing mission against ISIS. Instead it would increase its training of Kurdish anti-ISIS fighters and accept a larger number of Syrian refugees.

Turkey has not only attacked ISIS (and provided a base for U.S. bombing), but has also launched airstrikes against the Syrian Kurdish militia that has been the most successful group fighting ISIS. In October 2015, Russia began large-scale bombing, supposedly directed at ISIS, but also bombing other groups fighting against the Syrian government including rebel groups supported by the United States and its allies. The downing of a Russian war plane by Turkey near its border with Syria raised concerns about a serious broadening of the war. However, in December 2015, the US and Russia began to discuss ways to end the Syrian conflict and the UN Security Council unanimously endorsed a roadmap for a peace process in Syria.

As is frequently the case, the question of whether direct military action by the US, Canada and other Western democracies helps or hinders the effort to bring peace to a troubled region is difficult to determine.

NATIONAL SECURITY

Canada is fortunate in that its national security has not been seriously challenged. Although Canada is next to the world's superpower, Canada is an ally of the United States and the two countries share generally similar values and a largely integrated economy, and often cooperate militarily. Thus, Canada has not needed to guard against a threat of invasion in a very long time. Indeed, Canada's spending on the military as a proportion of gross national product declined significantly from 2009 to 2015.

Threats to the security of the North American continent from Soviet bombers and missiles during the Cold War and, more recently, from terrorist attacks led to concerns about Canada's security. However, by pursuing a strategy of "defence against help"—that is, taking sufficient measures to prevent gaps in North American security—Canada has avoided American unilateral action on Canadian territory to deal with potential threats (Legasse, 2010).

Nevertheless, Canada faces potential challenges to its sovereignty in the Arctic. Although Canada claims the Northwest Passage through the territorial waters of the Arctic, American ships have sailed through the passage without informing the Canadian government. Likewise, Russian submarines have entered the Canadian Arctic. As Arctic ice continues to thin because of global climate change, it may not be long before Canada's Northwest Passage becomes a major international shipping route. Plans by major petroleum companies to drill in Canada's Arctic have raised serious concerns about the potential for oil spills in the fragile northern environment. In addition, there are competing territorial claims by Russia, Canada, the United States, Denmark, and Norway to exploit the huge oil, gas, and mineral resources that lie under the seabed of the High Arctic.

Prime Minister Harper made well-publicized visits to the Arctic each summer to "show the flag." However, the Conservative party promise in the 2006 Canadian election to build three armed heavy icebreakers to enforce Canadian sovereignty in the Arctic was not fulfilled. Instead, in 2012 it was announced that six to eight light naval icebreakers would be built and fully operational by 2023. Unlike stronger icebreakers, they will be unable to operate between November and July because of ice conditions (Byers, 2012).

Terrorism

On October 22, 2014, Michael Zehaf-Bibeau shot Corporal Nathan Cirillo who was standing on guard at the National War Memorial. He then fled to the nearby Parliament buildings, wrestled with a guard who tried unsuccessfully to take his rifle, and entered the Centre Block. MPs locked themselves in their caucus rooms and the prime minister hid in a closet. Zehaf-Bibeau was killed in a shoot-out with Parliament's security personnel. Throughout the day, rumours of other terrorists raised fears throughout Ottawa and downtown Ottawa was locked down. With Maurice Couteau-Rouleau having run over two Canadian soldiers (killing one) two days earlier, fears about terrorism in Canada were heightened. However, the rumours proved false. Although both attacks in October were inspired by Islamic extremist ideas, they were apparently unconnected "lone wolf" attacks rather than organized or directed by a terrorist group domestic or foreign.

Zehaf-Bibeau, whose father was from Libya and whose Quebec mother was a high-ranking federal official, was a mentally disturbed drug addict. He wanted to go to an Islamic country but had been refused a Libyan passport and was seeking a Canadian one that he probably would not receive given his several convictions. In a short video left in his car, he explained that he wanted to retaliate for Canada's actions in Afghanistan and the prime minister's intention to send troops to Iraq.

Terrorism can be defined as the use of violence or the threat of violence to intimidate a population for political purposes.[9] Al-Qaeda's terrorist attacks on the United States on September 11, 2011—along with deadly suicide bombings of trains around Madrid (2004) and London's Underground (2005)—shocked the public of Western countries. In Canada, there have been some unsuccessful terrorist plots associated with Islamic extremism, most notably the plans by the "Toronto 18" (mainly involving young persons) in 2006 to use truck bombs to attack various Ontario targets. However, Canada's most deadly terrorist act involved Sikh extremists who planted explosives on an Air India flight from Montreal to London, killing all 329 persons on board. This was a response to an Indian government-sponsored attack on the sacred Golden Temple in Amritsar that killed as many as 1500 Sikhs occupying the temple.

Concerns about terrorism led the Conservative government to adopt a number of new laws that go much further than anti-terrorism legislation adopted after the terrorist attacks of 2011. In particular, Bill C-51 (the Anti-Terrorism Act) allows the Canadian Security Intelligence Service (CSIS) to take any action that CSIS considers reasonable to "reduce . . . threats to the security of Canada." This can include breaking laws and violating the Charter of Rights and Freedoms provided that there has been judicial permission after a secret hearing in which only the government can present its case (Forcese & Roach, 2015, April 15). Bill C-51 includes making it a serious criminal offence to advocate or promote "terrorism offences in general"—a rather broad category. It also has implications for privacy by facilitating the sharing of information among various departments of government and foreign agencies as well as making it easier for telecom companies to voluntarily provide information about their customers to the government. Limits to CSIS's law enforcement powers are not provided, thus potentially making it possible to use detention or rendition (Roach & Forcese, 2015, April 2).

Such broadly defined powers are very different from merely sending agents to speak "with the parents of radicalized youth" as the government claimed. Moreover, these new provisions will apply to CSIS's full security mandate, not just

---

[9]Although we sometimes think of terrorism as being conducted by extremist groups, many governments have used terror to intimidate their population. Terror directed against civilians is often used in warfare to try to demoralize the enemy and encourage surrender. For example, both Axis and Allied powers used terror extensively in World War II, which ended after the American use of atomic weapons on two Japanese cities.

anti-terrorism. The agency will be able to exercise these powers to reduce threats associated with sabotage, espionage, foreign-influenced activity, and subversion.

The anti-terrorism legislation passed easily in the House of Commons. The Liberals supported the bill but recommended that there be parliamentary oversight of CSIS. The NDP and the Green Party were strongly opposed, with NDP leader Thomas Mulcair arguing that "we cannot protect our freedoms by sacrificing them" (New Democratic Party News, 2015). The Organization for Security and Cooperation in Europe (OSCE), representing 57 countries including Canada and the United States, criticized Bill C-51 for violating the Universal Declaration of Human Rights (which Canada signed in 1948) because of its threats to privacy, freedom of expression, and freedom of movement.

HUMAN SECURITY

The realist perspective points out that the primary focus of the foreign and defence policies of all countries has typically been **national security**—that is, protecting the country from foreign threats to its population, territory, and independence (Sens & Stoett, 2005). However, building on a growing concern about human rights since World War II, the idea of "security" has been broadened from a focus on the security of the state from foreign aggression to include **human security**. As defined by the United Nations Human Development Report (1994), human security includes economic, food, health, environmental, community, and political security. In an address to the General Assembly of the United Nations in 1996, Canadian foreign affairs minister Lloyd Axworthy argued,

> At a minimum, human security requires that basic needs are met, but it also acknowledges that sustained economic development, human rights and fundamental freedoms, the rule of law, good governance, sustainable development and social equity are as important to global peace as arms control and disarmament. . . . Canada has both the capacity and the credibility to play a leadership role in support of human security in the developing world. (Axworthy, 1997, p. 183)

In Axworthy's view, values rather than national self-interest were coming to the fore in international politics and thus should be the focus of foreign policy. Canada's success in building a peaceful liberal democratic state that respected the diversity of its peoples could set a positive example for other countries. Thus, even though Canada did not possess a high level of "hard power" because its military capabilities were limited, the country could play a key role in international politics by drawing on its "soft power"—that is, leadership by its values and its example. The way for Canada to exert influence was not to rely on the power of the United States. Instead, Canada could play an independent role in world affairs by working with the growing number of non-governmental organizations that were pursuing peace and development goals, as well as by participating in multilateral forums with other middle

NATIONAL SECURITY
Protection of a country from foreign threats to its population, territory, and independence.

HUMAN SECURITY
A view of security that focuses on the protection of people from various threats to their well-being.

powers that shared similar values (Bernard, 2006). Reflecting this view, Canada played a leading role in the effort to ban anti-personnel landmines, which culminated in the 1997 signing of the Convention on the Prohibition of the Use, Stockpiling, Production and Transfer of Anti-Personnel Mines and on Their Destruction (known as the "Ottawa Treaty"). As well, Canada played a major role in the creation of the International Criminal Court, which can bring to trial those responsible for genocide and crimes against humanity. In both these initiatives, international agreements were reached despite the vehement objections of the leading powers (the United States, Russia, and China). Non-governmental organizations and cyberactivism proved important in mobilizing the popular support that led to these agreements.

International Campaign to Ban Landmines
www.icbl.org

International Criminal Court
www.icc-cpi.int

Canadians have also been important in raising the environmental concerns that seriously threaten human security. Specifically, Canada took centre stage in the UN-sponsored Conference on the Human Environment in 1972, and Canadian Maurice Strong chaired the UN Conference on Environment and Development (better known as the "Earth Summit") in 1992. Canada also played a key role in the development of the Montreal Protocol (1987), a treaty providing for the phasing out of ozone-depleting substances.

However, Canada later became a laggard rather than a leader in efforts to reduce the emission of greenhouse gases, which is potentially the most serious threat to the global environment. In 2011, Canada became the only country to withdraw from the Kyoto Protocol on climate change, joining only two United Nations members (the United States and South Sudan) who had not ratified the Protocol. Likewise, Canada's greenhouse gas emissions increased substantially while most other industrialized nations have reduced their emissions. In 2014, Canada was ranked as the worst climate change performer of the world's 58 industrialized countries (Huffington Post Canada, 2014, October 22).

HUMANITARIAN INTERVENTION AND THE RESPONSIBILITY TO PROTECT

During the 1990s, UN-backed peacekeeping missions failed to stop horrific human rights abuses in several countries. For example, during the genocide in Rwanda, Roméo Dallaire, the Canadian commander of the UN Assistance Mission, pleaded for more troops. However, the UN Security Council refused and instead severely cut back the number of UN troops in Rwanda.

In 1999, Canada was part of a NATO force that conducted 78 days of airstrikes against Yugoslavia to try to prevent a humanitarian catastrophe. This devastating attack was designed to persuade Serbian forces to stop their assaults on Albanian Muslims in the province of Kosovo where they formed a large majority and to withdraw their troops from that area. After a peace proposal was rejected by Serbia (then part of Yugoslavia), Serbian attacks on Albanians accelerated and about 800 000 Albanians fled from Kosovo. After 78 days of bombing, Serbian president Slobodan Milošević agreed to pull his

troops out of Kosovo.[10] Albanians returned to Kosovo while about 200 000
Serbs, fearing retribution, left Kosovo. Kosovo became a United Nations pro-
tectorate and in 2008 declared its independence.

The attack on Yugoslavia sparked controversy because it involved a foreign military intervention in the affairs of a sovereign state that was not authorized by the United Nations Security Council, thereby violating international
law. Supporters of the intervention argued that it was necessary on humanitarian grounds to protect the Albanian population that was in imminent danger;
Yugoslavia was violating the human rights that it had agreed to respect by
signing various international agreements. The United Nations could not effectively resolve the crisis because Russia and China would likely have wielded
their veto power to stop the UN Security Council from authorizing military
action.

To avoid the controversy often associated with the term "humanitarian
intervention," which highlights interference with state sovereignty, Lloyd
Axworthy promoted the concept of the **responsibility to protect**, which is
intended to focus on the responsibility of the government of each country to
protect its own people. This new terminology was adopted by the Canadian-
sponsored International Commission on Intervention and State Sovereignty
(ICISS). In its report, the ICISS laid out the basic principles of its view of the
responsibility to protect:

> *State sovereignty implies responsibility, and the primary responsibility
> for the protection of its people lies with the state itself. Where a popula-
> tion is suffering serious harm, as a result of internal war, insurgency,
> repression or state failure, and the state in question is unwilling or unable
> to halt or avert it, the principle of non-intervention yields to the interna-
> tional responsibility to protect. (International Commission on Interven-
> tion and State Sovereignty, 2001, p. xi)*

The responsibility to protect includes preventing crises that put populations at risk and responding with appropriate measures. In extreme cases
involving actual or apprehended large-scale loss of life or ethnic cleansing,
military intervention could be used as a last resort. The report argued that the
UN Security Council was the most appropriate body to authorize military
intervention and suggested ways to improve its performance. However, if the
Security Council failed in its duty, the report suggested two alternatives: The
of the UN General Assembly could recommend that the Security Council take
action, or regional organizations might take action within their regions and
later seek authorization from the Security Council. Finally, the report noted
that if the Security Council failed to act, "concerned states may not rule out
other means to meet the gravity and urgency of that situation."

RESPONSIBILITY TO PROTECT
The responsibility of a state to protect its population from genocide, war crimes, ethnic cleansing, and crimes against humanity and, as a last resort, the responsibility of the international community, particularly through the United Nations, to intervene if a state is unwilling or unable to protect its population.

[10]Milošević died before his trial for genocide, crimes against humanity, and war crimes could be completed.

International Coalition for the
Responsibility to Protect
www.responsibilitytoprotect.org

Global Centre for the Responsibility
to Protect
www.globalr2p.org

Group of 77
www.g77.org

The Darfur/Sudan Peace Network
www.sdcanada.org

At the UN World Summit in 2005, delegates agreed that there is a collective international responsibility to protect if genocide, war crimes, ethnic cleansing, and crimes against humanity are at stake. Timely and decisive action through the Security Council should be taken when "peaceful means prove inadequate and national authorities are manifestly failing to do it" (United Nations, 2005). The Security Council unanimously reaffirmed this agreement in 2006. However, the agreement did not authorize intervention without the approval of the United Nations.

Russia, China, and the Group of 77 (as of 2015, consisting of 134 developing countries) have voiced concerns that the responsibility to protect[11] could be used to justify self-interested interference, particularly by Western countries, in the affairs of other countries. This set off alarm bells in the many former colonies that have suffered from Western conquest and domination. Thus, the responsibility to protect has not been used by the Security Council, even after the High Commission of the UN's Human Rights Council reported that the government of Sudan had "manifestly failed to protect the population of Darfur" (Bellamy, 2009).

Canada's commitment to the responsibility to protect faded after John Manley replaced Lloyd Axworthy as Liberal minister of foreign affairs and the concern about terrorism took high priority. The Harper Conservative government further distanced itself from Axworthy's ideals—going so far as to direct foreign affairs personnel not to use terms such as "human security" and the "responsibility to protect" (Davis, 2009). Nevertheless, the responsibility to protect doctrine was invoked to justify intervention in Libya after protesters were massacred. However, whether this doctrine could be used to justify actions in support of rebel forces in a civil war aimed at regime change is controversial. Nevertheless, Canada's foreign affairs minister, John Baird, on a visit to eastern Libya, encouraged the rebel command to keep fighting rather than accept a ceasefire (Berthiaume, 2012).

DEVELOPMENT ASSISTANCE

Development assistance (foreign aid) had its origins in the Cold War, particularly as a tool to try to staunch the spread of communism among the newly decolonized countries. Under Prime Minister Pearson, Canadian policy shifted toward "humane internationalism"—that is, helping those in the poorest countries. However, many of the poorest countries have dismal human rights records and often have the weakest ability to make progress in reducing poverty. Canada's 2005 International Policy Statement recommended that good governance be a greater focus in development assistance. Specifically good governance involved democratization, human rights, the rule of law, public

[11]However, Russia's foreign minister claimed that Russia was exercising its responsibility to protect when it invaded Georgia in August 2008 after Georgia's attack on Russian forces in South Ossetia (a breakaway region of Georgia).

sector institution and capacity building, and conflict prevention, peace building, and security-sector reform (Canadian International Development Agency, 2005). Canada's Official Development Assistance Accountability Act (2008) states that official development assistance must contribute to poverty reduction, take into account the perspectives of the poor, and be consistent with international human rights standards.

The Canadian International Development Agency (CIDA), a government agency, was established in 1968, but lost its separate identity in 2013 as it was merged into the Department of Foreign Affairs, Trade, and Development (DFATD). Critics claimed that DFATD was more concerned with trade issues than with development. In fact, a substantial number of positions were cut when development became the responsibility of DFATD. (DFATD was renamed Global Affairs Canada by the Trudeau government in 2015.)

Canada's development projects have often worked through Canadian non-governmental organizations that have a significant presence in developing countries. For example, KAIROS Canada (representing 11 major churches and religious organizations) has projects related particularly to ecological justice and human rights in many developing countries. Although senior officials in CIDA in 2010 recommended continued government funding for its projects, then-international cooperation minister Bev Oda inserted the word "not" before "recommended," thus deliberately misleading Parliament about CIDA's recommendation. Oxfam Canada, a major development non-governmental organization, was warned by the Canada Revenue Agency that it could lose its charitable status because "alleviating poverty is charitable, but preventing it is not" (Canadian Press, 2014, July 25).

KAIROS
www.kairoscanada.org

In recent years, the Canadian government has indicated that it will increasingly use Canadian corporations (such as collaborating with Canadian mining companies) in projects and will focus more on promoting Canadian interests abroad.

Canada supported the Millennium Development Goals (MDG) adopted by the United Nations in 2000 and to be reached by 2015. These goals included achieving universal primary education, reducing child morality, combating HIV/AIDS, malaria, and other diseases, ensuring environmental sustainability, and devoping a global partnership for development. The MDG had considerable success in cutting the rate of poverty in half and providing basic education for nearly all children; however, it was less successful in achieving health goals and improving life in Africa (Bates-Earner, Carin, Lee, & Lim, 2012). In 2015, the United Nations adopted 17 sustainable development goals (including ending poverty and hunger, achieving gender equality, and stopping climate change) to be reached by 2030 (Open Working Group Proposal for Sustainable Development Goals, 2014).

The Commission on International Development (chaired by Lester B. Pearson) recommended that the developed countries dedicate 0.7 percent of their gross national income to assisting the development of poorer countries—a goal that the developed countries (including Canada) and the United Nations

Here, PO2 Stephan Belanger places bags of corn soya blend while *HMCS St John's* is being loaded with humanitarian supplies by local men and the ship's company, with the collaboration of the Canadian embassy and representatives of the World Food Program (WFP), September 2008 at Port au Prince, Haiti. Acting on a request from the UN WFP and UN International Maritime Organization, the Canadian government sent *HMCS St John's* to Haiti, the least developed country in the Americas, to provide humanitarian aid over several weeks.

© MCpl Eduardo Mora Pinede/Formation Imaging Services

adopted in 1970. However, Canada has never reached that goal and, in fact, the amount of assistance dropped in the 1990s as the Canadian government struggled to shrink its budgetary deficit and debt. Further cuts in assistance (as a proportion of Canada's gross national income) occurred from 2011 to 2014. As Figure 18-1 indicates, Canada's official development assistance is below the average of the donor countries.

The 2015 Canadian government budget did not increase its development assistance funding. However, it did announce that a Development Financing

Canadian Council for International Co-operation
www.ccic.ca

Initiative would be established "to support effective international development by providing financing, technical assistance, and business advisory services to firms operating in developing countries." In Europe, where development financing constitutes a sizable proportion of development aid,

FIGURE 18-1
OFFICIAL DEVELOPMENT
ASSISTANCE AS A
PERCENTAGE OF GROSS
NATIONAL INCOME AND
BILLIONS OF DOLLARS

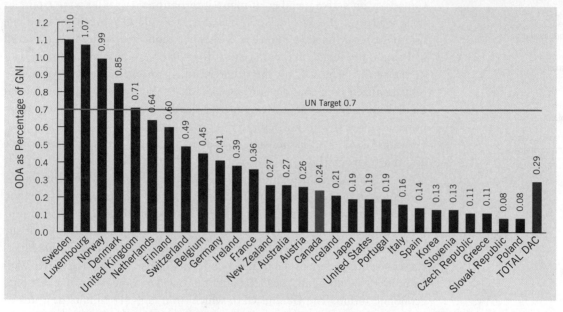

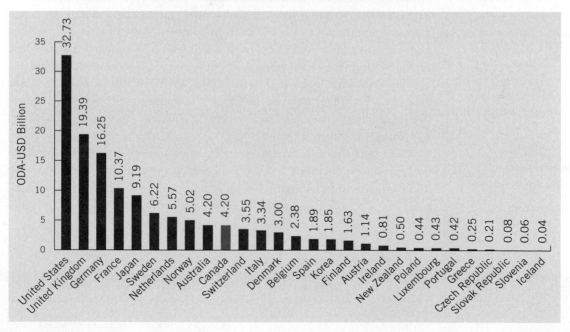

Source: Organisation for Economic Co-operation and development (2015). Net official development assistance in 2014. http://www.oecd.org/dac/stats/development-aid-stable-in-2014-but-flows-to-poorest-countries-still-falling.htm. Used with permission.

the countries receiving aid are generally not involved in investment decisions and only a small proportion of companies in poor countries are supported (Romero, 2014).

INTERNATIONAL ORGANIZATIONS

Canada is an active member of many international organizations. Some of these—such as the World Bank, the World Trade Organization, and the International Monetary Fund—are of great economic importance, as well as being quite inclusive organizations that involve many or most countries of the world. The G8, on the other hand, is an exclusive club of highly industrialized countries (including Canada).[12] In addition to its informal annual meetings of the eight countries' leaders (and invited leaders from other countries, who participate in some sessions), the G8 holds regular meetings of ministers responsible for particular policy areas, such as finance and the environment.

As Canadian finance minister, Paul Martin played a leading role in the formation of the G20, consisting of countries with major economies including major developing countries such as China, India, Brazil, and South Africa as well as the European Union. Formed in 1998, it originally consisted of the finance ministers of the member states. However, as a result of the 2008 financial crisis, the leaders of the member countries began meeting regularly. With its broader membership, the G20 could be considered the major international economic forum. The G8 and G20, which hold annual summits of heads of parliamentary governments and presidential states behind closed doors, do not have a permanent office or staff. In contrast, the Organisation for Economic Co-operation and Development (OECD) has a substantial staff that provides information and policy advice designed to promote economic growth and financial stability as well as providing advice on effective development assistance. The 34 members of the OECD are countries with developed economies (including Canada) and some emerging countries (such as Mexico, Chile, and Turkey) that meet its standards.[13]

Canada is also an active participant in two international organizations that reflect the country's British and French heritage: the Commonwealth and L'Organisation internationale de la Francophonie.[14] In both these organizations, Canada has, at times, pursued a democracy and human rights

World Bank
www.worldbank.org

World Trade Organization
www.wto.org

International Monetary Fund
www.imf.org

G8 Information Centre
www.g8.utoronto.ca

G20
G20.org

Organisation for Economic
Co-operation and Development
www.oecd.org

The Commonwealth
www.thecommonwealth.org

L'Organisation internationale de la
Francophonie
www.francophonie.org

---

[12]The G8 consists of Canada, France, Germany, Italy, Japan, Russia, the United Kingdom, and the United States, along with a representative of the European Union. Russia was suspended from the G8 beginning in 2014 after its seizure of Crimea from Ukraine. In effect, the G8 reverted to being the G7.

[13]In addition, Brazil, India, Indonesia, China, and South Africa are "key partners," while Russia's application for membership was stalled in 2014.

[14]Quebec, is also a full-fledged member of *la Francophonie*.

agenda. For example, Prime Minister Brian Mulroney led the fight to persuade the Commonwealth to impose economic sanctions on the apartheid regime in South Africa. In addition, Canada is a member of several regional organizations, including the Organization of American States (OAS), the Arctic Council, and Asia-Pacific Economic Cooperation (APEC). In total, Canada is a member of more than 80 international governmental organizations. Canada's involvement in a variety of international organizations is seen by some as a counterweight to Canada's strong ties to the United States. However, Canada often takes similar positions to the United States in these organizations.

TRADE POLICY

International trade has become a high priority for governments and is an important part of Canada's foreign policy. In particular, the pursuit of trade and investment agreements with a variety of other countries has been a major goal of Canadian governments.

Trade considerations sometimes outweigh other Canadian foreign policy objectives. For example, in its first years in office, Harper's Conservative government was critical of China's human rights record and angered China by bestowing honorary Canadian citizenship on the Dalai Lama, the exiled spiritual leader of Tibet. Harper's failure to visit China (Canada's second largest trading partner) while it was hosting the 2008 Olympics was viewed by the Chinese government as a deliberate snub. The resulting chill in Canada–China

Stephen and Laureen Harper with one of the two giant pandas on a 10-year loan from China.

© Xinhua/Li Jian/Landov

relations hurt various segments of the Canadian economy. Thus, Harper eventually made a trip to China in 2009. His second visit in 2012 included the signing of a Canada–China foreign investment promotion and protection agreement. In recognition of improving relations, China gave Canada a 10-year loan of two giant pandas.

Summary and Conclusion

Canada's foreign policy has to some extent reflected the liberal internationalist perspective. Canada built its international reputation through its role in peacekeeping, its tradition of "quiet diplomacy," its effectiveness as a "helpful fixer," and its commitment to international organizations. Canada has demonstrated leadership on such global problems as human rights, poverty, disease, conflict, and environmental sustainability. However, Canada is no longer a major player in United Nations peacekeeping operations, has not been a strong supporter of the United Nations in recent years, and is less generous with development assistance than many other comparable countries. As well, Canadian diplomacy—which once was highly respected—suffered from increased government direction and the government's focus on the Canadian economy and the interests of Canadian businesses. Canada's internationalist reputation was also weakened by its failure to live up to its commitments on global climate change. It remains to be seen to what extent foreign policy will be modified with the election of a Liberal government in 2015 that promised to focus on returning to a greater peacekeeping role and to take action on climate change.

Canada's foreign policies are strongly affected by its relationship to the United States. The integration of the economies of the two countries, the close relationship between the Canadian and American militaries, the influence of American media and cultural products, the generally similar perspective on international issues, and cross-border family and personal relations make it unlikely that the Canadian government would take a radically different course of action in world affairs from that of the American government. Nevertheless, Canadian governments avoided direct involvement with the United States in the Vietnam War, the 2003 invasion of Iraq, and the American ballistic missile defence system. Likewise, in recent years the Canadian government has tried to reduce Canadian economic dependence on the United States by negotiating trade and investment agreements with other countries.

The world has changed dramatically since the days of Lester Pearson and liberal internationalism. Yet the world still needs countries that can help resolve conflicts, advance human rights, and promote sustainable development. Canada's ability to meet the challenges of democracy, diversity, and good government gives Canada a "soft power" that can win respect and influence in the world.

Discussion Questions

1. Should there be a greater focus in Canadian politics on world affairs?

2. Should Canada increase its assistance to poor countries? Should aid only be given to countries that

demonstrate progress toward democracy and human rights?

3. Should Canada's foreign policy focus be on Canada's economic and security interests, maintaining its

close relationship with the United States, or pursuing humane internationalism?

4. Should Canada increase its involvement in peacekeeping operations? Should it only participate in military operations that are sanctioned by the United Nations?

5. Should Canada substantially increase the strength and capabilities of its military forces? If so, for what purposes? If not, why not?

Further Reading

Axworthy, L. (2003). *Navigating a new world: Canada's global future*. Toronto, ON: Knopf.

Bratt, D., & Kukucha, C.J. (Eds.). (2015). *Readings in Canadian foreign policy: Classic debates and new ideas* (3rd ed.). Toronto, ON: Oxford University Press.

Byers, M. (2007). *Intent for a nation*. Vancouver, BC: Douglas & McIntyre.

Clark, J. (2013). *How we lead. Canada in a century of change*. Toronto, ON: Random House Canada.

Dallaire, R. (2003). *Shake hands with the devil: The failure of humanity in Rwanda*. Toronto, ON: Random House.

Griffiths, F., Huebert, R., & Lackenbauer, P.W. (2011). *Canada and the changing Arctic. Sovereignty, security, and stewardship*. Waterloo, ON: Wilfrid Laurier University Press.

Heinbecker, P. (2011). *Getting back in the game: A foreign policy handbook for Canada* (2nd ed.). Toronto, ON: Dundurn.

Keating, T. (2012). *Canada and the world order: The multilateralist tradition in Canadian foreign policy* (3rd ed.). Toronto, ON: Oxford University Press.

Kirton, J. (2007). *Canadian foreign policy in a changing world*. Toronto, ON: Thomson Nelson.

Lui, A. (2012). *Why Canada cares: Human rights and foreign policy in theory and practice*. Montreal, QC: McGill-Queen's University Press.

McDonough, D.S. (Ed.). (2012). *Canada's national security in the post 9/11 world: Strategy, interests, and threats*. Toronto, ON: University of Toronto Press.

Nossal, K.R., Roussel, S., & Paquin, S. (2010). *International policy and politics in Canada*. Toronto, ON: Pearson Canada.

Potter, E. (2009). *Branding Canada: Projecting Canada's soft power through public diplomacy*. Montreal, QC: McGill-Queen's University Press.

Smith, H.A., & Sjolander, C.T. (Eds.) (2013). *Canada in the world. Internationalism in Canadian foreign policy*. Don Mills, ON: Oxford University Press.

Warner, R. (Ed.). (2015). *Unsettled balance. Ethics, security, and Canada's international relations*. Vancouver: UBC Press.

Welsh, J. (2004). *At home in the world: Canada's global vision for the 21st century*. Toronto, ON: HarperCollins.

GLOSSARY

Act of Union, 1840 An act that united Upper and Lower Canada, creating the United Province of Canada.

Alternative dispute resolution A process where disputing parties choose a third party (rather than a judge) to try to resolve the dispute.

Alternative service delivery Methods of delivering government services apart from the use of traditional departments and agencies, with the goal of making government more businesslike and responsive to the needs of the recipients of services.

Anti-dumping duties Duties imposed on imports of a particular product when a foreign producer sells the product in the importing country for less than its "fair value."

Assimilation The process through which groups of individuals with a different culture learn and adopt the values and norms of the host society.

Asylum seekers Individuals who have sought international protection and whose claim for refugee status has not yet been determined.

Asymmetrical federal system A federal system in which some subnational governments have a different relationship with the national government, including different powers, than other subnational governments.

Attitudinal model of judicial decision making The view that judges pursue their own policy preferences in interpreting the law, as well as being influenced by their attitudes toward the facts of the case.

Authority The right to exercise power.

Balanced budget The practice of government spending no more than the revenues it collects annually.

Balfour Declaration (1926) A resolution of the Imperial Conference that declared that Britain and the dominions are autonomous and equal communities in no way subordinate one to another.

Bicameral legislature A legislature with two chambers or houses.

Bill of Rights, 1689 The bill that followed the Glorious Revolution of 1688, which added protections for parliamentary free speech, regular sessions, and other protections, and is generally regarded as the stage of British history when the Crown accepted the supremacy of Parliament.

Block grant The unconditional transfer of a block of money from the federal government to a provincial government.

Branch plants Factories set up outside the United States by an American company to produce and sell products in a foreign market.

British North America Act, 1867 An act of the Parliament of the United Kingdom establishing the Dominion of Canada. In 1982 it was renamed the Constitution Act, 1867.

Brokerage theory A perspective that maintains that parties are not differentiated by ideology and that they do not adopt consistent policy positions over time.

Budget Government statement that proposes tax increases or decreases as well as other revenue and borrowing measures, outlines the state of the economy and government finances in general, and often includes announcements of major new programs.

Bureaucracy Rule by offices and officials.

Buycotting The act of buying goods and services based on political or ethical considerations, or both.

Cabinet The active part of the Queen's Privy Council for Canada. Composed of the prime minister and ministers, it controls most of the executive and legislative powers of government.

Cabinet committees Groups of cabinet ministers who examine policy proposals from related policy fields and recommend to the plenary (full) cabinet what action should be taken. Their recommendations generally are accepted.

Cabinet secrecy A convention that forbids the disclosure of the views expressed by particular ministers during cabinet (and cabinet committee) discussions, in order to encourage frankness.

Cabinet solidarity The basic principle that ministers must avoid public disagreements over policy once cabinet decides on it, and that they must vote in unison in the House on government business.

Canada–European Union Comprehensive Economic and Trade Agreement (CETA) An agreement between Canada and the European Union that was signed in 2014 and will be implemented in 2016 if formal agreement is approved.

Canada Health Transfer A block grant intended to fund medicare and hospital insurance, although some conditions are involved.

Canada Social Transfer A block grant intended to fund post-secondary education, social assistance, early childhood education, and childcare programs.

Canada–United States Automotive Agreement, 1965 An agreement (often referred to as the "Auto Pact") that eliminated tariffs between the two countries on new automobiles, trucks, buses, and original vehicle parts, while providing guarantees about the level of production in Canada.

Canadian Bill of Rights An act of Parliament passed in 1960 establishing various rights and freedoms that only applies to matters under federal jurisdiction.

Canadian Judicial Council A body of senior judges established to review complaints about federally appointed judges.

Caucus Parliamentary members who belong to a particular party.

Central agencies The Prime Minister's Office and the Privy Council Office, which provide direct assistance to the prime minister and facilitate the setting of objectives by cabinet.

Central departments The Department of Finance and the Treasury Board Secretariat, which, along with the central agencies, advise cabinet and its committees and influence the direction and policies of the government.

Charlottetown Accord An agreement in 1992 on a broad package of constitutional changes, including Aboriginal self-government, Senate reform, and a statement of the characteristics of Canada. The agreement, which had the support of the prime minister, all premiers and territorial leaders, and four national Aboriginal leaders, was defeated in a referendum.

Charlottetown Conference, 1864 A meeting of the leaders of Canada and the Maritimes at which it was decided to hold further discussions about uniting the British North American colonies.

Charter dialogue The view that the Charter has created a dialogue between the courts and legislatures.

Charter of Rights and Freedoms As part of the Constitution Act, 1982, the Charter is superior to ordinary legislation, allows the courts to invalidate legislation, and applies to the actions of all governments and organizations under the control of government.

Citizens plus The idea that Indians possess certain rights in addition to the normal rights and duties of citizens.

Civic engagement A set of activities in the community, such as joining a voluntary organization, volunteering for the organization, helping others directly, or giving financial donations to charitable causes.

Civic nation A community based on a common historic territory, a community of laws and institutions, a sense of legal equality among community members, and a measure of common values, sentiments, and aspirations that binds the population together.

Civil disobedience The deliberate and public breaking of a law to draw attention to injustice.

Civil society The voluntary associations and non-governmental organizations that bring people together to achieve a common goal.

Class consciousness The awareness within a social class of their common interests and a willingness to act collectively on those interests.

Classic peacekeeping Activities carried out under the United Nations banner to support a ceasefire between countries in conflict or to supervise the implementation of a peace agreement.

Classical democratic theory The belief that it is desirable to have a large number of citizens from different backgrounds participating in political affairs.

Classical elite theory The belief that only a small ruling class has the knowledge and skills necessary to decide what is in the public interest, and that mass political participation is undesirable.

Classical federalism The view that a federal system should be based on autonomous federal and provincial governments, each with its own specific areas of responsibility.

Classical liberalism An ideological perspective based on a belief in a minimal role for government, leaving individuals free to pursue their interests and follow their own beliefs as long as they do not seriously harm others.

Closure A motion in the House of Commons to limit debate on a bill.

Coalition government A government in which two or more parties agree to jointly govern and share the cabinet positions.

Code Civil du Québec A codified system of law that is the basis of private law in Quebec.

Codified civil law A system of private law used in Quebec based on a comprehensive set of legal principles.

Cold War The severe tensions between the Western countries (led by the United States) and communist countries (led by the Soviet Union) that developed after the end of World War II and ended with the collapse of the Soviet Union in 1991.

Collaborative family law A process in which each party hires their own lawyer (or other professional) who helps the parties reach an acceptable settlement without going to court.

Collaborative federalism A trend in contemporary federalism in which both levels of government try to work together as equals in deciding some major policies.

Collective benefits Benefits to society as a whole.

Collective responsibility The convention that the cabinet as a group is responsible to the House of Commons for the decisions and actions of the government.

Committees of the Whole Committees composed of all members of the House using relaxed rules of debate and procedure to deal with supply motions or other topics.

Common law A body of law developed through the accumulation of court decisions that become binding precedents for similar future cases.

Competitive federalism A feature of Canadian federalism, beginning in the early 1960s, in which provincial and national governments competed to maximize their autonomy, power, and popularity with voters.

Comprehensive land claims agreements Agreements involving First Nations that had not signed treaties giving up their land.

Conditional grants Federal grants to provincial governments for specific programs that have to meet conditions set by the Canadian government.

Confidence chamber A legislative body (in Canada, the House of Commons) whose continued majority support is necessary for the government to remain in office.

Conscription crisis The imposition of compulsory military service during World War I that sharply divided many English and French Canadians.

Conservatism An ideological perspective that generally looks to laws based on traditional (religious) moral values and established institutions to maintain an orderly society.

Constitution The fundamental rules by which a country is governed.

Constitution Act, 1867 An act of the Parliament of the United Kingdom that established Canada as a federal union of Ontario, Quebec, Nova Scotia, and New Brunswick.

Constitution Act, 1982 This act patriated the Constitution, established a formula for amending the Constitution, added the Charter of Rights and Freedoms, recognized the rights of Aboriginal peoples, and made a commitment to the principle of equalization payments.

Constitutional Act, 1791 An act that divided Quebec into two separate colonies: Upper Canada and Lower Canada.

Constitutional Amendments Act, 1996 An act of Parliament that sets out the combination of provinces and regions whose support is needed before the Canadian cabinet presents proposed constitutional changes to Parliament.

Constitutional conventions Widely accepted informal constitutional rules.

Constitutional government A government that consistently acts in keeping with established fundamental rules and principles.

Cooperative federalism The feature of Canadian federalism following World War II in which federal and provincial governments generally cooperated under federal leadership in developing the welfare state.

Council of the Federation An organization established by the premiers to enable cooperation among the provinces and territories.

Countervailing duties Duties imposed on imports of a particular product that have been subsidized by the exporting country in a way that harms the home producers of that same product.

Court Challenges Program A federal government program that provided some money for individuals and groups seeking to challenge Canadian laws and government actions that violate equality rights and minority language rights.

The Crown The repository of all of the executive powers of the state and the supreme authority for government.

Cyberactivism Political activism that employs online communications tools such as websites, emails, blogs, and social networking services.

Declaratory power The right of the Canadian Parliament to declare any "local works or undertakings" within a province to be "for the general Advantage of Canada or for the Advantage of Two or more of the Provinces" and then legislate on that matter.

Deliberative democracy A form of democracy in which governing decisions are made based on discussion by citizens.

Democracy Rule by the people either directly or through the election of representatives.

Departmentalized cabinet A form of cabinet organization that emphasizes ministerial autonomy and relies on the prime minister and full cabinet to achieve coordination.

Deputy minister The administrative head of a department and the link between the minister who is politically responsible for the department and the non-partisan public servants in the department.

Differentiated citizenship The granting of special group-based legal or constitutional rights to national minorities and ethnic groups.

Direct democracy A form of democracy in which citizens are directly involved in making the governing decisions.

Disallowance power The right of the Canadian cabinet to disallow provincial legislation within one year of its passage.

Discretionary prerogative powers Powers that the monarch's representative may exercise upon his or her own personal discretion. Also called *personal prerogatives* or *reserve powers.*

Distinct society clause A clause in the Meech Lake Accord that the constitution should be interpreted in a manner consistent with the recognition of Quebec as a distinct society.

Durham Report, 1839 A report by the British governor Lord Durham that recommended the union of Upper and Lower Canada and the adoption of responsible government.

Electoral district association An association of members of a political party in a territorial area that is represented by a member in the House of Commons.

Electoral system The system by which the votes that people cast are translated into the representation of political parties in the House of Commons.

Employment equity Programs that encourage or require the hiring and promotion of women (or other groups) for positions in which they are underrepresented.

Equalization payments Unconditional grants from the Canadian government to the governments of the poorer provinces to bring their revenue-raising capabilities up to a national standard.

Estimates The money the government says is needed by government departments and agencies for the next fiscal year.

Ethnic groups Groups of immigrants who have left their countries of origin to enter another society, but who do not occupy a separate territory in their new homeland.

Ethnic nation A community with a distinctive culture and history, which operates solely for the benefit of that cultural group. Members of the ethnic nation share common ancestry, language, customs, and traditions.

Executive departments Organizations headed by cabinet ministers.

Executive federalism The basic nature of federal–provincial interaction since the 1940s, involving the interaction of the executives of the federal and provincial governments.

Federal Court of Canada A court that hears cases related to certain acts of Parliament, such as laws concerning copyright and patents, citizenship and immigration, and access to information and privacy. As well it hears appeals against the rulings of national administrative tribunals.

Federal system A system of governing in which authority is divided and shared between the central government and provincial governments, with each deriving its authority from the constitution.

Feminism An ideology that seeks to define and achieve equal political, economic, social, cultural, and personal rights for women.

First Ministers conferences Formal meetings of the prime minister and premiers, along with large supporting delegations of ministers, aides, and officials.

First Ministers meetings Informal private meetings of the prime minister and premiers.

Foreign Investment Review Agency (FIRA) A Canadian government agency established in 1973 to review proposals from foreigners to take over Canadian businesses or to set up new businesses.

Formal executive That part of the executive consisting of the Queen, the governor general, and the Queen's Privy Council for Canada, which possesses formal constitutional authority and by convention acts on the advice of the political executive.

Formative events theory A theory that emphasizes the importance of a crucial formative event in establishing the basic character of a country's political culture.

Founding fragments theory The theory that in the founding of new societies, only a fragment of the political culture of the "mother country" formed the basis for the political culture of the new society.

Franchise The right to vote.

Free rider An individual who enjoys the benefits of group action without contributing.

Generational replacement The process through which younger-age cohorts enter the electorate and replace their older predecessors.

Gerrymandering The drawing of boundaries for partisan advantage, particularly for the advantage of the governing party.

Glorious Revolution The series of events that led to the removal of James II from the throne in 1688, his replacement by William and Mary, and their acceptance of the Bill of Rights, 1689.

Governance The sharing by government of the process of governing with societal partners such as private sector organizations and non-governmental organizations; governing changes from the "command and control" model to the "partnership" model.

Government The set of institutions that have the authority to make executive decisions; present proposed laws, taxes, and expenditures to the appropriate legislative body; and oversee the implementation of laws and policies.

Governor in Council The formal name given to cabinet in order to cloak its decisions with constitutional authority. The phrase means that the governor general is acting on the advice of the Queen's Privy Council for Canada, the active part of which is the cabinet.

Hawthorn Report A Canadian government report that recommended that Indians should have rights in addition to those of other citizens and not be forced to assimilate into the majority society.

Health policy A special type of social policy concerned with curative and preventive measures.

Heritage language All languages other than the Aboriginal languages of the First Nations and Inuit peoples and the official languages of English and French.

House leaders Members of each party who are responsible for their party's strategy in the House of Commons, including negotiating the parliamentary timetable with other House leaders.

House officers Political officers of the House of Commons.

Human security A view of security that focuses on the protection of people from various threats to their well-being.

Identities Individual and group self-understandings of their traits and characteristics.

Ideological party A party that articulates distinct and consistent worldviews.

Implied bill of rights The judicial theory that rights are implied by the preamble to the Constitution Act, 1867, and therefore could not be infringed upon by ordinary legislation.

Independent immigrants People with specific occupational skills, experience, and personal qualifications who are selected on the basis of criteria that assess their ability to adapt and contribute to the country.

Individual ministerial responsibility The responsibility of individual cabinet ministers to the House of Commons for the decisions and actions of the department they administer.

Inherent right of self-government The perspective that First Nations have the right to govern themselves based on their independence before European colonization, a right that was never ceded.

Inherent Right of Self-Government Policy A Canadian government policy adopted in 1995 recognizing an inherent right to Aboriginal self-government.

Initiative A proposed new law or changes to an existing law drafted by an individual or group rather than by a government or legislature. The proposal is put to a vote by the people after enough signatures have been collected.

Institutionalized cabinet A form of cabinet organization that emphasizes collective decision making and seeks to achieve it by a highly structured system of cabinet committees and central agencies.

Institutionalized interest group A group that has a formal organizational structure, a well-established membership base, paid professional staff, executive officers, permanent offices, and the capability to respond to the interests of its members by developing policy positions and promoting them through regular contact with government policy-makers.

Integration The multidimensional process through which an immigrant becomes a member of the host society.

Interest groups Organizations that pursue the common interests or values of groups of people, particularly by trying to influence the making and implementation of public policies.

Internationalism The idea that each country should take a constructive role in managing global disputes by working with other countries rather than acting unilaterally. This involves actively supporting international institutions and promoting international law.

Interstate federalism A federal system in which provincial interests are represented primarily by provincial governments.

Intrastate federalism A federal system in which provincial interests are represented in national political institutions.

Investment Canada A Canadian government agency established in 1985 with a mandate to attract foreign investment.

Issue-oriented group A group formed to express views on a particular issue, concern, or grievance, but with little organizational capacity and usually not long-lasting.

Joint committees Standing committees composed of members of both the House of Commons and the Senate.

Judicial Advisory Committee A committee that assesses candidates for appointment as superior court judges.

Judicial Committee of the Privy Council The highest court of appeal for Canada for constitutional and civil matters until 1949.

Judicial independence The principle that the courts are expected to be independent of government and its agencies, legislative bodies, and other influences.

Judicial review The authority of the courts to invalidate laws passed by Parliament or provincial legislatures that they deem to be in violation of the Constitution.

Keynesian economics A perspective on managing the economy through government stimulation of the economy when business investment is weak and cooling the economy when inflation is rampant.

Leader of Her Majesty's Loyal Opposition The person who usually leads the second-largest party in the House and who would normally be considered the most likely to be prime minister in the event of a change in government.

Leadership convention A meeting of party members to select a new leader.

Leadership review The formal process that sets out the procedures for evaluating and possibly replacing a party leader.

Legal model of judicial decision making The view that judges base their decisions on a careful reading of the relevant law.

Legislative committees Temporary committees of the House established primarily to review a specific bill.

Legitimacy The acceptance by the people that those in positions of authority have the right to govern.

Liberal democracy A political system in which the powers of government are limited by law, the rights of the people to freely engage in political activity are well established, and fair elections are held to choose those who make governing decisions.

Liberal internationalism The idea that the application of liberal values—including rights and freedoms, democracy, the rule of law, and justice, combined with the growing interaction and interdependence among the peoples, economies, and countries of the world—can make a peaceful world possible, particularly through the development of international institutions.

Liberalism An ideological perspective that emphasizes the value of individual freedom based on a belief that individuals are generally capable of using reason in pursuit of their own interests.

Life-cycle effects The tendency for people to vote at higher rates as they age.

Line departments Departments that deliver the basic programs and services of government.

Lobbying An effort to influence government decisions, particularly through direct personal communication with key government decision makers.

Loyalists Americans who remained loyal to the British Crown at the time of the War of Independence. Subsequently, many Loyalists migrated to the British North American colonies.

Macroeconomic policy Deals with the general health of the economy, in particular with monetary policy, economic stability, employment, the level of inflation, and with the overall level of spending, taxation, and deficits.

Majority government A governing party that has a majority of seats in the House of Commons regardless of whether it received a majority of votes in an election.

Maritime Rights Movement A political movement in the 1920s that sought better terms for the Maritime provinces within Canada.

Marxist theory A theory that views capitalist countries as inherently biased toward the interests of capitalism and the capitalist class.

Meech Lake Accord An agreement on constitutional change reached by the prime minister and premiers in 1987 that failed to be ratified by all provincial legislatures. The accord satisfied the conditions laid out by Quebec for signing the Constitution Act, 1982, while extending the powers granted to Quebec to all provinces.

Microeconomic policy Focuses on the behaviour of individual or smaller sets of actors like consumers, firms, unions, and local governments.

Millennium Development Goals Goals established by the United Nations for the development of poorer countries.

Minority government A single party forms the government, but does not have a majority of members in the House of Commons.

Mixed member proportional system An electoral system in which voters cast one vote for the party they prefer and one vote for the candidate they prefer. Some legislators represent the district in which they received the most votes, while other legislators are selected based on the proportion of votes received by their party.

Monetarism The perspective that autonomous central banks should limit the growth of the money supply and keep interest rates high when needed to prevent inflation.

Mother tongue The first language a person learned at home in childhood and still understands.

Multination state A state that contains more than one nation.

Multiparty system with a dominant party One large party receives about 40 percent of the vote, and the two largest parties together win about two-thirds of voter support.

Multiparty system without a dominant party Competition where there is no dominant party and three or four parties are well placed to form coalitions.

Nation A historical community with its own institutions, occupying a given territory or homeland, and sharing a distinct language and culture.

National Energy Program A Canadian government program adopted in 1980 that included keeping oil prices below the international level, increasing the Canadian government's share of oil revenues, establishing a federal Crown corporation to be involved in the oil industry, and encouraging and subsidizing oil exploration on federal lands in the Arctic and offshore Newfoundland.

National minority A culturally distinct and potentially self-governing society that has been incorporated into a larger state.

National Policy A Canadian government policy adopted in 1879 that included a high tariff on the import of manufactured products, railway construction, and the encouragement of immigration to Western Canada.

National security Protection of a country from foreign threats to its population, territory, and independence.

Nation-state A state in which the population shares a single ethnic culture.

Neoliberalism An ideological perspective based on a strong belief in a free market system with the role of government reduced to a bare minimum, individuals responsible for their own well-being, taxes substantially reduced, global free trade pursued and barriers to the international flow of finance and investment removed.

Neo-pluralism A modification of pluralist theory that views business interests as having a privileged position in influencing government policy-making.

New Public Management (NPM) The adoption of the practices of private business in the administrative activities of government.

New social movements Social movements concerned particularly with developing a collective sense of identity among those who are deemed to suffer from oppression, along with adopting new cultural values and lifestyles.

New social movement theory A theory that in post-industrial society new social movements have developed, particularly among the new middle class, which is interested in post-materialist values such as a concern for the quality of life, identity, participation, and individual freedom.

North American Aerospace Defense Command A joint American–Canadian organization that provides for the detection of and response to an attack on North America, particularly by aircraft and missiles.

North American Free Trade Agreement An agreement between Canada, the United States, and Mexico that established a high level of economic integration in North America.

North Atlantic Treaty Organization An alliance of the United States, Canada, and many European countries formed during the Cold War.

Notwithstanding clause A provision in the Charter of Rights and Freedoms that allows Parliament or a provincial legislature to explicitly declare that a particular law (related to some sections of the Charter) shall operate notwithstanding the provisions of the Charter.

Oakes test A Supreme Court of Canada ruling setting out basic principles in applying the reasonable limits clause.

Officers of Parliament Independent officials who assist Parliament in holding government accountable and protecting various rights of Canadians.

Official multiculturalism A policy introduced in 1971 that encouraged individuals to embrace the culture and tradition of their choice while retaining Canadian citizenship.

Omnibus bills Proposed laws changing legislation on a large number of unrelated topics.

Open federalism The Harper government's approach to federalism involving such measures as transferring more money to provincial governments, respecting the constitutional division of powers and provincial autonomy, and limiting the use of the federal spending power.

Parliamentary supremacy The principle that Parliament is the supreme law-making body whose ability to legislate has not been restricted by a superior constitutional document.

Party conventions Meetings of party members that are held to elect party officials and debate policy and amendments to the party's constitution.

Party discipline The expectation that parliamentary members will vote in keeping with the position that their party has adopted in caucus.

Party identification A sense of attachment to a particular political party.

Party system A pattern of electoral competition that emerges between two or more parties.

Party whips Members of each party who maintain party discipline and ensure that members attend votes.

Pay equity A requirement that equal pay be given for work of equal value, in particular by increasing the pay of those working in occupations staffed primarily by women to the level of pay of equivalent occupations primarily staffed by men.

Peace operations A wide range of activities with the aim of building and enforcing peace, including peacekeeping, peace building, and peace enforcement.

Peak associations Organizations representing a particular major interest based on a number of related interest groups rather than individual members.

Peripheral dependence perspective The view that Canada is unable or unwilling to develop independent foreign policies because of constraints imposed by the United States.

Permanent residents Immigrants who are allowed to live in Canada and receive certain rights and privileges, while remaining a citizen of their home country. Permanent residents must pay taxes and respect all Canadian laws.

Plebiscitary democracy The use of referendums, initiatives, and recall procedures as an alternative to what some view as the elite-oriented nature of representative democracy.

Pluralist theory The theory that the freedom of individuals to establish and join groups that are not controlled by the government results in a variety of groups having an ability to influence the decisions of government, with no group having a dominant influence.

Pluralization A new term to describe the increasing social divisions based on gender, ethnicity, sexual orientation, family form, age, or relation to the labour market.

Policy community Collaboration of government officials responsible for a particular policy area and relevant institutionalized interest groups in developing public policies.

Policy context Those multilayered, interactive and changeable elements connected with the policy process which bound the freedom of choice of policy actors, or compel certain options to be chosen, or establish what matters are under active consideration by political societies or political actors.

Policy paradigms The generally accepted norms for how the policy-making process takes place and what relevant questions and evidence are acceptable.

Political culture The fundamental political values, beliefs, and orientations that are widely held within a political community.

Political discourse The ways in which politics is discussed and the rhetoric that is used in political persuasion.

Political efficacy A belief that government is responsive to the people and that they can influence what government does.

Political executive The prime minister, cabinet, and ministers of state.

Political ideology A set of ideas, values, and beliefs about politics, society, and the economic system often based on assumptions about human nature.

Political participation Actions people take to raise awareness about issues, to influence the choice of government personnel, and to shape the content of legislation and public policies.

Political party An organization that endorses one or more of its members as candidates and supports their election.

Political socialization The process by which new generations and immigrants are socialized into the political culture.

Politics Activities related to influencing, making, and implementing collective decisions.

Polyethnic rights Group-based rights that allow ethnic groups and religious minorities to express their cultural distinctiveness without discrimination.

Polyethnic state A state that contains many ethnic groups.

Post-materialist theory A theory that those who have grown up in relative security and affluence are more likely to give priority to post-materialist values rather than materialist values.

Post-materialist values Values such as self-expression, participation in economic and political decisions, emphasis on the quality of life, tolerance of diversity, and concern for environmental protection.

Power The ability to affect the behaviour of others, particularly by getting them to act in ways that they would not otherwise have done.

Preferential voting An electoral system in which voters rank candidates in order of preference. If no candidate receives a majority of first preferences, the second preferences of the candidate with the least votes are added to the votes of the other candidates. The process continues until one candidate has a majority.

Prerogative power The powers the monarch once uniquely possessed that have not been taken away by Parliament.

Prime minister The head of government, meaning the person chosen by the governor general to form a government able to retain the confidence of a majority of the elected house of Parliament, the House of Commons.

Prime Minister's Office Provides partisan political advice to the prime minister and is staffed by supporters of the party in power.

Prime minister–centred cabinet A form of cabinet organization in which the first minister is so powerful that the nominal mechanisms for collective decision making, such as cabinet committees and central agencies, serve the prime minister's personal agenda.

Principal–agent theory A theory based on the idea that the bureaucrat, who is supposed to follow the will of the minister or the legislature, often uses specialized knowledge to thwart this arrangement.

Principal power perspective The view that changes in the international system have resulted in Canada's becoming a principal power able to independently assert its national values and interests in international politics.

Private bills Proposed laws that are of concern to a limited group.

Private law Areas of law dealing with the relationships among individuals, groups, and businesses that are primarily of private interest rather than general public interest.

Private members' bills A public bill put forward by a member of Parliament who is not in the cabinet.

Private sector The sector of economic society that exists in a competitive environment and strives to maximize profit for private owners, be they corporations, family-owned businesses, or self-employed individuals.

Privy Council Office The central agency that provides non-partisan policy advice to the prime minister and cabinet.

Procedural officers of Parliament The staff who provide services to the House of Commons and Senate.

Progressive movement A late nineteenth-century movement that sought to break the "spoils system" in government by making the public sector at all levels more businesslike and shielding it from the political realm.

Proportional representation system An electoral system in which the proportion of seats a party receives in the legislative body reflects the proportion of votes the party obtained.

Protest activities Political acts that include non-violent actions such as signing a petition, boycotts, peaceful marches, demonstrations, and strikes. They may sometimes involve the use of violence to damage property or harm the opponents of the cause.

Provincial courts Trial courts whose judges are appointed and paid by the provincial government.

Provincial/territorial nominees Permanent immigrants who are nominated by provinces or territories on the basis of their skills, education, and work experience.

Public bills Proposed laws that have an impact on the whole of society or are designed to promote the general welfare.

Public bureaucracy The staffs of a variety of governing institutions.

Public choice The model of the policy process whose basic assumption is that all actors in the public sphere are driven by self-interest and public policy reflects this.

Public interest group A group that pursues goals that can be viewed as being for the public good and do not benefit members of the group exclusively.

Public law Laws concerning the relationship of the state to individuals and laws concerning the authority and operations of the state.

Public policy What government does or does not do, purposefully, or what it compels or encourages others in society to do, or not to do.

Public sector The institutions and agencies of the state, ideally concerned with acting in the public interest.

Purposive incentives Incentives to join a group based on the satisfaction that is gained by expressing one's values or promoting a cause in which one believes.

Quasi-federalism A system in which the federal government dominates provincial governments, particularly through its use of the powers of reservation and disallowance to invalidate provincial legislation.

Quebec Act, 1774 An act of the British Parliament that guaranteed that Catholics would be able to freely practise their religion, the privileges of the Catholic Church would be maintained, and the French system of civil (private) law would be used alongside British criminal law.

Quebec Civil Code A codified system of law that is the basis of private law in Quebec.

Quiet Revolution A series of political, institutional, and social reforms ushered in under Quebec Liberal leader Jean Lesage beginning in 1960.

Rational choice theory A theory based on the assumption that individuals rationally pursue their own self-interest.

Rational model A model of the policy process that maintains decision makers are oriented toward achieving objectives and influenced by a desire to be as complete as possible with regard to examination of options to reach those objectives.

Realist perspective The view that in a world without a central authority able to impose order, each country is concerned primarily with survival, security, and promotion of its own national interests.

Reasonable limits clause A clause of the Charter of Rights and Freedoms that allows for reasonable limits on rights and freedoms, provided the limits can be demonstrably justified in a free and democratic society.

Recall A procedure that allows citizens to recall their representative and require that a new election be held, provided sufficient names are obtained on a petition.

References Opinions of the courts on questions asked by the federal or provincial government.

Referendum A vote by the people on a particular question asked by the government or legislative body.

Refugees People living in or outside Canada who fear persecution in their home country or whose removal from Canada to their country of origin would subject them to torture, a risk to their life, or a risk of cruel and unusual treatment.

Representative democracy A form of democracy in which citizens elect representatives to make governing decisions on their behalf.

Reservation power The right of a lieutenant governor to reserve the passage of provincial legislation until that legislation is approved by the Canadian cabinet.

Residual power Legislative power over matters not listed in the Constitution.

Responsibility to protect The responsibility of a state to protect its population from genocide, war crimes, ethnic cleansing, and crimes against humanity and, as a last resort, the responsibility of the international community, particularly through the United Nations, to intervene if a state is unwilling or unable to protect its population.

Responsible government A governing system in which the executive is responsible to an elected, representative legislative body and must retain its support to remain in office.

Restorative justice The perspective that justice should focus on offenders taking responsibility for their actions; repairing the harm that has been caused; and reconciling the offender, the victim, and the community.

Royal Commission on Aboriginal Peoples A Royal Commission established by the Canadian government that recommended a fundamental restructuring of the relationship between Aboriginal and settler societies based on the recognition of Aboriginal nationhood.

Royal Proclamation, 1763 Established British rule over the former French colonies and placed "Indians" under the protection of the British Crown.

Rule of law The principle that individuals should be subject only to known, predictable, and impartial rules, rather than to the arbitrary orders of those in governing positions.

Runoff election A second election that is held (often with only the top two candidates) if no candidate in the first election wins a majority of votes.

Scientific management A complex system of management of the production process, often popularly associated with time and motion studies, which maintains that there is one best way to increase output.

Security Council A key body of the United Nations responsible for maintaining international peace and security. It consists of 5 permanent members who each has a veto and 10 members elected by the UN General Assembly for two-year terms.

Selective benefits Particular benefits that are made available to the members of an interest group but are not available to the public as a whole.

Self-government rights Group-based rights that grant a national minority some kind of territorial jurisdiction or autonomy over its political and cultural affairs.

Self-interest groups Interest groups that are primarily concerned with selective benefits that are directed toward their members.

Semi-independent public agency A government organization that has a degree of independence from executive controls and parliamentary scrutiny.

Sentencing circles Groups that may include the guilty individual, the victim, their families, elders, and other interested members of the community, along with the prosecutor, defence lawyer, and police officers. The goal is to reach a consensus about what measures are needed to reintegrate the offender as a responsible member of the community and to assist the victim.

Shared-cost programs Provincial programs in which the Canadian government generally paid half the costs.

Single-member plurality electoral system (SMP) An electoral system in which voters in each district elect a single representative. The candidate with the most votes is elected, regardless of whether that candidate received the majority of votes.

Single transferable vote system An electoral system in which voters mark their preferences for a number of candidates in a multimember district with a certain percentage (quota) of votes needed for a candidate to win. The second preferences that are surplus to what the winning candidates need are transferred to candidates who have not reached the quota. This process continues until all the seats in the district are filled.

Social capital The networks, norms of generalized reciprocity, and trust that foster coordination and cooperation for mutual benefit.

Social class A large category of people who hold a similar position in the hierarchy of society and in the economy.

Social conservatism An ideology based on a commitment to traditional ideas about the family and morality.

Social democracy The perspective that greater social and economic equality is needed for a country to be fully democratic.

Social movement A network of groups and individuals that seeks major social and political changes, particularly by acting outside of established political institutions.

Social policy Commonly understood to include public policies that knit communities together in a sense of fraternity and mutual aid, such as income redistribution, work-related benefits, and fiscal transfers.

Social rights Rights that require government action, such as the right to education, housing, or employment.

Socialism An ideological perspective that emphasizes the value of social and economic equality and generally is critical of the capitalist economic system.

Socioeconomic status A combination of income (or wealth), education, and occupational status.

Solidary incentives Incentives to join a group for social reasons, such as the opportunities to attend meetings and interact with others.

Speaker The presiding officer of the House of Commons, who is responsible for applying the rules and procedures, maintaining order in debate, and overseeing the administration of the Commons.

Special committees Committees of the House established to study a particular issue.

Special representation rights The provision of guaranteed representation for particular groups in legislative bodies or other political institutions.

Specific claims Claims by Aboriginal groups based on allegations that treaties and other legal obligations of the Canadian government have not been fulfilled or that the Canadian government has not properly administered Aboriginal lands and other assets.

Speech from the Throne Government's indication of what it considers to be the state of the country, together with a general outline of the kinds of legislation that it has planned for the parliamentary session the speech introduces.

Spending power The ability of the Canadian government to spend money as it sees fit, even on matters under provincial jurisdiction.

Stages (or policy cycle) approach Sees the policy process as including a number of separate elements, or stages, that altogether add up to a sequence of events that unfold in logical succession in a more or less cyclical fashion.

Standing committees Permanent committees of the House whose responsibilities include detailed examination of proposed legislation and review of departmental estimates.

State An independent, self-governing country whose governing institutions are able to make and enforce rules that are binding on the people living within a particular territory.

State-centred theory The theory that the state is largely independent of social forces and thus state actors are relatively free to act on their own values and interests.

Status Indians Those of Indian ancestry who are listed in the official government registry and are entitled to certain benefits, including exemption from taxation on property or income earned on the reserve.

Statute of Westminster, 1931 An act of the Parliament of the United Kingdom ending British control of Canada.

Statutory law A law that has been passed by an act of Parliament or a provincial legislature.

Strategic model of judicial decision making The view that a bargaining process among the judges takes place for them to reach a majority or a unanimous decision.

Subcultures Variations on the national political culture.

Subordinate (delegated) legislation Authority for subordinate legislation that comes from a primary piece of legislation passed by

Parliament and takes the form of orders-in-council or regulations made by a minister or agency.

Superior courts Courts in each province whose judges are appointed and paid by the Canadian government.

Supply-side economics The perspective that reducing taxes on those who supply goods and services is the most effective way to achieve economic growth.

Supreme Court of Canada The highest judicial body in Canada since 1949.

Tariff A tax or customs duty on imported goods.

Third sector Voluntary, non-profit organizations that contribute to the general good of the public.

Time allocation A motion in the House of Commons that allocates the time that can be spent debating a bill.

Tort Harmful actions, negligence, or words that allow the injured party to sue for damages.

Tory touch An element of traditional conservatism that includes the defence of a hierarchical rule by a privileged elite on behalf of the collective good of the nation.

Trade in Services Agreement (TiSA) A potential agreement being negotiated by 24 countries including Canada, the United States, and the European Union that would establish free trade in services including a major reduction in government regulation of services.

Trans-Pacific Partnership (TPP) A proposed free trade agreement involving 12 countries including Canada.

Treaty federalism The view that First Nations and the Canadian government representing later settlers should establish nation-to-nation agreements that enable the nations as co-sovereigns to coexist peacefully as autonomous entities within Canada.

Triple-E Senate A proposal that the Senate be reformed to be elected and effective based on equal representation from each province regardless of population size.

Two-and-a-half party system Pattern of competition whereby two major parties win at least three-quarters of the vote, and a third party receives a much smaller share of the vote.

Two-party system A pattern of competition in which there are two, or primarily two, parties.

Two-party systems Two major parties win 90 percent or more of the popular vote and the gap between their vote shares is small.

Unitary system A system of governing in which authority rests with the central government; regional and local governments are subordinate to the central government.

Volunteering Providing unpaid service to help others.

Welfare state A country whose governments ensure that all people have a minimum standard of living and are provided protection from hardships, including those caused by unemployment, sickness, disability, and old age.

Westminster Model The model of representative and responsible government used in the United Kingdom and in other countries that emulate it.

White Paper on Indians A 1969 Canadian government discussion paper that proposed to end the different legal status of Indians.

Whitehall Model The traditional British style of public administration with such features as ministerial responsibility, public service anonymity and neutrality, secrecy, and the merit principle.

World Trade Organization (WTO) An organization of more than 150 countries (including Canada) that establishes global rules of trade, including the lowering of trade barriers and procedures for dispute settlements.

REFERENCES

A.-G. Canada v. Lavell; Isaac v. Bédard [1974] S.C.R.

Abdelal, R., Herrera, Y., Johnston, A., & McDermott, R. (2005, July 22). Identity as a variable. Retrieved from www.wcfia. harvard.edu/sites/default/files/1076__YH_identityvariable.pdf

Abele, F., & Prince, M.J. (2007). Constructing political spaces for aboriginal communities in Canada. In I. Peach (Ed.), *Constructing tomorrow's federalism: New perspectives on Canadian governance* (pp. 171–200). Winnipeg, MB: University of Manitoba Press.

Abella, I., & Troper, H. (2000). *None is too many. Canada and the Jews of Europe, 1933–1948*. Toronto, ON: Key Porter.

Aboriginal Affairs and Northern Development Canada (2010a). Canada's statement of support on the United Nations Declaration on the Rights of Indigenous Peoples. Retrieved from www. aandc-aadnc.gc.ca

Aboriginal Affairs and Northern Development Canada (2010b). *Registered Indian population by sex and residence 2010*. Retrieved from www.aandc-aadnc.gc.ca

Aboriginal Affairs and Northern Development Canada (2014). Urban Aboriginal Peoples. Retrieved from http://www.aadnc-aandc. gc.ca/eng/1100100014265/1369225120949

Aboriginal Affairs and Northern Development Canada (2015). Comprehensive claims. Retrieved from https://www.aadnc-aandc. gc.ca/eng/1100100030577/1100100030578

Access to Information Review Task Force (2002). Making it work for Canadians: Report of the Access to Information Review Task Force, June 2002. Her Majesty the Queen in Right of Canada, Catalogue Number: BT22-83/2002-MRC.

Adams, M. (2003). *Fire and ice: The United States, Canada and the myth of converging values*. Toronto: Penguin Canada.

Adams, M. (2007). *Unlikely utopia: The surprising triumph of Canadian pluralism*. Toronto, ON: Viking Canada.

Agocs, C. (2012). "Representative bureaucracy?" Employment equity in the public service of Canada. Paper presented at the 2012 Annual General Meeting of the Canadian Political Science Association, Edmonton, AB.

Ajzenstat, J. (2003). *The once and future democracy: An essay in political thought*. Montreal, QC: McGill-Queen's University Press.

Albrow, M. (1991). Bureaucracy. In V. Bogdanor (Ed.), *The Blackwell encyclopedia of political science* (pp. 61–64). Oxford, UK: Basil Blackwell.

Almond, G., & Verba, S. (1963). *The civic culture: Political attitudes and democracy in five nations*. Princeton, NJ: Princeton University Press.

Amnesty International (2014). Missing and murdered indigenous women and girls. Understanding the numbers. Retrieved from http://www.amnesty.ca/blog/missing-and-murdered-indigenous-women-and-girls-understanding-the-numbers

Andersen, R., Curtis, J., & Grabb, E. (2006). Trends in civic association activity in four democracies: The special case of women in the United States. *American Sociological Review, 71*, 376–400.

Anderson, C. (2010). Regional heterogeneity and policy preferences in Canada: 1979–2006. *Regional and Federal Studies, 20* (4–5), 447–468.

Atleo, S. (2011, October 10). It's time to reset the relationship between First Nations and Canada. *Globe and Mail*.

Aucoin, P. (1995). *The new public management: Canada in comparative perspective*. Montreal, QC: Institute for Research on Public Policy.

Aucoin, P., Smith, J., & Dinsdale, G. (2004). *Responsible government: Clarifying essentials, dispelling myths and exploring change*. Ottawa, ON: Canadian Centre for Management Development.

Axworthy, L. (1997). Canada and human security: The need for leadership. *International Journal, 52* (2), 183–196.

Axworthy, T.S. (2008). *Everything old is new again: Observations on parliamentary reform*. Kingston, ON: Centre for the Study of Democracy, Queen's University.

Bakvis, H., & Skogstad, G. (Eds.). (2008). *Canadian federalism: Performance, effectiveness, and legitimacy* (2nd ed.). Toronto, ON: Oxford University Press.

Bakvis, H., Baier, G., & Brown, D.M. (2009). *Contested federalism: Certainty and ambiguity in the Canadian federation*. Toronto, ON: Oxford University Press.

Ball, T., Dagger, R., Christian, W., & Campbell, C. (2010). *Political ideologies and the democratic ideal* (2nd Canadian ed.). Toronto, ON: Pearson Education Canada.

Bank of Canada (2015). Drilling down—Understanding oil prices and their economic impact. Remarks by Timothy Lane, Deputy Director, to the Madison International Trade Association, Madison Wisconsin, January 13, 2015.

Banting, K., & Myles, J. (2014). Introduction. In K. Banting & J. Myles (Eds.). *Inequality and the fading of redistributive politics*. Vancouver, BC: UBC Press.

Banting, K., & Myles, J. (2015). Framing the new inequality: The politics of income redistribution in Canada. In David A. Green, W. Craig Riddell, and France St-Hilaire (Eds.). *Income inequality: The Canadian story*. Montreal, QC: Institute for Research on Public Policy, 1–27.

Bantjes, R. (2007). *Social movements in a global context: Canadian perspectives*. Toronto, ON: Canadian Scholars' Press.

Baran, Y. (2011). Social media in campaign 2011: A noncanonical take on the Twitter effect. *Policy Options* (June–July), 82–85.

Bargiel, J.-S. (2012). Federal voter turnout in First Nations reserves. Ottawa, ON: Elections Canada. Retrieved from www.elections. ca/content.aspx?section=res&dir=rec/part/fvt&document=index& lang=e

Barney, D. (2000). *Prometheus wired: The hope for democracy in the age of network technology.* Vancouver, BC: UBC Press.

Barsh, R. (1994). Canada's Aboriginal peoples: Social integration or disintegration? *Canadian Journal of Native Studies, 14* (1), 1–46.

Barsh, R., Fraser, M., Bull, F., Provost, T., & Smith, K. (1997). The Prairie Indian vote in Canadian politics 1965–1993: A critical case study from Alberta. *Great Plains Research, 7* (1), 3–26.

Bates-Earner, N., Carin, B., Lee, M.H., & Lim, W. (2012). Post-2015 development agenda: Goals, targets and indicators. The Centre for International Governance Innovation and the Korea Development Institute. Retrieved from sustainabledevelopment.un.org/content/documents/775cigi.pdf

Batson, C.D., Janoski, M.L., & Hanson, M. (1978). Buying kindness: Effect of an extrinsic incentive for helping on perceived altruism. *Journal of Personality and Social Psychology, 40,* 86–91.

Batt, S. (2005). Marching to different drummers: Health advocacy groups in Canada and funding from the pharmaceutical industry. Retrieved from www.whp-apsf/pdf/corpfunding.pdf

Baum, M. (2002). Sex, lies, and war: How soft news brings foreign policy to the inattentive public. *American Political Science Review, 96,* 91–109.

BC Ministry of Education (2008). *Program guide for graduation transitions.* Victoria, BC: Author.

BC Treaty Commission (2008). Why treaties—a legal perspective. Retrieved from http://www.bctreaty.net/files/pdf_documents/why_treaties_update_Aug08.pdf

Beck, J.M. (1968). *Pendulum of power: Canada's general elections.* Toronto, ON: Prentice-Hall.

Bédard, M. (2012). Omnibus bills: Frequently asked questions. Legal and Legislative Affairs Division, Library of Parliament, October 1, 2012.

Bedford, D. (2003). Aboriginal voter participation in Nova Scotia and New Brunswick. *Electoral Insight, 5* (3), 16–20.

Bedford, D. (2010). Emancipation as oppression: The *Marshall* decision and self-government. *Journal of Canadian Studies 44* (1), 68–87.

Bedford, D., & Pobihushchy, S. (1996). On-reserve Status Indian voter participation in the Maritimes. *Canadian Journal of Native Studies, 15,* 255–278.

Beeby, D. (2014, October 16). Revenue Canada targets birdwatchers for political activity. Retrieved from http://www.cbc.ca/news/politics/revenue-canada-targets-birdwatchers-for-political-activity-1.2799546

Beeby, D. (2014, September 15). Open letter from academics calls for moratorium on CRA political audit. Retrieved from http://www.cbc.ca/news/politics/academics-open-letter-calls-for-moratorium-on-political-tax-audits-1.2765967

Beeby, D. (2015, September 24). Poll ordered by Harper found strong support for niqab ban at citizenship ceremonies. CBC News. Retrieved from: http://www.cbc.ca/news/politics/canada-election-2015-niqab-poll-pco-1.3241895

Bélanger, E., & Nadeau, R. (2011). The Bloc Québécois: Capsized by the orange wave. In J. Pammett & C. Dornan (Eds.), *The Canadian federal election of 2011* (pp. 111–137). Toronto, ON: Dundurn Press.

Bell, D.V.J. (1992). *The roots of disunity. A study of Canadian political culture* (rev. ed.). Toronto, ON: Oxford University Press.

Bellamy, A. (2009). Realizing the responsibility to protect. *International Studies Perspectives, 10,* 111–128.

Benoit, K., & Laver, M. (2006). Party Policy in Modern Democracies. New York: Routledge.

Benzie, R. (2015, October 21). Electoral reform looms for Canada. *The Toronto Star.*

Berdahl, L. (2010). *Whither Western alienation: Shifting patterns of Western Canadian discontent with the federal government.* Calgary, AB: Canada West Foundation.

Bernard, P., Jr. (2006). Canada and human security: From the Axworthy doctrine to middle power internationalism. *American Review of Canadian Studies, 36* (2), 233–261.

Berthiaume, L. (2012, April 27). Hawkish Baird urged Libyan rebels to keep up fight. *Montreal Gazette.*

Bevelander, P., & Pendakur, R. (2007). Minorities, social capital and voting. IZA Discussion Paper No. 2928. IZA. Bonn, Germany. Institute for the Study of Labor. Retrieved from http://ftp.iza.org/dp2928.pdf

Bevelander, P., & Pendakur, R. (2009). Social capital and voting participation of immigrants and minorities in Canada. *Ethnic and Racial Studies, 32* (8), 1406–1430.

Bilodeau, A., & Kanji, M. (2010). The new immigrant voter, 1965–2004. In C.D. Anderson & L. B. Stephenson (Eds.), *Voting behaviour in Canada* (pp. 107–136). Vancouver, BC: UBC Press.

Bittner, A. (2010). Personality matters: The evaluation of party leaders in Canadian elections. In C.D. Anderson & L.B. Stephenson (Eds.), *Voting behaviour in Canada* (pp. 183–207). Vancouver, BC: UBC Press.

Black, J. (2013). Racial diversity in the 2011 federal election: Visible minority candidates and MPs. *Canadian Parliamentary Review, 36* (3), 21–34.

Blackwell, R. (2014, December 2). Green energy sector jobs surpass total oil sands employment. *The Globe and Mail.* Report on Business.

Blais, A. (2000). *To vote or not to vote? The merits and limits of rational choice.* Pittsburgh, PA: University of Pittsburgh Press.

Blais, A. (2005). Accounting for the electoral success of the Liberal Party in Canada. *Canadian Journal of Political Science, 38,* 821–840.

Blais, A., & Carty, K. (1990). Does proportional representation foster voter turnout? *European Journal of Political Research, 18* (20), 167–182.

Blais, A., & Loewen, P. (2011). *Youth electoral engagement in Canada.* Ottawa, ON: Elections Canada.

Blais, A., Gidengil, E., Dobryznska, A., Nevitte, N., & Nadeau, R. (2003). Does the local candidate matter? Candidate effects in the Canadian election of 2000. *Canadian Journal of Political Science, 36,* 657–664.

Blais, A., Gidengil, E., Nadeau, R., & Nevitte, N. (2002). *Anatomy of a Liberal victory: Making sense of the vote in the 2000 Canadian election.* Peterborough, ON: Broadview Press.

Blais, A., Gidengil, E., Nevitte, N., & Nadeau, R. (2004). Where does turnout decline come from? *European Journal of Political Research, 43* (2), 221–236.

Block, S. (2015). A higher standard. The case for holding low-wage employers in Ontario to a higher standard. Canadian Centre for Policy Alternatives. Retrieved from www.policyalternatives.ca/publications/reports/higher-standard

Bloemraad, I. (2006). *Becoming a citizen: Incorporating immigrants and refugees in the United States and Canada.* Berkeley, CA: University of California Press.

Blondel, J. (1968). Party systems and patterns of government in western democracies. *Canadian Journal of Political Science 1* (2), 180–203. doi:10.1017/S0008423900036507

Boothe, K. (2015). *Ideas and the pace of change. National pharmaceutical insurance in Canada, Australia, and the United Kingdom.* Toronto, ON: University of Toronto Press.

Bothwell, R. (1998). *Canada and Quebec: One country, two histories.* Vancouver, BC: UBC Press.

Bothwell, R., Drummond, I., & English, J. (1989). *Canada since 1945: Politics, power and provincialism* (rev. ed.). Toronto, ON: University of Toronto Press.

Bourgault, J., & Dunn, C. Eds. (2014). *Deputy Ministers in Canada: Comparative and Jurisdictional Perspectives.* Toronto: University of Toronto Press.

Boyd, D.R. (2003). *Unnatural law: Rethinking Canadian environmental law and policy.* Vancouver, BC: UBC Press.

Boyd, D.R. (2012). The right to a healthy environment: Revitalizing Canada's constitution. Vancouver, BC: UBD Press.

Boyd, D.R. (2014). Enshrine our right to clear air and water in the Constitution. *Policy Options, 35* (3), 34–36.

Brewer, G.D., & DeLeon, P. (1983). *The foundations of policy analysis.* Pacific Grove, CA: Brooks/Cole Publishing.

Brodie, J., & Jenson, J. (1988). *Crisis, challenge and change: Party and class in Canada revisited.* Ottawa, ON: Carleton University Press.

Brodie, J., & Jenson, J. (2007). Piercing the smokescreen: Stability and change in brokerage politics. In A. Gagnon & B. Tanguay (Eds.), *Canadian parties in transition* (3rd ed., pp. 52–72). Toronto, ON: Broadview Press.

Brown, S., & Bean, F. (2006). *New immigrants, new models of assimilation.* Retrieved from www.cri.uci.edu/pdf/NewImmigrantsNewModelsOfAssimilation_082306.pdf.

Bumsted, J. M. (2003). *The peoples of Canada: A pre-Confederation history* (2nd ed.). Toronto, ON: Oxford University Press.

Bumsted, J. M. (2004). *The peoples of Canada: A post-Confederation history* (2nd ed.). Toronto, ON: Oxford University Press.

Bumsted, J. M. (2008). *The peoples of Canada: A post-Confederation history* (3rd ed.). Toronto, ON: Oxford University Press.

Bunsha, D. (2013). What Clayoquot faces. *The Tyee.* Retrieved from www.thetyee.ca/2013/08/19/Clayoquot-Faces-New

Burck, J., Marten, F., & Bals, C. (2014), Climate change performance index. Retrieved from germanwatch.org/en/download/8599.pdf

Byers, M. (2012, March 27). You can't replace real icebreakers. *Globe and Mail.*

Cairns, A.C. (1968). The electoral system and the party system in Canada, 1921–1965. *Canadian Journal of Political Science, 1,* 55–80.

Cairns, A.C. (1977). The governments and societies of Canadian federalism. *Canadian Journal of Political Science, 10,* 695–725.

Cairns, A.C. (1992). *The charter versus federalism: The dilemmas of constitutional reform.* Montreal, QC: McGill-Queen's University Press.

Cairns, A.C. (2000). *Citizens plus: Aboriginal peoples and the Canadian state.* Vancouver, BC: UBC Press.

Cairns, A.C. (2003). Aboriginal people's electoral participation in the Canadian community. *Electoral Insight, 5* (3), 2–9.

Cairns, A.C. (2004). First Nations and the Canadian nation: Colonization and constitutional alienation. In J. Bickerton & A.-G. Gagnon (Eds.), *Canadian politics* (4th ed.) (pp. 439–455) Peterborough, ON: Broadview Press.

Calder v. Attorney General of British Columbia. (1973). CanLII 4 (S.C.C.).

Cameron, D., & Simeon, R. (2002). Intergovernmental relations in Canada: The emergence of collaborative federalism. *Publius: The Journal of Federalism, 32* (2), 49–72.

Campbell et al. v. Nisga'a. (2000). BCSC 619 (CanLII).

Campbell, C. (1978). *The Canadian Senate: A lobby from within.* Toronto, ON: Macmillan.

Campion-Smith, B., & Woods, A. (2012, September5). PQ celebration ends in tragedy. *Toronto Star.*

Canada Revenue Agency (2003). *Political activities CPS-022.* Retrieved from www.cra.gc.ca

Canada v. City of Montreal et al. [1978] 2 S.C.R 770

Canada, Budget 2015. Retrieved from http://www.budget.gc.ca/2015/docs/themes/jobs-growth-emplois-croissance-eng.html

Canadian Association of Petroleum Producers (CAPP). (2012). Retrieved from www.capp.ca

Canadian Bar Association (2012). Bill C-304 Canadian Human Rights Act amendments (hate messages). Ottawa: Canadian Bar Association. Retrieved from http://www.cba.org/CBA/submissions/pdf/12-25-eng.pdf

Canadian Election Study (2004). Surveys. Retrieved from http://ces-eec.mcgill.ca/surveys.html

Canadian Election Study (2011). Surveys. Retrieved from http://ces-eec.mcgill.ca/surveys.html

Canadian Heritage/Decima (2006). *Official language annual report 2005–2006. Official languages support programs.* Ottawa, ON: Canadian Heritage.

Canadian Institute for Health Information (2015). Canada's health system: International comparisons. Retrieved from http://www.cihi.ca/CIHI-ext-portal/internet/EN/TabbedContent/health+system+performance/indicators/international/cihi014192

Canadian International Development Agency (2005). *Canada's international policy statement.* Retrieved from www.acdi-cida.gc.ca/ips-development#61a

Canadian International Development Platform (2013). Canadian mining in Africa. Retrieved from cidpnsi.ca/foreign-direct investment-about

Canadian Press (2014, December 11). Tory member Michael Chong's bill to re-empower MPs passes another hurdle. Retrieved from http://www.winnipegfreepress.com/canada/tory-member-michael-chongs-bill-to-re-empower-mps-passes-another-hurdle-285547491.html

Canadian Press (2014, July 25). "Preventing poverty" not a valid goal for tax purposes, CRA tells Oxfam Canada. Retrieved from www.cbc.ca/news/politics/preventing-poverty-not-a-valid-goal-for-tax-purposes-cra-tells-oxfam-canada-1.2717774

Canadian Press (2014, September 6). Quebec premier wants province to sign Constitution by 2017.

Canadian Press (2014a, September 7). Couillard backs away from comments on Quebec's need to sign the Constitution.

Canadian Press (2014b, September 7). Harper won't entertain Couillard's constitution talks.

Canadian Press (2015, April 21). By the numbers: Highlights of the 2015 federal budget. Retrieved from http://globalnews.ca/news/1952495/by-the-numbers-highlights-of-the-2015-federal-budget/

Carrigan, D.O. (1968). *Canadian party platforms 1867–1968.* Urbana, IL: University of Illinois Press.

Carroll, W.K. (2004). *Corporate power in a globalizing world: A study in elite social organization.* Toronto, ON: Oxford University Press.

Carty, K. (1991). *Canadian political parties in the constituencies.* Toronto, ON: Dundurn Press.

Carty, K. (2006). The shifting place of political parties in Canadian political life. *Choices, 12* (4), 3–13.

Carty, K., Cross, W., & Young, L. (2000). *Rebuilding Canadian party politics.* Vancouver, BC: UBC Press.

Carty, R.K. (2004). Parties and franchise systems: The stratarchical organizational imperative. Party Politics 10 (1), pp. 5–24.

Carty, R.K. (2015). *Big tent politics: The Liberal Party's long mastery of Canada's public life.* Vancouver, BC: UBC Press.

Castells, M. (1997). *The power of identity.* Cambridge, MA: Blackwell.

Cattaneo, C., & Lewis, J. (2014, June 27). *Financial Post.* Nexen letting staff go, slashing costs despite CNOOC's pledges to Ottawa to win takeover approval: sources. Retrieved from: http://business.financialpost.com/news/energy/nexen-cutting-jobs-slashing-costs-despite-cnoocs-pledges-to-ottawa-to-win-takeover-approval-sources

CBC (2004). CBC/RadioCanada pre-election poll. Retrieved from www.cbc.ca/canadavotes/thepolls/democracypoll.htm

CBC News (2006, November 27). House passes motion recognizing Québécois as nation. Retrieved from www.cbc.ca/news/canada/story/2006/11/27/nation-vote.html

CBC News (2007, April 13). $11-billion rift found on equalization: economist: Tougher interpretation could see Atlantic Accord benefits end in 2012. Retrieved from www.cbc.ca/canada/newfoundland-labrador/story/2007/04/13/equalization.html

CBC News (2008a, June 3). Almost a quarter of Canadians don't believe in a god.

CBC News (2008b, December 20). Canada, Ontario announces $4B auto aid package. Retrieved from www.cbc.ca/canada/story/2008/12/20/auto-package.html

CBC News (2008c, May 8). Ontario must fight equalization formula. Retrieved from www.cbc.ca/canada/ottawa/story/2008/05/08/ot-equalization-080508.html

CBC News (2011a, June 16). Human smuggling bill makes a return. Retrieved from www.cbc.ca/news/canada/story/2011/06/16/pol-human-smuggling.html?ref=rss

CBC News (2011b, December 8). Niqab case goes to Canada's top court. Retrieved from www.cbc.ca/news/politics/story/2011/12/08/niqab-supreme-court.html

CBC News (2012a). McGuinty wants conditions on health transfers. Federal government should set national standards, Ontario premier says. January 9.

CBC News (2012b). Old Age Security sustainable, says budget watchdog. February 8.

CBC News (2013, August 30). Parliamentary researcher appointed new budget watchdog. Retrieved from http://www.cbc.ca/news/politics/parliamentary-researcher-named-new-budget-watchdog-1.1396066

CBC News (2013, February 15). Aboriginal Affairs Minister John Duncan resigns from cabinet. Retrieved from http://www.cbc.ca/news/politics/aboriginal-affairs-minister-john-duncan-resigns-from-cabinet-1.1301619

CBC News (2013, January 1). Idle No More spreading beyond Canada's borders. Retrieved from http://www.cbc.ca/m/touch/news/story/1.1331096

CBC News (2013, July 12). Brad Wall says Senate atrophy "not a bad end game." Retrieved from http://www.cbc.ca/news/politics/brad-wall-says-senate-atrophy-is-not-a-bad-end-game-1.2704203

CBC News (2014, March 9). Poll finds 61 per cent of Quebecers opposed to sovereignty. Retrieved from http://www.cbc.ca/news/canada/montreal/quebec-votes-2014/poll-finds-61-per-cent-of-quebecers-opposed-to-sovereignty-1.2566062

CBC News (2015, April 17). Carding policy passed by Toronto police board, despite lingering concerns. Retrieved from http://www.cbc.ca/news/canada/toronto/carding-policy-passed-by-toronto-police-board-despite-lingering-concerns-1.3037125

CBC News (2015, March 13). Rania El-Alloul declines $50K crowdfunded donation. Retrieved from http://www.cbc.ca/news/canada/montreal/rania-el-alloul-declines-50k-crowd-funded-donation-1.2993505

CBC News (2015, September 20). Justin Trudeau vows to scrap F–35 fighter jet program. Retrieved from: http://www.cbc.ca/news/politics/canada-election-2015-trudeau-scrap-f35-halifax-1.3235791

Centre for Research and Information on Canada (2002). Portraits of Canada, 2002. Retrieved from www.cric.ca/pdf/cahiers/cricpapers_dec2002.pdf

Charlton, T. (2015). Wall floats notwithstanding clause in response to SCOC labour ruling. Retrieved from www.thestarphoenix.com/Wall+floats+notwithstanding+clause+response+SCOC+labour+ruling/10787534/story.html

Chase, S. (2010). Tories refuse to reverse census decision. Globe and Mail, July 15, 2010. Retrieved from http://www.theglobeandmail.com/news/politics/tories-refuse-to-reverse-census-decision/article1368462/

Chase, S., & Grant, T. (2010). Statistics Canada chief falls on sword over census. Globe and Mail, July 21, 2010. Retrieved from http://www.theglobeandmail.com/news/politics/statistics-canada-chief-falls-on-sword-over-census/article1320915/

Chase, S., & Perkins, T. (2009, October 8). How a scattered army of insurance brokers outmuscled the Big Five. Globe and Mail. Retrieved from www.theglobeandmail.com/report-onbusiness/how-a-scattered-army-of-insurance-brokersoutmuscled-the-big-five/article1317631

Chong, M. (2014). "Reform Act, 2014 Backgrounder" September 11, 2014. http://michaelchong.ca/2014/09/11/reform-act-2014-backgrounder/

Chowdhry, A. (2015, October 20). Record number of visible minority MPs elected to Commons. Retrieved from: http://www.theglobeandmail.com/news/politics/record-number-of-visible-minority-mps-elected-to-commons/article26892245/

Christian, W., & Campbell, C. (1990). Political parties and ideologies in Canada (3rd ed.). Toronto, ON: McGraw-Hill Ryerson.

Citizenship and Immigration Canada (2009). The multiculturalism program. Application guidelines for funding "promoting integration." Retrieved from www.cic.gc.ca/english/multiculturalism/funding/guide/101-eng.asp#a2

Citizenship and Immigration Canada (2011a). Backgrounder—Overview: Ending the abuse of Canada's immigration system by human smugglers. Retrieved from www.cic.gc.ca/english/department/media/backgrounders/2012/2012-06-29i.asp

Citizenship and Immigration Canada (2011b). Discover Canada: The rights and responsibilities of citizenship. Ottawa, ON: Citizenship and Immigration Canada.

Citizenship and Immigration Canada (2011c). Summary tables—Permanent and temporary residents, 2011. Retrieved from www.cic.gc.ca/english/resources/statistics/facts2011-summary/01.asp

Citizenship and Immigration Canada (2012). Backgrounder—Designated countries of origin. Retrieved from www.cic.gc.ca/english/department/media/backgrounders/2012/2012-06-29a.asp

Citizenship and Immigration Canada (2014a). Facts and figures 2013-Immigration overview: Temporary residents. Retrieved from http://www.cic.gc.ca/english/resources/statistics/menu-fact.asp

Citizenship and Immigration Canada (2014b). Welcoming more new Canadians. Retrieved from http://news.gc.ca/web/article-en.do?nid=820409

Clancy, P. (2008). Business interests and civil society in Canada. In M. Smith (Ed.), Group politics and social movements in Canada. Peterborough, ON: Broadview Press.

Clark, J. (2013). How we lead. Canada in a century of change. Toronto, ON: Random House Canada.

Clark, W. (2003). Immigrants and the American dream: Remaking the middle class. New York, NY: Guildford.

Clarke, H.D., Jenson, J., LeDuc, L., & Pammett, J. (1984). Absent mandate: The politics of discontent in Canada. Toronto, ON: Gage.

Clarke, H.D., Jenson, J., LeDuc, L., & Pammett, J. (1991). Absent mandate: Interpreting change in Canadian elections (2nd ed.). Toronto, ON: Gage Educational Publishing Co.

Clarke, H.D., Jenson, J., LeDuc, L., & Pammett, J. (1996). Absent mandate: Canadian electoral politics in an era of restructuring (3rd ed.). Toronto, ON: Gage.

Clarke, H.D., Kornberg, A., & Scotto, T.J. (2009). Making political choices: Canada and the United States. Toronto, ON: University of Toronto Press.

Clarke, H.D., LeDuc, L., Jenson, J., & Pammett, J. (1979). Political choice in Canada. Toronto, ON: McGraw-Hill.

Clarke, H.D., Scotto, T., Reifler, J., & Kornberg, A. (2011). Winners and losers: Voters in the 2011 federal election. In J. Pammett & C. Dornan (Eds.), *The Canadian Federal Election of 2011.* (pp. 271–301). Toronto, ON: Dundurn Press.

Clarkson, S. (1979). Democracy in the Liberal party: The experiment with citizen participation under Pierre Trudeau. In H. Thorburn, (Ed.), *Party Politics in Canada* (4th ed.). Toronto, ON: Prentice-Hall.

Clarkson, S. (2001). The Liberal threepeat: The multi-system party in the multi-party system. In J. Pammett & C. Dornan (Eds.), *The Canadian general election of 2000* (pp. 13–58). Toronto, ON: Dundurn Press.

Clarkson, S. (2008). *Does North America exist? Governing the continent after NAFTA and 9/11.* Toronto, ON: University of Toronto Press.

Clement, W. (1977). *Continental corporate power: Economic elite linkages between Canada and the United States.* Toronto, ON: McClelland & Stewart.

Cochrane, C. (2010). Left/right ideology and Canadian politics. *Canadian Journal of Political Science, 43* (3), 583–605.

Cochrane, C., & Perrella, A. (2012). Regions, regionalism and regional differences in Canada. *Canadian Journal of Political Science, 45* (4), 829–853.

Coleman, W.D., & Skogstad, G. (1990). Policy communities and policy networks in Canada: A structural approach. In W.D. Coleman & G. Skogstad (Eds.), *Policy communities and public policy in Canada: A structural approach* (pp. 14–33). Toronto, ON: Copp Clark Pitman.

Conference Board of Canada (2011). *Canadian income inequality: Is Canada becoming more unequal?* Retrieved from www.conferenceboard.ca/hcp/hottopics.CanInequality.aspx

Conrad, M., & Finkel, A. (2007). *Canada: A national history.* Toronto, ON: Pearson.

Consensus Report on the Constitution. (1992). Retrieved from www.solon.org/Constitutions/Canada/English/Proposals/CharlottetownConsensus.html

Cook, R., (with Ricker, J. & Saywell, J.). (1977). *Canada: A modern study.* Toronto, ON: Clarke Irwin.

Cooper, B. (1984). Western political consciousness. In S. Brooks (Ed.), *Political thought in Canada: Contemporary perspectives.* Toronto, ON: Irwin.

Corak, M. (2008). Immigration in the long run: The education and earnings mobility of second generation Canadians. *Choices, 14* (13).

Corbeil, J., & Blaser, C. (2007). *The evolving linguistic portrait, 2006 census: Findings.* Statistics Canada (Catalogue no. 97-555-XWE2006001). Retrieved from http://census2006.ca/census-recensement/2006/as-sa/97-555/index-eng.cfm

Cotler, I. (2014). The dismantling of Supreme Court reform. *The Globe and Mail,* November 28.

Council of Canadian Academies (2009). Innovation and business strategy: Why Canada falls short: Report of the expert panel on business innovation in Canada. Retrieved from www.scienceadvice.ca/documents/(2009-06-11)%20Innovation%20Report.pdf

Courtney, J. (1973). *The selection of national party leaders in Canada.* Toronto, ON: Macmillan.

Courtney, J.C. (1995). *Do conventions matter? Choosing national party leaders in Canada.* Montreal, QC: McGill-Queen's University Press.

Courtney, J.C. (2004). *Elections.* Vancouver, BC: UBC Press.

Crawford, A. (2015, October 20). What might a Trudeau cabinet look like? CBC News. Retrieved from: www.cbc.ca/news/politics/canada-election-2015-trudeau-cabinet-1.3278289

Crête, J., & Lachapelle, G. (2001). The Bloc Québécois. In H. Thorburn (Ed.), *Party politics in Canada* (8th ed., pp. 292–301) Toronto, ON: Prentice Hall.

Creutzberg, T. (2011). *Canada's innovation underperformance: Whose policy problem is it?* Toronto: Mowat Centre.

Cross, W. (2004). *Political parties.* Vancouver, BC: UBC Press.

Cross, W., & Young, L. (2006). Are Canadian political parties empty vessels? Membership, engagement and policy capacity. *Choices, 12* (4), 14–28.

CTV News (2006, May 27). Harper wants fixed dates for federal elections. Retrieved from www.ctv.ca/servlet/ArticleNews/story/CTVNews/20060526/harper_fixed_elexns_060526

CTV News (2011, April 15). Surprise "vote mobs" shaking up election campaigns. Retrieved from www.ctvnews.ca/surprise-vote-mobs-shaking-up-election-campaign-1.632112

CTV News (2013, November 6), Saskatchewan repeals elected Senate law and passes motion calling for abolition. Retrieved from http://www.ctvnews.ca/politics/saskatchewan-repeals-elected-senate-law-passes-motion-calling-for-abolition-1.1530432

Curry, B. (2011, December 15). Idea of private landownership on reserves gets mixed reviews. *Globe and Mail.*

Curry, B. (2013). Judge raps justice officials for treatment of whistle-blower. Retrieved from www.theglobeandmail.com/news/politics/judge-raps-justice-officials-for-treatment-of-whistle-blower/article7394559/

Curry, B. (2014, January 14). Government spends millions on ads for "Economic Action Plan" that ended two years ago. *Globe and Mail.*

Curry, B. (2015). Harper's pledged funding for Toronto's Smart Transit draws criticism. *Globe and Mail,* June 19.

D'Ombrain, N. (2007). Cabinet secrecy. *Canadian Public Administration, 47,* 332–359.

Dalton, R. (2000). The decline of party identifications. In R. Dalton & M. Wattenberg (Eds.), *Parties without partisans: Political change in advanced industrial democracies* (pp. 19–36). Oxford, UK: Oxford University Press.

Dalton, R.J. (2006). *Citizen politics: Public opinion and political parties in advanced industrial democracies* (4th ed.). Washington, DC: CQ Press.

Dalton, R.J., McAllister, I., & Wattenberg, M.P. (2000). The consequences of partisan dealignment. In R.J. Dalton & M.P. Wattenberg (Eds.), *Parties without partisans: Political change in advanced industrial democracies* (pp. 37–63). Oxford, UK: Oxford University Press.

Davis, J. (2009, July 1). Liberal-era diplomatic language killed off. Embassy. Retrieved from www.embassymag.ca/page/view/diplomatic_language-7-1-2009

Dawson, R.M. (1929). *The civil service of Canada.* London, UK: Oxford University Press.

Dayen, D. (2015). The scariest trade deal nobody's talking about just suffered a big leak. *The New Republic,* June 5. Retrieved from http://www.newrepublic.com/article/121967/whats-really-going-trade-services-agreement

de Toqueville, A. (1969). *Democracy in America* (Rev. ed., trans. H. Reeve). New York, NY: Colonial Press. (Original work published in 1900).

Deibert, R. (2002). The politics of internet design: securing the foundations for global civil society networks. Retrieved from www.pinkcandyproductions.com/portfolio/conferences/globalization/pdfs/deibert.pdf

Delgamuukw v. British Columbia. (1997). CanLII 302 (S.C.C.).

Democracy Watch (2011). Federal Conservatives' accountability and democratic reform record gets an "F" for breaking many promises and practising politics as usual. Retrieved from http://democracywatch.ca/20111212-relsdec1211/

Department of Justice (2009). *Employment Equity Act* (1995, c. 44). Ottawa, ON: Author. Retrieved from http://laws.justice.gc.ca/en/E-5.401/index.html

Deutsch, K., & Foltz, W. (Eds.) (1963). *Nation-building.* New York, NY: Atherton Press.

Dewing, M., & Leman, M. (2006). *Canadian multiculturalism.* Library of Parliament. Retrieved from www.parl.gc.ca/information/library/PRBpubs/936-e.htm

Dicey, A.V. (1965). *The law of the Constitution* (10th ed.). New York, NY: St. Martin's Press.

Dickason, O.P. (with McNab, D.T.). (2009). *Canada's first nations: A history of founding peoples from earliest times* (4th ed.). Toronto, ON: Oxford University Press.

DiGiacomo, G. (2010). The federal government is not simply one government among many. In G. DiGiacomo & M. Flumian (Eds.), *The case for centralized federalism* (pp. 251–259). Ottawa, ON: University of Ottawa Press.

DiGiacomo, G., & Flumian, M. (2010). Introduction. In G. DiGiacomo & M. Flumian (Eds.), *The case for centralized federalism.* Ottawa, ON: University of Ottawa Press.

Ditchburn, J. (2015). Census debate back in the House of Commons with dueling bills. *Huffington Post/Canadian Press.* February 2. Retrieved from http://www.huffingtonpost.ca/2015/02/02/census-canada-ted-hsu-joe-preston-stats_n_6595202.html

Dobrowolsky, A. (2008). The women's movement in flux: Feminism and framing, passion and politics. In M. Smith, (Ed.), *Group politics and social movements in Canada* (pp. 159–180). Peterborough, ON: Broadview Press.

Dobrowolsky, A. (2014). The women's movement in flux: Feminism and framing, passion, and politics. In M. Smith (Ed.), *Group politics and social movements in Canada*, 2nd ed. (pp. 151–177). Toronto: University of Toronto Press.

Docherty, D.C. (2002). Our changing understanding of representation in Canada. In N. Nevitte (Ed.), *Value change and governance in Canada* (pp. 165–206). Toronto, ON: University of Toronto Press.

Docherty, D.C. (2005). *Legislatures.* Vancouver, BC: UBC Press.

Doern, G.B., & Conway, T. (1994). *The greening of Canada: Federal institutions and decisions.* Toronto, ON: University of Toronto Press.

Dornan, C. (2011). From contempt of Parliament to majority mandate. In J. Pammett & C. Dornan (Eds.), *The Canadian federal election of 2011* (pp. 7–13). Toronto, ON: Dundurn Press.

Downs, A. (1972). Up and down with ecology. The issue attention cycle. *The Public Interest, 28* (Summer), 38–50.

Dunn, C. (1995). *The institutionalized cabinet: Governing the western provinces.* Montreal and Kingston: McGill-Queen's University Press.

Dunn, C. (2010). The federal spending power. In C. Dunn, ed. *The handbook of Canadian public administration.* Don Mills, ON: Oxford University Press.

Dunn, C., & Bierling, G. (2009). Les sous-ministres des gouvernements provinciax canadiens comme figures archétypales. *Télescope: Revue d'analyse comparée en administration publique, 15* (1), 65–78.

Dupré, J.S. (1985). Reflections on the workability of executive federalism. In R. Simeon (Ed.), *Intergovernmental relations* (pp. 1–32). Toronto, ON: University of Toronto Press.

Duverger, M. (1954). *Political parties.* London, UK: Methuen.

Duverger, M. (1959). *Political parties, their organization and activity in the modern state* (2nd ed., B. & R. North, Trans.). London, UK: Methuen.

Dye, T.R. (1998). *Understanding public policy* (9th ed.). Upper Saddle River, NJ: Prentice Hall.

Edwards v. A.G. of Canada. (1928). S.C.R. 276.

Edwards v. A.G. of Canada. (1930). A.C. 124.

Eidlin, B. (2015). Class vs special interest. Labor, power and politics in the US and Canada in the 20th century. *Politics and Society, 43* (2), 181–211.

Ekospolitics.com (2015). Tolerance under pressure? Retrieved from http://www.ekospolitics.com/index.php/2015/03/tolerance-under-pressure/

Elections BC (2005). *2005 provincial general election post event review—Executive summary.* Victoria, BC: Author.

Elections Canada (1997). A history of the vote in Canada. Retrieved from www.elections.ca

Elections Canada (2008). Estimation of voter turnout by age group at the 39th federal general election, January 23, 2006. Retrieved from www.elections.ca/loi/res/rep39ge/estimation39ge_e.pdf

Elections Canada (2012). *Estimates of voter turnout by age group, 2011 federal general election.* Retrieved from www.elections.ca/content.aspx?section=res&dir=rec/part/estim/41ge&document=report41&lang=e#p4

Elections Canada (2015). Contestant's Leadership Campaign Return. Database available at: http://www.elections.ca/WPAPPS/WPF/EN/LC/SummaryReport?act=C2&eventid=7073&returntype=1&option=1&period=3&queryid=ee997c8374a04d368ef708741f69879a

Electoral Commission (2005). *Understanding electoral registration: The extent and nature of non-registration in Britain.* Retrieved from www.electoralcommission.org.uk/templates/search/document.cfm/13545

Elevate Consulting (2011). *Student Vote program evaluation final evaluation report.* Victoria, BC: Elevate Consulting.

Elkins, D.J., & Simeon, R. (1980). *Small worlds: Provinces and parties in Canadian political life.* Toronto, ON: Methuen.

Ellis, F., & Woolstencroft, P. (2011). The Conservative campaign: Becoming the new natural governing party? In J. Pammett & C. Dornan (Eds.), *The Canadian federal election of 2011* (pp. 15–44). Toronto, ON: Dundurn Press.

Employment and Social Development Canada (2014). Ensuring Canadian workers come first: Restricting access to the temporary foreign worker program. Retrieved from http://www.esdc.gc.ca/eng/jobs/foreign_workers/reform/restrict.shtml

English, J. (2015). "Pearson, Lester Bowles," in *Dictionary of Canadian Biography*, vol. 20, University of Toronto/Université Laval, 2003, accessed July 10. Retrieved from http://www.biographi.ca/en/bio/pearson_lester_bowles_20E.html

Environics Institute. (2012a). AmericasBarometer. Canada 2012. Retrieved from www.vanderbilt.edu/lapop/Canada/Canada-2012-report.pdf

Environics Institute. (2012b). Focus Canada 2012. Retrieved from http://www.environicsinstitute.org/uploads/institute-projects/environics%20institute%20-%20focus%20canada%202012%20final%20report.pdf (p. 18). Reprinted with permission.

Environics Institute. (2014). AmericasBarometer. The public speaks on democracy and governance across the Americas. Canada 2014. Final Report. Retrieved from http://www.vanderbilt.edu/lapop/canada/Canada-2014-Report_120414_W.pdf

Equal Voice (2015). Despite dramatic results, no meaningful change in the percentage of women elected to Parliament. Retrieved from: http://us7.campaign-archive2.com/?u=edc96b30d97838f2d42e39fdf&id=cb1402fbdb&e=57aa973747

Erickson, L. (1998). Entry to the Commons: Parties, recruitment and the election of women in 1993. In M. Tremblay & C. Andrew (Eds.), *Women and political representation in Canada.* Ottawa, ON: University of Ottawa Press.

Esselment, A. (2010). Fighting elections: Cross-level political party integration in Canada. *Canadian Journal of Political Science, 43* (4), 871–892.

Eulau, H. (1978). Changing views of representation. In J. Walkhe & A. Abramowitz (Eds.), *The politics of representation: Continuities in theory and research* (pp. 31–53). Beverly Hills, CA: age.

Evans, B., & Shields, J. (2002). The third sector: Neo-liberal restructuring, governance, and the remaking of state–civil society relationships. In C. Dunn (Ed.), *The handbook of Canadian public administration.* Toronto, ON: Oxford University Press.

Farney, J., & Malloy, J. (2011). Ideology and discipline in the Conservative Party of Canada. In J. Pammett & C. Dornan (Eds.), *The Canadian federal election of 2011* (pp. 247–269). Toronto, ON: Dundurn Press.

Federation of Canadian Municipalities (2012). *Canadian infrastructure report card: Volume 1: 2012 municipal roads and water systems.* Retrieved from http://fcm.ca/Documents/reports/Canadian_Infrastructure_Report_Card_EN.pdf

Feehan, J. (2009) The Churchill Falls contract: What happened and what's to come. *Newfoundland Quarterly, 101* (4), 35–38.

Feldman Family Law Group (2012). Quebec Court of Appeal decides on alimony for common law spouses. Retrieved from blog. separation.ca/?p=866

Fierlbeck, K. (2013). *Health care in Canada. A citizen's guide to policy and politics.* Toronto, ON: University of Toronto Press.

Fine, S. (2014, April 10). Tories chastised for lack of racial diversity in judicial appointments. Retrieved from http://www.theglobeandmail.com/news/politics/tories-chastised-for-lack-of-racial-diversity-in-judge-ranks/article17909652/

Fine, S. (2014, July 4). Ottawa's refugee health-care cuts 'cruel and unusual,' court rules. *The Globe and Mail.* Retrieved from http://www.theglobeandmail.com/news/politics/ottawas-refugee-health-cuts-cruel-and-unusual-court-rules/article19459837/

Fine, S. (2015, July 25). Stephen Harper's courts: How the judiciary has been remade. *The Globe and Mail.*

Fine, S. (2015, July 31). Law school blog sheds light on Supreme Court's newest judge. *The Globe and Mail.*

Fine, S. (2015, September 4). Canada's response to refugee crises today a stark contrast to past efforts. *The Globe and Mail.* Retrieved from: http://www.theglobeandmail.com/news/national/canadas-response-to-refugee-crises-today-a-stark-contrast-to-past-efforts/article26223762/

Finer, H. (1940). Administrative responsibility in democratic government. *Public Administration Review 1* (4), 335–350.

Flanagan, T. (2000). *First nations? Second thoughts.* Montreal, QC: McGill-Queen's University Press.

Flanagan, T. (2001). From Reform to the Canadian Alliance. In H. Thorburn, (Ed.), *Party politics in Canada* (8th ed., pp. 280–291). Toronto, ON: Prentice Hall.

Flanagan, T. (2009, January 10). Only voters have the right to decide on the coalition. *Globe and Mail.*

Flanagan, T. (2014). *Winning power. Canadian campaigning in the twenty-first century.* Montreal, QC: McGill-Queen's University Press.

Flanagan, T., Alcantara, C., & Le Dressay, A. (2010). *Beyond the Indian Act: Restoring Aboriginal property rights.* Montreal, QC: McGill-Queen's University Press.

Fontaine, P. (1990, October 30). Shocking testimony of sexual abuse. *The Journal.* CBC Digital Archives. Retrieved from http://archives.cbc.ca/society/education/clips/11177

Fontaine, T. (2015, October 26). Record 10 indigenous MPs elected to the House of Commons. Retrieved from: http://www.cbc.ca/news/aboriginal/indigenous-guide-to-house-of-commons-1.3278957

Forbes, H.D. (1987). Hartz-Horowitz at twenty: Nationalism, toryism, and socialism in Canada and the United States. *Canadian Journal of Political Science, 20* (2), 287–315.

Forcese, C., & Roach, K. (2015, April 15). The real agenda behind C-51. *The Walrus.*

Forsey, E., & Eglington, G.C. (1985). *The question of confidence in responsible government.* Ottawa, ON: Special Committee on the Reform of the House of Commons.

Fortin, S. (2009). From the Canadian social union to the federal social union of Canada, 1990–2006. In A.-G. Gagnon (Ed.), *Contemporary Canadian federalism: Foundations, traditions, institutions* (pp. 303–329). Toronto, ON: University of Toronto Press.

Fournier, P., Cutler, F., Soroka, S., Stolle, D., & Bélanger, E. (2013). Riding the orange wave: Leadership, values, and issues in the 2011 Canadian election. *Canadian Journal of Political Science 46:4* (December).

Francoli, M., Greenberg, J., & Waddell, C. (2011). The campaign in the digital media. In J.H. Pammett & C. Dornan (Eds.). *The Canadian federal election of 2011.* Toronto, ON: Dundurn Press.

Franks, C.E.S. (1987). *The Parliament of Canada.* Toronto, ON: University of Toronto Press.

Frideres, J. (2008). Creating an inclusive society: Promoting social integration in Canada. In J. Biles, M. Burstein, & J. Frideres (Eds.), *Immigration and integration in Canada in the twenty-first century* (pp. 77–101). Montreal, QC: McGill-Queen's University Press.

Friedenberg, E.Z. (1980). *Deference to authority: The case of Canada.* White Plains, NY: Sharpe.

Friedrich, C.J. (1940). Public policy and the nature of administrative responsibility. In C.J. Friedrich & E.S. Mason (Eds.), *Public policy: A yearbook of the Graduate School of Public Administration, Harvard University* (pp. 3–24). Cambridge, MA: Harvard University Press.

Fukuyama, F. (1992). *The end of history and the last man.* New York, NY. Free Press.

Gagnon, A.-G. (2009). Taking stock of asymmetrical federalism in an era of exacerbated centralization. In A.-G. Gagnon (Ed.), *Contemporary Canadian federalism: Foundations, traditions, institutions.* Toronto, ON: University of Toronto Press.

Gainer, A. (2011). *Corporate headquarters in Canada.* Calgary, AB: Fraser Forum. Retrieved from www.fraserinstitute.org

Gall, G.I. (2004). *The Canadian legal system* (5th ed.). Toronto, ON: Thomson Carswell.

Galt, V. (2007, January 22). Most trusted professionals: The fire-fighters, not the CEO. *Globe and Mail.*

Geddes, J. (2012, October 29). The price of persuasion. The federal government is spending tens of millions on commercials that make the Tories look good. *Maclean's,* p. 22.

German Marshall Fund of the United States. (2011). *Transatlantic trends: Immigration 2011.* Retrieved from www.gmfus.org/archives/transatlantic-trends-immigration-2011

Gibbins, R. (2014). Constitutional politics. In J. Bickerton & A.-G. Gagnon (Eds.). *Canadian politics,* 6th ed. Toronto, ON: University of Toronto Press, pp. 47–64.

Gibbins, R., & Arrison, S. (1995). *Western visions: Perspectives on the west in Canada.* Peterborough, ON: Broadview Press.

Gibson, D. (2005). Bible Bill and the money barons: The Social Credit court references and their constitutional consequences. In R. Connors & J.M. Law (Eds.). *Forging Alberta's constitutional framework* (pp. 191–236). Edmonton, AB: University of Alberta Press.

Giddens, A. (1994). *Beyond left and right: The future of radical politics.* London, UK: Polity.

Gidengil, E., Blais, A., Everitt, J., Fournier, P., & Nevitte, N. (2005). Missing the message: Young adults and the election issues. *Electoral Insight, 7,* 6–11.

Gidengil, E., Blais, A., Nevitte, N., & Nadeau, R. (2004). *Citizens.* Vancouver, BC: UBC Press.

Gidengil, E., Nevitte, N., Blais, A., Everitt, J., & Fournier, P. (2012). *Dominance and decline: Making sense of recent Canadian elections.* Toronto, ON: University of Toronto Press.

Gillmor, D., & Turgeon, P. (2000). *Canada: A people's history* (Vol. 1). Toronto, ON: McClelland & Stewart.

Gillmor, D., Michaud, A., & Turgeon, P. (2001). *Canada: A people's history* (Vol. 2). Toronto, ON: McClelland & Stewart.

Globe and Mail (2012, June 11). Over the years: Omnibus budget bills at first reading. Retrieved from www.theglobeandmail.com/incoming/over-the-years-omnibus-budget-bills-at-first-reading/article4249868

Good, D.A. (2007). *The politics of public money: Spenders, guardians, priority setters, and financial watchdogs in the Canadian government*. Toronto, ON: University of Toronto Press.

Government of Canada (2000). Background to the introduction of Bill C-20, the Clarity Bill. Depository Services Program (PRB 99-42E). Retrieved from http://dsp-psd.pwgsc.gc.ca/Collection-R/LoPBdP/BP/prb9942-e.htm

Government of Canada (2007). Speech from the Throne, 2007. Retrieved from http://publications.gc.ca/collections/collection_2007/gg/SO1-1-2007E.pdf

Government of Canada (2015, June 18). Zero Tolerance for Barbaric Cultural Practices Act received Royal Assent. Retrieved from: http://news.gc.ca/web/article-en.do?nid=989099

Grabb, E., & Curtis, J. (2005). *Regions apart: The four societies of Canada and the United States*. Toronto, ON: Oxford University Press.

Graham, A. (2007). *Canadian public sector financial management*. Montreal, QC: McGill-Queen's University Press.

Graham, A. (2014). *Canadian public sector financial management* (2nd ed.). Montreal and Kingston: McGill-Queen's University Press.

Grant, H., & Sweetman, A. (2004). Introduction to economic and urban issues in Canadian immigration policy. *Canadian Journal of Urban Research/Revue canadienne de recherche urbaine, 13* (1), 1–45.

Grant, T. (2011, December 4). Black Canadians paid less on average than whites: Study. *Globe and Mail*.

Grant, T. (2014). Poloz's prescription for unemployed youth: Work for free. *Globe and Mail*, November 4.

Gratschew, M. (2002). Compulsory voting. In R. López Pintor & M. Gratschew (Eds.), *Voter turnout since 1945: A global report* (pp. 105–110). Stockholm, SE: International Institute for Electoral Democracy and Assistance.

Gray, J. (2015). Ottawa's national security review a warning to foreign investors. *The Globe and Mail*, July 1.

Green Party of Canada (2015). Democratic reform. http://www.greenparty.ca/en/democratic-reform

Greene, I. (2006). *The courts*. Vancouver, BC: UBC Press.

Greenwood, J. (2015). The services boom. *Maclean's* April 13, pp. 34–35.

Grenier, É. (2015). Éric Grenier's Poll Tracker. CBC News. Canada Votes. Retrieved from: http://www.cbc.ca/news2/interactives/poll-tracker/2015/

Guérin, D. (2003). Aboriginal participation in Canadian federal elections. *Electoral Insight, 5* (3), 10–15.

Haddow, R. (2014). Power resources and the Canadian welfare state: Unions, partisanship and interprovincial differences in inequality and poverty reduction. *Canadian Journal of Political Science, 47* (4), 717–739.

Haida Nation v. British Columbia (Minister of Forests). (2004). SCC 73 (CanLII).

Hall, M., Lasby, D., Ayer, S., & Gibbons, W. (2009). *Caring Canadians, involved Canadians: Highlights from the 2007 Canada Survey of Giving, Volunteering and Participating* (Catalogue no. 71-542-X). Ottawa, ON: Ministry of Industry.

Hall, M., Lasby, D., Gumulka, G., & Tryon, C. (2006). *Caring Canadians, involved Canadians: Highlights from the 2004 Canada Survey of Giving, Volunteering and Participating* (Catalogue no. 71-542-XIE). Ottawa, ON: Ministry of Industry.

Hall, P. (2002). The role of government and the distribution of social capital. In R. Putnam (Ed.), *Democracies in flux: The evolution of social capital in contemporary society* (pp. 21–58). Oxford, UK: Oxford University Press.

Hansen, J., et al. (2013). Assessing "dangerous climate change": Required reductions of carbon emissions to protect young people, future generations and nature. Retrieved from http://www.plosone.org/article/info%3Adoi%2F10.1371%2Fjournal.pone.0081648

Harada, S. (2006). Great expectations: The Green Party of Canada's 2006 campaign. In C. Dornan, & J. Pammett (Eds.), *The Canadian federal election of 2006* (pp. 143–170). Toronto, ON: Dundurn Press.

Harmes, A. (2007). The political economy of open federalism. *Canadian Journal of Political Science, 40* (2), 417–437.

Harper, S. (2008, June 11). Prime Minister Stephen Harper's statement of apology. CBC News. Retrieved from www.cbc.ca/canada/story/2008/06/11/pm-statement.html

Harrell, A., & Deschâtelets, L. (2014). Political culture(s) in Canada: Orientations to politics in a pluralist, multicultural federation. In J. Bickerton & A-G. Gagnon (Eds.). *Canadian politics*, 6th ed., Toronto, ON; University of Toronto Press. pp. 229–247.

Harris, M. (2014). *Party of one: Stephen Harper and Canada's radical makeover*. Toronto: Viking.

Hart, M. (2008). *From pride to influence: Towards a new Canadian foreign policy*. Vancouver, BC: UBC Press.

Hartz, L., McRae, K., et. al. (1964). *The founding of new societies*. New York, NY: Harcourt Brace.

Hausegger, L., Hennigar, M., & Riddell, T. (2015). *Canadian courts. Law, politics, and process* (2nd ed.). Don Mills, ON: Oxford University Press.

Hausegger, L., Riddell, T., & Hennigar, M. (2013). Does patronage matter? Connecting influences on judicial appointments with judicial decision making. *Canadian Journal of Political Science, 46* (3), 665–690.

Havro, S.L. (2004). Financial sector reform in Canada: Interests and the policy process. *Canadian Journal of Political Science 37* (1), 161–184.

Heard, A. (1991). *Canadian constitutional conventions: The marriage of law and politics*. Toronto, ON: Oxford University Press.

Hébert, C. (2012, May 16). Quebec's streets not unique in staging discontent. *Toronto Star*.

Hébert, C. (2014). Referendum on Senate reform a dead end: Hébert. *Toronto Star*. Retrieved from http://www.thestar.com/news/canada/2014/04/23/philippe_couillard_officially_becomes_quebec_premier.html

Heckmann, F. (1997). *Integration und Integrationspolitik in Deutschland* (Paper No. 11). EFMS. Retrieved from www.efms.uni-bamberg.de/pdf/efms_p11.pdf.

Hein, G. (2000). Interest group litigation and Canadian democracy. *Choices, 6* (2).

Henderson, A. (2004). Regional political cultures in Canada. *Canadian Journal of Political Science, 37* (3), 595–615.

Henderson, A. (2007). *Nunavut: Rethinking political culture*. Vancouver, BC: UBC Press.

Henderson, A. (2010). Why regions matter: Sub-state polities in comparative perspective. *Regional and Federal Studies 20*, 4–5, pp. 439–441.

Henderson, A., Brown, S., Pancer, S., & Ellis-Hale, K. (2007). Mandated community service in high school and subsequent civic engagement: The case of the "double cohort" in Ontario, Canada. *Journal of Youth and Adolescence, 36*, 849–860.

Hermanson, E.N. (1995). The Senate. In *House of Commons of Canada, 35th Parliament, 2nd Session, Journals (69)*, September 18, 1996.

Herschel, R. (2008). The judicialization of mega-politics and the rise of political courts. *Annual Review of Political Science, 11*, 93–118.

Hessing, M., Howlett, M., & Summerville, T. (2005). *Canadian natural resource and environmental policy: Political economy and public policy* (2nd ed.). Vancouver: UBC Press.

Heywood, A. (2002). *Politics* (2nd ed.). Basingstoke, UK: Palgrave.

Hiebert, D., Schuurman, N., & Smith, H. (2007). *Multiculturalism "on the ground": The social geography of immigrant and visible minority populations in Montreal, Toronto and Vancouver, projected to 2017 Metropolis British Columbia* (Working paper #07–12). Vancouver, BC: Metropolis British Columbia.

Hoberg, G., & Phillips, J. (2011). Playing defence: Early responses to conflict expansion in the oil sands policy subsystem. *Canadian Journal of Political Science, 44* (3), 483–506.

Hofferbert, R.I. (1974). *The study of public policy.* Indianapolis: Bobbs-Merrill.

Hogg, P.W. (2006). *Constitutional law of Canada* (Student ed.). Toronto, ON: Carswell.

Hogg, P.W. (2009). Appointment of Justice Marshall Rothstein to the Supreme Court of Canada. In M. Charlton & P. Barker (Eds.), *Crosscurrents: Contemporary political issues.* Toronto, ON: Nelson.

Hogg, P.W., & Thornton, A.A. (1997). The Charter dialogue between courts and legislatures. *Osgoode Hall Law Journal, 35.*

Hogg, P.W., & Thornton, A.A. (1999, April). The Charter dialogue between courts and legislatures. *Policy Options,* 19–22.

Hogg, P.W., Thornton, A.A., & Wright, W.K. (2007). Charter dialogue revisited—or "much ado about metaphors". *Osgoode Hall Law Journal, 45* (1), 1–65.

Hoggwood, B.W., & Gunn, L.A. (1984). *Policy analysis for the real world.* New York, NY: Oxford University Press.

Holloway, S.K. (2006). *Canadian foreign policy: Defining the national interest.* Peterborough, ON: Broadview Press.

Horowitz, G. (1966). Conservatism, liberalism, and socialism in Canada: An interpretation. *Canadian Journal of Economics and Political Science, 32,* 143–171.

House of Commons Journals (1971, January 26), pp. 284–285.

House of Commons Standing Committee on Human Resources, Skills and Social Development and the Status of Persons with Disabilities (2010). *Federal poverty reduction plan: Working in partnership towards reducing poverty in Canada, 2010.* Retrieved from www.parl.gc.ca/content/hoc/Committee/403/HUMA/Reports/RP4770921/humarp07/humarp07-e.pdf

Howard, R. (1998). "History stalks before it strikes": Tightened identity and the right to self-determination: Essays in honour of Peter Baehr. In M. Castermans-Holleman, F. van Hoof, & J. Smith (Eds.), *The role of the nation-state in the twenty-first century* (pp. 61–78). Cambridge, MA: Kluwer Law International.

Howe, P. (2003). Where have all the voters gone? *Inroads: The Canadian Journal of Opinion, 12* (Winter/Spring), 74–83.

Howe, P. (2006). Political knowledge and electoral participation in the Netherlands: Comparisons with the Canadian case. *International Political Science Review, 27* (2), 137–166. doi:10.1177/0192512110606014424

Howe, P., & Bedford, D. (2009). *Electoral participation of Aboriginals in Canada.* Ottawa, ON: Elections Canada. Retrieved from www.elections.ca/med/eve/APRC/abo_participation_e.pdf

Howe, P., & Northrup, D. (2000). Strengthening Canadian democracy: The views of Canadians. *Policy Matters 1* (5).

Howlett, M., Ramesh, R., & Perl, A. (2009). *Studying public policy.* Don Mills, ON: Oxford University Press.

Hueglin, T.O. (2008). Working around the American model: Canadian federalism and the European Union. In L.A. White, R. Simeon, R. Vipond, & J. Wallner (Eds.), *The comparative turn in Canadian political science* (pp. 140–157). Vancouver, BC: UBC Press.

Huffington Post Canada (2014, October 22). Harper named world's worst climate change villain after damning report. Retrieved from http://www.huffingtonpost.ca/2014/10/21/canada-climate-change-ranking-oecd-report_n_6024844.html

Human Resources and Skills Development Canada (2012). *Indicators of well-being in Canada.* Retrieved from http://www4.hrsdc.gc.ca/.3ndic.1t.4r@-eng.jsp?iid=13

Human Rights Watch (2014). World Report 2014: European Union. Retrieved from https://www.hrw.org/world-report/2014/country-chapters/european-union

Hunger Canada (2014). Hunger count 2014. Retrieved from http://www.foodbankscanada.ca/getmedia/7739cdff-72d5-4cee-85e9-54d456669564/HungerCount_2014_EN.pdf.aspx?ext=.pdf

Huntington, S.P. (2011). *The clash of civilizations and the remaking of the world order.* New York, NY: Simon & Schuster

Hurley, M.C. (2003). *Bill C-7: The First Nations Governance Act.* Library of Parliament. Parliamentary Information and Research Service. Retrieved from http://www2.parl.gc.ca/Sites/LOP/LegislativeSummaries/Bills_ls.asp?Parl=37&Ses=2&ls=c7#35

Ibbitson, J. (2015). *Stephen Harper.* Toronto: Signal.

Indian and Northern Affairs Canada. (1969). *Statement of the Government of Canada on Indian policy.* Retrieved from www.ainc-inac.gc.ca/ai/arp/ls/pubs/cp1969/cp1969-eng.asp

Inglehart, R. (1971). The silent revolution in Europe: Intergenerational change in post-industrial societies. *American Political Science Review, 65,* 991–1017.

Inglehart, R. (1977). *Silent revolution: Changing values and political styles among western publics.* Princeton, NJ: Princeton University Press.

Inglehart, R. (1990). *Culture shift in advanced industrial society.* Princeton, NJ: Princeton University Press.

Inglehart, R.I. (2009). *Inglehart-Welzel cultural map of the world.* Retrieved from www.worldvaluessurvey.org.

Innovative Research Group (2015). Retrieved from http://www.innovativeresearch.ca/sites/default/files/pdf,%20doc,%20docx,%20jpg,%20png,%20xls,%20xlsx/151009_IRG29%20Wave%206%20Hill%20Times%20Oct%209%20Release.pdf

Institute for Democracy and Electoral Assistance (2015). Voter turnout database. http://www.idea.int/db/fieldview.cfm?field=221&region=-1

International Commission on Intervention and State Sovereignty (2001). *The responsibility to protect.* Ottawa, ON: International Development Research Centre.

International Panel on Climate Change (IPCC) (2014). IPCC Fifth Assessment Synthesis Report. Adopted 1 November 2014. Climate Change 2014: Synthesis Report/Longer Report. Retrieved from www.ipcc.ch/report/ar5/syr/

Inwood, G.J. (2009). *Understanding Canadian public administration: An introduction to theory and practice* (3rd ed.). Toronto, ON: Pearson Prentice Hall.

Inwood, G.J., Johns, C.M., & O'Reilly, P.L. (2011. *Intergovernmental policy capacity in Canada. Inside the worlds of finance, environment, trade and health.* Montreal: McGill-Queen's University Press.

Isfeld, G. (2014, September 12). *Financial Post.* Ottawa ratifies contentious foreign investment deal with China despite tensions. Retrieved from: http://business.financialpost.com/news/economy/ottawa-ratifies-contentious-foreign-investment-deal-with-china-despite-tensions

Isfield, G. (2015). Low oil to have 'both positive and negative effects' on Canadian economy, Ottawa told. *National Post,* March 12.

Ivison, J. (2015). Federal budget spending on transportation infrastructure to reach nearly $1 billion for major cities. *National Post* (16 April).

Jackson, A. (2014). The depressing future of income inequality. *Globe and Mail,* October 2, 2014.

Jamieson, K.H. (1992). *Dirty politics: Deception, distraction, democracy.* New York, NY: Oxford University Press.

Janoski, T., Musick, M., & Wilson, J. (1998). Being volunteered? The impact of social participation and pro-social attitudes on volunteering. *Sociological Forum, 13* (3), 495–519.

Jedwab, J. (2005). Neither finding nor losing our way: The debate over Canadian multiculturalism. *Canadian Diversity, 4* (1), 95–102.

Jeffrey, B. (2011). The disappearing Liberals: Caught in the crossfire. In J. Pammett & C. Dornan, C. (Eds.), *The Canadian federal election of 2011* (pp. 45–75). Toronto, ON: Dundurn Press.

Johnson, S. (2015, June 20). Getting the Trans-Pacific Partnership right. Retrieved from www.project-syndicate.org/commentary/tpp-labor-environmental-standards-by-simon-johnson-2015-06

Johnston, R., Blais, A., Brady, H.E., & Crête, J. (1992). *Letting the people decide: Dynamics of a Canadian election.* Montreal, QC: McGill-Queen's University Press.

Jones, C.O. (1997). *An introduction to the study of public policy* (3rd ed.). Pacific Grove, CA: Brooks/Cole Publishing.

Kahn, S., & Saloojee, R. (2003). Muslims and citizenship in Canada. *Canadian Diversity, 2* (1), 52–54.

Kelley, N., & Trebilcock, M. (1998). T*he making of the mosaic: A history of Canadian immigration policy.* Toronto, ON: University of Toronto Press.

Kennett, S.A. (2000). Meeting the intergovernmental challenge of environmental assessment. In P.C. Fafard & K. Harrison (Eds.), *Managing the environmental union: Intergovernmental regulations and environmental policy in Canada.* Montreal, QC: McGill-Queen's University Press.

Kerr v. Baranow 2011 SCC10, [2011] 1 S.C.R. 269.

Kidd, K. (2010, June 27). Tear gas fired in downtown rampage. *Toronto Star.* Retrieved from www.thestar.com/news/torontog20summit/article/829238--tear-gas-fired-in-downtown-rampage

King, A. (1973). Ideas, institutions and the policies of governments: A comparative analysis: Part III. *British Journal of Political Science* 3:4 409–423.

Kirby, J. (2014, November 23). Behind closed doors: The 12 most powerful lobbyists in Canada. *Maclean's* magazine. Retrieved from: http://www.macleans.ca/news/canada/behind-closed-doors-the-12-most-powerful-lobbyists-in-ottawa/

Kirton, J. (2007). *Canadian foreign policy in a changing world.* Toronto, ON: Thomson Nelson.

Kirton, J. (2011). Canada as a principal power 2010. In D. Bratt & C.J. Kukucha (Eds.). *Readings in Canadian foreign policy. Classic debates and new ideas* (2nd ed.). (pp. 69–75). Don Mills, ON: Oxford University Press.

Krackle, J. (2015, August 11). Fair Elections Act may disenfranchise Aboriginal voters. Anishnabek News.ca. Retrieved from: http://anishinabeknews.ca/2015/08/11/fair-elections-act-may-disenfranchise-aboriginal-voters/

Kraft, M.E., & Furlong, S.R. (2015). *Public policy: Politics, analysis and alternatives.* Thousand Oaks, CA: SAGE/CQ Press.

Kronby, M.C. (2010). *Canadian family law* (10th ed.). Mississauga, ON: John Wiley & Sons Canada.

Kuhn, T.S. (1962). *The structure of scientific revolutions.* Chicago: University of Chicago Press. Available at http://projektintegracija.pravo.hr/_download/repository/Kuhn_Structure_of_Scientific_Revolutions.pdf

Kuhn, T.S. (2012). *The structure of scientific revolutions: 50th anniversary edition.* Chicago: University of Chicago Press.

Kushner, J., Siegel, D., & Stanwick, H. (1997). Ontario municipal elections: Voting trends and determinants of electoral success in a Canadian province. *Canadian Journal of Political Science, 30,* 539–559.

Kymlicka, W. (1995). *Multicultural citizenship: A liberal theory of minority rights.* Toronto, ON: Oxford University Press.

Kymlicka, W. (2009). The current state of multiculturalism in Canada. *Canadian Journal for Social Research 2* (1), 15–34.

Ladner, K.L. (2003). Treaty federalism: An indigenous vision of Canadian federalisms. In F. Rocher & M. Smith (Eds.), *New trends in Canadian federalism* (2nd ed.). Peterborough, ON: Broadview Press.

Laghi, B. (2009, August 14). The wizard of Ottawa, behind the curtain. *Globe and Mail.* Retrieved from www.theglobeandmail.com/news/politics/the-wizard-of-ottawabehind-the-curtain/article1246477

Land, L. (2011). Taking a second look at those Attawapiskat numbers. Retrieved from www.otklaw.com.blog

Lapp, M. (1999). Ethnic group leaders and the mobilization of voter turnout: Evidence from five Montreal communities. *Canadian Ethnic Studies, 31* (2), 17–42.

LaSelva, S. (1996). *The moral foundations of Canadian federalism: Paradoxes, achievements and tragedies of nationhood.* Montreal: McGill-Queen's University Press.

LaSelva, S.V. (2009). Understanding Canada's origins: Federalism, multiculturalism, and the will to live together. In J. Bickerton & A.-G. Gagnon (Eds.), *Canadian Politics* (5th ed.). Toronto, ON: University of Toronto Press.

Lasswell, H.D. (1935). *Who gets what, when, how.* Whitefish, MT: Reprinted by Literary Licensing LLC, 2011.

Lasswell, H.D. (1951). The policy orientation. In D. Lerner & H.D. Lasswell. *The policy sciences: Recent developments in scope and method.* Stanford CA: Stanford University Press.

Lasswell, H.D. 1971. *A pre-view of policy sciences.* New York, NY: American Elsevier.

LeBlanc, D. (2011, December 13). Watchdog calls for financial penalties against unregistered lobbyists. *Globe and Mail.*

LeBlanc, D., & Curry, B. (2015, September 15). The decisions behind the scenes of the Liberals' infrastructure plan. *The Globe and Mail.* Retrieved from: http://www.theglobeandmail.com/news/politics/the-decisions-behind-the-scenes-of-the-liberals-infrastructure-plan/article26375251/?click=sf_globefb

LeDuc, L. (2003). *The politics of direct democracy: Referendums in global perspective.* Peterborough, ON: Broadview Press.

LeDuc, L. (2005, January). Making votes count: How well did our electoral system perform? *Electoral Insight.* Retrieved from www.elections.ca/eca/eim/article_search/article.asp?id=128&lang=e&frmPageSize=&textonly=false

LeDuc, L., & Pammett, J. (2011). The evolution of the Harper dynasty. In J. Pammett & C. Dornan (Eds.), *The Canadian federal election of 2011.* Toronto, ON: Dundurn Press.

LeDuc, L., Pammett, J., & Bastedo, H. (2008, August). *The problem of young voters: A qualitative and quantitative analysis.* Prepared for presentation at the American Political Science Association annual meeting, Boston, MA.

Legasse, P. (2010). Nils Ørvik's "defence against help." *International Journal, 55* (2), 463–474.

Levy, G. (2009). A crisis not made in a day. In P.H. Russell and L. Sossin (Eds.), *Parliamentary democracy in crisis.* Toronto, ON: University of Toronto Press.

Levy, G. (2014, February 10). What's not to like about Justin Trudeau's Senate reform? *Toronto Star.* Retrieved from http://www.hilltimes.com/opinion-piece/2014/02/10/whats-not-to-like-about-justin-trudeaus-senate-reform/37382

Lewis, S. (2015). It's time to rethink Ottawa's role in health care. *Policy Options,* March.

Li, Peter. (1998). *Chinese in Canada* (2nd ed.). Toronto, ON: Oxford University Press.

Liberal Party of Canada (2012). *Liberal Party of Canada constitution.* Retrieved from http://djsvoutqo4b1q.cloudfront.net/files/2012/04/Liberal-Party-of-Canada-2012-Constitution-English.pdf

Liberal Party of Canada (2015a). Justin Trudeau on extending the combat mission in Iraq and expanding into Syria. Retrieved from https://www.liberal.ca/speech-justin-trudeau-hoc-2015-on-extending-the-combat-mission-in-iraq-and-expanding-into-syria/

Liberal Party of Canada (2015b). Liberal Party of Canada website: www.liberal.ca

Light, P.C. (1999). *The true size of government*. Washington, DC: Brookings Institution Press.

Lightman, E. (2003). *Social policy in Canada*. Don Mills, ON: Oxford University Press.

Lindblom, C.E. (1977). *Politics and markets: the world's political-economic systems*. New York, NY: Basic Books.

Lipset, S.M. (1990). *Continental divide: The values and institutions of the United States and Canada*. New York, NY: Routledge.

Lipset, S.M. (1996). *American exceptionalism: A double-edged sword*. New York, NY: Norton.

Literary Review of Canada (2011). *The rights of refugees: What Europe's problems can teach Canada about a growing international concern*. Toronto, ON: Literary Review of Canada. Retrieved from http://reviewcanada.ca/reviews/2011/07/01/the-rights-of-refugees

Lochead, K.E. (2004). Whose land is it anyway? The long road to the Nisga'a treaty. In R.M. Campbell, L.A. Pal, & M. Howlett (Eds.), *The real worlds of Canadian politics: Cases in process and policy* (4th ed.) (pp. 267–334). Peterborough, ON; Broadview Press.

Loewen, P., & Fournier, P. (2011). *Aboriginal electoral participation in Canada*. Ottawa, ON: Elections Canada.

Lott, S. (2004). *Corporate retaliation against consumers: The status of strategic lawsuits against public participation (SLAPPs) in Canada*. Ottawa, ON: Public Interest Advocacy Centre.

Lucas, A.L., & Shawitt, L. (2000). Underlying constraints on inter-governmental cooperation in setting and enforcing environmental standards. In P.C. Fafard & K. Harrison (Eds.), *Managing the environmental union: Intergovernmental regulations and environmental policy in Canada* (pp. 133–162). Montreal, QC: McGill-Queen's University Press.

Lukacs, M. (2013, October 21). New Brunswick fracking protests on the frontline of a democratic fight. *The Guardian*. Retrieved from www.theguardian.com/environment/2013/oct/21/new-brunswick-fracking-protests

Lum, Z.-A. (2014). Canada is the only UN member to reject landmark indigenous rights document. *Huffington Post Canada*, October 28.

MacCharles, T. (2012, December 20). Supreme Court niqab ruling: Veil can be worn to testify in some cases. Thestar.com. Retrieved from http://www.thestar.com/news/canada/2012/12/20/supreme_court_niqab_ruling_veil_can_be_worn_to_testify_in_some_cases.html

Macdonald, D. (2007). *Business and environmental politics in Canada*. Peterborough, ON: Broadview Press.

MacFarlane, E. (2013). *Governing from the bench. The Supreme Court of Canada and the judicial role*. Vancouver, BC: UBC Press.

MacFarlane, J. (2014). Women gain on corporate boards but visible minority representation slips. *Globe and Mail*, November 19. Retrieved from www.theglobeandmail.com/report-on-business/corporate-boards-now-have-more-women-fewer-minorities/article21641463/

MacIvor, H. (2006). *Canadian politics and government in the Charter era*. Toronto, ON: Thomson Nelson.

Mackenzie, H. (2014). All in a day's work? CEO pay in Canada. Canadian Centre for Policy Alternatives. Available at: http://policy-alternatives.ca/sites/default/files/uploads/publications/National%20Office/2014/01/All_in_a_Days_Work_CEO_%20Pay.pdf

Macklem, P. (2001). *Indigenous difference and the constitution of Canada*. Toronto, ON: University of Toronto Press.

MacLelland, L. (2015). Toronto police controversy: What is carding and is it legal? Retrieved from ca.news.yahoo.com/blogs/dailybrew/toronto-police-controversy--what-is--carding--and-is-it-legal-192840113.html

Maher, S. (2015). Harper not doing enough to end cozy relationship between lobbyists and politicians, critics say. Retrieved from http://news.nationalpost.com/2015/03/09/harper-not-doing-enough-to-keep-promise-to-end-cozy-relationship-between-lobbyists-and-politicians/

Mahtani, M. (2002). Interrogating the hyphen-nation: Canadian multicultural policy and "mixed race" identities. *Social Identities, 8* (1), 67–90. doi:10.1080/13504630220132026

Mair, P. (2002). Comparing party systems. In L. LeDuc, R. Niemi, & P. Norris, (Eds.), *Comparing democracies 2: New challenges in the study of elections and voting* (pp. 88–107). London, UK: Sage.

Makin, K. (2006, June 22). Prosecutors must share blame for botched cases, report says wrongful convictions in Newfoundland blamed on systemic lack of objectivity. *Globe and Mail*.

Makin, K. (2012a, January 17). Quebec case puts spotlight on economic rights of common-law partners. *Globe and Mail*.

Malenfant, E., Lebel, A., & Martel, L. (2010). *Projections of the diversity of the Canadian population 2006 to 2031* (Catalogue no. 91-551-X). Ottawa, ON: Statistics Canada. Retrieved from www.statcan.gc.ca/bsolc/olc-cel/olc-cel?catno=91-551-x&lang=eng. Reproduced and distributed on an "as is" basis with the permission of Statistics Canada.

Maloney, R. (2015). Bill C-51. Support for anti-terror legislation still dropping: Poll suggests. *The Huffington Post Canada* (April 10). Retrieved from www.huffingtonpost.ca/2015/04/10/bill-c-51-poll-anti-terror-legislation_n_7042460.html

Maloney, W. (2006). Political participation: Beyond the electoral arena. In P. Dunleavy, R. Hefferman, P. Cowley, & C. Hay (Eds.), *Developments in British politics*. Basingstoke, UK: Palgrave.

Mandel, M. (1994). *The Charter of Rights and the legalization of politics in Canada* (rev. ed.). Toronto, ON: Wall and Thompson.

Manfredi, C. (2001). *Judicial power and the Charter: Canada and the paradox of liberal constitutionalism* (2nd ed.). Toronto, ON: Oxford University Press.

Manfredi, C.P. (2003, October). Same-sex marriage and the notwithstanding clause. *Policy Options, 24* (9), 21–24.

Manzer, R. (1985). *Public policy and political development in Canada*. Toronto: University of Toronto Press.

Marchildon, G. (2015). Douglas versus Manning: "The political and religious battle over medicare in postwar Canada," unpublished ms.

Marland, A. (2011). Constituency campaigning in the 2011 Canadian general election. In J. Pammett & C. Dornan (Eds.), *The Canadian federal election of 2011*. Toronto, ON: Dundurn Press.

Martell, L. (1994). *Ecology and society: An introduction*. Amherst, MA: University of Massachusetts Press.

Martin, L. (1982). *The presidents and the prime ministers: Washington and Ottawa face to face: The myth of bilateral bliss, 1867–1982*.Toronto, ON: Doubleday Canada.

Martin, L. (2011). *Harperland: The politics of control*. Toronto: Penguin Canada.

Martin, L. (2012, October 23). Why aren't we debating the Canada–China investment pact? *The Globe and Mail*. Retrieved from: http://www.theglobeandmail.com/globe-debate/why-arent-we-debating-the-canada-china-investment-pact/article4629358/

Mas, S. (2013). Conservative MP Michael Chong makes a bid to fix Parliament. CBC News, December 3, 2013. Retrieved from http://www.cbc.ca/news/politics/conservative-mp-michael-chong-makes-bid-to-fix-parliament-1.2448922

Matas, R. (1998, January 13). A teacher relives a legal nightmare. *Globe and Mail*.

Mazereeuw, P. (2015, July 1). CETA: Caught between Canadian business, EU politicians. *Embassy*. Retrieved from www.embassynews.ca/news/2015/07/01/feds-caught-between-canadian-business-eu-politicians-on-isds/47330/?mlc=842&muid=4334

McCarthy, S. (2012b, April 17). Ottawa curbs ability of green groups to intervene in review process. *Globe and Mail.*

McCarthy, S. (2014, December 9). Harper: It would be "crazy" to impose climate change regulations on the oil industry. *The Globe and Mail.*

McGilly. F. (1998). *An introduction to Canada's public social services* (2nd ed.). Don Mills, ON: Oxford University Press.

McGrane, D. (2011). Political marketing and the NDP's historic breakthrough. In J. Pammett & C. Dornan (Eds.), *The Canadian federal election of 2011.* Toronto, ON: Dundurn Press.

McInturff, K., & Tulloch, P. (2014). Narrowing the gap: The difference that public sector wages makes. Retrieved from www.policyalternatives.ca/sites/default/files/uploads/publications/National%20Office/2014/10/Narrowing_the_Gap.pdf

McKenna, B. (2014, November 25). "Buy American" shuts out Canadian iron and steel from B.C. ferry terminal. *Globe and Mail,* November 25, 2014.

McKenzie, J.I. (2002). *Environmental politics in Canada.* Don Mills, ON: Oxford University Press.

McLachlin, B. (2005). *Medicine and the law: The challenge of mental illness.* Retrieved from www.scc-csc.gc.ca/court-cour/ju/spe-dis/bm05-02-17-eng.asp

McNaught, K. (1969). *The Pelican history of Canada.* Harmondsworth, UK: Penguin Books.

McNeil, K. (2007). *The jurisdiction of inherent right Aboriginal governments.* Research paper for the National Centre for First Nations Governance. Retrieved from http://fngovernance.org/ncfng_research/kent_mcneil.pdf

McRoberts, K. (1988). *Quebec: Social change and political crisis* (2nd ed.). Toronto, ON: McClelland & Stewart.

McRoberts, K. (1993). *Quebec: Social change and political crisis* (3rd ed.). Toronto, ON: Oxford University Press.

McWhinney, E. (1982). *Canada and the constitution 1979–1982: Patriation and the Charter of Rights.* Toronto, ON: University of Toronto Press.

Meinhard, A., & Foster, M. (1999). *The impact of volunteer community service programs on students in Toronto's secondary schools* (Working Paper Series No. 12). Toronto, ON: Centre for Voluntary Sector Studies.

Meinhard, A., & Foster, M. (2000). *Structuring student volunteering programs to the benefit of students and the community* (Working Paper Series No. 14). Toronto, ON: Centre for Voluntary Sector Studies.

Meisel, J., & Mendelsohn, M. (2001). Meteor? Phoenix? Chameleon? The decline and transformation of party in Canada. In H. Thorburn, (Ed.), *Party politics in Canada* (8th ed., pp. 163–178). Toronto, ON: Prentice Hall.

Mendelsohn, M., & Matthews, S. (2010). *The new Ontario: The shifting attitudes of Ontarians towards Confederation.* Toronto, ON: The Mowat Centre for Policy Innovation. Retrieved from www.mowatcentre.ca/pdfs/mowatResearch/8.pdf

Mendelsohn, M., & Parkin, A. (2001). Introducing direct democracy in Canada. *Choices, 7* (5), 3–38.

Mennie, J. (2014, June 2). Sovereignty, PQ off young Quebec's radar—poll. *Montreal Gazette.* Retrieved from http://montrealgazette.com/news/local-news/sovereignty-pq-off-young-quebecs-radar-poll

Merica, D., & Bradner, E. (2015, October 7). Hillary Clinton comes out against TPP trade deal. CNN Politics. Retrieved from: http://www.cnn.com/2015/10/07/politics/hillary-clinton-opposes-tpp/index.html

Michels, R. (1915). *Political parties: A sociological study of the oligarchical tendencies of modern democracy* (E. Paul & C. Paul, Trans.). New York, NY: Hearst.

Milan, A. (2011). *Migration: International, 2009* (Catalogue no. 91-209-X). Ottawa, ON: Statistics Canada.

Milbrath, L., & Goel, M.L. (1977). *How and why do people get involved in politics?* (2nd ed.). Lanham, MD: University Press of America.

Miljan, L. (2012). *Public policy in Canada: An introduction* (6th ed.). Don Mills ON: Oxford University Press.

Mill, J.S. (1872/1991). *Considerations on representative government.* London, UK: Longmans.

Milner, H. (2002). *Civic literacy: How informed citizens make democracy work.* Hanover, NH: University Press of New England.

Milner, H. (2005). Are young Canadians becoming political drop-outs? A comparative perspective. *Choices, 11* (3), 1–26.

Milner, H. (2008). *The informed political participation of young Canadians and Americans.* Maryland, MD: Centre for Information and Research on Civic Learning and Engagement.

Mishler, W. (1979). *Political participation in Canada: Prospects for democratic citizenship.* Toronto, ON: Macmillan Canada.

Monsebraaten, L. (2015). Homeless denied day in court. *Toronto Star* (June 15).

Montpetit, E. (2004). *Misplaced distrust: Policy networks and the environment in France, the United States, and Canada.* Vancouver, BC: UBC Press.

Montpetit, E. (2010). The deliberative and adversarial attitudes of interest groups. In J. Courtney & D. Smith (Eds.), *The Oxford Handbook of Canadian Politics.* Toronto, ON: Oxford University Press.

Morton, D. (2006). *A short history of Canada* (6th ed.). Toronto, ON: McClelland & Stewart.

Morton, D. (2007). *A military history of Canada* (5th ed.). Toronto, ON: McClelland & Stewart.

Morton, F.L. (1999, April). Dialogue or monologue? *Policy Options, 19* (3), 23–26.

Morton, F.L., & Knopff, R. (2000). *The Charter revolution and the court party.* Peterborough, ON: Broadview Press.

Mosca, G. (1965). *The ruling class* (A. Livingston, Ed., H.D. Kahn, Trans.). New York, NY: McGraw Hill.

Muldoon, P., Lucas, A., Gibson, R.P., Pickfield, P., & Williams, J. (2015). *An introduction to environmental law and policy in Canada* (2nd ed.) Toronto: Emond Montgomery.

Myers, A. (2015). For Harper appointed judges, "originalism" can be a form of activism. *The Globe and Mail* (June 24).

National Assembly (2015). *Bill 62 An Act to foster adherence to State religious neutrality, and in particular, to provide a framework for religious accommodation requests in certain bodies.* Retrieved from: https://www.google.ca/search?sourceid=ie7&q=bill+62+natio nal+assembly&rls=com.microsoft:en-CA:IE-Address&ie=UTF-8&oe=UTF-8&rlz=1I7TSCA_en&gfe_rd=cr&ei=h-wbVpe8JoOA2 AGa4YHYAQ&gws_rd=ssl

National Post (2011, October 22). Graphic: Follow the tweets of the Occupy movement. Retrieved from http://news.national-post.com/2011/10/22/follow-the-tweets-of-the-occupy-movement

Naumetz, T. (2013). Budget bill gives Harper Cabinet new powers over the CBC. Retrieved from http://www.hilltimes.com/news/politics/2013/04/30/budget-bill-gives-harper-cabinet-new-powers-over-cbc/34566

Nevitte, N. (1995). The dynamics of Canadian political culture(s). In R.M. Krause & R.H. Wagenberg (Eds.), *Introductory readings in Canadian government and politics* (2nd ed.). Mississauga, ON: Copp Clark.

Nevitte, N. (1996). *The decline of deference: Canadian value change in cross-national perspective.* Peterborough, ON: Broadview Press.

New Democratic Party of Canada (2011). *Constitution of the New Democratic Party of Canada.* Retrieved from http://xfer.ndp.ca/2011/2011-constitution/2011-11-CONSTITUTION-ENG.pdf

New Democratic Party of Canada (2013). NDP policy. Retrieved from http://xfer.ndp.ca/2012/2012-12-17-Email-Convention/Mtl2013_PolicyBook_E.pdf

Newfoundland and Labrador Executive Council (2007). Premier Williams says "a promise made is not a promise kept" for Newfoundland and Labrador (News release). Retrieved from www.releases.gov.nl.ca/releases/2007/exec/0320n04.htm

Nicol, J. (2015, July 17). Federal election 2015. Voter ID rules stand, judge rules. CBC News. Retrieved from: http://www.cbc.ca/news/politics/federal-election-2015-voter-id-rules-stand-judge-rules-1.3156519

Niemi, R., Hepburn, M., & Chapman, C. (2000). Community service by high school students: A cure for civic ills? *Political Behaviour, 22,* 45–69.

Nossal, K.R. (2013). The Liberal past in the Conservative present: Internationalism in the Harper era. In H.A. Smith & C.T. Sjolander (Eds.). *Canada in the world. Internationalism in Canadian foreign policy.* Don Mills, ON: Oxford University Press.

Nossal, K.R., Roussel, S., & Paquin, S. (2011). *International policy and politics in Canada.* Toronto, ON: Pearson Canada.

Nye, J.S, Jr. (2004). *Soft power: The means to success in world politics.* New York: Public Affairs.

O'Neill, B. (2002). Sugar and spice? Political culture and the political behaviour of Canadian women. In J. Everitt & B. O'Neill (Eds.), *Citizen politics: Research and theory in Canadian political behaviour* (pp. 40–55). Toronto: ON: Oxford University Press.

Office of the Auditor General of Canada (2011). 2011 June status report of the auditor general's report. Retrieved from http://www.oag-bvg.gc.ca/internet/English/parl_oag_201106_04_e_35372.html

Office of the Auditor General of Canada (2012). *2012 Spring report of the Auditor General of Canada,* Chapter 2. Retrieved from www.oag-bvg.gc.ca

Office of the Commissioner for Federal Judicial Affairs (2015, April 1). Retrieved from http://www.fja.gc.ca/appointments-nominations/judges-juges-eng.html

Office of the Independent Police Review Director (2012). *Policing the right to protest: G20 systemic review report.* Toronto, ON: Author.

Ogrodnik, I. (2014, November 24). 25 years since Canada vowed to end child poverty, where are we now? Retrieved from www.globalnews.ca/news/1685376/25-years-since-canada-vowed-to-end-child-poverty-where-are-we-now

Olsen, D. (1980). *The state elite.* Toronto, ON: McClelland & Stewart.

Olson, M. (1965). *The logic of collective action: Public goods and the theory of groups.* Cambridge, MA: Harvard University Press.

Ontario Ministry of Education and Training (1999). *Ontario secondary schools, grades 9 to 12: Program and diploma requirements.* Toronto, ON: Author.

Open Working Group Proposal for Sustainable Development Goals (2014). United Nations Department of Economic and Social Affairs. Retrieved from sustainabledevelopment.un.org/sdgsproposal

Organisation for Economic Co-operation and Development (2006). Where immigrant students succeed: A comparative review of performance and engagement in PISA 2003 (OECD, Program for International Student Assessment). Retrieved from: http://www.oecd.org/edu/school/programmeforinternationalstudentassessmentpisa/whereimmigrantstudentssucceed-acomparativereviewofperformanceandengagementinpisa2003.htm

Organisation for Economic Co-operation and Development (2011). *Divided we stand: Why inequality keeps rising.* Retrieved from www.oecd.org/els/social/inequality

Organisation for Economic Co-operation and Development (2014b). OECD2014-Focus on Top Incomes-Figures-Data.xlsx.

Osborne, D., & Gaebler, T. (1992). *Reinventing government: How the entrepreneurial spirit is transforming the public sector.* New York, NY: Basic Books.

Ostberg, C.L., & Wetstein, M.E. (2007). *Attitudinal decision making in the Supreme Court of Canada.* Vancouver, BC: UBC Press.

Page v. Mulcair (2013) FC 402 (CanLII) http://www.canlii.org/en/ca/fct/doc/2013/2013fc402/2013fc402.html

Pal, L.A. (1993). *Interests of state: The politics of language, multiculturalism, and feminism in Canada.* Montreal, QC: McGill-Queen's University Press.

Pammett, J. (2008). Elections. In M. Whittington & G. Williams (Eds.), *Canadian politics in the 21st century* (7th ed.) (pp. 153–157). Toronto, ON: Nelson.

Pammett, J., & LeDuc, L. (2006). Voter turnout in 2006: More than just the weather. In J. Pammett & C. Dornan (Eds.), *The Canadian federal election of 2006* (pp. 304–326). Toronto, ON: Dundurn Press.

Papillon, M. (2008). Canadian federalism and the emerging mosaic of Aboriginal multilevel governance. In H. Bakvis & G. Skogstad (Eds.), *Canadian federalism: Performance, effectiveness, and legitimacy* (2nd ed.) (pp. 291–313). Toronto, ON: Oxford University Press.

Parliament of Canada (2012). Bill C-38. *An act to amend certain provisions of the budget tabled in parliament on March 29, 2012 and other measures.* Retrieved from http://parl.gc.ca/LegisInfo/BillDetails.aspx?Language=E&Mode=1&billId=5514128&View=8

Parliament of Canada (2015). Women Candidates in General Elections—1921 to date. Retrieved from http://www.parl.gc.ca/about/parliament/federalridingshistory/hfer.asp?Language=E&Search=WomenElection

Parliamentary Debates on the Subject of the Confederation of the British North American Provinces (1865). 3rd Session, 8th Provincial Parliament of Canada. Quebec: Hunter, Rose & Co, Parliamentary Printers, 1985. Available at: http://books.google.ca/books?id=WQ4UAAAAYAAJ&printsec=frontcover&source=gbs_ge_summary_r&cad=0#v=onepage&q&f=false

Patriquin, M. (2009, February 19). A billionaire, the law, his Brazilian ex: The stormy breakup that may redefine marriage in Canada. *Maclean's.*

Patten, S. (2010). Democracy and the candidate selection process in Canadian elections. In H. MacIvor (Ed.), *Elections* (pp. 135–154). Toronto, ON: Emond Montgomery Publications.

Payton, L. (2012, May 15). Auditor takes on brass over F-35 cost calculation. CBC News. Retrieved from www.cbc.ca

Peach, I. (2014). *Reference re Supreme Court Act,* ss5 and ss6—Expanding the Constitution of Canada. *Alberta Law Review, 23* (3), 1–5.

Peach, I., & Mintz, A. (2013). *Daniels v. Canada:* The inevitable comes to pass, at last. *Alberta Law Review, 50* (4), 883–892.

Pelz, T., & Lehmann, V. (2007). The evolution of UN peacekeeping: Reforming DPKO (Fact sheet). *Dialogue on Globalization.* Retrieved from the ReliefWeb website: www.reliefweb.int/rw/lib.nsf/db900sid/PANA-7HRDVG/$file/fes_nov2007.pdf?openelement

Pérez, O.J. (2008). Measuring democratic political cultures in Latin America. In R. Millett, J.S. Holmes, & O.J. Pérez (Eds.), *Latin American democracy: Emerging reality or endangered species?* (pp. 21–41). New York, NY: Routledge.

Perkins, T. (2009, April 20). Nobody's saviour. *Globe and Mail.* Retrieved from www.theglobeandmail.com/report-on-business/article1138040

Perkins, T., & Carmichael, K. (2014). Jeremy Rudin to replace Julie Dickson as head of OSFI. *Globe and Mail,* 13 June. Retrieved from http://www.theglobeandmail.com/report-on-business/new-osfi-head/article19163329/

Petter, A. (1989). Federalism and the myth of the federal spending power. *Canadian Bar Review, 68* (1), 448–479.

Petter, A. (2010). Legalize this: The chartering of Canadian politics. In J.B. Kelly & C.P. Manfredi (Eds.), *Contested constitutionalism: Reflections on the Canadian Charter of Rights and Freedoms*. Vancouver, BC: UBC Press.

Philips, S. (2004). Interest groups, social movements, and the voluntary sector: En route to reducing the democratic deficit. In J. Bickerton & A.-G. Gagnon (Eds.), *Canadian Politics* (4th ed., pp. 323–347). Peterborough, ON: Broadview Press.

Pickersgill, J. (1962). *The Liberal Party*. Toronto, ON: McClelland & Stewart.

Picot, G., & Hou, F. (2003). *The rise in low-income rates among immigrants in Canada* (Analytical Studies Branch Research Paper Series No. 198). Ottawa, ON: Statistics Canada.

Plante, F. (2013). The curtailment of debate in the House of Commons. *Canadian Parliamentary Review*, Spring 2013: 28–36.

Plecash, C. (2012, April 2). Feds want to silence environmental "radicals" in budget cuts, say critics. *Hill Times*.

Porter, B., & Jackman, M. (2014). Introduction: Achieving social rights in Canada. In M. Jackman & B. Porter (Eds.). *Advancing social rights in Canada*. Toronto, ON: Irwin Law.

Porter, J. (1965). *The vertical mosaic: An analysis of social class and power in Canada*. Toronto, ON: University of Toronto Press.

Potvin, M. (2011). Interethnic relations and racism in Quebec. In S. Gervais, C. Kirkey, and J. Rudy (Eds.), Quebec questions: Quebec studies for the twenty-first century. Don Mills, ON: Oxford University Press.

Preston, J. (2011, November 24). Protesters look for ways to feed the web. *New York Times*. Retrieved from www.nytimes.com/2011/11/25/business/media/occupy-movement-focuses-on-staying-current-on-social-networks.html

Prince, M. (2007). *The electoral participation of people with special needs*. Ottawa, ON: Elections Canada.

Prince, M. (2015). The provinces and social policy: Canada's multiple welfare states. In Christopher Dunn (ed.), *Provinces: Canadian provincial politics*. Toronto, ON: University of Toronto Press.

Prince, M.J., & Abele, F. (2005). Paying for self-determination: Aboriginal peoples, self-government, and fiscal relations in Canada. In M. Murphy (Ed.), *Canada: The state of the federation 2003. Reconfiguring Aboriginal-state relations*. Montreal, QC: McGill-Queen's University Press.

Privy Council Office (2007, October 15). Learning from experience: Overview of past efforts at public service renewal and lessons learned. Draft internal paper.

Pross, A.P. (1992). *Group politics and public policy* (2nd ed.). Toronto, ON: Oxford University Press.

Proudfoot, S. (2010). "Count on it: Long-form census basic to decision-making in Canada. Postmedia News. July 17. Retrieved from http://www.canada.com/technology/Count+long+form+census+basic+decision+making+Canada/3288863/story.html

Pruysers, S. (2014). Reconsidering vertical integration: An examination of national political parties and their counterparts in Ontario. *Canadian Journal of Political Science, 47* (2), 237–258.

Public Service Commission (2007). *Employment equity. Appointment policy: Questions and answers*. Retrieved from www.psc-cfp.gc.ca/plcy-pltq/qa-qr/appointment-nomination/equityequite-eng.htm

Putnam, R. (with Leonardi, R.) (1993). *Making democracy work: Civic traditions in modern Italy*. Princeton, NJ: Princeton University Press.

Putnam, R.D. (2000). *Bowling alone: The collapse and revival of American community*. New York, NY: Simon & Schuster.

R. v Drybones [1970] S.C.R. 282

R. v. Big Drug Mart Ltd. (1985). 1 S.C.R 295.

R. v. Edwards Books and Art Ltd. [1986] 2 S.C.R. 713

R. v. Gladue [1999] 1 S.C.R. 688

R. v. Keegstra, [1990] 3 S.C.R. 697

R. v. Marshall. (1999). CanLII 665 (S.C.C.).

R. v. Oakes. (1986). 1 S.C.R 103.

R. v. Pamajewon. (1996). CanLII 161 (S.C.C.).

R. v. Powley. (2003). 2 S.C.R. 207.

R. v. Sparrow. (1990). CanLII 104 (S.C.C.).

R. v. Van der Peet [1996] 2 S.C.R. 507

Radmilovic, V. (2010). Strategic legitimacy cultivation at the Supreme Court of Canada: Quebec Secession Reference and Beyond. *Canadian Journal of Political Science, 43* (4), 843–869.

Rayside, D., & Wilcox, C. (2011). The difference that a border makes: The political intersection of sexuality and religion in Canada and the United States. In D. Rayside & C. Wilcox (Eds.), *Faith, politics and sexual diversity in Canada and the United States*. Vancouver, BC: UBC Press.

Reference re Secession of Quebec. (1998). 2 S.C.R. 217. Retrieved from http://csc.lexum.umontreal.ca/en/1998/1998rcs2-217/1998rcs2-217.html

Reference re Securities Act. (2011). SCC61 [2011] 3 S.C.R. 837.

Reference re Senate Reform, 2014 SCC32

Reference re Supreme Court Act 2014 SCC 21 [2014].

Reference re. Securities Act, 2011 3 S.C.R 837 [2011]

Reitz, J. (2011). *Pro-immigration Canada. Social and economic roots of popular views*. Montreal, QC: Institute for Research on Public Policy.

Reitz, J.G., & Banerjee, R. (2007). Racial inequality, social cohesion, and policy issues in Canada. In K. Banting, T.J. Courchene, & F.L. Seidle (Eds.), *Belonging? Diversity, recognition and shared citizenship in Canada*. Montreal, QC: Institute for Research on Public Policy.

Rempel, R. (2006). *Dreamland: How Canada's pretend foreign policy has undermined sovereignty*. Montreal, QC: McGill-Queen's University Press.

Resnick, P. (2005). *The European roots of Canadian identity*. Toronto, ON: Broadview Press.

Rice, J.J., & Prince, M.J. (2013). *Changing politics of Canadian social policy*. Toronto, ON: University of Toronto Press.

Richards, J. (2014). Why the First Nations Education Act deserves broad parliamentary support. *Globe and Mail*, May 1.

Richer, K. (2007). *The federal spending power*. Parliamentary Information and Research Section, Library of Parliament Publication PRB 07-36-ew. Retrieved from www.parl.gc.ca/content/LOP/ResearchPublications/prb0736-e.pdf

Roach, K., & Forcese, C. (2015, April 2). Submission to the Senate Standing Committee. Retrieved from www.antiterrorlaw.ca

Robertson and Rosetanni v. R [1963] S.Cd.R. 651.

Robin, M. (1992). *Shades of right. Nativist and fascist politics in Canada, 1920—1940*. Toronto, ON: University of Toronto Press.

Romanow, R., Whyte, J., & Leeson, H. (1984). *Canada . . . Notwithstanding: The making of the constitution 1976–1982*. Toronto, ON: Methuen.

Romero, M.J. (2014). A private affair. Shining a light on the shadowy institutions giving public support to private companies and taking over the development agenda. European network on debt and development. Retrieved from http://www.eurodad.org/files/pdf/53be474b0aefa.pdf

Royal Commission on Aboriginal Peoples. (1996). *Royal Commission Report on Aboriginal Peoples*. Volume 1. Retrieved from www.aadnc-aandc.gc.ca/eng/1307458586498

Ruspini, P. (2005). Public policies and community services for immigrant integration: Italy and the European Union. *Global Migration Perspectives, 45.* Retrieved from www.gcim.org/attachements/GMP%20No%2045.pdf

Russell, P.H. (2004) *Constitutional odyssey: Can Canadians become a sovereign people?* (3rd ed.). Toronto, ON: University of Toronto Press.

Russell, P.H. (2006). Constitutional politics: In a new era Canada returns to old methods. In H.J. Michelmann & C. DeClercy (Eds.), *Continuity and change in Canadian politics: Essays in honour of David E. Smith* (pp. 19–38). Toronto, ON: University of Toronto Press.

Russell, P.H. (2008). *Two cheers for minority government: The evolution of Canadian parliamentary democracy.* Toronto, ON: Emond Montgomery.

Russell, P.H. (2009). The unrealized benefits of Canada's unfederal judicial system. In D. Anastakis & P.E. Bryden (Eds.), *Framing Canadian federalism: Historical essays in honour of John T. Saywell.* Toronto, ON: University of Toronto Press.

Russell, P.H. (2010). The Charter and Canadian democracy. In J.B. Kelly & C.P. Manfredi (Eds.), *Contested constitutionalism: Reflections on the Canadian Charter of Rights and Freedoms.* Vancouver, BC: UBC Press.

Russell, P.H., Knopff, R., Bateman, M.J., & Hiebert, J.I. (2008). *The court and the constitution: Leading cases.* Toronto, ON: Emond Montgomery.

Ryan, C. (2003). *Quebec and interprovincial discussion and consultation.* Retrieved from the Institute for Research on Public Policy website: www.irpp.org/miscpubs/archive/federation/ryan.pdf

Said, T. (2013). Employment equity in the federal public service: The current status and critical perspective. Ottawa: The Professional Institute of the Public Service of Canada. Retrieved from http://www.pipsc.ca/portal/page/portal/website/aboutinstitute/contact

Samara Canada (2014). Lightweights? Political participation beyond the ballot box. Toronto: Samara Canada. Retrieved from http://www.samaracanada.com/docs/default-document-library/samara_lightweights.pdf

Sarin, P. (2015, July 30). Millions of Canadians denied the right to vote in 2015 federal election. Rabble.ca. Retrieved from http://rabble.ca/columnists/2015/07/millions-canadians-denied-right-to-vote-2015-federal-election

Saul, J.R. (2008). *A fair country: Telling truths about Canada.* Toronto, ON: Viking Canada.

Saul, J.R. (2014). *The comeback.* Toronto, ON: Penguin Canada.

Savoie, D. (1999). *Governing from the centre: The concentration of power in Canadian politics.* Toronto, ON: University of Toronto Press.

Savoie, D. (2008). *Court government and the collapse of accountability in Canada and the United Kingdom.* Toronto, ON: University of Toronto Press.

Scarrow, S. (2000). Parties without members? Party organizations in a changing political environment. In R.J. Dalton & M.P. Wattenberg (Eds.), *Parties without partisans: Political change in advanced industrial democracies* (pp. 79–101). Oxford, UK: Oxford University Press.

Schachter v. Canada. (1992). 2 S.C.R. 679.

Scharper, S. (2011, September 11). Civil disobedience goes green. *Toronto Star.* Retrieved from www.thestar.com/opinion/editorialopinion/article/1051885--civil-disobedience-goes-green

Schmitz, C. (2010). Timelines mar refugee system overhaul. *The Lawyer's Weekly.* Retrieved from http://oppenheimer.mcgill.ca/Timelines-mar-refugee-system?lang=fr

Schneiderman, D. (1991, November). On stacking the Senate. *Policy Options, 12* (9), 34–35.

Science, Technology and Innovation Council of Canada (2008). State of the Nation (2008). Retrieved from: http://www.stic-csti.ca/eic/site/stic-csti.nsf/eng/h_00011.html

Science, Technology and Innovation Council of Canada (2010). State of the Nation (2010). Retrieved from: http://www.stic-csti.ca/eic/site/stic-csti.nsf/eng/h_00038.html

Sebesta, K. (2012). Gladue principles not being met: SCC. *Canadian Lawyer.* Retrieved from www.canadianlawyermag.com/legalfeeds/759/gladue-principles-not-being-met-scc.html.

Séguin, R. (2012, April 12). On constitutional questions it's still Quebec vs. the rest of the country. *Globe and Mail.*

Sens, A., & Stoett, P. (2005). *Global politics: Origins, currents, directions* (3rd ed.). Toronto, ON: Thomson Nelson.

Sheikh, M. (2010). We still have time to change the census decision. *Globe and Mail,* August 10. Retrieved from http://www.theglobeandmail.com/globe-debate/we-still-have-time-to-reverse-the-census-decision/article1376478/

Siaroff, A. (2005). *Comparing political regimes: A thematic introduction to comparative politics.* Peterborough, ON: Broadview Press.

Siegfried, A. (1966). *The race question in Canada.* Toronto, ON: McClelland & Stewart.

Sierra Club BC (2012). New risk of logging in Clayoquot Sound biosphere reserve. Retrieved from www.sierraclub.bc.ca/media-centre/press-releases/new-risk-of-logging-in-clayoquot-sound-biosphere-reserve

Simeon, R. (1976). Studying public policy. *Canadian Journal of Political Science, 9* (4), 548–580.

Simeon, R. (2006). *Federal–provincial diplomacy: The making of recent policy in Canada.* Toronto, ON: University of Toronto Press.

Simeone, T., & Troniak, S. (2011). *Legislative summary of Bill C-27: An act to enhance the financial accountability and transparency of First Nations.* Parliamentary Information and Research Services, Library of Parliament. Publication No. 41-1-C27-E.

Simmons, J., & Graefe, P. (2013). Assessing the collaboration that was "collaborative federalism" 1996–2006. *Canadian Political Science Review, 7* (1), 25–36.

Simpson, G. (2001). *The friendly dictatorship.* Toronto, ON: McClelland & Stewart.

Simpson, J. (2011, October 15). Quebecers want power, not independence. *Globe and Mail.*

Small, T. (2010). Canadian politics in 140 characters: Party politics in the Twitterverse. *Canadian Parliamentary Review* (Autumn), 39–45.

Smart, M. (2009). *The evolution of federal transfers since the O'Brien Report.* Retrieved from http://jdi-legacy.econ.queensu.ca/Files/Conferences/Budget2009conferencepapers/Michael%20Smart-v2.pdf

Smith, A. (2009). *The roles and responsibilities of central agencies* (PRB 09-01E). Retrieved from the Library of Parliament website www.parl.gc.ca/information/library/PRBpubs/prb0901-e.htm#a15

Smith, J. (2004). *Federalism.* Vancouver, BC: UBC Press.

Smith, J. (2013). The Canadian government reimbursed Attawapiskat First Nation for third party manager costs. Retrieved from http://www.thestar.com/news/canada/2013/04/11/the_canadian_government_reimbursed_attawapiskat_first_nation_for_third_party_manager_costs.html

Smith, M. (Ed.). (2007). *Group politics and social movements in Canada.* Peterborough, ON: Broadview Press.

Sniderman, P.M., Fletcher, J.F., Russell, P.H., & Tetlock, P.E. (1996). *The clash of rights: Liberty, equality, and legitimacy in pluralist democracy.* New Haven, CT: Yale University Press.

Songer, D.R., & Siripurapu, J. (2009). The unanimous decisions of the Supreme Court of Canada as a test of the attitudinal model. *Canadian Journal of Political Science, 42,* 65–92.

Soroka, S., Cutler, F., Stolle, D., & Fournier, P. (2011). Capturing change (and stability) in the 2011 campaign. *Policy Options, 32* (June–July), 70–77.

Soroka, S., Penner, E., & Blidook, K. (2009). Constituency influence in Parliament. *Canadian Journal of Political Science, 42,* 563–591.

Sossin, L. (2013). Should Canada have a representative Supreme Court? In N. Verrelli, ed., *The democratic dilemma. Reforming Canada's Supreme Court*. Montreal, QC: McGill-Queen's University Press.

Soucy, J., & Wrobel, M.C. (2000). *Fiscal policy in Canada: The changing role of the federal and provincial governments*. Parliamentary Research Branch, Library of Parliament, March 27, 2000, Publication no. 91-2E.

St. John's Telegram (2011, December 13). Editorial.

Statistics Canada (2003). Ethnic diversity survey: Portrait of a multicultural society (Catalogue No. 89-593-XIE). Retrieved from www.statcan.gc.ca/bsolc/olc-cel/olc-cel?lang=eng&catno=89-593-X

Statistics Canada, National Household Survey (2011). Immigration and Ethnocultural Diversity in Canada, National Household Survey, 2011 (Catalogue number 99-010-X2011001. Retrieved from www12.statcan.gc.ca/nhs-enm/2011/as-sa/99-010-x/2011001/c-g/c-g02-eng.cfm. Reproduced and distributed on an "as is" basis with the permission of Statistics Canada.

Statistics Canada (2011a). Aboriginal people and the labour market: Estimates from the Labour Force Survey, 2008–2010. Retrieved from www.statcan.gc.ca/pub/71-588-x/2011003/tablestableaux-eng.htm

Statistics Canada (2011b). Women in Canada: Paid work. Retrieved from www.statcan.gc.ca/pub/89-503-x/2010001/article/11387-eng.htm#a17

Statistics Canada (2011c, July 5). Reasons for not voting in the May 2, 2011, federal election. *The Daily*. Retrieved from www.statcan.gc.ca/daily-quotidien/110705/dq110705a-eng.htm

Statistics Canada. (2013). Immigration and ethnocultural diversity in Canada, National Household Survey, 2011. Catalogue number 99-010-X2011001. Retrieved from http://www12.statcan.gc.ca/nhs-enm/2011/as-sa/99-010-x/2011001/c-g/c-g01-eng.cfm. This does not constitute an endorsement by Statistics Canada of this product.

Statistics Canada (2014, February 25). The Daily. Retrieved from www.statcan.gc.ca/daily-quotidiem/140225/t140225b003-eng.htm.

Statistics Canada (2014, November 18). High income trends among Canadian taxpayers, 1982–2012) The Daily. Retrieved from www.statcan.gc.ca/daily-quotidien/141118/t141118b001-eng.htm.

Statistics Canada (2015a). Export of goods on a balance of payments basis, by product. CANSIM, table 228-0059 http://www.statcan.gc.ca/tables-tableaux/sum-som/l01/cst01/gblec04-eng.htm.

Statistics Canada (2015b). Labour force characteristics by age and sex—seasonally adjusted. Retrieved from http://www.statcan.gc.ca/daily-quotidien/150410/t150410a001-eng.htm.

Statutes of Quebec (2000). *An act respecting the exercise of the fundamental rights and prerogatives of the Québec people and the Québec state* (ch. 46). Retrieved from http://www2.publicationsduquebec.gouv.qc.ca/dynamicSearch/telecharge.php?type=2&file=/E_20_2/E20_2_A.html

Stechyson, N. (2012, April 9). Accounting differences explain F-35 price: MacKay. *Vancouver Sun*.

Stewart, I. (2002). Vanishing points: Three paradoxes of political culture research. In J. Everitt & B. O'Neill (Eds.), *Citizen politics: Research and theory in Canadian political behaviour* (pp. 21–39). Toronto, ON: Oxford University Press.

Stiglitz, J.E., & Hersh, A.S. (2015, October 2). The Trans-Pacific free trade charade. Project Syndicate. Retrieved from: http://www.project-syndicate.org/commentary/trans-pacific-partnership-charade-by-joseph-e--stiglitz-and-adam-s--hersh-2015-10

Stolle, D., Hooghe, M., & Micheletti, M. (2005). Politics in the supermarket: Political consumerism as a form of political participation. *International Political Science Review, 26* (3), 245–269.

Strapagiel, L. (2013, October 22). New Brunswick fracking protests: An FAQ guide. Why First Nations are protesting shale gas exploration in the province. Retrieved from o.canada.com/news/new-brunswick-fracking-protests-a-faq-guide

Strategic Counsel (2008). A report to the *Globe and Mail* and CTV: 2008 federal election pre-election national poll. Retrieved from www.thestrategiccounsel.com/our_news/polls/2008-10-12%20National%20Poll%20f.pdf

Student Vote (2015). *Students in Toronto's secondary schools.* Working Paper Series No. 12. Toronto, ON: Centre for Voluntary Sector Studies.

Suny, R.G. (2006). Nationalism, nation making and the postcolonial states of Asia, Africa, and Eurasia. In L. Barrington (Ed.), *Making and protecting the nation in postcolonial and postcommunist states.* Ann Arbor, MI, University of Michigan Press.

Tanguay, A.B. (2014). The limits to democratic reform in Canada. In J. Bickerton & A.-G. Gagnon (Eds.). Canadian politics, 6th ed. Toronto, ON: University of Toronto Press, pp. 281–308.

Taylor, A. (2010). *The civil war of 1812. American citizens, British subjects, Irish rebels, and Indian allies.* Toronto, ON: Random House Canada.

Taylor, S. (2012). DND's own lobby group, Conference of Defence Associations, plugs the F-35. *The Sixth Estate* (February 7). Retrieved from sixthestate.net.

Temelini, M. (2008). The Canadian student movement and the January 25, 1995, "National Day of Strike and Action." In M.H. Callaghan & M. Hayday (Eds.), *Mobilizations, protests & engagements: Canadian perspectives on social movements* (pp. 222–243). Halifax, NS: Fernwood.

"Territorial Evolution of Canada, 1867," Atlas of Canada, Map Archives History, 1639-1949 Territorial Evolution of Canada (1667 to 1949). (c) Department of Natural Resources Canada. All rights reserved. Retrieved from http://atlas.nrcan.gc.ca/site/english/maps/archives/historical/mcr_2306.

Thomas, P.E.J., Loewen, P.J., & MacKenzie, M.K. (2013). Fair isn't always equal: Constituency population and the quality of representation in Canada. *Canadian Journal of Political Science 46:2* (June), pp. 273–294.

Thomas, P.G. (2002). Parliament and the public service. In C. Dunn (Ed.), *The handbook of Canadian public administration*. Toronto, ON: Oxford University Press.

Thompson, D. (1976). *John Stuart Mill and representative government*. Princeton, NJ: Princeton University Press.

Thorburn, H.G. (2001). The development of political parties in Canada. In H.G. Thorburn & A. Whitehord (Eds.), *Party politics in Canada* (pp. 1–8). Toronto, ON: Prentice Hall.

Thorburn, H.G. (Ed.). (1991). *Party politics in Canada* (6th ed.). Toronto, ON: Prentice-Hall Canada.

Tilly, C. (1975). *The formation of national states in Western Europe*. Princeton, NJ: Princeton University Press.

Timeline: The Quebec *kirpan* case. (2006, March 2). CBC News Online. Retrieved from www.cbc.ca/news/background/kirpan

Titmuss, R. (1956). *The social division of welfare: Essays on the welfare state*. London: Unwin.

Tomlin, B.W., Hillmer, N., & Hampson, F.O. (2008). *Canada's international policies: Agendas, alternatives, and politics*. Toronto, ON: Oxford University Press.

Torjman, S. (2010). *Poverty reduction in Quebec: The first five years*. Ottawa, ON: Caledon Institute of Social Policy.

Torrance, J. (1986). *Public violence in Canada, 1867–1982*. Montreal, QC: McGill-Queen's University Press.

Tossutti, L. (2007). *The electoral participation of ethnocultural communities*. Ottawa, ON: Elections Canada.

Tossutti, L., & Hilderman, J. (2015). Representing Canadians: Is the 41st Parliament still a vertical mosaic? In E. Gidengil and H. Bastedo (Eds.), Canadian democracy from the ground up: Perceptions and performance. Vancouver: UBC Press.

Treasury Board of Canada Secretariat (2007). *Quick facts about official languages*. Retrieved from www.tbs-sct.gc.ca/faq/fat-eng.asp

Treasury Board of Canada Secretariat (2011–2012). Annual report on official languages. Retrieved from http://www.tbs-sct.gc.ca/reports-rapports/ol-lo/11-12/arol-ralo/arol-ralo-eng.pdf

Treasury Board of Canada Secretariat (2013). Demographic snapshot of the federal public service 2012. Retrieved from http://www.tbs-sct.gc.ca/res/stats/demo12-eng.asp#toc222

Treasury Board of Canada Secretariat (2014a). *Quick facts about official languages.* Retrieved from www.tbs-sct.gc.ca/faq/fat-eng.asp

Treasury Board of Canada Secretariat (2014b). Parent Crown corporations grouped by ministerial portfolio. Retrieved from https://www.tbs-sct.gc.ca/reports-rapports/cc-se/crown-etat/ccmp-smpm-eng.asp

Treasury Board of Canada Secretariat (2015). Distribution of designated groups in the public service by type of employment and gender. Retrieved from http://www.tbs-sct.gc.ca/reports-rapports/ee/2013-2014/tab08-eng.asp

Trudeau, P.E. (1987, May 27). Say good-bye to the dream of one Canada. *Toronto Star.* Retrieved from www.solon.org/Constitutions/Canada/English/Arguments/trudeau-star-87.html

Turcotte, M. (2015). Volunteering and charitable giving in Canada. Catalogue no. 89-652-X2015001. Ottawa: Minister of Industry, (pp. 5–16). Statistics Canada: General Social Survey on Giving, Volunteering and Participating, 2013. This does not constitute an endorsement by Statistics Canada of this product.

Turnbull, L., & Aucoin, P. (2006). *Fostering Canadians' role in public policy: A strategy for institutionalizing public involvement in policy* (CCRN Research Report P07). Ottawa, ON: Canadian Policy Research Networks.

Uhr, J. (1998). *Deliberative democracy in Australia: The changing place of Parliament.* Cambridge, UK: Cambridge University Press.

United Nations (1994). *Human development report 1994.* Retrieved from http://hdr.undp.org/en/reports/global/hdr1994

United Nations (2005). 2005 World summit outcome. Retrieved from www.un.org/summit2005

United Nations Declaration on the Rights of Indigenous Peoples (2009). Available at www.un.org/esa/socdev/unpfii/documents/DRIPs_en.pdf

United Nations High Commission on Refugees (2014). Asylum levels and trends in industrialized countries, first half 2014. Retrieved from http://www.unhcr.org/5423f9699.html

United Nations Peacekeeping (2015). Retrieved from www.un.org/en/peacekeeping/resources/statistics/contributors.shtml

United States Census Bureau (2010). Voting and registration in the election of November 2008: Population characteristics. Washington, D.C: U.S. Department of Commerce, Economics and Statistics Administration, U.S. Census Bureau. Retrieved from http://www.census.gov/prod/2010pubs/p20-562.pdf

Uppal, S., & LaRochelle-Côté, S. (2012). Factors associated with voting. Component of Statistics Canada Catalogue no. 75-001-X, Perspectives on Labour and Income. Ottawa: Statistics Canada.

Uppal, S., & LaRochelle-Côté, S. (2014). Overqualification among recent university graduates in Canada. Statistics Canada. Retrieved from http://www.statcan.gc.ca/pub/75-006-x/2014001/article/11916-eng.htm

Valenti, J. (2011, June 3). SlutWalks and the future of feminism. *The Washington Post.* Retrieved from http://www.washingtonpost.com/opinions/slutwalks-and-the-future-of-feminism/2011/06/01/AGjB9LIH_story.html

Van Harten, G. (2012, October 23). What if the Canada–China investor treaty is unconstitutional? Retrieved from: http://www.theglobeandmail.com/globe-debate/what-if-the-canada-china-investment-treaty-is-unconstitutional/article4629972/

Van Harten, G. (2014, September 14). Breaking down the harm to Canada done by treaty with China. Retrieved from: http://thetyee.ca/Opinion/2014/09/15/ http://thetyee.ca/Opinion/2014/09/15/China-Investment-Treaty-Breakdown/China-Investment-Treaty-Breakdown/

Van Loon, R., & Whittington, M.S. (1987). *The Canadian political system: Environment, structure and process* (4th ed.). Toronto, ON: McGraw.

Verba, S., & Nie, N. (1972). *Participation in America: Political democracy and social inequality.* New York, NY: Harper and Row.

Verba, S., Nie, N., & Kim, J. (1971). *The modes of democratic participation: A cross-national comparison.* Beverly Hills, CA: Sage.

Vézina, M., & Crompton, S. (2012). Canadian social trends. Component of Statistics Canada Catalogue no. 11-008-X. Ottawa: Statistics Canada.

Vincent, D. (2015, March 17). Canadians oppose niqab during citizenship ceremony, poll suggests. Thestar.com. Retrieved from http://www.thestar.com/news/canada/2015/03/17/canadians-oppose-niqab-during-citizenship-ceremony-poll-suggests.html

Voices-voix.ca (2014). Edgar Schmidt. Retrieved from http://voices-voix.ca/en/facts/profile/edgar-schmidt.

Volunteer Canada (2006). *Volunteering and mandatory community service: Choice—incentive—coercion—obligation.* A discussion paper. Ottawa, ON: Author.

Vriend v. Alberta. (1998). 1 S.C.R. 493.

Waddell, C. (2009). The campaign in the media 2008. In J.H. Pammett & C. Dornan. (Eds.), *The Canadian federal election of 2008.* Toronto, ON: Dundurn Press.

Wallner, J. (2014). 19th century division of powers, 21st century problems. Understanding Canadian intergovernmental relations. Retrieved from www.Canada2020.ca

Walton, D. (2012, February 10). Alberta should have proof provinces spending equalization wisely: Finance Minister. *Globe and Mail.*

Watts, R.L. (2008). *Comparing federal systems* (3rd ed.). Montreal, QC: McGill-Queen's University Press.

Weibust, I. (2010). The great green north? Canada's bad environmental record and how to fix it. In G. DiGiacomo & M. Flumian (Eds.), *The case for centralized federalism* (pp. 215–250). Ottawa, ON: University of Ottawa Press.

Wells, P. (2011, December 26). First Nations: Amid an emergency-a strategy. *Macleans,* 14–15.

Wells, P. (2013). *The longer I'm prime minister.* Toronto, ON: Random House Canada.

Wheare, K.C. (1967). *Federal government.* New York, NY: Oxford University Press.

Wherry, A. (2013, March 21). How sprawling budget bills threaten parliamentary democracy. *Maclean's.* Retrieved from www.macleans.ca/politics/how-sprawling-budget-bills-threaten-parliamentary-democracy/. Used with permission.

White, G. (2006). *Cabinets and first ministers.* Vancouver, BC: UBC Press.

White, P. (2015). Families look for answers to death of 7 aboriginal children in Thunder Bay. *The Globe and Mail.* Retrieved from: http://www.theglobeandmail.com/news/national/families-look-for-answers-to-deaths-of-7-aboriginal-students-in-thunder-bay/article26645550/

Whitehorn, A. (2001). Alexa McDonough and NDP gains in Atlantic Canada. In H. Thorburn (Ed.), *Party politics in Canada* (8th ed., pp. 264–279). Toronto, ON: Prentice Hall.

Whitehorn, A. (2007). Social democracy and the New Democratic Party. In A.-G. Gagnon & B. Tanguay (Eds.), *Canadian parties in transition* (3rd ed.). Toronto, ON: University of Toronto Press.

Whyte, J.D. (2011, November 10). Trudeau's belated victory. *Toronto Star*.

Whyte, M. (2014, December 5). Anatomy of a protest: Wendy Coburn and the mechanics of SlutWalk. thestar.com. Retrieved from http://www.thestar.com/entertainment/visualarts/2014/12/05/anatomy_of_a_protest_wendy_coburn_and_the_mechanics_of_slutwalk.html

Wilder, M., & Howlett, M. (2015). Province-building below the radar: The continued relevance of the province-building concept in Canadian political science. In C. Dunn, *Provinces: Canadian provincial politics* (3rd ed.). Toronto, ON: University of Toronto Press.

Williams, R.A. (2009). Endogenous shocks in subsystem adjustment and policy change: The credit crunch and Canadian banking regulation. *Journal of Public Policy, 29,* 29–53. doi:10.1017/S0143814X09001007

Wilson, J. (2002). Continuity and change in the Canadian environmental movement: Assessing the effects of institutionalization. In. D.L. VanNijnatten & R. Boardman (Eds.). Canadian environmental policy. Context and Cases (pp. 46–65). Toronto: Oxford University Press.

Wingrove, J. (2014, January 22). Refugee claims hit 'historic low' as Ottawa's policy faces fresh criticism. Retrieved from http://www.theglobeandmail.com/news/politics/refugee-claims-hit-historic-low-as-ottawas-policy-faces-fresh-criticism/article16461486/

Wiseman, N. (1988). A Note on "Hartz-Horowitz at Twenty": The Case of French Canada. *Canadian Journal of Political Science, 21* (4), 795–806.

Wiseman, N. (2007). *In search of Canadian political culture.* Vancouver, BC: UBC Press.

Wood, G. (2015). What ISIS really wants. *The Atlantic*, March. Retrieved from http://www.theatlantic.com/features/archive/2015/02/what-isis-really-wants/384980/

World Bank Group (2014). Doing business. Measuring business regulations. Retrieved from http://www.doingbusiness.org/data/exploretopics/paying-taxes

World Health Organization (2010). Key components of a well-functioning health system. Retrieved from http://www.who.int/healthsystems/publications/hss_key/en/

World Values Survey (1982). Retrieved from www.worldvaluessurvey.org.

World Values Survey (2006). Retrieved from www.worldvaluessurvey.org.

Worms, J.-P. (2002). Old and new civic ties and social ties in France. In R. Putnam (Ed.). *Democracies in flux: The evolution of social capital in contemporary society* (pp. 137–188). Oxford, UK: Oxford University Press.

Wortley, S., & Tanner, J. (2004). Discrimination or "good" policing? The racial profiling debate in Canada. *Our Diverse Cities 1,* 97–201.

Wynne, K. (2014, April 25). Premier's statement on the Supreme Court of Canada's ruling on Senate reform. Retrieved from http://www.premier.gov.on.ca/en/news/29350

Yang, J. (2011a, November 2). Inside a G20 cell. *Toronto Star*, pp. A1, 14.

Young, I. (1989). Polity and group difference: A critique of the ideal of universal citizenship. *Ethics, 99,* 250–274.

Young, L., & Everitt, J. (2004). *Advocacy groups.* Vancouver, BC: UBC Press.

Young, L., & Everitt, J. (2010). Advocacy groups. In W. Cross (Ed.). *Auditing Canadian democracy.* Vancouver, BC: UBC Press.

Zakaras, A. (2007). John Stuart Mill, individuality and participatory democracy. In N. Urbinati & A. Zakaras (Eds.), *J.S. Mill's political thought: A bicentennial reassessment* (pp. 200–220). Cambridge, UK: Cambridge University Press.

INDEX

Page numbers followed by f indicate figures, those followed by b indicate boxes, those followed by t indicate tables, and those followed by n indicate footnotes.